ABAS II

Adaptive Behavior Assessment System

SECOND EDITION

Adaptive Behavior Assessment System
Second Edition

Manual

Patti L. Harrison
Thomas Oakland

PsychCorp

PsychCorp™
A brand of Harcourt Assessment, Inc.

Portions of this work were previously published.

ISBN 0158004515

6 7 8 9 10 11 12   B C D E

Printed in the United States of America

Visit our website at www.PsychCorp.com

Published by Harcourt Assessment, Inc., 19500 Bulverde Road,
San Antonio, TX 78259, USA, 1-800-211-8378.

Acknowledgements

The publication of the *Adaptive Behavior Assessment System–Second Edition* (ABAS–II) is a result of the hard work and commitment of a number of people. Throughout all phases of development Dr. Jianjun Zhu, senior research director, was the force behind the project with his tireless efforts and dedication. Dr. Zhu contributed his guidance and expertise to all aspects of the development process, and his influence is evident in all components of the published product. In addition to his contributions to the quality of development, Dr. Zhu was responsible for a majority of the substantial amount of statistical analysis required for the ABAS–II. Enough cannot be said about the tremendous energy and personal commitment of Dr. Zhu. The authors are honored to have experienced his extensive knowledge and experience, as well as his enthusiasm and support. The authors value Dr. Zhu's numerous contributions to the project and thank him for the many years of work that he has devoted to the ABAS–II.

Mary Sichi, research analyst, was invaluable to the project during standardization and the final stages of development. Her research into current developments in the field of mental retardation contributed to the expansion of the test framework. She collaborated with the authors to ensure that their vision of the ABAS–II was carried throughout the entire process of publication. Her supervision of case review and scoring assured the quality of the data. During the final phase of development, she drafted many sections of the manual and dedicated her efforts to increasing the overall quality and clarity of the entire manual and the rating forms. The authors feel very fortunate that she was assigned to the project and express their gratitude for her organization, patience and encouragement, in addition to her professional expertise.

Yvonne Elias, senior research analyst, was responsible for many aspects of the tryout phase of development. Tara Malec, senior research analyst, assisted with necessary scoring processes during tryout. Stephanie Tong, research analyst, offered crucial 11th hour support during the final phase of development by assisting with table formatting and quality assurance. She also provided a sharp-eyed review of the materials. Imelda G. Martinez, research analyst, lent her expertise to table and figures, allowing important project deadlines to be met. A special thanks is in order for Dr. Diane Coalson, research director, for contributing her writing talents to an important section of the manual.

Dr. Judith Treloar's leadership in supporting the development of the ABAS and the ABAS–II has been instrumental. She envisioned the need for such a scale and worked actively to help ensure its success. The work of Dr. David M. Schwartz, National Measurement Consultant, has also been critical.

Dr. Aurelio Prifitera, President of the The Psychological Corporation, and Dr. Lawrence G. Weiss, Director, Psychological Measurement Group, provided critical advice and support during key phases of the project. In particular, Dr. Weiss' support of the expansion of the test framework and other innovations was essential. Phillip Ray, project manager, lent his energy and enthusiasm during the standardization phase of the project. Pamela Parmer, project manger, jumped in with both feet during the final phase, and her commitment and determination propelled the project through to publication.

Dr. Charles Wilkins, senior psychometrician, was key to the analysis and preparation of the normative data. Dr. Anli Lin, statistical analyst, also contributed psychometric support, including the factor analysis and hand-smoothing of norms. Cleopatra DeLeon, senior data analyst, assisted with the preparation of data for statistical analysis.

Members of the editorial team deserve much credit for their part in shaping the complexities of ABAS–II content into a smooth finished product. Weslea Miller, editor, was instrumental in coordinating all aspects of editorial and production work. She dedicated many hours to editing the rating forms and all components of the manual. She also took on the difficult but important task of working with translators to assure the quality of the Spanish rating forms. Elizabeth Manclark, freelance editor, lent her expertise to a large portion of the manual. Margaret Young Cooley also provided editorial support during the final phases. Spanish translator Jennifer Meehan, along with members of Tri-Lin Integrated Services translated, back translated, and reviewed Spanish versions of rating forms. Special thanks are due to Dulce Mendoza and María Muñoz, research analysts, for conducting final reviews of all Spanish rating forms. Cynthia Sweet, Marian Zahora, Javier Flores, Robin Espiritu, and other members of the production team contributed their talents to the appearance, design, and production of all ABAS–II materials.

Victoria Locke, manager, clinical sampling, and her team worked very hard to collect an often elusive sample of young children from a variety of backgrounds. Joyce Townsend, supervisor, Examiner Relations/Recruiting, and her team, including Wesley King, Kristin Vega, Elsa Estorga, Becky Matanic, and Mari Martinez deserve mention for their efforts. Stephanie Torres, study manager, deserves special recognition for keeping all aspects of sampling on track to the end. Ruth Mendez, clinical sampling operations supervisor, Cynthia Jackson, and other members of the case review team had the difficult task of coordinating the collection and initial review of the data. Rene Martinez, senior associate, did an excellent job of tracking and reviewing all clinical cases. David Quintero, scoring supervisor, coordinated all aspects of data entry and protocol filing. Matt Morris, manager, System Software Development group and Glen Larson, programmer, performed the computer programming necessary for scoring and data entry. Jean Shimko, quality assurance supervisor, and her team of reviewers including Mary Mata and Evangelina Souza were responsible for the enormous task of checking the accuracy of the normative data and the tables in the manual.

Dr. Nancy Roser, Language and Literacy Studies, Flawn Professor of Early Childhood Education, The University of Texas at Austin conducted an impressively thorough readability study of items on the infant-preschool rating forms. Appreciation is also due to the many examiners, coordinators, reviewers, and consultants who provided data and feedback to make this project possible. Their names are listed in Appendix D of this manual. Equally important are the respondents who gave their time completing ABAS–II rating forms so that we could collect the necessary data. The publication and high level of quality of the ABAS–II are only possible due to the combined effort, talent, and professional dedication of everyone involved.

Patti L. Harrison
Thomas Oakland
July 2003

Contents

Figures

Tables

Appendix A. Norms Tables

Teacher/Daycare Provider and Teacher Forms

Parent/Primary Caregiver and Parent Forms

Appendix B. Supplementary Tables

Teacher/Daycare Provider and Teacher Forms

Parent/Primary Caregiver and Parent Forms

Adult Form, Self Report

Preface

Over a decade ago, Matarazzo (1992) predicted that in the new century "better developed successors to today's scales for assessing personal competency and adaptive behavior…will be in wide use in clinical settings." The *Adaptive Behavior Assessment System–Second Edition* (ABAS–II) fills this role by building on the strong psychometric and clinical foundation of ABAS while incorporating current theoretical and research perspectives in the field of adaptive behavior assessment.

ABAS–II retains all features of the original ABAS. These include an assessment of overall adaptive functioning (the General Adaptive Composite) as well as an assessment of the ten adaptive skill areas specified by the *Diagnostic and Statistical Manual of Mental Disorders–Fourth Edition–Text Revision* (*DSM–IV–TR*; American Psychiatric Association, 2000). ABAS–II retains the Parent and Teacher Forms for ages 5–21 years, and the Adult Form for ages 16–89 years. New features include the infant-preschool Parent/Primary Caregiver and Teacher/Daycare Provider rating forms and normative data for children ages birth–5 years. Additionally, the structure of the original ABAS has been expanded to incorporate current American Association on Mental Retardation (AAMR) guidelines for the diagnosis of mental retardation and includes an assessment of the Conceptual, Social, and Practical domains of adaptive behavior.

Also new to this edition are validity studies with measures of adaptive behavior for children age 5 and younger. The validity section now includes correlational studies looking at relationships with the *Wechsler Preschool and Primary Scale of Intelligence–Third Edition* and the *Wechsler Intelligence Scale for Children–Fourth Edition*. Clinical validity for children age 5 and younger is established through studies of children diagnosed with a variety of disorders including mental retardation, developmental delay, biological risk factors, and Autistic Disorder.

The expanded structure, downward extension of norms, and additional validity studies included in ABAS–II combine to create a valuable, versatile, and comprehensive assessment of adaptive behavior appropriate across a wide range of age groups and clinical settings.

Chapter 1

Introduction

The *Adaptive Behavior Assessment System®–Second Edition* (ABAS®–II) provides a comprehensive, norm-referenced assessment of adaptive skills for individuals ages birth to 89 years. The ABAS–II may be used to assess an individual's adaptive skills for diagnosis and classification of disabilities and disorders, identification of strengths and limitations, and to document and monitor an individual's progress over time. The comprehensive range of specific adaptive skills and broad adaptive domains measured by the ABAS–II correspond to the specifications identified by the American Association on Mental Retardation (AAMR; 1992, 2002b) and the *Diagnostic and Statistical Manual of Mental Disorders–Fourth Edition–Text Revision* (*DSM–IV–TR*; American Psychiatric Association [APA], 2000). The ABAS–II provides for assessment by multiple respondents, evaluates functioning across multiple settings, and contributes to a complete assessment of the daily, functional skills of an individual. The instrument's multidimensional quality is derived from five rating forms that are designed to evaluate individuals across various age ranges and environmental settings.

Components of the ABAS–II include this manual and five rating forms. Relevant respondents who can rate the daily adaptive skills of the individual being evaluated may complete these forms. Respondents may be parents, family members, teachers, daycare staff, supervisors, counselors, care providers, or others who are familiar with the daily activities of the individual. Another individual may rate an adult, or he or she may rate himself or herself. The rating forms may be completed independently by a respondent or may be read aloud to a respondent who has limited reading skills. Each rating form is easy to complete and score requiring approximately 20 minutes to complete, and 5–10 minutes to hand-score. Computer scoring software is also available.

Key Features

The ABAS–II is a multifunctional tool and can be used for several purposes. The information obtained by using this assessment can contribute to the comprehensive, diagnostic assessment of individuals who may be experiencing difficulties with the daily adaptive skills that are necessary for functioning effectively within their environments, given the typical demands placed on individuals of the same age. Results from the ABAS–II can be used in combination with other evaluation information to make diagnostic decisions and to plan interventions and services. Adaptive behavior assessment is required to meet international, national, and state requirements for identification, diagnosis, and classification of disabilities and disorders, such as those based on the Individuals with Disabilities Education Act Amendments of 1997 (IDEA; 1999), *DSM–IV–TR*, Social Security, and Medicaid. By providing comprehensive, diagnostic assessment information, the ABAS–II can be useful for individuals with a variety of disabilities, disorders, and health conditions, including mental retardation, developmental disabilities, developmental delays, learning and emotional disorders, and dementias. This type of information is essential when adaptive skill limitations are a concern and the goal of the intervention or treatment is to improve the daily adaptive functioning of an individual.

The five rating forms were developed during 8 years of research. Data collected during pilot and national tryout phases were analyzed to select items for the national standardization editions. The standardization samples for the Parent/Primary Caregiver and Teacher/Daycare Provider Forms for children ages birth to 5 years together comprised 2,100 individuals; the standardization samples for the Parent, Teacher, and Adult Forms together comprised 5,270 individuals. The composition of the standardization samples was representative of the U.S. population according to the following variables: gender, race/ethnicity, and parent education level (U.S. Bureau of the Census, 1999, 2000). These samples represented a continuum of development, including individuals with typically developing skills and individuals identified with disability in proportions representative of the general U.S. population (U.S. Bureau of the Census, 1999, 2000).

The normative data presented in this manual enable the professional user to obtain a normative comparison between an individual's adaptive skills and the adaptive skills of typically developing individuals of the same age in a representative national standardization sample. The ABAS–II also features validity data for special samples of individuals with disabilities, including mental retardation, developmental delay, and others.

Norm-referenced scores are provided for specific skill areas as specified by AAMR (1992) and *DSM–IV–TR* guidelines. Tables 1.1 and 1.2 provide a summary of the skill areas assessed by the ABAS–II. Norm-referenced scores are provided for three broad domains of adaptive behavior. These adaptive domains, as defined by the AAMR (2002b), were developed by combining skill areas and are described in Table 1.3. Norm-referenced scores are also provided for a total score, called the General Adaptive Composite (GAC). Norm-referenced scores for the skill areas include scaled scores ($M = 10$, $SD = 3$), average guessing rates, and age equivalents. Norm-referenced scores for the adaptive domains and for the GAC include standard scores ($M = 100$, $SD = 15$), critical values to calculate 90% and 95% confidence intervals, and percentile ranks. Descriptive classifications of *Extremely Low, Borderline, Below Average, Average, Above Average, Superior,* and *Very Superior* may be used for the skill areas, adaptive domains, and the GAC (see Table 3.1).

The skill areas, adaptive domains, and GAC have high internal consistency and test-retest reliability. Cross-form consistency studies enable comparisons for situations in which a parent and teacher rate the same child, and when self-ratings and other-respondent ratings are obtained for an adult. Tables 5.16 and 5.17 provide correlation data and compare means of skill area scaled scores, adaptive domain composite scores, and GAC scores obtained when different respondents rate the same individuals.

Due to the overlap of age ranges between the infant-preschool and school-age rating forms, a special cross-form consistency study compared the scores of children age 5 on the Teacher/Daycare Provider or Parent/Primary Caregiver Form with their scores on the corresponding school-age form (i.e. Teacher or Parent Form). Tables 5.18 and 5.19 provide correlation data and compare means of skill area scaled scores, adaptive domain composite scores, and GAC scores obtained from this study.

Extensive validity data were collected during development. Validity studies were conducted with samples of individuals with the following disabilities or disorders: mental retardation, learning disabilities, Attention-Deficit/Hyperactivity Disorder (ADHD), developmental delays, biological risk factors, language disorders, motor impairments, autistic disorders, emotional disturbances, behavior disorders, hearing impairment, physical impairments, Alzheimer's disease, and neuropsychological disorders. The validity studies with clinical samples provide useful data about the performance of individuals with various disabilities and disorders and include percentages of individuals in each sample that fell below designated cut-off scores.

Additional validity studies were conducted to investigate relationships between the ABAS–II and the *Vineland Adaptive Behavior Scales–Interview Edition* (VABS–IE; Sparrow, Balla, & Cicchetti, 1984); the *Vineland Adaptive Behavior Scales–Classroom Edition* (VABS–CE; Sparrow, Balla, & Cicchetti, 1985); the *Behavior Assessment System for Children–Teacher Rating Scales* (BASC; Reynolds & Kamphaus, 1998); the *Scales of Independent Behavior–Revised* (SIB–R; Bruininks, Woodcock, Weatherman, & Hill, 1996); the *Wechsler Preschool and Primary Scale of Intelligence–Third Edition* (WPPSI–III; Wechsler, 2002); the *Wechsler Intelligence Scale for Children–Third Edition* (WISC–III; Wechsler, 1991); the *Wechsler Intelligence Scale for Children–Fourth Edition* (WISC–IV; Wechsler, 2003); the *Wechsler Adult Intelligence Scale–Third Edition* (WAIS–III; Wechsler, 1997); the *Wechsler Abbreviated Scales of Intelligence* (WASI; The Psychological Corporation, 1999); *The Stanford Binet Intelligence Scale–Fourth Edition* (SB–IV; Thorndike, Hagen, & Sattler, 1986); and the *Wechsler Individual Achievement Test* (WIAT; The Psychological Corporation, 1992).

Nature of Adaptive Skills

The ABAS–II is based on three types of information: (a) a concept of adaptive behavior promoted for many years by the AAMR (1992, 2002b; Grossman, 1983; Heber, 1959); (b) legal and professional standards applicable to a number of special education and disability classification systems, such as federal and state special education and disability regulations, IDEA (1999), and the *DSM–IV–TR*; and (c) research investigating diagnosis, classification, and intervention for people with various disabilities. The three types of information are uniform in their conclusion that every individual requires a repertoire of skills in order to meet the daily demands and expectations of his or her environment. Examples of adaptive skills that individuals use on a daily basis include those related to eating, dressing, expressing needs, taking care of personal possessions, making purchases, interacting with peers, controlling one's behavior in a structured setting, following a schedule, communicating with other people, practicing safety, managing money, and holding a job.

The ABAS–II is designed to evaluate whether an individual displays various functional skills necessary for daily living without the assistance of others. Thus, this instrument focuses on independent behaviors and measures what an individual actually does, in addition to measuring what he or she may be able to do. In addition, the ABAS–II focuses on behaviors an individual displays on his or her own, without assistance from others.

Historically, two general aspects of adaptive skills have been described in the literature and measured with adaptive skill scales: personal independence and social responsibility (AAMR, 1992, 2002b; Grossman, 1983; Harrison, 1990; Horn & Fuchs, 1987). Grossman described these two aspects as "what people do to take care of themselves and relate to others" (p. 42). More recently, the AAMR (2002b) concluded that research investigating adaptive skills identifies three clusters and thus describes adaptive behavior as "the collection of conceptual, social, and practical skills that have been learned by people in order to function in their everyday lives" (p. 41).

The AAMR (2002b) identifies several important characteristics of adaptive behavior that relate to individuals with mental retardation; these aspects have significant implications for assessment, diagnosis, classification, and intervention for individuals who have other disabilities and disorders as well. The characteristics include:

- Adaptive skill limitations often coexist with strengths in other adaptive skill areas (p. 41).
- (A) person's strengths and limitations in adaptive skills should be documented within the context of community and cultural environments typical of the person's age peers and tied to the person's individualized need for supports (p. 41).

Thus, adaptive skills as measured by the ABAS–II are defined as those practical, everyday skills required to function and meet environmental demands, including effectively and independently taking care of oneself and interacting with other people. Specific skill areas included in the definitions of adaptive skills used by the AAMR (1992) and the *DSM–IV–TR*, and measured by the ABAS–II are: Communication, Community Use, Functional Academics, Home/School Living, Health and Safety, Leisure, Self-Care, Self-Direction, Social, and Work. This set of skills areas can be conceptually grouped into three broad categories of related skills. These categories, as defined by the AAMR (2002b), are represented by the following adaptive domains: Conceptual (communication and academic skills), Social (interpersonal and social competence skills), and Practical (independent living and daily living skills).

Table 1.1 Description and Sample Items of the Skill Areas for Teacher/Daycare Provider and Parent/Primary Caregiver Forms

Skill Area	Number of Items		Description	Sample Items
	Teacher/ Daycare Provider Form	Parent/ Primary Caregiver Form		
Communication	25	25	Speech, language, and listening skills needed for communication with other people, including vocabulary, responding to questions, conversation skills, nonverbal communication skills, etc.	Raises voice to get attention. Sings all or part of the words to songs. Speaks in sentences of six or more words.
Community Use	–	22	Skills needed for functioning and appropriate behavior in the community, including getting around in the community, expression of interest in activities outside the home, recognition of different facilities, etc.	Recognizes own home in his/her immediate neighborhood. Asks to go to a park or other favorite community place. Finds the restrooms in public places.
Functional Pre-Academics	24	23	Basic pre-academic skills that form the foundations for reading, writing, mathematics, and other skills needed for daily, independent functioning, including letter recognition, counting, drawing simple shapes, etc.	Holds crayon or pencil with point down when using paper. Sings the alphabet song. Reads his/her own written name.
School/Home Living[a]	23	25	Skills needed for basic care of a home or living setting or a school or classroom setting, including cleaning, straightening, helping adults with household tasks, taking care of personal possessions, etc.	Turns television on and off. Picks up and throws away trash. Wipes up spills at school or daycare.
Health and Safety	21	24	Skills needed for protection of health and to respond to illness and injury, including following safety rules, using medicines, showing caution, keeping out of physical danger, etc.	Acts startled or surprised when he/she hears a very loud sound. Refrains from putting dirt or sand in mouth. Carries scissors safely.
Leisure	23	22	Skills needed for engaging in and planning leisure and recreational activities, including playing with others, playing with toys, engaging in recreation at home, following rules in games, etc.	Shows interest in mobiles or other moving objects. Plays simple games like "peek-a-boo" or rolls a ball to others. Asks to be read to from a favorite book.
Self-Care	24	24	Skills needed for personal care including eating, dressing, bathing, toileting, grooming, hygiene, etc.	Nurses, drinks, or eats willingly, with little encouragement. Holds and drinks from a sipping cup. Washes hands with soap. Dresses himself/herself.
Self-Direction	24	25	Skills needed for independence, responsibility, and self-control, including making choices about food and clothing, starting and completing tasks, following a daily routine, following directions, etc.	Sits quietly for at least one minute without demanding an adult's attention. Resists pushing or hitting another child when angry or upset. Keeps working on hard tasks without becoming discouraged or quitting.
Social	25	24	Skills needed to interact socially and get along with other people, including expressing affection, having friends, showing and recognizing emotions, assisting others, using manners, etc.	Smiles when he/she sees parent. Shows sympathy for others when they are sad or upset. Apologizes if he/she hurts the feelings of others.
Motor	27	27	Basic fine and gross motor skills needed for locomotion, manipulation of the environment and the development of more complex activities such as sports, including sitting, pulling up to a standing position, walking, fine motor control, kicking, etc.	Shakes rattle or other toys. Stands up from a sitting position. Uses scissors to cut along a straight line.
Total Items	216	241		

[a]On the Teacher/Daycare Provider Form, the skill area is titled School Living; on the Parent/Primary Caregiver Form, the skill area is titled Home Living.

Adaptive Behavior Assessment System–Second Edition

Table 1.2   Description and Sample Items of the Skill Areas for Teacher, Parent, and Adult Forms

Skill Area	Number of Items			Description	Sample Items
	Teacher Form	Parent Form	Adult Form		
Communication	22	24	25	Speech, language, and listening skills needed for communication with other people, including vocabulary, responding to questions, conversation skills, etc.	Names 20 or more familiar objects. Ends conversations appropriately. Uses up-to-date information to discuss current events.
Community Use	15	23	24	Skills needed for functioning in the community, including use of community resources, shopping skills, getting around in the community, etc.	Mails letters at the postal box or local post office. Finds and uses a pay phone. Orders his/her own meals when eating out.
Functional Academics	22	23	27	Basic reading, writing, mathematics, and other academic skills needed for daily, independent functioning, including telling time, measurement, writing notes and letters, etc.	Reads his/her own written name. Finds somebody's telephone number in the phone book. Makes reminder notes or lists.
School/Home Living[a]	20	25	23	Skills needed for basic care of a home or living setting (or, for the Teacher Form, school and classroom setting), including cleaning, straightening, property maintenance and repairs, food preparation, performing chores, etc.	Wipes up spills at home. Takes out trash when can is full. Keeps toys, games, or other belongings neat and clean.
Health and Safety	16	22	20	Skills needed for protection of health and to respond to illness and injury, including following safety rules, using medicines, showing caution, etc.	Carries scissors safely. Follows general safety regulations at school. Tests hot foods before eating them.
Leisure	17	22	23	Skills needed for engaging in and planning leisure and recreational activities, including playing with others, engaging in recreation at home, following rules in games, etc.	Plays alone with toys, games, or other fun activities. Waits for his/her turn in games and other fun activities. Tries a new activity to learn about something new.
Self-Care	19	24	25	Skills needed for personal care including eating, dressing, bathing, toileting, grooming, hygiene, etc.	Buttons his/her own clothing. Uses public restroom alone. Keeps hair neat during the day by brushing or combing.
Self-Direction	21	25	25	Skills needed for independence, responsibility, and self-control, including starting and completing tasks, keeping a schedule, following time limits, following directions, making choices, etc.	Stops a fun activity, without complaints, when told that time is up. Controls temper when disagreeing with friends. Completes large home or school projects on time.
Social	20	23	23	Skills needed to interact socially and get along with other people, including having friends, showing and recognizing emotions, assisting others, and using manners.	Says "Thank you" when given a gift. Laughs in response to funny comments or jokes. Listens to friends or family members who need to talk about problems.
Work[b]	21	21	24	Skills needed for successful functioning and holding a part- or full-time job in a work setting, including completing work tasks, working with supervisors, and following a work schedule.	Shows positive attitude towards job. Starts back to work willingly after taking a break or lunch. Cares properly for work supplies and equipment.
Total Items	193	232	239		

[a]On the Teacher Form, the skill area is titled School Living; on the Parent and Adult Forms, the skill area is titled Home Living.
[b]The Work Skill Area is completed only when individuals have a part- or full-time job.

Table 1.3 Skill Areas Included in the GAC and Adaptive Domains

	Parent/Primary Caregiver Form		Teacher/Daycare Provider Form[b]	Parent Form	Teacher Form	Adult Form
	Ages 0–11 months[a]	Ages 1–5 years	Ages 2–5	Ages 5–21	Ages 5–21	Ages 16–89
GAC — Skill Areas	Communication Health and Safety Leisure Self-Care Self-Direction Social Motor[c]	Communication Community Use Functional Pre-Academics[f] Home Living Health and Safety Leisure Self-Care Self-Direction Social Motor[c]	Communication Functional Pre-Academics School Living Health and Safety Leisure Self-Care Self-Direction Social Motor[c]	Communication Community Use Functional Academics Home Living Health and Safety Leisure Self-Care Self-Direction Social Work[d]	Communication Community Use Functional Academics Home Living Health and Safety Leisure Self-Care Self-Direction Social Work[d]	Communication Community Use Functional Academics Home Living Health and Safety Leisure Self-Care Self-Direction Social Work[e]
Adaptive Domain — Skill Areas						
Conceptual	Communication Self-Direction	Communication Functional Pre-Academics[f] Self-Direction	Communication Functional Pre-Academics[f] Self-Direction	Communication Functional Academics Self-Direction	Communication Functional Academics Self-Direction	Communication Functional Academics Self-Direction
Social	Leisure Social	Leisure Social	Leisure Social	Leisure Social	Leisure Social	Leisure Social
Practical	Self-Care Health and Safety[g]	Self-Care Home Living[h] Community Use Health and Safety	Self-Care School Living[h] Community Use Health and Safety	Self-Care Home Living Community Use Health and Safety	Self-Care School Living Community Use Health and Safety	Self-Care Home Living Community Use Health and Safety Work[e]

Note. Shaded areas indicate the skill areas that are completed and scored for each form.

Note. The grouping of skill areas into adaptive domains is based on AAMR (2002b) guidelines.

[a] Functional Pre-Academics, Home living, and Community Use are not administered to children under 1 year of age.

[b] Community Use is not included on the Teacher/Daycare Provider Form.

[c] Motor is only included on the Parent/Primary Caregiver and Teacher/Daycare Provider Forms. The Motor Skill Area scaled score is included in the GAC but is not included in the adaptive domains.

[d] Work is optional on the Parent and Teacher Forms and is administered only if the individual is 17 years or older and has a part- or full-time job. It is not included in the GAC or any adaptive domains.

[e] Work is optional on the Adult Form and is administered only if the individual has a part- or full-time job. The Practical Domain composite score and the GAC can be derived either with or without the Work Skill Area scaled score.

[f] On the Parent/Primary Caregiver and Teacher/Daycare Provider Forms, Functional Academics is titled Functional Pre-Academics.

[g] Health and Safety was placed in both the Conceptual and Practical Domains by the AAMR (2002b). Based on the ABAS–II item content, Health and Safety is included in the Practical Domain.

[h] Home Living is on the Parent/Primary Caregiver, Parent, and Adult Forms; School Living is on the Teacher/Daycare Provider and Teacher Forms.

Focus and Content of the Rating Forms

The five rating forms provide for the measurement of adaptive skills of individuals through 89 years of age and across multiple environmental settings including home, preschool, school, daycare, community, and work. Some adaptive skills are only observable in certain settings and by some respondents. Therefore, separate rating forms are necessary to assess the adaptive skills most relevant for the specific setting and respondent. Each rating form is completed independently by the respondent, or may be read to the respondent if he or she does not have the reading skills to complete the rating form independently. A respondent completes the form by reading the instructions and responding to each item. The rating scale for the items allows respondents to indicate if the individual is able to independently perform an activity and, if so, how frequently (*always, sometimes,* or *never*) he or she performs the activity when it is needed. Because a respondent cannot observe all possible daily activities of the individual, respondents can identify which items he or she had less opportunity to observe and needed to guess or estimate about the rating. The guessing scores enable the professional user to compare the respondent's guessing rate to the average guessing rate in the standardization sample, and to use the guessing rate information when interpreting the results and making decisions about the individual.

Although it is possible to assess the adaptive skills of an individual with a single rating form, the use of multiple rating forms is recommended to provide a comprehensive assessment across a variety of settings. For example, professional users may solicit multiple ratings by requesting that a parent complete the Parent Form and the teacher complete the Teacher Form for an 8-year-old child. For a 30-year-old individual, for example, the Adult Form may be completed by three respondents: the individual himself or herself, a family member, and a work supervisor.

Parent/Primary Caregiver Form (Ages 0–5)

The Parent/Primary Caregiver Form is a comprehensive, diagnostic measure of the adaptive skills that have primary relevance for the functioning of infants, toddlers, and preschoolers in the home and other settings, and can be completed by parents or other primary care providers. The Parent/Primary Caregiver Form is used for children ages birth–5 years, and includes 241 items, with 22 to 27 items per skill area. This form is available in Spanish[1].

Parent Form (Ages 5–21)

The Parent Form is a comprehensive, diagnostic measure of the adaptive skills that have primary relevance for children's functioning in the home and community, and can be completed by parents or other primary care providers. The Parent Form is used for children in grades Kindergarten (K) through 12 or ages 5–21 years. The form extends through age 21 to include special education students and other students who continue to be served through a secondary school setting. This form includes 232 items, with 21 to 25 items per skill area. This form is available in Spanish[1].

Teacher/Daycare Provider Form (Ages 2–5)

The Teacher/Daycare Provider Form is a comprehensive, diagnostic measure of the adaptive skills that have primary relevance for toddler's and preschooler's functioning in a daycare center, home daycare, preschool, or school setting. Teachers, teacher's aides, daycare instructors, or other daycare or childcare providers can complete this form. The Teacher/Daycare Provider Form is used for children ages 2–5 years, and includes 216 items, with 21 to 27 items per skill area. This form is available in Spanish[1].

Teacher Form (Ages 5–21)

The Teacher Form is a comprehensive, diagnostic measure of the adaptive skills that have primary relevance for children's functioning in a school setting, and can be completed by teachers or teacher's aides. The Teacher Form is used for children in grades K through 12 or ages 5–21 years. The form extends through age 21 to include special education students and other students who continue to be served through a secondary school setting. This form includes 193 items, with 15 to 22 items per skill area.

Adult Form (Ages 16–89)

The Adult Form is a comprehensive, diagnostic measure of the adaptive skills that have primary relevance for an adult's functioning in home and community settings. The Adult Form may be completed by the individual being evaluated for a self-rating if his or her functional skills are judged to be adequate for providing valid responses to the items. Family members, supervisors, or other respondents who are familiar with the individual in his or her various environments can also complete this form. Two separate norms tables are provided for the Adult Form: Adult Form, Self Report and Adult Form, Rated by Others. The Adult Form is used for individuals ages 16–89 years, and includes 239 items, with 20 to 27 items per skill area.

[1]Spanish versions were translated from the English forms, back-translated, and then reviewed by a third party. Validity and reliability data do not currently exist for the ABAS–II Spanish rating forms. Therefore, results obtained from the Spanish forms should be interpreted with caution, and should always be used in conjunction with other standardized instruments as part of a comprehensive assessment.

Age Range Overlap Between Forms

The overlap of age ranges between the rating forms enables the user to select the most appropriate forms for use with individuals age 5 or ages 16–21. For children who are 5 years of age, users may choose either an infant-preschool or a school-age form. The infant-preschool forms (Teacher/Daycare Provider and Parent/Primary Caregiver Forms) generally should be used with 5-year-old children who may be lower functioning or have more serious disorders or disabilities. These forms can also be used with children whose initial referral for evaluation of a possible disability or eligibility for special education occurs at age 5, or with 5-year-old children for whom there is no prior knowledge regarding the level of functioning. Users also may choose the infant-preschool forms for 5-year-old children who were previously assessed with these forms to directly compare adaptive skill ratings between the two evaluations. The school-age forms (Teacher and Parent Forms) generally should be used with 5-year-old children who are thought to have higher functioning or less severe problems.

Note. Use only the infant-preschool forms with children younger than 5 (≤ 4:11) and only the school-age forms with children older than 5 (≥ 6:0).

For young adults who are ages 16–21 years, users may choose the school-age Parent and Teacher Forms or the Adult Form. The school-age forms are typically used with young adults who are still participating in some type of secondary educational program, such as high school or special education programs. The Adult Form generally is used with young adults who are no longer participating in secondary school settings, but may be participating in community or work settings, job training programs, or post-secondary institutions. The Adult Form is the only form that may be used to obtain a self rating.

Adaptive Skills and Mental Retardation

Adaptive skill measurement has traditionally been associated with the study, evaluation, and treatment of mental retardation. Assessment of adaptive behavior, along with assessment of intelligence, has been required for classification and diagnosis of mental retardation for many years. The official definition of mental retardation by the AAMR (Heber, 1959) indicated that adaptive behavior deficits, in addition to subaverage intelligence, were necessary for a classification of mental retardation. Deficits in adaptive behavior were included as part of subsequent definitions of mental retardation by the AAMR (Grossman, 1983) and other groups (*Diagnostic and Statistical Manual of Mental Disorders–3rd Edition Revised* [*DSM–IIIR*]; APA, 1987; *Diagnostic and Statistical Manual of Mental Disorders–4th Edition* [*DSM–IV*], APA, 1994).

Special education legislation, including the Education for All Handicapped Children Act of 1975, IDEA of 1991, and its amendments of 1997, required both subaverage intelligence and deficits in adaptive behavior for a classification of mental retardation. According to the IDEA, "Mental retardation means significantly subaverage general intellectual functioning, existing concurrently with deficits in adaptive behavior and manifested during the developmental period, that adversely affects a child's educational performance" (IDEA, Final Regulations, 1999, Sec. 300.7). Adaptive skill limitations are included in a number of other diagnostic or classification systems for mental retardation, including the *International Classification of Diseases* (World Health Organization, 1993); *International Classification of Functioning, Disability, and Health* (World Health Organization, 2001); and, as described by Reschley, Myers, and Hartel (2002), regulations and procedures for developmental disabilities, Social Security Disability Determination Services, and Medicaid include adaptive behavior criteria.

The 1992 definition of mental retardation from the AAMR placed considerably greater emphasis on adaptive skills than previous AAMR definitions:

> Mental retardation refers to substantial limitations in present functioning. It is characterized by significantly subaverage intellectual functioning, existing concurrently with related limitations in two or more of the following applicable skill areas: communication, self-care, home living, social skills, community use, self-direction, health and safety, functional academics, leisure, and work. Mental retardation manifests before age 18 (p. 5).

A comparable definition of mental retardation is used in the *DSM–IV–TR:*

> ...Significantly subaverage general intellectual functioning (Criterion A) that is accompanied by significant limitations in adaptive functioning in at least two of the following skill areas: communication, self-care, home living, social/interpersonal skills, use of community resources, self-direction, functional academics, work, leisure, health and safety (Criterion B). The onset must occur before age 18 years (Criterion C) (p. 41).

The most recent definition of mental retardation by the AAMR (2002b) emphasizes broad domains of adaptive behavior:

> Mental retardation is a disability characterized by significant limitations both in intellectual functioning and in adaptive behavior as expressed in conceptual, social, and practical adaptive skills. This disability originates before age 18 (p. 1).

The AAMR manual (2002b) also provides an operational definition for limitations in adaptive behavior:

> For the diagnosis of mental retardation, significant limitations in adaptive behavior should be established through the use of standardized measures normed on the general population, including people with disabilities and people without disabilities. On these standardized measures, significant limitations in adaptive behavior are operationally defined as performance that is at least two standard deviations below the mean of either (a) one of the following three types of adaptive behavior: conceptual, social, or practical, or (b) an overall score on a standardized measure of conceptual, social, and practical skills (p. 76).

Other professional associations (e.g., APA) as well as federal and state governments have not revised their policies to reflect current AAMR guidelines, though they may do so in the future. Professional users are advised to consult legal and professional standards when using adaptive behavior data for diagnosis, classification, or support planning.

Use of the ABAS–II With Individuals Other Than Those With Mental Retardation

Although the assessment of adaptive skills has traditionally been associated with the diagnosis and classification of mental retardation, the concept of adaptive skills is important for all individuals, including those with limitations and disabilities other than mental retardation. Adaptive skills should be assessed routinely for children or adults who have difficulties, disabilities, or disorders that interfere with daily functioning (Harrison, 1990; Harrison & Boney, 2002; Reschly, 1990). Adaptive skill assessment may provide important information for the diagnosis and planning of treatment or intervention for individuals with developmental delays, biological risk factors, traumatic brain injuries, Autistic

Disorder, ADHD, learning and behavior disorders, sensory impairments, physical disabilities or injuries, health impairments, motor impairments, emotional disorders, brain injuries, stroke, dementias, Alzheimer's disease, substance-related disorders, psychotic disorders, and multiple disabilities. Specific examples include the following:

- A pediatric neuropsychologist in a public health clinic evaluates a 1-year-old girl with Cerebral Palsy.

- A 2-year-old boy is referred to a pediatrician at a university hospital because of a possible Pervasive Developmental Disorder.

- The parents of a 3-year-old child request assessment by school psychologists at a state child development center because the child has not met major developmental milestones and may have significant delays in communication, social, and motor skill development.

- A school district requests adaptive behavior assessment data from parents and teachers of children eligible for special education programs to assist in planning and coordinating home-school programs.

- Parents of a child who is blind request consultation with his or her Individual Education Plan (IEP) committee on ways to best promote adaptive skill development.

- A third grade male student with a learning disability in reading displays a possible behavioral disorder and is referred to the school psychologist.

- A fourth grade female student diagnosed with an emotional disturbance disorder displays various problems at home for which the parents have requested help from a psychologist in private practice.

- A fifth grade male student diagnosed with Attention-Deficit/Hyperactivity Disorder is referred to a mental health center for comprehensive assessment of adaptive skills and behavior problems, based on reports of diminished self-direction, self-care, and school/home living skills and increased acting-out behaviors.

- The school district uses ABAS–II data to assist students with disabilities in their transition from school to work settings.

- A rehabilitation specialist is responsible for coordinating the rehabilitation of an adult with traumatic brain injury.

- A neuropsychologist routinely acquires ABAS–II data to better understand an individual's development in home, school and/or work settings.

- An assisted living facility for older adults uses ABAS–II data to assist the clinician when making decisions regarding program planning and monitoring.

- A woman concerned about her father's advanced stages of Alzheimer's disease requests an evaluation of his adaptive skills from a team of physicians and social workers to better understand the severity of his disorder and to implement a program designed to promote important functional behaviors.

- A clinical psychologist uses the ABAS–II with individuals with depression and anxiety to assess the impact of the mental disorders on daily functioning and to provide individuals and their families with intervention goals.

- A psychiatrist uses the ABAS–II to initially assess an individual's adaptive skills and to monitor behavioral and skill level changes in response to medication.

Applications of the ABAS–II

Uses of the ABAS–II include diagnostic assessment, identification of adaptive skill strengths and limitations, identification of service needs, program planning and monitoring, and research and evaluation. The ABAS–II may be used in many settings and agencies including settings that provide services for children, such as public or private schools, daycare programs, community agencies, and medical or residential settings. The ABAS–II may be used as part of the comprehensive assessment of children and adults who are being evaluated for possible diagnosis of disabilities or problems, in addition to those who have previously been diagnosed with disabilities or problems. Similarly, the ABAS–II may be used in a variety of programs and settings for adults including public and private service provider agencies, medical and health facilities, residential facilities or group homes, community programs and agencies, vocational and occupational training programs, and prisons.

Diagnosis and Classification

Disability and special education regulations as set forth by community, state, federal, and international classification systems routinely require a comprehensive adaptive behavior assessment as part of the multifactor, multimethod assessment conducted for individuals with mental retardation. The ABAS–II fulfills many of these requirements. It also assists in determining diagnoses and classifications other than mental retardation and in determining eligibility for special programs. Special education and other disability services often require the comprehensive assessment of adaptive skills and other qualities when determining diagnoses and eligibility for services for individuals with a wide variety of disabilities in special education or disability categories (e.g., serious emotional disturbances, traumatic brain injuries, pervasive developmental disorders, or other health impairments) and specific categories of mental disorders, such as those denoted in the *DSM–IV–TR*. For infants, toddlers, preschoolers, and school-age children through age 9, IDEA includes developmental delay as a disability and defines a child with developmental delay as one "who is experiencing developmental delays, as defined by the State and measured by appropriate diagnostic instruments and procedures, in one or more of the following areas: physical development, social or emotional development, cognitive development, social or emotional development, or adaptive development" (IDEA, Final Regulations, 1999, Sec. 300.7).

Identification of Strengths and Weaknesses in Adaptive Skills

The information obtained with the ABAS–II can be used by the clinician as part of a comprehensive assessment of adaptive skills and enables him or her to evaluate the extent to which an individual displays the skills necessary to meet environmental demands. The ABAS–II enables professional and other users to assess the extent to which individuals take care of themselves and relate to others during daily living in critical skill areas and in broad domains of adaptive behavior. Determination of adaptive skill strengths and limitations is important for individuals with mental retardation, developmental delays, and other disabilities or disorders. Although individuals with mental retardation are a primary target population for adaptive skill assessment, other individuals may also experience difficulties with adaptive skills. The ABAS–II should be considered for use when identifying strengths and weaknesses in adaptive skills for individuals who display characteristics of disabilities or disorders other than mental retardation.

Identifying Service Needs and Planning and Monitoring Programs

When the goal of treatment or intervention is to improve independent daily functioning and quality of life for an individual whose adaptive skill limitations are of concern, a comprehensive diagnostic assessment is essential. The ABAS–II provides an analysis of strengths and limitations in adaptive functioning that the professional user needs to develop appropriate intervention plans and support services for the individual. For example, an infant or toddler may need assistance with eating, drinking, and communicating skills. A school-age child may need interventions for dressing and grooming skills, and a teenager may need training related to the use of community resources and work skills. An adult may only need an intermittent level of support in managing money but an extensive level of support for transportation. After services and programs have been implemented, the ABAS–II is a useful tool for monitoring an individual's gains in adaptive skills and in evaluating his or her responses to different environments and support services.

The AAMR's manuals (1992, 2002b) on mental retardation place considerable emphasis on the need to consider the specific settings in which an individual lives, works, and receives services; the extent to which the characteristics of these environments facilitate or impede the individual's development and well-being; and the optimum environment that may facilitate an individual's independence/interdependence, productivity, community integration, social belonging, and well-being. As noted by the AAMR, there is a need for "an ecological approach to understanding behavior that depends on evaluating the discrepancy between a person's capabilities and skills and the adaptive skills and competencies required to function in an environment" (p. 147).

The detailed information obtained by the rating forms concerning important adaptive skills, combined with data related to the demands and expectations of the settings in which an individual must participate, facilitate the planning of services and interventions. For example, Seltzer (1997) described the importance of obtaining information about both the individual's skills and corresponding environments when identifying functional limitations of adults with disabilities. Dunn (1997) emphasized that, when planning transition programs for adolescents who are leaving a school program to move to a work or occupation program, it is important to analyze the adolescent's skills and integrate the assessment data with information about the new environmental demands.

Research and Evaluation

The ABAS–II measures a variety of adaptive skills and encompasses a wide age range, therefore it is useful for research and evaluation that describes or investigates the development and display of skills of many groups of people, including individuals with disabilities, individuals in special programs, and individuals receiving special services. The ABAS–II may be used to investigate the short- and long-term effects of intervention programs or other services, and facilitates institutional research and evaluation efforts. Features that make it especially useful for institutional research and evaluation include:

- Consistency between the ABAS–II and the AAMR (1992, 2002b) and the *DSM–IV–TR* definitions and conceptions of mental retardation;

- Up-to-date norms, including norms for various subgroups;

- Ease in use, administration, and scoring;

- Availability of separate forms and norms for the parents and teachers of individuals ages birth to 21 years; and

- Availability of separate norms for self-ratings and ratings by other respondents for individuals ages 16 to 89.

Qualifications of Users, Confidentiality, and Test Security

The professional user of the ABAS–II is responsible for selecting respondents, coordinating the completion of the rating forms, and scoring and interpreting the results. The user typically is involved, either individually or as a team member, in decision-making using the ABAS–II results in conjunction with other assessment results. Decisions may involve determining a diagnosis or classification and eligibility for special programs, planning interventions or treatment, and monitoring the effectiveness of a program. Individuals trained in the basic principles of psychological and educational assessment and test interpretation, the strengths and limitations of tests, and the use of assessment in data-based decision making are qualified to be professional users of the ABAS–II. The professional user should follow the practices described in the *Standards for Educational and Psychological Testing* (American Educational

Research Association, American Psychological Association, & National Council on Measurement in Education, 1999) and adhere to the ethical principles of associations of professionals that use educational and psychological tests.

The professional user may also supervise other service providers (e.g., paraprofessionals, aides) in the administration and scoring of the ABAS–II. Professional users are responsible for ensuring that other service providers have adequate training and supervision in administration and scoring, are able to provide appropriate answers to questions from the respondents, know when to refer questions to the professional users, and follow ethical and legal principles (e.g. confidentiality, test security). Professional users should provide structured and comprehensive training sessions prior to any administration and scoring activities by other service providers. The training sessions should provide many opportunities to discuss general assessment principles as well as ethical and legal standards, the purposes and uses of the ABAS–II, and specific techniques in administration and scoring. Administration and scoring activities should be carefully supervised at all times, and the work of other service providers should be checked to ensure that accurate results are obtained.

Although the respondent usually completes the rating forms independently, the professional user or another service provider may need to answer questions about the items. Rating forms facilitate communication between the professional user and the respondent by providing a place for the respondent to indicate that further comment is necessary on a particular item. Space is provided for respondents to record these comments or any other general comments they may have. This further communication between a respondent and assessment professional may afford an excellent opportunity to gain more clinical knowledge about the person being rated.

The application of professional ethical standards and principles for assessment practices is important for users of any psychological or educational assessment instrument, or any other technique for measuring human skills, behaviors, and traits. Protection of the individual's rights, use of valid and reliable assessment methods, and appropriate use of assessment results in decision-making are important principles for use of any assessment instrument, including the ABAS–II. Assessment results should be shared only with the individual being evaluated, his or her guardian(s), and/or others who have a legal right to know the information. Maintaining the security of the rating forms is important for maintaining the privacy of the individual being evaluated and for controlling the distribution of assessment items. Similarly, unused rating forms should be controlled by the professional user and should not be distributed without authorization.

Chapter 2

Administration and Scoring

The ABAS–II is easy to administer and score. The respondent may complete the rating forms independently or, if he or she does not have the skills necessary to read and rate the items independently, a trained service provider may administer the ABAS–II by reading the items aloud. After scoring a rating form, the professional user may obtain norm-referenced scores for the skill areas, adaptive domains, and the GAC (i.e., total score). This chapter provides information concerning the correct techniques to administer and score this assessment.

General Considerations

The professional user should initially consider several factors related to administration and interpretation, including selection of respondents, establishment of rapport and communication with respondents, use of other service providers for administering and scoring, and general issues in using behavior rating scales.

Selecting Respondents

The ABAS–II was designed to be completed by various respondents who have knowledge about the daily adaptive skills of an individual, and who have had extended and frequent opportunities to observe the individual's skills and responses to environmental demands. Careful selection of respondents is critical for obtaining valid ratings. Professional users should follow these guidelines when evaluating the qualifications of the respondent and his or her knowledge of the individual.

All Forms: Respondents generally should have the following qualifications: (a) frequent contact with the individual (e.g., almost everyday); (b) contacts of long duration (e.g., several hours for each contact); (c) recent contact (e.g., during the past 1 to 2 months); and (d) opportunities to observe the variety of skills measured by the ABAS–II.

Parent/Primary Caregiver Form (Ages 0–5): Respondents may include parents or other primary-care providers who are living with the child and are familiar with his or her daily activities. This could include grandparents, aunts or uncles, adult siblings, foster parents, and care providers from home living units in residential facilities.

Parent Form (Ages 5–21): Respondents may include parents or other primary-care providers who are living with the child and are familiar with his or her daily activities. This could include grandparents, aunts or uncles, adult siblings, foster parents, and care providers from home living units in residential facilities.

Teacher/Daycare Provider Form (Ages 2–5): Respondents may include teachers, daycare providers, nurses, or other personnel of daycares, schools, hospitals, or community programs for toddlers and young children. The respondent for the Teacher/Daycare Provider Form should be familiar with the child's adaptive skills in a structured school, daycare, or other service delivery setting.

Teacher Form (Ages 5–21): Respondents may include teachers, teacher's aides, or other school professionals or paraprofessionals. The respondent for the Teacher Form should be familiar with the child's adaptive skills in a structured classroom and school setting.

Adult Form (Ages 16–89): Respondents may include family members, counselors, professional caregivers in residential or non-residential facilities, work supervisors, aides, or other individuals in home or community settings who are familiar with the adult's daily activities. Individuals who display a high level of functioning may complete the form themselves.

Rapport and Communication With Respondents

Establishing and maintaining a rapport and communication with respondents is essential for obtaining valid results. The circumstances for administering the ABAS–II typically involve an individual who has been referred for assessment to determine if he or she has a disability or disorder and a need for intervention, such as special education, rehabilitation, treatment, or placement. Many respondents may not have previously participated in this type of assessment and may experience anxiety or have questions. The professional user should attempt to decrease a respondent's anxiety and provide information about the purpose of the assessment, the confidentiality of the respondent's ratings, how the results might be used to make diagnostic decisions about the individual, and who will have access to the results. Topics for discussion include:

Purpose of the overall assessment: Individuals who are rated with the ABAS–II are participating in a comprehensive assessment process to identify or diagnose a problem or disability, and to plan special services or programs. Explain the purpose of the overall assessment process to the respondent and answer his or her questions. For example, explain to a parent or family member by saying, "As you know, Jake has been experiencing difficulty in school. We are conducting a comprehensive assessment of Jake's skills in order to better understand his strengths and difficulties." Then provide details about the nature of the evaluation.

Reason for administering: Explain to the respondent the reason for administering the ABAS–II as part of the overall assessment. For example, say to a parent or family member, "An important part of Tonya's evaluation is to obtain information about the daily skills she has and needs to get along at home and other places, and you are an important person to give this type of information. We are asking you to complete the ABAS–II rating form so you can give us information about Tonya's daily skills."

Expectations for respondents: Determine if the respondent has sufficient knowledge of the individual's adaptive skills, is able to read and understand the directions and items, and will provide ratings that are honest and objective. Ask the respondent questions designed to determine if he or she understands the directions and has the knowledge and skills to rate the items appropriately. If the respondent does not have the necessary familiarity with the individual, the user should select one or more other respondents. If the respondent does not have the skills needed to read and respond to the items, administer the ABAS–II by reading the items aloud to the respondent. If a self rating on the Adult Form is being considered, it may be necessary to obtain background information or question the individual to determine if he or she is able to provide a valid rating of his or her own skills.

Explaining the instructions: provide a brief description of the items and instructions for completing the rating form, including the following points:

- The rating form describes many different types of skills, such as communication, eating, dressing, household, and safety skills. All of these skills are important for a person to take care of himself or herself and function well.

- Please read the directions on the form and mark your rating for each of the skills.

- Your ratings will tell us if (*individual's name*) is able to display these important daily skills independently and, if so, how often he or she does so when appropriate or needed.

- Circle **0** (*Is Not Able*), if (*individual's name*) cannot perform the activity or behavior described. Circle **0** if he/she cannot do it because he/she is not capable or does not have the ability.

- If (*individual's name*) is able to do it, then circle **1** (*Never or Almost Never When Needed*) to indicate that he/she never or almost never does it; or circle **2** (*Sometimes When Needed*) to indicate that he/she sometimes does it; or circle **3** (*Always or Almost Always When Needed*) to indicate that he/she always or almost always does it now, or that he/she accomplished it fully when younger.

- After you have circled **0**, **1**, **2**, or **3** for the item, evaluate whether you have observed (*individual's name*) perform the behavior or activity or if you are estimating or guessing about the frequency of the behavior. If your answer is based on an estimate or guess, place a check in the column under the heading **Check If You Guessed**.

- Please rate every item, even if some items do not seem to apply to (*individual's name*)'s age group or are difficult to rate.

- Please let me know if you have any questions or need my help while you are completing the form. If you have a question about an item, you may also put a check in the last column under the heading **Comments**, and talk to me about it when you are done. Also, feel free to put any comments you have in the **Notes** box on page 10 of the rating form.

- For some respondents, especially parents or primary care-providers for children, it may be important to add, "Please know that the items on this scale cover a wide age range. (*individual's name*) is not expected to have all the skills described in the items. It is important that you give factual information about the skills that he/she does and does not have."

Wait for the respondent to read the Directions on the second and third pages of the rating form and provide additional instruction and assistance if necessary.

Identify for the respondent those skill areas that should be completed, depending on which form is being used and the age of the individual being rated. Refer to the following guidelines:

- Explain to a respondent who is completing the Parent/Primary Caregiver Form for a child who is younger than 12 months old that he or she should complete only those skill areas specified for this age range. He or she should not provide ratings for the Community Use, Functional Pre-Academics, or Home Living skill areas.

- Remind a respondent who is completing the Teacher/Daycare Provider Form that he or she should provide ratings for all items in all skill areas.

- Remind respondents who are completing the Parent and Teacher Forms (Ages 5–21) and the Adult Form that he or she should provide ratings for all items with the exception of the Work Skill Area. The Work Skill Area is completed only if the individual is 17–21 years old (Parent and Teacher Forms) or 16–74 years old (Adult Form) and has a part- or full-time job.

Answering respondent's questions: Users may answer a respondent's questions before, during, and after completion of the rating form. Some questions may relate to the instructions for completing the rating forms; other questions may relate to the individual's problems or to services available for the individual and his or her family. Answer questions with as much detail as possible, and provide instruction that will allow the respondent to provide the most reliable and valid information about the individual's performance of the activities and behaviors as described in the assessment items. Refer to Table 2.1 for a list of frequently asked questions and appropriate answers.

Table 2.1   Frequently Asked Questions and Answers

Questions	Answers
If I am not sure how to rate an item, may I leave it blank?	No, please respond to *all* items. Evaluate if you have observed the behavior or whether you are estimating, or guessing, about the frequency of behavior. If your answer is based on an estimate, place a check in the column under the heading **Check If You Guessed**.
What if (*individual's name*) is too young to perform this activity?	Circle **0** (Is Not Able) if (*individual's name*) is too young to perform the activity.
What if (*individual's name*) has a disability or condition that prevents performance of this activity?	Circle **0** (Is Not Able) if (*individual's name*) has a disability or condition that prevents performance of the activity.
What if (*individual's name*) is able to perform this activity, but needs reminders or prompting to perform it?	Because he/she is able to perform the activity do not circle **0**. Circle **1** if he/she never or almost never performs it on his/her own without reminders or prompting. Circle **2** if he/she only sometimes performs it on his/her own without reminders or prompting. You should only circle **3** if he/she performs the activity most of the time on his/her own without reminders or prompting. (Professional users may elect to ask respondents to note if the individual needs reminding or prompting).
What if (*individual's name*) is not able to perform this activity by himself or herself, but needs help or assistance from another person?	Unless specifically noted otherwise in an item, the focus is on independent behavior, that is, when the individual is able to perform the activity or behavior without assistance or help. Thus, circle **0** if the individual is not able to perform this activity by himself or herself, but needs help or assistance from another person. (Professional users may elect to ask respondents to note if the client needs assistance or help).
What if (*individual's name*) performed this activity by himself or herself at a younger age, but now has outgrown it?	Circle **3** if he/she accomplished the activity fully when younger, but is now too old for the activity. However, if the activity is still appropriate for his/her age, rate the item according to what he/she does now.
What if (*individual's name*) has never had an opportunity to perform this activity?	There may be several reasons that a person does not have an opportunity to perform an activity, for example, the environment in which he/she is in does not have this type of activity or a parent does not allow the activity. In this case, the respondent should be instructed to estimate, or guess, about the individual's performance of the activity and to rate the item according to whether or not (*individual's name*) would be able to perform the activity or behavior described if given the opportunity, and if so, how often would he or she perform it when needed.
Some respondents may ask questions about an item itself, for example, if he or she does not understand the item.	Provide information that will enable a respondent to understand the meaning of an item, but be cautious not to provide information that may influence the respondent's ratings.

Completion of the rating form off-site: Although it is preferable for the rating form to be completed in a controlled setting such as a clinic, school, or agency office, some circumstances may require that the respondent complete the rating form off-site. Teachers, daycare providers, or other staff in classrooms, school libraries, or offices often complete the Teacher/Daycare Provider or Teacher Forms during free time. Respondents for the Parent/Primary Caregiver and Parent Forms and the Adult Form may need to complete the rating forms at home or another location.

Before forms are taken off-site, it is important to provide information, instructions, and safeguards to ensure that the off-site completion is valid and appropriate. Discuss all necessary instructions and provide contact information in case questions arise. Supply the respondent with information about when and where the rating form should be returned.

Remind respondents to indicate questions about an item by checking the **Comments** column, and by recording their comments in the **Notes** box on page 10 of the rating form. When the form is returned, review (in person or by telephone) any items the respondent has checked for comments, as well as any comments they have written.

If a rating form is to be mailed to a respondent, either write or verbally discuss the necessary information about the overall assessment and instructions for completing and returning the rating form.

Multiple Respondents

Whenever possible, professional users should obtain ratings from multiple respondents. Using multiple sources of information about an individual improves the validity of the assessment and can provide information about the individual's skills in a variety of settings and in response to various environmental demands. Use of multiple respondents can provide information about the degree of consistency of an individual's adaptive skills across settings, in response to different environmental demands, and from the unique perspectives of different respondents.

Information gathered from multiple respondents indicates the consistency or inconsistency of an individual's adaptive skills. This information improves decision-making about diagnosis of disabilities or disorders and assists in the planning of programs and services. The following examples demonstrate various assessments using multiple respondents.

- To assess a child using either the infant-preschool or school-age forms, obtain ratings from a parent or primary care provider and a teacher or daycare provider.
- To assess a child using the infant-preschool or school-age forms, obtain ratings from two or more teachers (e.g., general education teacher and special education teacher) and/or daycare providers.
- To assess an adult living at home, obtain a self-rating and ratings from a family member or other person living with or supervising the adult.
- To assess an adult living in a residential facility, obtain ratings from two or more care providers or supervisors (e.g., the care providers for the day and night shifts, or the work supervisor and the residential care provider).

When a Respondent Completes Rating Forms for More Than One Individual

It is possible that one respondent may be requested to rate multiple individuals. For example, a teacher may be asked to complete rating forms for several children in his or her classroom who have mental retardation or other disabilities. A care provider for adults in a residential-care facility or group home may be requested to complete rating forms for several adults in his or her care. If a respondent is asked to evaluate several individuals, instruct the respondent to complete the ratings for each individual independently and to focus carefully on only that individual's adaptive skills. It is recommended that a respondent take a break after the completion of each rating form to increase the independence of his or her rating for each individual.

General Issues in Rating Scale Assessment

The ABAS–II is designed to assess an individual's typical daily adaptive skills. The rating scale approach has many advantages for assessing adaptive skills: it provides for a comprehensive assessment of numerous adaptive skills, it involves relevant respondents in the assessment process, it obtains information from multiple perspectives and sources of information, and it focuses on adaptive skills occurring in naturalistic settings.

Another assessment technique, direct testing of an individual's abilities, is used for the evaluation of traits such as intelligence and academic ability. However, direct testing of adaptive skills would result in a measure of the individual's abilities in a structured-test environment only and, unlike a rating scale, would not provide information about the individual's actual behaviors in a home, school, community, or work setting. Structured observations of an individual's behavior by a trained observer provide another type of behavior assessment that can be used to evaluate some daily adaptive skills. However, numerous observations in multiple settings over a long period of time would be required to assess the comprehensive variety of adaptive skills used on a daily basis. Thus, a rating scale approach is considered to be the most valid, practical, and efficient technique for assessing adaptive skills. Users of such rating scales should be familiar with the important issues in rating scale assessment; should promote valid responses to the rating scale by respondents, and should take these issues into account when interpreting and using the results.

Gresham and Elliott (1990) provide an excellent summary of important issues regarding the administration, scoring, and interpretation of rating scales. A respondent's ratings for individual items on a rating scale reflect a summary of the relative frequency, rather than exact frequency, of the individual's skills. For example, if a respondent rates the item, "Controls temper when disagreeing with friends" as *Always When Needed*, the rating indicates the respondent's overall summary of this type of skill. A respondent's ratings reflect his or her own expectations and standards for skills, and these may differ from respondent to respondent and setting to setting. As a result, the use of multiple respondents will provide information from different perspectives. The ratings of a respondent may be influenced more by certain characteristics of the individual (e.g., appearance, ability, background) than by the trait being assessed. Above all, a respondent's ratings reflect his or her perceptions and willingness to be completely honest in communicating these perceptions. Careful administration combined with careful selection of respondents and properly established rapport and communication with the individual being evaluated will provide the most valid information.

Administration Guidelines

Materials and Setting

Administration requires the Parent/Primary Caregiver, Teacher/Daycare Provider, Parent, Teacher, or Adult Form and a pencil with an eraser. Provide the respondent with a chair and a table (or a clipboard or other writing surface). The respondent should complete the rating form in an environment as free from distractions as possible.

Completing the Demographics Section of the Rating Form

The demographics section located on the first page of the rating form provides important information about the individual being evaluated and about the respondent (see Figure 2.1). This section can be completed by the respondent or by the professional user. The professional user should verify the accuracy of the individual's date of birth and the current date.

ABAS® II
Adaptive Behavior
Assessment System®
SECOND EDITION

Patti L. Harrison
Thomas Oakland

Parent Form
Ages 5–21

CHILD INFORMATION

Child's Name: __Emily__ __R.__ __Sample__   Age: __9__   Grade: __4__
First   Middle   Last

School: __Larkspur Elementary__   City: __San Antonio__   State: __TX__

Sex: ☒ Female ☐ Male

	Month	Day	Year
Today's Date	10	15	2002
Date of Birth	5	4	1993

Does the child have any disabling conditions? ☐ Yes ☒ No

If yes, please describe: _____

Race/Ethnicity: ☐ African American   ☐ Asian   ☐ Native American
☐ Hispanic   ☒ White   ☐ Other: _____

The child has: ☒ No job   ☐ Part-time job   ☐ Full-time job

PARENT INFORMATION

Parent's Name: __Lauren__ __Sample__   Occupation: __Accountant__
First   Last

Number of siblings the child has at home:

☒ None   ☐ 1   ☐ 2   ☐ 3 or more

Your relationship to the child you are rating:

☒ Parent   ☐ Guardian   ☐ Other: _____

ISBN 015400461-8

Figure 2.1   Sample of the Demographic Section of the Parent Form (Ages 5–21)

Responding to and Recording Ratings for Items

Respondents should read and respond to all items and rate the extent to which the individual performs the adaptive skills when needed. The respondent should select and circle one of four ratings for each item: **0** (*Is Not Able*), **1** (*Never or Almost Never When Needed*), **2** (*Sometimes When Needed*), or **3** (*Always or Almost Always When Needed*). After the respondent provides a numeric rating for an item, he or she should place a check in the **Check if you Guessed** box if it was necessary to guess about the individual's performance for that item. A sample of a completed skill area of the Parent Form is shown in Figure 2.2.

Community Use						
1. Looks both ways before crossing a street or parking lot.	0	1	2	③	☐	○
2. Orders his/her own meals when eating out.	0	1	2	③	☐	○
3. Finds the restrooms in public places.	0	1	2	③	☐	○
4. Packs his/her own clothing and supplies for overnight trips.	0	1	②	3	☐	○
5. Uses the school or local library to check out books, use reference materials, or for other purposes.	0	1	2	③	☐	○
6. Follows another's directions to nearby places.	0	1	2	③	☐	○
7. Carries enough money to make small purchases, for example, a soft drink.	0	1	②	3	☐	○
8. Walks alone to friends' houses in the neighborhood.	0	1	2	③	☐	○
9. Mails letters at the postal box or local post office.	0	1	2	③	☐	○
10. Finds a specific department in a store or business, for example, customer service department in a bank or laundry supplies in a store.	0	1	2	③	☐	○
11. Walks or rides bike alone to locations within a one-mile or five-block radius of home or school.	0	1	2	③	☑	○
12. Carries personal identification when traveling to nearby places in the community.	0	①	2	3	☐	○
13. States general address of a travel destination, for example, "On Washington Avenue, near Lake Street."	0	1	②	3	☐	○
14. Asks other people's advice on where to shop.	0	1	②	3	☐	○
15. Finds and uses a pay phone.	0	1	②	3	☐	○
16. Asks store clerk for product information before buying an item.	0	1	②	3	☐	○
17. Relies on himself/herself for travel in the community, for example, walks or uses public transportation, a bicycle, or a car.	⓪	1	2	3	☐	○
18. Takes other people on trips to nearby places, for example, takes a younger child to a park.	⓪	1	2	3	☐	○
19. Tells others about a store's hours of operation, for example, "10 a.m. to 9 p.m."	0	1	②	3	☐	○
20. Shops for friends and family who may be unable to shop.	0	1	②	3	☐	○
21. Calls to find out if a repair or order is ready.	0	1	②	3	☐	○
22. Calls a repairperson if, for example, the air conditioner or heater is not working.	0	1	②	3	☐	○
23. Calls a doctor or hospital when ill or hurt.	0	1	②	3	☑	○

Total **50** / 69 Total Guessed **2**

④

Figure 2.2 Sample of a Completed Skill Area of the Parent Form (Ages 5–21)

Checking the Completed Rating Form

Following completion of the rating form by the respondent, the professional user should immediately check the form to determine that a rating was recorded for each item. If a respondent failed to record a rating for an item, the user should ask the respondent to provide a rating. All items in each appropriate skill area must be completed to compute the raw scores for the skill areas and to obtain normative scores. If a respondent indicates that he or she is uncertain about how to rate an item, tell the respondent to estimate or guess, and to place a check to indicate that he or she guessed on the item. Reassure respondents that guessing is appropriate and that many respondents guess about the ratings of a few items. If a respondent refuses to provide a rating even after encouragement, leave the rating blank and score the item **0** when raw scores are computed for the skill areas. Although not preferred, one or two items with no ratings per skill area may be allowed.

Administration by Reading the Items to Respondents

Most items on all rating forms require no more than a sixth-grade reading level. This is appropriate for the majority of the respondents. However, if a respondent does not have the skill to read and rate the items independently, read each item to the respondent and ask him or her to respond verbally. Many professional users may elect to read the items to respondents regardless of their reading level, especially if the respondents express anxiety about the individual being evaluated or nervousness about the assessment. Users may also wish to read items to a respondent as part of an overall interview about several aspects of the individual's adaptive skills. To administer the ABAS–II by reading the items to a respondent, refer to the following steps.

▶ **Step 1:** Ask the respondent the necessary questions to complete the demographic section of the rating form.

▶ **Step 2:** Read and explain the directions to the respondent. Answer the respondent's questions using the Explaining the Instructions section of this manual. Substitute phrases about the respondent reading and circling ratings for the items with phrases to indicate that the user will read and circle the ratings for each of the items. For example, the following are substitutions in the instructions used for the Parent Form.

> Instead of *Please read and answer all items,* say: **I will read the items to you.**

> Instead of *For each item, record your responses by circling one of the following,* say: **For each item, rate the child's skills by selecting one of the following ratings and telling me your rating. I will circle your rating in the rating form.**

> Instead of *If your answer is based on a guess, put a check in the column under the heading, Check if you Guessed,* say: **If your answer is based on a guess, tell me you guessed.**

▶ **Step 3:** Place an extra rating form, opened to the directions, in front of the respondent. As you read each rating, point to the ratings on the rating form. To ensure that the respondent understands the item ratings and other directions, it may be necessary to review the directions more than once.

▶ **Step 4:** Read each item verbatim and ask the respondent for his or her rating. For the first few items, point to the ratings on the respondent's rating form and say:

> **Would you say that** (*individual's name*) **is not able to do this, is able to but never does this, sometimes does this, or always does this? Please tell me if you needed to guess about this rating.**

When the respondent clearly understands how to rate the items and evaluate if he or she guessed, read each item and say: **Tell me (or point to) your rating.**

Scoring

Use the following procedures to obtain and record the scores for all five rating forms. (See Chapter 3 for information about interpretation and use of the scores.)

▶ **Step 1: Check the guessing factor**

Count the total number of guessed responses (as indicated by a check in the **Check if you Guessed** box next to the item rating) for each skill area and record the total in the box labeled Total Guessed. Most respondents in the national standardization sample guessed on 3 or fewer items for each skill area (refer to Tables A.3, A.7, A.11, and A.14). If the respondent guesses on four or more items in a skill area, interview the respondent to determine the reason for the large number of guessed responses and evaluate whether or not to continue scoring. If you decide to continue scoring and interpretation with the current respondent, report the higher than average number of guesses in all reports, multidisciplinary team discussions, and other venues in which the scores may be used to make decisions about the individual. If, after careful evaluation and interviewing of the respondent, you determine that the he or she does not have sufficient knowledge about the individual's skills, identify a new respondent who has more knowledge about the individual.

► Step 2: Add the item scores for each skill area to obtain the raw score

For *each* of the skill areas, sum the behavior frequencies (**1, 2,** or **3**) to obtain the raw score and record in the box labeled Total (see Figure 2.2). The total raw score should never be more than the maximum score indicated in this box. The number of skill areas to sum will vary depending on the type of rating form. Refer to Table 1.3 to determine the appropriate skill areas to sum.

► Step 3: Transfer the skill area raw scores to the Summary Page

Transfer the raw score for each skill area to the Raw Scores column of the Raw Score to Scaled Score Conversions table on the Summary Page of the rating form (**A** in Figure 2.3). Skill areas are listed in order of administration.

► Step 4: Obtain scaled scores for the skill areas

Using the individual's chronological age and the type of rating form, identify the appropriate norms table in Appendix A that contains the relevant scaled scores for the skill areas (Tables A.1, A.5, A.9, and A.12). For example, use Table A.1 to obtain the scaled scores for a child age 2 years 2 months whose respondent completed the Teacher/Daycare Provider Form. Use Table A.5 to obtain the scaled scores for a child age 10 years 3 months whose respondent completed the school-age Parent Form. Obtain the scaled scores for an adult age 30 years 8 months who completed a self report on the Adult Form by using Table A.9.

After identifying the appropriate table, locate the raw score for each skill area. Then, reading across from this raw score to the scaled score column, find the equivalent scaled score. Record the scaled score for each skill area on the Summary Page in the column to the right of the raw scores and in the remaining unshaded box in its row (**B** in Figure 2.3).

► Step 5: Obtain the standard scores for the GAC and adaptive domains

Sum the scaled scores of the skill areas used for the GAC and for each adaptive domain, and record in the Sums of Scaled Scores box (**C** in Figure 2.3). Transfer the sums of scaled scores to the Sum of Scaled Scores to Composite Score Conversions table on the Summary Page (**D** in Figure 2.3).

Note. The Parent/Primary Caregiver Form excludes the Community Use, Functional Pre-Academics, and Home Living Skill Areas for children ages birth–11 months. For this age range, adaptive domain composites and the GAC are calculated without these skill areas.

Note. The Work Skill Area is completed and scored only if the individual has a part- or full-time job. Scaled scores for Work are available for ages 17–21 years on the Parent and Teacher Forms as optional scores, but they are not included in the GAC. On these rating forms, the GAC is based on the remaining nine skill areas. The Work Skill Area scaled scores are available for ages 16–74 years on the Adult Form, and can be included in the GAC. On the Adult Form, the GAC may be based on ten skill areas (if the Work Skill Area was completed) or nine skill areas (if the Work Skill Area was not completed).

Note. The Work Skill Area scaled score is not included in the Practical Domain on the Parent or Teacher Forms. On the Adult Form, the Practical Domain may be based on five skill areas (if the Work Skill Area was completed) or four skill areas (if the Work Skill Area was not completed).

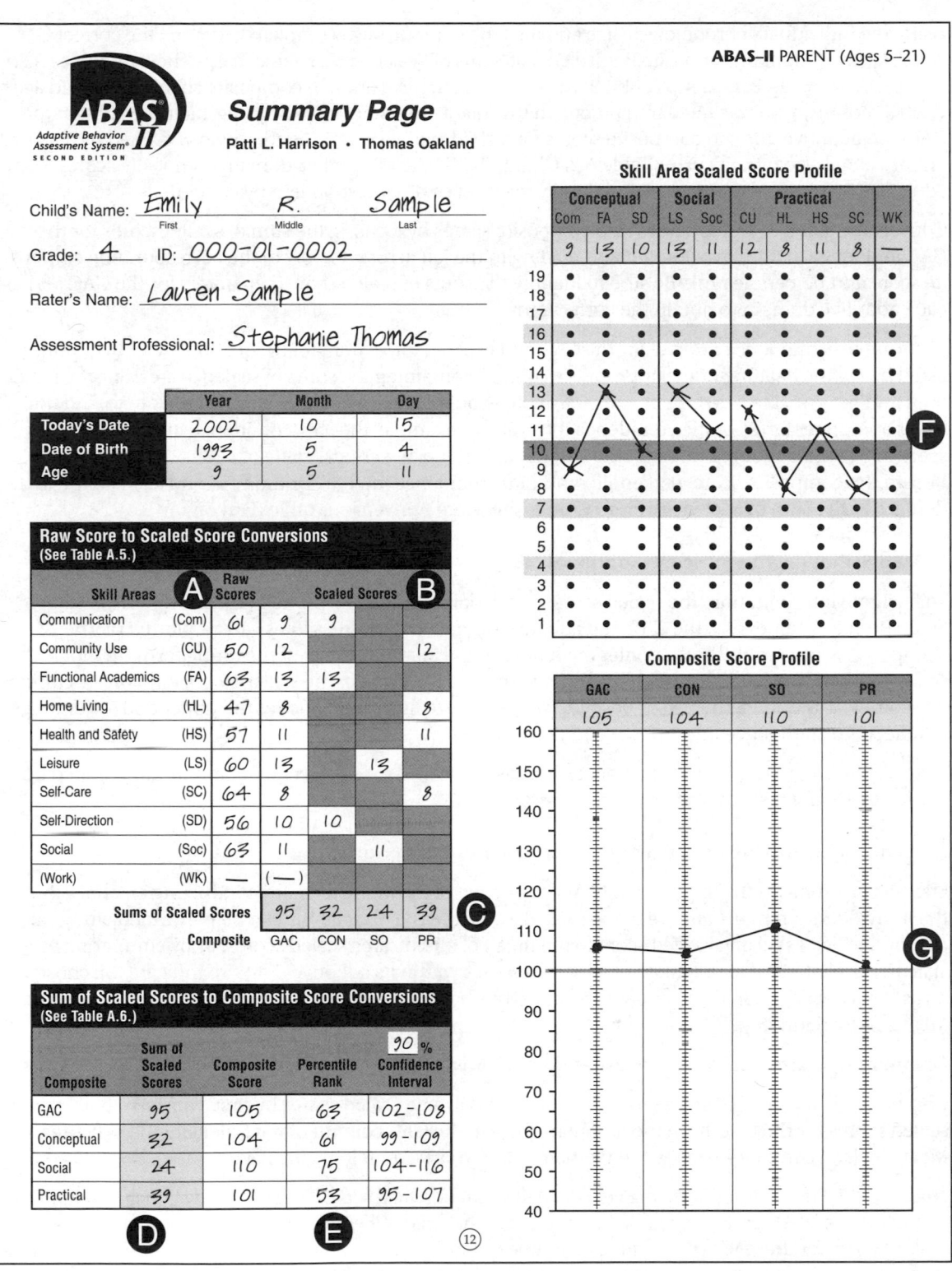

Figure 2.3 Sample of a Completed Summary Page of the Parent Form (Ages 5–21)

Using the individual's chronological age and the type of rating form completed, identify the correct GAC and Adaptive Domain Composite Equivalents of Sums of Scaled Scores Table in Appendix A (Tables A.2, A.6, A.10, and A.13). For example, obtain the GAC and adaptive domain composite scores for a child age 4 years 5 months, who was rated by a parent on the infant-preschool form by using Table A.6. Obtain the GAC and adaptive domain composite scores for a child age 14 years 5 months, who was rated by a teacher on the school-age form by using Table A.2. Obtain the GAC and adaptive domain composite scores for an adult, age 52 years, who was rated by a family member or other respondent by using Table A.13.

Convert the sums of scaled scores into composite scores by locating the sum of scaled scores for the GAC and for each adaptive domain and reading to the left across the row to the corresponding composite score and percentile rank. Be sure to identify the sums of scaled scores separately for the GAC and each adaptive domain to obtain the correct score.

Determine a confidence interval for the GAC and each adaptive domain by locating the critical values listed below the heading of the appropriate column containing the sums of scaled scores. Subtract and then add the critical value for either a 90% or 95% confidence level to the composite score to find the lower and upper limits of the confidence interval. For example, the 95% confidence interval of a GAC score of 93 for a 5 year old rated on the Parent Form is 93± the critical value of 4 (89–97; see Table A.6). Record the composite score, percentile rank, and confidence interval for the GAC and each adaptive domain in the Sum of Scaled Scores to Composite Score Conversions table (**E** in Figure 2.3).

▶ Step 6: Plot profiles of scores (optional)

To facilitate interpretation, the scaled scores of the skill areas can be plotted on the Skill Area Scaled Score Profile. Additionally, the GAC and adaptive domain composite scores can be plotted on the Composite Score Profile. Both profiles are found on the Summary Page of the rating form. To plot a score, mark the point on the graph that corresponds to the value of the skill area scaled score or composite score (**F** and **G** in Figure 2.3). If desired, you may place horizontal lines at the upper and lower ranges to reflect the confidence intervals for composite scores.

Note. To further assist in interpretation, skill areas in the Skill Area Scaled Score Profile are grouped by adaptive domain instead of administration order.

▶ Step 7: Identify skill area strengths and weaknesses (optional)

Space is provided on the Supplemental Analyses page of the rating form for conducting an analysis of the individual's strengths and weaknesses across skill areas. This analysis can be performed either by comparing each skill area scaled score to the mean of all skill area scaled scores, or by comparing each skill area scaled score to the mean of all scaled scores within its adaptive domain. Indicate the chosen basis for comparison in the Comparison Group box by marking the box next to GAC Mean or Domain Means (**A** in Figure 2.4).

Compare skill area scaled scores using the GAC Mean.

Compare skill area scaled scores to the mean of all skill area scaled scores by first transferring the sum of scaled scores for the GAC from the Summary Page to the GAC column of the Calculate the Skill Area Mean Scaled Scores table on the Supplemental Analyses page (**B** in Figure 2.4).

Note. For the Parent/Primary Caregiver Form, the sum of scaled scores for the GAC will include either seven or ten scaled scores, depending on the age of the child. When using the Adult Form, the sum of scaled scores for the GAC will include either nine or ten scaled scores, depending on whether or not Work was included. These rating forms provide alternate columns in which to transfer the sum of scaled scores for the GAC. Transfer the sum to the appropriate column depending on the number of skill areas included in the GAC.

Divide the sum of scaled scores by the total number of skill areas summed, indicated below the sum of scaled scores. Record the mean scaled score (*MSS*) in the last row of the Calculate the Skill Area Mean Scaled Scores table. Record the *MSS* to two decimal places.

Transfer the skill area scaled scores from the Summary Page to the Determining Strengths and Weaknesses table on the Supplemental Analyses page. Then transfer the *MSS* to the right of each skill area scaled score. For each skill area, compute the difference score by subtracting the *MSS* from the scaled score. Enter the difference score for each skill area in the Difference from Mean column (**C** in Figure 2.4).

Use Table B.1, B.8, B.15, or B.22 in Appendix B to evaluate the statistical and clinical significance of the difference score. These tables provide the critical values required for the difference score to be statistically significant at the .15 and .05 levels. Indicate the chosen level in the Statistical Significance Level box on the Supplemental Analyses page, and record the critical value for each skill area. If the absolute value of the difference score is equal to or greater than this critical value, it is considered statistically significant. Tables B.1, B.8, B.15, or B.22 also provide the frequencies of difference scores obtained by the standardization sample (base rates) by indicating the difference scores obtained by 1%, 2%, 5%, 10%, and 25% of the sample. When a difference score is both significant and infrequent, note whether the skill area reflects a relative strength (S) or weakness (W) (**D** in Figure 2.4). If the score is a positive value, it reflects a strength; if the score is a negative value, it reflects a weakness. Refer to Chapter 3 for a detailed description of this analysis.

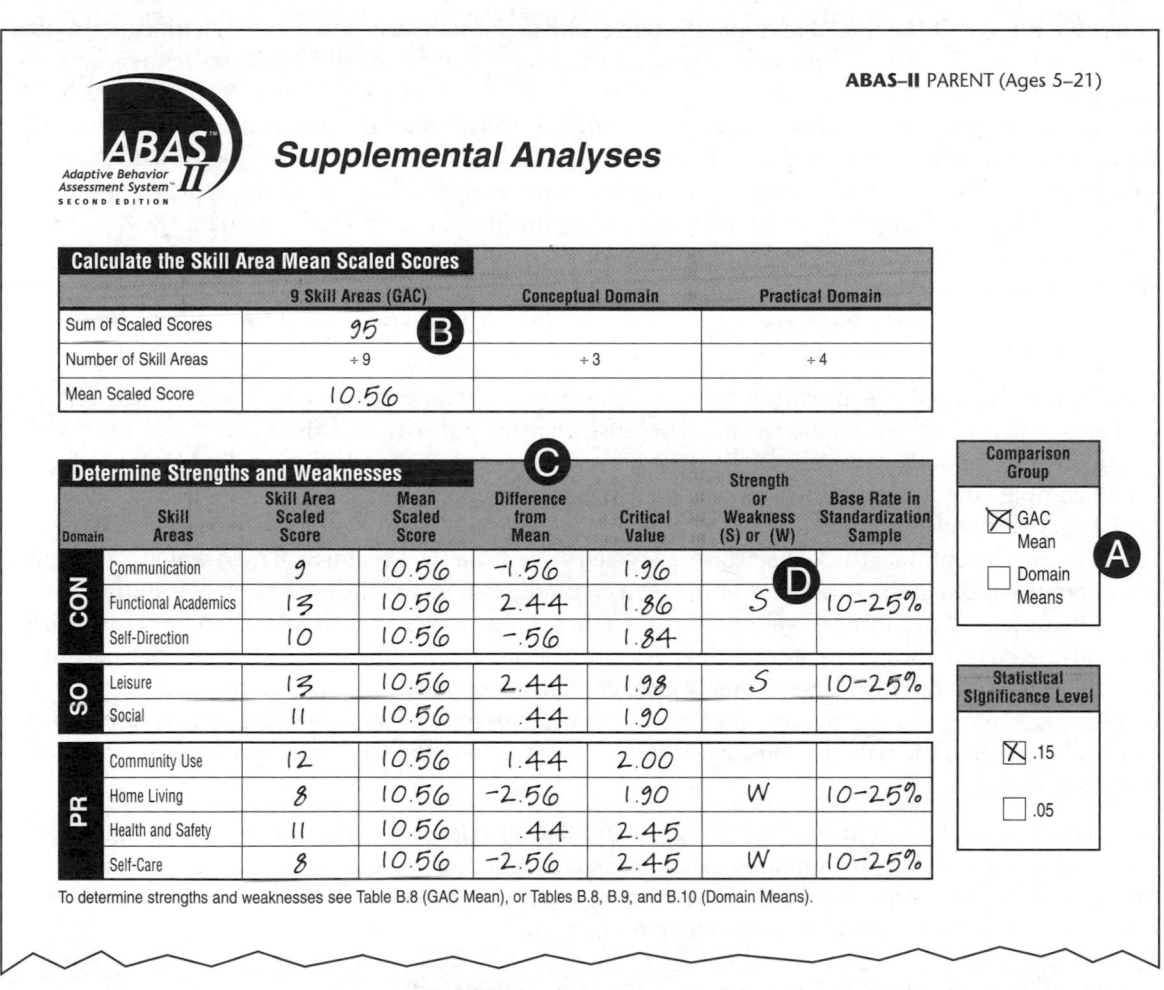

Figure 2.4   Sample of a Completed Strength/Weakness Analysis Using the GAC Mean

Compare skill area scaled scores using the domain means.

Compare each skill area scaled score to the mean of skill area scaled scores within its adaptive domain by first transferring the sum of scaled scores for the Conceptual (CON) and Practical (PR) Domains from the Summary Page to the appropriate columns of the Calculate the Skill Area Mean Scaled Scores table on the Supplemental Analyses page (**A** in Figure 2.5).

Note. When using the Adult Form, the sum of scaled scores for the Practical Domain will include either four or five scaled scores, depending on whether or not the Work Skill Area was included. Transfer the sum to the correct column, depending on the number of skill areas included in the Practical Domain.

Divide the sum of scaled scores by the total number of skill areas summed, indicated below each sum of scaled scores. Record the *MSS* in the last row of the Calculate the Skill Area Mean Scaled Scores table.

Transfer the skill area scaled scores from the Summary Page to the Determining Strengths and Weaknesses table. Then transfer the *MSS* for the Social and Practical domains to the right of the skill areas included in each domain. Each domain may have a different *MSS*. For *each* skill area, excluding Leisure and Social, compute the difference score by subtracting the *MSS* from the scaled score. Enter the difference score in the Difference from Mean column (**B** in Figure 2.5).

Use Table B.1, B.8, B.15, or B.22 in Appendix B to evaluate the statistical and clinical significance of the difference score. These tables provide the critical values required for the difference score to be statistically significant at the .15 and .05 levels. Indicate the chosen level in the Statistical Significance Level box on the Supplemental Analyses page, and record the critical value for each skill area. If the absolute value of the difference score is equal to or greater than this critical value, it is considered statistically significant. Tables B.1, B.8, B.15, and B.22 also provide the frequencies of difference scores obtained by the standardization sample (base rates) by indicating the difference scores obtained by 1%, 2%, 5%, 10%, and 25% of the sample. When a difference score is significant and infrequent, note whether the skill area reflects a relative strength (S) or weakness (W) (**C** in Figure 2.5). If the score is a positive value, it reflects a strength; if the score is a negative value, it reflects a weakness. Refer to Chapter 3 for a detailed description of this analysis.

On all forms, skill area scaled scores from the Social Domain (SO) cannot be compared to the mean of skill area scaled scores within their domain because there are only two skill areas in the Social Domain. Therefore, to conduct a domain-specific strength/weakness analysis for the Social and Leisure Skill Areas, compare the two subtests to each other. For example, to compare Leisure to Social, record the Social Skill Area scaled score in the *MSS* column of the Determining Strengths and Weaknesses table (**D** in Figure 2.5). Subtract the Social Skill Area scaled score from the Leisure Skill Area scaled score. Enter the difference score in the Difference from Mean column. Then record the critical value from Table B.2, B.9, B.16, or B.23. If the absolute value of the difference score is equal to or greater than this critical value, it is considered statistically significant. Tables B.3, B.10, B.17, and B.24 provide the cumulative percentages (base rates) of inter-skill area scatter within domains obtained by the standardization sample. When a difference score is significant and infrequent, note whether the skill area reflects a relative strength (S) or weakness (W). If the score is a positive value, it reflects a strength; if the score is a negative value, it reflects a weakness.

Note. When using the Parent/Primary Caregiver and Teacher/Daycare Provider Forms, a strength/weakness analysis using adaptive domain means cannot be conducted for the Motor Skill Area because it is not included in any adaptive domain. Therefore, a strength/weakness analysis for Motor can only be conducted using the GAC *MSS* as a basis for comparison.

▶ Step 8: Compare adaptive domain composite scores (optional)

Space is provided on the Supplemental Analyses page of the rating form for conducting an analysis of discrepancies in the individual's functioning in different adaptive domains.

Transfer the composite scores of the two domains being compared into the Score 1 and Score 2 columns of the Discrepancy Comparisons table (**E** in Figure 2.5). Subtract score 2 from score 1 and record the result in the Difference column.

Supplemental Analyses

Calculate the Skill Area Mean Scaled Scores

	9 Skill Areas (GAC)	Conceptual Domain 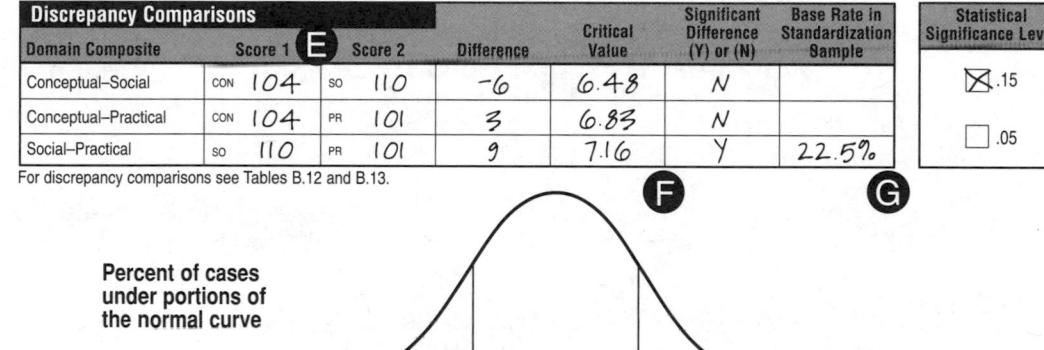	Practical Domain
Sum of Scaled Scores		32	39
Number of Skill Areas	÷ 9	÷ 3	÷ 4
Mean Scaled Score		10.67	9.75

Determine Strengths and Weaknesses

Domain	Skill Areas	Skill Area Scaled Score	Mean Scaled Score	Difference from Mean	Critical Value	Strength or Weakness (S) or (W)	Base Rate in Standardization Sample
CON	Communication	9	10.67	-1.67	1.36	W	25%
CON	Functional Academics	13	10.67	2.33	1.32	S	10%
CON	Self-Direction	10	10.67	-.67	1.31		
SO	Leisure	13	11	2	1.75		47.2%
SO	Social	11	13	-2	1.75		47.2%
PR	Community Use	12	9.75	2.25	1.66	S	10–25%
PR	Home Living	8	9.75	-1.75	1.61		>25%
PR	Health and Safety	11	9.75	1.25	1.94		
PR	Self-Care	8	9.75	-1.75	1.94		

Comparison Group
- ☐ GAC Mean
- ☒ Domain Means

Statistical Significance Level
- ☒ .15
- ☐ .05

To determine strengths and weaknesses see Table B.8 (GAC Mean), or Tables B.8, B.9, and B.10 (Domain Means).

Discrepancy Comparisons

Domain Composite	Score 1		Score 2		Difference	Critical Value	Significant Difference (Y) or (N)	Base Rate in Standardization Sample
Conceptual–Social	CON	104	SO	110	-6	6.48	N	
Conceptual–Practical	CON	104	PR	101	3	6.83	N	
Social–Practical	SO	110	PR	101	9	7.16	Y	22.5%

Statistical Significance Level
- ☒ .15
- ☐ .05

For discrepancy comparisons see Tables B.12 and B.13.

Percent of cases under portions of the normal curve

Percent of Cases	2.2	6.7	16.1	50	16.1	6.7	2.2
Standard Scores	70	80	90	100	110	120	130
Qualitative Descriptions	Extremely Low	Borderline	Below Average	Average	Above Average	Superior	Very Superior
GAC/Composite Score Ranges	≤70	71–79	80–89	90–109	110–119	120–129	≥130

⑪

Figure 2.5   Sample of a Completed Strength/Weakness Analysis Using Domain Means and a Completed Discrepancy Comparison

Evaluate the statistical and clinical significance of the difference. If the absolute value of the composite pair difference score is equal to or greater than the critical value in Table B.5, B.12, B.19, or B.26, it is considered statistically significant. Record the critical value, and indicate with a (Y) or (N) whether the discrepancy is statistically significant (**F** in Figure 2.5).

Tables B.6, B.13, B.20, and B.27 provide cumulative percentages (base rates) of the sample that obtained each difference score. Base rates are provided separately for each direction of the discrepancy (i.e., CON>PR and CON<PR). This is because the direction of the difference between scores influences interpretation, and given the same absolute value, the base rates for two directions may be quite different. Record the frequency of each statistically significant composite pair difference in the Base Rate in Standardization Sample column of the Discrepancy Comparisons table (**G** in Figure 2.5). Refer to Chapter 3 for a detailed description of this analysis.

►Step 9: Obtain the test-age equivalents of skill area raw scores (optional)

Use Table A.4 or A.8 to obtain the test-age equivalents of skill area raw scores for the infant-preschool or school-age forms. Locate the appropriate raw score for the skill area and read across from the raw score to the Test Age column of the table to identify the test-age equivalent. Repeat this procedure for each skill area. When using the infant-preschool forms, if an obtained raw score is beyond the limits found on the table, record the test age as "greater than 6 years" for a score greater than the upper limit of the raw score. When using the school-age forms, if an obtained raw score is beyond the limits found on the table, record the test age as "less than 5 years" for a score less than the lower limit of the raw score. In addition, record the test age as "greater than 21 years" for a score greater than the upper limit of the raw score.

To obtain a mean test age, sum the test ages and divide by the number of skill areas. To obtain a median test age, distribute the test ages in rank order and find the central value.

Note. Test ages are highly criticized and should be used with great caution, if at all. Refer to Chapter 3 for more information.

Chapter 3

Interpretations and Interventions

The ABAS–II measures skills that are important to everyday life. The need to communicate, display suitable social and academic skills, function effectively at home and in the community, engage in leisure and work, and care for individual health and safety needs begins early in life and remains important until death. Centuries ago, the Greeks believed that the skills required to care for one's self, engage in important life activities, and assist others represented an individual's level of intelligence and maturity (Clarke, Clarke, & Berg, 1985). These skills remain critical for everyday functioning today.

The range of adaptive skills displayed by individuals within a society is broad. Most individuals have sufficient adaptive skills necessary to function independently. Some individuals have one or more deficits that interfere with daily functions. Deficits in adaptive skills often are apparent in individuals diagnosed with medical problems (e.g., Alzheimer's disease, Autistic Disorder, brain injury, dementia, developmental delays, and heart/pulmonary disorders) and psychological disorders (e.g., attention-deficit disorders, behavior disorders, learning disabilities, psychoses, and substance abuse). Individuals diagnosed with mental retardation constitute a large and important segment of those with disorders who display deficiencies in adaptive behavior (AAMR, 1992, 2002b; *DSM–IV–TR*; IDEA, 1999).

A primary purpose of the ABAS–II is to comprehensively, validly, and reliably describe the degree to which individuals display normal adaptive behavior and skills. Thus, emphasis is placed on describing an individual's general adaptive behavior, behaviors associated with the three adaptive domains (e.g., conceptual, practical, and social), and ten skill areas. This information can be used to identify areas of strengths and weaknesses in addition to specific adaptive skills that need further development in order to advance independence and interdependence, increase productivity and effectiveness, and promote feelings of worth. Information from the ABAS–II also can assist in diagnosis and classification, program planning and monitoring, institutional planning, and research activities. This chapter discusses the types of scores used to describe ABAS–II data, provides descriptive classifications for different levels of development, outlines guidelines for interpreting scores, recommends strategies for using ABAS–II data, and provides case studies.

Description of Scores

Normative scores are provided for skill areas, adaptive domains, and the GAC. Scaled scores are derived from the raw scores of each of the skill areas. These scaled scores are used to derive standard scores for the adaptive domain scores and the GAC. The conversion of raw scores into normative scores enables users to interpret scores within the ABAS–II, and between the ABAS–II and other measures. Scaled scores of the skill areas and composite scores of the three adaptive domains and the GAC are age-corrected standard scores that enable the user to compare each individual's adaptive skill with other individuals in the same age group.

The GAC is derived from the sum of scaled scores from seven, nine, or ten skill areas, depending on the age of the individual and the type of rating form. The Conceptual Domain score is derived from the sum of scaled scores from the Communication, Functional Academics, and Self-Direction Skill Areas. The Social Domain score is derived from the sum of scaled scores from the Social and Leisure Skill Areas. The Practical Domain score is derived from the sum of scaled scores from the Self-Care, Home/School Living, Community Use, Health and Safety, and Work (if administered on the Adult Form) Skill Areas.

For children younger than 1 year, rated using the Parent/Primary Caregiver Form, the Conceptual Domain does not include the Functional Pre-Academics Skill Area and the Practical Domain does not include the Community Use and Home/School Living Skill Areas. The Teacher/Daycare Provider Form does not include the Community Use Skill Area for any age. For young children rated using either infant-preschool form, the Motor Skill Area scaled score contributes to the GAC but does not contribute to any of the adaptive domains. The Work scaled score does not contribute to the GAC or the Practical Domain on the Parent and Teacher Forms and is included in these scores on the Adult Form only when the individual being evaluated has a part- or full-time job (refer to Table 1.3).

Distribution of the Skill Area Scaled Scores

The distribution of scaled scores of each of the skill areas has a mean of 10 and a standard deviation of 3. A scaled score of 10 defines the average (mean) performance of a given age group. Scaled scores of 7 and 13 deviate 1 *SD* from the mean and scaled scores of 4 and 16 deviate 2 *SD*s from the mean. For example, individuals who obtain a scaled score of 7 for a skill area perform 1 *SD* below the mean of individuals in the same age group.

When interpreting scaled scores, professional users must be aware that the distributions of skill area raw scores are skewed due to the natural ceiling that is reached as skills are acquired throughout the lifespan. Although the theoretical floor and ceiling of the scaled scores are 1 and 19, the highest scaled scores obtainable on skill areas often are less than 19 due to the skewed nature of the distribution. Skewness is found in all measures of adaptive behavior (Reschly, Myers, & Hartel, 2002; Schalock, 1999).

Theoretically, if the skill area score distributions had met the properties of the normal curve and had not been skewed, about 68% of individuals assessed with the ABAS–II should have scaled scores within 1 *SD* of the mean and 95% should have scaled scores within 2 *SD*s of the mean (Anastasi & Urbina, 1997). Although necessary and conventional procedures were used to normalize the distribution of the standardization sample, only limited normalization corrections could be completed. Therefore, the percent of the standardization samples that falls within 1 or 2 *SD*s of the mean is not perfectly consistent with that of a normal distribution. Nevertheless, the validity and reliability studies reported in Chapter 5 indicate that the skill area scaled scores can accurately reflect an individual's adaptive skills and can be compared to those of his or her peers in the same age group. Many efforts were made to ensure that the skill area scaled scores are consistent with other measurements of adaptive skills and intelligence, especially at key clinical decision points (e.g., at 2 *SD*s below the mean).

Distributions of the Adaptive Domain and GAC Standard Scores

The distribution of scores of the three adaptive domains and the GAC has a mean of 100 and a standard deviation of 15. A score of 100 defines the average performance of a given age group. Scores of 85 and 115 deviate 1 *SD* from the mean and scores of 70 and 130 deviate 2 *SD*s from the mean. In contrast to the scaled scores of the skill areas, the distribution of scores on the three adaptive domains and the GAC closely approximates the normal distribution. For example, approximately 68% of individuals assessed with the ABAS–II should have a GAC score within 1 *SD* of the mean, and 95% should have GAC scores within 2 *SD*s of the mean.

Although the reliabilities of the adaptive domain and GAC scores generally are very high, the ability to determine differences between individuals with high scores decreases as the scores reach the ceiling of their scale. Because the adaptive skills of infants and younger children are still in the early stages of development, their adaptive domain and GAC scores do not show a ceiling effect, and can be classified as either *Superior* or *Very Superior*. However, adaptive domain and GAC scores of older children and adults cannot differentiate those with *Superior* and *Very Superior* adaptive skills with high accuracy. To prevent misinterpretation, this manual contains normative data only for the ranges of scores that have high accuracy and can be interpreted meaningfully. The highest adaptive domain/GAC score obtainable is 160 for ages 0–5 years on the infant-preschool forms; 130 for ages 5–7 years on the school-age forms; and 120 for ages 8–89 years on the school-age forms or Adult Form. The ABAS–II is not designed to assess adaptive skill levels above these score points.

The ABAS–II typically is used to assess the adaptive skill development of those who display below average to average development. The focus of the ABAS–II is on the assessment of the basic adaptive skills that are necessary for an individual to function effectively in most environments. Its purpose is not to assess talents or specialized skills needed in certain environments or in response to high-level or unusual expectations or demands. The ABAS–II, like other measures of adaptive behavior, is rarely used to identify individuals with superior levels of adaptive development or skills (Reschly, Myers, & Hartel, 2002). Thus, limiting standard scores on the ABAS–II to 120 or 130 does not compromise its typical use for diagnosis of disabilities or disorders.

In general, standard scores provide the most accurate description of test data. However, individuals who are inexperienced in interpreting test data may find standard scores difficult to understand. Thus, other methods (e.g., percentiles and test-age equivalents) often are used in conjunction with standard scores to describe an individual's performance.

Percentile Ranks

Age-based percentile ranks are provided for the adaptive domains and GAC. Percentile ranks indicate an individual's standing relative to other individuals of the same age. Percentile ranks reflect points on a scale below which a given percentage of scores fall, based on the standardization sample. Percentile ranks typically range from 1 to 99, with 50 as the mean and median. For example, individuals with a percentile rank of 15 obtain scores as high or higher than the scores of 15% of other individuals the same age.

Although easy to understand and useful for explaining an individual's performance relative to that of others, percentile ranks have various limitations. Percentile ranks do not have equal intervals. Percentile ranks in a normal distribution, such as the GAC, tend to cluster near the median (the 50th percentile). Therefore, for individuals who score within the average range, a change of one or two raw score points may produce a large change in their percentile ranks. However, for those with more extreme scores, a change of one or two raw score points is not likely to produce a sizable change in their percentile ranks.

Test-Age Equivalents

Test-age equivalents represent the average age in years and months at which a given raw score is typical. For example, on the Teacher Form, a raw score of 49 on the Communication Skill Area corresponds to a test-age equivalent of 5:8–5:11 (i.e. 5 years 8 months through 5 years 11 months). This means that a child who obtains this raw score is functioning at the level of a typical child in the 5:8–5:11 age range in this skill area. A higher raw score of 59 on the Communication Skill Area corresponds to a higher test-age equivalent of 10:8–10:11. Test-age equivalents are provided for the Teacher/Daycare Provider, Teacher, Parent/Primary Caregiver, and Parent Forms in Appendix A (Tables A.4 and A.8).

Although test-age equivalents help professional users compare an individual's adaptive skill development to adaptive skill levels typical of various ages, they have limitations when used as part of any assessment instrument (American Educational Research Association, 1999) Test-age equivalents may not be comparable across skill areas. For example, if an individual has test-age equivalents of 7:8–7:11 on the Community Use and Functional Academics Skill Areas, it does not indicate that the individual is equally proficient in both of these skill areas. In addition, test-age equivalents do not form equally spaced units or intervals throughout a scale. Thus, small raw score changes may result in large changes in test-age equivalents.

Clinical decisions about the equivalency of scores should be made from a review of the individual's scaled scores, not the test-age equivalents. Individuals should not be diagnosed or placed in schools or other environments based on their test-age equivalents. Diagnostic decisions typically consider standard scores and various other qualities of the individual (e.g., age, academic aptitude and achievement, physical or acuity limitations) combined with personal choices and environmental expectations and resources. Although notable differences between test-age equivalents and an individual's chronological age may be obtained, an interpretation of an individual's test-age equivalents such as "her adaptive skills are far below or above average for her age" are unwarranted. Test-age equivalents that are very low or high compared to an individual's chronological age do not indicate that the individual's adaptive skills resemble those of the much older or younger age group in every way.

Finally and most importantly, test-age equivalents provide little information about an individual's standing relative to other individuals the same age. A 9-year-old child who obtains a test-age equivalent of 7:4–7:7 may or may not be in the average range compared to other 9-year-old children. This test-age equivalent simply indicates that the child's performance was typical of children ages 7:4–7:7. It does not indicate that a score is atypical or unusually low for 9-year-old children. Standard scores or percentile ranks must be used to compare an individual's performance to that of other individuals the same age.

Be advised that test-age equivalents generally should not be used due to their psychometric limitations and the risk of misinterpretation. If it is decided that test-age equivalents should be used in very special circumstances, the assessment professional must understand and explain all limitations and ensure that others do not interpret the data incorrectly or inappropriately.

Standard Errors of Measurement and Confidence Intervals

Scores such as those derived from measures of adaptive skills, are based on observational data. Observed scores reflect an individual's true ability combined with some degree of measurement error. An observed score therefore is an *estimate* of an individual's true score. We can more accurately estimate an individual's true score by establishing a band of scores around the observed score. Scores that are less reliable have a broader band while those that are more reliable have a narrower band.

The standard error of measurement (*SEM*) is used to calculate the confidence interval, or band of scores, around the observed score within which an individual's true score is likely to fall. Confidence intervals provide another means of expressing the precision of test scores. The professional user can use confidence intervals to report an individual's score as an interval that is likely to contain the individual's true score. Confidence intervals also serve as a reminder that measurement error is inherent in all test scores and that the observed test score is only an estimate of the individual's true score. Users are encouraged to establish confidence intervals around adaptive domain and GAC scores and to use this information to ensure greater accuracy during interpretation. For example, if an 8-year-old child's observed GAC score is 97 on the Teacher Form, the user can be 90% confident that the child's true GAC score falls in the range of 95–99 and 95% confident that the child's true GAC score falls in the range of 94–100.

Tables A.2, A.6, A.10, and A.13 provide critical values for calculating confidence intervals of the adaptive domain and GAC scores. The *SEM* formula provided in Chapter 5 also can be used to calculate the confidence interval for the scaled scores of the skill areas.

Descriptive Classifications

The GAC and scores from the adaptive domains can be characterized as falling within a certain level of performance (e.g., *Very Superior, Superior, Above Average, Average, Below Average, Borderline,* and *Extremely Low*). Scaled scores from each of the skill areas can be characterized as falling within the *Superior, Above Average, Average, Below Average, Borderline,* and *Extremely Low* levels of performance. The level of performance refers to the rank (usually expressed as a scaled score or standard score, percentile rank, and descriptive classification) obtained by an individual on a given test compared to the performance of an appropriate normative group. Clinically speaking, level of performance is important for estimating the presence and severity of any impairment or presence of a relative strength. However, patterns of an individual's strengths and weaknesses often are emphasized without necessarily implying any type of impairment. Table 3.1 lists the descriptive classifications and corresponding percentiles for scores on the three adaptive domains and the GAC along with the classifications for the skill area scaled scores. Test results can be described in a manner similar to the following example:

> Relative to individuals of comparable age, the level of this individual's adaptive behavior currently falls in the (*descriptive classification*) range on a standardized measure of adaptive behavior.

Table 3.1   GAC Scores, Domain Composite Scores, Skill Area Scaled Scores, Percentiles, and Score Classifications

GAC/Domain Composite Scores	Percentiles	Classification
130 or more	≥98	Very Superior
120–129	91–97	Superior
110–119	75–90	Above Average
90–109	25–74	Average
80–89	9–24	Below Average
71–79	3–8	Borderline
70 or Less	≤2	Extremely Low

Skill Area Scaled Scores	Percentiles	Classification
15 or More	–	Superior
13–14	–	Above Average
8–12	–	Average
6–7	–	Below Average
4–5	–	Borderline
3 or Less	–	Extremely Low

Note. Because the distributions of the skill areas are skewed, percentiles are not provided for the scaled scores of the skill areas.

Interpretation of Scores

Interpretations of ABAS–II data are based on information about an individual's general adaptive skills, as represented in the GAC, composite scores from the three adaptive domains, and scores from each of the skill areas. This section provides some basic information for interpreting results.

Verify the Administration and Scoring of Rating Forms

Professional users should answer the respondent's questions, consider the effects of guessing, carefully review the accuracy of the data, resolve conflicting data, and consider information from other sources before beginning to interpret scores, describe an individual's overall adaptive behavior, or evaluate strengths and weaknesses.

Answer Respondent's Questions

Respondents who have completed a rating form may have questions about some items or the nature of their responses. Whenever possible, personally ask respondents if they have questions. Determine if the **Comments** column was checked for any items and review any comments written in the **Notes** box on page 10 of the rating form. Answer the respondent's questions and provide additional assistance as necessary to ensure the information provided is accurate and complete.

Consider the Effects of Guessing

As noted in Chapter 1, average rates of guessing were determined for each of the six standardization samples (Tables A.3, A.7, A.11, and A.14). If the guessing rate on a completed rating form exceeds average levels, obtain additional ABAS–II data from other respondents who are more familiar with the individual.

Review the Accuracy of the Data

Review and closely inspect the accuracy of the recording, scoring, and transferring of data. For example, were all the items completed? Were the raw scores, skill area scaled scores, adaptive domain scores, and the GAC calculated properly? Were the scores recorded correctly? If the GAC, adaptive domain, and skill area scores differ from expected levels for that individual, carefully evaluate the data for possible errors.

Items are presented in order of difficulty (i.e., items that appear in the beginning of a skill area generally are easier and intended to be more suitable for discriminating among younger individuals; items at the end of a skill area are more difficult and generally intended to discriminate among older individuals). Thus, an individual typically receives higher ratings (i.e., **3**s) on the earlier items and lower ratings (i.e., **1**s and **0**s) on later items. Some individuals will not display this profile because their adaptive skills are unevenly developed (i.e., an individual does not display some skills typically performed at younger ages but displays some skills typically performed at more advanced ages). Individuals who display this unusual profile may have GAC, adaptive domain, and skill area scores that do not accurately characterize their adaptive skill levels.

Resolve Conflicting Data

Multiple respondents completing rating forms for one individual may describe the individual in very different ways, resulting in significant score differences. It is necessary to resolve these differences to obtain an accurate description of an individual's adaptive behaviors and to make decisions regarding how best to use this information. Examples of some of these differences follow.

Discussions with respondents may reveal errors, confusion, or other factors that attenuated their responses. Often an individual's adaptive skills are displayed more prominently in one environment than in others. Thus, opportunities to observe adaptive skills may differ. In addition, some respondents are better observers, and may be more capable and prepared to complete a rating form. Respondents may have a personal interest in characterizing the data in one way or another (e.g., when the outcome of an evaluation may have legal or financial implications). Professional users should be vigilant to these possibilities.

The user can have a greater level of confidence in the data when two or more sources of information are available and provide generally similar ratings. The availability of only one rating form minimizes opportunities for a user to determine inter–rater or cross–form reliability. Using information from additional sources can help overcome this limitation.

Consider Information From Additional Sources

Information from alternative sources may help verify ABAS–II data. Obtain a history of the individual, examine existing documents, and interview individuals who are familiar with the individual. This type of information may serve as a substitute for not having multiple respondents. Additional information acquired generally should be consistent with that obtained from the ABAS–II.

Interpreting the GAC

The ABAS–II assesses a strong and unified single factor of adaptive skills. Empirical support exists for a trait of adaptive skills as assessed by the ABAS–II and, unless otherwise indicated, justifies the use of the GAC. The GAC represents a comprehensive and global estimate of an individual's adaptive functioning. The GAC describes the degree to which an individual's adaptive skills generally compare to the adaptive skills of other individuals within the same age group. Test results may be described in the following manner.

> John obtained a score of ____ on the General Adaptive Composite. His true score is likely to fall within the range of _____ to _____ at a _____ % level of confidence. Relative to individuals of comparable age, John currently is functioning at the _____ percentile and his overall level of adaptive behavior can be described as being in the _____ (*refer to Table 3.1 for descriptive classifications*) range of functioning.

The GAC is based on information obtained from all relevant skill areas (see Table 1.3). It generally provides the most complete measure of an individual's adaptive behavior and is likely to be the most reliable and accurate estimate of an individual's overall adaptive functioning. However, the GAC may not accurately reflect an individual's overall adaptive functioning if skill area scaled scores vary considerably (e.g., skill area scaled scores range from high to low). For example, although a GAC of 100 generally indicates that an individual displays average adaptive behavior compared to other individuals of the same age group, this score is not an accurate summary if it is derived from skill area scaled scores that range from 3 and less to 13 or more. Therefore, do not interpret the GAC if considerable scatter exists among the skill area scaled scores. Use the instructions in the following section to examine scatter and determine which level of scores to use as the basis of interpretation.

Examining Scatter

Determine the level of score variability (e.g., scatter) by examining skill area scaled scores. Variability is evident in scores that range from high to low. Profiles that have similar scores indicate considerable consistency of an individual's adaptive skills. If the scores do not differ significantly, the GAC and adaptive domain scores are likely to summarize an individual's adaptive behavior accurately, and a strengths and weaknesses analysis at the skill area level will not be meaningful.

However, if the skill area scaled scores demonstrate significant variability, the GAC may not accurately summarize an individual's adaptive skills and a strengths and weaknesses analysis is more likely to be meaningful. If an individual's scaled scores are variable, interpretations should rely on the significant differences in skill area scaled scores. Additionally, if skill area scaled scores within domains do not show significant variability with one another, interpretations also may rely on any significant differences that exist between adaptive domain composite scores. If an individual's skill area scaled scores appear to be variable, interpretations should rely on the methods described in the following sections.

Examining Overall Skill Area Scaled Score Scatter

Before conducting a skill area strengths and weaknesses analysis, follow these three steps to determine if the level of observed scatter is both significant and rare enough to make such an analysis meaningful.

Step 1. Determine if the skill area scaled scores differ significantly

Calculate the difference between the smallest and the largest skill area scaled score. Compare the absolute value of the difference with the related critical values provided in Tables B.2, B.9, B.16, and B.23 to determine if the difference between two scaled scores is significant at the .15 and .05 levels. A difference is statistically significant if it is *equal to or greater than* the related critical value. For example, on the Teacher Form, differences in scaled scores on the Communication and Community Use Skill Areas are significant at the .15 level if they differ by more than 1.82 points, and at the .05 level if they differ by more than 2.47 points (Table B.2).

Step 2. Determine if a difference between two skill area scaled scores is rare

A difference that is statistically significant may not be meaningful if it occurs frequently in the population. Refer to Tables B.3, B.10, B.17, and B.24 to determine if a statistically significant difference is also clinically significant. These tables provide the cumulative percentages (base rates) of inter-skill-area scatter for each rating form by age group. For example, a 3-point scaled score difference between any two skill areas on any rating form will be statistically significant at the .15 level. However, between 73% and 99% of the standardization sample obtained such a difference. In contrast, less than 3% of the standardization sample have two scores that differ by 11 or more points. Thus, a range of 11 points or more is relatively rare.

Step 3. Determine the level of occurrence to be considered rare

Professional users must decide what level of occurrence can be considered rare: 25%, 10%, 5%, 2% or 1%. This decision depends on institutional policy, the purposes of the assessment, and the degree of risk the user is willing to assume. Users are responsible for exercising sound professional judgment in their selection of the levels. Sattler (2001) suggests that differences between composite scores that occur in less than 10% to 15% of the standardization sample should be considered unusual.

Reliance on the GAC should be minimized when skill area scaled scores show significant and rare levels of scatter. In such a case, a more meaningful interpretation may be obtained by conducting a strengths and weaknesses analysis of the skill area scaled scores (use the Determining Strengths and Weaknesses table on the Supplemental Analyses page of the rating form). Emphasis also may be placed on the adaptive domain composite scores if skill area scaled scores *within* the adaptive domains do not show significant variability.

Examining Skill Area Scaled Score Scatter Within Adaptive Domains

Before conducting an analysis of discrepancies between adaptive domain composite scores, follow these three steps to determine if the skill area scaled scores show significant variability within the adaptive domains. The procedures used to determine scatter within the adaptive domains parallel the procedures used to determine overall scatter.

Step 1. Determine if the skill area scaled scores differ significantly within adaptive domains

Calculate the difference between the smallest and the largest skill area scaled score within an adaptive domain. Compare the absolute value of the difference with the related critical values provided in Tables B.2, B. 9, B. 16, and B.23 to determine if the difference between two scaled scores is significant at the .15 and .05 levels. For example, on the Teacher/Daycare Provider Form (Table B.2), differences in scaled scores on Health and Safety and Self-Care (within the Practical Domain) are significant at the .15 level if they differ by more than 2.48 points and are significant at the .05 level if they differ by more than 3.38 points.

Step 2. Determine if a difference between two skill areas scaled scores within an adaptive domain is rare

As previously noted, a difference that is statistically significant may not be clinically meaningful if it occurs frequently in the population. Refer to Tables B.3, B.10, B.17, and B.24 to determine if a statistically significant difference is also rare. For example, on the Teacher Form, a 2-point difference between any two skill area scaled scores within the Conceptual Domain will be statistically significant at the .15 level. However, 84% of the standardization sample obtained a difference of 2 or more points (Table B.3). In contrast, less than 5% of the standardization sample had a scatter of 8 or more points within the Conceptual Domain. Thus, a scatter of 8 points or more is relatively rare.

Step 3. Determine the level of occurrence to be considered rare

Professional users must decide what level of occurrence can be considered rare: 25%, 10%, 5%, 2% or 1%. This decision depends on institutional policy, the purposes of the assessment, and the degree of risk the user is willing to assume.

If scaled scores within adaptive domains do show significant differences, rely on a strengths and weaknesses analysis at the skill area level, and use caution when interpreting and comparing adaptive domain composite scores. When skill area scaled scores within adaptive domains do not show significant and rare levels of scatter, meaningful interpretations based on the differences between adaptive domain composite scores may be obtained by conducting a discrepancy analysis (use the Discrepancy Comparison table on the Supplemental Analyses page of the rating form).

Interpreting Strengths and Weaknesses

Skill Area Strengths and Weaknesses

Scoring steps (Chapter 2) prepare the professional user to examine scores from each of the relevant skill areas and to identify scores that are significantly higher or lower than others. Attempts to interpret skill area strengths and weaknesses will be of little value if the profile shows little variability. Refer to Table 3.2 for the following example.

Table 3.2   Scaled Scores for Joe and Mary on the Parent Form

Skill Area	Joe Scaled Scores	Mary Scaled Scores	Difference From *MSS*	Critical Value[a]	Percent in Standardization Sample	Strength or Weakness
Communication	1	5	**–3**	2.29	>5	
Community Use	2	8	0	2.33		
Functional Academics	1	2	**–6**	2.17	<1	W
Home Living	1	8	0	2.22		
Health and Safety	3	10	2	2.86		
Leisure	2	12	**4**	2.31	<2	S
Self-Care	1	12	**4**	2.86	>5	
Self-Direction	1	7	–1	2.15		
Social	1	8	0	2.22		

Note. Bold numbers indicate statistical significance. *MSS* = Mean Scaled Score.

[a]Critical values significant at the .05 level when comparing each scaled score to the mean of all nine skill areas.

On the Parent Form, the scaled scores for Joe show little variability. The user should report Joe's scaled scores as presenting a consistent profile, one in which his nine skill area scaled scores show considerable similarity and fall in the extremely low range. In contrast, 8-year-old Mary's scaled scores fall in the extremely low, borderline, and average range. The inter-skill area scatter of 10 points is significant at the .05 level and occurs in 6.7% of the standardization sample (Tables B.9 and B.10). Such variability renders the interpretation of the GAC less meaningful and increases the importance of determining strengths and weaknesses.

As described in Chapter 2, the first step of a strengths and weaknesses analysis is to determine if the differences between each skill area scaled score and the mean of all scaled scores or the mean of all scaled scores within its domain are statistically significant. Using data from the Parent Form, the user should compare the differences between each of Mary's skill area scaled scores and the mean of all nine skill area scores (*MSS* = 8) to the critical values found in Table B.8. Significantly higher skill areas are Leisure and Self-Care. Significantly lower skill areas are Communication and Functional Academics. This information provides the first indication of the differences between Mary's skill area scaled scores and *MSS*.

The user should then examine if these differences occur rarely. For example, Mary's Communication Skill Area scaled score (5) differs significantly from the mean of the nine skill areas (8) by 3 points. A difference of 3 occurs less than 10% of the time but more than 5% of the time. Therefore, depending on the standard selected by the user, the score difference of 3 points may be considered rare (if 10% is selected as a rare level of occurrence) or not very rare (if 5% is selected).

If the user decides on a 5% or less occurrence as rare for Mary, only two skill areas (Functional Academics and Leisure) out of the four that differ significantly from the *MSS* also demonstrate differences that are rare. Although Communication and Self-Care scaled scores differ significantly from the *MSS*, the degree to which they differ does not occur rarely.

Finally, the user should determine how many of an individual's skill area scores are deficits compared to the scores of individuals in the same age group. For this purpose, users may need to use additional methods of identifying deficits to fulfill the criteria required by state or federal agencies, boards, institutions, and other organizations. For example, *DSM–IV–TR* criteria for a diagnosis of mental retardation require significant limitations in at least two adaptive skill areas. A number of states also require documentation of deficits in two or more skill areas for a diagnosis of mental retardation. Although the *DSM–IV–TR* does not operationally define significant limitations in skill areas, one possible criterion is 2 or more standard deviations below the mean.

Tables B.4, B.11, B.18, and B.25 provide the percentage of individuals within the standardization samples who obtained two or more scaled scores equal to or less than 2 *SD*s below the mean (i.e., scaled scores of

4 or less). These tables enable users to evaluate how rarely individuals obtain a number of skill area scaled scores that are equal to or less than 2 SDs below the mean. For example, among 5-year-olds rated on the Teacher Form (Table B.4), 16% had two or more scaled scores equal to or less than 2 SDs below the mean, 10% have three or more scaled scores equal to or less than 2 SDs below the mean, and 1.3% had nine scaled scores equal to or less than 2 SDs below the mean.

Similarly, an analysis of the number of skill area deficits (i.e., scaled scores of 4 or less) in comparison with the standardization sample may assist professional users in the diagnosis or treatment planning of individuals with a variety of disabilities and disorders. Determining that an individual has deficits in an unusually large number skill areas in comparison to the national standardization sample will assist the user in documenting the extensiveness of the impact of the disability or disorder on the individual's daily functioning and in planning interventions and treatments for the individual. For example, if a 3-year-old child diagnosed with Autistic Disorder has scaled scores of 4 or less in five skill areas, compared to 3% of the standardization sample, the user will have additional documentation about the impact of Autistic Disorder on the child's functioning and can use this information to plan interventions accordingly. If a 72-year-old adult with symptoms of cognitive impairments and memory loss obtains deficits in six skill areas, compared to 2% of the standardization sample, the user will have important documentation about the impact of the impairment on the adult's functioning that may inform treatment and assistance plans.

Adaptive Domain Discrepancies

The scoring procedures described in Chapter 2 prepare the professional user to examine composite scores from each of the adaptive domains and to identify scores that are significantly higher or lower than others. Attempts to interpret adaptive domain discrepancies will be of little value if the differences between scores are not significant and rare. Refer to Table 3.3 for the following example.

Table 3.3   Adaptive Domain Composite and GAC Scores for Joe and Mary on the Parent Form

Adaptive Domain/GAC	Joe	Mary				
	Composite Scores	Composite Scores	Score 1 – Score 2 Difference	Critical Value[a]	Significant Difference (Y) or (N)	Percent in Standardization Sample
Conceptual	50	75	(CON – SO) = **–25**	8.31	Y	1.7
Social	58	100	(SO – PR) = 2	8.31	N	
Practical	46	98	(CON – PR) = **–23**	7.21	Y	2.9
GAC	44	89				

Note. Bold numbers indicate statistical significance.

[a]Critical values significant at the .05 level when comparing each adaptive domain to every other adaptive domain.

Composite scores for Joe show little variability. The user should not continue with a discrepancy analysis, but should instead report that Joe's functioning across all adaptive domains presents a consistent profile in which all composite scores and the GAC fall in the extremely low range. Mary's composite scores, however, display a more variable profile. While two adaptive domain scores fall in the average range, one falls in the borderline range of functioning, illustrating a large discrepancy and a possible focus of interpretation. Before conducting a discrepancy comparison, however, the user should determine the amount of scatter within the adaptive domains in order to decide whether an interpretation of discrepancies would be valuable. Within the Conceptual Domain, inter-skill area scatter is 5 points, within the Social Domain the scatter is 4 points, and within the Practical Domain the scatter is 4 points (using Mary's skill area scaled scores from Table 3.2). While the scatter within each domain is significant at the .05 level, the levels of scatter within the Conceptual and Social Domains occur 18.4% and 14.6% of the time, respectively, and the level of scatter within the Practical Domain occurs 52.4% of the time (Tables B.9 and B.10). Therefore, depending on the standard selected by the user, the score differences of 4 and 5 points within the Conceptual and Social Domains may be considered rare (if 25% is selected as a rare level of occurrence) or not very rare (if 10% is selected). The scatter within the Practical

Domain is not considered rare. The user may proceed with a discrepancy analysis, but should interpret discrepancy analysis results with caution if the scatter within domains is considered rare. The first step of a discrepancy analysis is to determine whether the differences between domains are statistically significant.

The user should compare the differences between Mary's adaptive domain scores to the critical values found in Table B.12. The discrepancy of 25 points between her Conceptual and Social Domain scores is significant at the .05 level, and the discrepancy of 23 points between her Conceptual and Practical Domain is also significant at the .05 level.

The user should then examine whether these differences occur rarely. Using Table B.13, and keeping in mind the direction of the discrepancies, the difference between her Conceptual and Social Domain scores occurs 1.7 % of the time, and the difference between her Conceptual and Practical Domain scores occurs 2.9% of the time. Therefore, the discrepancies between her Conceptual and Social Domains, and between her Conceptual and Practical Domains may be considered rare.

Finally, the user should determine how many of an individual's composite scores are deficits compared to the scores of others of the same age group. Once again, users may need to use additional methods of identifying deficits to fulfill the criteria required by states or federal agencies, institutions, and other organizations. For example, the AAMR manual (2002b) provides an operational definition for limitations in adaptive behavior: "For the diagnosis of mental retardation, significant limitations in adaptive behavior should be established through the use of standardized measures normed on the general population, including people with disabilities and people without disabilities. On these standardized measures, significant limitations in adaptive behavior are operationally defined as performance that is at least two standard deviations below the mean of either (a) one of the following three types of adaptive behavior: conceptual, social, or practical, or (b) an overall score on a standardized measure of conceptual, social, and practical skills" (p. 76).

Tables B.7, B.14, B.21, and B.28 provide the percentage of individuals within the standardization samples who obtained scores at least 2 *SD*s below the mean in at least one of the three adaptive domains, or a GAC score at least 2 *SD*s below the mean. For example, among 6-year-olds rated on the Parent Form (Table B.14), 5.4% had at least one adaptive domain or the GAC equal to or less than two *SD*s below the mean.

Developing Hypotheses About Strengths and Weaknesses

Skill Area Strengths and Weaknesses

Professional users can offer hypotheses about the nature of an individual's adaptive skills after evaluating the data and reviewing the individual's background. Profile analysis, a process that helps identify an individual's strengths and weaknesses within a set of scores, may provide information that can be used to test a hypothesis. Scores that are significantly higher than others suggest strengths, while scores that are significantly lower than others suggest weaknesses. Support for the hypothesis that some skill areas represent strengths and others weaknesses requires differences between skill area scaled scores to not only be statistically significant, but also rare. Additional support for the belief that some adaptive skills are stronger than others can be found in information from other sources (e.g., interviews, observations, and other test data).

The interpretation of individual adaptive skill deficits should be guided by an understanding that the 10 skill areas are relatively independent areas of behavior (see Chapter 5). Although they can be grouped into broad categories of functioning represented by the three adaptive domains, users may interpret the skill areas independently of one another. The following are examples of situations in which an individual may demonstrate deficits in skill areas.

> The individual's environment may not emphasize or reward the development of one skill area. Limitations in other areas (e.g., having a physical or sensory impairment) may impede its development or the individual may resist developing adaptive skills in a particular area (e.g., Functional Academics or Self-Care).

An individual may have deficits in two or more related skill areas. Children may have deficits in the Functional Academics and Social Skill Areas due to an underlying deficiency in the Communication Skill Area. Adults with deficits in Self-Direction also may have resulting deficits in Home Living and Work.

Deficits in two or more skill areas may occur independently of one another, may contribute to one another, or may be due to a pervasive influence from a third common cause (e.g., a physical or psychological disorder). Professional users working closely with other individuals who are familiar with the individual being assessed should strive to determine if deficits in skill areas are interrelated and have a common origin that needs attention.

Adaptive Domain Strengths and Weaknesses

The AAMR (2002b) emphasizes the importance of assessing conceptual, social, and practical skills in an assessment of adaptive behavior and the use of information in these three areas for diagnostic and intervention purposes. Significant limitations in adaptive behavior are defined as performance at least 2 SDs below the mean on (a) the Conceptual, Social, or Practical Domain or (b) an overall score on a standardized measure that assesses these three adaptive domains (e.g., GAC). The ABAS–II provides a standardized norm-referenced assessment of conceptual, social, and practical skills needed to perform daily life activities. It is normed on a representative population that includes people with and without disabilities. The skills it measures have been conceptually linked to these three adaptive domains. Thus, the comprehensive data provided by these three adaptive domains figures importantly in the diagnosis of mental retardation.

Conceptual skills include receptive and expressive language, reading and writing, money concepts, and self-direction. Social skills include interpersonal relationships, responsibility, self-esteem, gullibility, naiveté, following rules, obeying laws, and avoiding victimization. Practical skills include basic maintenance activities of daily living (e.g., eating, mobility, toileting, dressing), instrumental activities of daily living (e.g., meal preparation, housekeeping, transportation, taking medications, money management, telephone use) together with occupation skills and maintenance of safe environments (AAMR, 2002b, p. 42).

Within the context of an individual's particular score profile and environment, it may be helpful to focus on strengths and weaknesses between adaptive domains when working with individuals who display disorders other than mental retardation. For example, an individual may obtain average scores in the Social and Practical Domains but display a significant and rare deficit in the Conceptual Domain. This discrepancy may suggest a direction for further assessment and for program planning. Another individual may obtain adaptive domain scores 2 SDs below the mean in the Conceptual and Practical Domains, while obtaining an average score in the Social Domain. In this profile, the area of social adaptive functioning represents a strength and could lend support to a hypothesis that eliminates certain categories of disorders that typically affect social functioning.

When appropriate, the GAC also can be used to identify global limitations in adaptive behavior (AAMR, 2002b, p. 81). Thus, data from the Conceptual, Social, and Practical Domains and the GAC may be used to facilitate diagnostic, classification, or support planning efforts.

Summary of Guidelines for Interpreting Scores

Various methods exist to assist users in analyzing and interpreting test data. For example, in multifactor measures of intelligence, IQ scores may serve as the first level of interpretation followed by a review of index scores, subtest variability within factors, intersubtest variability, and qualitative analyses (Sattler, 2001; The Psychological Corporation, 1994). Many professional users are familiar with this method and use it routinely. Other users have acquired knowledge of different methods or have developed their own that allow them to analyze and interpret test data efficiently and effectively. Figure 3.1 summarizes the methods described in detail in this chapter that may be useful for analyzing and interpreting results. When interpreting ABAS–II scores, always consider important and prevailing environmental requirements.

Guidelines for Interpreting Scores

A. Determining Scatter

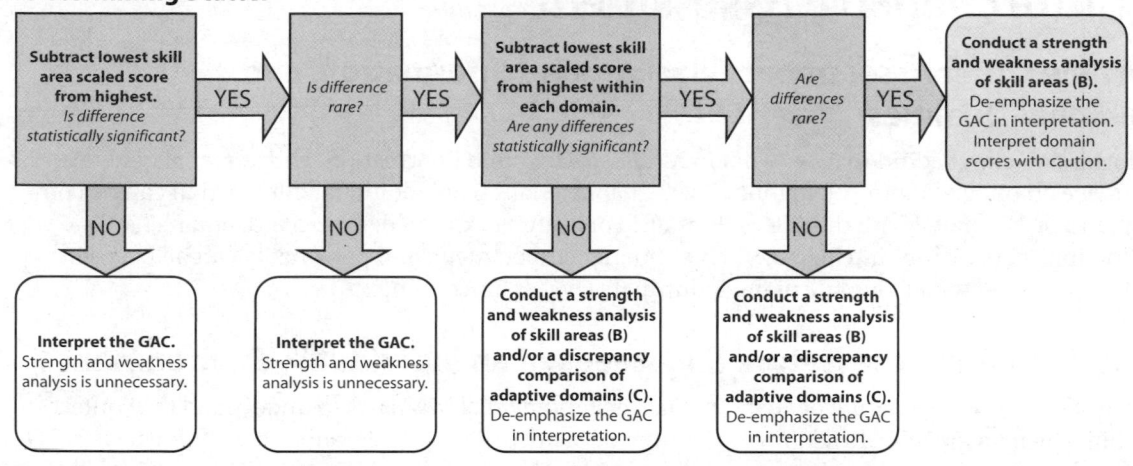

B. Skill Area Scaled Score Strength and Weakness Analysis

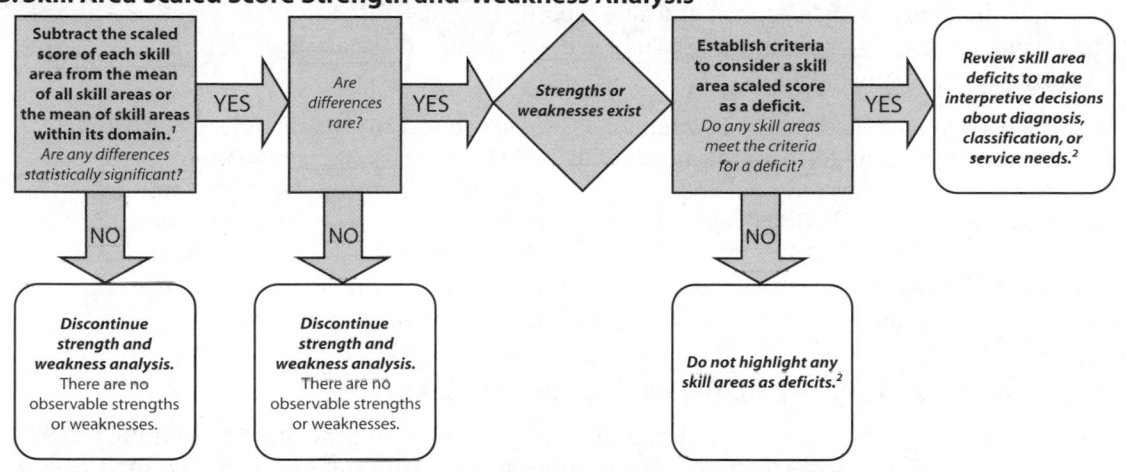

C. Discrepancy Comparison of Adaptive Domains

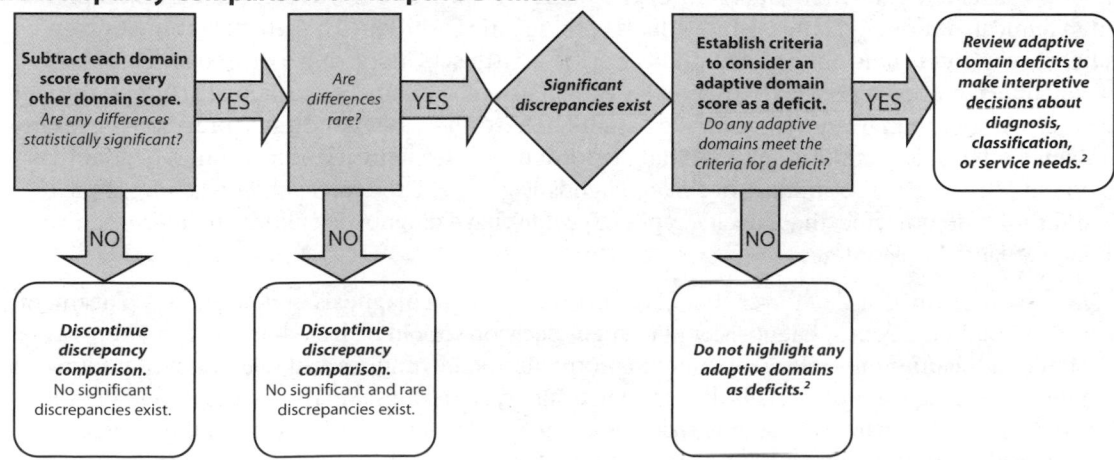

[1] In general, the mean of all skill areas should be used for the strength and weakness analysis if there are no significant discrepancies between adaptive domain composite scores.

[2] Relative strengths and weaknesses may be interpreted.

Figure 3.1   Guidelines for Interpreting Scores

Use of ABAS–II Scores Within a Comprehensive Assessment

Review Other Assessments, Background Information, and Personal Qualities

Information about additional assessment results, background information, and personal qualities enhance an understanding of an individual's adaptive skills. This additional information can be compared to or integrated with the ABAS–II results. For example, knowledge of an individual's family, schooling, work history, intelligence, achievement, temperament, and personality can help a user develop a broad understanding of the individual's level of functioning.

Understanding the Nature and Needs of an Individual's Environment

Information about the nature of an individual's environment allows users to understand the context within which an individual's adaptive skills were developed. For example, adolescents who have lived for some time in institutions for the severely impaired are likely to display differences in adaptive skills compared to other adolescents the same age who have lived with their families. In addition, individuals who live in families that have many resources and an established regimen for promoting adaptive skills are likely to be more advanced than other individuals living in families that have fewer resources and no regimen for promoting adaptive skills.

Professional users should incorporate information provided by the ABAS–II and other evaluative information with the current and forthcoming needs of the individual. This information prepares users to assist individuals in their development and to meet the needs that characterize their environment. For example, an emphasis on Functional Academic and Work Skill Areas may be necessary if an individual is preparing to enter the job market. An emphasis on Self-Care, Home Living, and Health and Safety Skill Areas may be needed if an individual is living alone. An emphasis on Communication and Social Skill Areas may be essential as an important part of rehabilitation following a stroke.

Avoid Relying Solely on ABAS–II Profiles to Diagnose

Professional users are encouraged to use profile analysis for clinical interpretation and for the generation of hypotheses in conjunction with other data gathered in the comprehensive evaluation. However, users are discouraged from using profile analysis to determine whether a pattern of strengths and weaknesses observed in an individual's ABAS–II scores corresponds to the average or common profiles found in clinical groups (e.g., among individuals with Autistic Disorder). This practice is not encouraged because more reliable and valid methods exist to assist users in making a diagnosis. Profiles of scores of clinical groups reported in Chapter 5 were collected on clinical populations acquired through convenience rather than from well-controlled studies. These and other conditions preclude the exclusive reliance on profile analysis of ABAS–II data to form diagnoses. Furthermore, profiles of adaptive skills do not adequately discriminate between diagnostic groups. Therefore, validity data from the clinical samples do not show that specific types of profiles have diagnostic validity in determining a disability category or disorder.

A *single* assessment instrument never should be used to develop a diagnosis or determine a placement for a child or adult. Instead, a diagnosis or placement decision should be based on a comprehensive evaluation that includes multiple assessment instruments and techniques and relies on many sources of information to evaluate adaptive skills displayed in a variety of settings and over some period of time. Although ABAS–II results may assist in decision-making about diagnoses or disorders, they always should be used in conjunction with other assessment results.

Utilize ABAS–II Information for Planning Interventions

The ABAS–II provides information important to the diagnosis of mental retardation as well as other mental, physical, social, and emotional difficulties. Professional users often employ the ABAS–II to enhance program planning and monitoring. Information from ratings on specific items, and scores from skill areas, adaptive domains, and the GAC may be used to support diagnoses, assist in decision-making, and serve as a benchmark for later evaluations.

ABAS–II Items in Program Planning

Item-level data can provide a basis for developing interventions. Each item identifies an important life skill. For example, individuals unable to state or write their home address, including zip code, should be taught these skills and encouraged to practice them. Individuals who do not complete routine tasks within a reasonable period or who do not clean up their work areas after completing work need assistance in acquiring these essential skills.

Skill Areas in Program Planning

Evaluate information from each of the skill areas for program planning. Identify strengths and weaknesses and the skill areas in which further development is most important. Program planning typically prioritizes the skill areas that are both low and immediately necessary for functioning.

Adaptive Domains in Program Planning

The AAMR (2002b) conceptualizes mental retardation along five dimensions: adaptive behavior; intellectual abilities; participation, interactions, and social roles; health; and context. "Adaptive behavior is a collection of conceptual, social, and practical skills that have been learned by people in order to function in their everyday lives" (AAMR, 2002b, p. 14). Limitations in adaptive behaviors can adversely impact a person's daily life, ability to respond to change, and environmental demands. Limitations should be evaluated in light of the four other dimensions (i.e., intellectual abilities; participation, interactions, and social roles; health; and context). Furthermore, the use of adaptive skill data differs, depending on the extent to which the data is important for diagnosis, classification, or support planning.

Knowledge of the level of development of conceptual, social, and practical skills may assist in program planning. When appropriate, adaptive domains may be used to conceptualize a general area of strength or limitation within an individual's profile and to guide program planning to meet personal needs and environmental expectations. For example, an individual functioning in a school or training setting will have more demands in the area of conceptual adaptive behavior. An individual transitioning to an independent living situation is likely to have environmental demands more associated with practical adaptive behavior. Additionally, the three adaptive domains may provide a framework in which to describe specific skill area strengths and weaknesses.

The AAMR (2002b) promotes the use of conceptual, social, and practical skills in diagnosis, classification, and program planning. However, other professional associations (e.g., APA) and the federal and state governments have not revised their policies to reflect the AAMR's policy recommendations. Users are advised to consult legal and professional standards that should guide their use of adaptive behavior data for diagnosis, classification, or support planning.

Guidelines for Program Planning and Monitoring

Program planning and monitoring involves five steps.

▶ **Step 1: Identify the skill levels needed for an individual's current environment or the environment into which the individual is moving**

Behavior is understood by recognizing the qualities displayed by an individual in response to environmental requirements within which his or her behavior occurs. This widely accepted belief within the behavioral sciences also applies to adaptive skills. A close examination of an environment helps define the qualities important to successful functioning within that environment and the degree to which support may be needed to help individuals succeed.

The skill areas constitute qualities important for successful functioning within most environments for most people. An understanding of both the skill areas required by an individual's environment and the level of his or her adaptive skill development is essential to successful planning. For example, adaptive skills commonly found in school environments generally are more important for students, while adaptive skills commonly found in work environments generally are more important for adults. The presence of deficits in critical skill areas typically warrants interventions in these areas.

Knowledge of the availability of support systems provided within families, schools, work, assisted living centers, and through community-supported services to help people function more effectively will contribute to program planning. Assistance commonly is provided to develop adaptive skills and to provide compensatory assistance when an individual's level of development is decreasing, slow to change, or lower than that required for successful functioning. The degree of support needed may range broadly, from intermittent to pervasive levels. The following are definitions of support (AAMR, 1992, 2002b).

Intermittent support is provided as needed. The support is short-term because the individual does not always require assistance. The support may be of high or low intensity. Intermittent support may be necessary during job changes or acute medical problems. The costs for and duration of services are minimal.

Limited support consists of time-limited services and focuses on specific goals (e.g., employment training, transitional support from school to work). Cost and duration generally exceed that of intermittent support but are less than other support levels.

Extensive support consists of long-term and regular involvement (e.g., daily) in one or more settings (e.g., home, school, and work).

Pervasive support involves consistent, highly intense services offered in various settings. The general goal of pervasive support is to help provide life-sustaining services. The cost for and duration of pervasive services exceed those for other levels.

Knowledge of an individual's specific environmental expectations, support services, level of support, skill strengths, and deficits is critical to program planning and monitoring.

▶ **Step 2: Identify current areas of strengths and weaknesses relative to environmental requirements**

A profile of the adaptive domains and skill areas may provide evidence about an individual's strengths and weaknesses. The adaptive skills assessed by the ABAS–II do not constitute personal traits that are pervasive and immutable. Instead, the ABAS–II measures adaptive skills that are developed, have been acquired, and thus often are modifiable to the degree homes, schools, work, and other important settings require, nurture, reinforce, and sustain their development. A score profile that describes an individual's strengths and weaknesses in various areas of adaptive functioning combined with information about the skill levels needed in his or her current or future environments will aid program planning and monitoring.

Adaptive Behavior Assessment System–Second Edition

► **Step 3: Identify and prioritize intervention objectives based on discrepancies between environmental needs and personal attainment**

General intelligence generally shows little substantial improvement following interventions. In contrast, adaptive skills are more amenable to change and thus more likely to show improvement. For example, an individual with deficits in the Communication and Self-Care Skill Areas is likely to display improvements in these skill areas following efforts to develop them and when his or her environment promotes and rewards the newly acquired skills. A review of an individual's profile of scores should be combined with a review of the requirements of his or her current or future environment. For example, an individual may display deficiencies in Communication, Community Use, and School Living Skill Areas. Adaptive skills associated with Communication and School Living may be especially critical to an individual's independent functioning. In contrast, adaptive skills associated with Community Use may be less critical. Thus, the most essential interventions will focus on promoting Communication and School Living.

► **Step 4: Implement interventions to achieve specific objectives**

The implementation of interventions to achieve desired objectives forms the core of professional service. Interventions are likely to be effective when developmental goals are clearly defined, suitable instructional strategies are implemented and sustained, and when the environment rewards an individual for using newly acquired skills.

Decisions regarding the degree of support each individual needs are based on ABAS–II data combined with additional information regarding personal and environmental characteristics (e.g., environmental demands and potential systems of support). Interventions should encourage individuals to display necessary adaptive skills that depend increasingly less on higher levels of support (e.g., extensive and pervasive levels) by enabling the individual to become more self-sufficient and thus require lower levels of support (e.g., limited and intermittent levels). Individuals whose adaptive skills are extremely deficient and are living in environments that require these skills may need extensive or pervasive support for long periods. The successful provision of support or services to individuals with mental retardation in order to maintain their functioning within a typical range does not eliminate a diagnosis of mental retardation (AAMR, 1992, 2002a).

► **Step 5: Monitor the implementation and effectiveness of the interventions**

A process that employs formative evaluation methods to monitor adaptive skill development is important to the monitoring of program success. Knowledge of change in skill development, acquired through the continued use of the ABAS–II and other assessment methods, can lead to continued modifications in program, support levels, training, and the further reinforcement of newly acquired skills. Improvements may be reflected in specific ABAS–II items (e.g., when the goals of training are more modest and the time periods brief), in scores on one or more of the skill areas or adaptive domains consistent with program goals, and in changes in the degree of support necessary (e.g., progressing from extensive to limited support).

As previously indicated, adaptive skills are not traits and are more subject to change than traits such as intelligence or personality. As a result, an assessment of adaptive skills may need to occur more frequently because the skills are more susceptible to change. Individuals typically function in two or more environments (e.g., home and work, or home and school), each of which may require different levels of adaptive skills to function effectively and independently. Frequent testing is likely to provide up-to-date information.

Case Studies

The following five case studies demonstrate various methods for using the ABAS–II in clinical practice. Each case study is drawn from clinical practice and names have been changed to ensure confidentiality.

Sample Case Report Using the ABAS–II

Chris: a 29-year-old adult with Mental Retardation

Psychological Report

Name: Chris Jones

Parents: Joe and Karen Jones

DOT: 1999/ 10/ 24

DOB: 1970/ 4/ 17

Age: 29:6

Sources of Information

Adaptive Behavior Assessment System–Second Edition

Guide To The Assessment of Test Session Behaviors

Matrix Analogies Test–Short Form

The Stanford Binet Intelligence Scale–Fourth Edition

Wide Range Achievement Test–3

School Records

Interviews:

Mr. and Mrs. Jones

Chris Jones

Referral

Chris, a 29-year-old male, was referred for testing in order to better understand his current levels of achievement, intellectual, and adaptive development. His parents, together with staff from a regional resource center that provides assistance to adults with mental retardation, requested current assessment data and assistance in developing an intervention program designed to increase Chris' independence.

Rapport was established and maintained with Mr. and Mrs. Jones and Chris during a home visit. They conveyed information in an open and friendly manner. Chris enjoyed showing me around his yard and room. Their home is located in an isolated rural area 20 miles from a city with a population of 18,000. Mr. Jones works irregular hours at an electric generation plant. Mrs. Jones has not worked outside their home since Chris' birth and has devoted most of her time to his care.

The following day, when testing Chris, rapport was again established and easily maintained. Data from the *Guide to the Assessment of Test Session Behaviors* (Glutting & Oakland, 1993) indicated Chris' test-taking behaviors were within the average range. Thus, the cognitive test data reported herein are considered to be a valid indication of his abilities.

Background Information

Mrs. Jones reported no prenatal, perinatal, or postnatal complication associated with her pregnancy with Chris. At about 6 months of age Chris appeared to have "spells" which were diagnosed, in part, through an abnormal EEG as petit mal seizures. At about that same time Chris was diagnosed with hemophilia. He has taken several medications in an attempt to control his seizures. However, his medications have had limited success, and he continues to have seizures one or more times during a 6 month interval. Chris' parents report that they have been over-protective of him since learning of these problems at the age of 6 months. Chris is their only child.

At age 4, Chris was enrolled in a private kindergarten. His parents were led to believe his development was normal at that time. At age 5, Chris entered a public kindergarten, was tested, and placed in a special education program for children with developmental delays. At age 6, Chris started first grade and received most of his classes in special education with some regular education experiences. He repeated first grade.

At age 7, Chris acquired HIV while receiving a transfusion and was put on AZT. Upon learning of his HIV, his parents discontinued his school attendance and restricted his interactions with others out of fear that Chris would be rejected. Chris received his education at home with assistance from the local school district. The parents explained to Chris that his seizures made him very special and, because of them, he would be kept at home.

On a typical day Chris gets up about 10:00 a.m., eats breakfast, and watches "The Price Is Right". He watches the news and weather at noon and may eat again. Mrs. Jones takes Chris to physical therapy on Tuesdays and Thursdays. Following therapy, they frequently shop and eat out. Evenings are typically spent at home playing Nintendo. Chris has his bath at 10:30 p.m. His bedtime varies, depending on the shift his father works. He may go to bed as late as 2:00 a.m. when his father returns after working the late shift. Chris takes medications five times daily.

Chris has no ongoing or regular peer relationships. Children of family friends come to Chris' home on occasion. Also, a 13-year-old boy who lives down the road sees Chris occasionally. Chris has some peer contact as a result of his attending local high school football games in the fall. However, none of these relationships can be considered strong and abiding friendships.

Test Results

Intellectual Abilities: Chris' general intellectual ability, as assessed by the SB–IV (Thorndike, Hagen, & Sattler, 1986), is at the 1st percentile, with a scaled score of 40. His scaled scores are 54 on Abstract Reasoning, 50 on Short Term Memory, 44 on Verbal Reasoning, and 42 on Quantitative Reasoning. No significant differences exist among these scores. His scores generally resemble those of average children 4:6 to 7 years of age. His short-term retention of visually presented information constitutes a strength. His short-term attention of auditory information constitutes a weakness.

Given Chris' apparent strength in processing visual information, the *Matrix Analogies Test–Short Form* (Naglieri, 1985) was also administered. This test assesses intellectual abilities of a visual processing nature. His score on this measure, at the 1st percentile, is consistent with those from the SB–IV (Thorndike, Hagen, & Sattler, 1986).

Achievement: Chris' achievement, as measured by the *Wide Range Achievement Test–Revision 3* (Wilkinson, 1993), is consistent with his intellectual abilities. Chris' standard scores are 54 on Spelling, 52 on Reading Recognition, and less than 46 on Arithmetic. All scores are at the 1st percentile.

Adaptive Behavior and Skills: Chris' adaptive skills were assessed using the ABAS–II Adult Form. Mrs. Jones served as the respondent. (Chris' scores are reported in Table 3.4.)

Chris' GAC and Conceptual, Practical, and Social Domain-related qualities are below the 1st percentile and consistent with his intelligence. The data supports a continued diagnosis of mental retardation. Chris' adaptive skills are in the extremely low range. The profile is flat, with no significant differences between the scores.

Interventions

During the discussion of Chris' profile, Mr. and Mrs. Jones admitted that their desire to shelter and restrict Chris' social interactions and to personally provide for his daily needs has resulted in the restricted development of his adaptive skills. Although Mr. And Mrs. Jones suspected this before the assessment, the ABAS–II data confirmed their belief and motivated a commitment to an intervention plan leading to increased independence.

A meeting with staff from the regional resource center helped identify specific long-term and behavioral goals. The most important long-term goal was to prepare Chris for work and for living in an intermediate care facility after his parents are unable to care for him. The center staff agreed to have Chris attend a daily program that focuses on the use of community resources and the development of communication and social skills, largely in a work context.

Table 3.4   Chris' ABAS–II Scores

Skill Area/Adaptive Domain/GAC	Scaled Scores Adult Form, Rated by Others
Communication	3
Community Use	1
Functional Academics	1
Home Living	1
Health and Safety	2
Leisure	3
Self-Care	3
Self-Direction	1
Social	1
Conceptual Domain	53
90% Confidence Interval	50–56
Social Domain	60
90% Confidence Interval	56–64
Practical Domain	49
90% Confidence Interval	46–52
GAC	47
90% Confidence Interval	45–49

Lewis: Diagnosed with Pervasive Developmental Disorder/Autistic Disorder at age 3 years 10 months

Lewis, a 46-month-old male, was referred by his parents for an evaluation. He lives with his biological mother, stepfather, 14-year-old stepsister, and 65-year-old maternal grandmother. Lewis' mother remains at home to care for him. His stepfather is employed framing houses.

Lewis was born full-term, of average height and weight, and, except for a C-section, the delivery was normal. His mother was 27, in good health, reportedly consumed no alcohol or illegal drugs during her pregnancy, and smoked about 8 cigarettes a day.

Lewis' gross motor development generally was normal. For example, he sat at 7 months and walked at 12 months. He displayed oral/sensory sensitivity. He has restricted his diet to a limited range of foods, preferring peanut butter and jelly sandwiches, grilled cheese, and toast. He currently eats with his hands, and smells his food before eating it.

Lewis displays no fears and shows minimal awareness of danger. His mother describes him as "bouncing off the walls," displaying potentially dangerous behaviors (e.g., looking at the TV screen after climbing on top of the TV), almost always in action, and able to sustain his active behavior over a long period of time. At home, when Lewis is told "no" he runs, throws tantrums, bangs his head, twirls, and kicks and hits. He does not throw tantrums on the bus ride to school or at school. There are no reports of serious injuries, illnesses, allergies, and visual or auditory acuity problems. He takes 100 mg. of Zoloft® twice daily to improve his concentration and attention. Lewis goes to bed at 8:00 p.m. and, after taking Clonodine (.1 mg) at bedtime, sleeps through the night. There are no indications that he experiences nightmares.

He enjoys placing objects (e.g., blocks, magnets, colors) in a line, spinning toys, and watching television programs that present captioned information at the bottom of the screen (e.g., CNN, The Weather Channel). Lewis does not interact with family members, has no neighborhood friends, and displays limited interaction with peers at school.

Lewis attends school daily, from 9:00 a.m.–3:00 p.m., at a school for children diagnosed with autism. His teacher reports considerable improvement in Lewis' behavior and achievement during the last six months following the use of applied behavior management principles. In addition, Lewis is beginning to exhibit parallel play, a condition considered a precursor to the development of advanced social skills.

The ABAS–II was used to describe the development of Lewis' adaptive skills in specific areas and his adaptive behavior in conceptual, practical, and social domains and to assist in program planning for his home and school environments. ABAS–II data was also used to establish a baseline for the continued monitoring of his progress in the program. The ten skill areas were perceived by Lewis' teachers and parents as being central to his further development and important components of his school and home program.

Lewis' mother and grandmother completed the Parent/Primary Caregiver Form together and his teacher completed the Teacher/Daycare Provider Form. Lewis' scores are reported in Table 3.5.

Table 3.5   Lewis' ABAS–II Scores

Skill Area/Adaptive Domain/GAC	Scaled Scores	
	Parent/Primary Caregiver Form	Teacher/Daycare Provider Form
Communication	1	4
Community Use	1	–
Functional Pre-Academics	7	10
Home/School Living	1	3
Health and Safety	2	4
Leisure	1	4
Self-Care	1	3
Self-Direction	3	3
Social	2	1
Motor	6	7
Conceptual Domain	57	72
90% Confidence Interval	51–63	67–77
Social Domain	50	55
90% Confidence Interval	43–57	48–62
Practical Domain	43	56
90% Confidence Interval	37–49	49–63
GAC	49	61
90% Confidence Interval	46–52	58–64

Lewis' adaptive behavior, as reflected in scores from the GAC and the three adaptive domains, is extremely low and generally consistent at home and school. The adaptive skill profiles reveal considerable consistency in parent and teacher ratings. Both sets of ratings indicate that his Functional Pre-Academics Skill Area is the most advanced followed by the Motor Skill Area. Scores from both forms indicate that the Communication, Home/School Living, and Social Skill Area development should be emphasized at home and school.

Lewis' intelligence was assessed with the *Bayley Scales of Infant Development–Second Edition* (Bayley, 1993). His Mental Development Index was less than 50 and he displayed little meaningful language during the test. Lewis' speech and language development are delayed. He does not converse verbally with other individuals and when he vocalizes, his words are unrelated to questions or comments made by others or the nature of his activities. Lewis' Receptive (standard score of 38), Expressive (standard score of 47) and Total Language (standard score of 43) development is significantly delayed, as measured by the *Clinical Evaluation of Language Fundamentals—Third Edition* (Semel, Wiig, & Secord, 1994). His language age scores lie between 16 and 20 months. His language and intellectual development are consistent.

An evaluation by an occupational therapist indicated that Lewis displays delays in fine motor, self-care, and play skills; and has decreased attention, limited communication, and sensory integration issues. His gross motor skills, including mobility, constituted strengths.

Results from an assessment for Autistic Disorder, completed by the parents, and evaluated in combination with other information, support a diagnosis of a Pervasive Developmental Disorder/Autistic Disorder.

Lewis' parents and teachers agreed that Lewis' skill development and program implementation must focus on developing more control of his behaviors (e.g., eliminating running, head-banging, twirling, hitting, and kicking). The use of applied behavior management principles at school has resulted in important behavioral improvements. Lewis' mother, father, and grandmother agreed to observe the demonstration of these principles at school and to work with the school psychologist, a behavior specialist, to implement a similar program at home.

Additionally, the school's pre-academic program is producing positive results, supported in part by the ABAS–II data, and will continue to be utilized. Further efforts to promote Communication, School Living, and Social Skill Area development also were added to Lewis' IEP.

Lewis' family agreed to implement a home-based program that also emphasized the Communication and Social Skill Area development and used behavior management principles to promote better eating habits and home living skills (e.g., bathing, tooth brushing). The family agreed to readminister the ABAS–II in 6 months to determine if changes occurred in these skill areas.

Nona: Evaluation for services associated with a diagnosis of Mental Retardation

Nona, a 9-year-old female student in third grade, was born three months prematurely. She displayed developmental disabilities during infancy and early childhood, especially in communication and cognitive skills. Nona began to receive special education preschool services for children with developmental delays at age 3. School reports indicated that she was diagnosed with a speech and language impairment at age 7 and has been receiving special educational services. However, the school district she previously attended did not provide test records. Nona's current school district conducted its own evaluation and believes that Nona displays lower mental abilities than other students.

Nona's WISC–III standard scores were reported as follows: Verbal IQ was 62, Performance IQ was 66, and Full Scale IQ was 61. Her standard scores in math and reading, as measured by the WIAT, were in the low 70s. Teacher reports indicate that Nona's achievement resembles that of a kindergarten or first grade student.

Nona attends school regularly, generally is well behaved but often distracted, and displays problems retaining what she learns. Nona comes from a large and loving family. Her father, mother, and three older sisters are attentive to her needs and have worked consistently to help Nona develop social skills. Table 3.6 details Nona's ABAS–II scores.

Table 3.6   Nona's ABAS–II Scores

Skill Area/Adaptive Domain/GAC	Scaled Scores	
	Teacher Form	Parent Form
Communication	1	2
Community Use	2	5
Functional Academics	1	1
School/Home Living	1	8
Health and Safety	3	2
Leisure	2	4
Self-Care	1	3
Self-Direction	1	2
Social	1	7
Conceptual Domain	50	53
90% Confidence Interval	47–53	47–59
Social Domain	58	75
90% Confidence Interval	54–62	69–81
Practical Domain	49	62
90% Confidence Interval	45–53	57–67
GAC	44	58
90% Confidence Interval	42–47	55–61

The results listed in Table 3.6 provide a profile of a student who displays extremely low to borderline adaptive skills. Nona's overall adaptive skills, as measured by the GAC, are below the 1st percentile as reported by both her teacher and parent. Nona's conceptual, social, and practical composite scores also are low. They fall below the 1st percentile at school. They are somewhat higher at home where her Social Domain composite falls in the 5th percentile, showing an area of relative strength. Scores from the Teacher Form generally are the same, and suggest no notable skill areas that are relative strengths or weaknesses. The profile from the Parent Form is more variable and amenable to identifying strengths and weaknesses. Information from Table B.8 was used to further investigate if the skill area scaled scores differ significantly from Nona's mean scaled score of 3.8 on the Parent Form (using .05 as the standard) and if the differences occur rarely (using 5% as the standard).

Nona's scaled scores on the Parent Form associated with Communication, Functional Academics, and Health and Safety are significantly lower than her average skill area score while those associated with Home Living and Social are significantly advanced compared to her average skill area scaled score. Although these scores differ significantly from her mean, none of the differences occur rarely. The reports from the Teacher and Parent Forms display differences: the GACs differ considerably (i.e., a discrepancy of 14 points), but the percentile ranks of <1 for each form are consistent. In addition, considerable agreement exists in scores from seven of the nine skill areas.

During a meeting arranged to discuss these results, Nona's teacher and mother confirmed that Nona's adaptive skill development in the Communication, Functional Academics, Health and Safety, Leisure, Self-Care, and Self-Direction Skill Areas was low. They also discussed the apparent differences between School and Home Living and Social Skill Areas. Nona's mother indicated that she and Nona's older sisters have a close and loving relationship. Her sisters often serve as surrogate mothers and encourage her in various ways. Furthermore, they accompany and supervise her when she uses community resources.

At home, Nona must follow a set schedule to perform various chores and is closely supervised by her older sisters. Thus, her sisters' supervision seemingly is the catalyst for Nona to perform her home chores. In contrast, at school, Nona rarely displays the initiative to help care for her learning environments. Nona's teacher realized she should require and encourage her to assume more age-related responsibilities at school (e.g., throwing trash away, bringing needed books and supplies).

At school, Nona rarely seeks friendship with others, says "thank you," offers to assist others, or displays other social skills common for children her age. In contrast, Nona displays suitable social skills at home because her family has insisted and worked with Nona since she was 4 years old to develop social skills that enable her to "blend in." This information indicates that Nona may need additional opportunities at school to be with other students in non-self contained settings that provide opportunities for her to display current social skills and to acquire new social skills.

A meeting of the child study team was held at the conclusion of the school year to consider special education eligibility and programming issues. Members agreed that Nona meets eligibility for services, given a classification of mental retardation based in part on her scores from the ABAS–II, WISC–III, and WIAT. The ABAS–II scores also provided a basis for prioritizing emphasis on further development of her adaptive skills. Of course, considerable discussion focused on advancing Nona's functional academic skills. In addition, Nona's mother agreed to encourage Nona to become more independent in her use of community resources.

Nona's teacher recommended more time next year in integrated settings at school to better use and advance Nona's social skills. She also recommended that her next classroom teacher place higher expectations on using and further developing her School Living Skill Area. The child study team recommended that a more thorough evaluation of Nona's language skills, including pragmatic language, be obtained and, if necessary, services provided to promote her language development.

Information from the ABAS–II was instrumental in helping Nona's family and school officials better understand her adaptive skills at home and school. The results supported a diagnosis of mental retardation and helped identify the specific adaptive skills to which efforts from the home and school should be directed.

Rodney: A diagnosis of Traumatic Brain Injury

Rodney, a 48-year-old male, was hospitalized following a motorcycle accident. His development during infancy, childhood, and adulthood reportedly were normal. He completed high school and later took courses in trade school. He was married for 12 years, divorced 5 years ago, and has 3 children. Prior to his accident, Rodney was employed in the home building industry as a mason. He has been unable to work since his accident and is beginning to participate in rehabilitation services at a local medical center.

Tests conducted in the hospital following his accident led the physicians to conclude that Rodney exhibits traumatic brain injury (TBI), principally in the right hemisphere. The prognosis was guarded, given the severity of his internal head injuries. His WAIS–III Full Scale IQ was 65, Verbal IQ was 74, and Performance IQ was 60. His WAIS–III Block Design subtest was lowest, with a scaled score of 1. The ABAS–II was administered during this same period. Rodney's rehabilitation specialists served as the respondents. The results of the assessment of Rodney's adaptive skills are provided in Table 3.7.

Table 3.7   Rodney's ABAS–II Scores Before and After the Accident

Skill Area/Adaptive Domain/GAC	Scaled Scores Adult Form, Rated by Others	
	Before Accident	**After Accident**
Communication	9	4
Community Use	11	3
Functional Academics	10	4
Home Living	11	2
Health and Safety	10	5
Leisure	12	4
Self-Care	11	2
Self-Direction	10	2
Social	9	1
Work	9	–
Conceptual Domain	94	63
90% Confidence Interval	91–97	60–66
Social Domain	99	62
90% Confidence Interval	95–103	58–66
Practical Domain	97	59[a]
90% Confidence Interval	94–100	56–62
GAC	97	54[b]
90% Confidence Interval	95–99	52–56

[a]Based on 4 skill areas
[b]Based on 9 skill areas

Rodney's adaptive skills are in the extremely low range, with a GAC of 54, which lies below the 1st percentile. His three adaptive domain scores also are at or below the 1st percentile. He displays borderline abilities in four skill areas: Communication, Functional Academics, Health and Safety, and Leisure. His skill areas are extremely low in Community Use, Home Living, Self-Care, Self-Direction, and Social.

Information from Table B.22 was used to further investigate if the scaled scores differ significantly from his mean scaled score of 3 (using .05 as the standard) and if the differences occur rarely (using 5% as the standard). Relative to his average skill level, Rodney's adaptive skills are highest on Health and Safety and lowest on Social. However, none of the differences is rare.

Rodney's initial recovery has been somewhat slow. His rehabilitation initially focused on the development of skills associated with Communication and Functional Academics. Having achieved some success in these two areas, Rodney and his rehabilitation specialists are considering other areas that need to be addressed. His rehabilitation specialists were interested in discovering the level and nature of Rodney's adaptive skills before the accident. This information often helps establish a standard against which recovery is evaluated. Therefore, with Rodney's permission, additional ABAS–II data about his adaptive functioning before the accident were acquired from a male friend with whom he previously lived and worked. These scores are provided in Table 3.7.

Before Rodney's accident, his GAC score falls in the average range, with a corresponding percentile rank of 42. His conceptual, social, and practical domain-related abilities also were in the average range. All scaled scores of the skill areas are in the average range. This information helped assure the therapists that Rodney's adaptive skills were in the average range before the accident. These data help set a goal and standard for therapy.

Before the accident, Rodney lived alone and was employed as a mason. He would like to return home and to work as soon as possible. Based on his ABAS–II profile and other supporting information, Rodney and his therapists decided to focus on the development of the Home Living, Self-Care, Self-Direction, and Social Skill Areas. Adaptive skills in these four areas are required if Rodney is to enjoy greater degrees of independent living and to eventually return to work.

An initial goal of therapy will be to help Rodney return home and receive daily assistance from home-based rehabilitation specialists. Extensive support services are likely to be necessary at first. Progress toward limited, then intermittent, and finally no support services is expected. Everyone agrees that rehabilitation provided in the home is likely to be more beneficial than that provided exclusively in a hospital setting. Rodney also will receive rehabilitation services on an outpatient basis to help promote his physical and language development. Arrangements were made to readminister the ABAS–II in three months to help evaluate the effectiveness of and/or modify Rodney's program.

Information from the ABAS–II was instrumental in helping Rodney and his medical team better understand his adaptive skills, examine the effects of the TBI, identify specific adaptive skills to which efforts would be directed, and create two baselines (i.e., one premorbid and the other postmorbid) against which progress will be measured.

Mary: A diagnosis of later onset of Alzheimer's disease

Mary was a homemaker and assisted in performing various farm-related chores throughout her adult life. She married her childhood sweetheart at age 18 soon after they both graduated from high school. Her husband, a farmer, died 9 years ago. Mary remained in her farm home until one month ago. Mary, age 80, recently moved into an assisted-living center. Her only daughter arranged for Mary to live there after the daughter became concerned that her mother's life was endangered due to her failing health, particularly memory and aphasia-related difficulties. Mary also displays signs of dementia. An evaluation confirmed later onset of Alzheimer's disease. Mary's daughter served as the respondent for the ABAS–II. The assessment of Mary's adaptive skills is provided in Table 3.8.

Table 3.8   Mary's ABAS–II Scores

Skill Area/Adaptive Domain/GAC	Scaled Scores
	Adult Form, Rated by Others
Communication	3
Community Use	3
Functional Academics	2
Home Living	3
Health and Safety	3
Leisure	5
Self-Care	2
Self-Direction	3
Social	5
Conceptual Domain	61
90% Confidence Interval	59–63
Social Domain	75
90% Confidence Interval	72–78
Practical Domain	61
90% Confidence Interval	59–63
GAC	59
90% Confidence Interval	57–61

Mary's adaptive skills are extremely low, with a GAC of 59, a score that falls below the 1st percentile. Behaviors associated with Mary's Social Domain are at the 5th percentile while those associated with her Conceptual and Practical Domains are below the 1st percentile. In addition, seven skill area scaled scores lie in the extremely low level. The skill areas of Leisure and Social fall in the borderline range. Information from Table B.22 was used to further investigate if Mary's scaled scores differ significantly from her mean scaled score of 3.2 (using .05 as the standard) and if the differences occurred rarely (using 5% as the standard). Her Leisure and Social skill areas fall significantly above her mean of 3.2. However, these differences from the mean should not be considered rare.

Mary's daughter and the staff at the assisted-living center discussed the ABAS–II results and profile. This information helped verify the prior diagnosis of later onset of Alzheimer's disease. More importantly, the ABAS–II data enabled Mary's daughter and the staff to identify program goals that may promote the development and minimize the deterioration of adaptive skills, and allow Mary to remain as safe and independent as possible. Mary's daughter became aware that further deterioration of her mother's adaptive skills might jeopardize her being allowed to remain in the assisted-living center.

Mary's daughter and the staff agreed that Mary would benefit from a daily program that focused on three skill areas considered to be essential to Mary's immediate and long term needs: Health and Safety, Home Living, and Self-Care. These skill areas contribute to the daily activities vital to Mary's basic needs and independence, but her scores in these areas were low. Many of the residents at the center have similar needs; therefore, the center offers a daily regimen involving group and individual programs that focus on these three skills areas. Mary soon became involved in these programs. Her daughter and staff agreed to readminister the ABAS–II in four months to determine if Mary's adaptive skills had improved, remained the same, or declined. Program revisions would be considered at that time.

Information from the ABAS–II was instrumental in helping Mary, her daughter, and the staff understand her adaptive skills, compare them with current personal and center-based needs, identify specific adaptive skills to which efforts will be directed, examine the effects of later onset of Alzheimer's disease on her adaptive skills, and create a baseline to measure progress.

Chapter 4

Development and Standardization

Development of the ABAS–II

ABAS–II items were developed according to a systematic method involving multiple steps as described in Chapter 5 of this manual. Items were written at a fifth-grade reading level, on average. Most items require no more than a sixth-grade reading level. All items included on the rating forms were reviewed by an independent consultant and edited as necessary to meet this goal.

Pilot and Tryout Studies

One pilot study and one national tryout study were conducted to evaluate the psychometric properties of the school-age forms and the Adult Form items and scales. Approximately 92 parents, 63 teachers, and 273 adults participated in the pilot study of the Parent, Teacher, and Adult Forms, respectively. During the nationwide tryout study, 1,045 parents, 980 teachers, and 1,406 adults completed the Parent, Teacher, and Adult Forms, respectively. After preliminary focus group reviews of items, a nationwide tryout study of the Parent/Primary Caregiver and Teacher/Daycare Provider Forms was conducted in which 1,520 forms were completed. For all forms, the data from tryout studies were used to evaluate item statistics, differential item functioning, item guessing rate, item bias, skill area reliability and validity, clarity of the instructions, and clinical usefulness. On the basis of tryout data analysis, 272, 242, and 275 items were selected for the standardization editions of the Parent, Teacher, and Adult Forms, respectively, and 344 and 342 items were chosen for the standardization editions of the Parent/Primary Caregiver and Teacher/Daycare Provider Forms, respectively.

Standardization

Description of the Sample

Normative information presented in this manual is based on national standardization samples representative of the English-speaking U.S. population ages 0 through 89 years. Standardization samples of the school-age and Adult Form were stratified by sex, race/ethnicity, and educational level parameters according to census data from 1999, and standardization samples of the infant-preschool forms were stratified by the same variables according to 2000 census data (U.S. Bureau of the Census, 2000). In addition, efforts were made to ensure that the samples were representative by geographical regions. The following sections present the demographic characteristics and composition details of the standardization sample.

> **Age:** The standardization sample of the Parent/Primary Caregiver Form was divided into thirteen age groups spanning birth to age 5 years. The standardization sample of the Teacher/Daycare Provider Form was divided into seven age groups spanning ages 2–5 years. The standardization samples of the school-age Teacher and Parent Forms were divided into eleven age groups spanning ages 5–21 years. The standardization samples of the Adult Form (self report and rated by others) were each divided into seven age groups spanning ages 16–89 years. The size of each age group is presented in Table 4.1 for each of the six standardization samples.

Table 4.1   Standardization Sample by Age Group

Infant-Preschool Forms			School-Age Forms			Adult Form		
Ages	Teacher/ Daycare Provider	Parent/ Primary Caregiver	Ages	Teacher	Parent	Ages	Self Report	Rated by Others
0:0–0:3	–	100	5	150	120	16–21	150	100
0:4–0:7	–	100	6	140	130	22–29	150	140
0:8–0:11	–	100	7	140	120	30–39	180	160
1:0–1:3	–	100	8	150	150	40–49	180	180
1:4–1:7	–	100	9	150	150	50–64	110	150
1:8–1:11	–	100	10	150	150	65–74	120	100
2:0–2:5	100	100	11	150	150	75–89	100	90
2:6–2:11	100	100	12	150	150			
3:0–3:5	100	100	13–14	250	150			
3:6–3:11	100	100	15–16	140	200			
4:0–4:5	100	100	17–21	120	200			
4:6–4:11	100	100						
5:0–5:11	150	150						
Total	750	1350	**Total**	1690	1670	**Total**	990	920

Sex: The standardization samples consisted of equal numbers of male and female participants in each age group from 0 to 64 years. The two oldest age groups included more women than men, in proportions consistent with census data.

Race/Ethnicity: For each age group in the standardization samples, the proportions of Whites, African Americans, Hispanics, and other racial/ethnic groups were based on the racial/ethnic proportions of individuals within each age group of the U.S. population according to the census data.

Education Level: The standardization sample was stratified according to the following five education levels based on the number of years of school completed. For participants ages 0–21 years, highest parent education was used; for participants ages 22–89 years, participant education was used.

≤8 years

9–11 years

12 years

13–15 years

≥16 years

Geographic Region: The United States was divided into the four major geographic regions specified by the census reports (see Figures 4.1 and 4.2): Northeast, North Central, South, and West. The number of participants from each region was closely proportionate to the population percentages in each region.

Locating and Testing the Sample

The standardization data of the school-age forms and Adult Form were collected by 139 independent examiners in 107 cities in the United States. The standardization data of the infant-preschool forms were collected by 214 independent examiners in 184 cities in the United States. Various methods were used to recruit participants to fit within the sampling matrix. These methods included random telephone calls and flyers placed in schools, preschools, daycare centers, military bases, senior centers, churches, parent-teacher associations and various community organizations. The data collection of the standardization samples of the school-age forms and Adult Forms took place from December 1998 to

December 1999; data collection of the standardization samples of the infant-preschool forms occurred from November 2001 to October 2002.

Representativeness of the Sample

Detailed demographic information of the U.S. population and the standardization samples is provided by age, race/ethnicity, and education in Tables 4.2, 4.3, and 4.4, respectively; by age, sex, and education in Tables 4.5, 4.6, and 4.7; and by age, sex, and race/ethnicity in Tables 4.8, 4.9, and 4.10.

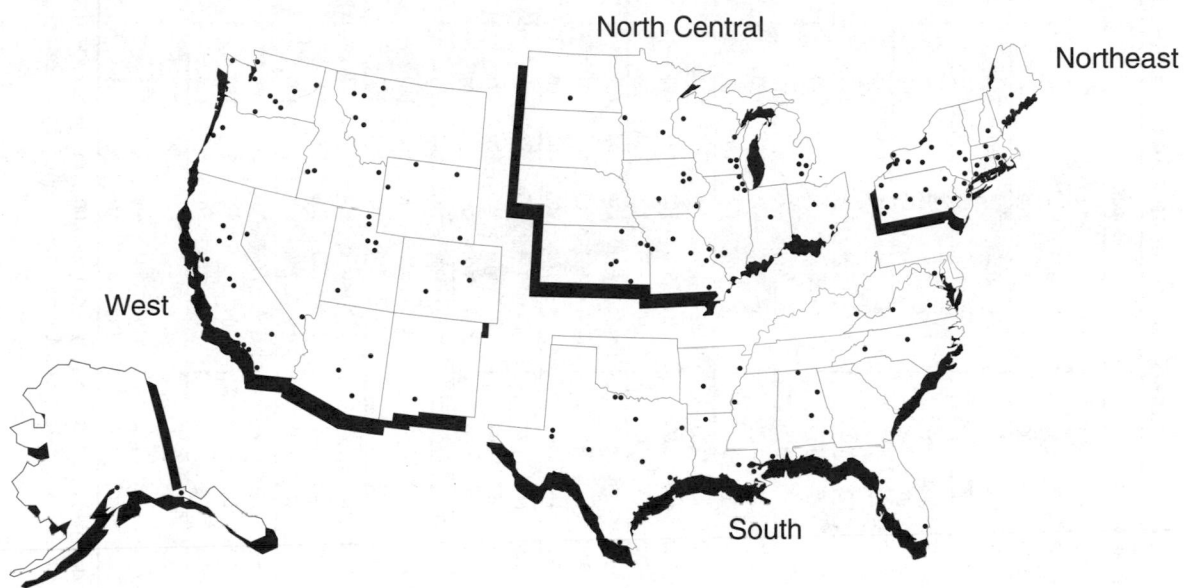

Figure 4.1   Standardization Sampling Sites for Infant-Preschool Forms

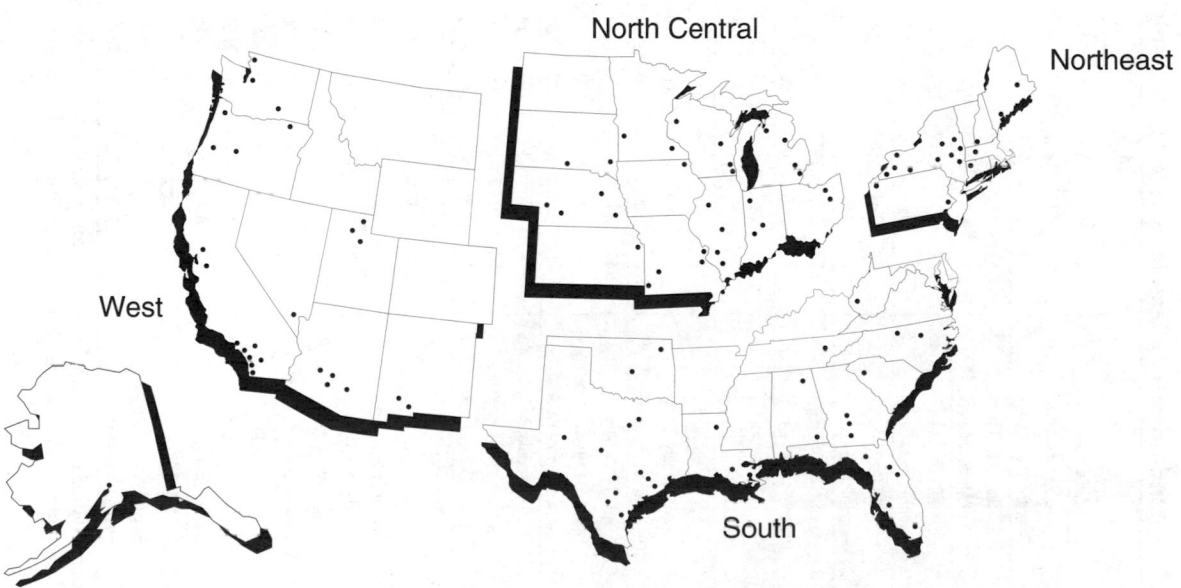

Figure 4.2   Standardization Sampling Sites for School-Age and Adult Forms

Table 4.2 Standardization Sample by Age, Race/Ethnicity, and Education: Parent/Primary Caregiver and Teacher/Daycare Provider Forms

Ages	Sample	White					African American					Hispanic					Other				
		≤8	9–11	12	13–15	≥16	≤8	9–11	12	13–15	≥16	≤8	9–11	12	13–15	≥16	≤8	9–11	12	13–15	≥16
0:0–0:3	U.S. Population	0.62	3.19	14.02	20.33	22.07	0.29	1.87	4.59	4.55	2.09	3.44	6.69	5.06	3.99	2.42	0.03	0.34	1.01	0.91	2.48
	Parent/Primary Caregiver	1.00	3.00	15.00	20.00	25.00	1.00	2.00	3.00	6.00	2.00	2.00	7.00	7.00	4.00	–	–	–	–	1.00	1.00
0:4–0:7	U.S. Population	0.62	3.19	14.02	20.33	22.07	0.29	1.87	4.59	4.55	2.09	3.44	6.69	5.06	3.99	2.42	0.03	0.34	1.01	0.91	2.48
	Parent/Primary Caregiver	–	4.00	14.00	20.00	22.00	–	3.00	4.00	3.00	3.00	4.00	6.00	5.00	5.00	2.00	–	–	1.00	2.00	2.00
0:8–0:11	U.S. Population	0.62	3.19	14.02	20.33	22.07	0.29	1.87	4.59	4.55	2.09	3.44	6.69	5.06	3.99	2.42	0.03	0.34	1.01	0.91	2.48
	Parent/Primary Caregiver	–	3.00	14.00	20.00	22.00	1.00	2.00	4.00	6.00	2.00	1.00	8.00	5.00	4.00	2.00	–	–	1.00	2.00	3.00
1:0–1:3	U.S. Population	1.02	2.63	13.17	21.09	22.69	0.53	2.72	5.38	5.83	1.88	2.78	5.08	4.75	2.91	1.70	0.21	0.30	1.02	1.85	2.49
	Parent/Primary Caregiver	–	4.00	13.00	22.00	23.00	–	3.00	4.00	5.00	2.00	3.00	5.00	6.00	5.00	2.00	–	–	–	1.00	2.00
1:4–1:7	U.S. Population	1.02	2.63	13.17	21.09	22.69	0.53	2.72	5.38	5.83	1.88	2.78	5.08	4.75	2.91	1.70	0.21	0.30	1.02	1.85	2.49
	Parent/Primary Caregiver	–	4.00	11.00	21.00	22.00	–	3.00	5.00	6.00	4.00	3.00	5.00	6.00	3.00	2.00	–	–	1.00	1.00	3.00
1:8–1:11	U.S. Population	1.02	2.63	13.17	21.09	22.69	0.53	2.72	5.38	5.83	1.88	2.78	5.08	4.75	2.91	1.70	0.21	0.30	1.02	1.85	2.49
	Parent/Primary Caregiver	1.00	3.00	14.00	21.00	23.00	–	4.00	4.00	5.00	–	3.00	5.00	5.00	5.00	1.00	–	–	1.00	1.00	5.00
2:0–2:5	U.S. Population	0.65	2.10	14.94	22.74	21.18	0.06	2.58	5.00	4.08	2.68	2.56	5.00	5.39	3.60	1.53	0.24	0.53	1.15	1.77	2.23
	Parent/Primary Caregiver	–	3.00	15.00	23.00	21.00	–	3.00	5.00	4.00	3.00	3.00	5.00	5.00	4.00	3.00	–	1.00	1.00	2.00	2.00
	Teacher/Daycare Provider	–	3.00	17.00	23.00	21.00	1.00	4.00	5.00	5.00	2.00	2.00	5.00	4.00	2.00	3.00	–	1.00	1.00	–	2.00
2:6–2:11	U.S. Population	0.65	2.10	14.94	22.74	21.18	0.06	2.58	5.00	4.08	2.68	2.56	5.00	5.39	3.60	1.53	0.24	0.53	1.15	1.77	2.23
	Parent/Primary Caregiver	–	3.00	15.00	24.00	20.00	–	3.00	5.00	4.00	3.00	4.00	5.00	4.00	4.00	1.00	–	1.00	1.00	1.00	2.00
	Teacher/Daycare Provider	–	2.00	15.00	23.00	21.00	2.00	5.00	5.00	4.00	3.00	2.00	3.00	5.00	4.00	1.00	–	–	2.00	2.00	1.00
3:0–3:5	U.S. Population	0.74	2.57	13.92	22.06	21.24	0.45	1.90	5.57	5.88	2.24	3.19	5.34	4.03	3.92	1.15	0.14	0.38	1.31	1.40	2.56
	Parent/Primary Caregiver	1.00	2.00	15.00	22.00	22.00	–	2.00	6.00	6.00	2.00	3.00	6.00	4.00	4.00	1.00	–	–	–	2.00	2.00
	Teacher/Daycare Provider	–	3.00	14.00	22.00	22.00	–	6.00	6.00	6.00	2.00	1.00	5.00	5.00	5.00	1.00	–	–	2.00	2.00	2.00
3:6–3:11	U.S. Population	0.74	2.57	13.92	22.06	21.24	0.45	1.90	5.57	5.88	2.24	3.19	5.34	4.03	3.92	1.15	0.14	0.38	1.31	1.40	2.56
	Parent/Primary Caregiver	1.00	2.00	15.00	22.00	22.00	–	3.00	6.00	6.00	2.00	3.00	6.00	4.00	4.00	1.00	–	–	–	2.00	2.00
	Teacher/Daycare Provider	1.00	3.00	14.00	22.00	22.00	–	5.00	5.00	7.00	2.00	–	4.00	4.00	5.00	2.00	–	–	2.00	–	4.00
4:0–4:5	U.S. Population	0.59	2.29	15.40	20.23	22.07	0.27	2.36	5.06	5.36	1.21	3.54	6.07	4.51	3.63	1.18	0.22	0.34	1.55	1.46	2.68
	Parent/Primary Caregiver	1.00	1.00	16.00	20.00	22.00	–	3.00	5.00	6.00	1.00	2.00	7.00	5.00	4.00	1.00	–	1.00	2.00	2.00	3.00
	Teacher/Daycare Provider	1.00	2.00	16.00	20.00	22.00	–	3.00	5.00	5.00	1.00	3.00	7.00	4.00	4.00	2.00	–	1.00	2.00	2.00	3.00
4:6–4:11	U.S. Population	0.59	2.29	15.40	20.23	22.07	0.27	2.36	5.06	5.36	1.21	3.54	6.07	4.51	3.63	1.18	0.22	0.34	1.55	1.46	2.68
	Parent/Primary Caregiver	1.00	2.00	16.00	20.00	22.00	–	3.00	5.00	5.00	1.00	3.00	7.00	4.00	4.00	1.00	–	1.00	2.00	2.00	3.00
	Teacher/Daycare Provider	1.00	4.00	15.00	20.00	22.00	–	2.00	5.00	5.00	1.00	5.00	5.00	4.00	4.00	1.00	–	–	2.00	1.00	3.00
5:0–5:11	U.S. Population	0.74	2.59	13.58	20.23	23.57	0.41	2.01	5.56	5.60	1.55	3.24	4.95	4.49	4.87	1.25	0.23	0.19	1.60	1.67	1.67
	Parent/Primary Caregiver	0.67	2.67	13.33	19.33	24.00	–	2.67	5.33	5.33	1.33	2.67	5.33	4.00	5.33	1.33	0.67	0.67	2.00	1.33	2.00
	Teacher/Daycare Provider	0.67	2.67	13.33	20.00	24.00	–	2.67	5.33	6.00	1.33	3.33	4.67	4.00	5.33	1.33	0.67	–	2.00	1.33	1.33

Note. U.S. population data are from *Current Population Survey, October 2000* [Machine-readable data file] by U.S. Bureau of the Census, 2000, Washington, DC: U.S. Bureau of the Census (Producer/Distributor). For individuals ages 0–21, education is based on parent education; for individuals ages 22–89, education is the number of years completed.

Table 4.3 Standardization Sample by Age, Race/Ethnicity, and Education: Parent and Teacher Forms

Ages	Sample	White					African American					Hispanic					Other				
		≤8	9–11	12	13–15	≥16	≤8	9–11	12	13–15	≥16	≤8	9–11	12	13–15	≥16	≤8	9–11	12	13–15	≥16
5	U.S. Population	0.80	2.66	14.74	18.58	23.68	0.49	3.14	4.50	5.49	2.06	3.67	3.81	4.77	3.86	1.91	0.23	0.56	1.42	1.34	2.25
	Parent	0.83	2.50	15.83	16.67	23.33	0.83	1.67	4.17	4.17	3.33	0.83	2.50	8.33	6.67	1.67	0.83	0.83	2.50	1.67	0.83
	Teacher	0.67	2.67	15.33	18.67	24.00	–	4.00	5.33	5.33	1.33	4.00	4.00	5.33	2.00	1.33	–	0.67	1.33	1.33	2.67
6	U.S. Population	0.67	2.46	16.27	20.53	23.39	0.54	2.82	4.94	4.52	1.68	3.44	3.18	4.57	3.60	1.94	0.31	0.59	1.30	1.43	1.81
	Parent	–	–	18.46	20.77	23.08	1.54	0.77	5.38	3.85	3.08	0.77	2.31	6.92	4.62	2.31	–	1.54	1.54	1.54	1.54
	Teacher	0.71	4.29	17.86	15.00	24.29	0.71	3.57	5.71	4.29	1.43	3.57	4.29	5.00	2.14	1.43	0.71	–	1.43	1.43	2.14
7	U.S. Population	0.77	2.57	15.85	19.56	23.64	0.42	3.35	6.89	4.61	2.07	3.64	3.03	4.27	3.41	1.72	0.23	0.13	0.92	0.78	2.12
	Parent	0.83	3.33	15.83	16.67	25.00	1.67	2.50	6.67	5.00	1.67	0.83	3.33	5.00	5.00	1.67	–	1.67	0.83	0.83	1.67
	Teacher	0.71	3.57	15.71	18.57	23.57	0.71	1.43	7.14	5.00	2.86	3.57	3.57	3.57	4.29	1.43	–	–	1.43	0.71	2.14
8	U.S. Population	0.86	2.76	15.41	21.31	22.69	0.39	2.57	5.62	6.16	2.42	3.45	2.77	3.77	3.12	1.79	0.30	0.32	0.96	1.53	1.80
	Parent	0.67	2.67	17.33	19.33	22.67	1.33	1.33	3.33	8.00	2.67	2.67	3.33	4.00	3.33	2.00	–	0.67	1.33	2.00	1.33
	Teacher	0.67	2.67	16.00	18.67	24.67	–	2.67	6.00	5.33	3.33	2.67	2.00	4.67	2.00	2.00	–	–	2.67	2.00	2.00
9	U.S. Population	0.73	2.20	16.59	21.55	23.26	0.38	2.59	5.17	4.94	2.50	3.28	2.99	3.52	3.50	1.70	0.30	0.26	0.61	1.69	2.25
	Parent	1.33	2.67	17.33	17.33	25.33	0.67	2.67	4.67	4.67	3.33	2.00	2.67	6.00	3.33	1.33	–	0.67	0.67	2.00	1.33
	Teacher	1.33	3.33	16.67	21.33	22.00	0.67	2.00	6.00	4.00	2.67	4.00	0.67	5.33	2.67	2.00	–	0.67	1.33	2.00	1.33
10	U.S. Population	0.72	3.14	15.22	20.73	22.74	0.36	3.09	6.21	5.59	2.55	3.17	2.48	4.24	3.37	1.43	0.26	0.53	1.13	1.36	1.68
	Parent	2.00	3.33	14.00	20.67	22.00	0.67	4.00	6.00	5.33	2.67	0.67	3.33	5.33	2.67	2.00	0.67	0.67	1.33	0.67	2.00
	Teacher	2.00	3.33	14.67	20.00	22.67	–	3.33	6.00	6.00	2.67	3.33	2.00	5.33	1.33	2.00	–	0.67	1.33	2.00	1.33
11	U.S. Population	0.68	2.90	18.20	20.45	23.94	0.66	2.47	4.51	4.47	2.27	0.01	0.33	0.19	0.55	0.06	0.23	0.54	0.99	1.03	2.24
	Parent	2.00	2.67	18.00	20.67	22.67	1.33	2.00	2.00	5.33	2.67	3.33	2.00	4.00	4.00	2.00	–	0.67	1.33	1.33	2.00
	Teacher	0.67	3.33	18.00	18.00	25.33	0.62	2.67	6.67	2.00	2.67	4.00	1.33	3.33	4.67	1.33	–	0.67	1.33	1.33	2.00
12	U.S. Population	0.58	2.58	17.51	21.24	22.84	0.44	1.86	5.55	4.31	2.23	3.41	2.85	3.85	3.21	1.78	0.49	0.58	1.44	1.53	1.72
	Parent	1.33	1.33	17.33	21.33	23.33	1.33	2.00	2.67	6.67	1.33	2.00	3.33	4.00	3.33	2.00	–	0.67	2.67	2.00	1.33
	Teacher	3.33	1.33	18.00	16.00	24.00	0.67	2.00	5.33	4.67	2.67	3.33	2.00	5.33	3.33	2.00	0.67	–	2.00	1.33	2.00
13–14	U.S. Population	0.77	2.77	18.09	20.07	23.66	0.76	3.12	5.14	4.53	2.53	2.93	2.14	3.51	3.04	1.49	0.78	0.39	1.49	1.21	1.56
	Parent	1.33	2.67	18.67	20.67	24.00	–	3.33	2.67	2.67	3.33	3.33	2.00	5.33	3.33	1.33	0.67	0.67	1.33	1.33	1.33
	Teacher	0.80	2.80	18.00	18.80	24.40	0.80	3.20	5.20	4.40	2.40	3.20	2.40	4.40	1.60	1.60	0.80	0.40	1.60	1.20	2.00
15–16	U.S. Population	0.92	3.33	17.75	19.94	23.17	0.55	2.46	5.56	4.59	2.75	3.50	2.91	3.31	2.53	1.57	0.43	0.31	1.33	1.37	1.74
	Parent	1.00	3.00	20.00	21.50	23.00	0.50	2.00	2.50	3.50	3.50	2.00	4.00	3.50	2.50	1.50	0.50	1.00	1.50	2.00	1.00
	Teacher	1.43	5.00	20.71	12.86	25.00	–	2.86	7.14	2.14	2.86	2.86	5.00	3.57	2.14	0.71	0.71	0.71	0.71	1.43	2.14
17–21	U.S. Population	0.59	3.91	19.65	19.79	21.31	0.53	2.51	5.79	4.37	2.11	3.68	3.09	4.01	2.58	1.28	0.33	0.42	1.16	1.10	1.79
	Parent	0.50	5.00	20.00	20.00	21.00	0.50	1.50	4.00	4.50	3.50	1.50	4.00	6.00	1.50	1.50	–	0.50	1.50	1.00	2.00
	Teacher	–	5.00	23.33	11.67	25.00	–	2.50	5.83	5.00	1.67	3.33	3.33	4.17	4.17	0.83	0.83	0.83	1.67	–	0.83

Note. U.S. population data are from *Current Population Survey, March 1999* [Machine-readable data file] by U.S. Bureau of the Census, 1999, Washington, DC: U.S. Bureau of the Census (Producer/Distributor). For individuals ages 0–21, education is based on parent education; for individuals ages 22–89, education is the number of years completed.

Table 4.4 Standardization Sample by Age, Race/Ethnicity, and Education: Adult Form, Self Report and Rated by Others

Ages	Sample	White ≤8	White 9-11	White 12	White 13-15	White ≥16	African American ≤8	AA 9-11	AA 12	AA 13-15	AA ≥16	Hispanic ≤8	Hisp 9-11	Hisp 12	Hisp 13-15	Hisp ≥16	Other ≤8	Other 9-11	Other 12	Other 13-15	Other ≥16
16-21	U.S. Population	0.59	3.91	19.65	19.79	21.31	0.53	2.51	5.79	4.37	2.11	3.68	3.09	4.01	2.58	1.28	0.33	0.42	1.16	1.10	1.79
	Self Report	0.67	5.33	19.33	20.00	20.00	–	3.33	5.33	4.67	1.33	3.33	2.67	4.00	3.33	2.00	–	0.67	2.00	0.67	1.33
	Rated by Others	2.00	5.00	20.00	24.00	19.00	–	2.00	2.00	4.00	1.00	1.00	5.00	6.00	3.00	2.00	1.00	–	–	2.00	1.00
22-29	U.S. Population	0.68	6.16	17.12	26.03	18.49	–	–	2.74	1.37	1.37	0.68	3.42	10.27	4.11	1.37	–	1.37	0.68	1.37	2.74
	Self Report	–	4.67	20.00	22.67	18.67	–	–	5.33	5.33	2.00	0.67	4.00	6.00	4.00	1.33	1.33	0.67	0.67	0.67	2.00
	Rated by Others	0.71	6.43	17.86	27.14	18.57	–	–	2.86	1.43	0.71	0.71	3.57	7.86	3.57	2.14	–	1.43	0.71	1.43	2.86
30-39	U.S. Population	2.44	2.44	24.39	20.73	19.51	–	–	3.66	1.22	2.44	2.44	4.88	4.27	3.05	4.27	–	–	1.22	0.61	2.44
	Self Report	0.56	3.89	23.33	18.89	22.22	–	2.22	4.44	3.89	2.22	2.78	2.78	3.33	2.78	1.67	0.56	0.56	0.56	1.11	2.22
	Rated by Others	2.50	2.50	25.00	21.25	20.00	–	–	3.75	1.25	2.50	2.50	5.00	3.75	3.13	2.50	–	–	1.25	0.63	2.50
40-49	U.S. Population	1.09	1.09	24.59	23.50	23.50	0.55	0.55	2.19	1.09	1.64	3.28	0.55	6.01	3.28	2.73	–	–	0.55	1.64	2.19
	Self Report	0.56	2.22	26.11	21.67	23.33	–	1.11	3.89	3.89	2.78	1.11	1.67	3.33	1.67	1.67	–	0.56	1.67	1.11	1.67
	Rated by Others	1.11	1.11	25.00	23.89	23.89	0.56	0.56	2.22	1.11	1.67	3.33	0.56	5.00	3.33	2.22	–	–	0.56	1.67	2.22
50-64	U.S. Population	1.83	1.83	27.44	17.68	28.05	1.22	–	0.61	–	1.83	6.10	3.05	4.27	4.27	0.61	0.61	–	0.61	–	–
	Self Report	1.82	5.45	30.00	20.00	21.82	–	0.91	–	3.64	0.91	2.73	1.82	2.73	0.91	1.82	0.91	0.91	0.91	0.91	1.82
	Rated by Others	2.00	1.33	30.67	19.33	30.00	1.33	–	0.67	–	2.00	2.67	3.33	2.00	2.67	0.67	0.67	–	0.67	–	–
65-74	U.S. Population	6.86	6.86	36.27	14.71	16.67	0.98	0.98	–	0.98	0.98	4.90	1.96	0.98	1.96	0.98	–	0.98	1.96	0.98	–
	Self Report	5.83	12.50	32.50	15.83	15.83	0.83	0.83	1.67	3.33	0.83	2.50	0.83	1.67	0.83	0.83	–	0.83	1.67	–	0.83
	Rated by Others	6.00	6.00	39.00	15.00	17.00	1.00	1.00	–	1.00	1.00	5.00	2.00	1.00	1.00	–	–	1.00	2.00	1.00	–
75-89	U.S. Population	12.22	7.78	31.11	15.56	15.56	–	–	5.56	1.11	2.22	3.33	2.22	1.11	1.11	–	1.11	–	–	–	–
	Self Report	14.00	11.00	31.00	16.00	15.00	2.00	2.00	3.00	1.00	–	3.00	–	1.00	1.00	–	–	1.00	1.67	–	–
	Rated by Others	12.22	7.78	31.11	15.56	15.56	–	–	5.56	1.11	2.22	3.33	2.22	1.11	1.11	–	1.11	–	–	–	–

Note. U.S. population data are from *Current Population Survey, March 1999* [Machine-readable data file] by U.S. Bureau of the Census, 1999, Washington, DC: U.S. Bureau of the Census (Producer/Distributor). For individuals ages 0–21, education is based on parent education; for individuals ages 22–89, education is the number of years completed.

Table 4.5 Standardization Sample by Age, Sex, and Education: Parent/Primary Caregiver and Teacher/Daycare Provider Forms

Ages	Sample	Female					Male					Total				
		≤8	9-11	12	13-15	≥16	≤8	9-11	12	13-15	≥16	≤8	9-11	12	13-15	≥16
0:0-0:3	U.S. Population	2.16	6.13	10.93	13.95	15.60	2.22	5.95	13.76	15.84	13.45	4.38	12.08	24.69	29.79	29.05
	Parent/Primary Caregiver	3.00	5.00	8.00	17.00	17.00	1.00	7.00	17.00	14.00	11.00	4.00	12.00	25.00	31.00	28.00
0:4-0:7	U.S. Population	2.16	6.13	10.93	13.95	15.60	2.22	5.95	13.76	15.84	13.45	4.38	12.08	24.69	29.79	29.05
	Parent/Primary Caregiver	3.00	6.00	12.00	14.00	15.00	1.00	7.00	12.00	16.00	14.00	4.00	13.00	24.00	30.00	29.00
0:8-0:11	U.S. Population	2.16	6.13	10.93	13.95	15.60	2.22	5.95	13.76	15.84	13.45	4.38	12.08	24.69	29.79	29.05
	Parent/Primary Caregiver	2.00	6.00	13.00	14.00	15.00	–	7.00	11.00	18.00	14.00	2.00	13.00	24.00	32.00	29.00
1:0-1:3	U.S. Population	1.78	5.19	12.25	14.81	14.73	2.76	5.53	12.06	16.88	14.03	4.54	10.72	24.31	31.69	28.76
	Parent/Primary Caregiver	2.00	6.00	12.00	16.00	14.00	1.00	6.00	11.00	17.00	15.00	3.00	12.00	23.00	33.00	29.00
1:4-1:7	U.S. Population	1.78	5.19	12.25	14.81	14.73	2.76	5.53	12.06	16.88	14.03	4.54	10.72	24.31	31.69	28.76
	Parent/Primary Caregiver	1.00	8.00	14.00	16.00	11.00	2.00	4.00	9.00	15.00	20.00	3.00	12.00	23.00	31.00	31.00
1:8-1:11	U.S. Population	1.78	5.19	12.25	14.81	14.73	2.76	5.53	12.06	16.88	14.03	4.54	10.72	24.31	31.69	28.76
	Parent/Primary Caregiver	–	5.00	14.00	16.00	15.00	4.00	7.00	9.00	16.00	14.00	4.00	12.00	23.00	32.00	29.00
2:0-2:5	U.S. Population	2.16	5.37	11.63	15.99	14.15	1.35	4.84	14.86	16.19	13.47	3.51	10.21	26.49	32.18	27.62
	Parent/Primary Caregiver	2.00	4.00	13.00	15.00	16.00	1.00	7.00	13.00	18.00	11.00	3.00	11.00	26.00	33.00	27.00
	Teacher/Daycare Provider	1.00	5.00	14.00	13.00	17.00	2.00	7.00	13.00	17.00	11.00	3.00	12.00	27.00	30.00	28.00
2:6-2:11	U.S. Population	2.16	5.37	11.63	15.99	14.15	1.35	4.84	14.86	16.19	13.47	3.51	10.21	26.49	32.18	27.62
	Parent/Primary Caregiver	2.00	7.00	13.00	15.00	13.00	2.00	4.00	13.00	18.00	13.00	4.00	11.00	26.00	33.00	26.00
	Teacher/Daycare Provider	3.00	6.00	12.00	16.00	13.00	1.00	4.00	15.00	17.00	13.00	4.00	10.00	27.00	33.00	26.00
3:0-3:5	U.S. Population	2.45	4.67	11.78	17.11	13.05	2.08	5.53	13.05	16.14	14.14	4.53	10.20	24.83	33.25	27.19
	Parent/Primary Caregiver	2.00	8.00	10.00	15.00	15.00	2.00	2.00	15.00	19.00	12.00	4.00	10.00	25.00	34.00	27.00
	Teacher/Daycare Provider	–	9.00	13.00	13.00	15.00	1.00	5.00	12.00	20.00	12.00	1.00	14.00	25.00	33.00	27.00
3:6-3:11	U.S. Population	2.45	4.67	11.78	17.11	13.05	2.08	5.53	13.05	16.14	14.14	4.53	10.20	24.83	33.25	27.19
	Parent/Primary Caregiver	2.00	7.00	14.00	14.00	13.00	2.00	3.00	12.00	19.00	14.00	4.00	10.00	26.00	33.00	27.00
	Teacher/Daycare Provider	–	8.00	12.00	13.00	17.00	1.00	3.00	14.00	20.00	12.00	1.00	11.00	26.00	33.00	29.00
4:0-4:5	U.S. Population	2.47	5.47	12.94	14.29	13.68	2.14	5.60	13.58	16.39	13.44	4.61	11.07	26.52	30.68	27.12
	Parent/Primary Caregiver	2.00	7.00	13.00	15.00	13.00	1.00	4.00	14.00	17.00	14.00	3.00	11.00	27.00	32.00	27.00
	Teacher/Daycare Provider	2.00	9.00	12.00	17.00	10.00	2.00	3.00	14.00	14.00	17.00	4.00	12.00	26.00	31.00	27.00
4:6-4:11	U.S. Population	2.47	5.47	12.94	14.29	13.68	2.14	5.60	13.58	16.39	13.44	4.61	11.07	26.52	30.68	27.12
	Parent/Primary Caregiver	1.00	8.00	12.00	15.00	14.00	3.00	4.00	15.00	16.00	12.00	4.00	12.00	27.00	31.00	26.00
	Teacher/Daycare Provider	4.00	6.00	11.00	15.00	14.00	2.00	5.00	15.00	15.00	13.00	6.00	11.00	26.00	30.00	27.00
5:0-5:11	U.S. Population	2.71	5.19	12.17	14.88	13.46	1.91	4.54	13.06	17.50	14.57	4.62	9.73	25.23	32.38	28.03
	Parent/Primary Caregiver	3.33	6.00	10.67	15.33	14.67	0.67	5.33	14.00	16.00	14.00	4.00	11.33	24.67	31.33	28.67
	Teacher/Daycare Provider	2.67	4.00	11.33	16.67	15.33	2.00	6.00	13.33	16.00	12.67	4.67	10.00	24.66	32.67	28.00

Note. U.S. population data are from *Current Population Survey, October 2000* [Machine-readable data file] by U.S. Bureau of the Census, 2000, Washington, DC: U.S. Bureau of the Census (Producer/Distributor). For individuals ages 0–21, education is based on parent education; for individuals ages 22–89, education is the number of years completed.

Table 4.6 Standardization Sample by Age, Sex, and Education: Parent and Teacher Forms

Ages	Sample	Female					Male					Total				
		≤8	9-11	12	13-15	≥16	≤8	9-11	12	13-15	≥16	≤8	9-11	12	13-15	≥16
5	U.S. Population	2.70	5.18	12.98	13.88	14.14	2.50	5.00	12.45	15.41	15.77	5.20	10.18	25.43	29.29	29.91
	Parent	0.83	3.33	17.50	18.33	10.00	2.50	4.17	13.33	10.83	19.17	3.33	7.50	30.83	29.16	29.17
	Teacher	3.33	8.67	12.67	12.67	12.67	1.33	2.67	14.67	14.67	16.67	4.66	11.34	27.34	27.34	29.34
6	U.S. Population	2.23	4.46	12.34	15.96	14.30	2.74	4.59	14.74	14.12	14.53	4.97	9.05	27.08	30.08	28.83
	Parent	1.54	3.08	15.38	14.62	15.38	0.77	1.54	16.92	16.15	14.62	2.31	4.62	32.30	30.77	30.00
	Teacher	1.43	7.14	17.86	9.29	14.29	4.29	5.00	12.14	13.57	15.00	5.72	12.14	30.00	22.86	29.29
7	U.S. Population	2.91	4.27	14.13	13.72	13.81	2.15	4.82	13.81	14.64	15.74	5.06	9.09	27.94	28.36	29.55
	Parent	2.50	5.00	13.33	11.67	17.50	0.83	5.83	15.00	15.83	12.50	3.33	10.83	28.33	27.50	30.00
	Teacher	4.29	3.57	12.14	17.14	12.86	0.71	5.00	15.71	11.43	17.14	5.00	8.57	27.85	28.57	30.00
8	U.S. Population	2.24	4.37	13.01	15.67	13.82	2.76	4.06	12.74	16.45	14.88	5.00	8.43	25.75	32.12	28.70
	Parent	2.00	3.33	11.33	18.00	15.33	2.67	4.67	14.67	14.67	13.33	4.67	8.00	26.00	32.67	28.66
	Teacher	1.33	3.33	15.33	14.00	16.00	2.00	4.00	14.00	14.00	16.00	3.33	7.33	29.33	28.00	32.00
9	U.S. Population	2.50	4.56	11.51	15.16	14.69	2.19	3.48	14.38	16.51	15.02	4.69	8.04	25.89	31.67	29.71
	Parent	0.67	4.67	14.00	16.00	14.67	3.33	4.00	14.67	11.33	16.67	4.00	8.67	28.67	27.33	31.34
	Teacher	2.00	4.00	16.67	18.00	9.33	4.00	2.67	12.67	12.00	18.67	6.00	6.67	29.34	30.00	28.00
10	U.S. Population	2.27	4.72	13.92	14.20	14.26	2.23	4.53	12.88	16.84	14.14	4.50	9.25	26.80	31.04	28.40
	Parent	2.67	7.33	14.00	14.00	12.00	1.33	4.00	12.67	15.33	16.67	4.00	11.33	26.67	29.33	28.67
	Teacher	2.67	5.33	14.67	11.33	16.00	2.67	4.00	12.67	18.00	12.67	5.34	9.33	27.34	29.33	28.67
11	U.S. Population	2.83	4.22	13.37	14.13	13.82	2.62	4.28	13.42	15.39	15.93	5.45	8.50	26.79	29.52	29.75
	Parent	4.67	3.33	14.00	14.67	13.33	2.00	4.00	11.33	16.67	16.00	6.67	7.33	25.33	31.34	29.33
	Teacher	3.33	4.67	14.67	12.00	15.33	2.00	3.33	14.67	14.00	16.00	5.33	8.00	29.34	26.00	31.33
12	U.S. Population	2.22	3.81	13.24	14.75	13.56	2.70	4.06	15.11	15.54	15.00	4.92	7.87	28.35	30.29	28.56
	Parent	2.67	3.33	14.00	16.00	14.00	2.00	4.00	12.67	17.33	14.00	4.67	7.33	26.67	33.33	28.00
	Teacher	5.33	4.00	17.33	8.67	14.67	2.67	1.33	13.33	16.67	16.00	8.00	5.33	30.66	25.34	30.67
13-14	U.S. Population	2.51	3.99	13.78	14.54	14.61	2.73	4.43	14.46	14.32	14.63	5.24	8.42	28.24	28.86	29.24
	Parent	3.33	4.67	15.33	13.33	13.33	2.00	4.00	12.67	14.67	16.67	5.33	8.67	28.00	28.00	30.00
	Teacher	2.80	4.80	15.20	13.20	14.00	2.80	4.00	14.00	12.80	16.40	5.60	8.80	29.20	26.00	30.40
15-16	U.S. Population	2.39	4.45	13.62	13.72	14.20	3.01	4.55	14.32	14.71	15.02	5.40	9.00	27.94	28.43	29.22
	Parent	2.00	5.50	12.00	15.50	15.00	2.00	4.50	15.50	14.00	14.00	4.00	10.00	27.50	29.50	29.00
	Teacher	4.29	5.71	14.29	9.29	16.43	0.71	7.86	17.86	9.29	14.29	5.00	13.57	32.15	18.58	30.72
17-21	U.S. Population	2.35	5.37	15.30	13.94	12.66	2.77	4.55	15.31	13.90	13.83	5.12	9.92	30.61	27.84	26.49
	Parent	1.00	5.50	17.00	14.00	12.50	1.50	5.50	14.50	13.00	15.50	2.50	11.00	31.50	27.00	28.00
	Teacher	1.67	5.83	17.50	9.17	15.83	2.50	5.83	17.50	11.67	12.50	4.17	11.66	35.00	20.84	28.33

Note. U.S. population data are from *Current Population Survey, March 1999* [Machine-readable data file] by U.S. Bureau of the Census, 1999, Washington, DC: U.S. Bureau of the Census (Producer/Distributor). For individuals ages 0–21, education is based on parent education; for individuals ages 22–89, education is the number of years completed.

Table 4.7   Standardization Sample by Age, Sex, and Education: Adult Form, Self Report and Rated by Others

Ages	Sample	Female					Male					Total				
		≤8	9-11	12	13-15	≥16	≤8	9-11	12	13-15	≥16	≤8	9-11	12	13-15	≥16
16-21	U.S. Population	2.35	5.37	15.30	13.94	12.66	2.77	4.55	15.31	13.90	13.83	5.12	9.92	30.61	27.84	26.49
	Self Report	1.33	5.33	19.33	13.33	10.67	2.67	6.67	11.33	15.33	14.00	4.00	12.00	30.66	28.66	24.67
	Rated by Others	1.00	5.00	16.00	16.00	12.00	3.00	7.00	12.00	17.00	11.00	4.00	12.00	28.00	33.00	23.00
22-29	U.S. Population	1.38	4.11	14.66	17.30	13.29	1.85	5.09	15.92	15.63	10.76	3.23	9.20	30.58	32.93	24.05
	Self Report	2.00	6.00	19.33	14.00	8.67	–	3.33	12.67	18.67	15.33	2.00	9.33	32.00	32.67	24.00
	Rated by Others	1.43	8.57	10.71	15.00	14.29	–	2.86	18.57	18.57	10.00	1.43	11.43	29.28	33.57	24.29
30-39	U.S. Population	1.81	3.98	15.96	14.48	14.31	2.08	4.47	17.24	12.01	13.68	3.89	8.45	33.20	26.49	27.99
	Self Report	2.22	3.33	12.78	15.56	16.11	1.67	6.11	18.89	11.11	12.22	3.89	9.44	31.67	26.67	28.33
	Rated by Others	1.25	2.50	11.25	13.75	21.25	3.75	5.00	22.50	12.50	6.25	5.00	7.50	33.75	26.25	27.50
40-49	U.S. Population	2.13	3.50	17.29	14.11	13.85	2.07	3.51	15.42	13.51	14.60	4.20	7.01	32.71	27.62	28.45
	Self Report	0.56	1.67	18.89	16.11	12.78	1.11	3.89	16.11	12.22	16.67	1.67	5.56	35.00	28.33	29.45
	Rated by Others	2.78	0.56	15.56	16.11	15.00	2.22	1.67	17.22	13.89	15.00	5.00	2.23	32.78	30.00	30.00
50-64	U.S. Population	3.32	5.04	19.98	12.45	11.09	3.47	4.44	14.66	11.12	14.43	6.79	9.48	34.64	23.57	25.52
	Self Report	3.64	8.18	16.36	10.00	11.82	1.82	0.91	17.27	15.45	14.55	5.46	9.09	33.63	25.45	26.37
	Rated by Others	4.67	4.00	18.00	12.67	10.67	2.00	0.67	16.00	9.33	22.00	6.67	4.67	34.00	22.00	32.67
65-74	U.S. Population	6.74	8.13	23.25	10.14	6.75	7.11	5.62	13.46	8.44	10.36	13.85	13.75	36.71	18.58	17.11
	Self Report	6.67	11.67	26.67	8.33	2.50	2.50	3.33	10.83	11.67	15.83	9.17	15.00	37.50	20.00	18.33
	Rated by Others	4.00	6.00	22.00	10.00	9.00	8.00	4.00	20.00	8.00	9.00	12.00	10.00	42.00	18.00	18.00
75-89	U.S. Population	12.99	9.71	21.31	10.39	5.90	8.56	5.27	12.02	6.92	6.92	21.55	14.98	33.33	17.31	12.82
	Self Report	12.00	10.00	24.00	10.00	4.00	7.00	4.00	11.00	7.00	11.00	19.00	14.00	35.00	17.00	15.00
	Rated by Others	6.67	5.56	26.67	15.56	5.56	10.00	4.44	11.11	2.22	12.22	16.67	10.00	37.78	17.78	17.78

Note. U.S. population data are from *Current Population Survey, March 1999* [Machine-readable data file] by U.S. Bureau of the Census, 1999, Washington, DC: U.S. Bureau of the Census (Producer/Distributor). For individuals ages 0–21, education is based on parent education; for individuals ages 22–89, education is the number of years completed.

Table 4.8 Standardization Sample by Age, Sex, and Race/Ethnicity: Parent/Primary Caregiver and Teacher/Daycare Provider Forms

Ages	Sample	Female White	Female African American	Female Hispanic	Female Other	Male White	Male African American	Male Hispanic	Male Other	Total White	Total African American	Total Hispanic	Total Other
0:0–0:3	U.S. Population	29.60	6.61	10.27	2.31	30.64	6.78	11.34	2.47	60.24	13.39	21.61	4.78
	Parent/Primary Caregiver	29.00	10.00	10.00	1.00	35.00	4.00	10.00	1.00	64.00	14.00	20.00	2.00
0:4–0:7	U.S. Population	29.60	6.61	10.27	2.31	30.64	6.78	11.34	2.47	60.24	13.39	21.61	4.78
	Parent/Primary Caregiver	29.00	6.00	12.00	3.00	31.00	7.00	10.00	2.00	60.00	13.00	22.00	5.00
0:8–0:11	U.S. Population	29.60	6.61	10.27	2.31	30.64	6.78	11.34	2.47	60.24	13.39	21.61	4.78
	Parent/Primary Caregiver	28.00	9.00	10.00	3.00	31.00	6.00	10.00	3.00	59.00	15.00	20.00	6.00
1:0–1:3	U.S. Population	29.72	7.62	8.24	3.18	30.89	8.71	8.97	2.67	60.61	16.33	17.21	5.85
	Parent/Primary Caregiver	29.00	9.00	10.00	2.00	33.00	5.00	11.00	1.00	62.00	14.00	21.00	3.00
1:4–1:7	U.S. Population	29.72	7.62	8.24	3.18	30.89	8.71	8.97	2.67	60.61	16.33	17.21	5.85
	Parent/Primary Caregiver	31.00	9.00	9.00	1.00	27.00	9.00	10.00	4.00	58.00	18.00	19.00	5.00
1:8–1:11	U.S. Population	29.72	7.62	8.24	3.18	30.89	8.71	8.97	2.67	60.61	16.33	17.21	5.85
	Parent/Primary Caregiver	37.00	4.00	6.00	3.00	25.00	9.00	13.00	3.00	62.00	13.00	19.00	6.00
2:0–2:5	U.S. Population	30.09	7.27	8.98	2.96	31.54	7.13	9.10	2.94	61.63	14.40	18.08	5.90
	Parent/Primary Caregiver	28.00	9.00	10.00	3.00	34.00	6.00	8.00	2.00	62.00	15.00	18.00	5.00
	Teacher/Daycare Provider	27.00	12.00	10.00	1.00	37.00	5.00	6.00	2.00	64.00	17.00	16.00	3.00
2:6–2:11	U.S. Population	30.09	7.27	8.98	2.96	31.54	7.13	9.10	2.94	61.63	14.40	18.08	5.90
	Parent/Primary Caregiver	32.00	6.00	10.00	2.00	30.00	9.00	8.00	3.00	62.00	15.00	18.00	5.00
	Teacher/Daycare Provider	31.00	10.00	7.00	2.00	30.00	9.00	8.00	3.00	61.00	19.00	15.00	5.00
3:0–3:5	U.S. Population	29.92	7.96	8.15	3.03	30.60	8.08	9.48	2.78	60.52	16.04	17.63	5.81
	Parent/Primary Caregiver	31.00	6.00	11.00	2.00	31.00	10.00	7.00	2.00	62.00	16.00	18.00	4.00
	Teacher/Daycare Provider	35.00	8.00	6.00	1.00	26.00	12.00	11.00	1.00	61.00	20.00	17.00	2.00
3:6–3:11	U.S. Population	29.92	7.96	8.15	3.03	30.60	8.08	9.48	2.78	60.52	16.04	17.63	5.81
	Parent/Primary Caregiver	31.00	8.00	7.00	4.00	29.00	9.00	10.00	2.00	60.00	17.00	17.00	6.00
	Teacher/Daycare Provider	28.00	8.00	8.00	6.00	32.00	11.00	7.00	–	60.00	19.00	15.00	6.00
4:0–4:5	U.S. Population	28.65	6.83	9.87	3.50	31.92	7.43	9.06	2.75	60.57	14.26	18.93	6.25
	Parent/Primary Caregiver	29.00	8.00	10.00	3.00	31.00	7.00	9.00	3.00	60.00	15.00	19.00	6.00
	Teacher/Daycare Provider	28.00	9.00	10.00	3.00	33.00	5.00	9.00	3.00	61.00	14.00	19.00	6.00
4:6–4:11	U.S. Population	28.65	6.83	9.87	3.50	31.92	7.43	9.06	2.75	60.57	14.26	18.93	6.25
	Parent/Primary Caregiver	30.00	7.00	10.00	3.00	31.00	7.00	9.00	3.00	61.00	14.00	19.00	6.00
	Teacher/Daycare Provider	30.00	7.00	10.00	3.00	32.00	6.00	9.00	3.00	62.00	13.00	19.00	6.00
5:0–5:11	U.S. Population	29.29	7.47	9.42	2.23	31.41	7.66	9.39	3.13	60.70	15.13	18.81	5.36
	Parent/Primary Caregiver	30.67	7.33	10.00	2.00	29.33	7.33	8.67	4.67	60.00	14.66	18.67	6.67
	Teacher/Daycare Provider	30.67	7.33	9.33	2.67	30.00	9.33	9.33	2.67	60.67	15.33	18.66	5.34

Note. U.S. population data are from Current Population Survey, October 2000 [Machine-readable data file] by U.S. Bureau of the Census, 2000, Washington, DC: U.S. Bureau of the Census (Producer/Distributor).

Table 4.9 Standardization Sample by Age, Sex, and Race/Ethnicity: Parent and Teacher Forms

Ages	Sample	Female				Male				Total			
		White	African American	Hispanic	Other	White	African American	Hispanic	Other	White	African American	Hispanic	Other
5	U.S. Population	29.21	7.73	8.98	2.91	31.09	7.95	9.22	2.91	60.30	15.68	18.20	5.82
	Parent	30.00	6.67	10.83	2.50	29.17	7.50	9.17	4.17	59.17	14.17	20.00	6.67
	Teacher	28.67	8.00	8.67	4.67	32.67	8.00	8.00	1.33	61.34	16.00	16.67	6.00
6	U.S. Population	31.30	7.22	7.84	3.06	32.10	7.16	9.00	2.33	63.40	14.38	16.84	5.39
	Parent	27.69	10.00	9.23	3.08	34.62	4.62	7.69	3.08	62.31	14.62	16.92	6.16
	Teacher	32.14	7.14	7.86	2.86	30.00	8.57	8.57	2.86	62.14	15.71	16.43	5.72
7	U.S. Population	30.00	8.41	8.42	1.99	32.28	8.95	7.77	2.17	62.28	17.36	16.19	4.16
	Parent	26.67	8.33	10.00	5.00	35.00	9.17	5.83	–	61.67	17.50	15.83	5.00
	Teacher	28.57	9.29	10.00	2.14	33.57	7.86	6.43	2.14	62.14	17.15	16.43	4.28
8	U.S. Population	30.72	8.99	7.38	2.22	32.33	8.17	7.47	2.72	63.05	17.16	14.85	4.94
	Parent	31.33	10.00	8.00	0.67	31.33	6.67	7.33	4.67	62.66	16.67	15.33	5.34
	Teacher	29.33	8.00	9.33	3.33	33.33	9.33	4.00	3.33	62.66	17.33	13.33	6.66
9	U.S. Population	30.98	6.92	7.75	2.87	33.46	8.48	7.35	2.18	64.44	15.40	15.10	5.05
	Parent	34.00	7.33	5.33	3.33	30.00	8.67	10.00	1.33	64.00	16.00	15.33	4.66
	Teacher	31.33	12.00	6.00	0.67	33.33	3.33	8.67	4.67	64.66	15.33	14.67	5.34
10	U.S. Population	31.34	8.06	7.30	2.61	31.27	9.58	7.54	2.30	62.61	17.64	14.84	4.91
	Parent	29.33	10.00	9.33	1.33	32.67	8.67	4.67	4.00	62.00	18.67	14.00	5.33
	Teacher	28.00	8.00	10.67	3.33	34.67	10.00	3.33	2.00	62.67	18.00	14.00	5.33
11	U.S. Population	31.17	7.75	7.17	2.40	35.09	6.70	7.09	2.63	66.26	14.45	14.26	5.03
	Parent	33.33	8.00	7.33	1.33	32.67	5.33	8.00	4.00	66.00	13.33	15.33	5.33
	Teacher	28.67	8.67	10.67	2.00	36.67	6.00	4.00	3.33	65.34	14.67	14.67	5.33
12	U.S. Population	30.73	7.45	6.93	2.38	34.12	6.91	8.13	3.35	64.85	14.36	15.06	5.73
	Parent	30.67	7.33	8.00	4.00	34.00	6.67	6.67	2.67	64.67	14.00	14.67	6.67
	Teacher	34.00	6.67	8.00	1.33	28.67	8.67	8.00	4.67	62.67	15.34	16.00	6.00
13–14	U.S. Population	32.53	7.80	6.35	2.63	32.71	8.29	6.87	2.82	65.24	16.09	13.22	5.45
	Parent	32.00	6.67	8.67	2.67	35.33	5.33	6.67	2.67	67.33	12.00	15.34	5.34
	Teacher	32.00	7.60	8.00	2.40	32.80	8.40	5.20	3.60	64.80	16.00	13.20	6.00
15–16	U.S. Population	31.87	7.76	6.36	2.37	33.17	8.08	7.51	2.89	65.04	15.84	13.87	5.26
	Parent	37.50	3.00	7.00	2.50	31.00	9.00	6.50	3.50	68.50	12.00	13.50	6.00
	Teacher	29.29	6.43	10.00	4.29	35.71	8.57	4.29	1.43	65.00	15.00	14.29	5.72
17–21	U.S. Population	32.49	7.57	6.91	2.54	33.54	7.15	7.45	2.34	66.03	14.72	14.36	4.88
	Parent	31.00	10.00	7.00	2.00	35.50	4.00	7.50	3.00	66.50	14.00	14.50	5.00
	Teacher	29.17	9.17	9.17	2.50	35.83	5.83	6.67	1.67	65.00	15.00	15.84	4.17

Note. U.S. population data are from *Current Population Survey, March 1999* [Machine-readable data file] by U.S. Bureau of the Census, 1999, Washington, DC: U.S. Bureau of the Census (Producer/Distributor).

Table 4.10 Standardization Sample by Age, Sex, and Race/Ethnicity: Adult Form, Self Report and Rated by Others

Ages	Sample	Female White	Female African American	Female Hispanic	Female Other	Male White	Male African American	Male Hispanic	Male Other	Total White	Total African American	Total Hispanic	Total Other
16–21	U.S. Population	32.49	7.57	6.91	2.54	33.54	7.15	7.45	2.34	66.03	14.72	14.36	4.88
	Self Report	32.00	8.67	6.67	2.67	33.33	6.00	8.67	2.00	65.33	14.67	15.34	4.67
	Rated by Others	35.00	5.00	9.00	1.00	35.00	4.00	8.00	3.00	70.00	9.00	17.00	4.00
22–29	U.S. Population	32.81	7.66	7.32	2.94	32.65	5.99	7.69	2.93	65.46	13.65	15.01	5.87
	Self Report	32.00	7.33	7.33	3.33	34.00	5.33	8.67	2.00	66.00	12.66	16.00	5.33
	Rated by Others	34.29	1.43	10.71	3.57	36.43	3.57	7.14	2.86	70.72	5.00	17.85	6.43
30–39	U.S. Population	34.89	6.83	6.22	2.60	34.73	5.79	6.48	2.46	69.62	12.62	12.70	5.06
	Self Report	37.22	6.11	5.00	1.67	31.67	6.67	8.33	3.33	68.89	12.78	13.33	5.00
	Rated by Others	38.13	3.13	7.50	1.25	33.13	4.38	9.38	3.13	71.26	7.51	16.88	4.38
40–49	U.S. Population	37.48	6.36	4.49	2.56	37.29	5.36	4.37	2.09	74.77	11.72	8.86	4.65
	Self Report	38.89	5.56	3.89	1.67	35.00	6.11	5.56	3.33	73.89	11.67	9.45	5.00
	Rated by Others	36.11	2.78	9.44	1.67	38.89	3.33	5.00	2.78	75.00	6.11	14.44	4.45
50–64	U.S. Population	40.08	5.53	4.18	2.09	38.33	4.31	3.47	2.02	78.41	9.84	7.65	4.11
	Self Report	42.73	1.82	4.55	0.91	36.36	3.64	5.45	4.55	79.09	5.46	10.00	5.46
	Rated by Others	35.33	2.67	11.33	0.67	48.00	1.33	–	0.67	83.33	4.00	11.33	1.34
65–74	U.S. Population	44.55	5.23	3.33	1.89	37.19	3.65	2.79	0.18	81.74	8.88	6.12	2.07
	Self Report	47.50	3.33	4.17	0.83	35.00	4.17	2.50	2.50	82.50	7.50	6.67	3.33
	Rated by Others	44.00	2.00	3.00	2.00	39.00	2.00	6.00	2.00	83.00	4.00	9.00	4.00
75–89	U.S. Population	52.11	4.64	2.48	1.07	34.23	2.76	1.70	1.02	86.34	7.40	4.18	2.09
	Self Report	50.00	6.00	3.00	1.00	37.00	2.00	1.00	–	87.00	8.00	4.00	1.00
	Rated by Others	52.22	6.67	1.11	–	30.00	2.22	6.67	1.11	82.22	8.89	7.78	1.11

Note. U.S. population data are from *Current Population Survey, March 1999* [Machine-readable data file] by U.S. Bureau of the Census, 1999, Washington, DC: U.S. Bureau of the Census (Producer/Distributor).

Efforts were made to ensure that a representative proportion of individuals across the entire range of adaptive skill was sampled during standardization. To prevent truncated norms, whenever possible, individuals with specific clinical diagnoses were included in the normative sample according to the percentages reported by the U.S. Department of Education (1998, 2001) and the theoretical distribution. Table 4.11 reports the detailed percentages of the clinical cases in the standardization samples. Finally, information regarding respondents who completed the rating forms during the standardization studies is reported in Table 4.12.

Table 4.11 Percentage of Clinical Cases Included in the Standardization Samples

Clinical Group	Teacher/Daycare Provider	Parent/Primary Caregiver	Teacher	Parent	Adult, Rated by Others	Adult, Self Report
Biological Risk Factors	0.53	0.81	–	–	–	–
Language Disorders	0.13	0.52	–	–	–	–
PDD-NOS	–	0.07	–	–	–	–
Developmental Delay	1.20	0.89	–	–	–	–
Motor Impairment	–	0.22	–	–	–	–
ADHD	–	–	0.41	1.02	0.22	0.10
Alzheimer's Disease	–	–	–	–	0.76	0.20
Autistic Disorder	0.13	0.07	0.41	0.24	–	–
Behavior Disorder	–	–	0.71	0.12	–	–
Emotional Disturbance	–	–	0.59	0.12	–	–
Epilepsy	–	–	–	–	–	0.30
Deaf and Hard of Hearing	–	–	0.36	0.06	0.11	0.71
Learning Disability	–	–	3.08	1.08	–	0.81
Mental Retardation	0.93	0.30	2.01	1.26	1.63	0.51
Parkinson's Disease	–	–	–	–	–	0.30
Speech Impairment	–	–	0.47	0.36	–	–
Stroke	–	–	–	–	–	0.91
Brain Injury	–	–	0.12	–	0.33	0.81
Visual Impairment	–	–	–	0.12	0.11	0.91
Other	–	–	0.30	0.42	0.43	1.31
Total	**2.93**	**2.89**	**8.46**	**4.97**	**4.24**	**7.17**

Note. PDD-NOS = Pervasive Developmental Disorder Not Otherwise Specified; ADHD = Attention-Deficit/Hyperactivity Disorder.

Table 4.12 Information Regarding the Respondents of the Standardization Samples

Teacher/Daycare Provider Sample		Parent/Primary Caregiver Sample		Adult Sample, Rated By Others	
Category of Respondent	Percent	Category of Respondent	Percent	Category of Respondent	Percent
General Education Teacher	9.47	Mother	89.26	Mother	11.63
Preschool Teacher	37.07	Father	7.93	Father	1.96
Special Education Teacher/Teacher's Aide	5.33	Grandparent	1.41	Husband	20.33
Daycare or Child Care Provider	33.33	Other Relative	1.26	Brother	1.20
Other Service Provider	11.60	Unknown	0.14	Son	4.24
Unknown	3.20			Daughter	11.09
				Wife	22.39

Teacher Sample		Parent Sample			
Category of Respondent	Percent	Category of Respondent	Percent	Sister	4.13
General Education Teacher	68.52	Mother	82.22	Other Relative	6.30
Teacher's Aide	8.82	Father	11.08	Roommate	1.74
Special Education Teacher	10.00	Grandparent	3.23	Romantic Friend	4.24
Other Teacher	12.01	Other Relative	3.23	Non-romantic Friend	4.02
Unknown	0.65	Unknown	0.24	Work Supervisor	0.33
				Professional Caregiver	1.20
				Teacher	0.65
				Teacher's Aide	0.11
				Other	2.61
				Unknown	1.83

Norms Development

Derivation of Skill Area Scaled Scores

For each age group, the total raw scores of each skill area were converted to percentiles and then converted into scaled scores with a mean of 10 and a standard deviation of 3. This conversion was accomplished by preparing a cumulative frequency distribution of raw scores for each age group, normalizing these distributions where possible, and calculating the appropriate scaled score for each raw score. For each skill area, the progression of means, skewness, and variance values across the age groups were examined and minor sampling fluctuations smoothed. The progression of scaled scores within each age group and across age groups was then examined. Further smoothing eliminated minor irregularities. The scaled score equivalents of skill area raw scores are provided in Tables A.1, A.5, A.9, and A.12.

Norms for the Community Use, Functional Pre-Academics and Home Living Skill Areas are not developed for ages younger than 1 year, because children this age have not yet reached the developmental stage necessary to perform most of the activities described in these areas. The Community Use Skill Area is not included in the Teacher/Daycare Provider norms because most teachers do not regularly observe their students outside of the classroom and the ratings would produce an unacceptably high average guess rate. On the infant-preschool forms, the Motor Skill Area, which assesses fine and gross motor development, replaces the Work Skill Area. The norms for the Work Skill Area are not developed for ages 5–16 years on the Parent and Teacher Forms or for ages 75–89 years on the Adult Form because the majority of children or adults in these age ranges are not employed.

Derivation of Average Guessing

For each age group, the average number of items guessed by the respondents was calculated for each skill area and reported in Tables A.3, A.7, A.11, and A.14 for each normative sample. The standard error of the means, also reported in these tables, allows the test user to calculate the confidence interval of the mean number of items guessed.

Derivation of Adaptive Domain Composite Scores

The sums of skill area scaled scores for each adaptive domain were calculated by summing each individual's actual age-corrected scaled scores on the skill areas included in the adaptive domain (refer to Table 1.3).

For each age group and rating form, the means and standard deviations of the sums of scaled score distributions were calculated and are reported in Tables C.1, C.2, C.3, and C.4. Due to a ceiling effect, the range of scaled scores and the sum of scaled scores vary by age group.

For each standardization sample, the distribution of the sums of scaled scores was converted to a scale with a mean of 100 and a standard deviation of 15 for each age group independently. This conversion was accomplished by preparing a cumulative frequency distribution of actual sums of scaled scores for each age group, smoothing and normalizing these distributions, and then calculating the appropriate adaptive domain composite score equivalent for each sum of scaled scores. Successive adjustments were based on computerized smoothing and visual inspection of the distributions. The adaptive domain composite score equivalents of sums of scaled scores are provided in Tables A.2, A.6, A.10, and A.13 for each of the standardization samples.

Due to the nature of adaptive skills, the distributions of the standardization data are skewed for the skill areas. Therefore, even though the reliabilities of the adaptive domain composite scores are generally very high, the differential ability decreases when the score reaches the natural ceiling of the scale. To prevent misinterpretation of the adaptive domain composites for the school-age forms and Adult Form, this manual provides normative data only for the range of scores that closely approximates the normal distribution and can be meaningfully interpreted. The range of obtainable adaptive domain scores is 40–160 on infant-preschool forms, 40–130 for ages 5–7 years on the school-age forms, and 40–120 for ages 8–89 years on school-age forms or the Adult Form.

Derivation of the GAC

The sums of skill area scaled scores for the GAC were calculated by summing each individual's actual age-corrected scaled scores on the relevant skill areas. For the Parent/Primary Caregiver Form, the sums of scaled scores for children ages birth–11 months were calculated using only seven skill areas because three of the ten skill areas are not administered to this age group. For ages 1–5 years using the Parent/Primary Caregiver Form, the GAC is calculated using all 10 skill areas. The sums of scaled scores for the Teacher/Daycare Provider Form were calculated using all nine of the skill areas included on the form. For the school-age Parent and Teacher Forms, the sums of the scaled scores were calculated using only nine of the ten skill areas. The Work Skill Area is not included in the GAC because it is irrelevant for most school-aged children. For the adult norms, the sums of the scaled scores were calculated with and without the Work Skill Area, depending on whether or not the individual being rated was employed (refer to Table 1.3).

For each age group, the means and standard deviations of the sums of scaled score distributions were calculated and are reported in Tables C.1, C.2, C.3, and C.4. Due to a ceiling effect, the range of scaled scores and the sum of scaled scores vary by age group. An analysis of variance revealed statistically significant variation by age group in the mean scores for the scales. Moreover, the results of Bartlett's test for homogeneity of variance indicated that the variance across ages was significant. Consequently, GAC score equivalents of sums of scaled scores also were derived separately by age group.

For each standardization sample, the distribution of the sums of scaled scores was converted to a scale with a mean of 100 and a standard deviation of 15 separately for each age group. This conversion was accomplished by preparing a cumulative frequency distribution of actual sums of scaled scores for each age group, smoothing and normalizing these distributions, and then calculating the appropriate GAC score equivalent for each sum of scaled scores. Successive adjustments were based on computerized smoothing and visual inspection of the distributions. The GAC score equivalents of sums of scaled scores are provided Tables A.2, A.6, A.10, and A.13 in Appendix A for each of the standardization samples.

Due to the nature of adaptive skills, the distributions of the standardization data are skewed for the skill areas. Therefore, even though the reliability of the GAC scale is very high, the differential ability decreases when the score reaches the natural ceiling of the scale. To prevent misinterpretation, this manual provides normative data only for the range of scores that closely approximates the normal distribution and can be meaningfully interpreted. The range of obtainable GAC scores is 40–160 on infant-preschool forms, 40–130 for ages 5–7 years on school-age forms, and 40–120 for ages 8–89 years on school-age forms and the Adult Form.

Derivation of Test-Age Equivalents

The ABAS–II provides the test-age equivalents of skill area raw scores for individuals ages 0–21 years who are rated using the infant-preschool or school-age forms (Tables A.4 and A.8). The test-age equivalents represent the average performance of each age group on each skill area. Tables A.4 and A.8 were developed in the following manner. For each age interval, the raw score (or scores) corresponding to a scaled score of 10 represents the mean test performance for that particular age. For each skill area, the tables show these raw scores for the indicated test ages. If the same raw score appeared at two successive test ages, it was assigned to the middle age. If the raw score bands overlapped by more than 1 point, the overlap was divided evenly between the adjacent test ages. The test-age distributions of some skill areas were smoothed.

Chapter 5

Reliability and Validity

The statistical properties of the ABAS–II presented in this chapter determine the confidence clinicians can have in the accuracy of obtained scores. The psychometric properties that are critical to the interpretation of scores are reliability coefficients, standard errors of measurement, confidence intervals, statistical significance of the differences between scores (critical values), frequency of score differences (base rates), and the validity of the instrument. This chapter reports and discusses these statistics as they relate to the quantitative interpretation of ABAS–II scores. This chapter extends an understanding of the ABAS–II by summarizing considerable empirical evidence that informs professional users about the instrument's psychometric qualities that should guide its use. ABAS–II is a relatively new measure for which prior research is unavailable. The authors encourage additional research that will provide further empirical evidence of its statistical properties.

Evidence of Reliability

Reliability refers to consistency in behavior. When behaviors are quantified as test scores, reliability refers to the consistency or stability of such scores. Behavior itself, however, is rarely entirely consistent. Even the most habitual behaviors display differences from time to time. Furthermore, respondents may view and rate behaviors differently, or may be more attentive on some days than others. Thus, while the goal to develop perfectly reliable rating scales is laudatory, realistically it is unattainable. Some degree of error exists in every measurement. Moreover, measurement error tends to be random and difficult to predict for any given individual.

A relatively high degree of reliability is essential when making decisions that may impact an individual's life (e.g., making a diagnosis of mental retardation). Error in classification and diagnosis is most likely to occur when scores are close to a cut score (a specific point on a scale at which scores at or above are interpreted or acted upon differently than scores below). Estimates of a test's reliability should be considered when attempting to classify or diagnose behaviors based on one or more scores that are close to a cut score. Fortunately, a statistic is available to inform test users of the degree of error in scores that may be expected. This statistic, the standard error of measurement (*SEM*), provides test users with a band of scores that surrounds an observed score and likely includes the true score. This error score reflects the size of a test's measurement error (as reflected in a test's reliability coefficients) combined with its standard deviation. The use of the *SEM* is intended to increase the accuracy of descriptions of an individual's test behaviors, to establish confidence intervals around the observed scores, and to assist in comparing scores from different tests. Information on measurement error is essential to the use of the ABAS–II.

This chapter examines the following four forms of reliability: internal consistency, test-retest reliability, inter-rater reliability, and cross-form consistency. In addition, standard errors of measurement are provided to assist in increasing the accuracy of test interpretations. The data included in these analyses were obtained during standardization.

Internal Consistency

Estimates of internal consistency are typically displayed through correlation coefficients that reflect relationships among scores derived from individual items or subsets of items within a test following a single administration of the test (American Educational Research Association et al., 1999). For the ABAS–II, the internal consistency reliability was estimated using coefficient alpha and is reported in Tables 5.1–5.4 for each of the six standardization samples by age group. The average internal consistency reliability coefficients of the skill areas, adaptive domains, and the GAC were calculated using Fisher's z transformation.

In addition, the tables provide the internal consistency reliability by level of performance and by clinical groups whenever available. For the purposes of this data analysis, the levels of performance were classified by the GAC scores. Individuals with GAC scores of 89 or less were classified as *below average*, individuals with GAC scores of 90–109 were classified as *average*, and individuals with GAC scores of 110 or higher were classified as *above average*. However, due to the limited ceilings and significant restriction of range, internal consistency reliability data were not reported for the *above average* level. For both *average* and *below average* levels, reliability coefficients were calculated by 3, 4, 5, or 6 age bands (4 age bands for the Teacher/Daycare Provider Form, 6 age bands for the Parent/Primary Caregiver Form, 5 age bands for the Teacher and Parent Forms, and 3 age bands for the Adult Form). Because the variability of the samples analyzed by performance level differs from that of the overall standardization samples, reliability coefficients corrected for the variability of each performance level sample are also reported. The corrected reliability coefficients were calculated using the method developed by Allen and Yen (1979).

The reliability coefficients for the GAC were consistent across the six standardization samples; average reliability coefficients ranged from .97–.99. Average reliability coefficients of the adaptive domains ranged from .91–.98. Average reliability coefficients of the skill areas were typically in the .90s, ranging from .80 to .97. When analyzed by levels of performance, the average corrected reliability coefficients for the GAC of individuals with average or below average performance were in the .90s, ranging from .92–.99. Average corrected reliability coefficients for the adaptive domains were typically in the .90s for individuals with average or below average performance, ranging from .80–.98. The average corrected reliability coefficients of the skill areas of each performance level were mostly in .80s and .90s, ranging from .78–.98.

Tables 5.1–5.4 also indicate that the reliability coefficients of the samples with different clinical diagnoses ranged from .96–.99 for the GAC, from .86–.98 for the adaptive domains, and from .67–.98 for the skill areas. In addition, when analyzed by age bands, the reliability coefficients of the samples with mixed clinical diagnoses ranged from .97–.99 for the GAC, from .90–.99 for the adaptive domains, and from .79–.98 for the skill areas.

Overall, the reliability data suggest that the scaled scores for the skill areas, as well as the adaptive domain and GAC scores, reflect a high degree of internal consistency in the items and that the ABAS–II is equally reliable for assessing individuals with different levels of adaptive functioning or individuals with different clinical diagnoses.

Standardization Sample by Age Group: Teacher/Daycare Provider Form

Skill Area/Composite	Age Group							Average r_{xx}
	2:0-2:5	2:6-2:11	3:0-3:5	3:6-3:11	4:0-4:5	4:6-4:11	5:0-5:11	
Communication	.91	.92	.95	.93	.93	.91	.92	.93
Functional Pre-Academics	.89	.91	.94	.92	.94	.93	.93	.92
School Living	.94	.95	.95	.94	.94	.93	.93	.94
Health and Safety	.83	.88	.88	.85	.86	.83	.89	.86
Leisure	.89	.86	.92	.87	.89	.89	.92	.89
Self-Care	.84	.84	.90	.78	.85	.73	.72	.82
Self-Direction	.90	.87	.94	.92	.92	.93	.94	.92
Social	.87	.86	.93	.90	.93	.94	.94	.91
Motor	.82	.85	.84	.76	.83	.87	.88	.84
Conceptual Domain	.95	.95	.97	.96	.97	.96	.97	.96
Social Domain	.93	.92	.96	.93	.95	.95	.96	.94
Practical Domain	.93	.95	.96	.93	.94	.92	.93	.94
GAC	.97	.98	.99	.98	.98	.98	.98	.98

Standardization Sample by Age Group: Teacher Form

Skill Area/Composite	Age Group											Average r_{xx}
	5	6	7	8	9	10	11	12	13-14	15-16	17-21	
Communication	.91	.93	.93	.95	.94	.95	.96	.94	.94	.96	.93	.94
Community Use	.79	.85	.84	.88	.85	.88	.94	.93	.91	.93	.91	.89
Functional Academics	.93	.95	.95	.96	.96	.95	.98	.97	.95	.97	.96	.96
School Living	.90	.93	.92	.95	.94	.95	.96	.95	.95	.95	.95	.94
Health and Safety	.87	.93	.89	.94	.94	.94	.96	.96	.95	.95	.94	.94
Leisure	.91	.93	.92	.94	.95	.93	.95	.95	.94	.95	.94	.94
Self-Care	.85	.95	.92	.95	.93	.94	.94	.93	.94	.95	.88	.93
Self-Direction	.92	.94	.94	.96	.96	.97	.98	.97	.97	.97	.96	.96
Social	.94	.96	.93	.96	.96	.96	.97	.95	.95	.96	.94	.95
Work	-	-	-	-	-	-	-	-	-	-	.96	.96
Conceptual Domain	.96	.97	.97	.98	.98	.98	.99	.98	.98	.99	.98	.98
Social Domain	.96	.97	.96	.97	.97	.97	.98	.97	.97	.98	.97	.97
Practical Domain	.95	.97	.96	.98	.97	.97	.98	.98	.98	.98	.97	.97
GAC	.98	.99	.99	.99	.99	.99	.99	.99	.99	.99	.99	.99

Note. Average reliability coefficients (r_{xx}) were calculated using Fisher's z transformation.

Table 5.1 Reliability Coefficients of Skill Areas, Adaptive Domains, and the GAC: Teacher/Daycare Provider and Teacher Forms *(continued)*

Standardization Sample by Level of Performance[a]: Teacher/Daycare Provider Form

Average (GAC = 90–109)

Skill Area/Composite	Age 2 (n = 110)			Age 3 (n = 102)			Age 4 (n = 98)			Age 5 (n = 81)			Average r_{xx}	
	SD	r	r^c	SD	r	r^c	SD	r	r^c	SD	r	r^c	r	r^c
Communication	2.20	.88	.93	2.20	.92	.95	2.40	.88	.92	2.10	.70	.85	.86	.92
Functional Pre-Academics	2.30	.88	.93	2.30	.91	.95	2.60	.90	.92	2.50	.91	.93	.90	.93
School Living	2.20	.90	.95	2.00	.88	.95	2.00	.85	.93	2.20	.78	.88	.86	.93
Health and Safety	2.20	.78	.88	2.00	.76	.89	2.10	.61	.81	2.20	.72	.85	.72	.86
Leisure	2.10	.78	.89	1.80	.75	.91	2.10	.69	.85	1.90	.62	.85	.72	.88
Self-Care	2.30	.78	.87	2.40	.82	.88	2.50	.62	.73	2.50	.22	.46	.66	.78
Self-Direction	2.10	.76	.88	1.90	.86	.94	1.80	.82	.93	2.10	.85	.93	.83	.92
Social	2.00	.70	.87	2.00	.83	.92	2.20	.88	.94	1.90	.84	.93	.82	.92
Motor	2.70	.79	.83	2.20	.67	.83	2.60	.75	.82	2.30	.78	.87	.75	.84
Conceptual Domain		.87	.93		.89	.94		.86	.92		.81	.90	.86	.92
Social Domain		.80	.91		.82	.93		.81	.91		.76	.90	.80	.91
Practical Domain		.85	.92		.86	.93		.73	.84		.65	.78	.79	.88
GAC		.88	.93		.89	.95		.83	.90		.84	.91	.86	.92

Below Average (GAC = 89 or Less)

Skill Area/Composite	Age 2 (n = 39)			Age 3 (n = 46)			Age 4 (n = 53)			Age 5 (n = 33)			Average r_{xx}	
	SD	r	r^c	SD	r	r^c	SD	r	r^c	SD	r	r^c	r	r^c
Communication	2.00	.87	.94	2.80	.92	.93	2.60	.91	.93	2.50	.90	.93	.90	.93
Functional Pre-Academics	2.10	.81	.90	2.70	.93	.94	2.90	.95	.95	2.30	.93	.96	.92	.94
School Living	2.50	.90	.93	2.70	.95	.96	2.00	.89	.95	2.60	.92	.94	.92	.95
Health and Safety	2.50	.79	.85	2.20	.87	.93	1.90	.74	.90	2.40	.85	.90	.82	.90
Leisure	2.60	.88	.91	2.30	.91	.95	2.10	.86	.93	2.10	.90	.95	.89	.94
Self-Care	2.30	.81	.89	2.20	.91	.95	2.70	.87	.90	2.30	.82	.89	.86	.91
Self-Direction	2.30	.83	.90	2.50	.93	.95	1.80	.81	.93	2.20	.91	.95	.88	.94
Social	2.00	.80	.91	2.30	.91	.94	2.10	.86	.93	2.60	.93	.95	.88	.93
Motor	2.40	.82	.88	1.90	.82	.93	2.40	.85	.90	2.40	.88	.92	.84	.91
Conceptual Domain		.87	.93		.95	.96		.93	.96		.95	.97	.93	.96
Social Domain		.88	.94		.94	.96		.90	.95		.95	.97	.92	.96
Practical Domain		.90	.93		.95	.97		.91	.95		.91	.94	.92	.95
GAC		.95	.97		.98	.99		.96	.98		.97	.98	.97	.98

Note. SD = standard deviation; *r* = internal consistency reliability coefficient (coefficient alpha); *r^c* = corrected internal consistency reliability.
Average reliability coefficients (r_{xx}) were calculated using Fisher's z transformation.

[a]Conditional reliability coefficients for the above average level are not reported due to significant restriction of the range.

Adaptive Behavior Assessment System–Second Edition

Table 5.1 Reliability Coefficients of Skill Areas, Adaptive Domains, and the GAC: Teacher/Daycare Provider and Teacher Forms (continued)

Standardization Sample by Level of Performance[a]: Teacher Form

Average (GAC = 90–109)

Skill Area/Composite	Ages 5–6 (n = 132)			Ages 7–8 (n = 130)			Ages 9–10 (n = 109)			Ages 11–12 (n = 100)			Ages 13–21 (n = 219)			Average r_{xx}	
	SD	r	r^c	SD	r	r^c	SD	r	r^c	SD	r	r^c	SD	r	r^c	r	r^c
Communication	2.10	.75	.88	1.66	.79	.94	1.64	.72	.92	2.00	.79	.91	2.06	.84	.93	.81	.92
Community Use	2.30	.59	.76	2.12	.63	.82	2.23	.68	.82	2.24	.68	.82	1.81	.74	.91	.81	.83
Functional Academics	2.86	.91	.92	2.02	.91	.96	2.16	.90	.95	1.52	.76	.94	1.64	.85	.95	.81	.95
School Living	2.02	.81	.91	1.75	.77	.92	1.84	.79	.92	1.79	.72	.90	1.56	.83	.95	.84	.92
Health and Safety	1.83	.66	.88	1.67	.67	.90	1.86	.73	.90	2.02	.68	.85	1.40	.74	.94	.65	.90
Leisure	1.86	.75	.90	1.88	.81	.93	1.92	.80	.92	1.67	.80	.94	1.69	.81	.94	.89	.93
Self-Care	2.01	.72	.87	1.54	.77	.94	1.97	.70	.87	1.49	.56	.89	1.85	.77	.91	.69	.90
Self-Direction	1.87	.76	.91	1.67	.85	.95	2.03	.86	.94	2.21	.88	.93	1.99	.90	.95	.78	.94
Social	2.06	.86	.94	1.71	.85	.95	2.02	.90	.96	1.78	.85	.95	1.75	.85	.95	.81	.95
Conceptual Domain		.80	.90		.87	.96		.87	.95		.85	.94		.90	.96	.86	.95
Social Domain		.86	.94		.89	.96		.88	.95		.86	.96		.88	.96	.87	.95
Practical Domain		.80	.90		.80	.93		.78	.90		.67	.87		.85	.95	.79	.91
GAC		.86	.93		.90	.96		.87	.94		.83	.94		.91	.97	.85	.95

Below Average (GAC = 89 or Less)

Skill Area/Composite	Ages 5–6 (n = 80)			Ages 7–8 (n = 75)			Ages 9–10 (n = 77)			Ages 11–12 (n = 84)			Ages 13–21 (n = 139)			Average r_{xx}	
	SD	r	r^c	SD	r	r^c	SD	r	r^c	SD	r	r^c	SD	r	r^c	r	r^c
Communication	2.63	.89	.92	3.14	.89	.88	2.53	.89	.92	2.96	.95	.95	2.77	.91	.93	.88	.92
Community Use	2.94	.72	.73	3.07	.85	.84	2.66	.82	.86	3.19	.93	.92	3.29	.88	.86	.85	.85
Functional Academics	2.78	.88	.90	2.71	.96	.97	2.65	.96	.97	3.15	.97	.97	2.84	.95	.96	.91	.96
School Living	2.33	.87	.92	2.67	.91	.93	2.86	.93	.94	3.35	.95	.94	3.29	.91	.89	.84	.93
Health and Safety	2.86	.89	.90	2.57	.91	.93	2.93	.94	.94	3.09	.95	.95	3.53	.93	.90	.78	.93
Leisure	2.81	.85	.87	2.32	.86	.91	2.27	.86	.92	2.50	.91	.94	2.79	.90	.91	.83	.91
Self-Care	3.43	.91	.89	3.43	.93	.90	3.90	.93	.88	3.85	.93	.89	4.02	.94	.88	.86	.89
Self-Direction	3.10	.89	.88	2.89	.92	.92	2.86	.94	.94	2.81	.96	.96	3.07	.94	.94	.88	.93
Social	2.81	.93	.94	2.64	.90	.92	2.86	.93	.93	2.96	.94	.94	2.96	.92	.92	.89	.93
Conceptual Domain		.93	.94		.96	.96		.96	.97		.98	.98		.96	.97	.96	.97
Social Domain		.93	.94		.92	.94		.93	.95		.95	.96		.93	.94	.93	.95
Practical Domain		.92	.93		.95	.95		.95	.95		.97	.96		.96	.94	.95	.95
GAC		.97	.97		.98	.98		.98	.98		.99	.99		.98	.97	.95	.98

Note. SD = standard deviation; r = internal consistency reliability coefficient (coefficient alpha); r^c = corrected internal consistency reliability.
Average reliability coefficients (r_{xx}) were calculated using Fisher's z transformation.
[a]Conditional reliability coefficients for the above average level are not reported due to significant restriction of the range.

▲ Clinical Sample by Diagnoses: Teacher/Daycare Provider Form

Skill Area/Composite	Autistic Disorder (n = 35)	Developmental Delay (n = 48)	Motor Impairment (n = 32)	Mild Mental Retardation (n = 31)	Moderate Mental Retardation (n = 19)	PDD-NOS (n = 19)	Rec./Exp. Language Disorder (n = 52)	Biological Risk Factors (n = 30)	Average r_{xx}
Communication	.90	.94	.96	.91	.91	.95	.94	.92	.93
Functional Pre-Academics	.94	.96	.97	.94	.95	.95	.95	.97	.96
School Living	.93	.95	.96	.94	.91	.94	.95	.96	.94
Health and Safety	.84	.92	.89	.89	.86	.84	.91	.89	.88
Leisure	.84	.89	.93	.93	.75	.90	.88	.85	.88
Self-Care	.71	.86	.89	.88	.67	.83	.87	.75	.82
Self-Direction	.90	.94	.95	.94	.82	.94	.93	.91	.92
Social	.92	.92	.94	.94	.84	.93	.93	.89	.92
Motor	.74	.89	.91	.82	.82	.81	.87	.82	.84
Conceptual Domain	.95	.97	.98	.96	.95	.98	.97	.97	.97
Social Domain	.93	.94	.96	.96	.88	.95	.95	.92	.94
Practical Domain	.92	.96	.96	.95	.86	.94	.96	.89	.94
GAC	.97	.99	.99	.98	.96	.98	.98	.97	.98

▲ Clinical Sample by Diagnoses: Teacher Form

Skill Area/Composite	ADHD (n = 30)	Autistic Disorder (n = 32)	Emotional Disturbance (n = 73)	Deaf and Hard of Hearing (n = 19)	Learning Disability (n = 248)	Mental Retardation (n = 199)	Physical Impairment (n = 52)	Behavior Disorder (n = 56)	Average r_{xx}
Communication	.94	.95	.95	.94	.93	.94	.97	.94	.95
Community Use	.92	.93	.91	.86	.91	.91	.96	.90	.92
Functional Academics	.98	.97	.97	.97	.97	.97	.98	.95	.97
School Living	.95	.95	.93	.96	.93	.95	.98	.95	.95
Health and Safety	.92	.96	.94	.94	.93	.94	.97	.92	.94
Leisure	.95	.95	.92	.93	.93	.91	.96	.94	.94
Self-Care	.93	.89	.92	.90	.92	.95	.95	.91	.92
Self-Direction	.93	.93	.95	.95	.95	.95	.97	.95	.95
Social	.95	.96	.94	.96	.94	.94	.98	.95	.95
Conceptual Domain	.98	.98	.98	.98	.98	.98	.99	.98	.98
Social Domain	.97	.97	.96	.97	.96	.96	.98	.97	.97
Practical Domain	.98	.98	.97	.97	.97	.98	.99	.92	.97
GAC	.99	.99	.99	.99	.99	.99	.99	.99	.99

Note. Average reliability coefficients (r_{xx}) were calculated using Fisher's z transformation.

Adaptive Behavior Assessment System–Second Edition

Table 5.1 Reliability Coefficients of Skill Areas, Adaptive Domains, and the GAC: Teacher/Daycare Provider and Teacher Forms (continued)

Mixed Clinical Sample by Age: Teacher/Daycare Provider Form

Skill Area/Composite	2 (n = 42)	3 (n = 66)	4 (n = 81)	5 (n = 77)	Average r_{xx}
Communication	.92	.93	.94	.93	.93
Functional Pre-Academics	.93	.93	.94	.94	.94
School Living	.94	.94	.94	.93	.94
Health and Safety	.88	.88	.84	.89	.87
Leisure	.83	.89	.90	.90	.88
Self-Care	.81	.84	.83	.79	.82
Self-Direction	.84	.94	.93	.93	.92
Social	.85	.92	.93	.94	.92
Motor	.82	.81	.82	.91	.85
Conceptual Domain	.94	.97	.97	.97	.96
Social Domain	.90	.95	.95	.95	.94
Practical Domain	.92	.95	.94	.94	.94
GAC	.97	.98	.98	.98	.98

Mixed Clinical Sample by Age: Teacher Form

Skill Area/Composite	5–6 (n = 75)	7–8 (n = 99)	9–10 (n = 131)	11–12 (n = 124)	13–14 (n = 146)	15–21 (n = 165)	Average r_{xx}
Communication	.93	.95	.95	.96	.96	.96	.95
Community Use	.85	.92	.90	.95	.93	.95	.92
Functional Academics	.92	.97	.97	.97	.97	.98	.97
School Living	.96	.96	.95	.97	.96	.96	.96
Health and Safety	.95	.94	.95	.97	.96	.96	.96
Leisure	.91	.92	.94	.96	.94	.94	.94
Self-Care	.95	.95	.94	.95	.95	.95	.95
Self-Direction	.91	.95	.95	.97	.96	.96	.95
Social	.96	.96	.96	.96	.96	.95	.96
Conceptual Domain	.96	.98	.98	.99	.98	.99	.98
Social Domain	.96	.97	.97	.98	.97	.97	.97
Practical Domain	.98	.98	.98	.99	.98	.99	.98
GAC	.99	.99	.99	.99	.99	.99	.99

Note. Average reliability coefficients (r_{xx}) were calculated using Fisher's z transformation.

Table 5.2 Reliability Coefficients of Skill Areas, Adaptive Domains, and the GAC: Parent/Primary Caregiver and Parent Forms

Standardization Sample by Age Group: Parent/Primary Caregiver Form

Skill Area/Composite	Age Group													Average r_{xx}
	0:0–0:3	0:4–0:7	0:8–0:11	1:0–1:3	1:4–1:7	1:8–1:11	2:0–2:5	2:6–2:11	3:0–3:5	3:6–3:11	4:0–4:5	4:6–4:11	5:0–5:11	
Communication	.66	.74	.79	.87	.86	.88	.92	.91	.94	.91	.85	.87	.86	.87
Community Use	–	–	–	.89	.89	.87	.92	.91	.92	.85	.91	.88	.84	.89
Functional Pre-Academics	–	–	–	.86	.92	.88	.90	.89	.92	.92	.90	.93	.90	.90
Home Living	–	–	–	.93	.92	.91	.92	.92	.94	.91	.91	.92	.89	.92
Health and Safety	.48	.72	.75	.81	.84	.87	.87	.88	.89	.83	.83	.83	.82	.82
Leisure	.68	.80	.82	.87	.85	.83	.89	.84	.91	.88	.86	.86	.91	.85
Self-Care	.53	.84	.79	.78	.80	.77	.86	.76	.87	.82	.84	.80	.78	.80
Self-Direction	.60	.78	.78	.84	.85	.84	.89	.82	.90	.88	.88	.90	.90	.85
Social	.75	.86	.79	.85	.82	.86	.90	.87	.90	.88	.87	.86	.88	.86
Motor	.65	.86	.82	.85	.81	.75	.88	.80	.80	.81	.81	.73	.84	.81
Conceptual Domain	.70	.79	.84	.92	.94	.93	.96	.94	.96	.95	.94	.95	.94	.92
Social Domain	.81	.88	.89	.91	.89	.90	.94	.91	.94	.92	.92	.91	.94	.91
Practical Domain	.65	.86	.82	.94	.95	.94	.96	.95	.97	.94	.96	.94	.94	.93
GAC	.86	.94	.94	.97	.98	.97	.98	.97	.98	.98	.98	.97	.98	.97

Standardization Sample by Age Group: Parent Form

Skill Area/Composite	Age Group											Average r_{xx}
	5	6	7	8	9	10	11	12	13–14	15–16	17–21	
Communication	.90	.91	.91	.93	.89	.91	.91	.94	.91	.92	.95	.92
Community Use	.92	.93	.88	.92	.91	.89	.91	.91	.92	.91	.94	.91
Functional Academics	.94	.93	.92	.94	.90	.92	.90	.94	.92	.92	.96	.93
Home Living	.89	.92	.91	.93	.90	.92	.93	.93	.92	.94	.95	.92
Health and Safety	.86	.85	.84	.87	.82	.84	.82	.90	.88	.87	.92	.86
Leisure	.89	.91	.90	.91	.90	.91	.91	.94	.92	.92	.94	.91
Self-Care	.90	.87	.86	.88	.79	.85	.80	.91	.84	.86	.91	.87
Self-Direction	.91	.93	.89	.91	.91	.94	.93	.94	.93	.95	.95	.93
Social	.90	.91	.90	.92	.92	.93	.91	.94	.93	.94	.94	.92
Work	–	–	–	–	–	–	–	–	–	–	.92	.92
Conceptual Domain	.96	.97	.96	.97	.96	.96	.96	.97	.97	.97	.98	.97
Social Domain	.94	.95	.94	.95	.95	.95	.95	.96	.96	.96	.96	.95
Practical Domain	.96	.96	.95	.97	.94	.95	.95	.97	.96	.96	.98	.96
GAC	.98	.98	.98	.99	.98	.98	.98	.99	.98	.98	.99	.98

Note. Average reliability coefficients (r_{xx}) were calculated using Fisher's z transformation.

Table 5.2 Reliability Coefficients of Skill Areas, Adaptive Domains, and the GAC: Parent/Primary Caregiver and Parent Forms *(continued)*

Standardization Sample by Level of Performance[a]: Parent/Primary Caregiver Form

Average (GAC = 90–109)

Skill Area/Composite	Age 0 (n = 150)			Age 1 (n = 155)			Age 2 (n = 97)			Age 3 (n = 108)			Age 4 (n = 97)			Age 5 (n = 63)			Average r_{xx}	
	SD	r	r^c	SD	r	r^c	SD	r	r^c	SD	r	r^c	SD	r	r^c	SD	r	r^c	r	r^c
Communication	2.30	.75	.85	2.00	.87	.94	2.20	.89	.94	1.90	.78	.91	2.20	.77	.87	1.90	.66	.86	.80	.90
Community Use	–	–	–	2.00	.83	.92	2.20	.84	.91	1.90	.76	.91	2.20	.70	.84	1.90	.76	.90	.78	.90
Functional Pre-Academics	–	–	–	2.20	.79	.89	2.10	.85	.92	2.50	.89	.93	2.40	.87	.92	2.50	.88	.92	.86	.92
Home Living	–	–	–	2.10	.93	.97	2.10	.84	.92	2.00	.77	.90	2.00	.77	.90	1.90	.76	.90	.83	.92
Health and Safety	2.20	.69	.84	2.00	.84	.93	2.00	.76	.89	2.00	.73	.88	2.20	.75	.86	1.60	.64	.90	.74	.89
Leisure	2.10	.85	.93	2.20	.83	.91	2.00	.79	.91	2.00	.73	.88	2.10	.72	.86	2.10	.78	.89	.79	.90
Self-Care	1.80	.85	.95	2.10	.79	.90	2.50	.79	.86	2.40	.59	.74	2.20	.50	.73	2.10	.76	.88	.73	.86
Self-Direction	2.10	.76	.88	1.80	.79	.92	1.40	.67	.93	1.80	.64	.87	2.00	.75	.89	1.90	.78	.91	.74	.90
Social	1.70	.81	.94	1.80	.83	.94	2.00	.79	.91	1.90	.66	.86	1.90	.73	.89	2.00	.74	.89	.77	.91
Motor	2.00	.90	.96	2.20	.85	.92	2.00	.68	.86	2.30	.69	.82	2.30	.67	.81	2.40	.77	.86	.78	.89
Conceptual Domain		.68	.82		.80	.91		.84	.94		.76	.90		.81	.90		.68	.85	.77	.89
Social Domain		.85	.94		.86	.94		.83	.93		.71	.88		.77	.89		.81	.91	.81	.92
Practical Domain		.78	.90		.88	.94		.86	.93		.77	.88		.73	.86		.74	.90	.80	.91
GAC		.75	.88		.89	.95		.87	.94		.80	.91		.81	.90		.82	.92	.83	.92

Below Average (GAC = 89 or Less)

Skill Area/Composite	Age 0 (n = 68)			Age 1 (n = 70)			Age 2 (n = 45)			Age 3 (n = 46)			Age 4 (n = 52)			Age 5 (n = 42)			Average r_{xx}	
	SD	r	r^c	SD	r	r^c	SD	r	r^c	SD	r	r^c	SD	r	r^c	SD	r	r^c	r	r^c
Communication	2.40	.72	.82	2.50	.83	.88	2.40	.91	.94	2.50	.92	.95	2.40	.80	.87	3.00	.88	.88	.86	.90
Community Use	–	–	–	2.50	.78	.85	2.40	.87	.92	2.50	.89	.92	2.40	.90	.94	3.00	.74	.74	.85	.89
Functional Pre-Academics	–	–	–	2.10	.50	.75	2.60	.87	.90	2.50	.93	.95	2.20	.88	.93	2.30	.89	.94	.85	.91
Home Living	–	–	–	1.80	.91	.97	2.30	.92	.95	2.10	.91	.96	2.50	.91	.94	2.40	.86	.91	.90	.95
Health and Safety	2.70	.78	.82	2.20	.84	.91	2.40	.87	.92	2.20	.85	.92	2.10	.68	.84	2.20	.74	.86	.80	.88
Leisure	1.90	.81	.92	2.30	.86	.92	2.00	.85	.94	2.60	.88	.91	2.40	.84	.90	2.70	.87	.90	.85	.92
Self-Care	2.50	.87	.91	2.00	.77	.90	2.50	.87	.91	2.50	.86	.90	2.40	.81	.88	2.80	.70	.74	.82	.88
Self-Direction	2.40	.74	.83	2.30	.83	.90	2.10	.84	.92	2.10	.83	.92	1.80	.76	.91	1.70	.69	.90	.79	.90
Social	2.30	.84	.91	2.10	.77	.89	2.10	.88	.94	2.40	.88	.93	2.00	.76	.89	2.20	.78	.88	.83	.91
Motor	2.20	.91	.95	2.00	.85	.93	2.70	.91	.93	2.70	.83	.86	2.20	.73	.85	3.10	.83	.82	.85	.90
Conceptual Domain		.72	.82		.78	.88		.93	.95		.94	.96		.87	.93		.82	.91	.86	.92
Social Domain		.86	.93		.86	.93		.91	.96		.91	.94		.83	.91		.87	.92	.88	.93
Practical Domain		.86	.89		.90	.95		.95	.97		.95	.97		.90	.94		.84	.88	.91	.94
GAC		.87	.92		.94	.97		.97	.98		.97	.98		.94	.97		.90	.93	.94	.96

Note. SD = standard deviation; *r* = internal consistency reliability coefficient (coefficient alpha); r^c = corrected internal consistency reliability.

Average reliability coefficients (r_{xx}) were calculated using Fisher's *z* transformation.

[a]Conditional reliability coefficients for the above average level are not reported due to significant restriction of the range.

Table 5.2 Reliability Coefficients of Skill Areas, Adaptive Domains, and the GAC: Parent/Primary Caregiver and Parent Forms *(continued)*

Standardization Sample by Level of Performance[a]: Parent Form

Average (GAC = 90–109)

Skill Area/Composite	Ages 5–6 (n = 113)			Ages 7–8 (n = 129)			Ages 9–10 (n = 137)			Ages 11–12 (n = 127)			Ages 13–21 (n = 219)			Average r_{xx}	
	SD	r	r^c	SD	r	r^c	SD	r	r^c	SD	r	r^c	SD	r	r^c	r	r^c
Communication	2.00	.79	.91	1.89	.76	.90	2.10	.82	.91	2.00	.82	.92	1.80	.83	.94	.81	.92
Community Use	2.61	.84	.88	2.02	.77	.90	1.69	.78	.93	1.96	.77	.90	1.69	.85	.95	.81	.92
Functional Academics	2.41	.91	.94	2.01	.86	.94	2.08	.82	.91	1.67	.67	.90	1.76	.71	.90	.81	.92
Home Living	2.01	.79	.91	2.89	.86	.87	2.71	.82	.85	2.79	.86	.87	2.52	.87	.91	.84	.88
Health and Safety	2.36	.75	.85	1.88	.60	.84	1.91	.61	.84	1.97	.65	.85	1.62	.62	.89	.65	.86
Leisure	1.90	.76	.91	1.97	.78	.91	2.15	.78	.89	2.06	.84	.92	1.79	.77	.92	.89	.91
Self-Care	2.39	.85	.90	2.00	.64	.84	2.54	.68	.77	1.97	.68	.86	1.75	.52	.83	.69	.85
Self-Direction	1.87	.84	.94	2.11	.70	.85	2.01	.76	.89	1.74	.73	.91	1.83	.85	.95	.78	.92
Social	2.32	.82	.89	2.21	.79	.89	2.28	.80	.88	2.19	.77	.88	2.02	.84	.93	.81	.90
Conceptual Domain		.88	.95		.83	.92		.82	.91		.80	.93		.85	.95	.84	.93
Social Domain		.85	.93		.83	.92		.85	.92		.83	.91		.82	.93	.84	.84
Practical Domain		.86	.92		.79	.90		.79	.89		.78	.89		.78	.92	.80	.80
GAC		.89	.94		.84	.92		.81	.90		.83	.93		.85	.94	.85	.93

Below Average (GAC = 89 or Less)

Skill Area/Composite	Ages 5–6 (n = 60)			Ages 7–8 (n = 70)			Ages 9–10 (n = 84)			Ages 11–12 (n = 79)			Ages 13–21 (n = 149)			Average r_{xx}	
	SD	r	r^c	SD	r	r^c	SD	r	r^c	SD	r	r^c	SD	r	r^c	r	r^c
Communication	2.79	.88	.90	3.02	.87	.87	2.34	.84	.90	2.53	.91	.94	2.48	.90	.93	.88	.91
Community Use	2.87	.78	.80	3.22	.86	.84	1.98	.84	.93	2.29	.85	.91	2.24	.91	.95	.85	.90
Functional Academics	2.83	.87	.88	2.95	.91	.91	2.19	.87	.93	1.87	.92	.97	2.47	.95	.96	.91	.94
Home Living	2.18	.80	.89	2.97	.77	.78	3.55	.86	.80	3.23	.86	.83	3.57	.90	.85	.84	.83
Health and Safety	2.69	.75	.80	2.63	.76	.81	2.09	.69	.85	2.56	.81	.86	2.78	.85	.87	.78	.84
Leisure	2.01	.80	.91	2.60	.83	.87	2.13	.78	.89	2.22	.87	.93	2.04	.86	.94	.83	.91
Self-Care	2.14	.84	.92	2.69	.88	.90	2.78	.81	.83	2.87	.87	.88	3.46	.89	.85	.86	.88
Self-Direction	1.89	.84	.93	3.31	.84	.80	2.91	.88	.89	2.97	.92	.92	2.71	.89	.91	.88	.90
Social	2.03	.83	.92	3.15	.87	.86	2.99	.91	.91	3.18	.90	.89	3.05	.90	.89	.89	.90
Conceptual Domain		.92	.95		.92	.91		.91	.94		.95	.96		.95	.96	.93	.95
Social Domain		.87	.94		.91	.92		.88	.93		.91	.93		.91	.94	.90	.93
Practical Domain		.84	.88		.90	.91		.87	.90		.91	.92		.94	.93	.90	.91
GAC		.93	.95		.95	.95		.92	.94		.96	.97		.97	.97	.95	.96

Note. SD = standard deviation; *r* = internal consistency reliability coefficient (coefficient alpha); r^c = corrected internal consistency reliability.

Average reliability coefficients (r_{xx}) were calculated using Fisher's *z* transformation.

[a]Conditional reliability coefficients for the above average level are not reported due to significant restriction of the range.

Table 5.2   Reliability Coefficients of Skill Areas, Adaptive Domains, and the GAC: Parent/Primary Caregiver and Parent Forms *(continued)*

Clinical Sample by Diagnoses: Parent/Primary Caregiver Form

Skill Area/Composite	Autistic Disorder (n = 34)	Developmental Delay (n = 78)	Motor Impairment (n = 50)	Mild Mental Retardation (n = 27)	Moderate Mental Retardation (n = 22)	PDD-NOS (n = 18)	Rec./Exp. Language Disorder (n = 52)	Biological Risk Factors (n = 66)	Average r_{xx}
Communication	.86	.95	.96	.83	.86	.75	.89	.97	.91
Community Use	.93	.97	.97	.85	.91	.90	.92	.98	.94
Functional Pre-Academics	.96	.97	.97	.92	.95	.92	.94	.97	.95
Home Living	.93	.96	.98	.87	.93	.92	.85	.98	.94
Health and Safety	.93	.94	.96	.86	.79	.80	.86	.97	.91
Leisure	.88	.93	.95	.87	.87	.89	.86	.96	.91
Self-Care	.75	.92	.96	.70	.83	.86	.75	.95	.87
Self-Direction	.86	.94	.95	.87	.88	.88	.89	.96	.91
Social	.87	.93	.95	.86	.89	.88	.82	.96	.91
Motor	.81	.91	.94	.75	.79	.80	.83	.95	.87
Conceptual Domain	.92	.98	.98	.94	.95	.93	.95	.98	.96
Social Domain	.92	.96	.97	.92	.93	.94	.90	.97	.94
Practical Domain	.96	.98	.99	.94	.95	.94	.93	.99	.97
GAC	.98	.99	.99	.97	.98	.98	.97	.99	.98

Clinical Sample by Diagnoses: Parent Form

Skill Area/Composite	ADHD (n = 49)	Learning Disability (n = 26)	Mental Retardation (n = 40)	Average r_{xx}
Communication	.93	.94	.96	.94
Community Use	.96	.96	.97	.96
Functional Academics	.95	.97	.97	.96
Home Living	.95	.92	.96	.95
Health and Safety	.91	.95	.95	.94
Leisure	.94	.94	.94	.94
Self-Care	.88	.92	.96	.93
Self-Direction	.95	.92	.96	.95
Social	.92	.94	.96	.94
Conceptual Domain	.97	.98	.99	.98
Social Domain	.96	.97	.97	.97
Practical Domain	.97	.98	.99	.98
GAC	.99	.99	.99	.99

Note. Average reliability coefficients (r_{xx}) were calculated using Fisher's z transformation.

Table 5.3   Reliability Coefficients of Skill Areas, Adaptive Domains, and the GAC: Adult Form, Self Report

Standardization Sample by Age Group

Skill Area/Composite	Age Group							Average r_{xx}
	16–21	22–29	30–39	40–49	50–64	65–74	75–89	
Communication	.91	.91	.93	.93	.92	.93	.91	.92
Community Use	.90	.90	.93	.93	.92	.93	.95	.92
Functional Academics	.90	.90	.93	.92	.92	.93	.94	.92
Home Living	.90	.92	.92	.93	.93	.94	.95	.93
Health and Safety	.89	.86	.90	.91	.85	.92	.90	.89
Leisure	.94	.94	.95	.95	.97	.96	.96	.95
Self-Care	.93	.90	.86	.86	.82	.87	.87	.88
Self-Direction	.94	.94	.93	.95	.94	.95	.94	.94
Social	.93	.91	.93	.91	.91	.92	.95	.92
Work	.90	.92	.89	.88	.89	.94	–	.92
Conceptual Domain	.96	.96	.97	.97	.97	.97	.97	.97
Social Domain	.96	.96	.97	.96	.96	.97	.97	.96
Practical Domain (without Work)	.96	.96	.97	.97	.96	.97	.97	.97
Practical Domain (with Work)	.97	.97	.97	.97	.97	.98	–	.97
GAC (without Work)	.99	.98	.99	.99	.99	.99	.99	.99
GAC (with Work)	.99	.99	.99	.99	.99	.99	–	.99

Note. Average reliability coefficients (r_{xx}) were calculated using Fisher's *z* transformation.

Table 5.3   Reliability Coefficients of Skill Areas, Adaptive Domains, and the GAC: Adult Form, Self Report (continued)

Standardization Sample By Level of Performance[a]

Skill Area/Composite	Average (GAC = 90–109)										
	Ages 16–29 (n = 145)			Ages 30–49 (n = 152)			Ages 50–89 (n = 160)			Average r_{xx}	
	SD	r	r^c	SD	r	r^c	SD	r	r^c	r	r^c
Communication	2.20	.81	.90	2.29	.81	.89	2.40	.86	.91	.86	.90
Community Use	2.03	.80	.91	2.00	.83	.92	2.17	.85	.92	.87	.92
Functional Academics	2.13	.75	.87	2.02	.77	.89	2.02	.77	.89	.85	.88
Home Living	2.24	.81	.90	2.27	.87	.93	2.34	.88	.93	.88	.92
Health and Safety	2.21	.78	.88	1.43	.59	.91	1.77	.63	.87	.78	.89
Leisure	2.16	.85	.92	2.41	.91	.94	2.06	.91	.96	.90	.94
Self-Care	1.56	.56	.88	1.49	.44	.86	1.43	.62	.91	.64	.89
Self-Direction	2.20	.85	.92	1.98	.78	.90	1.92	.79	.91	.87	.91
Social	2.30	.82	.90	2.02	.72	.87	2.06	.79	.90	.84	.89
Work	2.39	.83	.89	2.28	.69	.82	2.30	.85	.91	.80	.88
Conceptual Domain		.85	.92		.86	.93		.89	.94	.87	.93
Social Domain		.86	.93		.85	.92		.88	.95	.86	.93
Practical Domain (without Work)		.79	.92		.78	.93		.81	.93	.79	.93
Practical Domain (with Work)		.82	.92		.79	.93		.86	.94	.83	.93
GAC (without Work)		.89	.95		.89	.96		.92	.97	.90	.96
GAC (with Work)		.91	.95		.89	.95		.93	.97	.91	.96

Skill Area/Composite	Below Average (GAC = 89 or Less)										
	Ages 16–29 (n = 72)			Ages 30–49 (n = 91)			Ages 50–89 (n = 80)			Average r_{xx}	
	SD	r	r^c	SD	r	r^c	SD	r	r^c	r	r^c
Communication	2.21	.84	.91	2.28	.88	.93	2.44	.87	.91	.86	.92
Community Use	1.63	.65	.90	2.02	.85	.93	1.96	.89	.95	.82	.93
Functional Academics	1.79	.82	.93	1.95	.86	.94	2.26	.89	.94	.86	.94
Home Living	2.37	.87	.92	2.32	.88	.93	2.25	.91	.95	.89	.94
Health and Safety	1.95	.80	.91	2.67	.86	.89	2.31	.86	.92	.84	.91
Leisure	1.90	.83	.93	2.12	.84	.92	2.25	.89	.94	.86	.93
Self-Care	3.45	.93	.91	2.91	.82	.83	2.74	.78	.82	.86	.86
Self-Direction	2.07	.89	.95	2.09	.88	.94	1.98	.89	.95	.89	.95
Social	2.54	.89	.92	2.24	.86	.92	2.59	.89	.92	.88	.92
Work	3.07	.92	.92	3.18	.87	.85	2.68	.94	.95	.91	.92
Conceptual Domain		.89	.95		.93	.96		.93	.96	.92	.96
Social Domain		.89	.94		.89	.94		.91	.95	.93	.94
Practical Domain (without Work)		.87	.94		.93	.95		.92	.95	.93	.95
Practical Domain (with Work)		.91	.95		.94	.95		.94	.96	.93	.95
GAC (without Work)		.93	.97		.96	.98		.96	.97	.96	.97
GAC (with Work)		.95	.97		.96	.98		.96	.98	.96	.98

Note. SD = standard deviation; r = internal consistency reliability coefficient (coefficient alpha); r^c = corrected internal consistency reliability.

Average reliability coefficients (r_{xx}) were calculated using Fisher's z transformation.

[a]Conditional reliability coefficients for the above average level are not reported due to significant restriction of the range.

Table 5.4   Reliability Coefficients of Skill Areas, Adaptive Domains, and the GAC: Adult Form, Rated by Others

Standardization Sample by Age Group

Skill Area/Composite	Age Group 16–21	22–29	30–39	40–49	50–64	65–74	75–89	Average r_{xx}
Communication	.95	.93	.92	.93	.93	.91	.97	.94
Community Use	.95	.94	.95	.94	.93	.93	.98	.95
Functional Academics	.96	.96	.96	.96	.97	.97	.99	.97
Home Living	.94	.95	.94	.95	.95	.94	.98	.95
Health and Safety	.91	.93	.91	.94	.93	.86	.98	.93
Leisure	.93	.95	.95	.95	.95	.95	.97	.95
Self-Care	.94	.91	.91	.93	.94	.82	.98	.93
Self-Direction	.96	.95	.95	.95	.96	.92	.98	.96
Social	.95	.93	.92	.93	.95	.95	.96	.94
Work	.95	.97	.92	.94	.97	.99	–	.97
Conceptual Domain	.98	.98	.98	.98	.98	.97	.99	.98
Social Domain	.96	.97	.96	.97	.97	.97	.98	.97
Practical Domain (without Work)	.98	.98	.98	.98	.98	.96	.99	.98
Practical Domain (with Work)	.98	.98	.98	.98	.98	.97	–	.98
GAC (without Work)	.99	.99	.99	.99	.99	.99	.99	.99
GAC (with Work)	.99	.99	.99	.99	.99	.99	–	.99

Note. Average reliability coefficients (r_{xx}) were calculated using Fisher's *z* transformation.

Table 5.4   Reliability Coefficients of Skill Areas, Adaptive Domains, and the GAC: Adult Form, Rated by Others *(continued)*

Standardization Sample By Level of Performance[a]

Average (GAC = 90–109)

Skill Area/Composite	Ages 16–29 (n = 106)			Ages 30–49 (n = 149)			Ages 50–89 (n = 153)			Average r_{xx}	
	SD	r	r^c	SD	r	r^c	SD	r	r^c	r	r^c
Communication	2.11	.86	.93	2.16	.82	.91	1.96	.85	.94	.84	.93
Community Use	1.85	.79	.92	1.95	.77	.90	2.02	.88	.95	.82	.93
Functional Academics	1.95	.85	.94	1.98	.74	.89	2.17	.88	.94	.83	.93
Home Living	2.08	.90	.95	2.36	.88	.93	2.45	.90	.94	.89	.94
Health and Safety	1.97	.69	.87	1.51	.53	.88	1.57	.58	.89	.60	.88
Leisure	2.16	.88	.94	2.08	.87	.94	1.98	.91	.96	.89	.95
Self-Care	2.03	.68	.86	1.86	.75	.91	1.64	.68	.91	.71	.90
Self-Direction	1.97	.86	.94	2.09	.83	.92	1.89	.85	.94	.85	.93
Social	2.21	.83	.91	2.04	.81	.91	1.79	.84	.94	.83	.92
Work	2.24	.92	.96	2.12	.87	.94	2.07	.95	.98	.92	.96
Conceptual Domain		.90	.95		.86	.94		.90	.96	.89	.95
Social Domain		.89	.94		.88	.94		.89	.96	.89	.94
Practical Domain (without Work)		.84	.93		.83	.94		.83	.95	.83	.95
Practical Domain (with Work)		.87	.94		.84	.94		.86	.95	.86	.95
GAC (without Work)		.92	.97		.91	.96		.92	.97	.92	.97
GAC (with Work)		.93	.97		.92	.97		.93	.97	.93	.97

Below Average (GAC = 89 or Less)

Skill Area/Composite	Ages 16–29 (n = 72)			Ages 30–49 (n = 91)			Ages 50–89 (n = 80)			Average r_{xx}	
	SD	r	r^c	SD	r	r^c	SD	r	r^c	r	r^c
Communication	1.99	.90	.96	2.35	.87	.92	2.38	.95	.97	.91	.95
Community Use	2.29	.93	.96	1.99	.92	.96	2.17	.97	.99	.95	.98
Functional Academics	2.60	.96	.97	2.61	.96	.97	2.57	.98	.98	.97	.97
Home Living	2.18	.90	.95	2.66	.93	.95	2.93	.97	.97	.94	.96
Health and Safety	2.37	.90	.94	2.99	.91	.91	2.41	.97	.98	.94	.95
Leisure	2.14	.90	.95	1.84	.86	.95	1.92	.95	.98	.91	.96
Self-Care	2.40	.93	.95	2.79	.92	.93	3.32	.98	.97	.95	.95
Self-Direction	1.91	.91	.97	2.14	.92	.96	2.12	.97	.99	.94	.98
Social	2.32	.92	.95	2.12	.87	.93	2.42	.95	.97	.92	.95
Work	3.04	.94	.94	2.80	.93	.94	3.71	.99	.98	.97	.96
Conceptual Domain		.96	.98		.95	.97		.98	.99	.97	.98
Social Domain		.93	.96		.91	.96		.97	.98	.94	.97
Practical Domain (without Work)		.97	.98		.96	.97		.99	.99	.98	.98
Practical Domain (with Work)		.97	.98		.97	.98		.99	.99	.98	.98
GAC (without Work)		.98	.99		.98	.99		.99	.99	.98	.99
GAC (with Work)		.98	.99		.98	.99		.99	.99	.98	.99

Note. SD = standard deviation; r = internal consistency reliability coefficient (coefficient alpha); r^c = corrected internal consistency reliability.

Average reliability coefficients (r_{xx}) were calculated using Fisher's z transformation.

[a]Conditional reliability coefficients for the above average level are not reported due to significant restriction of the range.

Table 5.4   Reliability Coefficients of Skill Areas, Adaptive Domains, and the GAC: Adult Form, Rated by Others (continued)

Clinical Sample by Diagnoses

Skill Area/Composite	Alzheimer's Disease (*n* = 25)	Mental Retardation (*n* = 30)	Neuropsychological Disorders (*n* = 20)	Average r_{xx}
Communication	.96	.94	.94	.95
Community Use	.96	.96	.97	.96
Functional Academics	.97	.97	.98	.97
Home Living	.95	.93	.97	.95
Health and Safety	.93	.91	.96	.94
Leisure	.95	.94	.95	.95
Self-Care	.97	.94	.97	.96
Self-Direction	.93	.95	.95	.94
Social	.95	.95	.94	.95
Work	.86	.95	.98	.95
Conceptual Domain	.98	.98	.98	.98
Social Domain	.97	.97	.97	.97
Practical Domain (without Work)	.98	.98	.99	.98
Practical Domain (with Work)	.98	.98	.99	.98
GAC (without Work)	.99	.99	.99	.99
GAC (with Work)	.99	.99	.99	.99

Note. Average reliability coefficients (r_{xx}) were calculated using Fisher's *z* transformation.

Standard Errors of Measurement

The *SEM* provides an estimate of the amount of error in an individual's observed score. The *SEM* is inversely related to the reliability of a scale. Therefore, greater reliability means a smaller *SEM*, and increases the amount of confidence the clinician can have in the precision of the observed test score. The *SEM* is calculated with the following formula:

$$SEM = SD \sqrt{1 - r_{xx}}$$

where *SD* is the standard deviation unit of the scale, and r_{xx} is the reliability coefficient of the scale. Comparisons between the *SEM*s of the skill area scaled scores and GAC or adaptive domain scores should not be made because they are based on different standard deviation units. Because the standard deviation for the skill area scaled scores is 3 and for the GAC and adaptive domain scores is 15, the *SEM*s of the skill area scaled scores usually appear smaller than those of the GAC and adaptive domain scores. In fact, GAC and adaptive domain scores are actually more reliable measures than any of the individual skill area scaled scores. The *SEM*s for the skill area, adaptive domain and GAC scores, based on the internal consistency reliability coefficients for the six standardization samples, are shown in Tables 5.5–5.8. As demonstrated by internal consistency data, the ABAS–II reliability coefficients range from good to excellent for assessing individuals with different adaptive levels and individuals with different clinical diagnoses. Therefore, the *SEM*s provided in Tables 5.5–5.8 for the standardization samples may also be used for individuals with related adaptive levels or clinical diagnoses.

The *SEM* is used to calculate the confidence interval of the expected true score. Confidence intervals provide another means of expressing the precision of test scores. The clinician can use confidence intervals to report an individual's score as an interval that is likely to contain the individual's true score. Confidence intervals also serve as a reminder that measurement error is inherent in all test scores and that the observed test score is only an estimate of true ability or skill. Confidence intervals based on the *SEM* are calculated using the following formula:

Confidence Interval of *p*% = Observed Score ± *Zp* (*SEM*)

where *p* is the confidence level, such as 90% or 95%, and *Zp* is the *Z* value associated with the confidence level, which can be located in the normal probability tables. Critical values for calculating 90% and 95% confidence intervals are reported in Appendix Tables A.2, A.6, A.10, and A.13.

Table 5.5   Standard Errors of Measurement of Skill Areas, Adaptive Domains, and the GAC by Age: Teacher/Daycare Provider and Teacher Forms

Teacher/Daycare Provider Form

Skill Area/Composite	Age Group							Average SEM
	2:0–2:5	2:6–2:11	3:0–3:5	3:6–3:11	4:0–4:5	4:6–4:11	5:0–5:11	
Communication	0.90	0.85	0.67	0.79	0.79	0.90	0.85	0.82
Functional Pre-Academics	0.99	0.90	0.73	0.85	0.73	0.79	0.79	0.83
School Living	0.73	0.67	0.67	0.73	0.73	0.79	0.79	0.73
Health and Safety	1.24	1.04	1.04	1.16	1.12	1.24	0.99	1.12
Leisure	0.99	1.12	0.85	1.08	0.99	0.99	0.85	0.99
Self-Care	1.20	1.20	0.95	1.41	1.16	1.56	1.59	1.31
Self-Direction	0.95	1.08	0.73	0.85	0.85	0.79	0.73	0.86
Social	1.08	1.12	0.79	0.95	0.79	0.73	0.73	0.90
Motor	1.27	1.16	1.20	1.47	1.24	1.08	1.04	1.22
Conceptual Domain	3.35	3.35	2.60	3.00	2.60	3.00	2.60	2.95
Social Domain	3.97	4.24	3.00	3.97	3.35	3.35	3.00	3.58
Practical Domain	3.97	3.35	3.00	3.97	3.67	4.24	3.97	3.76
GAC	2.60	2.12	1.50	2.12	2.12	2.12	2.12	2.12

Teacher Form

Skill Area/Composite	Age Group											Average SEM
	5	6	7	8	9	10	11	12	13–14	15–16	17–21	
Communication	0.90	0.79	0.79	0.67	0.73	0.67	0.60	0.73	0.73	0.60	0.79	0.73
Community Use	1.37	1.16	1.20	1.04	1.16	1.04	0.73	0.79	0.90	0.79	0.90	1.03
Functional Academics	0.79	0.67	0.67	0.60	0.60	0.67	0.42	0.52	0.67	0.52	0.60	0.62
School Living	0.95	0.79	0.85	0.67	0.73	0.67	0.60	0.67	0.67	0.67	0.67	0.73
Health and Safety	1.08	0.79	0.99	0.73	0.73	0.73	0.60	0.60	0.67	0.67	0.73	0.77
Leisure	0.90	0.79	0.85	0.73	0.79	0.79	0.67	0.73	0.73	0.67	0.73	0.76
Self-Care	1.16	0.67	0.85	0.67	0.79	0.73	0.73	0.79	0.73	0.67	1.04	0.82
Self-Direction	0.85	0.73	0.73	0.60	0.60	0.52	0.42	0.52	0.52	0.52	0.60	0.61
Social	0.73	0.60	0.79	0.60	0.60	0.60	0.52	0.67	0.67	0.60	0.73	0.65
Work	–	–	–	–	–	–	–	–	–	–	0.60	0.60
Conceptual Domain	3.00	2.60	2.60	2.12	2.12	2.12	1.50	2.12	2.12	1.50	2.12	2.22
Social Domain	3.00	2.60	3.00	2.60	2.60	2.60	2.12	2.60	2.60	2.12	2.60	2.60
Practical Domain	3.35	2.60	3.00	2.12	2.60	2.60	2.12	2.12	2.12	2.12	2.60	2.52
GAC	2.12	1.50	1.50	1.50	1.50	1.50	1.50	1.50	1.50	1.50	1.50	1.57

Note. The average *SEM*s were calculated by averaging the sum of the squared *SEM*s for each age group and obtaining the square root of the result.

Table 5.6 Standard Errors of Measurement of Skill Areas, Adaptive Domains, and the GAC by Age: Parent/Primary Caregiver and Parent Forms

Parent/Primary Caregiver Form

Skill Area/Composite	0:0–0:3	0:4–0:7	0:8–0:11	1:0–1:3	1:4–1:7	1:8–1:11	2:0–2:5	2:6–2:11	3:0–3:5	3:6–3:11	4:0–4:5	4:6–4:11	5:0–5:11	Average SEM
Communication	1.75	1.53	1.37	1.08	1.12	1.04	0.85	0.90	0.73	0.90	1.16	1.08	1.12	1.16
Community Use	–	–	–	0.99	0.99	1.08	0.85	0.90	0.85	1.16	0.90	1.04	1.20	1.00
Functional Pre-Academics	–	–	–	1.12	0.85	1.04	0.95	0.99	0.85	0.85	0.95	0.79	0.95	0.94
Home Living	–	–	–	0.79	0.85	0.90	0.85	0.85	0.73	0.90	0.90	0.85	0.99	0.86
Health and Safety	2.16	1.59	1.50	1.31	1.20	1.08	1.08	1.04	0.99	1.24	1.24	1.24	1.27	1.34
Leisure	1.70	1.34	1.27	1.08	1.16	1.24	0.99	1.20	0.90	1.04	1.12	1.12	0.90	1.18
Self-Care	2.06	1.20	1.37	1.41	1.34	1.44	1.12	1.47	1.08	1.27	1.20	1.34	1.41	1.38
Self-Direction	1.90	1.41	1.41	1.20	1.16	1.20	0.99	1.27	0.95	1.04	1.04	0.95	0.95	1.22
Social	1.50	1.12	1.37	1.16	1.27	1.12	0.95	1.08	0.95	1.04	1.08	1.12	1.04	1.15
Motor	1.77	1.12	1.27	1.16	1.31	1.50	1.04	1.34	1.34	1.31	1.31	1.56	1.20	1.34
Conceptual Domain	8.22	6.87	6.00	4.24	3.67	3.97	3.00	3.67	3.00	3.35	3.67	3.35	3.67	4.63
Social Domain	6.54	5.20	4.97	4.50	4.97	4.74	3.67	4.50	3.67	4.24	4.24	4.50	3.67	4.63
Practical Domain	8.87	5.61	6.36	3.67	3.35	3.67	3.00	3.35	2.60	3.67	3.00	3.67	3.67	4.52
GAC	5.61	3.67	3.67	2.60	2.12	2.60	2.12	2.60	2.12	2.12	2.12	2.60	2.12	2.94

Parent Form

Skill Area/Composite	5	6	7	8	9	10	11	12	13–14	15–16	17–21	Average SEM
Communication	0.95	0.90	0.90	0.79	0.99	0.90	0.90	0.73	0.90	0.85	0.67	0.87
Community Use	0.85	0.79	1.04	0.85	0.90	0.99	0.90	0.90	0.85	0.90	0.73	0.89
Functional Academics	0.73	0.79	0.85	0.73	0.95	0.90	0.95	0.73	0.85	0.85	0.60	0.82
Home Living	0.99	0.85	0.90	0.79	0.95	0.85	0.79	0.79	0.85	0.73	0.67	0.84
Health and Safety	1.12	1.16	1.20	1.08	1.27	1.20	1.27	0.95	1.04	1.08	0.85	1.12
Leisure	0.99	0.90	0.95	0.90	0.95	0.90	0.90	0.73	0.85	0.85	0.73	0.88
Self-Care	0.95	1.08	1.12	1.04	1.37	1.16	1.34	0.90	1.20	1.12	0.90	1.12
Self-Direction	0.90	0.79	0.99	0.90	0.90	0.73	0.79	0.73	0.79	0.67	0.67	0.81
Social	0.95	0.90	0.95	0.85	0.85	0.79	0.90	0.73	0.79	0.73	0.73	0.84
Work	–	–	–	–	–	–	–	–	–	–	0.85	0.85
Conceptual Domain	3.00	2.60	3.00	2.60	3.00	3.00	3.00	2.60	2.60	2.60	2.12	2.75
Social Domain	3.67	3.35	3.67	3.35	3.35	3.35	3.35	3.00	3.00	3.00	3.00	3.29
Practical Domain	3.00	3.00	3.35	2.60	3.67	3.35	3.35	2.60	3.00	3.00	2.12	3.03
GAC	2.12	2.12	2.12	1.50	2.12	2.12	2.12	1.50	2.12	2.12	1.50	1.97

Note. The average *SEM*s were calculated by averaging the sum of the squared *SEM*s for each age group and obtaining the square root of the result.

Table 5.7   Standard Errors of Measurement of Skill Areas, Adaptive Domains, and the GAC by Age: Adult Form, Self Report

Skill Area/Composite	16–21	22–29	30–39	40–49	50–64	65–74	75–89	Average SEM
Communication	0.90	0.90	0.79	0.79	0.85	0.79	0.90	0.85
Community Use	0.95	0.95	0.79	0.79	0.85	0.79	0.67	0.85
Functional Academics	0.95	0.95	0.79	0.85	0.85	0.79	0.73	0.85
Home Living	0.95	0.85	0.85	0.79	0.79	0.73	0.67	0.79
Health and Safety	0.99	1.12	0.95	0.90	1.16	0.85	0.95	0.99
Leisure	0.73	0.73	0.67	0.67	0.52	0.60	0.60	0.67
Self-Care	0.79	0.95	1.12	1.12	1.27	1.08	1.08	1.04
Self-Direction	0.73	0.73	0.79	0.67	0.73	0.67	0.73	0.73
Social	0.79	0.90	0.79	0.90	0.90	0.85	0.67	0.85
Work	0.95	0.85	0.99	1.04	0.99	0.73	–	0.85
Conceptual Domain	3.00	3.00	2.60	2.60	2.60	2.60	2.60	2.72
Social Domain	3.00	3.00	2.60	3.00	3.00	2.60	2.60	2.84
Practical Domain (without Work)	3.00	3.00	2.60	2.60	3.00	2.60	2.60	2.78
Practical Domain (with Work)	2.60	2.60	2.60	2.60	2.60	2.12	–	2.47
GAC (without Work)	1.50	2.12	1.50	1.50	1.50	1.50	1.50	1.60
GAC (with Work)	1.50	1.50	1.50	1.50	1.50	1.50	–	1.50

Note. The average *SEM*s were calculated by averaging the sum of the squared *SEM*s for each age group and obtaining the square root of the result.

Table 5.8   Standard Errors of Measurement of Skill Areas, Adaptive Domains, and the GAC by Age: Adult Form, Rated by Others

Skill Area/Composite	16–21	22–29	30–39	40–49	50–64	65–74	75–89	Average SEM
Communication	0.67	0.79	0.85	0.79	0.79	0.90	0.52	0.73
Community Use	0.67	0.73	0.67	0.73	0.79	0.79	0.42	0.67
Functional Academics	0.60	0.60	0.60	0.60	0.52	0.52	0.30	0.52
Home Living	0.73	0.67	0.73	0.67	0.67	0.73	0.42	0.67
Health and Safety	0.90	0.79	0.90	0.73	0.79	1.12	0.42	0.79
Leisure	0.79	0.67	0.67	0.67	0.67	0.67	0.52	0.67
Self-Care	0.73	0.90	0.90	0.79	0.73	1.27	0.42	0.79
Self-Direction	0.60	0.67	0.67	0.67	0.60	0.85	0.42	0.60
Social	0.67	0.79	0.85	0.79	0.67	0.67	0.60	0.73
Work	0.67	0.52	0.85	0.73	0.52	0.30	–	0.52
Conceptual Domain	2.12	2.12	2.12	2.12	2.12	2.60	1.50	2.12
Social Domain	3.00	2.60	3.00	2.60	2.60	2.60	2.12	2.66
Practical Domain (without Work)	2.12	2.12	2.12	2.12	2.12	3.00	1.50	2.19
Practical Domain (with Work)	2.12	2.12	2.12	2.12	2.12	2.60	–	2.12
GAC (without Work)	1.50	1.50	1.50	1.50	1.50	1.50	1.50	1.50
GAC (with Work)	1.50	1.50	1.50	1.50	1.50	1.50	–	1.50

Note. The average *SEM*s were calculated by averaging the sum of the squared *SEM*s for each age group and obtaining the square root of the result.

Test-Retest Reliability

Test-retest reliability was investigated by asking teachers, daycare providers, parents, and adults to each rate a child, adult, or themselves two times using the same form. The test-retest interval for the Teacher/Daycare Provider Form ranged from 2 days to 6 weeks, with a mean retest interval of 13 days and standard deviation of 10 days. The test-retest interval for the Parent/Primary Caregiver Form ranged from 2 days to 5 weeks, with a mean retest interval of 12 days and standard deviation of 10 days. The test-retest interval for the Teacher Form ranged from 3 days to 3 weeks, with a mean retest interval of 11 days and standard deviation of 3 days. The test-retest interval for the Parent Form ranged from 5 days to 6 weeks, with a mean retest interval of 11 days and standard deviation of 5 days. The test-retest interval for the Adult Form, Self Report ranged from 6 days to 3 weeks and 4 days, with a mean retest interval of 10 days and standard deviation of 3 days. The test-retest interval for the Adult Form, Rated by Others ranged from 3 days to 6 weeks, with a mean retest interval of 12 days and standard deviation of 6 days. The infant-preschool teacher/daycare and parent/primary caregiver samples included 115 and 207 children, respectively. School-age teacher and parent samples included 143 and 104 children, respectively. The two adult samples included 66 adults (self report) and 52 adults (rated by others).

Test-retest reliability was estimated using Pearson's product-moment correlation coefficient and is reported in Tables 5.9–5.12 for the six standardization samples by age group. The tables report the standardized differences between the first and second administrations. In this manual Cohen's *d* is used to report standardized differences (Cohen, 1996). The tables also report the correlation coefficients corrected for the variability of the standardization sample. References made in text are to corrected correlations.

The test-retest reliability coefficients of the GAC, mostly in the .90s, are consistent across all six samples. The mean GAC scores of the two administrations are also consistent, with mean retest scores being slightly higher. The test-retest reliability coefficients of the adaptive domains are generally in the upper .80s land .90s. As expected, the test-retest reliability coefficients of the skill areas are slightly lower, mainly in the .70s, .80s, and .90s on the infant-preschool forms, and in the .80s and .90s on the school-age and adult forms.

Table 5.9   Test-Retest Reliability Coefficients of Skill Areas, Adaptive Domains, and the GAC: Teacher/Daycare Provider and Teacher Forms

▶ **Teacher/Daycare Provider Form**

Ages 2–3 (n = 59)	First Testing		Second Testing				
Skill Area/Composite	Mean	SD	Mean	SD	Cohen's d	r_{12}	Corrected r^a
Communication	10.9	2.9	10.9	2.8	.00	.87	.87
Functional Pre-Academics	10.7	3.1	10.5	2.7	−.07	.76	.75
School Living	11.0	2.8	11.1	2.5	.04	.83	.85
Health and Safety	10.8	2.7	10.5	2.6	−.11	.82	.86
Leisure	10.3	2.9	10.4	2.9	.03	.85	.86
Self-Care	10.4	2.6	10.3	2.5	−.04	.81	.85
Self-Direction	10.7	2.7	10.8	2.4	.04	.81	.85
Social	10.8	3.2	10.8	2.8	.00	.83	.81
Motor	11.0	3.0	11.0	2.9	.00	.88	.88
Conceptual Domain	103.7	15.1	103.5	14.3	−.01	.88	.88
Social Domain	102.0	16.3	102.6	15.0	.04	.87	.85
Practical Domain	103.3	13.8	102.5	12.2	−.06	.86	.88
GAC	103.6	15.5	103.3	14.3	−.02	.91	.90

Ages 4–5 (n = 56)	First Testing		Second Testing				
Skill Area/Composite	Mean	SD	Mean	SD	Cohen's d	r_{12}	Corrected r^a
Communication	11.1	2.3	11.6	2.6	.20	.66	.80
Functional Pre-Academics	9.5	2.8	9.6	2.7	.04	.92	.93
School Living	10.6	2.3	10.8	2.6	.08	.79	.88
Health and Safety	10.0	2.5	10.1	2.6	.04	.70	.79
Leisure	10.1	2.6	9.9	2.4	−.08	.79	.84
Self-Care	10.6	2.7	10.5	2.5	−.04	.85	.87
Self-Direction	10.1	2.5	10.2	2.5	.04	.83	.88
Social	11.0	2.3	11.1	2.4	.04	.79	.88
Motor	10.8	2.6	10.9	2.4	.04	.75	.81
Conceptual Domain	100.0	13.1	101.6	13.5	.12	.87	.90
Social Domain	102.0	12.7	101.3	12.6	−.06	.86	.90
Practical Domain	101.3	12.0	101.7	12.8	.03	.87	.92
GAC	101.3	12.9	101.8	13.2	.04	.90	.92

All Ages[b] (n = 115)	First Testing		Second Testing				
Skill Area/Composite	Mean	SD	Mean	SD	Cohen's d	r_{12}	Corrected r^a
Communication	11.0	2.6	11.3	2.7	.11	.79	.84
Functional Pre-Academics	10.1	3.0	10.1	2.8	.00	.86	.87
School Living	10.8	2.6	11.0	2.5	.08	.81	.87
Health and Safety	10.4	2.6	10.3	2.6	−.04	.77	.83
Leisure	10.2	2.8	10.1	2.7	−.04	.82	.85
Self-Care	10.5	2.6	10.4	2.5	−.04	.83	.86
Self-Direction	10.4	2.6	10.5	2.5	.04	.82	.87
Social	10.9	2.8	10.9	2.6	.00	.81	.85
Motor	10.9	2.8	10.9	2.7	.00	.83	.85
Conceptual Domain	101.9	14.2	102.5	13.9	.04	.88	.89
Social Domain	102.0	14.6	102.0	13.8	.00	.87	.88
Practical Domain	102.3	12.9	102.1	12.5	−.02	.87	.90
GAC	102.4	14.3	102.6	13.8	.01	.91	.91

[a]Correlations were corrected for the variability of the standardization sample (Guilford & Fruchter, 1978).

[b]Reliability coefficients for the overall sample were calculated using Fisher's z transformation.

Table 5.9   Test-Retest Reliability Coefficients of Skill Areas, Adaptive Domains, and the GAC: Teacher/Daycare Provider and Teacher Forms *(continued)*

Teacher Form

Ages 5–9 ($n = 39$)	First Testing		Second Testing				
Skill Area/Composite	Mean	SD	Mean	SD	Cohen's d	r_{12}	Corrected r[a]
Communication	8.7	3.1	9.0	3.0	.10	.95	.95
Community Use	8.6	3.0	8.7	2.9	.03	.95	.95
Functional Academics	9.2	3.2	9.2	3.3	.00	.96	.96
School Living	9.2	2.4	9.3	2.2	.04	.97	.98
Health and Safety	9.3	3.0	9.3	3.1	.00	.96	.96
Leisure	9.4	2.7	9.4	2.8	.00	.97	.97
Self-Care	8.6	3.4	8.7	3.2	.03	.98	.98
Self-Direction	8.9	3.2	8.9	3.0	.00	.95	.94
Social	9.3	2.2	9.3	2.2	.00	.97	.99
Conceptual Domain	97.4	16.7	98.4	16.3	.06	.98	.97
Social Domain	97.2	12.5	97.3	12.8	.01	.99	.99
Practical Domain	94.9	15.6	95.3	14.4	.03	.99	.99
GAC	96.4	16.0	96.8	15.2	.03	.99	.99

Ages 10–12 ($n = 50$)	First Testing		Second Testing				
Skill Area/Composite	Mean	SD	Mean	SD	Cohen's d	r_{12}	Corrected r[a]
Communication	7.9	3.4	8.3	3.8	.11	.82	.76
Community Use	6.7	3.7	7.0	3.8	.08	.80	.70
Functional Academics	7.9	3.8	7.9	3.7	.00	.95	.92
School Living	7.9	3.5	8.0	3.8	.03	.88	.84
Health and Safety	8.0	3.5	8.0	3.5	.00	.88	.83
Leisure	8.4	3.3	8.2	3.4	−.06	.94	.93
Self-Care	8.3	3.6	8.5	3.4	.06	.95	.93
Self-Direction	7.6	3.8	7.5	4.0	−.03	.87	.79
Social	8.7	3.6	8.7	3.5	.00	.86	.80
Conceptual Domain	91.8	19.0	93.0	20.8	.06	.94	.90
Social Domain	94.3	18.0	93.5	18.0	−.04	.92	.89
Practical Domain	91.2	20.2	92.3	21.6	.05	.92	.86
GAC	91.9	20.4	92.9	21.1	.05	.95	.91

[a]Correlations were corrected for the variability of the standardization sample (Guilford & Fruchter, 1978).

Table 5.9 Test-Retest Reliability Coefficients of Skill Areas, Adaptive Domains, and the GAC: Teacher/Daycare Provider and Teacher Forms (continued)

Teacher Form

Ages 13–21 (n = 54) Skill Area/Composite	First Testing Mean	SD	Second Testing Mean	SD	Cohen's d	r_{12}	Corrected r[a]
Communication	8.2	3.5	8.5	3.4	.09	.83	.77
Community Use	8.8	3.0	8.8	3.1	.00	.91	.91
Functional Academics	9.1	2.8	9.2	2.7	.04	.94	.95
School Living	8.3	3.5	8.7	3.2	.12	.84	.79
Health and Safety	9.7	2.6	9.4	2.8	−.11	.90	.92
Leisure	9.0	3.0	9.2	2.8	.07	.85	.85
Self-Care	9.4	3.2	9.5	2.9	.03	.96	.95
Self-Direction	8.5	3.3	8.7	3.1	.06	.92	.90
Social	9.1	3.1	9.4	3.0	.10	.81	.80
Conceptual Domain	97.1	16.4	98.1	16.5	.06	.95	.94
Social Domain	97.4	16.9	98.7	16.4	.08	.91	.88
Practical Domain	96.5	16.2	97.5	16.1	.06	.97	.96
GAC	96.0	17.6	97.1	17.8	.06	.96	.94

All Ages[b] (n = 143) Skill Area/Composite	First Testing Mean	SD	Second Testing Mean	SD	Cohen's d	r_{12}	Corrected r[a]
Communication	8.2	3.4	8.6	3.4	.12	.88	.86
Community Use	8.0	3.4	8.1	3.4	.03	.90	.89
Functional Academics	8.7	3.3	8.8	3.3	.03	.95	.95
School Living	8.4	3.3	8.6	3.2	.06	.92	.91
Health and Safety	9.0	3.1	8.9	3.2	−.03	.92	.92
Leisure	8.9	3.1	8.9	3.0	.00	.93	.93
Self-Care	8.8	3.4	8.9	3.2	.03	.97	.96
Self-Direction	8.3	3.5	8.3	3.5	.00	.92	.89
Social	9.0	3.1	9.1	3.0	.03	.91	.92
Conceptual Domain	95.3	17.5	96.4	18.1	.06	.96	.94
Social Domain	96.3	16.2	96.5	16.1	.01	.96	.95
Practical Domain	94.2	17.6	95.1	17.9	.05	.97	.96
GAC	94.7	18.2	95.6	18.4	.05	.97	.96

[a]Correlations were corrected for the variability of the standardization sample (Guilford & Fruchter, 1978).

[b]Reliability coefficients for the overall sample were calculated using Fisher's z transformation.

Table 5.10   Test-Retest Reliability Coefficients of Skill Areas, Adaptive Domains, and the GAC: Parent/Primary Caregiver and Parent Forms

Parent/Primary Caregiver Form

Ages 0:0–0:11 (n = 43)

Skill Area/Composite	First Testing Mean	First Testing SD	Second Testing Mean	Second Testing SD	Cohen's d	r_{12}	Corrected r^a
Communication	9.5	3.2	9.9	2.6	.14	.75	.71
Health and Safety	9.7	3.1	9.6	2.9	−.03	.75	.73
Leisure	10.1	2.7	10.4	2.1	.12	.70	.76
Self-Care	9.8	2.5	9.3	2.4	−.20	.78	.85
Self-Direction	10.3	2.9	10.4	2.4	.04	.79	.80
Social	10.5	2.6	10.6	2.2	.04	.76	.82
Motor	9.9	2.3	9.8	2.2	−.04	.71	.83
Conceptual Domain	99.0	16.4	101.0	14.4	.13	.85	.82
Social Domain	100.3	13.2	101.8	11.5	.12	.82	.86
Practical Domain	97.6	15.5	95.8	13.9	−.12	.82	.81
GAC	98.2	15.7	98.4	13.8	.01	.89	.88

Age 1 (n = 41)

Skill Area/Composite	First Testing Mean	First Testing SD	Second Testing Mean	Second Testing SD	Cohen's d	r_{12}	Corrected r^a
Communication	9.6	2.5	9.8	2.6	.08	.83	.88
Community Use	9.8	2.8	10.2	2.7	.15	.70	.74
Functional Pre-Academics	9.9	2.8	9.7	2.7	−.07	.75	.78
Home Living	10.5	3.0	10.6	3.1	.03	.89	.89
Health and Safety	9.9	2.5	10.0	2.6	.04	.85	.89
Leisure	10.4	2.7	10.6	2.4	.08	.74	.79
Self-Care	10.1	3.1	10.2	3.2	.03	.89	.88
Self-Direction	10.0	3.1	10.6	3.2	.19	.76	.74
Social	9.5	3.0	10.0	2.9	.17	.79	.79
Motor	10.5	3.0	10.4	2.9	−.03	.77	.77
Conceptual Domain	97.4	14.2	98.6	15.4	.08	.82	.84
Social Domain	98.2	15.0	100.3	14.6	.14	.81	.81
Practical Domain	98.9	14.7	100.0	15.3	.07	.90	.90
GAC	98.4	15.0	99.6	15.3	.08	.86	.86

Ages 2–3 (n = 61)

Skill Area/Composite	First Testing Mean	First Testing SD	Second Testing Mean	Second Testing SD	Cohen's d	r_{12}	Corrected r^a
Communication	10.5	2.7	11.1	3.1	.21	.81	.84
Community Use	10.5	2.6	10.6	3.0	.04	.81	.86
Functional Pre-Academics	10.5	3.0	10.3	3.2	−.06	.92	.92
Home Living	10.7	2.9	10.9	2.9	.07	.81	.82
Health and Safety	10.3	2.6	10.5	2.7	.08	.72	.79
Leisure	10.8	2.7	10.8	3.0	.00	.83	.86
Self-Care	10.9	2.9	10.9	2.9	.00	.76	.78
Self-Direction	10.4	2.8	10.9	3.1	.17	.84	.86
Social	10.7	2.4	10.8	2.8	.04	.79	.87
Motor	10.7	3.1	10.6	3.3	−.03	.83	.82
Conceptual Domain	101.5	14.9	103.4	16.6	.12	.90	.90
Social Domain	102.6	13.4	103.1	16.0	.03	.88	.90
Practical Domain	102.4	14.3	103.2	15.5	.05	.85	.86
GAC	102.4	14.4	103.3	16.3	.06	.91	.92

aCorrelations were corrected for the variability of the standardization sample (Guilford & Fruchter, 1978).

Table 5.10 Test-Retest Reliability Coefficients of Skill Areas, Adaptive Domains, and the GAC: Parent/Primary Caregiver and Parent Forms (continued)

▶ **Parent/Primary Caregiver Form**

Ages 4–5 (n = 62)

Skill Area/Composite	First Testing Mean	SD	Second Testing Mean	SD	Cohen's d	r_{12}	Corrected r[a]
Communication	11.0	2.5	11.7	2.6	.27	.71	.80
Community Use	10.1	2.8	10.3	2.6	.07	.73	.76
Functional Pre-Academics	10.0	3.1	10.3	2.8	.10	.83	.82
Home Living	9.8	2.7	10.6	2.8	.29	.69	.75
Health and Safety	10.9	2.7	10.9	2.7	.00	.74	.79
Leisure	9.9	3.1	10.3	3.1	.13	.80	.78
Self-Care	9.9	2.8	10.4	2.7	.18	.67	.71
Self-Direction	10.2	2.7	10.7	2.7	.19	.71	.77
Social	10.2	2.7	10.5	2.8	.11	.67	.74
Motor	11.0	2.4	11.4	2.5	.16	.68	.79
Conceptual Domain	100.9	14.7	104.2	13.0	.24	.85	.85
Social Domain	98.9	15.7	100.9	15.6	.13	.79	.77
Practical Domain	99.7	14.1	102.1	13.8	.17	.82	.84
GAC	100.5	14.1	103.3	13.5	.20	.84	.86

All Ages[c] (n = 207)

Skill Area/Composite	First Testing Mean	SD	Second Testing Mean	SD	Cohen's d	r_{12}	Corrected r[a]
Communication	10.3	2.8	10.8	2.8	.18	.78	.82
Community Use[b]	10.1	2.7	10.4	2.8	.11	.75	.79
Functional Pre-Academics[b]	10.2	3.0	10.2	2.9	.00	.85	.85
Home Living[b]	10.3	2.9	10.7	2.9	.14	.81	.83
Health and Safety	10.3	2.7	10.3	2.7	.00	.77	.81
Leisure	10.3	2.8	10.5	2.8	.07	.77	.80
Self-Care	10.2	2.9	10.3	2.8	.04	.79	.81
Self-Direction	10.3	2.8	10.7	2.8	.14	.78	.80
Social	10.3	2.7	10.5	2.7	.07	.76	.81
Motor	10.6	2.7	10.6	2.8	.00	.75	.80
Conceptual Domain	100.0	15.0	102.2	14.9	.15	.86	.86
Social Domain	100.1	14.4	101.6	14.7	.10	.83	.84
Practical Domain	99.9	14.6	100.7	14.8	.05	.85	.86
GAC	100.1	14.7	101.6	14.8	.10	.88	.88

[a]Correlations were corrected for the variability of the standardization sample (Guilford & Fruchter, 1978).

[b]Based on 164 observations.

[c]Reliability coefficients for the overall sample were calculated using Fisher's z transformation.

Table 5.10   Test-Retest Reliability Coefficients of Skill Areas, Adaptive Domains, and the GAC: Parent/Primary Caregiver and Parent Forms (continued)

Parent Form

Ages 5–9 (n = 30) Skill Area/Composite	First Testing Mean	SD	Second Testing Mean	SD	Cohen's d	r_{12}	Corrected r^a
Communication	8.4	3.9	8.9	3.8	.13	.88	.79
Community Use	9.0	3.6	8.4	4.0	−.16	.89	.84
Functional Academics	8.5	3.9	8.7	4.0	.05	.93	.89
Home Living	9.0	3.8	9.2	3.5	.05	.93	.89
Health and Safety	9.5	3.9	9.4	3.7	−.03	.89	.81
Leisure	9.3	3.6	8.9	4.0	−.11	.88	.82
Self-Care	9.3	3.1	9.4	3.2	.03	.91	.90
Self-Direction	8.7	4.0	8.3	4.1	−.10	.90	.83
Social	8.6	4.2	8.5	4.0	−.02	.96	.93
Conceptual Domain	92.6	19.9	92.9	20.1	.01	.96	.92
Social Domain	95.0	19.3	93.6	20.3	−.07	.95	.91
Practical Domain	97.0	18.5	96.0	18.1	−.05	.95	.92
GAC	93.8	20.5	93.0	20.7	−.04	.95	.91

Ages 10–12 (n = 31) Skill Area/Composite	First Testing Mean	SD	Second Testing Mean	SD	Cohen's d	r_{12}	Corrected r^a
Communication	11.2	2.0	11.8	1.7	.32	.56	.80
Community Use	11.2	2.2	11.6	2.1	.19	.85	.92
Functional Academics	11.4	2.7	11.4	2.5	.00	.90	.92
Home Living	9.5	4.0	10.0	3.9	.13	.92	.85
Health and Safety	10.7	2.5	11.2	2.1	.22	.81	.87
Leisure	11.0	2.1	11.5	2.2	.23	.82	.91
Self-Care	10.7	2.0	11.0	1.8	.16	.77	.90
Self-Direction	10.7	2.6	11.4	2.3	.29	.87	.90
Social	10.6	3.1	11.2	2.5	.21	.86	.85
Conceptual Domain	106.3	10.7	108.2	9.9	.18	.87	.93
Social Domain	104.8	12.8	107.3	11.4	.21	.84	.89
Practical Domain	104.6	12.8	107.2	12.0	.21	.91	.93
GAC	105.3	11.2	107.9	11.0	.23	.90	.94

[a]Correlations were corrected for the variability of the standardization sample (Guilford & Fruchter, 1978).

Table 5.10   Test-Retest Reliability Coefficients of Skill Areas, Adaptive Domains, and the GAC: Parent/Primary Caregiver and Parent Forms (continued)

▶ **Parent Form**

Ages 13–21 (*n* = 43)	First Testing		Second Testing				
Skill Area/Composite	Mean	SD	Mean	SD	Cohen's *d*	r_{12}	Corrected *r*[a]
Communication	10.8	2.4	11.2	2.1	.18	.85	.90
Community Use	11.6	2.5	11.7	2.4	.04	.92	.95
Functional Academics	10.7	2.3	10.9	2.4	.09	.90	.94
Home Living	10.0	3.3	10.5	3.1	.16	.90	.87
Health and Safety	10.7	2.3	11.0	2.1	.14	.90	.94
Leisure	10.9	2.5	11.3	2.3	.17	.84	.89
Self-Care	11.1	2.0	11.1	2.2	.00	.76	.89
Self-Direction	10.5	2.6	11.0	2.6	.19	.86	.90
Social	10.3	2.4	10.9	2.4	.25	.87	.92
Conceptual Domain	104.8	14.3	106.4	13.4	.12	.91	.92
Social Domain	104.3	12.7	107.3	12.4	.24	.83	.88
Practical Domain	103.4	15.0	104.7	14.5	.09	.95	.95
GAC	105.3	14.9	107.3	13.9	.14	.93	.93

All Ages[b] (*n* = 104)	First Testing		Second Testing				
Skill Area/Composite	Mean	SD	Mean	SD	Cohen's *d*	r_{12}	Corrected *r*[a]
Communication	10.3	3.0	10.7	2.9	.14	.80	.84
Community Use	10.8	3.0	10.7	3.2	−.03	.89	.91
Functional Academics	10.3	3.2	10.4	3.2	.03	.91	.92
Home Living	9.6	3.6	10.0	3.5	.11	.92	.87
Health and Safety	10.3	2.9	10.6	2.7	.11	.87	.89
Leisure	10.5	2.8	10.7	3.1	.07	.85	.88
Self-Care	10.5	2.5	10.6	2.5	.04	.83	.90
Self-Direction	10.1	3.1	10.3	3.3	.06	.88	.88
Social	9.9	3.3	10.3	3.2	.12	.91	.91
Conceptual Domain	101.7	16.2	103.1	16.1	.09	.92	.92
Social Domain	101.8	15.4	103.4	16.0	.10	.89	.89
Practical Domain	101.9	15.7	102.9	15.5	.06	.94	.93
GAC	102.0	16.5	103.4	16.7	.08	.93	.93

[a]Correlations were corrected for the variability of the standardization sample (Guilford & Fruchter, 1978).

[b]Reliability coefficients for the overall sample were calculated using Fisher's *z* transformation.

Table 5.11 Test-Retest Reliability Coefficients of Skill Areas, Adaptive Domains, and the GAC: Adult Form, Self Report

Ages 16–89 (*n* = 66)	First Testing		Second Testing				
Skill Area/Composite	Mean	SD	Mean	SD	Cohen's *d*	r_{12}	Corrected r^a
Communication	10.5	3.1	10.7	3.3	.06	.92	.91
Community Use	10.3	3.2	10.5	3.3	.06	.93	.92
Functional Academics	10.2	3.3	10.3	3.5	.03	.97	.96
Home Living	10.4	3.2	10.5	3.1	.03	.94	.93
Health and Safety	9.9	3.1	10.2	3.0	.10	.94	.94
Leisure	9.9	3.2	10.1	3.1	.06	.95	.94
Self-Care	10.3	2.7	10.3	2.7	.00	.92	.93
Self-Direction	10.2	3.2	10.2	3.3	.00	.96	.95
Social	10.3	3.1	10.5	2.9	.07	.93	.92
Work[b]	10.2	3.6	10.4	3.6	.06	.97	.96
Conceptual Domain	101.4	16.6	102.2	18.0	.05	.96	.95
Social Domain	101.1	15.8	102.1	15.9	.06	.95	.95
Practical Domain (without Work)	100.9	16.6	102.0	17.0	.07	.96	.95
Practical Domain (with Work)[b]	102.7	17.2	104.0	16.8	.08	.99	.98
GAC (without Work)	100.6	16.4	101.5	16.9	.05	.97	.96
GAC (with Work)[b]	102.3	15.5	103.3	15.6	.06	.99	.99

[a]Correlations were corrected for the variability of the standardization sample (Guilford & Fruchter, 1978).

[b]Based on 47 observations.

Table 5.12 Test-Retest Reliability Coefficients of Skill Areas, Adaptive Domains, and the GAC: Adult Form, Rated by Others

Ages 16–89 (*n* = 52)	First Testing		Second Testing				
Skill Area/Composite	Mean	SD	Mean	SD	Cohen's *d*	r_{12}	Corrected r^a
Communication	10.7	2.6	10.8	2.7	.04	.87	.91
Community Use	10.8	2.4	11.0	2.4	.08	.91	.94
Functional Academics	10.8	2.4	11.0	2.3	.09	.88	.92
Home Living	10.7	2.8	11.0	2.7	.11	.95	.96
Health and Safety	10.8	1.9	10.9	1.8	.05	.80	.92
Leisure	10.7	2.4	10.8	2.6	.04	.92	.95
Self-Care	10.7	2.0	10.8	2.0	.05	.89	.95
Self-Direction	10.6	2.6	10.7	2.8	.04	.89	.92
Social	10.5	2.7	10.6	2.7	.04	.90	.92
Work[b]	10.5	2.3	10.5	2.3	.00	.86	.91
Conceptual Domain	102.7	11.9	103.6	12.7	.07	.91	.94
Social Domain	102.3	13.3	103.2	13.8	.07	.95	.96
Practical Domain (without Work)	103.3	11.8	104.6	11.5	.11	.94	.96
Practical Domain (with Work)[b]	103.2	11.9	104.0	11.8	.07	.92	.95
GAC (without Work)	101.8	12.9	103.2	13.3	.11	.93	.95
GAC (with Work)[b]	101.7	11.7	102.9	11.9	.10	.94	.96

[a]Correlations were corrected for the variability of the standardization sample (Guilford & Fruchter, 1978).

[b]Based on 43 observations.

Inter-Rater Reliability

This estimate of reliability is based on correlations between scores obtained from different respondents (e.g., two teachers) who rated the same individual using the same form. Reliability estimates using this method can be expected to reflect more measurement error than the two previously discussed forms of reliability due to additional sources of error (e.g., errors due to differences in the levels of familiarity the two respondents have with the individual, and to ratings completed at slightly different times).

Inter-rater reliability was evaluated using five samples. The teacher/daycare provider sample included 42 children ages 2 years 0 months–5 years 9 months, each rated by two teachers or daycare providers. The parent/primary caregiver sample included 56 children ages 0 months–5 years 10 months, each rated by two parents. The teacher sample included 84 children, ages 5–18 years, each rated by two teachers; the parent sample consisted of 75 children, ages 5–21 years, each rated by two parents; the adult sample included 52 adults each rated by two other respondents.

Inter-rater reliability was estimated using Pearson's product-moment correlation coefficient and is reported in Tables 5.13–5.15 by age group and standardization sample. The tables also present the standardized differences (Cohen's d) between the two ratings and the correlation coefficients corrected for the variability of the standardization sample. References made in text are to corrected correlations.

Table 5.13 Inter-Rater Reliability Coefficients of Skill Areas, Adaptive Domains, and the GAC: Teacher/Daycare Provider and Teacher Forms

Teacher/Daycare Provider Form

Ages 2–5 ($n = 42$)	First Respondent		Second Respondent				
Skill Area/Composite	Mean	SD	Mean	SD	Cohen's d	r_{12}	Corrected r[a]
Communication	11.5	2.9	10.7	2.7	−.29	.72	.74
Functional Pre-Academics	10.8	2.8	10.5	2.7	−.11	.82	.85
School Living	10.2	2.2	10.6	2.9	.16	.46	.71
Health and Safety	10.8	2.4	10.5	2.9	−.11	.64	.77
Leisure	10.6	2.6	10.5	3.2	−.03	.44	.58
Self-Care	11.2	2.4	11.0	3.0	−.07	.46	.66
Self-Direction	11.0	3.0	11.1	2.9	.03	.53	.53
Social	11.3	2.6	10.8	2.8	−.19	.67	.75
Motor	12.2	2.3	11.2	3.1	−.37	.48	.70
Conceptual Domain	105.4	14.9	103.5	15.0	−.13	.83	.83
Social Domain	104.2	12.8	102.8	15.7	−.10	.65	.74
Practical Domain	103.5	8.8	102.3	14.4	−.10	.62	.87
GAC	105.3	12.2	104.0	15.9	−.09	.74	.83

[a]Correlations were corrected for the variability of the standardization sample (Guilford & Fruchter, 1978).
Pooled standard deviation was used as the estimate of variability of the current sample.

Table 5.13 Inter-Rater Reliability Coefficients of Skill Areas, Adaptive Domains, and the GAC: Teacher/Daycare Provider and Teacher Forms (continued)

Teacher Form

Ages 5–9 ($n = 34$) Skill Area/Composite	First Respondent Mean	SD	Second Respondent Mean	SD	Cohen's d	r_{12}	Corrected r[a]
Communication	6.3	3.6	5.3	3.4	−.29	.83	.75
Community Use	7.4	3.6	6.7	3.3	−.20	.73	.61
Functional Academics	7.0	3.5	6.4	3.3	−.18	.74	.65
School Living	8.1	3.3	7.7	3.5	−.12	.85	.82
Health and Safety	8.3	3.4	7.3	3.2	−.30	.86	.82
Leisure	7.9	3.8	7.1	3.5	−.22	.76	.62
Self-Care	9.1	3.6	8.8	3.9	−.08	.83	.75
Self-Direction	7.1	3.7	6.5	3.5	−.17	.85	.77
Social	7.7	3.5	7.2	3.8	−.14	.81	.74
Conceptual Domain	84.3	19.0	77.2	15.5	−.41	.74	.58
Social Domain	88.7	17.8	85.8	17.9	−.16	.82	.74
Practical Domain	91.3	18.4	87.8	17.9	−.19	.95	.92
GAC	88.2	19.3	84.2	17.7	−.22	.93	.89

Ages 10–18 ($n = 50$) Skill Area/Composite	First Respondent Mean	SD	Second Respondent Mean	SD	Cohen's d	r_{12}	Corrected r[a]
Communication	7.0	4.1	6.8	3.9	−.05	.81	.65
Community Use	8.0	3.9	6.8	3.8	−.31	.80	.66
Functional Academics	8.2	3.7	7.3	3.5	−.25	.90	.85
School Living	8.1	3.5	7.0	3.8	−.30	.81	.74
Health and Safety	8.6	3.8	8.0	3.6	−.16	.81	.69
Leisure	8.3	3.8	7.3	3.4	−.28	.83	.73
Self-Care	8.4	3.8	8.2	3.6	−.05	.85	.76
Self-Direction	7.8	3.4	7.2	3.6	−.17	.87	.83
Social	9.2	3.1	8.1	3.3	−.34	.86	.85
Conceptual Domain	90.1	22.1	85.5	20.1	−.22	.92	.82
Social Domain	96.3	19.3	89.3	17.2	−.38	.85	.75
Practical Domain	93.5	20.4	90.2	17.7	−.17	.90	.82
GAC	91.7	20.8	89.2	18.6	−.13	.95	.90

All Ages[b] ($n = 84$) Skill Area/Composite	First Respondent Mean	SD	Second Respondent Mean	SD	Cohen's d	r_{12}	Corrected r[a]
Communication	6.7	3.9	6.2	3.8	−.13	.82	.70
Community Use	7.7	3.8	6.8	3.6	−.24	.77	.64
Functional Academics	7.8	3.7	6.9	3.4	−.25	.84	.77
School Living	8.1	3.4	7.3	3.7	−.23	.83	.78
Health and Safety	8.5	3.6	7.7	3.5	−.23	.84	.76
Leisure	8.2	3.8	7.2	3.4	−.28	.80	.68
Self-Care	8.7	3.7	8.5	3.7	−.05	.84	.76
Self-Direction	7.5	3.5	6.9	3.6	−.17	.86	.80
Social	8.6	3.3	7.8	3.5	−.24	.84	.80
Conceptual Domain	87.8	21.0	82.1	18.7	−.29	.85	.72
Social Domain	93.3	19.0	87.9	17.5	−.30	.84	.75
Practical Domain	92.6	19.5	89.3	17.7	−.18	.93	.88
GAC	90.3	20.2	87.4	18.3	−.15	.94	.90

[a]Correlations were corrected for the variability of the standardization sample (Guilford & Fruchter, 1978). Pooled standard deviation was used as the estimate of variability of the current sample.

[b]Reliability coefficients for the overall sample were calculated using Fisher's z transformation.

Table 5.14 Inter-Rater Reliability Coefficients of Skill Areas, Adaptive Domains, and the GAC: Parent/Primary Caregiver and Parent Forms

Parent/Primary Caregiver Form

Ages 0–5 (n = 56) Skill Area/Composite	First Respondent		Second Respondent		Cohen's d	r_{12}	Corrected r^a
	Mean	SD	Mean	SD			
Communication	9.8	2.3	10.2	2.0	.19	.64	.79
Community Use[b]	10.2	2.7	9.5	2.5	–.27	.50	.59
Functional Pre-Academics[b]	9.8	2.7	9.4	2.5	–.15	.82	.85
Home Living[b]	9.9	2.9	9.4	3.0	–.17	.69	.71
Health and Safety	10.3	2.9	9.4	2.6	–.33	.61	.63
Leisure	10.0	2.8	9.5	3.4	–.16	.71	.75
Self-Care	10.4	2.4	9.9	2.7	–.20	.71	.81
Self-Direction	10.0	3.3	9.6	3.0	–.13	.73	.67
Social	10.3	2.6	9.8	2.7	–.19	.57	.68
Motor	11.0	2.4	10.2	2.7	–.31	.63	.76
Conceptual Domain	97.7	13.6	96.9	12.4	–.06	.83	.86
Social Domain	99.4	14.2	96.6	16.5	–.18	.69	.72
Practical Domain	100.1	14.3	96.0	13.7	–.29	.74	.77
GAC	99.7	13.3	96.4	13.1	–.25	.77	.82

[a]Correlations were corrected for the variability of the standardization sample (Guilford & Fruchter, 1978). Pooled standard deviation was used as the estimate of variability of the current sample.

[b]Based on 49 observations.

Table 5.14 Inter-Rater Reliability Coefficients of Skill Areas, Adaptive Domains, and the GAC: Parent/Primary Caregiver and Parent Forms (continued)

Parent Form

Ages 5–9 (n = 32)

Skill Area/Composite	First Respondent Mean	SD	Second Respondent Mean	SD	Cohen's d	r_{12}	Corrected r^a
Communication	9.8	2.8	9.5	2.6	–.11	.89	.90
Community Use	10.3	3.0	9.3	2.4	–.37	.73	.73
Functional Academics	10.3	3.1	9.3	2.6	–.35	.69	.67
Home Living	9.7	3.2	8.7	3.4	–.30	.78	.74
Health and Safety	10.0	2.8	9.0	2.5	–.38	.68	.72
Leisure	10.0	3.4	9.2	2.9	–.25	.78	.72
Self-Care	10.8	3.2	10.4	2.9	–.13	.88	.87
Self-Direction	9.7	3.9	9.0	4.0	–.18	.86	.77
Social	10.4	3.2	9.3	3.3	–.34	.64	.59
Conceptual Domain	98.8	16.5	95.9	13.5	–.19	.88	.85
Social Domain	100.3	16.1	95.3	15.2	–.32	.76	.73
Practical Domain	100.8	14.2	95.3	14.2	–.39	.89	.90
GAC	101.8	15.8	96.7	13.3	–.35	.90	.88

Ages 10–21 (n = 43)

Skill Area/Composite	First Respondent Mean	SD	Second Respondent Mean	SD	Cohen's d	r_{12}	Corrected r^a
Communication	10.6	2.2	10.3	2.2	–.14	.46	.71
Community Use	11.5	2.4	10.5	2.4	–.42	.71	.81
Functional Academics	10.9	2.4	10.2	2.2	–.30	.70	.81
Home Living	9.8	3.0	8.0	3.4	–.56	.74	.74
Health and Safety	10.6	2.8	10.1	2.8	–.18	.74	.77
Leisure	11.3	2.1	10.1	2.8	–.48	.78	.89
Self-Care	10.7	2.5	9.9	2.7	–.31	.85	.89
Self-Direction	10.0	3.0	9.1	3.4	–.28	.82	.82
Social[b]	10.0	3.0	9.5	3.2	–.16	.61	.61
Conceptual Domain	102.6	14.8	98.1	15.1	–.30	.82	.83
Social Domain	104.4	14.4	99.5	16.1	–.32	.77	.79
Practical Domain	103.1	14.7	96.4	16.1	–.43	.92	.92
GAC	104.8	13.5	98.8	15.8	–.41	.91	.93

All Ages[b] (n = 75)

Skill Area/Composite	First Respondent Mean	SD	Second Respondent Mean	SD	Cohen's d	r_{12}	Corrected r^a
Communication	10.2	2.5	9.9	2.3	–.12	.74	.83
Community Use	11.0	2.7	10.0	2.4	–.39	.72	.77
Functional Academics	10.7	2.7	9.8	2.4	–.35	.70	.75
Home Living	9.7	3.1	8.3	3.4	–.43	.76	.74
Health and Safety	10.3	2.8	9.6	2.7	–.25	.71	.75
Leisure	10.7	2.8	9.7	2.9	–.35	.78	.82
Self-Care	10.7	2.8	10.1	2.8	–.21	.87	.88
Self-Direction	9.8	3.4	9.0	3.6	–.23	.84	.80
Social	10.2	3.1	9.4	3.2	–.25	.63	.60
Conceptual Domain	101.1	15.5	97.2	14.4	–.26	.85	.84
Social Domain	102.7	15.2	97.7	15.7	–.32	.77	.76
Practical Domain	102.1	14.4	96.0	15.2	–.41	.91	.91
GAC	103.6	14.4	97.9	14.8	–.39	.91	.91

[a]Correlations were corrected for the variability of the standardization sample (Guilford & Fruchter, 1978). Pooled standard deviation was used as the estimate of variability of the current sample.

[b]Reliability coefficients for the overall sample were calculated using Fisher's z transformation.

Table 5.15   Inter-Rater Reliability Coefficients of Skill Areas, Adaptive Domains, and the GAC: Adult Form, Rated by Others

Ages 16–89 ($n = 52$)	First Respondent		Second Respondent				
Skill Area/Composite	Mean	SD	Mean	SD	Cohen's d	r_{12}	Corrected r[a]
Communication	10.9	2.7	10.5	3.0	–.14	.76	.80
Community Use	11.2	2.5	10.4	2.7	–.31	.77	.84
Functional Academics	11.4	2.5	11.0	2.5	–.16	.66	.76
Home Living	10.6	3.0	9.5	3.2	–.35	.76	.76
Health and Safety	10.8	2.5	10.0	2.9	–.30	.72	.81
Leisure	11.0	2.5	10.1	2.9	–.33	.73	.81
Self-Care	10.9	2.5	10.3	2.6	–.24	.84	.89
Self-Direction	10.9	2.5	9.8	2.7	–.42	.78	.85
Social	11.0	2.8	10.4	3.0	–.21	.74	.78
Work[b]	11.3	2.2	10.8	2.4	–.22	.74	.86
Conceptual Domain	104.4	12.7	101.0	13.4	–.26	.82	.87
Social Domain	103.8	13.3	99.7	13.5	–.31	.81	.85
Practical Domain (without Work)	104.5	14.2	99.7	14.1	–.34	.85	.87
Practical Domain (with Work)[b]	106.0	11.6	100.5	13.0	–.45	.83	.90
GAC (without Work)	103.8	13.7	99.1	15.1	–.33	.86	.89
GAC (with Work)[b]	104.6	10.7	99.9	12.3	–.41	.86	.93

[a]Correlations were corrected for the variability of the standardization sample (Guilford & Fruchter, 1978). Pooled standard deviation was used as the estimate of variability of the current sample.

[b]Based on 37 observations.

On the Teacher/Daycare Provider Form, the inter-rater reliability coefficient of the GAC was .83. The mean GAC score difference between two respondents was approximately 1 point. The corrected reliability coefficients for the adaptive domains averaged .81. The inter-rater reliability coefficients for the skill areas averaged .70. The corrected inter-rater reliability coefficients of the GAC, adaptive domains, and skill areas are relatively higher than the uncorrected coefficients due to the low variability of the sample.

On the Teacher Form, the inter-rater reliability coefficient of the GAC was .90 for students from all age groups. The mean GAC score difference between two respondents was approximately 3 points. The inter-rater reliability coefficients for the adaptive domains averaged .78 for students from all age groups. The inter-rater reliability coefficients for the skill areas averaged .74 for students from all age groups. The corrected inter-rater reliability coefficients of the GAC, adaptive domains, and skill areas are relatively lower than the uncorrected coefficients due to the high variability of the sample.

On the Parent/Primary Caregiver Form, the inter-rater reliability coefficient of the GAC was .82. The mean GAC score difference between two respondents was approximately 3 points. The inter-rater reliability coefficients for the adaptive domains averaged .78. Inter-rater reliability coefficients for the skill areas averaged .72. The corrected inter-rater reliability coefficients of the GAC, adaptive domains and skill areas are generally higher than the uncorrected coefficients due to the low variability of the sample.

On the Parent Form, the inter-rater reliability coefficient of the GAC was .91 for the combined age group. The mean GAC score difference between two respondents was approximately 6 points. The inter-rater reliability coefficients for the adaptive domains averaged .84 for children from all age groups. The inter-rater reliability coefficients for the skill areas averaged .77 for children from all age groups.

On the Adult Form, the inter-rater reliability coefficient of the GAC scores of 52 adults rated by two respondents was .89 when calculated without the Work Skill Area and .93 when calculated with the Work Skill Area. The mean GAC score difference between the two respondents was approximately 5 points. The inter-rater reliability coefficient of the adaptive domain scores averaged .87. Inter-rater reliability coefficients for the skill areas averaged .82. Overall, the corrected inter-rater reliability coefficients of the GAC, adaptive domains and skill areas are slightly higher than the uncorrected coefficients due to the low variability of the sample.

Cross-Form Consistency

Correlations Between the Ratings of Different Respondents Using Different Forms

The consistency between teacher and parent ratings for children, and between self-report and the rating of others for adults was estimated using Pearson's product-moment correlation coefficient. Samples consisted of 130 children for the infant-preschool forms, 30 children for the school-age forms, and 105 individuals for the Adult Form. The results are reported in Tables 5.16–5.17. The tables also present the standardized differences (Cohen's d) between the two ratings and the correlation coefficients corrected for the variability of the standardization sample. References made in text are to corrected correlations.

Table 5.16 Consistency Between the Ratings of Teachers and Parents

Teacher/Daycare Provider and Parent/Primary Caregiver Forms

Ages 2–5 ($n = 130$)	Teacher/Daycare Provider		Parent/Primary Caregiver				
Skill Area/Composite	Mean	SD	Mean	SD	Cohen's d	r_{12}	Corrected r[a]
Communication	10.3	3.0	9.9	2.7	–.14	.64	.64
Functional Pre-Academics	10.0	3.0	10.1	2.8	.03	.62	.62
School/Home Living	10.4	2.8	10.0	2.9	–.14	.44	.51
Health and Safety	10.2	3.0	9.7	2.7	–.18	.39	.39
Leisure	10.1	2.8	10.0	2.8	–.04	.60	.65
Self-Care	10.0	3.0	10.0	2.8	.00	.42	.42
Self-Direction	10.1	3.0	9.9	2.8	–.07	.43	.43
Social	10.0	3.1	10.0	2.9	.00	.46	.42
Motor	10.4	2.8	10.2	2.9	–.07	.39	.47
Conceptual Domain	99.8	15.2	98.0	13.8	–.12	.70	.69
Social Domain	99.3	15.3	98.5	14.7	–.05	.60	.58
Practical Domain	100.3	14.6	98.4	14.1	–.13	.56	.58
GAC	99.9	14.8	98.3	14.2	–.11	.68	.68

Teacher and Parent Forms

Ages 5–21 ($n = 30$)	Teacher		Parent				
Skill Area/Composite	Mean	SD	Mean	SD	Cohen's d	r_{12}	Corrected r[a]
Communication	8.6	3.7	9.4	3.3	.23	.70	.54
Community Use	9.3	2.9	10.2	3.0	.31	.66	.68
Functional Academics	9.4	3.3	9.6	3.8	.06	.84	.81
School/Home Living	9.5	3.0	9.3	4.1	–.06	.51	.51
Health and Safety	9.8	2.8	9.9	3.5	.03	.59	.64
Leisure	9.8	2.9	10.1	3.4	.09	.70	.72
Self-Care	10.1	2.9	9.5	3.5	–.19	.53	.56
Self-Direction	9.1	3.2	10.2	3.5	.33	.82	.80
Social	9.6	3.1	10.0	3.2	.13	.67	.65
Conceptual Domain	99.2	18.0	99.2	18.0	.00	.85	.79
Social Domain	100.3	16.4	100.6	16.9	.02	.73	.67
Practical Domain	100.4	17.8	98.5	18.4	–.10	.73	.63
GAC	99.7	18.6	98.6	19.4	–.06	.81	.70

[a]Correlations were corrected for the variability of the standardization sample (Allen & Yen, 1979).
 Pooled standard deviation was used as the estimate of variability of the current sample.

Table 5.17 Consistency Between the Adult Form, Self Report and the Adult Form, Rated by Others

Ages 16–49 (*n* = 41)	Self Report		Rated by Others				
Skill Area/Composite	Mean	SD	Mean	SD	Cohen's *d*	r_{12}	Corrected *r*[a]
Communication	11.2	2.7	11.3	2.6	.04	.69	.75
Community Use	10.7	2.6	10.8	2.8	.04	.76	.82
Functional Academics	10.9	2.5	11.4	2.4	.20	.59	.71
Home Living	10.2	2.8	10.1	2.9	–.04	.77	.80
Health and Safety	10.9	1.9	10.7	2.4	–.09	.75	.90
Leisure	9.9	2.8	10.2	3.0	.10	.71	.75
Self-Care	10.5	2.0	10.7	2.0	.10	.66	.85
Self-Direction	10.9	2.3	11.0	2.7	.04	.80	.88
Social	10.9	2.4	10.7	2.8	–.08	.81	.88
Work[b]	11.6	1.8	11.7	2.6	.04	.71	.89
Conceptual Domain	105.6	11.9	106.2	13.5	.05	.81	.88
Social Domain	101.4	13.6	101.5	13.9	.01	.82	.85
Practical Domain (without Work)	102.3	12.6	102.2	13.6	–.01	.85	.90
Practical Domain (with Work)[b]	102.3	12.7	103.8	13.6	.11	.84	.89
GAC (without Work)	103.3	11.7	103.8	13.5	.04	.87	.92
GAC (with Work)[b]	102.6	11.7	103.4	13.5	.06	.88	.93

Ages 50–89 (*n* = 64)	Self Report		Rated by Others				
Skill Area/Composite	Mean	SD	Mean	SD	Cohen's *d*	r_{12}	Corrected *r*[a]
Communication	12.3	1.4	12.3	1.6	.00	.74	.94
Community Use	12.4	1.3	12.2	1.6	–.14	.53	.91
Functional Academics	12.0	1.5	12.0	1.5	.00	.47	.87
Home Living	11.8	2.0	11.7	2.1	–.05	.73	.88
Health and Safety	11.8	1.5	12.0	1.4	.14	.63	.91
Leisure	11.8	1.4	11.7	1.4	–.07	.68	.93
Self-Care	11.8	0.7	11.9	0.8	.13	.40	.97
Self-Direction	12.2	1.6	12.4	1.3	.14	.54	.87
Social	12.3	0.8	12.1	1.2	–.20	.60	.97
Work	–	–	–	–	–	–	–
Conceptual Domain	111.5	8.1	111.9	8.4	.05	.71	.92
Social Domain	111.5	6.7	108.2	6.4	–.50	.82	.96
Practical Domain (without Work)	111.8	8.8	112.4	8.7	.07	.73	.91
Practical Domain (with Work)	–	–	–	–	–	–	–
GAC (without Work)	109.9	6.4	110.0	6.6	.02	.82	.97
GAC (with Work)	–	–	–	–	–	–	–

[a]Correlations were corrected for the variability of the standardization sample (Allen & Yen, 1979). Pooled standard deviation was used as the estimate of variability of the current sample.

[b]Based on 38 observations.

Table 5.17 Consistency Between the Adult Form, Self Report and the Adult Form, Rated by Others *(continued)*

All Ages[c] (*n* = 105)	Self Report		Rated by Others				
Skill Area/Composite	Mean	SD	Mean	SD	Cohen's *d*	r_{12}	Corrected *r*[a]
Communication	11.9	2.1	11.9	2.1	.00	.72	.88
Community Use	11.7	2.1	11.7	2.2	.00	.66	.87
Functional Academics	11.6	2.0	11.8	1.9	.10	.53	.80
Home Living	11.2	2.4	11.1	2.6	−.04	.75	.84
Health and Safety	11.4	1.7	11.5	1.9	.06	.69	.91
Leisure	11.0	2.2	11.1	2.3	.04	.70	.87
Self-Care	11.3	1.5	11.4	1.5	.07	.54	.93
Self-Direction	11.7	2.0	11.9	2.1	.10	.69	.88
Social	11.7	1.7	11.6	2.1	−.05	.72	.94
Work[b]	11.6	1.8	11.7	2.6	.04	.71	.89
Conceptual Domain	109.2	10.1	109.7	11.0	.05	.76	.90
Social Domain	107.5	11.0	105.6	10.5	−.18	.82	.92
Practical Domain (without Work)	108.1	11.4	108.4	11.9	.03	.80	.91
Practical Domain (with Work)[b]	105.7	13.1	106.9	12.9	.09	.80	.90
GAC (without Work)	107.3	9.4	107.6	10.3	.03	.85	.95
GAC (with Work)[b]	102.6	11.7	103.4	13.5	.06	.88	.93

[a]Correlations were corrected for the variability of the standardization sample (Allen & Yen, 1979). Pooled standard deviation was used as the estimate of variability of the current sample.

[b]Based on 38 observations.

[c]Reliability coefficients for the overall sample were calculated using Fisher's *z* transformation.

For the infant-preschool sample, the correlation between the teacher/daycare provider and parent/primary caregiver ratings was .68 for the GAC. Mean GAC scores differed by approximately 2 points. The correlations for the adaptive domain scores averaged .62. Mean adaptive domain scores differed by approximately 2 points. The correlations for the skill areas averaged .51. Mean skill area scaled scores differed by less than 1 scaled score.

For the school-age sample, the correlation between the teacher and parent ratings was .70 for the GAC. Mean GAC scores differed by approximately 1 point. The correlations for the adaptive domain scores averaged .70. Mean adaptive domain scores differed by approximately 2 points or less. The correlations for the skill areas averaged .66. Mean skill area scaled scores differed by approximately 1 scaled score or less.

The moderate to high correlations between parent and teacher scores on both infant-preschool and school-age forms suggest good consistency between these primary respondents for children. Past research, summarized by Boan and Harrison (1997), has found generally low to moderate correlations between parent and teacher scores on adaptive skill instruments, perhaps because of different expectations of different respondents and because children display different behaviors in home and school settings. ABAS–II results show somewhat higher correlations between the ratings of parents and teachers than found in previous research. However, the correlations, especially for the skill areas, emphasize the potential distinctions between respondents' ratings and the importance of using both parents and teachers as respondents to obtain information about the child's skills in multiple settings.

For the adult sample, the correlation between self report and the ratings of others for the GAC was .95 without the Work Skill Area and .93 with the Work Skill Area for the overall sample. Mean GAC scores differed by less than 1 point. The correlations for the adaptive domain scores averaged .91. Mean adaptive domain scores differed by approximately 2 points or less. The correlations for the skill areas averaged .88. Mean skill area scaled scores displayed minimal differences between the two respondents. The results for the adult sample suggest that there is considerable consistency when adults rate themselves and when others rate them. However, the distinction between information provided by the two respondents (i.e., self and others) may provide important clinical data for decision-making.

Correlations Between the Ratings of the Same Respondent Using Alternate Forms for Children Age 5 Years

Because of the overlap in age ranges at 5 years, correlations between the Teacher/Daycare Provider Form and Teacher Form were investigated using a nonclinical sample of 49 children ages 5 years 0 months–5 years 11 months, with a mean age of 5 years 5 months. Each child in the sample was rated by the same respondent on both forms. The sample had the following composition: 51% female and 49% male; 57% White, 14 % African American, 23% Hispanic, and 6% of other racial/ethnic origin. Table 5.18 reports the mean scores and correlations between the two forms. References made in text are to corrected correlations.

Table 5.18   Correlation Between the Teacher/Daycare Provider and Teacher Forms: Age 5

(n = 49) Skill Area/Composite	Teacher/Daycare Provider		Teacher		Cohen's d	r_{12}	Corrected r^a
	Mean	SD	Mean	SD			
Communication	10.8	3.4	10.2	3.2	–.18	.78	.72
Functional (Pre-)Academics	10.4	3.0	9.8	3.0	–.20	.32	.32
School Living	11.2	3.0	10.8	2.5	–.14	.57	.57
Health and Safety	11.0	2.8	11.1	2.9	.04	.75	.78
Leisure	11.4	3.1	11.2	3.1	–.06	.63	.60
Self-Care	11.7	2.3	10.8	2.1	–.41	.62	.78
Self-Direction	11.2	3.2	10.2	2.4	–.35	.61	.56
Social	11.1	3.2	11.4	2.8	.10	.74	.70
Conceptual Domain	103.9	16.6	104.6	12.7	.05	.73	.67
Social Domain	105.7	16.6	106.6	15.1	.06	.75	.70
Practical Domain	105.9	14.4	105.4	11.6	–.04	.73	.75
GAC	105.7	16.4	105.7	13.1	.00	.78	.74

[a]Correlations were corrected for the variability of the standardization sample (Allen & Yen, 1979).
Pooled standard deviation was used as the estimate of variability of the current sample.

The correlation between the Teacher/Daycare Provider Form GAC and the Teacher Form GAC was .74. Mean GAC scores did not differ. Correlations between adaptive domain scores averaged .71. Mean adaptive domain scores differed by 1 point or less. Skill area correlations were in the .70s and below, with an average of .63. Mean skill area scaled scores differed by 1 scaled score or less. The correlations between the two forms are substantial and provide evidence for the use of either form for 5-year-old children, based on results from this sample of children with no known disabilities or disorders.

Relationships between the Parent/Primary Caregiver Form and Parent Form ages were investigated using a nonclinical sample of 51 children ages 5 years 0 months–5 years 11 months, with a mean age of 5 years 6 months, rated by the same respondent on each form. The sample had the following composition: 56% female and 44% male; 46% White, 17% African American, 31% Hispanic, and 6% of other racial/ethnic origin. Table 5.19 reports the mean scores and correlations between the two forms.

The correlation between the Parent/Primary Caregiver GAC and the Parent Form GAC was .71. Mean GAC scores differed by approximately 3 points. Correlations between adaptive domain scores averaged .63. Mean adaptive domain scores differed by 2 points, on average. Skill area correlations averaged .50. Mean skill area scaled scores differed by 1 scaled score or less, on average. The correlations between the two forms, though slightly lower than those between the Teacher/Daycare Provider and Teacher Forms, ranged from moderate to high and support the use of either form for 5 year old children, based on results from this sample of children with no known disabilities or disorders.

Table 5.19   Correlation Between the Parent/Primary Caregiver and Parent Forms: Age 5

(n = 51) Skill Area/Composite	Parent/Primary Caregiver Mean	SD	Parent Mean	SD	Cohen's d	r_{12}	Corrected r^a
Communication	10.8	3.3	11.3	3.2	.15	.61	.53
Community Use	10.4	3.8	10.4	3.0	.00	.50	.19
Functional (Pre-)Academics	10.4	3.4	9.4	4.2	−.26	.68	.59
Home Living	11.3	2.8	10.4	3.3	−.29	.63	.68
Health and Safety	10.2	3.4	10.8	3.0	.19	.57	.44
Leisure	10.8	3.2	11.3	3.1	.16	.53	.47
Self-Care	9.7	3.0	10.7	2.7	.35	.32	.32
Self-Direction	10.8	2.9	10.7	3.2	−.03	.53	.56
Social	10.6	2.7	10.5	3.4	−.03	.69	.75
Conceptual Domain	102.5	16.6	102.7	16.8	.01	.69	.62
Social Domain	102.6	15.5	104.8	16.4	.14	.70	.68
Practical Domain	100.8	16.8	104.6	13.7	.25	.68	.60
GAC	102.0	16.4	104.6	15.3	.16	.76	.71

[a]Correlations were corrected for the variability of the standardization sample (Allen & Yen, 1979).
Pooled standard deviation was used as the estimate of variability of the current sample.

Evidence of Validity

Validity refers to the degree to which the accumulated evidence supports the interpretations of a test's scores for its intended purpose. This evidence is found in two forms: a test's theory and the empirical evidence that informs interpretations of test scores (American Educational Research Association et al., 1999). Test validation is the joint responsibility of test developers and test users. The test developer is responsible for providing relevant evidence that supports its use. Evidence that informs ABAS–II users and should help guide their use of the instrument is discussed in the following sections. However, professional users of the ABAS–II are responsible for evaluating this and other evidence in various applied and research settings. They are encouraged to examine the relevance of the ABAS–II in response to clinical needs and practices. Whenever possible, additional data should be acquired that examines the validity of the ABAS–II in various settings and for various purposes.

Validity cannot be summarized using only data. Instead, a test's validity is found in the viability of its theory and the relevance and richness of its empirical data. Both theory and empirical data impact the various ways in which a test is used. The ABAS–II developers and professional users have an ongoing responsibility to acquire, share, and examine evidence that informs the profession as to ways in which this instrument can and should be used. The various forms of evidence that are relevant to the validity of the ABAS–II include test content, response process, internal structure, internal consistency, age group differences, clinical validity, and the consequences of testing.

Test Content

An analysis of the test content should begin with an examination of test items to determine if they adequately represent and relate to the traits or skills that are being measured. The theory and constructs of the ABAS–II are derived from the AAMR's (1992) premise that ten skill areas are important to successful and independent functioning. These skill areas are: Communication, Community Use, Functional Academics, Health and Safety, Home or School Living, Leisure, Self-Care, Self-Direction, Social, and Work. More recent AAMR (2002b) guidelines that specify the grouping of the ten skill areas into three broad domains of adaptive behavior have also informed the structure of the ABAS–II. The ABAS–II addresses both skill areas and adaptive domains, and is highly relevant to its intended use.

The items in each of the skill areas reflect adaptive skills important in the lives of individuals who differ by age, gender, race/ethnicity, social status, and other demographic qualities. The authors conducted a comprehensive review of research concerning developmental skills in children, youth, and adults; functional skills necessary in home, school, community, work, and other settings; and individuals with disabilities and other mental or physical health problems. Guided by AAMR (1992) descriptions, the goal was to identify categories of important adaptive skills, (e.g., eating, dressing) and then develop test items that addressed those categories. An initial item pool of almost 1,500 items was developed and reviewed by individuals knowledgeable in developmental psychology, education, mental retardation, and related areas. This review led to the selection of 460 items for the infant-preschool forms and 789 items for the school-age and adult forms. These two item sets were each subject to reviews through data collected during field trials and standardization.

During the initial field-testing, data was collected from more than 428 individuals for the school-age and adult forms. Infant-preschool forms were reviewed by focus groups. Following an analysis of the data from all forms, items were selected for inclusion in more extensive field trials. These field trials obtained information from nationally stratified samples of 1520 parents and teachers for the infant-preschool forms; and 1,045 parents, 980 teachers, and 1,406 adults for the school-age and adult forms. Again, the most promising items were selected and included in standardization. Item selection led to the identification of 342, 344, 242, 272, and 275 standardization items for the Teacher/Daycare Provider, Parent/Primary Caregiver, Teacher, Parent, and Adult Forms, respectively. Following the collection and thorough review of standardization data, the final items were selected (see Table 1.1): 216 on the Teacher/Daycare Provider Form, 241 on the Parent/Primary Caregiver Form, 193 on the Teacher Form, 232 on the Parent Form, and 239 on the Adult Form. More than 95% of the items are consistent between two or more forms.

Final item selection was guided by four principles: (1) to measure adaptive skills relevant to clinical and applied practice; (2) to ensure sufficient numbers of items to provide a comprehensive and robust measure of each skill area while not making the test too long (e.g., to not have more items than needed); (3) to measure qualities that could be readily observed; and (4) to ensure that the test displays suitable psychometric qualities.

The first principle was achieved by selecting items on which clinicians often rely. The second principle was achieved by ensuring that each rating form had a sufficient number of items (i.e., a mean of 23 items per skill area) and an acceptable level of internal consistency (e.g., the coefficient alpha of the GAC score should be at least .90 for each age group on all rating forms). The ABAS–II achieves this level of internal consistency except for the age group of 0:0–0:3 rated on the Parent/Primary Caregiver Form, which has a reliability coefficient of .86 for the GAC. Furthermore, the recommended use of two or more rating forms provides at least twice the amount of information about an individual's adaptive behavior. The third principle was addressed by designing items with strong behavior references and by eliminating items that had high rates of guessing. Average rates of guessing were determined for each of the six standardization samples (Tables A.3, A.7, A.11, and A.14). Teachers and daycare providers, on average, guessed at two or fewer items per skill area. Parents, on average, guessed less than once per skill area. Adults rating others, on average, guessed less than once per skill area. Adults providing self-ratings rarely guessed. The fourth principle, suitable psychometric qualities, is discussed later in this chapter.

Response Process

A primary purpose of this assessment instrument is to accurately describe the degree to which individuals display normal adaptive skills. A description of adaptive skills is enhanced when pertinent information is acquired from two or more knowledgeable respondents about the presence of desired behaviors as displayed in two or more settings. The ABAS–II uses a four-point response option that allows respondents to indicate either the presence or absence of skills and the frequency (never, sometimes, or always) of their display.

During standardization, respondents were asked to comment on the ease of completing the rating forms. The information they provided indicated that the items are easy to complete, the response options are clear, and there is little need for guessing.

The ABAS–II is often completed by more than one respondent. The use of different respondents across home, school, work, and other settings and the use of multiple sources of information is an important principle in the comprehensive, clinical assessment of which the ABAS–II is intended to be a part. For example, it is not unusual for a clinician to request that two or more teachers and one or both parents (or grandparents) complete rating forms for a child. Information from two or more respondents may or may not agree. High inter-rater agreement provides some evidence about the accuracy of the assessment. Differences may be the result of the individual displaying different levels of adaptive skills in the various environments, failure of a respondent to accurately record ratings, or administrative or scoring difficulties. Furthermore, correlations between parent and teacher ratings on behavior rating scales are often low to moderate (Kamphaus & Frick, 1996). Consistency of results from two or more respondents is improved when the following standards apply to the measure: the behaviors being assessed are externalized and readily observable, the rating forms that are completed by the various respondents measure the same qualities, and the majority of the items are consistent between the various rating forms (Kamphaus & Frick, 1996). The ABAS–II meets these standards. Items measure only behaviors that are directly observable, and all five rating forms have at least eight out of the ten skill areas in common. These qualities are intended to ensure that the response processes enhance the quality of the data and the test's validity.

Internal Structure

Evidence of a test's internal structure is found in the degree to which relationships among test items and other test components conform to the construct on which score interpretations are based (American Education Research Association, et al., 1999). The AAMR (1992, 2002b) and *DSM–IV–TR* provided the internal theoretical structure of the ABAS–II by defining adaptive skill areas; domains of conceptual, social, and practical adaptive functioning; and overall adaptive behavior important in the assessment of individuals with mental retardation.

The theoretical structure of the ABAS–II outlines ten skill areas, all of which display considerable internal consistency, exhibit differences sensitive to age range, and are independent of one another yet assess common adaptive skills. These skill areas collectively form conceptual, social, and practical composites of adaptive functioning, as well as an overall construct of adaptive behavior (the GAC).

Internal Consistency

Internal consistency refers to relationships among scores derived from individual items or subsets of items within a test following a single administration of the test. All ABAS–II scores indicate considerable internal consistency, and are described in the reliability section of this chapter (see Tables 5.1–5.4).

Age Group Differences

Adaptive skills are acquired during the course of an individual's development and can be expected to vary with age. For example, many adaptive skills are acquired somewhat early in life (e.g., tying one's shoes), while others are acquired later in life (e.g., balancing a checkbook). Adaptive skills are often well developed before adulthood. Therefore, adults generally do not display significant increases in adaptive skills as they become older.

ABAS–II items are sensitive to age differences (i.e., persons who are older tend to display a behavior more frequently than those who are younger). Differences on the various items can be translated into age differences on each of the skill areas (see Tables A.4 and A.8). For example, on the Teacher Form (Table A.4), a raw score of 48 on Communication is equivalent to the average performance of children ages 5 years 4 months–5 years 7 months. A raw score of 58 on Communication is equivalent to the average performance of children ages 9 years 4 months–9 years 7 months. A raw score of 62 on Communication is equivalent to the average performance of children 15 years of age. All items in each of the skill areas display age differences.

Intercorrelations Among the Skill Areas

The theoretical structure of the ABAS–II suggests that the skill areas will be somewhat independent of one another and have low to moderate intercorrelations. However, all skill areas are expected to show a higher correlation with their respective adaptive domain and to correlate strongly with the GAC. Data examining these intercorrelations are provided in Tables 5.20–5.23 (all ages) and C.1–C.4 (by age group).

Table 5.20 Intercorrelations of Skill Area Scaled Scores and Sums of Scaled Scores for Adaptive Domains and the GAC: Teacher/Daycare Provider and Teacher Forms (All Ages)

Teacher/Daycare Provider Form

Skill Area/Composite	Com	FA	SL	HS	LS	SC	SD	Soc	MO	CON[a]	SO[a]	PR[a]	GAC[b]
Communication										.56			.65
Functional Pre-Academics	.47									.57			.60
School Living	.47	.51										.68	.76
Health and Safety	.54	.43	.66									.66	.75
Leisure	.57	.47	.62	.67							.69		.77
Self-Care	.42	.43	.53	.51	.50							.57	.62
Self-Direction	.51	.52	.75	.68	.71	.54				.60			.80
Social	.60	.49	.70	.65	.69	.49	.75				.69		.79
Motor	.52	.46	.45	.53	.53	.47	.47	.49					.63
Conceptual Domain	.81	.81	.70	.67	.71	.57	.83	.75	.60				.84
Social Domain	.63	.52	.72	.72	.92	.54	.80	.92	.56	.80			.84
Practical Domain	.57	.55	.86	.86	.71	.80	.78	.72	.58	.77	.78		.82
GAC	.73	.69	.82	.81	.83	.70	.85	.84	.71	.93	.91	.92	
Mean[c]	10.16	10.13	10.19	10.22	10.22	10.25	10.21	10.17	10.31	30.50	20.39	30.66	91.86
SD	3.00	3.01	2.99	3.04	2.96	2.96	3.00	3.00	2.98	7.36	5.47	7.57	20.87

Teacher Form

Skill Area/Composite	Com	CU	FA	SL	HS	LS	SC	SD	Soc	CON[a]	SO[a]	PR[a]	GAC[b]
Communication										.80			.85
Community Use	.74											.72	.78
Functional Academics	.73	.74								.76			.77
School Living	.71	.67	.65									.78	.84
Health and Safety	.69	.68	.63	.76								.80	.82
Leisure	.75	.69	.66	.75	.72						.78		.84
Self-Care	.61	.54	.53	.60	.62	.56						.65	.67
Self-Direction	.74	.63	.68	.77	.74	.77	.56			.76			.84
Social	.74	.62	.60	.74	.74	.78	.60	.81			.78		.83
Conceptual Domain	.92	.78	.89	.79	.76	.81	.63	.90	.80				.89
Social Domain	.79	.69	.66	.79	.77	.94	.62	.84	.95	.85			.87
Practical Domain	.80	.85	.75	.88	.89	.80	.80	.79	.79	.87	.84		.89
GAC	.88	.83	.82	.87	.86	.88	.73	.88	.87	.96	.92	.96	
Mean[c]	8.83	8.92	9.23	9.38	9.14	9.46	9.55	8.66	9.38	26.71	18.84	36.99	82.54
SD	3.40	3.25	3.14	3.19	3.13	3.06	2.97	3.38	3.14	8.88	5.85	10.69	24.16

Note. **Com** = Communication; **CU** = Community Use; **FA** = Functional (Pre-)Academics; **SL** = School Living; **HS** = Health and Safety; **LS** = Leisure; **SC** = Self-Care; **SD** = Self-Direction; **Soc** = Social; **MO** = Motor; **CON** = Conceptual Domain; **SO** = Social Adaptive Domain; **PR** = Practical Adaptive Domain.
[a]Adaptive Domain correlations corrected by removing the skill area scaled score from the sum of the scaled scores.
[b]GAC correlations corrected by removing the skill area scaled score(s) from the sum of the scaled scores.
[c]Means and SDs reported under corrected adaptive domains and GAC were calculated using all skill areas included in the composite.

Adaptive Behavior Assessment System–Second Edition

Table 5.21 Intercorrelations of Skill Area Scaled Scores and Sums of Scaled Scores for Adaptive Domains and the GAC: Parent/Primary Caregiver and Parent Forms (All Ages)

Parent/Primary Caregiver Form

Skill Area/Composite	Com	CU	FA	HL	HS	LS	SC	SD	Soc	MO	CON[a]	SO[a]	PR[a]	GAC[b]
Communication											.52			.64
Community Use	.38												.53	.59
Functional Pre-Academics	.39	.57									.45			.47
Home Living	.36	.65	.49										.58	.59
Health and Safety	.51	.61	.45	.61									.64	.69
Leisure	.54	.56	.46	.51	.56							.61		.71
Self-Care	.42	.44	.36	.55	.51	.48							.55	.62
Self-Direction	.46	.64	.49	.68	.55	.62	.53				.50			.73
Social	.57	.63	.49	.64	.56	.61	.53	.66				.61		.75
Motor	.49	.44	.44	.49	.47	.48	.44	.43	.45					.58
Conceptual Domain	.82	.69	.82	.67	.60	.66	.53	.81	.70	.55				
Social Domain	.62	.66	.52	.64	.62	.90	.57	.71	.90	.51	.76			
Practical Domain	.55	.82	.57	.85	.85	.62	.78	.69	.68	.53	.73	.73		.78
GAC	.73	.79	.68	.79	.77	.78	.71	.80	.82	.68	.91	.89	.91	
Mean[c]	10.21	10.25	10.22	10.23	10.16	10.29	10.24	10.26	10.29	10.23	28.42	20.57	36.32	95.54
SD	2.92	2.96	2.97	2.96	2.89	2.92	2.84	2.93	2.91	2.81	8.03	5.24	12.24	24.44

Parent Form

Skill Area/Composite	Com	CU	FA	HL	HS	LS	SC	SD	Soc	CON[a]	SO[a]	PR[a]	GAC[b]
Communication										.72			.75
Community Use	.61											.67	.73
Functional Academics	.68	.70								.74			.77
Home Living	.47	.58	.55									.67	.67
Health and Safety	.63	.64	.65	.62								.74	.79
Leisure	.69	.62	.64	.54	.68						.71		.79
Self-Care	.52	.47	.52	.56	.60	.53						.63	.67
Self-Direction	.64	.62	.66	.59	.66	.69	.60			.71			.81
Social	.66	.50	.55	.50	.64	.71	.56	.71			.71		.75
Conceptual Domain	.87	.73	.89	.61	.73	.76	.62	.88	.73				.86
Social Domain	.73	.61	.65	.56	.72	.92	.59	.76	.93	.81			.81
Practical Domain	.67	.81	.73	.85	.86	.71	.79	.74	.66	.81	.75		.82
GAC	.81	.79	.82	.76	.84	.84	.74	.85	.81	.94	.89	.94	
Mean[c]	9.76	10.07	9.93	9.39	9.87	9.96	9.87	9.72	9.50	29.41	19.46	39.19	88.07
SD	2.96	3.00	3.03	3.57	3.09	2.98	2.90	3.27	3.31	8.13	5.81	10.33	22.50

Note. **Com** = Communication; **CU** = Community Use; **FA** = Functional (Pre-)Academics; **HL** = Home Living; **HS** = Health and Safety; **LS** = Leisure; **SC** = Self-Care; **SD** = Self-Direction; **Soc** = Social; **MO** = Motor; **CON** = Conceptual Adaptive Domain; **SO** = Social Adaptive Domain; **PR** = Practical Adaptive Domain.

[a] Adaptive Domain correlations corrected by removing the skill area scaled score from the sum of the scaled scores.

[b] GAC correlations corrected by removing the skill area scaled score(s) from the sum of the scaled scores.

[c] Means and *SD*s reported under corrected adaptive domains and GAC were calculated using all skill areas included in the composite.

Table 5.22 Intercorrelations of Skill Area Scaled Scores and Sums of Scaled Scores for Adaptive Domains and the GAC: Adult Form, Self Report: (All Ages)

Skill Area/Composite	Com	CU	FA	HL	HS	LS	SC	SD	Soc	WK	CON[a]	SO[a]	PR-4[a]	PR-5[a]	GAC-9[b]	GAC-10[b]
Communication											.75				.77	.76
Community Use	.80												.75	.73	.85	.83
Functional Academics	.75	.81									.82				.84	.83
Home Living	.51	.64	.67										.74	.73	.73	.74
Health and Safety	.63	.70	.71	.67									.77	.76	.80	.79
Leisure	.68	.74	.73	.60	.66							.71			.81	.81
Self-Care	.52	.59	.58	.60	.62	.57							.69	.69	.70	.69
Self-Direction	.65	.73	.74	.68	.72	.74	.62				.75				.85	.85
Social	.62	.67	.66	.61	.65	.71	.63	.77				.71			.79	.81
Work	.53	.56	.58	.56	.58	.60	.56	.69	.65					.66		.70
Conceptual Domain	.89	.86	.92	.69	.76	.80	.64	.89	.76	.66					.89	.90
Social Domain	.70	.76	.75	.66	.71	.92	.65	.81	.92	.68	.84				.85	.87
Practical Domain-4	.72	.87	.81	.86	.87	.76	.81	.80	.75	.66	.87	.81			.88	
Practical Domain-5	.73	.83	.81	.84	.85	.78	.79	.84	.80	.80	.88	.85	.98			.90
GAC-9	.82	.89	.88	.79	.84	.86	.75	.88	.84	.70	.96	.91	.96	.96		
GAC-10	.82	.86	.87	.79	.83	.85	.75	.89	.85	.76	.95	.92	.96	.97	1.00	
Mean[c]	9.98	9.85	9.93	10.05	10.17	9.60	10.39	10.08	10.15	10.42	29.99	19.75	40.47	51.35	90.20	101.52
SD	2.97	2.98	3.01	2.97	2.75	3.04	2.53	2.97	2.99	2.92	8.04	5.55	9.58	11.21	21.92	23.20

Note. **Com** = Communication; **CU** = Community Use; **FA** = Functional Academics; **HL** = Home Living; **HS** = Health and Safety; **LS** = Leisure; **SC** = Self-Care; **SD** = Self-Direction; **Soc** = Social; **WK** = Work; **CON** = Conceptual Adaptive Domain; **SO** = Social Adaptive Domain; **PR-4** = Practical Adaptive Domain without Work; **PR-5** = Practical Adaptive Domain with Work; **GAC-9** = GAC without Work; **GAC-10** = GAC with Work.

[a] Adaptive Domain correlations corrected by removing the skill area scaled score from the sum of the scaled scores.

[b] GAC correlations corrected by removing the skill area scaled score(s) from the sum of the scaled scores.

[c] Means and SDs reported under corrected adaptive domains and GAC were calculated using all skill areas included in the composite.

Adaptive Behavior Assessment System–Second Edition

Table 5.23 Intercorrelations of Skill Area Scaled Scores and Sums of Scaled Scores for Adaptive Domains and the GAC: Adult Form, Rated by Others (All Ages)

Skill Area/Composite	Com	CU	FA	HL	HS	LS	SC	SD	Soc	WK	CON[a]	SO[a]	PR-4[a]	PR-5[a]	GAC-9[b]	GAC-10[b]
Communication											.78				.80	.81
Community Use	.78												.79	.84	.87	.88
Functional Academics	.75	.85									.82				.85	.85
Home Living	.61	.67	.67										.75	.73	.76	.75
Health and Safety	.71	.79	.79	.71									.84	.83	.86	.85
Leisure	.70	.78	.75	.63	.72							.75			.82	.81
Self-Care	.61	.65	.63	.64	.70	.60							.74	.77	.74	.75
Self-Direction	.72	.75	.78	.71	.78	.75	.68				.80				.87	.90
Social	.71	.71	.68	.66	.72	.75	.64	.80				.75			.82	.83
Work	.67	.66	.66	.55	.65	.62	.60	.76	.74					.69		.75
Conceptual Domain	.90	.87	.93	.73	.84	.80	.70	.91	.80	.76					.91	.92
Social Domain	.75	.79	.77	.69	.77	.93	.67	.83	.94	.73	.86				.87	.87
Practical Domain-4	.77	.89	.83	.87	.91	.78	.85	.83	.78	.69	.89	.83		.98	.90	
Practical Domain-5	.79	.90	.84	.83	.90	.78	.85	.88	.81	.81	.92	.85	.98			.93
GAC-9	.85	.90	.89	.82	.89	.87	.79	.90	.86	.75	.96	.92	.97	.98		.99
GAC-10	.85	.91	.88	.80	.88	.85	.80	.92	.86	.80	.96	.92	.96	.97	.99	
Mean[c]	10.11	9.76	10.06	10.10	9.98	10.05	10.26	10.02	10.21	10.16	30.19	20.26	40.10	50.40	90.55	100.92
SD	2.92	3.03	3.12	3.06	2.87	2.96	2.65	3.02	2.99	2.92	8.22	5.54	10.12	11.85	22.77	24.18

Note. **Com** = Communication; **CU** = Community Use; **FA** = Functional Academics; **HL** = Home Living; **HS** = Health and Safety; **LS** = Leisure; **SC** = Self-Care; **SD** = Self-Direction; **Soc** = Social; **WK** = Work; **CON** = Conceptual Adaptive Domain; **SO** = Social Adaptive Domain; **PR-4** = Practical Adaptive Domain without Work; **PR-5** = Practical Adaptive Domain with Work; **GAC-9** = GAC without Work; **GAC-10** = GAC with Work.

[a] Adaptive Domain correlations corrected by removing the skill area scaled score from the sum of the scaled scores.

[b] GAC correlations corrected by removing the skill area scaled score(s) from the sum of the scaled scores.

[c] Means and SDs reported under corrected adaptive domains and GAC were calculated using all skill areas included in the composite.

On the Teacher/Daycare Provider Form, intercorrelations among the skill areas generally were in the .50s. Corrected intercorrelations between the skill areas and their respective adaptive domains averaged .63. Corrected intercorrelations between the skill areas and the GAC averaged .71. All skill areas displayed higher correlations with the GAC than with other skill areas. Corrected intercorrelations between adaptive domains and the GAC averaged .83.

On the Teacher Form, intercorrelations among the skill areas generally were in the high .60s and .70s. Corrected intercorrelations between the skill areas and their respective adaptive domains averaged .76, and corrected intercorrelations between the skill areas and the GAC averaged .80. All skill areas displayed higher correlations with the GAC than with other skill areas. Corrected intercorrelations between adaptive domains and the GAC averaged .88.

On the Parent/Primary Caregiver Form, intercorrelations among the skill areas generally were in the .40s and .50s. Corrected intercorrelations between the skill areas and their respective adaptive domains averaged .55. In contrast, corrected intercorrelations between the skill areas and the GAC averaged .64. Skill areas typically displayed higher correlations with the GAC than with other skill areas.

Note. Mean sums of scaled scores for the GAC and adaptive domains of the Parent/Primary Caregiver Form reported in Table 5.21 are lower than average due to the inclusion of age groups younger than 1 year. These age groups include fewer skill areas in their composite scores than the older age groups in the sample, leading to lower sums of scaled scores.

On the Parent Form, intercorrelations among the skill areas generally were in the .60s. In contrast, the corrected intercorrelations between the skill areas and their respective adaptive domains averaged .70, and corrected intercorrelations between the skill areas and the GAC averaged .75. All skill areas displayed higher correlations with the GAC than with other skill areas. Corrected intercorrelations between adaptive domains and the GAC averaged .83.

On the Adult Form, Self Report, intercorrelations among the skill areas generally were in the .60s. In contrast, corrected intercorrelations between the skill areas and their respective adaptive domains averaged .74 (without Work) and .73 (with Work). Corrected intercorrelations between the skill areas and the GAC averaged .79 (without Work) and .78 (with Work). All skill areas displayed higher correlations with the GAC than with other skill areas. Corrected intercorrelations between adaptive domains and the GAC averaged .87 (without Work) and .89 (with Work).

On the Adult Form, Rated by Others, intercorrelations among the skill areas generally were in the .60s and .70s. Corrected intercorrelations between the skill areas and their respective adaptive domains averaged .78 (both with and without Work). Corrected intercorrelations between the skill areas and the GAC averaged .82 (both with and without Work). All skill areas displayed higher correlations with the GAC than with other skill areas. Corrected intercorrelations between adaptive domains and the GAC averaged .89 (without Work) and .91 (with Work).

Across all forms, trends observed in the data for all ages (Tables 5.20–5.23) exist in the data for each of the age groups within the sample (Tables C.1–C.4). Intercorrelations among the skill areas are moderate and lower than those between the skill areas and the GAC. Intercorrelations between the skill areas and adaptive domains are generally higher than those among skill areas, but lower than those between the skill areas and the GAC. Adaptive domains correlate most highly with the GAC. In summary, support for the theoretical structure of the ABAS–II is found in the intercorrelation data.

Factor Structure

Evidence of a test's factor structure is integral to examining a test's validity (American Educational Research Association, et al., 1999). Factor analysis is a principle means of determining a test's factor structure. In factor analysis, refined statistical techniques are used to analyze the interrelationships among behavioral data. The goal is to reduce a relatively large set of data to a smaller number of factors or common traits that best describe the qualities measured by the data set. The number of factors identified depends on the size and complexity of the data and the degree to which a test measures one or more traits (Anastasi & Urbina, 1997). In confirmatory factor analysis, the specific relationships between observed variables (e.g., adaptive skill areas) and a latent variable (e.g., GAC) are specified in advance by the researcher. The model is then tested to determine if the relationships between observed and latent variables confirm the hypothesized structure.

Results from factor-analytic research of adaptive behavior scales offer evidence in support of both a unidimensional and multidimensional structure, and may differ by such variables as sample characteristics, scale content, and method of analysis (e.g., Bruininks, McGrew, Maruyama, 1988; Jacobson & Mulick, 1996). Although the controversy regarding the structure of adaptive behavior is likely to continue as more comprehensive measures such as the ABAS–II are developed and more advanced psychometric procedures are applied, the practical benefits of obtaining information about an individual's adaptive functioning in the ten skill areas have obvious implications for clinical decision-making and treatment planning.

The theoretical foundations of the ABAS–II assert that the ten skill areas constitute important aspects of adaptive behavior. Although the skill areas are assumed to be somewhat independent of one another, recent revisions to the AAMR's 1992 criteria for the assessment of mental retardation suggest that the skill areas may be grouped into three domains of conceptual, social, and practical adaptive behavior (AAMR, 2002b; see Table 1.3 for the skill areas included within each of the three adaptive domains). Based on these theoretical foundations, both a one-factor and three-factor structural model for the ABAS–II were tested and compared to a model with no common factors (null model). It was expected that both models would produce a superior fit to the data than the null model.

Confirmatory factor analysis was conducted with data from the entire standardization sample for each of the five rating forms. Because the Adult Form may be completed by the individual or by other respondents, confirmatory factor analysis was conducted separately for this form based on the respondent (i.e. self-report or rated by others). The factor models were evaluated using a number of goodness-of-fit measures, including the Tucker-Lewis Index (TLI; Tucker & Lewis, 1973) and the Adjusted Goodness-of-Fit Index (AGFI; Jöreskog & Sörbom, 1993). The TLI and AGFI provide values between 0 and 1, with a value of 1 indicating a perfect model fit. Model fit was also evaluated with Steiger's (1990) Root Mean Square Error of Approximation (RMSEA). RMSEA values ≤ .05 indicate a close model fit, and values up to .08 represent an adequate model fit with reasonable errors of approximation in the population (Browne & Cudeck, 1993).

The results shown in Table 5.24 confirm that a conservative one-factor model provides a good fit to the observed data from the standardization samples. These data confirm that the ABAS–II assesses a strong and unified single factor of adaptive skill. The confirmation of a one-factor model on the ABAS–II is consistent with research by McGrew and Bruininks (1989) that suggested that most adaptive functioning instruments measure a general, global factor. Although the one-factor model provided the most parsimonious fit to the data, results also indicate that the three-factor model produces a close fit to the data, providing support for the AAMR's (2002b) categorization of adaptive skill areas into three more general domains. Because the ABAS–II is designed to provide a more comprehensive measure of adaptive behavior than many existing measures, it is expected that future investigations utilizing this instrument with clinical samples will provide additional information regarding the structure of adaptive behavior.

Table 5.24 Goodness-of-Fit Statistics for Confirmatory Factor Analysis

Standardization Sample	n	Goodness-of-Fit Indices of the One-Factor and Three-Factor Models					Improvement		
		x^2	df	x^2/df	AGFI	RMSEA	x^2	df	TLI
Teacher/Daycare Provider	750								
Null Model		3659.9	28	130.7					
Model 1 (one factor)		142.1	20	7.1	.92	.09	3517.9	8	.95
Model 2 (three factors)		127.1	17	7.5	.91	.09	15.0	3	.95
Parent/Primary Caregiver	1050								
Null Model		5421.8	36	150.6					
Model 1 (one factor)		278.6	27	10.3	.91	.09	5143.2	9	.94
Model 2 (three factors)		245.9	24	10.3	.91	.09	32.7	3	.94
Teacher	1690								
Null Model		13220.7	36	367.2					
Model 1 (one factor)		753.9	27	27.9	.85	.13	12466.8	9	.93
Model 2 (three factors)		706.6	24	29.4	.84	.13	47.3	3	.92
Parent	1670								
Null Model		10129.3	36	281.4					
Model 1 (one factor)		687.3	27	25.5	.86	.12	9442.0	9	.91
Model 2 (three factors)		552.2	24	23.0	.87	.11	135.1	3	.92
Adult, Self Report	990								
Null Model		7401.8	36	205.6					
Model 1 (one factor)		502.7	27	18.6	.83	.13	6899.1	9	.91
Model 2 (three factors)		482.5	24	20.1	.82	.14	20.2	3	.91
Adult, Rated by Others	920								
Null Model		7699.7	36	213.9					
Model 1 (one factor)		428.0	27	15.9	.84	.13	7271.8	9	.93
Model 2 (three factors)		407.7	24	17.0	.83	.13	2.3	3	.92

Note. The Motor Skill Area was not included in factor analysis because AAMR (2002b) guidelines do not include this skill area in any of the three adaptive domains.

Note. The Work Skill Area was not included in factor analysis because too few cases had scores in this skill area.

Note. Results for Parent/Primary Caregiver sample do not include ages 0:0–0:11 because adaptive domain and GAC scores for this age group include fewer skill areas.

Correlations With Other Variables

A test's validity is traditionally evaluated, in part, by evidence that examines relationships between the test and other variables such as additional test scores or other types of information. *Concurrent validity* refers to the relationship between two sets of data obtained at or about the same time. *Predictive validity* indicates the accuracy of test data to predict performance some time in the future. Information on the ABAS–II's concurrent validity included in this manual provides evidence important to understanding the test's convergent and discriminant validity. Evidence of a test's convergent and discriminant validity is found in the degree to which it shows higher correlations with qualities thought to be more related to it and lower correlations with qualities thought to be less related to it. The predictive validity of ABAS–II will be determined based on results of forthcoming studies that will provide evidence for the various ways in which the test is likely to be used.

Note. All correlations reported in the following validity studies are *corrected* correlations, unless otherwise noted in table or text.

Correlations With Measures of Adaptive Behavior and Other Types of Behavior Rating Scales

Validity data concerning the ABAS–II and other behavior rating scales is described below. Relationships between the ABAS–II and comprehensive adaptive behavior scales, as well as brief scales of adaptive behavior and problem behavior scales, were examined.

Correlations With the Vineland Adaptive Behavior Scale

Relationships between the ABAS–II Teacher/Daycare Provider Form and the VABS–*Classroom Edition* (VABS–CE) were examined with a nonclinical sample of 44 students ages 3 years 3 months–5 years 11 months, with a mean age of 4 years 7 months. The sample had the following composition: 59% female and 41% male; 57% White, 7% African American, 32% Hispanic, and 4% of other racial/ethnic origin. Table 5.25 reports the mean scores and correlations between the two measures.

The adaptive skills of the sample generally fell within the average range; means and standard deviations were 103 and 11 on the GAC and 100 and 12 on the VABS–CE Adaptive Behavior Composite. The correlation between these overall composite scores was .75. The adaptive domains of the ABAS–II correlated from .58–.73 with the VABS–CE Adaptive Behavior Composite. The ABAS–II Motor Skill Area correlated .61 with the VABS–CE Motor Skills Domain. The correlations between these two comprehensive measures of adaptive behavior are substantial and add support to ABAS–II validity.

Further relationships between the ABAS–II Teacher Form and the VABS–CE were examined with a nonclinical sample of 57 students ages 5–12 years, with a mean age of 8 years 7 months. The sample had the following composition: 42% female and 58% male; 90% White, 5% African American, 3% Hispanic, and 2% of other racial/ethnic origin. The sample was rated by teachers using both the ABAS–II Teacher Form and the VABS–CE. Table 5.25 reports the mean scores and correlations between the two measures.

The adaptive skills of this sample generally fell within the average range; means and standard deviations of overall composite scores were 102 and 14 on the ABAS–II and 100 and 13 on the VABS–CE. The correlation between the GAC and the VABS–CE Adaptive Behavior Composite was .84. Furthermore, scores from all three ABAS–II adaptive domains correlated significantly (.53–.82) with the three VABS–CE domains and Adaptive Behavior Composite. Data from the ABAS–II Work Skill Area and the VABS–CE measure of Motor Skills are not reported because the skills are not common to both measures. The ABAS–II skill areas generally correlated significantly with the VABS–CE domains and Adaptive Behavior Composite. As with the previous sample of children ages 3–5 years, the correlations between the school-age measures are substantial and add additional support to ABAS–II validity.

Table 5.25 Correlation Between the ABAS–II and the VABS–CE

Teacher/Daycare Provider Form (*n* = 44) (Non-Clinical Sample)

| | Vineland Scores | | | | | ABAS–II | |
	Communication Domain	Daily Living Skills Domain	Socialization Domain	Motor Skills Domain	Adaptive Behavior Composite	Mean	SD
ABAS–II							
Communication	.49	.27	.39	.50	.53	11.0	2.8
Functional Pre-Academics	.50	.69	.55	.41	.63	10.2	2.5
School Living	.38	.37	.49	.56	.54	10.9	2.2
Health and Safety	.30	.26	.50	.47	.47	11.0	2.4
Leisure	.39	.43	.60	.51	.58	10.3	2.2
Self-Care	.29	.26	.24	.54	.44	11.1	2.6
Self-Direction	.27	.17	.41	.31	.35	10.8	2.4
Social	.44	.29	.58	.61	.60	10.9	1.7
Motor	.51	.40	.45	.61	.61	10.7	2.6
Conceptual Domain	.63	.58	.65	.61	.73	103.0	11.6
Social Domain	.45	.40	.62	.59	.62	102.3	10.0
Practical Domain	.38	.35	.52	.63	.58	104.6	11.8
GAC	.59	.54	.67	.71	.75	103.3	11.0
Vineland							
Mean	96.6	98.7	99.1	108.1	100.3		
SD	13.8	10.2	9.5	16.6	11.9		

Table 5.25   Correlation Between the ABAS–II and the VABS–CE (continued)

Teacher Form (n = 57) (Non-Clinical Sample)

	Vineland Scores				ABAS–II	
	Communication Domain	Daily Living Skills Domain	Socialization Domain	Adaptive Behavior Composite	Mean	SD
ABAS–II						
Communication	.75	.68	.55	.74	9.2	3.1
Community Use	.64	.64	.49	.69	9.4	3.1
Functional Academics	.72	.71	.45	.74	9.2	3.2
School Living	.59	.79	.70	.80	10.2	2.1
Health and Safety	.38	.51	.48	.52	10.2	2.1
Leisure	.71	.75	.67	.72	9.7	2.5
Self-Care	.75	.79	.79	.79	10.4	1.3
Self-Direction	.75	.76	.61	.76	9.4	3.0
Social	.65	.77	.60	.72	10.1	2.2
Conceptual Domain	.76	.75	.53	.77	99.9	17.1
Social Domain	.71	.82	.71	.77	100.4	11.9
Practical Domain	.59	.77	.69	.81	103.0	11.9
GAC	.73	.83	.69	.84	102.3	13.8
Vineland						
Mean	95.7	102.6	99.2	99.8		
SD	16.0	13.3	12.4	13.4		

Relationships between the ABAS–II Parent/Primary Caregiver Form and the VABS–*Interview Edition* (VABS–IE) were examined with a nonclinical sample of 45 children ages 1 month–5 years 9 months with a mean age of 2 years 10 months. The sample had the following composition: 49% female and 51% male; 73% White, 7% African American, 18% Hispanic, and 2% of other racial/ethnic origin. Table 5.26 reports the mean scores and correlations between the two measures.

The adaptive skills of the sample ranged from average to above average; means and standard deviations of overall composite scores were 104 and 16 on the ABAS–II and 112 and 19 on the VABS–IE. The correlation between the GAC and the VABS–IE Adaptive Behavior Composite was .70. Scores from three ABAS–II adaptive domains correlated .49–74 with the four VABS–IE domains. The ABAS–II skill areas in general showed moderate correlations with the VABS–IE domains and Adaptive Behavior Composite. The correlation between the ABAS–II Motor Skill Area and the VABS–IE Motor Skills Domain was .62. As with the teacher forms, the correlations between the ABAS–II and Vineland parent measures are substantial and add further support to ABAS–II validity.

Table 5.26 Correlation Between the ABAS–II and the VABS–IE

▶ **Parent/Primary Caregiver Form (*n* = 45)** (Non-Clinical Sample)

	Vineland Scores					ABAS–II	
	Communication Domain	Daily Living Skills Domain	Socialization Domain	Motor Skills Domain	Adaptive Behavior Composite	Mean	SD
ABAS–II							
Communication	.64	.38	.45	.36	.54	10.8	2.8
Community Use[a]	.64	.47	.47	.54	.63	11.0	2.7
Functional Pre-Academics[a]	.50	.48	.40	.49	.53	10.0	2.4
Home Living[a]	.45	.54	.54	.70	.65	11.3	2.8
Health and Safety	.51	.44	.39	.49	.53	10.8	3.2
Leisure	.68	.57	.63	.47	.68	10.5	2.9
Self-Care	.30	.39	.34	.43	.41	11.0	2.8
Self-Direction	.50	.57	.57	.56	.65	10.9	3.3
Social	.53	.64	.63	.59	.69	11.2	2.5
Motor	.47	.51	.40	.62	.57	10.8	2.6
Conceptual Domain	.61	.55	.57	.50	.66	102.5	15.5
Social Domain	.66	.65	.68	.56	.74	103.6	14.2
Practical Domain	.52	.49	.49	.58	.61	104.4	16.4
GAC	.61	.58	.58	.61	.70	103.9	15.8
Vineland							
Mean	103.5	114.3	112.0	108.2	111.7		
SD	15.3	19.7	20.0	14.6	18.5		

[a]Based on 36 observations.

Correlations With the Scales of Independent Behavior–Revised

Relationships between the ABAS–II and two forms of the SIB–R (*Early Development Form* and *Short Form*) were investigated. The ABAS–II is a comprehensive, diagnostic measure of adaptive behavior designed to measure the skill areas and domains specified by the AAMR (2002b) and *DSM–IV–TR*. It is not a brief form or screener. In contrast, the SIB–R forms used in the study are brief versions, have only 40 items each, and are more limited in the number and type of scores that they provide. The validity studies between the ABAS–II and SIB–R forms described below provide general information about how a more limited assessment, such as an SIB–R brief form, may relate to the comprehensive, detailed assessment provided by the ABAS–II. The SIB–R brief forms used in the present studies had low correlations with the ABAS–II, compared to the higher correlations between the ABAS–II and the Vineland, a comprehensive measure of adaptive behavior.

Relationships between the ABAS–II Parent/Primary Caregiver Form and the SIB–R: *Early Development Form* were evaluated with a nonclinical sample of 34 children ages 2 months–1 year 11 months, with a mean age of 1 year 2 months. The sample had the following composition: 56% female and 44% male; 50% White, 23% African American, 21% Hispanic, and 6% of other racial/ethnic origin. Table 5.27 reports the mean scores and correlations between the two measures.

The adaptive skills of the sample generally fell within the average range; the mean and standard deviation of the GAC were 102 and 14, and the mean and standard deviation of the SIB–R: *Early Development Form* Broad Independence Scale were 110 and 12. The SIB–R: *Early Development Form* Broad Independence standard score correlated .18 with the GAC, and also had low correlations with the adaptive domains and skill areas.

Table 5.27 Correlation Between the ABAS–II and the SIB–R

Parent/Primary Caregiver Form and SIB–R: *Early Development Form* (*n* = 34) (Non-Clinical Sample)

	SIB–R	ABAS–II	
	Broad Independence Score	Mean	SD
ABAS–II			
Communication	.41	10.4	2.6
Community Use[a]	-.04	10.5	2.9
Functional Pre-Academics[a]	.16	10.7	3.2
Home Living[a]	.07	10.7	2.6
Health and Safety	.16	9.8	3.2
Leisure	.15	10.6	2.6
Self-Care	.04	10.5	2.2
Self-Direction	.00	10.6	2.5
Social	.23	10.6	2.1
Motor	.21	10.5	2.0
Conceptual Domain	.25	102.2	13.9
Social Domain	.20	101.9	12.1
Practical Domain	.10	100.4	14.4
GAC	.18	101.8	13.8
SIB–R			
Mean	109.9		
SD	12.1		

Teacher/Daycare Provider Form and SIB–R: *Short Form* (*n* = 35) (Non-Clinical Sample)

	SIB–R	ABAS–II	
	Broad Independence Score	Mean	SD
ABAS–II			
Communication	.50	10.4	3.5
Functional Pre-Academics	.32	10.1	2.8
School Living	.55	11.3	2.3
Health and Safety	.51	10.6	2.7
Leisure	.36	10.6	2.7
Self-Care	.67	11.1	2.2
Self-Direction	.45	10.7	3.1
Social	.36	10.5	3.1
Motor	.14	11.5	2.4
Conceptual Domain	.56	101.3	15.2
Social Domain	.40	102.1	14.6
Practical Domain	.63	104.5	12.2
GAC	.59	103.5	13.5
SIB–R			
Mean	111.6		
SD	13.6		

[a]Based on 20 observations.

Further relationships between the ABAS–II Teacher/Daycare Provider Form and the SIB–R: *Short Form* were evaluated with a nonclinical sample of 35 children ages 2 years 0 months–5 years 11 months with a mean age of 4 years 0 months. The sample had the following composition: 47% female and 53% male; 31% White, 36% African American, 28% Hispanic, and 5% of other racial/ethnic origin. Table 5.27 reports the mean scores and correlations between the two measures.

The adaptive skills of the sample generally fell within the average to above average range; the mean and standard deviation of the GAC were 104 and 14, and the mean and standard deviation of the SIB–R Broad Independence Scale were 112 and 14. The correlation between the GAC and the SIB–R Broad Independence standard score is .59.

Correlation With the Behavior Assessment Scale for Children

The BASC is a behavior rating scale that measures primarily negative (clinical) dimensions of behavior and personality. It is designed for the differential diagnosis and educational classification of a variety of children's emotional and behavioral disorders. Adaptive behavior, as measured by the ABAS–II, may be inversely related to negative behaviors, as measured by the BASC, especially for children diagnosed with emotional or behavior disorders, or with co-morbidity of mental retardation and emotional or behavior disorders. For this reason, a study examining correlations between the Teacher/Daycare Provider Form and the BASC Teacher Rating Scale was conducted with a nonclinical sample of 37 children ranging in age from 4 years 0 months–5 years 10 months with a mean age of 4 years 11 months. The sample had the following composition: 49% female and 51% male; 49% White, 32% African American, 16% Hispanic, and 3% of other racial/ethnic origin. Table 5.28 reports the mean scores and correlations between the two measures.

The scores for the sample generally fell within the average range. The mean GAC was 107, and the mean *T* scores of the BASC problem behavior composites ranged from 45–46. The correlations between the GAC and BASC Externalizing Problems, Internalizing Problems, and Behavior Symptoms Index composites were –.49, –.39, and –.66 respectively.

Although the primary emphasis of the BASC is on negative dimensions of personality and behavior, it also includes a few specific scales of positive behaviors (i.e., adaptability and social skills) as well as an adaptive skill composite. However, the BASC scales do not measure the comprehensive adaptive behavior and adaptive skill areas assessed by the ABAS–II and required by the AAMR (2002b), *DSM–IV–TR* and IDEA (1999) for the diagnosis of mental retardation. The positive behavior scales of the BASC are intended to assist in the interpretation of its problem behavior scales. The correlation between the GAC and the BASC Adaptive Skills Composite was .80.

Correlations With Measures of Intelligence and Achievement

Although instruments that assess adaptive skills and instruments that measure intelligence or achievement (cognitive measures) are often used together in clinical assessment, the two general types of instruments are quite different and serve separate assessment purposes. Adaptive behavior assessment generally involves the use of behavior rating scales and focuses on typical, everyday activities. Measures of intelligence and achievement emphasize internal cognitive processes, are directly administered to examinees through ability test items, and focus on correct or incorrect answers in a testing situation. As summarized by Boan and Harrison (1997), previous research has found generally moderate correlations between adaptive skill scales and intelligence tests. Keith, Fehrmann, Harrison, and Pottebaum (1987) explored several models to explain the relationship between adaptive skill and intelligence and found the most support for the model explaining that adaptive skill and intelligence are separate but related constructs. The results described in the next section correlating the ABAS–II and cognitive assessments are consistent with this model.

Table 5.28 Correlation Between the ABAS–II and the BASC

Teacher/Daycare Provider Form (n = 37) (Non-Clinical Sample)

	BASC Behavior Scales										BASC Composite Scores				ABAS–II	
	Hyperactivity	Aggression	Anxiety	Depression	Somatization	Atypicality	Withdrawal	Attention Problems	Adaptability	Social Skills	Externalizing Problems Composite	Internalizing Problems Composite	Adaptive Skills Composite	Behavioral Symptoms Index	Mean	SD
ABAS–II																
Communication	-.23	-.15	-.17	-.28	-.29	-.47	-.40	-.36	.42	.29	-.18	-.28	.39	-.36	11.6	3.1
Functional Pre-Academics	-.06	.00	-.22	-.26	.12	-.20	-.52	-.40	.40	.52	-.02	-.11	.51	-.26	10.4	2.7
School Living	-.62	-.58	-.60	-.73	-.23	-.64	-.46	-.80	.70	.64	-.63	-.56	.72	-.80	11.6	1.8
Health and Safety	-.25	-.59	-.01	-.45	.00	.04	-.29	-.28	.67	.55	-.48	-.13	.65	-.31	11.5	2.0
Leisure	-.39	-.43	-.24	-.50	-.09	-.41	-.54	-.56	.66	.71	-.43	-.27	.74	-.54	10.9	2.4
Self-Care	.07	.10	-.20	-.29	.03	.04	-.11	-.23	.14	.07	.07	-.16	.13	-.13	11.6	2.1
Self-Direction	-.55	-.59	-.08	-.38	.03	-.33	-.28	-.74	.74	.65	-.60	-.12	.74	-.58	11.5	2.3
Social	-.51	-.37	-.32	-.63	-.19	-.73	-.49	-.72	.58	.61	-.46	-.40	.64	-.70	11.5	2.0
Motor	-.24	-.35	-.30	-.42	-.27	-.42	-.33	-.40	.52	.40	-.31	-.36	.50	-.45	11.3	2.6
Conceptual Domain	-.36	-.30	-.23	-.43	-.11	-.47	-.57	-.65	.70	.63	-.35	-.26	.73	-.53	106.2	12.7
Social Domain	-.46	-.43	-.29	-.60	-.15	-.60	-.54	-.67	.66	.69	-.46	-.35	.72	-.66	105.8	11.1
Practical Domain	-.43	-.57	-.43	-.72	-.08	-.28	-.46	-.64	.73	.64	-.54	-.43	.73	-.63	107.8	7.8
GAC	-.44	-.49	-.36	-.63	-.15	-.51	-.59	-.70	.77	.73	-.49	-.39	.80	-.66	107.2	10.6
BASC																
Mean	45.4	45.3	48.5	42.5	49.4	46.7	45.0	48.6	51.9	52.4	45.1	45.9	52.4	45.0		
SD	6.5	7.0	9.4	5.5	9.8	8.5	8.4	11.6	9.3	9.9	6.8	9.0	9.8	8.1		

Note. BASC means and standard deviations based on *T* scores. Higher problem behavior scale *T* scores indicate a greater frequency of the problem behaviors included in the scale; higher positive behavior scale *T* scores indicate a greater frequency of the positive behaviors included in the scale.

Correlations With the Wechsler Preschool and Primary Scale of Intelligence–Third Edition

Correlations between the ABAS–II and the WPPSI–III were investigated using two samples. Each sample was administered the WPPSI–III and rated on the Teacher/Daycare Provider Form (sample 1) or Parent/Primary Caregiver Form (sample 2).

Table 5.29 Correlation Between the ABAS–II and the WPPSI–III

Sample 1

Teacher/Daycare Provider Form (Non-Clinical Sample)	n	WPPSI–III Scores					ABAS–II	
		VIQ	PIQ	PSQ	FSIQ	GLC	Mean	SD
ABAS–II								
Communication	229	.58	.41	.40	.53	.51	8.2	3.8
Functional Pre-Academics	229	.57	.53	.54	.60	.58	8.6	3.6
School Living	229	.52	.46	.41	.51	.47	9.0	3.4
Health and Safety	229	.60	.47	.46	.58	.57	8.7	3.5
Leisure	229	.52	.44	.45	.51	.50	9.1	3.3
Self-Care	229	.57	.49	.41	.56	.52	8.9	3.2
Self-Direction	229	.58	.46	.45	.57	.52	9.1	3.4
Social	229	.51	.40	.42	.50	.45	8.5	3.6
Motor	229	.50	.45	.35	.51	.45	8.9	3.4
Conceptual Domain	229	.65	.51	.50	.63	.59	90.5	19.4
Social Domain	229	.53	.41	.44	.51	.48	92.1	18.6
Practical Domain	229	.60	.50	.45	.59	.56	91.5	18.7
GAC	229	.62	.50	.47	.61	.57	90.7	19.3
WPPSI–III								
n		225	223	152	218	229		
Mean		92.5	93.2	92.5	92.3	94.0		
SD		19.0	18.2	18.3	19.4	18.0		

Sample 2

Parent/Primary Caregiver Form (Non-Clinical Sample)	n	WPPSI–III Scores					ABAS–II	
		VIQ	PIQ	PSQ	FSIQ	GLC	Mean	SD
ABAS–II								
Communication	306	.56	.47	.46	.54	.54	9.0	3.7
Community Use	306	.54	.46	.45	.53	.50	9.0	3.4
Functional Pre-Academics	306	.56	.58	.59	.62	.58	9.1	3.3
Home Living	306	.31	.32	.46	.34	.31	9.3	3.0
Health and Safety	306	.40	.40	.43	.42	.36	9.3	3.6
Leisure	306	.49	.49	.51	.53	.45	9.3	3.6
Self-Care	306	.44	.42	.46	.46	.41	9.4	3.3
Self-Direction	306	.47	.44	.49	.49	.46	9.4	3.3
Social	306	.43	.41	.44	.44	.42	9.3	3.4
Motor	306	.42	.46	.50	.47	.40	9.2	3.3
Conceptual Domain	306	.58	.53	.55	.60	.57	93.0	19.0
Social Domain	306	.46	.44	.48	.49	.43	94.2	19.4
Practical Domain	306	.47	.43	.48	.48	.42	93.7	18.3
GAC	306	.51	.48	.52	.54	.47	92.9	19.6
WPPSI–III								
n		306	303	185	297	312		
Mean		94.2	94.4	93.6	94.1	95.1		
SD		18.8	18.5	19.0	19.3	18.2		

Note. **VIQ** = Verbal IQ; **PIQ** = Performance IQ; **PSQ** = Processing Speed Quotient; **FSIQ** = Full Scale IQ; **GLC** = General Language Composite.

Sample 1 consisted of 229 children ages 2 years 6 month–5 years 11 months, with a mean age of 4 years 6 months, with no reported disabilities. The sample had the following composition: 40% female and 60% male; 67% White, 18% African American, 9% Hispanic, and 6% of other racial/ethnic origin.

Sample 2 consisted of 306 children ages 2 years 6 months–5 years 11 months, with a mean age of 4 years 4 months, with no reported disabilities. The sample had the following composition: 40% female and 60% male; 68% White, 18% African American, 8% Hispanic, and 6% of other racial/ethnic origin. Table 5.29 reports the mean scores and correlations between the measures.

The results for Sample 1 show that the mean of the Teacher/Daycare Provider Form GAC was 91, and the mean of the WPPSI–III Full Scale IQ (FSIQ) was 92. The GAC correlated .61 with the WPPSI–III FSIQ. Correlations between the GAC and the WPPSI–III Verbal IQ (VIQ), Performance IQ (PIQ) and General Language Composite (GLC) were .62, .50 and .57, respectively. The FSIQ scores of the WPPSI–III showed the highest correlations with the Conceptual Adaptive Domain (.63) and the Functional Pre-Academics Skill Area (.60). In addition, the WPPSI–III VIQ correlated .65 with the Conceptual Adaptive Domain.

For Sample 2, the mean of the GAC on the Parent/Primary Caregiver Form was 93, and the mean of the WPPSI–III FSIQ was 94. The GAC correlated .54 with the WPPSI–III FSIQ. Correlations between the GAC and WPPSI –III scores were .51, .48 and .47 for VIQ, PIQ, and GLC, respectively. As found in Sample 1, the FSIQ scores of the WPPSI–III showed the highest correlations with the Conceptual Adaptive Domain (.60) and the Functional Pre-Academics Skill Area (.62). Also similar to Sample 1, the WPPSI–III VIQ correlated .58 with the Conceptual Adaptive Domain. Overall, the correlations between the WPPSI–III and parent ratings are moderate, and slightly lower than those of the teacher ratings.

Results from both samples suggest generally moderate levels of correlation between ABAS–II and WPPSI–III IQ scores. Among the skill areas, Functional Pre-Academics generally displayed the highest correlation with WPPSI–III FSIQ. Among the adaptive domains, Conceptual displayed the highest correlation with the WPPSI–III FSIQ. Correlations generally were in the .50s and .60s, suggesting that for preschool ages, adaptive skills, as measured by the ABAS–II, are related to intelligence, as measured by the WPPSI–III, though the two constructs are somewhat distinct. These results are expected when comparing an adaptive behavior assessment that requires a parent or teacher to rate the degree to which a child independently uses adaptive skills in daily life, and a cognitive assessment that requires a child to answer questions and solve problem in a structured testing situation.

Correlations With the Wechsler Intelligence Scale for Children–Third Edition

Correlations between the ABAS–II and the WISC–III were investigated using three samples. Each sample was administered the WISC–III and rated on the Parent Form (sample 1) or Teacher Form (samples 2 and 3).

Sample 1 consisted of 49 children ages 7–17 years, with a mean age of 12 years, with no reported disabilities. The sample had the following composition: 46% female and 54% male; 75% White, 4% African American, 18% Hispanic, and 3% of other racial/ethnic origin.

Sample 2 was a mixed-clinical sample that included 116 children with different clinical diagnoses. Most (46%) were classified as exhibiting mild mental retardation; other classifications included moderate mental retardation (23%), speech/language impairment (11%), as well as ADHD , emotional disturbance, learning disabilities, and severe mental retardation (categories that constituted the remaining 20%). The children's ages ranged from 6–16 years, with a mean age of 11 years. The sample had the following composition: 40% female and 60% male; 67% White, 6% African American, 17% Hispanic, and 10% of other racial/ethnic origin.

Sample 3 included 21 children ages 7–16 years, with a mean age of 11 years, with no reported disabilities. The sample had the following composition: 42% female and 58% male; 75% White, 17% Hispanic, and 8% of other racial/ethnic origin. Table 5.30 reports the mean scores and correlations between the measures.

Table 5.30 Correlation Between the ABAS–II and the WISC–III

Sample 1 (n = 49)

Parent Form	WISC–III Scores			ABAS–II	
(Non-Clinical Sample)	VIQ	PIQ	FSIQ	Mean	SD
ABAS–II					
Communication	.34	.31	.36	10.4	2.3
Community Use	.46	.47	.52	10.4	2.3
Functional Academics	.55	.56	.61	10.2	2.6
Home Living	.22	.29	.29	9.7	3.4
Health and Safety	.37	.42	.45	10.3	2.8
Leisure	.27	.35	.33	9.9	2.4
Self-Care	.12	.05	.11	10.4	2.2
Self-Direction	.23	.26	.27	10.1	2.8
Social	.25	.24	.28	9.5	3.0
Conceptual Domain	.44	.46	.50	102.0	12.1
Social Domain	.31	.31	.34	98.6	12.6
Practical Domain	.41	.43	.48	101.8	12.3
GAC	.42	.45	.48	101.5	13.3
WISC–III					
Mean	106.6	104.4	106.0		
SD	12.6	12.4	12.4		

Sample 2

Teacher Form		WISC–III Scores			ABAS–II	
(Clinical Sample)	n	VIQ	PIQ	FSIQ	Mean	SD
ABAS–II						
Communication	116	.47	.34	.43	4.4	3.6
Community Use	114	.41	.32	.43	4.5	3.6
Functional Academics	115	.50	.46	.54	3.9	3.3
Home Living	115	.13	.16	.20	6.2	3.9
Health and Safety	115	.28	.31	.34	5.4	3.6
Leisure	115	.38	.30	.38	6.5	3.2
Self-Care	116	.23	.34	.32	5.9	4.2
Self-Direction	116	.22	.17	.26	4.8	3.5
Social	116	.25	.19	.25	6.4	3.8
Conceptual Domain	115	.41	.32	.43	72.7	18.8
Social Domain	115	.36	.29	.36	82.9	17.0
Practical Domain	114	.29	.34	.38	75.4	20.6
GAC	114	.35	.35	.40	72.6	19.7
WISC–III						
n		107	107	116		
Mean		69.6	70.9	66.8		
SD		14.4	16.0	15.8		

Note. **VIQ** = Verbal IQ; **PIQ** = Performance IQ; **FSIQ** = Full Scale IQ.

Table 5.30 Correlation Between the ABAS–II and the WISC–III (*continued*)

Sample 3 (*n* = 21)

Teacher Form	WISC–III Scores			ABAS–II	
(Non-Clinical Sample)	VIQ	PIQ	FSIQ	Mean	SD
ABAS–II					
Communication	.35	.39	.40	9.5	2.7
Community Use	.37	.51	.48	10.5	2.2
Functional Academics	.49	.53	.56	10.5	2.3
School Living	.73	.77	.81	10.6	2.0
Health and Safety	.55	.44	.55	10.6	1.5
Leisure	.54	.63	.61	11.0	1.3
Self-Care	.44	.51	.51	10.3	1.6
Self-Direction	.79	.76	.83	10.5	1.6
Social	.56	.44	.56	10.7	2.2
Conceptual Domain	.47	.55	.56	106.8	11.2
Social Domain	.46	.48	.52	106.6	11.2
Practical Domain	.61	.67	.69	106.3	10.8
GAC	.60	.63	.67	106.8	10.9
WISC–III					
Mean	104.4	103.5	104.3		
SD	14.0	13.8	13.8		

Note. **VIQ** = Verbal IQ; **PIQ** = Performance IQ; **FSIQ** = Full Scale IQ.

The results for Sample 1 show that the mean of the Parent Form GAC and the WISC–III FSIQ were 102 and 106, respectively. The GAC correlated .48 with the WISC–III FSIQ. Its correlations with the VIQ and PIQ were .42 and .45 respectively. As expected, FSIQ scores of the WISC–III correlated most highly with the Conceptual Adaptive Domain (.50) and the Functional Academics Skill Area (.61).

For Sample 2, the mean scores were 73 for the Teacher Form GAC and 67 for the WISC–III FSIQ. The GAC correlated .40 with the WISC–III FSIQ. The WISC–III VIQ and PIQ both correlated .35 with the GAC. The Conceptual Adaptive Domain and the Functional Academics Skill Area displayed the highest correlations with the WISC–III FSIQ (.43 and .54 respectively).

The results for Sample 3 show that the mean of the Teacher Form GAC and the WISC–III FSIQ were 107 and 104, respectively. The GAC correlated .67 with the WISC–III FSIQ. Correlations with the WISC–III VIQ and PIQ were .60 and .63, respectively. The FSIQ of the WISC–III showed the highest correlation with the School Living (.81) and Self-Direction (.83) Skill Areas. Interestingly, among the adaptive domains, the Practical Domain displayed the highest correlation with the WISC–III FSIQ (.69).

The results are similar to those found in the WPPSI–III study and suggest generally moderate levels of correlation between the GAC and the WISC–III IQ scores. Out of the three adaptive domains, the Conceptual Domain generally correlated most highly with the WISC–III FSIQ, and among the skill areas, Functional Academics generally correlated most highly with the WISC–III FSIQ. The Teacher Form correlated more highly with the WISC–III than did the Parent Form. The non-clinical sample rated by teachers showed the highest correlations, which were typically in the .60s. Correlations on the other two samples generally were in the .30s and .40s, suggesting that adaptive skills, as measured by the ABAS–II, and intelligence, as measured by the WISC–III, are relatively distinct but related constructs.

Correlations With the Wechsler Intelligence Scale for Children–Fourth Edition

Correlations between the ABAS–II and the WISC–IV were investigated using two samples. Each sample was administered the WISC–IV and rated on the Parent Form (sample 1) or Teacher Form (sample 2).

Sample 1 consisted of 122 children ages 6–16 years, with a mean age of 11 years, with no reported disabilities. The sample had the following composition: 52% female and 48% male; 54% White, 32% African American, 8% Hispanic, and 6% of other racial/ethnic origin.

Sample 2 included 145 children ages 6–16 years, with a mean age of 10 years, with no reported disabilities. The sample had the following composition: 56% female and 44% male; 57% White, 30% African American, 6% Hispanic, and 7% of other racial/ethnic origin. Table 5.31 reports the mean scores and correlations between the measures.

Table 5.31 Correlation Between the ABAS–II and the WISC–IV

Sample 1

| Parent Form | | WISC–IV Scores | | | | | ABAS–II | |
(Non-Clinical sample)	n	VCI	PRI	WMI	PSI	FSIQ	Mean	SD
ABAS–II								
Communication	122	.47	.42	.48	.25	.54	10.4	3.1
Community Use	122	.29	.11	.31	.12	.28	10.1	3.3
Functional Academics	122	.43	.29	.44	.13	.43	10.1	3.2
Home Living	122	.15	.11	.19	.21	.22	9.1	3.8
Health and Safety	122	.30	.20	.20	.08	.27	10.3	2.7
Leisure	122	.46	.36	.45	.27	.48	9.9	3.1
Self-Care	122	.12	.19	.14	.21	.16	9.4	2.8
Self-Direction	122	.30	.28	.26	.27	.35	9.8	3.4
Social	122	.23	.20	.22	.11	.20	9.3	3.6
Conceptual Domain	122	.45	.37	.45	.25	.49	101.1	15.7
Social Domain	122	.36	.27	.35	.18	.35	98.3	15.8
Practical Domain	122	.25	.16	.25	.18	.28	99.3	15.5
GAC	122	.39	.30	.38	.23	.41	99.4	16.9
WISC–IV								
n		120	121	118	119	112		
Mean		99.7	100.2	100.4	98.5	99.7		
SD		14.3	13.7	14.1	12.5	13.3		

Sample 2

| Teacher Form | | WISC–IV Scores | | | | | ABAS–II | |
(Non-Clinical sample)	n	VCI	PRI	WMI	PSI	FSIQ	Mean	SD
ABAS–II								
Communication	145	.37	.37	.20	.30	.50	9.9	2.4
Community Use	145	.36	.26	.27	.30	.47	10.2	2.4
Functional Academics	145	.36	.39	.39	.40	.57	10.2	2.5
School Living	145	.28	.26	.38	.27	.47	10.1	2.9
Health and Safety	145	.37	.31	.34	.27	.52	9.9	2.5
Leisure	145	.24	.19	.24	.22	.37	10.5	2.3
Self-Care	145	.39	.34	.22	.16	.46	10.0	2.5
Self-Direction	144	.39	.41	.30	.34	.57	10.0	2.6
Social	145	.27	.28	.24	.25	.43	10.5	2.4
Conceptual Domain	144	.44	.45	.34	.39	.63	104.9	12.7
Social Domain	145	.29	.26	.26	.26	.43	104.8	13.7
Practical Domain	145	.41	.35	.32	.27	.53	103.4	14.0
GAC	144	.42	.39	.35	.34	.58	104.8	14.2
WISC–IV								
n		142	145	141	145	139		
Mean		100.6	99.3	101.0	99.3	100.5		
SD		11.0	11.8	13.4	13.8	11.1		

Note. **VCI** = Verbal Comprehension Index; **PRI** = Perceptual Reasoning Index; **WMI** = Working Memory Index; **PSI** = Processing Speed Index; **FSIQ** = Full Scale IQ.

The results for Sample 1 show that the mean of the Parent Form GAC and the WISC–IV FSIQ were 99 and 100, respectively. The GAC correlated .41 with the WISC–IV FSIQ. Its correlations with the VCI and PRI were .39 and .30 respectively. The FSIQ scores of the WISC–IV correlated most highly with the Conceptual Adaptive Domain (.49) and the Communication Skill Area (.54).

For Sample 2, the mean scores were 105 for the Teacher Form GAC and 101 for the WISC–IV FSIQ. The WISC–IV FSIQ correlated .58 with the GAC. Correlations between the GAC and the WISC–IV VCI and PRI were .42 and .39, respectively. As expected, the Conceptual Adaptive Domain and the Functional Academics Skill Area displayed the highest correlations with the WISC–IV FSIQ, correlating .63 and .57 respectively.

Overall results suggest moderate levels of correlation between the GAC and the WISC–IV scores. Out of the three adaptive domains, the Conceptual Domain generally correlated most highly with the WISC–IV FSIQ. Correlations generally were in the .40s and .50s, suggesting that adaptive skills as measured by the ABAS–II, and intelligence as measured by the WISC–IV, are related but certainly distinct. As in WPPSI–III and WISC–III studies, teacher ratings correlated more highly with the WISC–IV scores than did parent ratings.

Correlations With the Wechsler Adult Intelligence Scale–Third Edition

Relationships between the ABAS–II and the WAIS–III were evaluated with a nonclinical sample of 37 adults ages 16–71 years, with a mean age of 33 years. The sample had the following composition: 70% female and 30% male; 91% White, 3% African American, 3% Hispanic, and 3% of other racial/ethnic origin. The sample was administered the WAIS–III and asked to rate themselves using the Adult Form. The mean scores and correlations between the measures are reported in Table 5.32.

Table 5.32   Correlation Between the ABAS–II and the WAIS–III

Adult Form, Self Report (n = 37)	WAIS–III Scores			ABAS–II	
(Non-Clinical Sample)	VIQ	PIQ	FSIQ	Mean	SD
ABAS–II					
Communication	.41	.41	.45	11.9	2.0
Community Use	.45	.38	.46	11.7	2.4
Functional Academics	.38	.45	.46	11.9	2.3
Home Living	.36	.39	.41	11.4	2.3
Health and Safety	.19	.28	.24	11.5	1.7
Leisure	.45	.31	.43	11.1	2.5
Self-Care	.63	.52	.65	11.2	1.5
Self-Direction	.45	.38	.47	11.4	2.2
Social	.59	.60	.63	11.6	1.7
Work[a]	.49	.11	.38	12.3	1.1
Conceptual Domain	.46	.41	.48	109.8	11.6
Social Domain	.54	.44	.54	106.7	11.0
Practical Domain (Without Work)	.47	.35	.47	108.4	11.3
Practical Domain (With Work)[a]	.57	.33	.52	109.6	10.2
GAC (Without Work)	.55	.50	.58	108.5	10.3
GAC (With Work)[a]	.72	.50	.67	109.4	9.0
WAIS–III					
Mean	111.4	110.6	111.4		
SD	11.9	10.6	11.0		

Note. **VIQ** = Verbal IQ; **PIQ** = Performance IQ; **FSIQ** = Full Scale IQ.

[a]Based on 34 observations.

The mean GAC was 109 and the mean WAIS–III FSIQ was 111. The GAC correlated .67 with the WAIS–III FSIQ. The WAIS–III VIQ and PIQ correlated .72 and .50, respectively, with the GAC. Correlations between the WAIS–III FSIQ and the adaptive domains generally were in the .40s and .50s. Correlations between the WAIS–III FSIQ and the skill areas generally were in the .40s.

Correlations With the Wechsler Abbreviated Scale of Intelligence

Relationships between the ABAS–II and the WASI were evaluated with a sample of 72 individuals ages 7–21 years, with a mean age of 12 years, with no reported disabilities. The sample had the following composition: 51% female and 49% male; 75% White, 17% African American, 3% Hispanic, and 5% of other racial/ethnic origin. The sample was administered the WASI and rated using the Parent Form. The mean scores and correlations between the measures are reported in Table 5.33.

Table 5.33   Correlation Between the ABAS–II and the WASI

Parent Form (*n* = 72) (Non-Clinical Sample)	WASI Scores				ABAS–II	
	VIQ	**PIQ**	**FSIQ (2 Subtests)**	**FSIQ (4 Subtests)**	**Mean**	**SD**
ABAS–II						
Communication	.39	.40	.40	.44	10.0	2.4
Community Use	.32	.34	.31	.36	10.6	2.6
Functional Academics	.29	.40	.36	.38	10.4	2.7
Home Living	.13	.16	.21	.15	9.8	3.3
Health and Safety	.33	.39	.35	.39	10.3	2.9
Leisure	.33	.40	.35	.40	10.0	2.8
Self-Care	.23	.34	.30	.31	10.3	2.8
Self-Direction	.22	.39	.29	.34	9.7	3.3
Social	.31	.42	.38	.41	9.4	3.4
GAC	.32	.43	.39	.42	100.4	15.1
WASI						
Mean	99.0	99.5	98.7	99.4		
SD	10.6	11.5	11.4	10.9		

Note. Adaptive Domain correlations not available for WASI data.

Note. **VIQ** = Verbal IQ; **PIQ** = Performance IQ; **FSIQ** = Full Scale IQ.

Mean scores were 99 for the WASI 4-subtest FSIQ and 100 for the GAC. The GAC correlated .42 with the WASI 4-subtest FSIQ, and correlated .32, .43, and .39 with the WASI VIQ, PIQ, and 2-subtest FSIQ, respectively. These results suggest a moderate relationship between the ABAS–II and the WASI.

Correlations With The Stanford Binet Intelligence Scale–Fourth Edition

Correlations between the ABAS–II and the SB–IV were evaluated with a mixed clinical sample of 19 individuals who had diagnoses of Autistic Disorder (15%) and mental retardation (85%). The sample ranged in age from 6–21 years, with a mean age of 11 years, and had the following composition: 42% female and 58% male; 68% White, 21% African American, and 11% Hispanic. The sample was administered the SB–IV and rated using the Teacher Form. The mean scores and correlations between the two measures are reported in Table 5.34.

As expected, the performance of the sample on both measures is low. Mean scores were 51 on the SB–IV Standard Age Score (SAS) and 61 on the GAC. The correlation between the GAC and the SB–IV SAS is .39. The Social Domain showed the highest correlation (.73) with the SB–IV SAS. This pattern of correlation was to be expected with this sample because it consisted primarily of individuals with mental retardation whose scores on the Conceptual Domain were significantly more restricted than their scores on the Social Domain.

Table 5.34   Correlation Between the ABAS–II and the SB–IV

Teacher Form (*n* = 19) (Clinical Sample)	SB–IV Composite SAS	ABAS–II Mean	SD
ABAS–II			
Communication	.43	2.7	2.3
Community Use	.34	2.7	3.0
Functional Academics	.48	2.3	2.3
School Living	.40	5.0	3.9
Health and Safety	.31	4.0	3.5
Leisure	.67	4.9	3.3
Self-Care	.10	4.1	3.7
Self-Direction	.34	3.6	3.0
Social	.56	4.4	3.3
Conceptual Domain	.44	62.4	15.0
Social Domain	.73	73.4	15.1
Practical Domain	.34	64.0	19.9
GAC	.39	61.2	18.1
SB–IV			
Mean	50.8		
SD	*12.3*		

Note. **SAS** = Standard Age Score.

Correlations With the Wechsler Individual Achievement Test

Correlations between the ABAS–II and the WIAT were examined with a mixed clinical sample of 44 children diagnosed with mental retardation (68%), learning disabilities (18%), ADHD (9%), and speech/language impairments (5%), ages 7–15 years, with a mean age of 13 years. The sample had the following composition: 32% female and 68% male; 86% White, 9% African American, and 5% of other racial/ethnic origin. The sample was administered the WIAT and rated using the Teacher Form. The mean scores and correlations between the measures are reported in Table 5.35.

Table 5.35   Correlation Between the ABAS–II and the WIAT

Teacher Form (*n* = 44) (Clinical Sample)	WIAT Scores Basic Reading	Math Reasoning	Reading Comprehension[a]	Numerical Operations[b]	ABAS–II Mean	SD
ABAS–II						
Communication	.51	.60	.55	.63	4.6	4.1
Community Use[a]	.53	.58	.53	.63	4.8	3.7
Functional Academics	.45	.60	.56	.70	5.0	4.2
School Living	.40	.54	.45	.65	5.3	3.9
Health and Safety[a]	.35	.48	.48	.49	4.7	3.9
Leisure	.52	.63	.62	.72	6.7	3.5
Self-Care	.44	.48	.39	.52	4.9	4.3
Self-Direction	.34	.47	.39	.56	5.3	4.0
Social	.41	.52	.45	.58	6.2	4.2
Conceptual Domain	.41	.54	.49	.67	75.2	24.1
Social Domain	.44	.57	.53	.68	83.8	21.1
Practical Domain[a]	.39	.53	.44	.67	74.1	21.5
GAC[a]	.39	.52	.46	.63	71.4	24.1
WIAT						
Mean	74.6	74.0	76.1	73.0		
SD	16.2	13.3	15.2	15.7		

[a]Based on 43 observations.

[b]Based on 40 observations.

Complete WIAT data were available on four composites: Basic Reading ($n = 44$), Reading Comprehension ($n = 43$), Numerical Operations ($n = 40$), and Math Reasoning ($n = 44$). Correlations between the GAC and the four WIAT composites follow: Numerical Operations .63; Math Reasoning, .52; Reading Comprehension .46; and Basic Reading .39. The Conceptual, Social, and Practical Adaptive Domains correlated most highly with Numerical Operations (.67, .68, and .67 respectively). Overall correlations between the ABAS–II and the WIAT are moderate for this mixed clinical sample.

Summary of Comparison Studies

Evidence of convergent validity is found in relationships between the ABAS–II and the VABS, which are both comprehensive measures of adaptive behavior. In contrast with its generally high correlations with the VABS, the ABAS–II displays lower correlations with brief behavior rating scales (generally in the .50s and lower), measures of problem behavior (ranging from the –.30s to the –.60s), measures of intelligence (generally in the .40s and .50s.), and measures of achievement (generally in the .60s).

Clinical Validity Studies

In addition to correlations with other measures, important evidence of the convergent and discriminant validity of the ABAS–II is found in its ability to distinguish between individuals with and without disabilities. The ABAS–II is designed to be used in diagnostic assessment, intervention planning and treatment programs for individuals with various disabilities and mental and physical disorders. Data were collected for individuals diagnosed with biological risk factors, motor impairments, language disorders, developmental delays, pervasive developmental disorders, mental retardation, Attention-Deficit/Hyperactivity Disorder, behavior disorders, emotional disturbances, hearing impairments, physical impairments, learning disabilities, Alzheimer's disease, and neuropsychological disorders. For each of the clinical samples a matched control group was selected from the related standardization sample. Each member of the control group was matched with one member of the clinical group in reference to the following demographic variables: age, sex, education (parent or self), race/ethnicity, and geographic region. Mean scores of clinical samples were compared to mean scores of their matched control group; a conservative alpha level of .01 was used to identify significant differences between clinical samples and control groups.

Independent researchers collected data, and potential participants were drawn from a variety of clinical settings. However, it is important to note the limitations of these studies. The samples were not randomly selected but were selected by convenience. Therefore, these samples may not be statistically representative. Because data in each clinical sample were collected in a variety of clinical settings, the diagnoses of different cases might be made on the basis of different criteria and procedures. The sample sizes for some studies were relatively small. Only group performance was reported. For these reasons the performance data from these samples are presented as examples and are not intended to be definitive representations of the diagnostic groups. The purpose of these clinical studies is to demonstrate that the ABAS–II can provide a valid assessment of adaptive skills for individuals in these special groups. All clinical validity tables summarize the performance of the clinical groups and matched control groups. These tables provide means and *SD*s of both groups, difference scores between the two groups, *t* values, *p* values, Cohen's *d*, and percentages of the sample that obtained various scores equal to or less than 2 *SD*s below the mean. The demographic data for the clinical samples are reported in Tables 5.36–5.38.

Table 5.36 Demographic Data of the Clinical Samples: Teacher/Daycare Provider and Parent/Primary Caregiver Forms

▶ **Teacher/Daycare Provider Form**

	Mild Mental Retardation	Moderate Mental Retardation	Developmental Delay	Biological Risk Factors	Motor Impairments	Language Disorders	PDD-NOS	Autistic Disorder
n	31	19	48	22	32	52	19	35
Age								
Mean	53.7	53.1	52.6	32.5	50.0	52.4	50.8	53.4
SD	10.7	13.7	10.5	2.6	12.3	11.8	10.8	10.5
Sex								
Female	32.3	52.6	31.3	54.6	21.9	32.7	15.8	8.6
Male	67.7	47.4	68.8	45.5	78.1	67.3	84.2	91.4
Race/Ethnicity								
White	64.5	52.6	79.2	68.2	65.6	73.1	79.0	85.7
African American	19.4	26.3	12.5	13.6	21.9	19.2	5.3	2.9
Hispanic	16.1	21.1	4.2	18.2	12.5	7.7	10.5	8.6
Other	–	–	4.2	–	–	–	5.3	2.9
Education								
≤8	3.2	–	–	–	–	1.9	–	–
9–11	9.7	15.8	4.2	4.6	3.1	9.6	–	–
12	35.5	42.1	33.3	13.6	37.5	28.9	10.5	31.4
13–15	32.3	15.8	47.9	36.4	34.4	25.0	42.1	25.7
≥16	19.4	26.3	14.6	45.5	25.0	34.6	47.4	42.9

▶ **Parent/Primary Caregiver Form**

	Mild Mental Retardation	Moderate Mental Retardation	Developmental Delay	Biological Risk Factors	Motor Impairments	Language Disorders	PDD-NOS	Autistic Disorder
n	27	22	78	57	50	52	18	34
Age								
Mean	53.9	52.6	47.4	20.3	35.1	51.8	49.0	54.4
SD	11.7	13.3	17.2	9.7	17.2	12.5	10.3	11.0
Sex								
Female	29.6	50.0	37.2	57.9	42.0	30.8	11.1	8.8
Male	70.4	50.0	62.8	42.1	58.0	69.2	88.9	91.2
Race/Ethnicity								
White	74.1	59.1	79.5	80.7	78.0	76.9	83.3	88.2
African American	11.1	18.2	12.8	15.8	12.0	19.2	–	–
Hispanic	14.8	18.2	5.1	1.8	8.0	3.9	11.1	8.8
Other	–	4.6	2.6	1.8	2.0	–	5.6	2.9
Education								
≤8	–	–	1.3	–	–	–	–	–
9–11	7.4	9.1	5.1	1.8	4.0	9.6	–	2.9
12	40.7	45.5	38.5	24.6	26.0	25.0	11.1	26.5
13–15	29.6	22.7	32.1	36.8	36.0	26.9	44.4	23.5
≥16	22.2	22.7	23.1	36.8	34.0	38.5	44.4	47.1

Note. Except for sample size (*n*) and age, data are reported as percentages. Sums of percentages in each category may not equal 100% due to rounding. Means and standard deviations of age are reported in months.

Table 5.37   Demographic Data of the Clinical Samples: Teacher Form

| | Mental Retardation Groups | | | | | | | | | | |
	Down Syndrome	Mental Retardation Unspecified	Mild Mental Retardation	Moderate Mental Retardation	ADHD	Behavior Disorder	Emotional Disturbance	Deaf and Hard of Hearing	Physical Impairment	Learning Disability	Autistic Disorder
n	21	84	66	27	30	56	73	19	52	248	32
Age											
Mean	11.3	11.8	10.9	13.9	10.0	13.6	11.3	11.0	10.9	11.6	9.8
SD	4.2	3.9	3.1	5.1	3.1	3.3	3.2	3.9	4.7	3.3	4.1
Sex											
Female	43.5	40.4	38.2	39.3	16.4	30.4	35.6	52.6	42.3	40.3	21.9
Male	56.5	59.6	61.8	60.7	83.6	69.6	64.4	47.4	57.7	59.7	78.1
Race/Ethnicity											
White	65.2	61.7	60.5	32.1	65.6	82.1	58.9	63.2	55.8	55.2	81.3
African American	8.7	6.4	13.2	3.6	14.8	7.1	8.2	5.3	7.7	11.3	6.3
Hispanic	17.4	20.2	18.4	57.1	14.8	8.9	27.4	15.8	15.4	22.2	6.3
Other	8.7	11.7	7.9	7.1	4.9	1.8	5.5	15.8	21.2	11.3	6.3
Education											
≤8	8.7	18.1	14.5	7.1	9.8	1.8	6.9	15.8	5.8	9.3	–
9–11	8.7	11.7	21.1	14.3	14.8	17.9	21.9	15.8	11.5	17.3	44.3
12	17.4	54.3	50.0	57.1	44.3	57.1	53.4	31.6	44.2	49.6	46.9
13–15	26.1	5.3	5.3	14.3	13.1	7.1	11.0	10.5	7.7	14.9	15.6
≥16	39.1	10.6	9.2	7.1	18.0	16.1	6.9	26.3	30.8	8.9	31.3

Note. Except for sample size (*n*) and age, data are reported as percentages. Sums of percentages in each category may not equal 100% due to rounding.

Table 5.38 Demographic Data of the Clinical Samples: Parent and Adult Forms

	Parent Form			Adult Form, Rated by Others			Adult Form, Self Report
	Mental Retardation Unspecified	ADHD	Learning Disability	Mental Retardation Unspecified	Alzheimer's Disease	Neuropsychological Disorders	Neuropsychological Disorders
n	41	49	26	30	25	20	18
Age							
Mean	11.2	11.9	13.3	37.3	77.2	62.8	45.2
SD	4.5	3.7	4.4	17.5	8.8	20.1	21.0
Sex							
Female	43.9	24.5	26.9	46.7	52.0	35.0	55.6
Male	56.1	75.5	73.1	53.3	48.0	65.0	44.4
Race/Ethnicity							
White	34.2	87.8	65.4	80.0	84.0	90.0	83.3
African American	7.3	4.1	3.9	6.7	4.0	–	11.1
Hispanic	53.7	6.1	19.2	13.3	12.0	10.0	–
Other	4.9	2.0	11.5	–	–	–	5.6
Education							
≤8	17.1	2.0	3.9	33.3	20.0	15.0	–
9–11	4.9	4.1	19.2	13.3	8.0	5.0	5.6
12	34.2	30.6	26.9	33.3	40.0	55.0	55.6
13–15	12.2	22.5	26.9	–	12.0	15.0	22.2
≥16	31.7	40.8	23.1	20.0	20.0	10.0	16.7

Note. Except for sample size (*n*) and age, data are reported as percentages. Sums of percentages in each category may not equal 100% due to rounding.

Individuals With Mental Retardation

According to the AAMR (2002b), the *DSM–IV–TR,* and the IDEA (1999), mental retardation is defined by deficits in both intelligence and adaptive behavior. The diagnosis and classification of mental retardation is an important use of a comprehensive measure of adaptive behavior such as the ABAS–II. Therefore, the performance on the ABAS–II of individuals diagnosed with mental retardation provides important evidence of the measure's validity. Means and standard deviation for the GAC, adaptive domains and skill areas, and the percentage in the samples that scored at least two *SD*s below the mean are reported to provide an indication of performance of the samples across all areas. It was expected that most individuals diagnosed with mental retardation would score significantly below the mean in most skill areas, on one or more adaptive domains, and on the GAC. AAMR (2002b, 1992) recognizes that individuals diagnosed with mental retardation can exhibit strengths as well as weaknesses in adaptive functioning. It was therefore anticipated that the samples would exhibit varying scores in different domains and skill areas, and that not all individuals in the samples would score at least 2 *SD*s below the mean on the GAC or on all domains and skill areas.

In addition to means, standard deviations, and percentages of the sample that scored two or more *SD*s below the normative mean on each skill area scaled score, adaptive domain composite score, and the GAC, the tables for clinical validity studies also provide percentages of each sample that correspond to criteria regarding adaptive behavior deficits specified by AAMR (2002b), *DSM–IV–TR,* and IDEA (1999). AAMR (2002b) specifies that adaptive behavior deficits required for a diagnosis of mental retardation are defined by a score at least two *SD*s below the mean on one or more adaptive domains or on an overall score such as the GAC. *DSM–IV–TR* specifies that deficits in at least two adaptive skill areas are necessary for a diagnosis of mental retardation. IDEA (1999) simply specifies deficits in adaptive behavior for a classification of mental retardation. Thus, the following data are reported for each of the clinical validity samples:

- Percentage of the sample obtaining a composite score that is at least two *SD*s below the mean in one or more of the adaptive domains.

- Percentage of the sample obtaining a composite score that is at least two *SD*s below the mean in one or more of the adaptive domains or in the GAC.
- Percentage of the sample obtaining scaled scores that are at least two *SD*s below the mean in two or more skill areas.

The clinical validity tables report the above data based on the definition of a deficit as a score that is at least two *SD*s below the mean. AAMR (2002b) uses a similar definition for a deficit, but *DSM–IV–TR*, and IDEA do not include a specific cut score for adaptive behavior deficits in their definitions for mental retardation. Thus, it was expected that most, but not all, individuals in the samples diagnosed with mental retardation would exhibit deficits of this magnitude on the GAC, at least one of three adaptive domains *or* the GAC, or on at least two skill areas.

The performance of individuals with mental retardation and matched control groups is reported in Table 5.39 by rating forms and groups. 10 groups of individuals with mental retardation were rated. Two groups rated on the Teacher/Daycare Provider Form were composed of children with mild ($n = 31$) and moderate ($n = 19$) mental retardation; Two groups rated on the Parent/Primary Caregiver Form were composed of children with mild ($n = 23$) and moderate ($n = 22$) mental retardation; Four groups rated on the Teacher Form included individuals with Down Syndrome ($n = 21$), mental retardation unspecified ($n = 84$), mild mental retardation ($n = 66$), and moderate mental retardation ($n = 27$). The Parent Form ($n = 41$) and Adult Form, Rated by Others ($n = 30$) each had one group of individuals whose level of mental retardation was unspecified.

The results across the four infant-preschool samples of children diagnosed with mental retardation are very consistent. The mean GAC scores of the clinical samples with mental retardation ranged from 63–67, which was significantly lower than those of the matched control groups, which ranged from 98–101 points. The mean scores of the adaptive domains for children with mental retardation ranged from 63–71 points, and were also significantly lower than those of the control group, which ranged from 97–104. The mean scaled scores for the skill areas were very low and much lower than those of the control group. Furthermore, 58% –73% of the samples of individuals diagnosed with mental retardation scored at least two *SD*s below the mean on the GAC. Of the four samples, 77%–86% scored at least two *SD*s below the mean on one or more adaptive domains or the GAC, and 84%–94% scored at least two *SD*s below the mean on at least two of the skill areas. For the matched control groups, the percentages scoring at least two *SD*s below the mean on the GAC were 0%–5%, the percentages scoring at least two *SD*s below the mean on one or more adaptive domains or the GAC were 3%–19%, and the percentages scoring at least two *SD*s below the mean on at least two of the skill areas were 10%–30%.

Among the adaptive domains, individuals with mental retardation displayed the greatest deficits in the Conceptual Domain, although all three domains showed significantly low scores. Infant-preschool samples of children with mental retardation showed significant deficits in all skill areas when compared to matched controls.

The results across the five school-age samples and one adult sample of individuals diagnosed with mental retardation were also very consistent. The mean GAC scores of the clinical samples with mental retardation ranged from 56–73, which was significantly lower than those of the matched control groups, which ranged from 93–101. The mean scores of the adaptive domains ranged from 56–82, and were significantly lower than those of the control groups. The mean scaled scores for the skill areas were very low and much lower than those of the control groups. Furthermore, 50%–87% of the samples of individuals diagnosed with mental retardation scored at least two *SD*s below the mean on the GAC. Of the six samples, 62%–100% scored at least two *SD*s below the mean on one or more adaptive domains or the GAC, and 76%–100% scored at least two *SD*s below the mean on two or more skill areas. For the matched control groups, the percentages scoring at least two *SD*s below the mean on the GAC were 0%–17%, the percentages scoring at least two *SD*s below the mean on one or more adaptive domains or the GAC were 5%–19%, and the percentages scoring at least two *SD*s below the mean on two or more skill areas were 5%–32%. In addition, significant differences were displayed between the mean GAC scores of the mild and moderate mental retardation samples, indicating that the ABAS–II has good specificity in differentiating school-age and older individuals who display different levels of mental retardation.

Table 5.39 Mean Performance of Individuals With Mental Retardation and Matched Control Groups

Teacher/Daycare Provider Form

Ages 2:6–5:10 (n = 31)	Individuals With Mild Mental Retardation			Matched Control Group			Mean Difference of the Two Samples			
	Mean	SD	% of Scores – 2 SD	Mean	SD	% of Scores – 2 SD	Difference	t value	p value	Cohen's d
Communication	4.0	2.1	58.06	10.9	2.6	.00	6.94	10.88	<.01	2.94
Functional Pre-Academics	4.6	2.7	64.52	9.6	2.8	6.45	5.03	7.18	<.01	1.83
School Living	6.2	3.0	25.81	10.0	2.5	.00	3.84	5.53	<.01	1.39
Health and Safety	5.0	2.8	41.94	10.4	2.7	.00	5.39	8.10	<.01	1.96
Leisure	5.6	2.0	22.58	10.7	2.8	.00	5.13	8.01	<.01	2.11
Self-Care	5.4	2.7	41.94	9.6	2.8	3.23	4.23	6.15	<.01	1.54
Self-Direction	6.0	2.6	25.81	10.8	2.8	.00	4.74	6.63	<.01	1.75
Social	4.7	2.9	48.39	11.0	2.6	.00	6.23	8.64	<.01	2.26
Motor	5.0	2.4	48.39	10.2	2.8	.00	5.19	8.14	<.01	1.99
Conceptual Domain	67.3	12.1	64.52	101.2	13.5	.00	33.90	10.04	<.01	2.64
Social Domain	71.1	13.1	58.06	103.7	13.6	.00	32.58	9.61	<.01	2.44
Practical Domain	70.5	16.5	51.61	98.7	12.8	3.23	28.26	7.77	<.01	1.91
GAC	67.1	13.4	58.06	100.8	13.4	.00	33.71	10.01	<.01	2.52
Cases with ≥ 2 skill areas – 2SD			93.55			9.68				
Cases with ≥ 1 adaptive domain – 2SD			77.42			3.23				
Cases with ≥ 1 adaptive domain or the GAC – 2SD			77.42			3.23				

Ages 2:7–5:11 (n = 19)	Individuals With Moderate Mental Retardation			Matched Control Group			Mean Difference of the Two Samples			
	Mean	SD	% of Scores – 2 SD	Mean	SD	% of Scores – 2 SD	Difference	t value	p value	Cohen's d
Communication	3.5	2.2	68.42	9.6	3.3	5.26	6.05	5.84	<.01	2.16
Functional Pre-Academics	4.4	3.1	57.89	10.5	2.9	5.26	6.11	6.82	<.01	2.04
School Living	5.4	3.3	47.37	10.0	2.9	.00	4.58	3.77	<.01	1.47
Health and Safety	4.6	2.4	52.63	10.8	2.8	.00	6.21	6.03	<.01	2.38
Leisure	4.5	2.5	52.63	9.4	2.5	.00	4.84	5.49	<.01	1.94
Self-Care	5.5	2.6	42.11	10.3	2.6	.00	4.84	5.07	<.01	1.86
Self-Direction	5.8	3.0	26.32	10.2	2.5	.00	4.32	4.37	<.01	1.56
Social	4.6	2.7	47.37	10.1	2.4	.00	5.47	6.22	<.01	2.14
Motor	5.2	2.9	42.11	9.7	3.5	5.26	4.58	4.79	<.01	1.43
Conceptual Domain	65.8	14.7	73.68	99.0	14.9	5.26	33.16	6.28	<.01	2.24
Social Domain	67.7	13.3	63.16	97.7	12.7	.00	29.95	6.54	<.01	2.30
Practical Domain	68.4	17.1	68.42	101.5	10.1	.00	33.11	6.08	<.01	2.36
GAC	64.6	15.2	63.16	98.9	13.2	.00	34.26	6.49	<.01	2.41
Cases with ≥ 2 skill areas – 2SD			84.21			10.53				
Cases with ≥ 1 adaptive domain – 2SD			84.21			5.26				
Cases with ≥ 1 adaptive domain or the GAC – 2SD			84.21			5.26				

Note. – 2 SD = 2 or more SDs below the mean.

Table 5.39 Mean Performance of Individuals With Mental Retardation and Matched Control Groups (continued)

▲ **Parent/Primary Caregiver Form**

Ages 2:6–5:10 (n =27)	Individuals With Mild Mental Retardation			Matched Control Group			Mean Difference of the Two Samples			
	Mean	SD	% of Scores – 2 SD	Mean	SD	% of Scores – 2 SD	Difference	t value	p value	Cohen's d
Communication	4.8	2.6	47.83	11.0	3.3	0.00	6.22	9.52	<.01	2.09
Community Use	4.7	2.9	65.22	10.4	2.4	0.00	5.70	8.06	<.01	2.14
Functional Pre-Academics	5.1	2.8	39.13	10.0	2.3	4.35	4.87	6.43	<.01	1.90
Home Living	6.7	2.9	21.74	9.4	2.7	4.35	2.65	3.46	<.01	.95
Health and Safety	5.3	2.6	34.78	10.0	3.1	4.35	4.70	5.74	<.01	1.64
Leisure	4.8	2.6	39.13	10.4	3.5	7.41	5.87	8.15	<.01	1.90
Self-Care	6.2	3.6	30.43	10.6	2.4	0.00	4.43	5.51	<.01	1.45
Self-Direction	6.0	2.6	30.43	9.7	3.4	0.00	3.78	4.80	<.01	1.25
Social	5.9	3.0	39.13	10.4	3.1	0.00	4.43	5.11	<.01	1.45
Motor	5.2	3.1	34.78	10.8	2.9	0.00	5.61	7.96	<.01	1.87
Conceptual Domain	68.0	12.8	69.57	99.7	16.5	0.00	31.78	8.77	<.01	2.15
Social Domain	70.5	12.0	52.17	101.4	17.2	4.35	30.96	8.22	<.01	2.09
Practical Domain	70.9	15.4	43.48	99.0	13.9	0.00	28.17	7.74	<.01	1.92
GAC	66.0	13.2	69.57	100.3	15.9	0.00	34.26	9.80	<.01	2.34
Cases with ≥ 2 skill areas – 2SD			92.59			29.63				
Cases with ≥ 1 adaptive domain – 2SD			77.78			18.52				
Cases with ≥ 1 adaptive domain or the GAC – 2SD			77.78			18.52				

Ages 2:6–5:11 (n =22)	Individuals With Moderate Mental Retardation			Matched Control Group			Mean Difference of the Two Samples			
	Mean	SD	% of Scores – 2 SD	Mean	SD	% of Scores – 2 SD	Difference	t value	p value	Cohen's d
Communication	2.7	1.6	81.82	9.6	2.9	9.09	6.91	10.16	<.01	2.95
Community Use	4.1	2.5	68.18	10.2	2.3	0.00	6.05	8.30	<.01	2.52
Functional Pre-Academics	4.2	2.8	68.18	9.8	2.5	0.00	5.59	7.32	<.01	2.11
Home Living	6.6	4.5	36.36	9.6	2.7	0.00	3.09	2.74	.01	.83
Health and Safety	4.4	3.4	59.09	10.0	2.8	0.00	5.64	6.48	<.01	1.81
Leisure	5.1	3.4	45.45	9.6	2.8	0.00	4.50	5.61	<.01	1.44
Self-Care	5.5	2.9	40.91	9.4	3.6	9.09	3.86	3.80	<.01	1.18
Self-Direction	5.8	3.1	45.45	10.4	2.6	0.00	4.59	5.05	<.01	1.60
Social	4.6	3.1	54.55	9.9	2.9	4.55	5.32	6.02	<.01	1.77
Motor	5.1	3.4	45.45	10.2	2.8	4.55	5.18	6.03	<.01	1.66
Conceptual Domain	62.5	13.0	72.73	98.0	14.2	4.55	35.55	8.84	<.01	2.61
Social Domain	68.5	18.0	54.55	97.2	15.1	4.55	28.68	6.37	<.01	1.73
Practical Domain	67.7	17.8	59.09	97.4	14.3	4.55	29.68	5.80	<.01	1.84
GAC	62.8	16.4	72.73	97.6	14.1	4.55	34.77	7.70	<.01	2.27
Cases with ≥ 2 skill areas – 2SD			90.91			13.64				
Cases with ≥ 1 adaptive domain – 2SD			86.36			4.55				
Cases with ≥ 1 adaptive domain or the GAC – 2SD			86.36			4.55				

Note. – 2 SD = 2 or more SDs below the mean.

Table 5.39 Mean Performance of Individuals With Mental Retardation and Matched Control Groups *(continued)*

Teacher Form

Ages 5–21 (n =21)	Individuals With Down Syndrome			Matched Control Group			Mean Difference of the Two Samples			
	Mean	SD	% of Scores – 2 SD	Mean	SD	% of Scores – 2 SD	Difference	t value	p value	Cohen's d
Communication	1.9	1.7	90.48	8.3	3.4	23.81	6.43	7.72	<.01	2.39
Community Use	2.1	2.3	85.71	8.5	3.0	14.29	6.38	7.69	<.01	2.39
Functional Academics	1.7	1.4	95.24	9.0	3.6	14.29	7.33	7.85	<.01	2.68
School Living	3.9	3.4	66.67	9.0	3.2	14.29	5.10	4.82	<.01	1.54
Health and Safety	2.4	2.0	85.71	8.7	3.8	19.05	6.29	6.92	<.01	2.07
Leisure	4.1	2.9	61.90	8.8	3.0	9.52	4.76	5.77	<.01	1.61
Self-Care	2.6	3.1	85.71	9.5	3.2	9.52	6.90	7.70	<.01	2.19
Self-Direction	2.9	2.7	85.71	8.5	3.3	23.81	5.57	7.07	<.01	1.85
Social	4.1	2.8	52.38	9.4	3.1	14.29	5.33	5.87	<.01	1.80
Conceptual Domain	57.8	9.6	90.48	96.8	17.7	9.52	39.00	9.34	<.01	2.74
Social Domain	70.4	13.2	52.38	96.8	16.0	9.52	26.33	6.22	<.01	1.80
Practical Domain	56.4	17.0	80.95	96.3	15.7	9.52	39.86	7.82	<.01	2.44
GAC	56.1	14.9	80.95	96.6	16.5	4.76	40.57	8.55	<.01	2.58
Cases with ≥ 2 skill areas – 2SD			100.00			28.57				
Cases with ≥ 1 adaptive domain – 2SD			90.48			19.05				
Cases with ≥ 1 adaptive domain or the GAC – 2SD			90.48			19.05				

Ages 5–21 (n =84)	Individuals With Mental Retardation (Unspecified)			Matched Control Group			Mean Difference of the Two Samples			
	Mean	SD	% of Scores – 2 SD	Mean	SD	% of Scores – 2 SD	Difference	t value	p value	Cohen's d
Communication	2.5	2.1	86.90	9.0	3.2	15.48	6.55	16.58	<.01	2.42
Community Use	2.5	2.0	85.71	9.4	2.6	10.71	6.92	20.86	<.01	2.98
Functional Academics	2.1	1.8	90.48	9.5	2.8	7.14	7.36	20.39	<.01	3.13
School Living	5.1	3.7	54.76	9.9	2.8	8.33	4.80	10.77	<.01	1.46
Health and Safety	3.9	3.1	71.43	9.7	2.8	8.33	5.81	13.29	<.01	1.97
Leisure	4.7	2.9	55.95	10.2	2.6	3.57	5.49	13.35	<.01	1.99
Self-Care	4.6	3.8	64.29	9.8	2.9	11.90	5.20	10.48	<.01	1.54
Self-Direction	3.6	2.9	70.24	9.1	2.9	11.90	5.50	12.78	<.01	1.90
Social	4.7	3.3	59.52	10.0	2.8	9.52	5.25	11.37	<.01	1.72
Conceptual Domain	61.8	11.3	83.33	100.1	14.8	7.14	38.29	20.20	<.01	2.91
Social Domain	73.7	14.3	53.57	102.7	14.7	4.76	28.98	13.17	<.01	2.00
Practical Domain	65.4	16.7	64.29	101.4	15.4	5.95	35.99	16.16	<.01	2.24
GAC	61.9	15.1	70.24	101.3	15.7	7.14	39.43	18.23	<.01	2.56
Cases with ≥ 2 skill areas – 2SD			97.62			20.24				
Cases with ≥ 1 adaptive domain – 2SD			90.48			9.52				
Cases with ≥ 1 adaptive domain or the GAC – 2SD			90.48			9.52				

Note. –2 SD = 2 or more SDs below the mean.

Table 5.39 Mean Performance of Individuals With Mental Retardation and Matched Control Groups *(continued)*

Teacher Form

Ages 5–21 (*n* =66)	Individuals With Mild Mental Retardation			Matched Control Group			Mean Difference of the Two Samples			
	Mean	SD	% of Scores – 2 SD	Mean	SD	% of Scores – 2 SD	Difference	t value	p value	Cohen's d
Communication	4.1	3.2	65.15	8.2	3.9	28.79	4.17	6.07	<.01	1.17
Community Use	4.4	3.0	63.64	8.6	3.4	18.18	4.21	7.27	<.01	1.31
Functional Academics	3.5	2.4	75.76	9.0	3.1	9.09	5.50	11.35	<.01	1.98
School Living	6.5	3.7	40.91	9.3	3.6	16.67	2.82	4.42	<.01	.77
Health and Safety	6.3	3.4	37.88	8.6	3.7	24.24	2.32	3.57	<.01	.65
Leisure	6.4	2.9	28.79	9.3	3.3	15.15	2.89	4.91	<.01	.93
Self-Care	5.6	4.2	51.52	9.4	3.3	13.64	3.74	5.73	<.01	.99
Self-Direction	5.3	3.8	54.55	8.4	3.6	22.73	3.14	4.93	<.01	.85
Social	6.3	3.3	40.91	8.9	3.6	16.67	2.68	4.41	<.01	.78
Conceptual Domain	72.1	15.9	54.55	96.9	17.7	10.61	24.82	8.15	<.01	1.48
Social Domain	81.6	13.6	30.30	97.2	18.2	12.12	15.52	5.27	<.01	.97
Practical Domain	76.5	19.2	43.94	96.8	18.8	13.64	20.29	5.87	<.01	1.07
GAC	72.9	17.6	50.00	96.6	20.1	13.64	23.64	6.79	<.01	1.25
Cases with ≥2 skill areas – 2SD			75.76			31.82				
Cases with ≥1 adaptive domain – 2SD			60.61			15.15				
Cases with ≥1 adaptive domain or the GAC – 2SD			62.12			15.15				

Ages 5–21 (*n* =27)	Individuals With Moderate Mental Retardation			Matched Control Group			Mean Difference of the Two Samples			
	Mean	SD	% of Scores – 2 SD	Mean	SD	% of Scores – 2 SD	Difference	t value	p value	Cohen's d
Communication	1.6	0.8	100.00	8.6	3.4	14.81	7.07	9.88	<.01	2.86
Community Use	2.0	1.7	92.59	8.6	3.0	14.81	6.56	9.28	<.01	2.69
Functional Academics	1.5	0.8	100.00	9.2	2.9	7.41	7.70	13.02	<.01	3.62
School Living	4.7	3.4	59.26	9.0	3.2	22.22	4.33	4.38	<.01	1.31
Health and Safety	3.8	3.3	66.67	9.3	2.7	14.81	5.48	6.09	<.01	1.82
Leisure	4.1	3.0	59.26	9.1	3.1	7.41	5.00	5.20	<.01	1.64
Self-Care	3.5	2.8	66.67	9.7	2.7	11.11	6.26	9.28	<.01	2.28
Self-Direction	3.6	3.2	74.07	8.9	3.3	22.22	5.30	6.57	<.01	1.63
Social	4.7	3.5	51.85	9.4	3.0	7.41	4.70	5.35	<.01	1.44
Conceptual Domain	57.6	7.5	96.30	99.0	17.3	11.11	41.33	11.00	<.01	3.10
Social Domain	72.0	13.3	48.15	98.3	16.5	3.70	26.33	5.73	<.01	1.76
Practical Domain	62.6	17.4	59.26	97.4	13.9	3.70	34.81	7.03	<.01	2.21
GAC	59.3	14.7	70.37	98.0	15.5	3.70	38.74	8.33	<.01	2.56
Cases with ≥2 skill areas – 2SD			100.00			29.63				
Cases with ≥1 adaptive domain – 2SD			96.30			14.81				
Cases with ≥1 adaptive domain or the GAC – 2SD			100.00			14.81				

Note. – 2 *SD* = 2 or more *SD*s below the mean.

Table 5.39 Mean Performance of Individuals With Mental Retardation and Matched Control Groups *(continued)*

Parent Form

Ages 5–21 (n =41)	Individuals With Mental Retardation (Unspecified)			Matched Control Group			Mean Difference of the Two Samples			
	Mean	SD	% of Scores – 2 SD	Mean	SD	% of Scores – 2 SD	Difference	t value	p value	Cohen's d
Communication	3.7	3.3	65.85	10.0	2.5	0.00	6.27	8.99	<.01	2.14
Community Use	4.1	3.4	65.85	9.7	2.5	2.44	5.56	8.29	<.01	1.86
Functional Academics	2.7	2.3	80.49	9.9	2.6	2.44	7.20	13.82	<.01	2.93
Home Living	5.5	4.3	51.22	9.3	3.8	14.63	3.76	4.43	<.01	.93
Health and Safety	4.2	3.6	60.98	9.6	2.7	4.88	5.44	7.89	<.01	1.71
Leisure	4.8	3.5	53.66	9.9	2.8	2.44	5.05	7.29	<.01	1.59
Self-Care	4.7	3.7	58.54	10.6	2.7	0.00	5.90	7.99	<.01	1.82
Self-Direction	4.3	3.4	60.98	10.1	2.8	2.44	5.73	8.08	<.01	1.84
Social	4.8	4.2	63.41	9.8	3.0	7.32	5.00	5.73	<.01	1.37
Conceptual Domain	64.2	15.9	73.17	100.4	12.6	0.00	36.22	11.13	<.01	2.52
Social Domain	73.9	17.9	63.41	99.6	14.2	4.88	25.73	6.73	<.01	1.59
Practical Domain	65.7	21.9	60.98	99.2	11.9	0.00	33.56	8.67	<.01	1.90
GAC	63.7	19.8	70.73	99.4	13.4	0.00	35.71	9.48	<.01	2.11
Cases with ≥ 2 skill areas – 2SD			82.93			4.88				
Cases with ≥ 1 adaptive domain – 2SD			80.49			4.88				
Cases with ≥ 1 adaptive domain or the GAC – 2SD			80.49			4.88				

Adult Form, Rated by Others

Ages 17–72 (n=30)	Individuals With Mental Retardation (Unspecified)			Matched Control Group			Mean Difference of the Two Samples			
	Mean	SD	% of Scores – 2 SD	Mean	SD	% of Scores – 2 SD	Difference	t value	p value	Cohen's d
Communication	3.9	2.9	70.00	9.4	3.4	6.67	5.53	7.13	<.01	1.75
Community Use	2.6	2.4	83.33	9.0	3.0	6.67	6.40	10.40	<.01	2.36
Functional Academics	2.2	1.9	80.00	9.0	3.6	13.33	6.80	10.33	<.01	2.36
Home Living	4.9	2.6	53.33	9.6	2.7	3.33	4.70	7.54	<.01	1.77
Health and Safety	2.7	2.5	86.67	9.5	3.3	13.33	6.87	10.93	<.01	2.35
Leisure	4.4	2.5	50.00	8.7	3.0	3.33	4.33	6.79	<.01	1.57
Self-Care	4.3	3.3	56.67	9.3	2.9	6.67	4.97	6.74	<.01	1.60
Self-Direction	3.3	2.4	73.33	9.4	2.9	0.00	6.03	11.23	<.01	2.27
Social	3.9	3.0	66.67	9.3	2.9	6.67	5.43	9.26	<.01	1.84
Conceptual Domain	61.5	12.9	76.67	95.0	16.0	10.00	33.50	10.91	<.01	2.31
Social Domain	69.7	12.7	66.67	93.7	14.5	3.33	23.97	8.42	<.01	1.76
Practical Domain (without Work)	61.7	15.3	66.67	94.5	14.3	6.67	32.77	10.71	<.01	2.21
GAC (without Work)	57.8	14.1	86.67	92.5	17.0	16.67	34.67	11.09	<.01	2.22
Cases with ≥ 2 skill areas – 2SD			86.67			16.67				
Cases with ≥ 1 adaptive domain – 2SD			80.00			13.33				
Cases with ≥ 1 adaptive domain or the GAC – 2SD			86.67			16.67				

Note. –2 SD = 2 or more SDs below the mean.

Among the adaptive domains, individuals with mental retardation showed the greatest deficits in Conceptual and Practical. Among the nine skill areas, the samples of individuals with mental retardation performed most poorly in Functional Academics and Communication. About 65%–100% of the samples with mental retardation scored at least two *SD*s below the mean on Functional Academics and Communication, while only 0%–29% of the matched control group did so.

In conclusion, the data indicate that all samples of individuals with mental retardation scored significantly lower on the ABAS–II than the matched control groups and demonstrated deficits in skill areas, adaptive domains, and overall adaptive functioning as described in the definitions of mental retardation by the AAMR (2002b), the *DSM–IV–TR*, and IDEA (1999).

Children Diagnosed With Developmental Delays

IDEA legislation identifies a child with a developmental delay as a child with a disability and establishes developmental delay as a special education eligibility category for infants, toddlers, and children ages 3–9 years. A child may be diagnosed and determined eligible for special education services in the category of developmental delay if he or she "is experiencing developmental delays, as defined by the State and as measured by appropriate diagnostic instruments and procedures, in one or more of the following areas: physical development, cognitive development, communication development, social or emotional development, or adaptive development." (IDEA, Final Regulations, 1999; Sec. 300.7). Some state regulations require identification of significant delays in at least two of the developmental areas mentioned above for a diagnosis of developmental delay. For children ages 3–9 years, IDEA allows states to determine if children may be classified as having a developmental delay or classified as having mental retardation, a learning disability, or another disability. The category of developmental delay for special education eligibility is used in some states where the classifications of mental retardation and learning disability is restricted to children of a specific, older age. In these states, the diagnosis of developmental delay may be used to help ensure that younger children in need of special education services can receive them before they have reached the age at which a classification of mental retardation or a learning disability is allowed. It was expected that children with developmental delays in the present studies would show significantly lower mean scores in one or more skill areas or adaptive domains, compared to a matched control group. The differences were not expected to be as large as those found between children with mild mental retardation and their matched control group, however.

The present samples of children diagnosed with developmental delays primarily comprise children with significant delays in two or more areas of development, or children with significant cognitive delays who were given the diagnosis of developmental delay, instead of mental retardation, according to the policies of their school district or agency setting. Additionally, children exhibiting only physical or language delays were placed in alternate clinical studies. IDEA criteria identify children younger than 3 years who experience developmental delays as "infants or toddlers with a disability", and children ages 3–9 years who experience developmental delays as "children with a disability" (IDEA, Final Regulations, 1999, Sec. 300.7). In our study, no significant differences were found when we examined the scores of these two age groups separately, so the groups were combined and reported together. The study includes two samples, one composed of 48 children ages 2 years 3 months–5 years 9 months rated on the Teacher/Daycare Provider Form, and one that included 78 children ages 8 months–5 years 11 months rated on the Parent/Primary Caregiver Form. Table 5.40 presents the means and standard deviations of the skill area, adaptive domain, and GAC scores for the samples of children with developmental delays and matched control groups.

Table 5.40 Mean Performance of Children With Developmental Delay and Matched Control Groups

Teacher/Daycare Provider Form

Ages 2:3–5:9 (n = 48)	Children With Developmental Delay			Matched Control Group			Mean Difference of the Two Samples			
	Mean	SD	% of Scores – 2 SD	Mean	SD	% of Scores – 2 SD	Difference	t value	p value	Cohen's d
Communication	6.8	3.4	32.61	10.5	3.2	4.35	3.65	5.16	<.01	1.11
Functional Pre-Academics	7.4	2.7	15.22	10.2	3.0	4.35	2.83	4.54	<.01	.99
School Living	8.5	2.7	6.52	9.6	2.7	4.35	1.07	2.07	.04	.40
Health and Safety	7.3	3.0	19.57	9.7	3.3	8.70	2.39	3.61	<.01	.76
Leisure	8.1	2.8	12.50	9.8	2.9	2.17	1.76	2.59	.01	.62
Self-Care	8.1	3.2	13.04	9.8	2.9	2.17	1.70	2.58	.01	.56
Self-Direction	8.6	3.1	10.87	9.4	2.9	4.35	.85	1.30	.20	.28
Social	7.5	3.1	21.74	9.5	2.6	2.17	1.98	3.21	<.01	.69
Motor	7.5	3.1	17.39	9.5	2.9	6.52	2.04	3.14	<.01	.68
Conceptual Domain	83.9	14.8	26.09	99.1	14.4	4.35	15.28	4.76	<.01	1.05
Social Domain	86.3	15.2	17.39	97.1	14.1	2.17	10.83	3.24	<.01	.74
Practical Domain	86.0	15.9	19.57	96.5	15.9	8.70	10.43	3.28	<.01	.66
GAC	84.0	14.5	21.74	97.0	14.9	4.35	12.96	4.08	<.01	.88
Cases with ≥ 2 skill areas – 2SD			52.08			20.83				
Cases with ≥ 1 adaptive domain – 2SD			33.33			12.50				
Cases with ≥ 1 adaptive domain or the GAC – 2SD			33.33			12.50				

Parent/Primary Caregiver Form

Ages 0:8–5:11 (n = 78)	Children With Developmental Delay			Matched Control Group			Mean Difference of the Two Samples			
	Mean	SD	% of Scores – 2 SD	Mean	SD	% of Scores – 2 SD	Difference	t value	p value	Cohen's d
Communication	6.6	3.4	24.00	10.6	3.1	4.00	4.03	6.91	<.01	1.24
Community Use	7.5	3.1	14.86	10.6	3.1	2.70	3.03	5.63	<.01	.98
Functional Pre-Academics	7.1	3.0	18.92	10.5	3.0	2.70	3.43	6.99	<.01	1.14
Home Living	8.4	2.9	9.46	10.6	3.1	2.70	2.24	5.00	<.01	.75
Health and Safety	8.0	3.1	16.00	10.3	2.7	2.67	2.36	4.76	<.01	.81
Leisure	7.3	3.0	14.67	10.2	3.1	3.85	2.92	5.78	<.01	.96
Self-Care	8.0	3.4	12.00	9.9	3.5	10.67	1.92	3.50	<.01	.56
Self-Direction	8.2	3.2	13.33	10.6	3.1	4.00	2.41	4.40	<.01	.76
Social	7.7	3.0	9.33	10.2	3.1	4.00	2.43	4.47	<.01	.80
Motor	7.6	3.2	12.00	10.4	3.1	5.33	2.80	5.59	<.01	.89
Conceptual Domain	81.3	17.3	28.00	102.0	16.7	1.33	20.77	6.93	<.01	1.22
Social Domain	83.8	16.1	20.00	99.8	16.2	8.00	16.01	5.69	<.01	.99
Practical Domain	85.5	16.1	18.67	100.9	16.5	5.33	15.39	5.72	<.01	.94
GAC	82.1	17.1	25.33	101.2	16.6	4.00	19.07	6.70	<.01	1.13
Cases with ≥ 2 skill areas – 2SD			42.31			19.23				
Cases with ≥ 1 adaptive domain – 2SD			34.62			12.82				
Cases with ≥ 1 adaptive domain or the GAC – 2SD			34.62			12.82				

Note. – 2 SD = 2 or more SDs below the mean.

Children with developmental delays across both samples performed significantly lower than their matched control groups. The differences, as expected, were not as great as those between children with mental retardation and their matched controls. The mean GAC across samples ranged from 82–84 for the children with developmental delays, and from 97–101 for the matched control groups. Mean adaptive domain scores for the clinical groups ranged from 81–86, while those of controls ranged from 97–102. Skill area scaled scores were generally lower for the clinical groups, although some fell within normal range, and some skill areas in the sample rated by teachers did not show significant deficits when compared to matched control groups. Parent and teacher clinical samples both displayed the greatest deficits in the Communication Skill Area.

Furthermore, 22% –25% of the samples of children with developmental delays scored at least two SDs below the mean on the GAC, while 42%–52% scored at least two SDs below the mean on two or more of the skill areas. 33%–35% scored at least two SDs below the mean on one or more adaptive domains or the GAC. For the matched control groups, 4% scored at least two SDs below the mean on the GAC, while 19%–21% scored at least two SDs below the mean on two or more skill areas. 13% scored at least two SDs below the mean on or more adaptive domains or the GAC. Results from these samples indicate that children with developmental delays do show overall deficits in adaptive skills. However, children with developmental delays may show deficits in different skill areas.

Children With Known Biological Risk Factors

The IDEA (1999) defines infant and toddlers with disabilities as those birth through age two who need early intervention services because they are experiencing developmental delays, as established by appropriate diagnostic instruments and procedures. IDEA also defines infants and toddlers with disabilities as those children who "Have a diagnosed physical or mental condition that has a high probability of resulting in developmental delay," and "at a State's discretion…are at risk of having substantial developmental delays if early intervention services are not provided (IDEA, Final Regulations, 1999, Sec. 300.16). The IDEA identifies some of the known biological and environmental factors associated with developmental disabilities or disorders as low birth weight; respiratory distress as a newborn; chromosomal abnormalities; genetic or congenital disorders; brain hemorrhage; infection; nutritional deprivation; a history of abuse or neglect; congenital infections; disorders secondary to exposure to toxic substances, including fetal alcohol syndrome; inborn errors of metabolism; disorders reflecting disturbance of the development of the nervous system; and severe attachment disorders. Additional studies have found links between specific risk factors such as low birth weight and fetal alcohol syndrome and later deficits in adaptive behavior (Hack, Taylor, Klein, & Eiben, 1994; Niccols, 1994) and support IDEA's focus on infants and toddlers with various conditions that have strong associations with significant delays.

The present samples of children in this eligibility category included those who had experienced biological or physical conditions identified by IDEA (1999) such as low birth weight, perinatal respiratory distress, chromosomal abnormalities, fetal alcohol syndrome and prenatal drug exposure. Children diagnosed with Down Syndrome were also included in this sample due to the fact that they had a chromosomal abnormality associated with significant delays. They were not included in the validity samples of individuals with mental retardation because they had not been diagnosed as having mental retardation due to their age or agency policy. The study includes two samples, one of 22 children age 2 years 2 months–2 years 11 months who were rated on the Teacher/Daycare Provider Form, and one of 57 children ages birth–2 years 11 months who were rated on the Parent/Primary Caregiver Form. The two samples of infants and toddlers with known biological or physical conditions were expected to have significantly lower mean scores than a matched control group on the GAC and adaptive domains. Skill areas were not expected to display consistent deficits due to the variety of biological and physical factors included in the sample. Table 5.41 presents the means and standard deviations of skill area, adaptive domain, and GAC scores for the two samples of infants and toddlers with known biological or physical conditions and matched control groups.

Table 5.41 Mean Performance of Children With Biological Risk Factors and Matched Control Groups

Teacher/Daycare Provider Form

Ages 2:2–2:11 (n = 22)	Children With Biological Risk Factors			Matched Control Group			Mean Difference of the Two Samples			
	Mean	SD	% of Scores – 2 SD	Mean	SD	% of Scores – 2 SD	Difference	t value	p value	Cohen's d
Communication	7.3	3.1	18.18	11.4	2.7	0.00	4.14	4.14	<.01	1.42
Functional Pre-Academics	7.4	3.3	18.18	10.7	3.6	4.55	3.36	2.84	<.01	.97
School Living	6.1	3.1	27.27	10.1	3.1	4.55	4.09	3.88	<.01	1.32
Health and Safety	6.3	3.3	27.27	11.5	2.7	0.00	5.23	5.89	<.01	1.73
Leisure	6.5	3.3	22.73	11.0	2.4	0.00	4.55	5.21	<.01	1.58
Self-Care	5.9	4.3	36.36	12.0	2.3	0.00	6.05	5.58	<.01	1.75
Self-Direction	6.6	3.2	31.82	10.8	2.8	0.00	4.18	3.97	<.01	1.39
Social	6.5	2.6	13.64	10.6	2.6	0.00	4.09	4.47	<.01	1.57
Motor	7.0	4.4	27.27	11.5	2.4	0.00	4.50	3.94	<.01	1.39
Conceptual Domain	80.9	17.6	31.82	105.2	16.2	0.00	24.27	3.89	<.01	1.43
Social Domain	78.8	16.3	22.73	103.5	11.7	0.00	24.68	5.19	<.01	1.74
Practical Domain	73.4	20.7	50.00	106.1	8.4	0.00	32.73	6.45	<.01	2.07
GAC	76.6	20.2	36.36	105.3	11.6	0.00	28.77	4.94	<.01	1.75
Cases with ≥ 2 skill areas – 2SD			36.36			0.00				
Cases with ≥ 1 adaptive domain – 2SD			59.09			0.00				
Cases with ≥ 1 adaptive domain or the GAC – 2SD			59.09			0.00				

Parent/Primary Caregiver Form

Ages 0:0–2:11 (n = 57)	Children With Biological Risk Factors			Matched Control Group			Mean Difference of the Two Samples			
	Mean	SD	% of Scores – 2 SD	Mean	SD	% of Scores – 2 SD	Difference	t value	p value	Cohen's d
Communication	7.8	3.0	12.28	10.7	2.8	0.00	2.89	5.92	<.01	1.00
Community Use[a]	7.3	2.7	16.67	10.6	3.0	0.00	3.38	5.19	<.01	1.18
Functional Pre-Academics[a]	7.7	2.9	14.29	11.0	2.9	0.00	3.26	5.69	<.01	1.12
Home Living[a]	6.6	2.9	26.19	10.8	2.7	2.38	4.24	7.85	<.01	1.52
Health and Safety	7.3	3.2	19.30	10.6	2.8	1.75	3.35	6.17	<.01	1.11
Leisure	8.5	2.4	5.26	10.9	3.0	1.75	2.40	5.15	<.01	.89
Self-Care	7.5	3.1	19.30	10.8	2.3	1.75	3.33	7.35	<.01	1.22
Self-Direction	8.1	3.0	7.02	10.8	2.5	0.00	2.70	5.65	<.01	.99
Social	7.6	3.1	17.54	10.6	3.1	1.75	3.00	5.24	<.01	.97
Motor	6.8	3.7	24.56	10.1	2.9	3.51	3.26	5.60	<.01	.98
Conceptual Domain	85.8	15.5	15.79	103.0	14.2	0.00	17.16	6.86	<.01	1.15
Social Domain	87.0	14.8	14.04	102.8	15.4	1.75	15.84	5.85	<.01	1.05
Practical Domain	82.1	17.0	24.56	103.3	13.1	1.75	21.25	8.06	<.01	1.40
GAC	81.6	17.5	26.32	102.8	14.4	0.00	21.19	7.86	<.01	1.32
Cases with ≥ 2 skill areas – 2SD			50.88			29.82				
Cases with ≥ 1 adaptive domain – 2SD			24.56			3.51				
Cases with ≥ 1 adaptive domain or the GAC – 2SD			26.32			3.51				

Note. –2 SD = 2 or more SDs below the mean.

[a]Based on 42 observations.

Results show that very young children with known biological and physical conditions display significant deficits on the GAC and adaptive domains. Their mean GACs were 77 for the teacher/daycare provider sample and 82 for the parent/primary caregiver sample. Matched controls had mean GACs of 105 and 103 for the teacher/daycare and parent/primary caregiver samples, respectively. Adaptive domains showed deficits of a similar magnitude, with the Practical Adaptive Domain displaying the greatest deficit across both samples. Similar to the skill area scaled scores of the groups with developmental delays, the scaled scores of the children with biological and physical conditions were generally lower than those of their matched controls, though no consistent pattern of deficits emerged. All skill area and adaptive domains means were found to be significantly lower than those of the matched control groups.

Additionally, 26%–36% of the samples of children with biological or physical conditions scored at least two *SD*s below the mean on the GAC, 26%–59% scored at least two *SD*s below the mean on one or more adaptive domains or the GAC, and 36%–51% scored at least two *SD*s below the mean on two or more skill areas. For the matched control groups, 0% scored at least two *SD*s below the mean on the GAC, 0%–4% scored at least two *SD*s below the mean on one or more adaptive domains or the GAC, and 0%–30% scored at least two *SD*s below the mean on two or more skill areas.

In conclusion, these results suggest that this sample of children identified with known biological or physical conditions already shows deficits in overall adaptive functioning as well as in different skill areas. The results also suggest that comprehensive assessment of adaptive behavior, along with diagnostic assessment and evaluation of other developmental areas, including medical evaluation, may assist in the diagnosis of developmental disabilities and disorders such as mental retardation, and assist in planning interventions for infants and toddlers.

Children With Motor and Physical Impairments

Motor and physical impairments in young children have been linked to later delays in fine and gross motor development (Bouffard, Watkinson, Thompson, Dunn, & Romanow, 1996; Geuze & Boerger, 1993). It was predicted that children with significant motor impairments would have lower scores in the Motor Skill Area, and possibly in other skill areas dependent on motor functioning, while obtaining low average to average scores in other areas such as conceptual and social functioning. Several samples of children with motor or physical impairments were investigated.

A study of infant-preschool aged children with motor impairments included one sample of 32 children ages 2 years 6 months–5 years 11 months who were rated on the Teacher/Daycare Provider Form, and a second sample of 50 children ages 4 months–5 years 3 months rated on the Parent/Primary Caregiver Form. Children included in the samples either had significantly low scores on standardized measures of motor development, or had a physical condition resulting in significant motor impairment. Children with Cerebral Palsy with significant motor impairments and no concurrent diagnosis of mental retardation were included in the study. Table 5.42 presents the means and standard deviations of skill area, adaptive domain, and GAC scores for the motor impaired and matched control groups.

Results show that young children with motor impairments displayed significant deficits on the GAC and some adaptive domains. Mean GACs were 76 for the teacher/daycare provider sample and 79 for the parent/primary caregiver sample. Matched controls had mean GACs of 97 and 98 for the teacher/daycare provider and parent/primary caregiver samples, respectively. As expected, children with motor impairments performed significantly lower on the Motor Skill Area than their matched controls. They also showed large deficits in the Self-Care Skill Area and in the Practical Adaptive Domain when compared to matched controls, most likely because motor skills are needed to perform activities included in these areas.

Teacher/Daycare Provider Form

Ages 2:6–5:11 (n = 32)	Children With Motor Impairments			Matched Control Group			Mean Difference of the Two Samples			
	Mean	SD	% of Scores – 2 SD	Mean	SD	% of Scores – 2 SD	Difference	t value	p value	Cohen's d
Communication[a]	7.4	3.6	23.33	9.2	3.4	10.00	1.73	2.11	.04	.49
Functional Pre-Academics	6.6	3.6	22.58	10.1	3.8	12.90	3.48	4.84	<.01	.94
School Living	5.8	4.2	41.94	9.5	3.3	6.45	3.68	4.76	<.01	.97
Health and Safety	6.3	3.9	35.48	9.7	2.9	3.23	3.45	4.65	<.01	1.00
Leisure	7.3	3.5	19.35	9.9	3.4	9.38	2.68	3.73	<.01	.78
Self-Care	4.6	3.1	61.29	9.7	3.8	9.68	5.13	6.29	<.01	1.48
Self-Direction	8.4	3.6	22.58	10.1	3.5	6.45	1.68	2.22	.03	.47
Social	7.4	4.0	25.81	9.7	3.4	6.45	2.35	2.78	<.01	.63
Motor	3.3	3.3	67.74	9.8	3.4	6.45	6.55	8.61	<.01	1.96
Conceptual Domain[a]	84.0	19.8	30.00	97.6	20.3	13.33	13.63	3.21	<.01	.68
Social Domain	83.7	20.9	29.03	97.9	17.7	9.68	14.19	3.38	<.01	.73
Practical Domain	70.8	22.1	58.06	96.3	17.6	12.90	25.48	6.09	<.01	1.28
GAC[a]	75.5	21.3	40.00	97.1	19.5	10.00	21.53	4.99	<.01	1.05
Cases with ≥ 2 skill areas – 2SD			78.12			25.00				
Cases with ≥ 1 adaptive domain – 2SD			59.37			21.87				
Cases with ≥ 1 adaptive domain or the GAC – 2SD			59.37			21.87				

Parent/Primary Caregiver Form

Ages 0:4–5:3 (n = 50)	Children With Motor Impairments			Matched Control Group			Mean Difference of the Two Samples			
	Mean	SD	% of Scores – 2 SD	Mean	SD	% of Scores – 2 SD	Difference	t value	p value	Cohen's d
Communication	8.3	3.4	16.33	10.0	2.9	4.08	1.69	2.89	<.01	.53
Community Use[b]	7.6	2.9	15.91	10.2	2.6	2.27	2.64	5.32	<.01	.96
Functional Pre-Academics[b]	7.6	2.8	11.36	10.1	2.6	0.00	2.57	4.56	<.01	.95
Home Living[b]	6.6	3.0	15.91	9.8	2.8	4.55	3.20	5.20	<.01	1.10
Health and Safety	6.9	3.1	22.45	9.7	2.9	2.04	2.80	4.91	<.01	.93
Leisure	8.0	3.2	14.29	10.2	2.9	2.00	2.14	3.85	<.01	.70
Self-Care	6.3	3.4	30.61	9.5	3.1	6.12	3.22	5.07	<.01	.99
Self-Direction	8.1	3.0	14.29	9.5	2.6	4.08	1.41	2.60	.01	.50
Social	7.9	3.2	12.24	10.1	2.9	2.04	2.14	3.88	<.01	.70
Motor	5.1	3.6	48.98	10.3	2.7	0.00	5.20	9.12	<.01	1.63
Conceptual Domain	86.3	16.5	18.37	98.0	13.3	4.08	11.69	4.03	<.01	.78
Social Domain	86.5	17.6	16.33	99.1	14.8	0.00	12.67	4.40	<.01	.78
Practical Domain	78.9	16.7	24.49	97.0	13.8	2.04	18.10	6.13	<.01	1.18
GAC	79.4	17.0	32.65	98.2	13.7	0.00	18.80	6.56	<.01	1.22
Cases with ≥ 2 skill areas – 2SD			64.00			26.00				
Cases with ≥ 1 adaptive domain – 2SD			30.00			8.00				
Cases with ≥ 1 adaptive domain or the GAC – 2SD			38.00			8.00				

Note. – 2 SD = 2 or more SDs below the mean.
[a]Based on 30 observations.
[b]Based on 44 observations.

Data were also collected for a sample of 52 school-age children with various physical impairments to identify the degree to which the impairments may affect daily adaptive functioning. The performance of the group of children with physical impairments and a matched control group are reported in Table 5.43.

The mean GAC of the clinical group using the Teacher Form was 62, which was significantly lower than the mean GAC of 102 for the matched control group. Significant differences were found on all skill areas, adaptive domains, and the GAC. 62% of the clinical sample had GAC scores at least two *SD*s below the mean. In contrast, 2% of the matched control group had GAC scores at least two *SD*s below the mean. 83% of the clinical sample scored at least two *SD*s below the mean on one or more adaptive domains or the GAC, compared to only 12% of the matched control group. In addition, 88% of the clinical group scored at least two *SD*s below the mean on two or more skill areas, while only 19% of the matched control group did so. Children with physical impairments showed the greatest deficits in the Community Use, Functional Academics, and Self-Care Skill Areas, when compared to matched controls.

Children With Receptive and/or Expressive Language Disorders

Children meeting *DSM–IV–TR* criteria for a Receptive or Expressive Language Disorder obtain significantly lower scores on measures of receptive or expressive language ability than scores on nonverbal measures of intelligence. Therefore, it was expected that children with Receptive and/or Expressive Language Disorder would demonstrate deficits in adaptive skills, including communication.

The present study of children with Receptive or Expressive Language Disorder included one sample of 52 children ages 2 years 6 months–5 years 11 months who were rated on the Teacher/Daycare Provider Form, and a second sample of 52 children ages 2 years 6 months–5 years 11 months rated on the Parent/Primary Caregiver Form. Children in the language disorder samples met *DSM–IV–TR* criteria for either Receptive or Expressive Language Disorder, or both. Children who were totally nonverbal were excluded from the study. Table 5.44 shows the means and standard deviations of skill area, adaptive domain, and GAC scores for the children with language disorders and matched control groups.

Results show that young children with Receptive and/or Expressive Language Disorder displayed significant deficits on the GAC and some adaptive domains. The mean GAC across samples was 84 for the children with language disorders, and ranged from 99–102 for the control groups. As predicted, children with Receptive and/or Expressive Language Disorder exhibited the greatest deficits in the Communication Skill Area. They also showed a large deficit in the Functional Pre-Academics Skill Area when compared to their matched controls. Almost all skill area scaled scores were significantly lower than those of matched controls.

Children With Pervasive Developmental Disorder Not Otherwise Specified

Children diagnosed with Pervasive Developmental Disorder Not Otherwise Specified (PDD-NOS) experience symptoms that are similar to typical pervasive developmental disorders (i.e., Autistic Disorder, Asperger's Disorder); however, these symptoms do not meet the criteria necessary for confirming a more specific diagnosis. The development of social interaction and verbal and nonverbal communication is often severely impaired. In addition, these children may exhibit characteristic symptoms of autism such as stereotyped movements, repetitive activities, and resistance to change (*DSM–IV–TR*). A diagnosis of PDD-NOS includes "atypical autism", in which diagnostic criteria for Autistic Disorder are not met due to a late age of onset, atypical symptomology and/or subthreshold symptomology.

Children diagnosed with PDD-NOS may have a variety of developmental impairments and deficits in daily functioning, including those skills assessed by the ABAS–II. According to the *DSM–IV–TR* classification of the disorder, a child having this diagnosis would be expected to have difficulty in several daily adaptive skills, especially communication, leisure activities, self-care, and social competence. Consequently, lower mean scores on the Communication, Leisure, Self-Care, and Social Skill Areas were expected.

The present study of children diagnosed with PDD-NOS included one sample of 19 children ages 3 years 0 months–5 years 8 months who were rated on the Teacher/Daycare Provider Form, and a second sample of 18 children ages 3 years 0 months–5 years 9 months rated on the Parent/Primary Caregiver Form. Table 5.45 presents the means and standard deviations of skill area, adaptive domain, and GAC scores for the samples of children with PDD-NOS and the matched control groups.

Table 5.43 Mean Performance of Children With Physical Impairments and a Matched Control Group

Teacher Form

Ages 5–20 (n = 52)	Children With Physical Impairments			Matched Control Group			Mean Difference of the Two Samples			
	Mean	SD	% of Scores – 2 SD	Mean	SD	% of Scores – 2 SD	Difference	t value	p value	Cohen's d
Communication	3.4	3.2	73.08	9.3	3.4	17.31	5.92	8.99	<.01	1.79
Community Use	3.1	3.2	76.92	9.8	2.8	9.62	6.67	11.52	<.01	2.22
Functional Academics	3.1	2.8	76.92	9.8	2.8	5.77	6.73	12.33	<.01	2.40
School Living	4.0	3.8	63.46	9.6	3.0	9.62	5.58	9.11	<.01	1.63
Health and Safety	4.1	3.9	63.46	10.1	2.6	7.69	5.92	9.04	<.01	1.79
Leisure	4.8	3.7	50.00	10.0	2.9	5.77	5.17	7.57	<.01	1.56
Self-Care	3.3	3.6	75.00	9.9	2.5	5.77	6.60	12.04	<.01	2.13
Self-Direction	3.7	3.2	67.31	9.4	2.8	13.46	5.63	9.43	<.01	1.87
Social	4.7	3.9	57.69	10.0	2.8	7.69	5.29	8.08	<.01	1.56
Conceptual Domain	65.0	16.7	69.23	102.0	15.8	3.85	37.02	11.11	<.01	2.28
Social Domain	73.6	18.3	48.08	101.5	15.5	3.85	27.92	8.15	<.01	1.65
Practical Domain	61.2	21.1	71.15	101.3	15.3	5.77	40.08	11.42	<.01	2.17
GAC	61.6	20.6	61.54	102.2	15.1	1.92	40.67	11.16	<.01	2.25
Cases with ≥ 2 skill areas – 2SD			88.46			19.23				
Cases with ≥ 1 adaptive domain – 2SD			82.69			11.54				
Cases with ≥ 1 adaptive domain or the GAC – 2SD			82.69			11.54				

Note. – 2 SD = 2 or more SDs below the mean.

Table 5.44 Mean Performance of Children With Receptive and/or Expressive Language Disorder and Matched Control Groups

Teacher/Daycare Provider Form

Ages 2:6–5:11 (n = 52)	Children With Language Disorders			Matched Control Group			Mean Difference of the Two Samples			
	Mean	SD	% of Scores – 2 SD	Mean	SD	% of Scores – 2 SD	Difference	t value	p value	Cohen's d
Communication	6.5	2.9	26.92	10.3	3.3	3.85	3.85	6.22	<.01	1.24
Functional Pre-Academics	7.3	2.7	19.23	10.1	2.7	0.00	2.77	6.20	<.01	1.03
School Living	8.0	2.9	13.46	9.8	3.4	9.62	1.83	3.15	<.01	.58
Health and Safety	8.0	2.7	11.54	9.7	3.4	5.77	1.71	2.82	<.01	.56
Leisure	7.8	2.7	9.62	10.5	3.1	1.92	2.73	4.59	<.01	.94
Self-Care	8.3	2.8	7.69	9.4	3.2	7.69	1.17	2.02	.05	.39
Self-Direction	8.0	2.8	15.38	9.9	3.2	5.77	1.87	3.41	<.01	.62
Social	7.8	3.1	13.46	9.8	3.3	5.77	2.02	3.15	<.01	.63
Motor	8.4	2.9	11.54	10.3	3.3	3.85	1.90	2.98	<.01	.61
Conceptual Domain	81.7	13.6	25.00	99.4	15.2	3.85	17.73	6.69	<.01	1.23
Social Domain	86.4	14.2	11.54	99.8	16.8	3.85	13.42	4.24	<.01	.86
Practical Domain	87.4	15.4	17.31	96.0	17.8	13.46	8.65	2.68	<.01	.52
GAC	84.2	14.0	13.46	98.6	16.9	3.85	14.40	4.76	<.01	.93
Cases with ≥ 2 skill areas – 2SD			50.00			23.08				
Cases with ≥ 1 adaptive domain – 2SD			32.69			13.46				
Cases with ≥ 1 adaptive domain or the GAC – 2SD			32.69			13.46				

Parent/Primary Caregiver Form

Ages 2:6–5:11 (n = 52)	Children With Language Disorders			Matched Control Group			Mean Difference of the Two Samples			
	Mean	SD	% of Scores – 2 SD	Mean	SD	% of Scores – 2 SD	Difference	t value	p value	Cohen's d
Communication	6.3	3.0	25.00	10.8	2.8	1.92	4.48	7.65	<.01	1.54
Community Use	7.6	2.7	9.62	10.8	2.9	0.00	3.19	5.46	<.01	1.14
Functional Pre-Academics	7.6	2.9	17.31	10.8	2.6	0.00	3.21	5.55	<.01	1.17
Home Living	8.4	2.5	3.85	10.4	2.5	0.00	2.04	4.33	<.01	.82
Health and Safety	8.1	3.0	9.62	10.1	2.5	0.00	2.00	3.82	<.01	.72
Leisure	7.8	2.7	9.62	10.9	2.7	1.92	3.06	5.74	<.01	1.13
Self-Care	8.4	2.7	7.69	10.2	2.8	1.92	1.77	3.15	<.01	.64
Self-Direction	8.2	2.4	5.77	10.3	2.9	1.92	2.12	4.53	<.01	.80
Social	8.2	3.0	7.69	10.2	2.7	1.92	1.96	3.67	<.01	.69
Motor	8.5	3.1	11.54	10.2	2.9	1.92	1.69	2.88	<.01	.56
Conceptual Domain	81.3	14.1	26.92	102.3	13.6	1.92	21.02	7.85	<.01	1.52
Social Domain	86.6	15.1	9.62	101.5	13.9	1.92	14.88	5.42	<.01	1.03
Practical Domain	86.5	14.5	11.54	101.2	13.0	0.00	14.69	5.32	<.01	1.07
GAC	83.6	15.2	23.08	101.5	12.9	1.92	17.92	6.58	<.01	1.27
Cases with ≥ 2 skill areas – 2SD			38.46			3.85				
Cases with ≥ 1 adaptive domain – 2SD			32.69			1.92				
Cases with ≥ 1 adaptive domain or the GAC – 2SD			32.69			1.92				

Note. –2 SD = 2 or more SDs below the mean.

Table 5.45 Mean Performance of Children With Pervasive Developmental Disorder Not Otherwise Specified and Matched Control Groups

Teacher/Daycare Provider Form

Ages 3:0–5:8 (n = 19)	Children With PDD-NOS			Matched Control Group			Mean Difference of the Two Samples			
	Mean	SD	% of Scores – 2 SD	Mean	SD	% of Scores – 2 SD	Difference	t value	p value	Cohen's d
Communication	3.8	2.7	61.11	10.8	3.2	5.56	7.00	7.45	<.01	2.36
Functional Pre-Academics	6.2	3.2	38.89	10.5	2.8	5.56	4.33	5.04	<.01	1.44
School Living	5.6	3.5	50.00	9.7	3.4	11.11	4.11	3.40	<.01	1.19
Health and Safety	4.2	3.0	61.11	9.0	2.7	0.00	4.83	4.81	<.01	1.69
Leisure	4.8	2.3	38.89	10.5	3.4	0.00	5.67	6.35	<.01	1.95
Self-Care	4.8	2.9	50.00	9.2	2.9	0.00	4.39	4.69	<.01	1.51
Self-Direction	5.1	2.5	44.44	9.3	3.0	11.11	4.22	4.26	<.01	1.53
Social	3.6	2.9	66.67	9.1	3.2	11.11	5.50	5.48	<.01	1.80
Motor	6.3	3.2	27.78	10.7	2.5	0.00	4.33	4.91	<.01	1.51
Conceptual Domain	68.5	13.5	50.00	100.2	16.5	11.11	31.67	7.03	<.01	2.10
Social Domain	65.8	14.2	61.11	97.4	17.4	11.11	31.56	6.24	<.01	1.99
Practical Domain	66.3	18.6	72.22	94.3	16.8	11.11	28.06	4.65	<.01	1.58
GAC	65.7	16.5	55.56	97.6	16.8	11.11	31.83	6.23	<.01	1.91
Cases with ≥ 2 skill areas – 2SD			78.95			15.79				
Cases with ≥ 1 adaptive domain – 2SD			78.95			15.79				
Cases with ≥ 1 adaptive domain or the GAC – 2SD			78.95			15.79				

Parent/Primary Caregiver Form

Ages 3:0–5:9 (n = 18)	Children With PDD-NOS			Matched Control Group			Mean Difference of the Two Samples			
	Mean	SD	% of Scores – 2 SD	Mean	SD	% of Scores – 2 SD	Difference	t value	p value	Cohen's d
Communication	4.5	3.0	50.00	11.2	2.8	0.00	6.72	6.86	<.01	2.32
Community Use	4.9	3.0	44.44	11.2	2.9	0.00	6.28	6.07	<.01	2.13
Functional Pre-Academics	7.3	3.6	22.22	10.8	3.0	0.00	3.56	3.42	<.01	1.07
Home Living	6.3	3.3	33.33	10.7	2.9	0.00	4.39	4.01	<.01	1.41
Health and Safety	4.9	3.0	44.44	11.1	2.6	0.00	6.11	6.71	<.01	2.18
Leisure	5.9	3.4	33.33	11.1	2.8	0.00	5.17	4.90	<.01	1.66
Self-Care	5.8	3.6	38.89	10.2	2.7	5.56	4.39	4.21	<.01	1.38
Self-Direction	6.3	2.9	27.78	10.3	2.7	0.00	4.06	4.19	<.01	1.45
Social	5.2	3.2	38.89	10.6	2.8	0.00	5.44	5.37	<.01	1.81
Motor	6.7	3.1	22.22	10.3	1.9	0.00	3.67	3.86	<.01	1.43
Conceptual Domain	73.4	17.4	38.89	103.2	15.6	0.00	29.78	5.52	<.01	1.80
Social Domain	72.0	18.3	44.44	103.2	15.1	0.00	31.22	5.50	<.01	1.86
Practical Domain	69.6	18.0	50.00	103.4	13.4	0.00	33.89	6.35	<.01	2.14
GAC	69.4	18.2	50.00	103.2	14.8	0.00	33.78	5.93	<.01	2.04
Cases with ≥ 2 skill areas – 2SD			55.56			5.56				
Cases with ≥ 1 adaptive domain – 2SD			50.00			0.00				
Cases with ≥ 1 adaptive domain or the GAC – 2SD			50.00			0.00				

Note. – 2 SD = 2 or more SDs below the mean.

Children with PDD-NOS showed significant deficits in all skill areas, adaptive domains, and on the GAC. The mean GAC across samples ranged from 66–69 for the samples of children with PDD-NOS, and from 98–103 for the matched control groups. As expected, children with PDD-NOS displayed the most significant deficits in the Communication skill area. Within the parent/primary caregiver clinical sample, the skill area of Functional Pre-Academics was a relative strength, displaying the highest mean of all skill areas, and one of the smallest deficits when compared to matched controls. Results from this study indicate that children with PDD-NOS show global deficits in adaptive functioning, and are most affected in the area of communication.

Children With Autistic Disorder

Children diagnosed with Autistic Disorder, a specific Pervasive Developmental Disorder, are characterized by deficits in verbal and nonverbal communication and social interaction, and may exhibit stereotyped movements, repetitive activities, and resistance to change (IDEA, 1999; *DSM–IV–TR*). Children diagnosed with Autistic Disorder may have a number of developmental difficulties and deficits in daily functioning, such as those skills assessed by the ABAS–II. Shriver, Allen, and Mathews (1999) listed several core domains related to daily adaptive skills that are important in assessing and treating children with Autistic Disorder, including social competence, play/leisure skills, and self-help/independent living skills.

Present samples included one of 35 children with Autistic Disorder ages 3 years 2 months–5 years 11 months rated on the Teacher/Daycare Provider Form, and a second sample of 34 children ages 3 years 1 month–5 years 11 months rated on the Parent/Primary Caregiver Form. The performance of these samples of children with Autistic Disorder and their matched control groups is reported in Table 5.46.

The mean GAC of children with Autistic Disorder assessed using the Teacher/Daycare Provider Form was 67, which was significantly lower than the mean GAC of 102 for the matched control group. The mean GAC of children with Autistic Disorder assessed using the Parent/Primary Caregiver Form was 64, which was also significantly lower than the mean GAC of 98 for the matched control group. Significant differences were found on all skill areas, adaptive domains, and on the GAC, with the exception of the Functional Pre-Academics Skill Area on the parent sample. Both samples of children with Autistic Disorder exhibited the greatest deficits in the Communication, Health and Safety, Leisure, and Social Skill Areas. Similar to the sample of children with PDD-NOS, the skill area showing the least deficit in the samples with Autistic Disorder was Functional Pre-Academics. Within the clinical samples, the Conceptual Adaptive Domain was the only adaptive domain that did not fall two *SD*s below the mean of the matched control groups.

Furthermore, 71% of the clinical samples had GAC scores at least two *SD*s below the mean. In contrast, only 0%–6% of the matched control groups had GAC scores at least two *SD*s below mean. 71%–77% of the clinical samples had one or more adaptive domain scores or the GAC at least two *SD*s below the mean, while only 3%–6% of the matched control groups did so. In addition, 71%–80% of the clinical samples scored at least two *SD*s below the mean on two or more skill areas, in contrast to only 3%–9% of the matched control groups.

Teacher Form data were also collected for a sample of 32 children ages 5–18 years diagnosed with Autistic Disorder. The performance of the sample of children with Autistic Disorder and a matched control group is reported in Table 5.46. The mean GAC scores of the children with Autistic Disorder rated using the Teacher Form was 54, which was significantly lower than the mean GAC of 101 for the matched control group. Significant differences were found on all skill areas, adaptive domains, and on the GAC. 84% of the clinical sample had GAC scores at least two *SD*s below the mean, in contrast to only 3% of the matched control group. 84% of the clinical sample had one or more adaptive domains or the GAC at least two *SD*s below the mean, compared to 9% of the control group. In addition, 92% of the clinical sample scored at least two *SD*s below the mean on two or more skill areas, while only 16% of the matched control group did so.

Table 5.46 Mean Performance of Children With Autistic Disorder and Matched Control Groups

Teacher/Daycare Provider Form

Ages 3:2–5:11 (n = 35)	Children With Autistic Disorder			Matched Control Group			Mean Difference of the Two Samples			
	Mean	SD	% of Scores − 2 SD	Mean	SD	% of Scores − 2 SD	Difference	t value	p value	Cohen's d
Communication	4.6	3.8	61.76	10.7	2.5	2.94	6.09	7.21	<.01	1.89
Functional Pre-Academics	7.4	3.9	14.71	11.1	2.8	2.94	3.62	4.53	<.01	1.07
School Living	5.4	3.5	47.06	9.8	2.8	0.00	4.41	5.78	<.01	1.39
Health and Safety	4.4	3.8	70.59	10.8	3.2	0.00	6.41	6.95	<.01	1.82
Leisure	4.9	3.4	62.86	10.4	2.5	0.00	5.50	7.22	<.01	1.84
Self-Care	4.9	3.4	64.71	10.0	2.6	0.00	5.18	6.91	<.01	1.71
Self-Direction	5.3	3.1	52.94	10.0	2.5	0.00	4.68	6.66	<.01	1.66
Social	4.1	3.8	67.65	10.2	3.1	0.00	6.06	7.16	<.01	1.75
Motor	6.4	2.6	20.59	11.0	2.2	0.00	4.62	7.31	<.01	1.92
Conceptual Domain	73.0	20.0	61.76	102.2	12.6	0.00	29.21	7.11	<.01	1.75
Social Domain	67.3	19.7	73.53	100.5	14.7	0.00	33.21	7.72	<.01	1.91
Practical Domain	65.9	21.1	73.53	100.5	15.7	0.00	34.65	7.25	<.01	1.86
GAC	67.2	21.2	70.59	101.5	14.0	0.00	34.26	7.51	<.01	1.91
Cases with ≥ 2 skill areas − 2SD			80.00			2.86				
Cases with ≥ 1 adaptive domain − 2SD			77.14			2.86				
Cases with ≥ 1 adaptive domain or the GAC − 2SD			77.14			2.86				

Parent/Primary Caregiver Form

Ages 3:1–5:11 (n = 34)	Children With Autistic Disorder			Matched Control Group			Mean Difference of the Two Samples			
	Mean	SD	% of Scores − 2 SD	Mean	SD	% of Scores − 2 SD	Difference	t value	p value	Cohen's d
Communication	4.4	3.7	58.82	10.4	2.7	0.00	6.03	7.55	<.01	1.86
Community Use	4.1	2.4	61.76	9.5	2.6	8.82	5.41	8.54	<.01	2.16
Functional Pre-Academics	7.8	3.9	20.59	9.3	3.0	2.94	1.47	1.88	.07	.42
Home Living	5.4	2.7	38.24	9.7	3.4	11.76	4.26	5.77	<.01	1.39
Health and Safety	4.2	2.9	58.82	9.8	3.6	5.88	5.68	6.49	<.01	1.74
Leisure	4.5	3.3	52.94	10.4	2.5	2.94	5.85	7.58	<.01	2.00
Self-Care	4.9	3.3	55.88	10.3	2.6	0.00	5.32	7.16	<.01	1.79
Self-Direction	5.2	3.1	38.24	10.1	2.6	0.00	4.88	8.22	<.01	1.71
Social	3.9	2.8	58.82	9.8	2.8	2.94	5.97	9.36	<.01	2.13
Motor	5.9	2.6	26.47	10.4	2.8	0.00	4.41	6.70	<.01	1.63
Conceptual Domain	71.7	20.1	55.88	97.9	11.8	0.00	26.18	6.80	<.01	1.59
Social Domain	64.6	16.4	64.71	99.2	13.3	5.88	34.62	9.25	<.01	2.32
Practical Domain	64.8	15.6	64.71	97.5	16.2	5.88	32.71	8.07	<.01	2.06
GAC	64.2	17.2	70.59	98.1	13.8	5.88	33.85	8.80	<.01	2.17
Cases with ≥ 2 skill areas − 2SD			70.59			8.82				
Cases with ≥ 1 adaptive domain − 2SD			70.59			5.88				
Cases with ≥ 1 adaptive domain or the GAC − 2SD			70.59			5.88				

Note. − 2 SD = 2 or more SDs below the mean.

Table 5.46 Mean Performance of Children With Autistic Disorder and Matched Control Groups *(continued)*

▲ **Teacher Form**

Ages 5–18 (n = 32)	Children With Autistic Disorder			Matched Control Group			Mean Difference of the Two Samples			
	Mean	SD	% of Scores – 2 SD	Mean	SD	% of Scores – 2 SD	Difference	t value	p value	Cohen's d
Communication	2.7	2.6	81.25	8.7	3.8	21.88	6.03	6.68	<.01	1.85
Community Use	2.6	2.4	81.25	9.4	2.7	9.38	6.84	9.34	<.01	2.68
Functional Academics	3.9	3.6	68.75	9.7	2.7	6.25	5.78	7.11	<.01	1.82
School Living	3.1	2.7	71.88	9.9	2.5	3.13	6.78	9.23	<.01	2.61
Health and Safety	2.2	2.0	81.25	9.8	2.2	6.25	7.59	12.72	<.01	3.61
Leisure	3.2	3.1	71.88	9.9	2.6	6.25	6.78	8.29	<.01	2.37
Self-Care	2.3	2.3	87.50	9.6	3.0	12.50	7.25	8.98	<.01	2.71
Self-Direction	2.3	2.5	84.38	8.7	3.1	12.50	6.41	8.75	<.01	2.28
Social	2.6	2.5	84.38	9.4	3.4	12.50	6.78	8.93	<.01	2.27
Conceptual Domain	62.7	16.5	81.25	98.9	16.1	6.25	36.19	8.27	<.01	2.22
Social Domain	64.7	13.1	75.00	101.0	16.4	6.25	36.25	8.82	<.01	2.44
Practical Domain	55.1	15.1	81.25	102.1	12.5	0.00	46.97	11.09	<.01	3.39
GAC	54.2	15.8	84.38	100.6	14.8	3.13	46.41	10.27	<.01	3.03
Cases with ≥ 2 skill areas – 2SD			91.62			15.62				
Cases with ≥ 1 adaptive domain – 2SD			84.37			9.37				
Cases with ≥ 1 adaptive domain or the GAC – 2SD			84.37			9.37				

Note. – 2 SD = 2 or more SDs below the mean.

The combined data from these studies suggest that children diagnosed with Autistic Disorder generally have significant deficits in adaptive skills. Assessment of adaptive skills may aid in the identification of specific deficits related to Autistic Disorder in the context of a comprehensive diagnostic assessment, and may also assist in the planning of treatment programs to increase the daily functioning of children with this disorder.

Children With Attention-Deficit/Hyperactivity Disorder

The performance of the samples of children diagnosed with ADHD and matched control groups is reported in Table 5.47. Although diagnostic criteria for ADHD do not specify that individuals exhibit adaptive skill deficits, many of the behavioral characteristics of ADHD may be associated with adaptive skill deficits. Comprehensive assessment of adaptive behavior may contribute to the broad evaluation needed for diagnosis. Intervention programs for children with ADHD may focus on increasing their daily adaptive skills. Two groups of individuals with ADHD were rated using Teacher or Parent Forms. The group rated on the Teacher Form included 30 children ages 5–9 years. The group rated on the Parent Form included 49 children ages 6–21 years.

For the sample of children ages 5–9 years and diagnosed with ADHD the mean GAC on the Teacher Form was 77, which was significantly lower than the mean GAC of 101 for the matched control group. Significant differences between the ADHD samples and control group were found on all skill areas, adaptive domains, and the GAC. 43% of the sample of children with ADHD had GAC scores at least two *SD*s below the mean. In contrast, 7% of individuals in the matched control group had GAC scores at least two *SD*s below the mean. 57% of the clinical sample had one or more adaptive domain scores or the GAC at least two *SD*s below the mean, compared to 10% of the matched control group. In addition, 63% of the clinical sample scored at least two *SD*s below the mean on two or more skill areas, while only 20% of the matched control group did so. Among the nine skill areas, the sample of children with ADHD rated by teachers showed the greatest deficits in the Self-Direction Skill Area, consistent with other typical behavioral characteristics of children with ADHD such as impulsivity and problems with concentration. 73% of the sample scored at least two *SD*s below the mean on Self-Direction, while only 17% of the matched control group did so.

For the sample of children ages 6–21 years diagnosed with ADHD, the mean GAC on the Parent Form was 91, which was significantly lower than the mean GAC of 100 for the matched control group. Significant differences were found in three of the nine skill areas. 14% of those with ADHD had GAC scores at least two *SD*s below the mean. In contrast, only 2% of children in the matched control group had GAC scores at least two *SD*s below the mean. 18% of the clinical sample had one or more adaptive domain scores or the GAC at least two *SD*s below the mean, compared to 4% of the matched control group. Consistent with the results from the sample of children with ADHD rated by teachers, this sample rated by parents displayed the greatest deficits in the Self-Direction Skill Area. 24% percent of the clinical sample scored at least two *SD*s below the mean on Self-Direction, while only 2% of the matched control group did so.

In conclusion, the samples of children diagnosed with ADHD exhibited deficits in adaptive skills when compared to matched controls. The samples rated by teachers had mean scores in all skill areas and adaptive domains that were significantly lower than those of children with typical functioning, whereas the sample rated by parents did not show significant deficits in all scores. These differences between the ratings of teachers and parents possibly reflect the tendency of children with ADHD to display more obvious behavior problems in situations such as a classroom where self-control is required. Both clinical samples obtained the lowest scores on the Self-Direction Skill Area. The findings of this study suggest that comprehensive assessment of the adaptive skills of children with ADHD may provide useful information for identifying the impact of attention problems on adaptive functioning in various settings and in planning intervention goals.

Table 5.47 Mean Performance of Children With ADHD and Matched Control Groups

Teacher Form

Ages 5–9 (n = 30)	Children With ADHD			Matched Control Group			Mean Difference of the Two Samples			
	Mean	SD	% of Scores – 2 SD	Mean	SD	% of Scores – 2 SD	Difference	t value	p value	Cohen's d
Communication	5.6	3.9	46.67	9.0	3.1	13.33	3.37	4.32	<.01	.96
Community Use	6.4	3.6	40.00	9.3	2.9	10.00	2.93	3.48	<.01	.90
Functional Academics	6.9	3.8	33.33	9.4	3.1	3.33	2.47	2.77	<.01	.71
School Living	6.7	3.2	30.00	10.5	2.8	3.33	3.80	5.17	<.01	1.26
Health and Safety	6.0	3.1	40.00	9.9	2.4	3.33	3.87	5.44	<.01	1.40
Leisure	6.7	3.2	33.33	9.8	3.3	10.00	3.07	3.91	<.01	.94
Self-Care	5.8	4.2	50.00	9.4	3.3	16.67	3.57	4.02	<.01	.95
Self-Direction	3.7	3.0	73.33	9.2	3.3	16.67	5.43	7.37	<.01	1.72
Social	5.1	3.2	50.00	10.1	2.4	3.33	5.00	7.73	<.01	1.77
Conceptual Domain	78.2	18.6	40.00	99.6	15.3	6.67	21.43	5.36	<.01	1.26
Social Domain	80.5	15.3	36.67	100.7	15.4	10.00	20.27	5.67	<.01	1.32
Practical Domain	79.6	19.4	36.67	101.0	15.0	3.33	21.40	5.14	<.01	1.23
GAC	76.8	18.2	43.33	100.6	15.9	6.67	23.77	5.93	<.01	1.39
Cases with ≥ 2 skill areas – 2SD			63.33			20.00				
Cases with ≥ 1 adaptive domain – 2SD			56.67			10.00				
Cases with ≥ 1 adaptive domain or the GAC – 2SD			56.67			10.00				

Parent Form

Ages 6–21 (n = 49)	Children With ADHD			Matched Control Group			Mean Difference of the Two Samples			
	Mean	SD	% of Scores – 2 SD	Mean	SD	% of Scores – 2 SD	Difference	t value	p value	Cohen's d
Communication	8.6	3.1	8.16	10.2	2.4	0.00	1.59	2.99	<.01	.57
Community Use	9.8	3.2	6.12	10.4	2.5	4.08	.59	1.14	.26	.21
Functional Academics	8.8	2.9	10.20	10.6	2.5	0.00	1.73	3.49	<.01	.64
Home Living	7.7	3.8	28.57	8.5	3.4	20.41	.80	1.14	.26	.22
Health and Safety	8.8	3.4	12.24	9.9	2.9	6.12	1.16	1.70	.10	.37
Leisure	9.2	3.2	6.12	10.4	2.5	2.04	1.14	2.03	.05	.40
Self-Care	8.7	3.1	18.37	9.2	2.4	2.04	.57	.97	.34	.21
Self-Direction	7.0	3.4	24.49	10.5	2.5	2.04	3.49	6.30	<.01	1.17
Social	8.2	3.6	16.33	9.4	3.0	8.16	1.14	1.55	.13	.34
Conceptual Domain	90.7	14.9	12.24	102.5	11.7	2.04	11.78	4.67	<.01	.88
Social Domain	94.4	16.1	8.16	100.2	13.0	4.08	5.84	1.84	.07	.40
Practical Domain	93.2	15.9	10.20	97.8	12.6	2.04	4.63	1.51	.14	.32
GAC	91.1	16.5	14.29	99.9	13.3	2.04	8.84	2.83	<.01	.59
Cases with ≥ 2 skill areas – 2SD			26.53			12.24				
Cases with ≥ 1 adaptive domain – 2SD			16.33			4.08				
Cases with ≥ 1 adaptive domain or the GAC – 2SD			18.37			4.08				

Note. – 2 SD = 2 or more SDs below the mean.

Children With Behavior Disorders and Emotional Disturbance

Children diagnosed with behavior disorders and emotional disturbance may have deficits in adaptive skills associated with the impact of their behavior or emotional problems on their daily activities (Sparrow & Cicchetti, 1987). The performance of 56 children ages 6–21 years diagnosed with behavior disorders and a matched control group is reported in Table 5.48. The mean GAC of the sample of children with behavior disorders on the Teacher Form was 77, which was significantly lower than the mean GAC of 92 for the matched control group. Children with behavior disorders also displayed lower scores in all three adaptive domains and eight of the nine skill areas. 39% of the children with behavior disorders had GAC scores at least two SDs below the mean, in contrast to 16% of the matched control group. 52% of the clinical sample scored at least two SDs below the mean on one or more adaptive domains or the GAC, compared to only 27% of the matched control group. In addition, 73% of the clinical group scored at least two SDs below the mean on two or more skill areas, while only 36% of the matched control group did so. Similar to the sample of children with ADHD, the children with behavior disorders showed the greatest deficits in the Self-Direction Skill Area. 75% of the clinical sample scored at least two SDs below the mean on Self-Direction, while 32% of the matched control group did so.

Data on a sample of 73 children ages 5–18 years diagnosed with emotional disturbances and a matched control group is presented in Table 5.49. The mean GAC of the clinical sample on the Teacher Form was 78, which was significantly lower than the mean GAC of 99 for the matched control group. Significant differences were found in all skill areas, adaptive domains, and the GAC. 37% of the clinical sample had GAC scores at least two SDs below the mean, in contrast to only 10% of children in the matched control group. 49% of the clinical sample scored at least two SDs below the mean on one or more adaptive domains or the GAC, compared to only 14% of the matched control group. In addition, 70% of the clinical group scored at least two SDs below the mean on two or more skill areas, while only 25% of the matched control group did so.

The data for children diagnosed with behavior disorders and emotional disturbance were similar to those for children diagnosed with ADHD and demonstrate important differences in comparison to individuals diagnosed with mental retardation. Children with behavior and emotional problems scored significantly lower in adaptive skills than did matched controls. However, children with mental retardation scored lower in all skill areas, adaptive domains, and the GAC than did the children with ADHD, behavior disorders, or emotional disturbance. Children with ADHD, behavior disorders, and emotional disturbance exhibited their lowest performance on the Self-Direction Skill Area. In comparison, individuals with mental retardation generally exhibited their lowest performance on the Communication and Functional Academics Skill Areas. The data suggest that comprehensive adaptive skill assessment for children with attention, behavior, or emotional problems, in addition to those with mental retardation, may be important in diagnosis, in identifying important strengths and weaknesses in their adaptive skills and in formulating interventions.

Teacher Form

Table 5.48 Mean Performance of Children With Behavior Disorders and a Matched Control Group

Ages 6–21 (n = 56)	Children With Behavior Disorders			Matched Control Group			Mean Difference of the Two Samples			
	Mean	SD	% of Scores – 2 SD	Mean	SD	% of Scores – 2 SD	Difference	t value	p value	Cohen's d
Communication	5.8	3.2	46.43	7.7	3.5	28.57	1.89	3.19	<.01	.56
Community Use	6.6	3.2	32.14	8.6	3.4	17.86	1.98	3.51	<.01	.60
Functional Academics	6.6	3.0	25.00	8.4	3.2	16.07	1.73	3.24	<.01	.56
School Living	6.1	3.7	46.43	8.5	3.6	19.64	2.41	3.54	<.01	.66
Health and Safety	5.5	3.3	48.21	8.5	3.8	25.00	3.02	4.60	<.01	.85
Leisure	6.7	3.2	28.57	8.7	3.2	14.29	2.04	3.70	<.01	.64
Self-Care	7.5	3.9	32.14	8.4	4.0	26.79	.89	1.09	.28	.23
Self-Direction	3.8	3.0	75.00	7.0	3.8	32.14	3.29	5.68	<.01	.96
Social	5.0	3.6	60.71	8.5	3.6	19.64	3.52	4.97	<.01	.98
Conceptual Domain	78.0	15.0	44.64	91.6	18.3	21.43	13.55	4.77	<.01	.81
Social Domain	79.8	16.5	33.93	94.5	18.2	14.29	14.75	4.49	<.01	.85
Practical Domain	81.3	15.7	25.00	93.1	19.9	16.07	11.86	3.52	<.01	.66
GAC	76.9	16.5	39.29	92.1	20.0	16.07	15.21	4.51	<.01	.83
Cases with ≥ 2 skill areas – 2SD			73.21			35.71				
Cases with ≥ 1 adaptive domain – 2SD			50.00			26.79				
Cases with ≥ 1 adaptive domain or the GAC – 2SD			51.79			26.79				

Note. –2 SD = 2 or more SDs below the mean.

Teacher Form

Table 5.49 Mean Performance of Children With Emotional Disturbance and a Matched Control Group

Ages 5–18 (n = 73)	Children With Emotional Disturbance			Matched Control Group			Mean Difference of the Two Samples			
	Mean	SD	% of Scores – 2 SD	Mean	SD	% of Scores – 2 SD	Difference	t value	p value	Cohen's d
Communication	5.3	3.8	54.79	8.8	3.6	20.55	3.44	5.47	<.01	.93
Community Use	5.2	3.8	54.79	9.0	3.0	10.96	3.75	6.89	<.01	1.10
Functional Academics	6.2	3.6	39.73	8.9	3.1	13.70	2.74	4.97	<.01	.82
School Living	6.4	3.8	39.73	9.2	3.3	12.33	2.85	4.51	<.01	.80
Health and Safety	5.9	3.7	46.58	9.3	3.1	13.70	3.34	5.51	<.01	.98
Leisure	6.7	3.0	26.03	9.7	2.8	6.85	3.04	6.27	<.01	1.05
Self-Care	7.5	3.6	30.14	9.3	3.1	15.07	1.79	3.18	<.01	.53
Self-Direction	4.7	3.3	54.79	8.7	3.3	17.81	3.99	6.66	<.01	1.21
Social	5.7	3.3	46.58	9.6	2.8	8.22	3.89	7.26	<.01	1.27
Conceptual Domain	78.8	18.2	41.10	97.8	17.1	12.33	19.03	6.34	<.01	1.08
Social Domain	81.6	14.8	31.51	100.4	15.2	6.85	18.81	7.41	<.01	1.25
Practical Domain	80.4	16.6	32.88	98.1	15.5	10.96	17.64	6.29	<.01	1.10
GAC	77.5	17.4	36.99	98.5	17.1	9.59	21.00	7.05	<.01	1.22
Cases with ≥ 2 skill areas – 2SD			69.86			24.66				
Cases with ≥ 1 adaptive domain – 2SD			49.32			13.70				
Cases with ≥ 1 adaptive domain or the GAC – 2SD			49.32			13.70				

Note. –2 SD = 2 or more SDs below the mean.

Children who are Deaf or Hard of Hearing

An adaptive skill assessment for individuals diagnosed as deaf or hard of hearing, or with other sensory or physical impairments typically is not necessary for diagnosis or classification of the disability. However, an assessment of adaptive skills may assist in evaluating the impact of the disability on daily functioning and in identifying areas of needed skill development and support (Meacham, Kline, Stovall, & Sands, 1987). The performance of a sample of 19 children ages 5–19 years diagnosed as deaf or hard of hearing and a matched control group is reported in Table 5.50.

The mean GAC of the deaf and hard of hearing sample using the Teacher Form was 93 and does not differ significantly from the mean GAC of 99 for the matched control group. Significant differences were also not apparent on the adaptive domains or skill areas. However, 16% of the deaf and hard of hearing group had GAC scores at least two *SD*s below the mean. In contrast, 5% of children in the control group did so. 26% of the clinical sample scored at least two *SD*s below the mean on one or more adaptive domains or the GAC, compared to only 5% of the matched control group. Skill area scaled scores for the deaf and hard of hearing group did not display significant differences from those of the matched control group, although as expected, the Communication Skill Area showed the greatest deficit when compared to matched controls. Results from this study suggest that children who are deaf or hard of hearing, on average, do not exhibit major deficits in adaptive skills on the ABAS–II. However, these children may demonstrate deficits in specific skill areas and have slightly lower adaptive functioning than typically is found among children with no identified disabilities or disorders.

Children With Learning Disabilities

According to IDEA (1999), one of the criteria for identifying a specific learning disability is a severe discrepancy between achievement and intellectual ability in one or more of the following areas: oral expression, listening comprehension, written expression, basic reading skill, reading comprehension, mathematics calculation, and mathematics reasoning. A child diagnosed with a learning disability also may have deficits in adaptive skills because the learning disability may affect daily functioning (Weller & Strawser, 1987). Data were gathered for samples of children diagnosed with learning disabilities to identify typical areas in which adaptive skills may be affected by the disability. The performance of the children with learning disabilities and matched control groups is reported in Table 5.51. Four groups of children with learning disabilities were rated using Teacher or Parent forms. The three groups rated on the Teacher Form were organized by age as follows: 5–9 years (*n* = 72), 10–12 years (*n* = 62), and 13–21 years (*n* = 114). One group (ages 7–21 years, *n* = 26) was rated on the Parent Form.

Consistent across the four samples, the clinical groups displayed significantly lower scores than the matched control groups. The mean GACs of the children with learning disabilities ranged from 84–91, and were significantly lower than the mean GACs of the matched control groups, which ranged from 94–103. Adaptive domain scores ranged from 81–96 across clinical samples, and from 95–105 for matched control groups. The samples of children with learning disabilities displayed significantly lower scores on as few as two to as many as eight out of the nine skill areas, depending on the sample. 11%–29% of individuals with learning disabilities had GAC scores at least two *SD*s below the mean, in contrast to 3%–11% of those in the control groups. 28%–44% of the clinical sample scored at least two *SD*s below the mean on one or more adaptive domains or the GAC, compared to only 4%–18% of the matched control group. In addition, 42%–61% of the samples of children with learning disabilities scored at least two *SD*s below the mean on two or more skill areas, while only 15%–36% of the matched control group did so. Overall, the four clinical groups performed most poorly on the Communication, Functional Academics, and Self-Direction Skill Areas. Results from this sample of children with learning disabilities suggest that the disability may have an impact on adaptive skills, that adaptive behavior assessment may assist in diagnosis and classification, and that intervention programs focused on increasing adaptive functioning may be important.

Table 5.50 Mean Performance of Children who are Deaf or Hard of Hearing and a Matched Control Group

Teacher Form

Ages 5–19 (n = 19)	Deaf and Hard of Hearing Sample			Matched Control Group			Mean Difference of the Two Samples			
	Mean	SD	% of Scores – 2 SD	Mean	SD	% of Scores – 2 SD	Difference	t value	p value	Cohen's d
Communication	7.2	4.1	36.84	9.5	3.0	5.26	2.26	1.98	.06	.63
Community Use	7.7	3.5	26.32	9.2	2.3	5.26	1.47	1.57	.13	.50
Functional Academics	8.0	3.7	26.32	9.0	2.6	10.53	.95	.88	.39	.30
School Living	9.7	3.5	15.79	9.4	3.6	15.79	-.26	-.22	.83	-.07
Health and Safety	9.2	3.5	15.79	9.7	2.9	10.53	.53	.50	.63	.16
Leisure	9.2	3.4	10.53	9.4	3.4	10.53	.21	.21	.84	.06
Self-Care	9.0	3.2	15.79	10.1	2.5	5.26	1.11	1.18	.25	.39
Self-Direction	8.2	3.6	15.79	8.9	3.5	15.79	.68	.56	.58	.19
Social	8.2	3.8	26.32	9.4	3.2	10.53	1.21	1.29	.21	.34
Conceptual Domain	90.6	19.5	21.05	98.4	13.4	0.00	7.79	1.44	.17	.47
Social Domain	93.4	17.8	15.79	98.8	16.9	0.00	5.47	1.14	.27	.32
Practical Domain	94.4	18.8	15.79	98.2	13.5	5.26	3.84	.72	.48	.23
GAC	93.2	20.4	15.79	99.2	14.8	5.26	6.00	1.03	.32	.34
Cases with ≥ 2 skill areas – 2SD			26.32			21.05				
Cases with ≥ 1 adaptive domain – 2SD			26.32			5.26				
Cases with ≥ 1 adaptive domain or the GAC – 2SD			26.32			5.26				

Note. –2 SD = 2 or more SDs below the mean.

Table 5.51　Mean Performance of Children With Learning Disabilities and Matched Control Groups

Teacher Form

Ages 5–9 (n = 72)

	Children With Learning Disabilities			Matched Control Group			Mean Difference of the Two Samples			
	Mean	SD	% of Scores – 2 SD	Mean	SD	% of Scores – 2 SD	Difference	t value	p value	Cohen's d
Communication	6.8	3.6	30.56	9.4	3.1	13.89	2.60	4.82	<.01	.77
Community Use	7.6	3.4	25.00	9.7	2.6	6.94	2.04	3.75	<.01	.67
Functional Academics	6.4	2.7	29.17	9.7	2.4	1.39	3.31	8.33	<.01	1.30
School Living	9.3	2.6	4.17	10.1	2.9	2.78	.81	1.83	.07	.29
Health and Safety	8.9	2.6	8.33	9.9	2.8	5.56	1.06	2.32	.02	.39
Leisure	8.8	3.4	15.28	10.1	2.7	4.17	1.33	2.88	<.01	.43
Self-Care	8.9	3.4	18.06	9.7	2.8	11.11	.76	1.52	.13	.24
Self-Direction	7.4	3.4	25.00	9.7	2.9	9.72	2.38	4.29	<.01	.75
Social	9.2	2.6	6.94	9.8	2.8	8.33	.64	1.56	.12	.24
Conceptual Domain	86.3	15.2	22.22	101.9	14.0	1.39	15.54	6.51	<.01	1.06
Social Domain	95.7	14.8	5.56	101.7	15.1	2.78	6.00	2.64	.01	.40
Practical Domain	93.7	13.5	8.33	101.4	14.7	2.78	7.71	3.15	<.01	.55
GAC	91.1	14.2	11.11	102.1	15.1	2.78	10.99	4.59	<.01	.75
Cases with ≥ 2 skill areas – 2SD			41.67			16.67				
Cases with ≥ 1 adaptive domain – 2SD			27.78			4.17				
Cases with ≥ 1 adaptive domain or the GAC – 2SD			27.78			4.17				

Ages 10–12 (n = 62)

	Children With Learning Disabilities			Matched Control Group			Mean Difference of the Two Samples			
	Mean	SD	% of Scores – 2 SD	Mean	SD	% of Scores – 2 SD	Difference	t value	p value	Cohen's d
Communication	6.2	4.1	46.77	8.6	3.3	19.35	2.47	3.92	<.01	.66
Community Use	6.5	3.8	43.55	9.0	2.6	12.90	2.45	4.23	<.01	.75
Functional Academics	5.4	3.5	59.68	9.2	2.8	8.06	3.85	6.61	<.01	1.21
School Living	7.2	3.9	35.48	9.1	3.2	17.74	1.94	2.94	<.01	.54
Health and Safety	7.2	3.7	30.65	8.9	3.1	14.52	1.66	2.91	<.01	.49
Leisure	8.2	3.3	14.52	9.3	3.1	9.68	1.06	1.88	.07	.33
Self-Care	7.6	3.7	32.26	9.6	2.7	11.29	1.97	3.34	<.01	.61
Self-Direction	6.0	3.5	45.16	8.5	3.5	19.35	2.48	4.53	<.01	.71
Social	7.1	3.8	33.87	9.2	2.9	11.29	2.10	3.97	<.01	.62
Conceptual Domain	81.0	18.1	38.71	97.3	16.0	11.29	16.37	5.51	<.01	.96
Social Domain	88.9	17.4	22.58	98.2	15.9	9.68	9.21	3.29	<.01	.55
Practical Domain	86.3	19.1	20.97	98.6	14.3	6.45	12.29	3.98	<.01	.73
GAC	83.8	19.6	29.03	99.1	16.5	8.06	15.32	4.85	<.01	.85
Cases with ≥ 2 skill areas – 2SD			61.29			27.42				
Cases with ≥ 1 adaptive domain – 2SD			43.55			12.90				
Cases with ≥ 1 adaptive domain or the GAC – 2SD			43.55			12.90				

Note. – 2 SD = 2 or more SDs below the mean.

Table 5.51 Mean Performance of Children With Learning Disabilities and Matched Control Groups (continued)

Teacher Form (continued)

Ages 13–21 (n = 114)	Children With Learning Disabilities			Matched Control Group			Mean Difference of the Two Samples			
	Mean	SD	% of Scores – 2 SD	Mean	SD	% of Scores – 2 SD	Difference	t value	p value	Cohen's d
Communication	7.0	3.7	33.33	8.0	3.3	24.56	.95	2.15	.03	.27
Community Use	7.5	3.5	30.70	8.5	3.3	21.05	1.01	2.48	.01	.30
Functional Academics	7.3	3.2	17.54	8.7	3.0	10.53	1.45	3.66	<.01	.47
School Living	8.0	3.5	24.56	8.6	3.2	17.54	.63	1.55	.12	.19
Health and Safety	8.1	3.7	25.44	8.6	3.5	21.93	.50	1.18	.24	.14
Leisure	7.6	3.3	18.42	8.6	3.2	14.04	1.05	2.53	.01	.32
Self-Care	8.9	3.3	15.79	9.5	2.9	9.65	.61	1.50	.14	.20
Self-Direction	6.6	3.7	42.11	7.7	3.5	27.19	1.17	2.59	.01	.32
Social	7.5	3.8	30.70	9.1	3.2	14.91	1.59	3.68	<.01	.45
Conceptual Domain	87.3	17.6	24.56	94.7	16.6	10.53	7.36	3.44	<.01	.43
Social Domain	88.5	17.6	19.30	96.0	16.5	8.77	7.50	3.61	<.01	.44
Practical Domain	91.2	17.4	14.91	95.8	16.7	12.28	4.58	2.22	.03	.27
GAC	87.3	18.7	23.68	94.2	17.4	11.40	6.89	3.14	<.01	.38
Cases with ≥ 2 skill areas – 2SD			48.25			35.96				
Cases with ≥ 1 adaptive domain – 2SD			30.70			17.54				
Cases with ≥ 1 adaptive domain or the GAC – 2SD			30.70			17.54				

Parent Form

Ages 7–21 (n = 26)	Children With Learning Disabilities			Matched Control Group			Mean Difference of the Two Samples			
	Mean	SD	% of Scores – 2 SD	Mean	SD	% of Scores – 2 SD	Difference	t value	p value	Cohen's d
Communication	7.3	3.8	23.08	9.5	3.4	15.38	2.23	2.71	.01	.62
Community Use	8.9	3.7	11.54	10.4	3.0	0.00	1.50	1.76	.09	.45
Functional Academics	7.2	3.8	23.08	10.6	3.1	3.85	3.42	4.65	<.01	.99
Home Living	8.5	4.0	23.08	11.0	2.3	0.00	2.46	2.90	<.01	.75
Health and Safety	8.8	4.5	26.92	11.0	2.0	0.00	2.27	2.74	.01	.65
Leisure	8.2	4.2	19.23	10.2	3.1	3.85	2.04	1.96	.06	.55
Self-Care	8.6	4.0	19.23	10.4	2.2	3.85	1.77	2.30	.03	.55
Self-Direction	7.8	3.1	11.54	10.2	3.5	11.54	2.38	2.71	.01	.72
Social	7.2	4.3	34.62	9.8	3.7	11.54	2.58	2.49	.02	.64
Conceptual Domain	85.9	17.5	23.08	101.2	16.7	11.54	15.35	3.71	<.01	.90
Social Domain	88.2	19.7	23.08	100.3	17.0	7.69	12.04	2.44	.02	.65
Practical Domain	91.6	19.4	11.54	104.8	11.7	0.00	13.19	3.50	<.01	.82
GAC	87.6	20.5	15.38	102.5	15.2	7.69	14.88	3.39	<.01	.82
Cases with ≥ 2 skill areas – 2SD			42.31			15.38				
Cases with ≥ 1 adaptive domain – 2SD			34.62			11.54				
Cases with ≥ 1 adaptive domain or the GAC – 2SD			34.62			11.54				

Note. –2 SD = 2 or more SDs below the mean.

Adults With Alzheimer's Disease

Identification of deficits in the daily skills necessary to care for oneself and get along with others may be useful in the selection of treatment programs and identification of supports for adults diagnosed with Alzheimer's disease. Data were collected for a sample of 25 adults ages 43–88 years diagnosed with Alzheimer's disease. The performance of the adults diagnosed with Alzheimer's disease and a matched control group is reported in Table 5.52.

The mean GAC of the group of adults with Alzheimer's disease rated by other respondents on the Adult Form was 61, and was significantly lower than the mean GAC of 104 for the matched control group. Adaptive domain scores also showed significant differences, ranging from 66–75 for the clinical sample, and from 104–105 for matched control group. Significant differences were found in all nine skill areas as well. 80% of the clinical sample had GAC scores at least two *SD*s below the mean compared to only 8% of the matched control group. 80% of the clinical sample scored at least two *SD*s below the mean on one or more adaptive domains or the GAC, in contrast to 8% of the matched control group. In addition, 80% of the clinical group scored at least two *SD*s below the mean on two or more skill areas, while only 8% of the matched control group did so. The data illustrate the impact of Alzheimer's disease on daily functioning and support the use of an adaptive behavior assessment for individuals diagnosed with the disease.

Adults With Neuropsychological Disorders

Adults diagnosed with neuropsychological disorders may have problems that influence daily functioning and justify the administration of an adaptive skill assessment. The performance of two samples of adults diagnosed with neuropsychological disorders and matched control groups are reported in Table 5.53 by rating forms. The first sample of 18 adults ages 18–85 rated on the Adult Form, Self Report included individuals with brain injury (39%), stroke (33%), Parkinson disease (11%), epilepsy (11%), and sclerosis (6%). The second sample of 20 adults ages 28–85 rated on the Adult Form, Rated by Others included individuals with brain injury (20%), stroke (60%), Parkinson disease (5%), epilepsy (10%), and unspecified neuropsychological disorder (5%).

Consistent across the two samples, adults diagnosed with neuropsychological disorders displayed lower scores when compared to the matched control groups. The mean GAC for the self-rated sample was 82, compared to the mean GAC of 100 for the matched control group. For the sample rated by others, the mean GAC was 67, which was significantly lower than the mean GAC of 101 for the matched control group. Adaptive domain scores ranged from 67–86 for the clinical samples, and from 99–103 for matched control groups. The sample of adults rated by others displayed significantly lower scores in all nine skill areas.

Furthermore, 28%–75% of the clinical groups had GACs at least two *SD*s below the mean, in contrast to 0%–5% of the matched control groups. 39%–80% of the clinical samples scored at least two *SD*s below the mean on one or more adaptive domains or the GAC, compared to 0%–5% of the matched control groups. In addition, 50%–75% of the clinical groups scored at least two *SD*s below the mean on two or more skill areas, while only 6%–10% of the matched control group did so. Although the samples of adults diagnosed with neuropsychological disorders did not have scores as low as the sample of adults diagnosed with Alzheimer's disease, most exhibited significant impairments in adaptive skills.

Table 5.52 Mean Performance of Adults With Alzheimer's Disease and a Matched Control Group

Adult Form, Rated by Others

Ages 43–88 (n = 25)	Adults With Alzheimer's Disease			Matched Control Group			Mean Difference of the Two Samples			
	Mean	SD	% of Scores – 2 SD	Mean	SD	% of Scores – 2 SD	Difference	t value	p value	Cohen's d
Communication	4.1	2.6	68.00	10.2	2.7	0.00	6.08	8.97	<.01	2.29
Community Use	3.4	1.8	84.00	10.5	3.1	8.00	7.16	10.46	<.01	2.82
Functional Academics	3.2	1.9	76.00	10.9	3.3	8.00	7.72	10.79	<.01	2.87
Home Living	3.4	1.7	76.00	11.0	2.5	4.00	7.60	11.33	<.01	3.56
Health and Safety	3.4	1.7	76.00	10.5	2.5	8.00	7.12	12.25	<.01	3.33
Leisure	5.5	2.1	32.00	11.3	3.2	0.00	5.76	7.81	<.01	2.13
Self-Care	3.8	3.2	64.00	10.9	2.0	0.00	7.16	9.38	<.01	2.68
Self-Direction	3.9	1.7	72.00	11.2	3.1	4.00	7.32	10.43	<.01	2.93
Social	4.2	2.3	60.00	10.8	3.2	4.00	6.56	8.44	<.01	2.35
Conceptual Domain	67.4	12.6	72.00	103.7	15.1	8.00	36.28	10.05	<.01	2.61
Social Domain	74.7	9.9	44.00	104.4	14.7	0.00	29.76	8.59	<.01	2.37
Practical Domain	66.2	14.5	64.00	105.2	12.5	4.00	38.96	10.56	<.01	2.88
GAC	61.4	11.6	80.00	103.6	16.6	8.00	42.16	10.68	<.01	2.94
Cases with ≥ 2 skill areas – 2SD			80.00			8.00				
Cases with ≥ 1 adaptive domain – 2SD			72.00			8.00				
Cases with ≥ 1 adaptive domain or the GAC – 2SD			80.00			8.00				

Note. –2 SD = 2 or more SDs below the mean.

Table 5.53 Mean Performance of Adults With Neuropsychological Disorders and Matched Control Groups

Adult Form, Self Report

Ages 18–85 (n = 18)	Adults With Neuropsychological Disorders			Matched Control Group			Mean Difference of the Two Samples			
	Mean	SD	% of Scores – 2 SD	Mean	SD	% of Scores – 2 SD	Difference	t value	p value	Cohen's d
Communication	8.2	3.5	16.67	10.3	2.6	0.00	2.11	1.92	.07	.68
Community Use	7.3	4.4	33.33	9.8	2.7	5.56	2.44	2.00	.06	.67
Functional Academics	7.2	3.9	27.78	9.8	2.5	0.00	2.67	2.39	.03	.82
Home Living	7.1	4.3	27.78	10.4	2.2	0.00	3.33	2.85	.01	.97
Health and Safety	7.0	4.3	33.33	10.2	2.4	0.00	3.17	2.66	.02	.91
Leisure	7.7	3.4	16.67	10.1	2.3	0.00	2.39	2.26	.04	.82
Self-Care	7.4	4.2	27.78	10.6	2.5	5.56	3.17	2.57	.02	.92
Self-Direction	6.8	4.2	33.33	10.1	2.7	0.00	3.28	2.46	.02	.93
Social	7.3	3.8	22.22	9.9	2.7	0.00	2.56	2.00	.06	.78
Conceptual Domain	85.1	19.7	27.78	99.5	12.5	0.00	14.44	2.50	.02	.88
Social Domain	86.0	17.6	22.22	99.1	13.0	0.00	13.11	2.29	.04	.85
Practical Domain	81.9	23.4	33.33	99.6	12.7	0.00	17.72	2.65	.02	.94
GAC	82.2	21.6	27.78	99.6	12.3	0.00	17.39	2.74	.01	.99
Cases with ≥ 2 skill areas – 2SD			50.00			5.56				
Cases with ≥ 1 adaptive domain – 2SD			38.89			0.00				
Cases with ≥ 1 adaptive domain or the GAC – 2SD			38.89			0.00				

Adult Form, Rated by Others

Ages 28–85 (n = 20)	Adults With Neuropsychological Disorders			Matched Control Group			Mean Difference of the Two Samples			
	Mean	SD	% of Scores – 2 SD	Mean	SD	% of Scores – 2 SD	Difference	t value	p value	Cohen's d
Communication	5.7	2.9	35.00	10.5	2.8	0.00	4.80	5.56	<.01	1.68
Community Use	4.4	2.7	65.00	10.0	3.0	5.00	5.65	6.46	<.01	1.98
Functional Academics	5.1	3.4	50.00	10.3	3.0	5.00	5.15	6.15	<.01	1.61
Home Living	4.1	3.0	70.00	11.5	2.2	0.00	7.40	8.77	<.01	2.81
Health and Safety	4.0	2.9	70.00	10.3	2.6	10.00	6.35	7.12	<.01	2.31
Leisure	6.4	2.7	25.00	10.4	3.4	5.00	4.00	4.46	<.01	1.30
Self-Care	4.4	3.8	65.00	10.5	2.3	0.00	6.10	5.68	<.01	1.94
Self-Direction	4.7	2.8	40.00	10.7	3.4	5.00	5.95	6.54	<.01	1.91
Social	6.1	3.3	30.00	10.8	2.5	0.00	4.75	5.48	<.01	1.62
Conceptual Domain	74.4	16.2	45.00	102.2	16.2	5.00	27.85	6.76	<.01	1.72
Social Domain	80.0	13.2	40.00	101.7	14.4	0.00	21.75	5.59	<.01	1.57
Practical Domain	67.0	16.7	65.00	103.0	14.0	0.00	36.00	7.89	<.01	2.34
GAC	67.4	15.2	75.00	101.4	16.2	5.00	34.05	7.48	<.01	2.17
Cases with ≥ 2 skill areas – 2SD			75.00			10.00				
Cases with ≥ 1 adaptive domain – 2SD			70.00			5.00				
Cases with ≥ 1 adaptive domain or the GAC – 2SD			80.00			5.00				

Note. – 2 SD = 2 or more SDs below the mean.

Summary of Clinical Validity Studies

The results of the clinical validity studies suggest that the ABAS–II demonstrates good levels of sensitivity in differentiating between clinical and nonclinical samples. The mean GACs of most clinical samples were significantly lower than those of the matched control groups. Furthermore, the percentages of individuals who scored at least two SDs below the mean of one or more adaptive domains or on the GAC, or on at least two skill areas were significantly higher for the clinical samples than for the matched control groups. In addition, the results of the clinical studies indicate that the ABAS–II has good specificity in differentiating individuals with different levels of disabilities. For example, there were significant differences between mean GAC scores of the school-age and adult samples of individuals diagnosed with mild and moderate mental retardation. Overall, the validity data with clinical samples suggest that adaptive skill assessment is important in the comprehensive assessment of individuals with a number of different disabilities and disorders. Adaptive skill assessment is required for the diagnosis and classification of individuals with mental retardation. It should also be considered for use in the comprehensive assessment of individuals being evaluated for other disabilities or disorders to aid in diagnoses, to identify strengths and limitations in adaptive skills, and to help develop needed interventions.

Consequences of Using the ABAS–II

Tests are commonly administered with the belief that the individual being assessed will derive some benefit from the test results. Tests can also assist professionals and institutions in meeting professional and legal standards governing diagnosis and classification, program planning and monitoring, institutional planning, and research and evaluation activities. The authors and publisher believe that tests are technical resources intended to assist professionals and parents or others involved in the care of the individual being assessed in accurately describing behaviors and improving decisions based on test results. We trust the consequences of using the ABAS–II are beneficial for those being tested as well as those using the results.

Professionals must be alert to intended and unintended consequences of test use. Professionals should also acknowledge intended and unintended consequences of relying on informal judgments instead of those informed by test results. Although information concerning the consequences of testing may influence the decision to use tests, such consequences alone do not detract from the validity of the intended test interpretations (American Education Research Association, et al., 1999).

Appendix A

Norms Tables

When consulting data tables, refer carefully to the table subheadings (upper left side of tables) to ensure that you are consulting the correct section of the table for the rating form you are using.

Table A.1 Scaled Score Equivalents of Skill Area Raw Scores: Teacher/Daycare Provider and Teacher Forms

Teacher/Daycare Provider Form

Ages 2:0–2:2

ss	Com	FA	SL	HS	LS	SC	SD	Soc	MO	ss
1	0-9	0	0-1	0-7	0-20	0-25	0-6	0-13	0-26	1
2	10-15	1	2-4	8-12	21-25	26-30	7-10	14-19	27-33	2
3	16-20	2	5-7	13-17	26-29	31-34	11-14	20-25	34-39	3
4	21-25	3	8-10	18-21	30-33	35-38	15-19	26-30	40-44	4
5	26-29	4	11-13	22-24	34-36	39-41	20-24	31-34	45-48	5
6	30-32	5	14-17	25-26	37-39	42-43	25-28	35-37	49-51	6
7	33-35	6-7	18-22	27-28	40-41	44-46	29-32	38-39	52-53	7
8	36-39	8-9	23-27	29-30	42-44	47-48	33-36	40-42	54-55	8
9	40-43	10-12	28-32	31-33	45-47	49-51	37-40	43-45	56-57	9
10	44-47	13-15	33-37	34-36	48-51	52-54	41-43	46-49	58-59	10
11	48-51	16-18	38-43	37-39	52-54	55-56	44-46	50-53	60-61	11
12	52-55	19-22	44-48	40-41	55-57	57-59	47-49	54-56	62-63	12
13	56-59	23-27	49-53	42-44	58-60	60-61	50-52	57-58	64-65	13
14	60-62	28-32	54-57	45-47	61-62	62-63	53-55	59-61	66-68	14
15	63-65	33-37	58-60	48-50	63-64	64	56-58	62-64	69-70	15
16	66-68	38-43	61-63	51-53	65	65	59-61	65-67	71-72	16
17	69-71	44-50	64-66	54-56	66	66-67	62-65	68-71	73-74	17
18	72-73	51-58	67-69	57-60	67-68	68	66-70	72-74	75-76	18
19	74-75	59-72	-	61-63	69	69-72	71-72	75	77-81	19

Ages 2:3–2:5

ss	Com	FA	SL	HS	LS	SC	SD	Soc	MO	ss
1	0-9	0	0-1	0-7	0-20	0-25	0-6	0-13	0-26	1
2	10-16	1	2-4	8-12	21-25	26-31	7-13	14-20	27-33	2
3	17-22	2	5-8	13-17	26-29	32-36	14-19	21-26	34-39	3
4	23-27	3	9-12	18-21	30-33	37-40	20-24	27-31	40-44	4
5	28-31	4-5	13-17	22-24	34-37	41-43	25-28	32-35	45-48	5
6	32-35	6-7	18-22	25-27	38-41	44-46	29-32	36-38	49-52	6
7	36-39	8-10	23-27	28-30	42-44	47-48	33-36	39-42	53-55	7
8	40-44	11-13	28-32	31-33	45-47	49-51	37-40	43-45	56-57	8
9	45-49	14-17	33-37	34-36	48-51	52-54	41-43	46-49	58-59	9
10	50-53	18-21	38-43	37-39	52-54	55-57	44-46	50-53	60-61	10
11	54-57	22-26	44-48	40-42	55-57	58-60	47-49	54-56	62-64	11
12	58-61	27-31	49-53	43-45	58-59	61-62	50-52	57-58	65-66	12
13	62-64	32-36	54-57	46-48	60-62	63-64	53-55	59-61	67-68	13
14	65-67	37-40	58-60	49-51	63-64	65	56-58	62-64	69-71	14
15	68-69	41-44	61-63	52-53	65	66-67	59-61	65-67	72-73	15
16	70-71	45-50	64-66	54-56	66	68	62-64	68-70	74	16
17	72-73	51-57	67-69	57-59	67	-	65-67	71-72	75-76	17
18	74	58-65	-	60-61	68	69-70	68-70	73-74	77-79	18
19	75	66-72	-	62-63	69	71-72	71-72	75	80-81	19

Ages 2:6–2:8

ss	Com	FA	SL	HS	LS	SC	SD	Soc	MO	ss
1	0-14	0-1	0-4	0-9	0-22	0-26	0-13	0-20	0-30	1
2	15-20	2	5-8	10-14	23-27	27-33	14-19	21-25	31-37	2
3	21-26	3	9-12	15-19	28-32	34-39	20-24	26-30	38-43	3
4	27-31	4-5	13-17	20-24	33-37	40-43	25-28	31-35	44-48	4
5	32-35	6-7	18-22	25-27	38-41	44-46	29-32	36-38	49-52	5
6	36-39	8-10	23-27	28-30	42-44	47-48	33-36	39-42	53-55	6
7	40-44	11-13	28-32	31-33	45-47	49-51	37-40	43-45	56-57	7
8	45-49	14-17	33-37	34-36	48-51	52-54	41-43	46-49	58-59	8
9	50-53	18-21	38-43	37-39	52-54	55-57	44-46	50-53	60-61	9
10	54-57	22-26	44-48	40-42	55-57	58-60	47-49	54-56	62-64	10
11	58-61	27-31	49-53	43-45	58-59	61-62	50-52	57-58	65-66	11
12	62-64	32-36	54-57	46-48	60-62	63-64	53-55	59-61	67-68	12
13	65-67	37-40	58-60	49-51	63-64	65-66	56-58	62-64	69-71	13
14	68-69	41-44	61-63	52-53	65	67	59-61	65-67	72-73	14
15	70-71	45-50	64-66	54-56	66	68	62-64	68-70	74	15
16	72-73	51-57	67-69	57-59	67	-	65-67	71-72	75-76	16
17	74	58-62	-	60-61	68	69-70	68-69	73	77-79	17
18	75	63-67	-	62	69	71	70-71	74-75	80-81	18
19	-	68-72	-	63	-	72	72	-	-	19

Ages 2:9–2:11

ss	Com	FA	SL	HS	LS	SC	SD	Soc	MO	ss
1	0-14	0-1	0-4	0-9	0-22	0-26	0-15	0-20	0-30	1
2	15-20	2	5-9	10-14	23-27	27-33	16-21	21-25	31-37	2
3	21-26	3-4	10-14	15-19	28-32	34-39	22-26	26-30	38-43	3
4	27-32	5-7	15-19	20-24	33-37	40-44	27-31	31-35	44-48	4
5	33-38	8-10	20-24	25-28	38-42	45-48	32-35	36-40	49-52	5
6	39-44	11-13	25-30	29-32	43-46	49-51	36-38	41-44	53-56	6
7	45-49	14-17	31-36	33-36	47-49	52-54	39-42	45-48	57-59	7
8	50-53	18-21	37-42	37-39	50-52	55-57	43-46	49-51	60-61	8
9	54-57	22-26	43-48	40-42	53-55	58-60	47-49	52-55	62-64	9
10	58-61	27-31	49-53	43-45	56-58	61-62	50-52	56-58	65-66	10
11	62-64	32-36	54-57	46-48	59-60	63-64	53-55	59-60	67-68	11
12	65-67	37-40	58-60	49-51	61-62	65-66	56-58	61-63	69-71	12
13	68-69	41-44	61-63	52-53	63-64	67	59-61	64-66	72-73	13
14	70-71	45-48	64-66	54-55	65-66	68	62-63	67-68	74	14
15	72-73	49-52	67-68	56-57	67	-	64-66	69-70	75-76	15
16	74	53-57	69	58-59	68	69	67-68	71-72	77-78	16
17	-	58-62	-	60-61	-	70	69	73	79-80	17
18	75	63-67	-	62	69	71	70-71	74-75	81	18
19	-	68-72	-	63	-	72	72	-	-	19

Note. **Com** = Communication; **FA** = Functional Pre-Academics; **SL** = School Living; **HS** = Health and Safety; **LS** = Leisure; **SC** = Self-Care; **SD** = Self-Direction; **Soc** = Social; **MO** = Motor.

Table A.1 Scaled Score Equivalents of Skill Area Raw Scores: Teacher/Daycare Provider and Teacher Forms (continued)

Teacher/Daycare Provider Form

Ages 3:0–3:2

ss	Com	FA	SL	HS	LS	SC	SD	Soc	MO	ss
1	0-18	0-2	0-9	0-13	0-24	0-28	0-17	0-25	0-36	1
2	19-25	3-4	10-14	14-19	25-29	29-34	18-22	26-30	37-41	2
3	26-31	5-6	15-19	20-24	30-34	35-40	23-27	31-34	42-46	3
4	32-37	7-8	20-24	25-28	35-39	41-45	28-32	35-38	47-51	4
5	38-42	9-11	25-30	29-32	40-44	46-50	33-36	39-42	52-55	5
6	43-46	12-15	31-36	33-36	45-48	51-54	37-39	43-46	56-58	6
7	47-50	16-19	37-42	37-39	49-52	55-57	40-43	47-50	59-61	7
8	51-54	20-24	43-46	40-42	53-55	58-60	44-47	51-54	62-64	8
9	55-59	25-30	47-51	43-45	56-58	61-62	48-51	55-58	65-66	9
10	60-63	31-36	52-56	46-48	59-60	63-64	52-55	59-60	67-68	10
11	64-67	37-40	57-60	49-51	61-62	65-66	56-58	61-63	69-71	11
12	68-69	41-44	61-63	52-53	63-64	67	59-61	64-66	72-73	12
13	70-71	45-48	64-65	54-55	65-66	68	62-63	67-68	74	13
14	72-73	49-52	66-67	56-57	67	–	64-66	69-70	75-76	14
15	74	53-57	68-69	58-59	68	69	67-68	71-72	77-78	15
16	–	58-62	–	60-61	–	70	69	73	79-80	16
17	75	63-65	–	62	69	71	70-71	74-75	81	17
18	–	66-69	–	63	–	72	72	–	–	18
19	–	70-72	–	–	–	–	–	–	–	19

Ages 3:3–3:5

ss	Com	FA	SL	HS	LS	SC	SD	Soc	MO	ss
1	0-18	0-2	0-13	0-13	0-24	0-28	0-17	0-25	0-36	1
2	19-25	3-4	14-19	14-19	25-29	29-34	18-22	26-30	37-41	2
3	26-31	5-6	20-24	20-25	30-34	35-40	23-27	31-36	42-46	3
4	32-37	7-8	25-29	26-30	35-39	41-45	28-32	37-39	47-51	4
5	38-42	9-13	30-34	31-34	40-44	46-50	33-37	40-42	52-55	5
6	43-46	14-18	35-39	35-38	45-49	51-55	38-42	43-46	56-58	6
7	47-50	19-23	40-44	39-41	50-53	56-59	43-46	47-50	59-63	7
8	51-54	24-28	45-49	42-45	54-56	60-62	47-50	51-54	64-67	8
9	55-59	29-34	50-53	46-48	57-59	63-64	51-53	55-58	68-69	9
10	60-63	35-39	54-56	49-51	60-61	65-66	54-56	59-61	70-72	10
11	64-67	40-44	57-60	52-53	62-63	67	57-59	62-65	73	11
12	68-70	45-49	61-63	54-55	64-65	68	60-63	66-68	74-75	12
13	71-72	50-53	64-65	56-57	66-67	–	64-66	69-70	76	13
14	73	54-56	66-67	58	68	69	67-68	71-72	77	14
15	74	57-59	68-69	59	–	70	69	73	78-79	15
16	75	60-62	–	60-61	69	71	70	74	80	16
17	–	63-65	–	62	–	–	71-72	75	81	17
18	–	66-69	–	63	–	72	–	–	–	18
19	–	70-72	–	–	–	–	–	–	–	19

Ages 3:6–3:8

ss	Com	FA	SL	HS	LS	SC	SD	Soc	MO	ss
1	0-24	0-3	0-18	0-19	0-29	0-34	0-22	0-30	0-41	1
2	25-31	4-6	19-24	20-25	30-34	35-40	23-27	31-36	42-46	2
3	32-37	7-8	25-29	26-30	35-39	41-45	28-32	37-39	47-51	3
4	38-42	9-13	30-34	31-34	40-44	46-50	33-37	40-42	52-55	4
5	43-46	14-18	35-39	35-38	45-49	51-55	38-42	43-46	56-58	5
6	47-50	19-23	40-44	39-41	50-53	56-59	43-46	47-50	59-63	6
7	51-54	24-28	45-49	42-45	54-56	60-62	47-50	51-54	64-67	7
8	55-59	29-34	50-53	46-48	57-59	63-64	51-53	55-58	68-70	8
9	60-63	35-39	54-56	49-51	60-61	65-66	54-56	59-61	71-72	9
10	64-67	40-44	57-60	52-53	62-63	67	57-59	62-65	73	10
11	68-70	45-49	61-63	54-55	64-65	68	60-63	66-68	74-75	11
12	71-72	50-53	64-65	56-57	66-67	–	64-66	69-70	76	12
13	73	54-56	66-67	58	68	69	67-68	71-72	77	13
14	74	57-59	68-69	59	–	70	69	73	78-79	14
15	–	60-62	–	60-61	69	71	70	74	80	15
16	75	63-65	–	62	–	72	71-72	75	81	16
17	–	66-69	–	63	–	–	–	–	–	17
18	–	70-71	–	–	–	–	–	–	–	18
19	–	72	–	–	–	–	–	–	–	19

Ages 3:9–3:11

ss	Com	FA	SL	HS	LS	SC	SD	Soc	MO	ss
1	0-24	0-3	0-18	0-22	0-31	0-37	0-24	0-36	0-42	1
2	25-31	4-8	19-26	23-28	32-38	38-44	25-31	37-39	43-48	2
3	32-37	9-13	27-33	29-33	39-44	45-50	32-37	40-42	49-53	3
4	38-43	14-18	34-39	34-37	45-49	51-55	38-42	43-46	54-58	4
5	44-49	19-23	40-44	38-41	50-53	56-59	43-46	47-50	59-63	5
6	50-54	24-28	45-49	42-45	54-56	60-62	47-50	51-54	64-67	6
7	55-59	29-34	50-53	46-48	57-59	63-64	51-53	55-58	68-70	7
8	60-63	35-39	54-56	49-51	60-61	65-66	54-56	59-61	71-72	8
9	64-66	40-44	57-59	52-53	62-63	67	57-59	62-64	73	9
10	67-68	45-49	60-62	54-55	64-65	–	60-62	65-66	74-75	10
11	69-70	50-53	63-65	56-57	66	68	63-65	67-69	76	11
12	71-72	54-56	66-67	58	67	–	66-67	70-71	77	12
13	73	57-59	68	59	68	69	68-69	72-73	78	13
14	74	60-62	69	60-61	–	70	70	74	79	14
15	–	63-65	–	62	69	71	71-72	75	80	15
16	75	66-68	–	63	–	72	–	–	81	16
17	–	69-70	–	–	–	–	–	–	–	17
18	–	71	–	–	–	–	–	–	–	18
19	–	72	–	–	–	–	–	–	–	19

Note. **Com** = Communication; **FA** = Functional Pre-Academics; **SL** = School Living; **HS** = Health and Safety; **LS** = Leisure; **SC** = Self-Care; **SD** = Self-Direction; **Soc** = Social; **MO** = Motor.

Table A.1 Scaled Score Equivalents of Skill Area Raw Scores: Teacher/Daycare Provider and Teacher Forms *(continued)*

Teacher/Daycare Provider Form

Ages 4:0–4:2

ss	Com	FA	SL	HS	LS	SC	SD	Soc	MO	ss
1	0–30	0–5	0–24	0–25	0–35	0–42	0–25	0–36	0–46	1
2	31–36	6–10	25–30	26–31	36–41	43–47	26–32	37–39	47–51	2
3	37–42	11–16	31–36	32–36	42–46	48–52	33–38	40–43	52–56	3
4	43–47	17–22	37–41	37–40	47–50	53–57	39–43	44–46	57–61	4
5	48–52	23–28	42–45	41–43	51–53	58–61	44–47	47–50	62–65	5
6	53–56	29–34	46–50	44–46	54–56	62–64	48–51	51–54	66–68	6
7	57–60	35–39	51–54	47–49	57–59	65–66	52–54	55–58	69–71	7
8	61–64	40–44	55–57	50–51	60–62	67	55–57	59–61	72–73	8
9	65–67	45–49	58–60	52–54	63–64	–	58–60	62–64	74–75	9
10	68–69	50–53	61–63	55–56	65	68	61–63	65–67	76	10
11	70–71	54–56	64–65	57–58	66	–	64–66	68–70	77	11
12	72	57–59	66–67	59	67	69	67–68	71–72	78	12
13	73	60–62	68	60–61	68	70	69	73	79	13
14	74	63–65	69	62	69	71	70–71	74–75	80	14
15	75	66–68	–	63	–	–	72	–	81	15
16	–	69–70	–	–	–	72	–	–	–	16
17	–	71	–	–	–	–	–	–	–	17
18	–	72	–	–	–	–	–	–	–	18
19	–	–	–	–	–	–	–	–	–	19

Ages 4:3–4:5

ss	Com	FA	SL	HS	LS	SC	SD	Soc	MO	ss
1	0–30	0–5	0–24	0–25	0–35	0–42	0–25	0–36	0–46	1
2	31–36	6–10	25–30	26–31	36–41	43–47	26–32	37–39	47–51	2
3	37–42	11–17	31–36	32–36	42–46	48–52	33–38	40–43	52–56	3
4	43–47	18–22	37–41	37–40	47–50	53–57	39–43	44–46	57–61	4
5	48–52	23–28	42–45	41–43	51–53	58–61	44–47	47–50	62–65	5
6	53–56	29–34	46–50	44–46	54–56	62–64	48–51	51–54	66–68	6
7	57–60	35–39	51–54	47–49	57–59	65–66	52–54	55–58	69–71	7
8	61–64	40–44	55–57	50–51	60–62	67	55–57	59–61	72–73	8
9	65–67	45–50	58–60	52–54	63–64	–	58–60	62–64	74–75	9
10	68–69	51–55	61–63	55–56	65	68	61–63	65–67	76–77	10
11	70–71	56–59	64–65	57–58	66	69	64–66	68–70	78	11
12	72	60–62	66–67	59	67	–	67–68	71–72	79	12
13	73	63–65	68	60–61	68	70	69	73	80	13
14	74	66–68	69	62	69	71	70–71	74–75	–	14
15	75	69–70	–	–	–	–	72	–	81	15
16	–	71	–	63	–	72	–	–	–	16
17	–	72	–	–	–	–	–	–	–	17
18	–	–	–	–	–	–	–	–	–	18
19	–	–	–	–	–	–	–	–	–	19

Ages 4:6–4:8

ss	Com	FA	SL	HS	LS	SC	SD	Soc	MO	ss
1	0–35	0–10	0–27	0–27	0–38	0–46	0–26	0–38	0–49	1
2	36–42	11–17	28–34	28–33	39–42	47–52	27–33	39–41	50–55	2
3	43–47	18–22	35–40	34–38	43–47	53–57	34–39	42–45	56–60	3
4	48–52	23–28	41–45	39–42	48–51	58–61	40–44	46–49	61–64	4
5	53–56	29–34	46–49	43–45	52–55	62–64	45–48	50–53	65–68	5
6	57–60	35–39	50–53	46–48	56–58	65–66	49–51	54–56	69–71	6
7	61–63	40–44	54–56	49–51	59–60	67	52–54	57–59	72–73	7
8	64–66	45–50	57–59	52–53	61–63	–	55–57	60–61	74–75	8
9	67–68	51–55	60–62	54–55	64–65	68	58–60	62–64	76–77	9
10	69–70	56–59	63–65	56–57	66	–	61–63	65–67	78	10
11	71	60–62	66–67	58	–	69	64–66	68–70	79	11
12	72	63–65	68	59	67	–	67–68	71–72	80	12
13	73	66–68	–	60–61	68	70	69–70	73–74	–	13
14	74	69–70	69	62	69	71	71	75	81	14
15	75	71	–	63	–	72	72	–	–	15
16	–	72	–	–	–	–	–	–	–	16
17	–	–	–	–	–	–	–	–	–	17
18	–	–	–	–	–	–	–	–	–	18
19	–	–	–	–	–	–	–	–	–	19

Ages 4:9–4:11

ss	Com	FA	SL	HS	LS	SC	SD	Soc	MO	ss
1	0–35	0–17	0–27	0–27	0–38	0–46	0–26	0–38	0–49	1
2	36–42	18–21	28–34	28–33	39–42	47–52	27–33	39–41	50–55	2
3	43–48	22–25	35–40	34–38	43–47	53–57	34–39	42–45	56–60	3
4	49–53	26–30	41–45	39–42	48–51	58–61	40–44	46–49	61–64	4
5	54–57	31–35	46–49	43–45	52–55	62–64	45–48	50–53	65–68	5
6	58–60	36–41	50–53	46–48	56–58	65–66	49–51	54–56	69–71	6
7	61–63	42–46	54–56	49–51	59–60	67	52–54	57–59	72–74	7
8	64–66	47–51	57–59	52–53	61–63	–	55–57	60–61	75–76	8
9	67–68	52–55	60–62	54–55	64–65	68	58–60	62–64	77	9
10	69–70	56–59	63–65	56–57	66	–	61–63	65–67	78	10
11	71	60–63	66–67	58	–	69	64–66	68–70	79	11
12	72	64–66	68	59	67	–	67–68	71–72	80	12
13	73	67–69	–	60–61	68	70	69–70	73–74	–	13
14	74	70–71	69	62	69	71–72	71	75	81	14
15	75	72	–	63	–	–	72	–	–	15
16	–	–	–	–	–	–	–	–	–	16
17	–	–	–	–	–	–	–	–	–	17
18	–	–	–	–	–	–	–	–	–	18
19	–	–	–	–	–	–	–	–	–	19

Note. **Com** = Communication; **FA** = Functional Pre-Academics; **SL** = School Living; **HS** = Health and Safety; **LS** = Leisure; **SC** = Self-Care; **SD** = Self-Direction; **Soc** = Social; **MO** = Motor.

Table A.1 Scaled Score Equivalents of Skill Area Raw Scores: Teacher/Daycare Provider and Teacher Forms (continued)

Teacher/Daycare Provider Form

Ages 5:0–5:2

ss	Com	FA	SL	HS	LS	SC	SD	Soc	MO
1	0-35	0-17	0-27	0-27	0-38	0-46	0-26	0-38	0-49
2	36-42	18-22	28-34	28-33	39-42	47-52	27-33	39-41	50-55
3	43-48	23-28	35-40	34-38	43-47	53-57	34-39	42-45	56-60
4	49-53	29-34	41-45	39-42	48-51	58-61	40-44	46-49	61-64
5	54-57	35-40	46-49	43-45	52-55	62-64	45-48	50-53	65-68
6	58-60	41-46	50-54	46-48	56-58	65-66	49-51	54-56	69-71
7	61-63	47-51	55-58	49-51	59-60	67	52-54	57-59	72-74
8	64-66	52-55	59-61	52-53	61-63	68	55-57	60-61	75-76
9	67-68	56-59	62-63	54-55	64-65	–	58-60	62-64	77
10	69-70	60-63	64-65	56-57	66	69	61-63	65-67	78
11	71	64-66	66-67	58-59	–	–	64-66	68-70	79
12	72	67-68	68	60	67	70	67-68	71-72	80
13	73	69-70	–	61	68	71	69-70	73-74	–
14	74	71-72	69	62	69	72	71	75	81
15	75	–	–	63	–	–	72	–	–
16	–	–	–	–	–	–	–	–	–
17	–	–	–	–	–	–	–	–	–
18	–	–	–	–	–	–	–	–	–
19	–	–	–	–	–	–	–	–	–

Ages 5:3–5:5

ss	Com	FA	SL	HS	LS	SC	SD	Soc	MO
1	0-37	0-22	0-29	0-29	0-40	0-51	0-29	0-39	0-53
2	38-43	23-28	30-36	30-35	41-43	52-56	30-36	40-42	54-59
3	44-49	29-34	37-43	36-40	44-47	57-60	37-42	43-46	60-64
4	50-54	35-40	44-49	41-44	48-51	61-63	43-47	47-50	65-68
5	55-58	41-46	50-54	45-47	52-55	64-65	48-51	51-54	69-71
6	59-61	47-51	55-58	48-49	56-58	66-67	52-54	55-57	72-74
7	62-64	52-55	59-61	50-52	59-61	68	55-57	58-60	75-76
8	65-67	56-59	62-63	53-55	62-63	–	58-60	61-63	77
9	68-69	60-63	64	56-57	64-65	69	61-63	64-66	78
10	70	64-66	65	58-59	66	–	64-66	67-69	79
11	71	67-68	66-67	60	67	70	67-68	70-71	80
12	72-73	69-70	68	61	68	71	69	72-73	–
13	74	71-72	69	62	–	72	70-71	74	81
14	–	–	–	63	69	–	72	75	–
15	75	–	–	–	–	–	–	–	–
16	–	–	–	–	–	–	–	–	–
17	–	–	–	–	–	–	–	–	–
18	–	–	–	–	–	–	–	–	–
19	–	–	–	–	–	–	–	–	–

Ages 5:6–5:8

ss	Com	FA	SL	HS	LS	SC	SD	Soc	MO
1	0-37	0-22	0-29	0-29	0-40	0-51	0-29	0-39	0-53
2	38-43	23-28	30-36	30-35	41-43	52-56	30-36	40-42	54-59
3	44-49	29-34	37-43	36-40	44-47	57-60	37-42	43-46	60-64
4	50-54	35-40	44-49	41-44	48-51	61-63	43-47	47-50	65-68
5	55-58	41-46	50-54	45-47	52-55	64-65	48-51	51-54	69-71
6	59-61	47-51	55-58	48-49	56-58	66-67	52-54	55-57	72-74
7	62-64	52-55	59-61	50-52	59-61	68	55-57	58-60	75-76
8	65-67	56-59	62-63	53-55	62-63	–	58-60	61-63	77
9	68-69	60-63	64	56-57	64-65	69	61-63	64-66	78
10	70	64-66	65	58-59	66	–	64-66	67-69	79
11	71	67-68	66-67	60	67	70	67-68	70-71	80
12	72-73	69-70	68	61	68	71	69	72-73	–
13	74	71-72	69	62	–	72	70-71	74	81
14	–	–	–	63	69	–	72	75	–
15	75	–	–	–	–	–	–	–	–
16	–	–	–	–	–	–	–	–	–
17	–	–	–	–	–	–	–	–	–
18	–	–	–	–	–	–	–	–	–
19	–	–	–	–	–	–	–	–	–

Ages 5:9–5:11

ss	Com	FA	SL	HS	LS	SC	SD	Soc	MO
1	0-37	0-28	0-29	0-29	0-40	0-51	0-29	0-39	0-53
2	38-43	29-34	30-36	30-35	41-43	52-56	30-36	40-42	54-59
3	44-49	35-40	37-43	36-40	44-47	57-60	37-42	43-46	60-64
4	50-54	41-46	44-49	41-44	48-51	61-63	43-47	47-50	65-68
5	55-58	47-51	50-54	45-47	52-55	64-65	48-51	51-54	69-71
6	59-61	52-55	55-58	48-49	56-58	66-67	52-54	55-57	72-74
7	62-64	56-59	59-61	50-52	59-61	68	55-57	58-60	75-76
8	65-67	60-63	62-63	53-55	62-63	69	58-60	61-63	77
9	68-69	64-66	64	56-58	64-65	–	61-63	64-66	78
10	70	67-68	65	59-60	66	70	64-66	67-69	79
11	71	69-70	66-67	61	67	71	67-68	70-71	80
12	72-73	71-72	68	62	68	–	69	72-73	–
13	74	–	69	63	–	72	70-71	74	81
14	–	–	–	–	69	–	72	75	–
15	75	–	–	–	–	–	–	–	–
16	–	–	–	–	–	–	–	–	–
17	–	–	–	–	–	–	–	–	–
18	–	–	–	–	–	–	–	–	–
19	–	–	–	–	–	–	–	–	–

Note. **Com** = Communication; **FA** = Functional Pre-Academics; **SL** = School Living; **HS** = Health and Safety; **LS** = Leisure; **SC** = Self-Care; **SD** = Self-Direction; **Soc** = Social; **MO** = Motor.

Table A.1 Scaled Score Equivalents of Skill Area Raw Scores: Teacher/Daycare Provider and Teacher Forms (continued)

Teacher Form

Ages 5:0–5:3

ss	Com	CU	FA	SL	HS	LS	SC	SD	Soc	ss
1	0-25	0-8	–	0-11	0-19	0-18	0-32	0-21	0-16	1
2	26-29	9-12	0-1	12-15	20-23	19-22	33-36	22-25	17-22	2
3	30-32	13-15	2-4	16-18	24-26	23-25	37-39	26-28	23-27	3
4	33-34	16-17	5-6	19-20	27-28	26-27	40-41	29-30	28-31	4
5	35	18	7	21-23	29	28	42	31	32-34	5
6	36-37	19	8	24-27	30	29	43	32-33	35-38	6
7	38-40	–	9	28-32	31-32	30-31	44-45	34-35	39-41	7
8	41-43	20	10	33-37	33-35	32-33	46-47	36-38	42-44	8
9	44-46	21-23	11-12	38-42	36-38	34-36	48-50	39-42	45-47	9
10	47-50	24-26	13-16	43-46	39-40	37-39	51-52	43-47	48-50	10
11	51-54	27-30	17-22	47-50	41-42	40-42	53-54	48-52	51-53	11
12	55-58	31-34	23-34	51-53	43-45	43-45	55	53-57	54-56	12
13	59-61	35-38	35-42	54-55	45-46	46-48	56-57	58-62	57-58	13
14	62-64	39-42	43-51	56-58	47-48	49-51	–	63	59-60	14
15	65-66	43-45	–	59-60	–	–	–	–	–	15
16	–	–	52-61	–	–	–	–	–	–	16
17	–	–	62-66	–	–	–	–	–	–	17
18	–	–	–	–	–	–	–	–	–	18
19	–	–	–	–	–	–	–	–	–	19

Ages 5:4–5:7

ss	Com	CU	FA	SL	HS	LS	SC	SD	Soc	ss
1	0-25	0-8	–	0-11	0-19	0-18	0-32	0-21	0-16	1
2	26-29	9-12	0-1	12-15	20-23	19-22	33-36	22-25	17-22	2
3	30-32	13-15	2-4	16-18	24-26	23-25	37-39	26-28	23-27	3
4	33-34	16-17	5-6	19-20	27-28	26-27	40-41	29-30	28-31	4
5	35	18	7	21-23	29	28	42	31	32-34	5
6	36-37	19	8	24-27	30	29	43	32-33	35-38	6
7	38-40	20	9	28-32	31-32	30-31	44-45	34-35	39-41	7
8	41-43	21	10	33-37	33-35	32-33	46-47	36-38	42-44	8
9	44-46	22-23	11-12	38-42	36-38	34-36	48-50	39-42	45-47	9
10	47-50	24-26	13-16	43-46	39-40	37-39	51-52	43-47	48-50	10
11	51-54	27-30	17-21	47-50	41-42	40-42	53-54	48-52	51-53	11
12	55-58	31-34	22-27	51-53	43-44	43-45	55	53-57	54-56	12
13	59-61	35-38	28-34	54-55	45-46	46-48	56-57	58-62	57-58	13
14	62-64	39-42	35-42	56-58	47-48	49-51	–	63	59-60	14
15	65-66	43-45	43-51	59-60	–	–	–	–	–	15
16	–	–	52-61	–	–	–	–	–	–	16
17	–	–	62-66	–	–	–	–	–	–	17
18	–	–	–	–	–	–	–	–	–	18
19	–	–	–	–	–	–	–	–	–	19

Ages 5:8–5:11

ss	Com	CU	FA	SL	HS	LS	SC	SD	Soc	ss
1	0-25	0-8	–	0-11	0-19	0-18	0-32	0-21	0-16	1
2	26-29	9-12	0-1	12-18	20-23	19-22	33-36	22-25	17-22	2
3	30-32	13-15	2-4	19-20	24-26	23-25	37-39	26-29	23-27	3
4	33-34	16-18	5-6	21-23	27-28	26-27	40-41	30-31	28-31	4
5	35-36	19	7	24-27	29	28	42-43	32-33	32-34	5
6	37-38	20	8-9	28-30	30	29	44	34-35	35-38	6
7	39-40	21	10	31-34	31-32	30-31	45	36	39-41	7
8	41-43	22-23	11-12	35-38	33-35	32-33	46-47	37-38	42-44	8
9	44-46	24	13-16	39-42	36-38	34-36	48-50	39-42	45-47	9
10	47-50	25-26	17-21	43-46	39-40	37-39	51-52	43-47	48-50	10
11	51-54	27-30	22-27	47-50	41-42	40-42	53-54	48-52	51-53	11
12	55-58	31-34	28-34	51-53	43-45	43-45	55	53-57	54-56	12
13	59-61	35-38	35-39	54-55	46-48	46-48	56-57	58-62	57-58	13
14	62-65	39-42	40-44	56-58	49-51	49-51	–	63	59-60	14
15	66	43-45	45-51	59-60	–	–	–	–	–	15
16	–	–	52-61	–	–	–	–	–	–	16
17	–	–	62-66	–	–	–	–	–	–	17
18	–	–	–	–	–	–	–	–	–	18
19	–	–	–	–	–	–	–	–	–	19

Ages 6:0–6:3

ss	Com	CU	FA	SL	HS	LS	SC	SD	Soc	ss
1	0-27	0-11	–	0-15	0-20	0-18	0-34	0-25	0-22	1
2	28-31	12-15	0-1	16-18	21-24	19-22	35-38	26-28	23-27	2
3	32-34	16-17	2-4	19-22	25-27	23-25	39-41	29-30	28-31	3
4	35	18	5-6	23-25	28-29	26-27	42	31-32	32-34	4
5	36-37	19-20	7-8	26-27	30	28	43	33-34	35-36	5
6	38-40	21	9	28-32	31	29	44-45	35	37-38	6
7	41-42	22	10-13	33-37	32-33	30-31	46	36-38	39-41	7
8	43-45	23	14-17	38-42	34-36	32-33	47-48	39-41	42-44	8
9	46-48	24-26	18-22	43-46	37-39	34-36	49-51	42-45	45-47	9
10	49-51	27-29	23-26	47-49	40-42	37-39	52-53	46-48	48-50	10
11	52-55	30-32	27-30	50-52	43-44	40-43	54-55	49-52	51-54	11
12	56-60	33-35	31-34	53-54	45-46	44-47	56-57	53-57	55-58	12
13	61-64	36-39	35-42	55-57	47-48	48-51	–	58-62	59-60	13
14	65-66	40-43	43-50	58-59	–	–	–	63	–	14
15	–	44-45	51-55	60	–	–	–	–	–	15
16	–	–	56-61	–	–	–	–	–	–	16
17	–	–	62-66	–	–	–	–	–	–	17
18	–	–	–	–	–	–	–	–	–	18
19	–	–	–	–	–	–	–	–	–	19

Note. **Com** = Communication; **CU** = Community Use; **FA** = Functional Academics; **SL** = School Living; **HS** = Health and Safety; **LS** = Leisure; **SC** = Self-Care; **SD** = Self-Direction; **Soc** = Social.

Table A.1 Scaled Score Equivalents of Skill Area Raw Scores: Teacher/Daycare Provider and Teacher Forms (continued)

Teacher Form

Ages 6:4–6:7

ss	Com	CU	FA	SL	HS	LS	SC	SD	Soc	ss
1	0-27	0-11	–	0-18	0-20	0-18	0-34	0-25	0-26	1
2	28-31	12-15	0-1	19-22	21-24	19-22	35-38	26-29	27-30	2
3	32-34	16-18	2-4	23-25	25-27	23-25	39-41	30-32	31-33	3
4	35-36	19-20	5-6	26-27	28-29	26-27	42-43	33-34	34-35	4
5	37-38	21	7-9	28-30	30	28	44	35	36	5
6	39-40	22	10-13	31-34	31	29	45	36	37-38	6
7	41-42	23	14-17	35-38	32-33	30-31	46	37-38	39-41	7
8	43-45	24	18-22	39-42	34-36	32-33	47-48	39-41	42-44	8
9	46-48	25-26	23-26	43-46	37-39	34-36	49-51	42-45	45-47	9
10	49-51	27-29	27-30	47-49	40-42	37-39	52-53	46-48	48-50	10
11	52-55	30-32	31-34	50-52	43-45	40-43	54-55	49-52	51-54	11
12	56-60	33-35	35-39	53-54	46-48	44-47	56-57	53-57	55-58	12
13	61-65	36-39	40-44	55-57	–	48-51	–	58-62	59-60	13
14	66	40-43	45-50	58-59	–	–	–	63	–	14
15	–	44-45	51-55	60	–	–	–	–	–	15
16	–	–	56-61	–	–	–	–	–	–	16
17	–	–	62-66	–	–	–	–	–	–	17
18	–	–	–	–	–	–	–	–	–	18
19	–	–	–	–	–	–	–	–	–	19

Ages 6:8–6:11

ss	Com	CU	FA	SL	HS	LS	SC	SD	Soc	ss
1	0-27	0-11	–	0-18	0-20	0-18	0-34	0-25	0-26	1
2	28-31	12-16	0-1	19-25	21-24	19-22	35-38	26-29	27-30	2
3	32-35	17-20	2-5	26-27	25-27	23-25	39-41	30-33	31-33	3
4	36-38	21	6-9	28-30	28-29	26-27	42-43	34-35	34-36	4
5	39-40	22	10-13	31-34	30-31	28	44-45	36	37-38	5
6	41	23	14-17	35-36	32-33	29	46	37-38	39-40	6
7	42-43	24-25	18-22	37-39	34-35	30-31	47	39-41	41-42	7
8	44-46	26	23-26	40-42	36-37	32-34	48	42-43	43-44	8
9	47-49	27-29	27-30	43-46	38-39	35-37	49-51	44-46	45-47	9
10	50-52	30-32	31-34	47-49	40-42	38-39	52-53	47-50	48-50	10
11	53-55	33-34	35-39	50-52	43-45	40-43	54-55	51-54	51-54	11
12	56-60	35-36	40-44	53-55	46-48	44-47	56-57	55-58	55-58	12
13	61-65	37-39	45-50	56-57	–	48-51	–	59-62	59-60	13
14	66	40-43	51-55	58-59	–	–	–	63	–	14
15	–	44-45	56-60	60	–	–	–	–	–	15
16	–	–	61-63	–	–	–	–	–	–	16
17	–	–	64-66	–	–	–	–	–	–	17
18	–	–	–	–	–	–	–	–	–	18
19	–	–	–	–	–	–	–	–	–	19

Ages 7:0–7:3

ss	Com	CU	FA	SL	HS	LS	SC	SD	Soc	ss
1	0-31	0-15	–	0-22	0-22	0-19	0-36	0-29	0-29	1
2	32-34	16-18	0-4	23-25	23-26	20-23	37-40	30-32	30-33	2
3	35-36	19-20	5-6	26-29	27-29	24-26	41-43	33-34	34-35	3
4	37-38	21-23	7-11	30-32	30	27-28	44	35-36	36	4
5	39-40	24	12-17	33-34	31	29	45	37-38	37-38	5
6	41-42	25-26	18-23	35-38	32-33	30-31	46	39	39-41	6
7	43-45	27	24-28	39-42	34-36	32-33	47-48	40-41	42-44	7
8	46-48	28	29-33	43-46	37-39	34-36	49	42-45	45-47	8
9	49-51	29-30	34-39	47-49	40-41	37-39	50-51	46-48	48-50	9
10	52-55	31-32	40-44	50-52	42-43	40-42	52-54	49-52	51-53	10
11	56-58	33-35	45-48	53-54	44-45	43-44	55-56	53-57	54-55	11
12	59-60	36-39	49-51	55-57	46-48	45-47	57	58-62	56-58	12
13	61-65	40-42	52-54	58	–	48-51	–	63	59-60	13
14	66	43-45	55-57	59-60	–	–	–	–	–	14
15	–	–	58-61	–	–	–	–	–	–	15
16	–	–	62-66	–	–	–	–	–	–	16
17	–	–	–	–	–	–	–	–	–	17
18	–	–	–	–	–	–	–	–	–	18
19	–	–	–	–	–	–	–	–	–	19

Ages 7:4–7:7

ss	Com	CU	FA	SL	HS	LS	SC	SD	Soc	ss
1	0-31	0-16	–	0-25	0-22	0-19	0-36	0-29	0-29	1
2	32-35	17-20	0-5	26-29	23-26	20-23	37-40	30-33	30-33	2
3	36-38	21-23	6-11	30-32	27-29	24-26	41-43	34-36	34-36	3
4	39-40	24-25	12-17	33-34	30-31	27-28	44-45	37-38	37-38	4
5	41	26	18-23	35-36	32-33	29	46	39	39-40	5
6	42-43	27	24-28	37-39	34-35	30-31	47	40-41	41-42	6
7	44-46	28	29-33	40-42	36-37	32-34	48	42-43	43-44	7
8	47-49	29-30	34-39	43-46	38-39	35-37	49	44-46	45-47	8
9	50-52	31-32	40-44	47-49	40-41	38-39	50-51	47-50	48-50	9
10	53-55	33-34	45-48	50-52	42-43	40-42	52-54	51-54	51-53	10
11	56-58	35-36	49-51	53-55	44-45	43-44	55-56	55-58	54-55	11
12	59-60	37-39	52-54	56-57	46-48	45-47	57	59-62	56-58	12
13	61-65	40-42	55-57	58	–	48-51	–	63	59-60	13
14	66	43-45	58-60	59-60	–	–	–	–	–	14
15	–	–	61-63	–	–	–	–	–	–	15
16	–	–	64-66	–	–	–	–	–	–	16
17	–	–	–	–	–	–	–	–	–	17
18	–	–	–	–	–	–	–	–	–	18
19	–	–	–	–	–	–	–	–	–	19

Note. **Com** = Communication; **CU** = Community Use; **FA** = Functional Academics; **SL** = School Living; **HS** = Health and Safety; **LS** = Leisure; **SC** = Self-Care; **SD** = Self-Direction; **Soc** = Social.

Table A.1 Scaled Score Equivalents of Skill Area Raw Scores: Teacher/Daycare Provider and Teacher Forms (continued)

Teacher Form

Ages 7:8–7:11

ss	Com	CU	FA	SL	HS	LS	SC	SD	Soc	ss
1	0–31	0–16	–	0–25	0–22	0–19	0–36	0–29	0–29	1
2	32–36	17–20	0–11	26–29	23–26	20–23	37–40	30–33	30–33	2
3	37–40	21–23	12–17	30–32	27–29	24–26	41–43	34–36	34–36	3
4	41	24–25	18–23	33–35	30–31	27–28	44–45	37–38	37–38	4
5	42–43	26–27	24–28	36–37	32–33	29	46–47	39	39–40	5
6	44–46	28	29–33	38–39	34–35	30–31	48	40–41	41–42	6
7	47	29	34–39	40–42	36–37	32–34	49	42–43	43–44	7
8	48–49	30–31	40–44	43–46	38–40	35–37	50	44–46	45–47	8
9	50–52	32–33	45–48	47–49	41–43	38–39	51	47–50	48–50	9
10	53–55	34–36	49–51	50–52	44–45	40–42	52–54	51–54	51–53	10
11	56–58	37–39	52–54	53–55	46	43–44	55–56	55–58	54–55	11
12	59–62	40–41	55–57	56–57	47–48	45–47	57	59–62	56–58	12
13	63–66	42–43	58–60	58	–	48–51	–	63	59–60	13
14	–	44–45	61–63	59–60	–	–	–	–	–	14
15	–	–	64–66	–	–	–	–	–	–	15
16	–	–	–	–	–	–	–	–	–	16
17	–	–	–	–	–	–	–	–	–	17
18	–	–	–	–	–	–	–	–	–	18
19	–	–	–	–	–	–	–	–	–	19

Ages 8:0–8:3

ss	Com	CU	FA	SL	HS	LS	SC	SD	Soc
1	0–35	0–18	0–5	0–28	0–24	0–20	0–38	0–30	0–30
2	36–38	19–22	6–14	29–32	25–28	21–24	39–42	31–34	31–34
3	39–40	23–25	15–21	33–34	29–31	25–27	43–45	35–37	35–37
4	41–43	26	22–27	35–36	32–33	28–29	46	38–39	38–39
5	44–45	27	28–32	37–38	34–35	30	47	40	40
6	46	28	33–36	39–40	36–37	31–32	48	41	41–42
7	47–49	29–30	37–41	41–43	38–39	33–35	49	42–43	43–44
8	50–51	31–32	42–46	44–47	40–41	36–38	50–51	44–46	45–47
9	52–54	33–34	47–51	48–50	42–43	39–41	52–53	47–50	48–51
10	55–58	35–36	52–55	51–53	44–45	42–43	54–55	51–55	52–54
11	59–60	37–39	56–58	54–56	46–47	44–45	56	56–60	55–57
12	61–65	40–42	59–60	57–58	48	46–48	57	61–63	58–60
13	66	43–45	61–63	59–60	–	49–51	–	–	–
14	–	–	64–65	–	–	–	–	–	–
15	–	–	66	–	–	–	–	–	–
16	–	–	–	–	–	–	–	–	–
17	–	–	–	–	–	–	–	–	–
18	–	–	–	–	–	–	–	–	–
19	–	–	–	–	–	–	–	–	–

Ages 8:4–8:7

ss	Com	CU	FA	SL	HS	LS	SC	SD	Soc
1	0–36	0–18	0–14	0–28	0–24	0–20	0–38	0–30	0–30
2	37–40	19–22	15–21	29–32	25–28	21–24	39–42	31–34	31–34
3	41–43	23–25	22–27	33–35	29–31	25–27	43–45	35–37	35–37
4	44–45	26–27	28–32	36–37	32–33	28–29	46–47	38–39	38–39
5	46	28	33–36	38	34–35	30	48	40	40
6	47	29	37–41	39–40	36–37	31–32	49	41	41–42
7	48–49	30–31	42–46	41–43	38–40	33–35	50	42–43	43–44
8	50–51	32–33	47–51	44–47	41–43	36–38	51	44–46	45–47
9	52–54	34–36	52–55	48–50	44–45	39–41	52–53	47–50	48–51
10	55–58	37–39	56–58	51–53	46	42–43	54–55	51–55	52–54
11	59–62	40–41	59–60	54–56	47	44–45	56	56–60	55–57
12	63–66	42–43	61–63	57–58	48	46–48	57	61–63	58–60
13	–	44–45	64–65	59–60	–	49–51	–	–	–
14	–	–	66	–	–	–	–	–	–
15	–	–	–	–	–	–	–	–	–
16	–	–	–	–	–	–	–	–	–
17	–	–	–	–	–	–	–	–	–
18	–	–	–	–	–	–	–	–	–
19	–	–	–	–	–	–	–	–	–

Ages 8:8–8:11

ss	Com	CU	FA	SL	HS	LS	SC	SD	Soc
1	0–36	0–18	0–14	0–28	0–24	0–20	0–38	0–30	0–30
2	37–40	19–22	15–21	29–32	25–28	21–24	39–42	31–34	31–34
3	41–43	23–25	22–27	33–35	29–31	25–27	43–45	35–37	35–37
4	44–46	26–27	28–32	36–38	32–33	28–29	46–47	38–39	38–39
5	47	28	33–36	39–40	34–35	30	48–49	40–41	40
6	48–49	29	37–41	41	36–37	31–32	50	42	41–42
7	50	30–31	42–46	42–43	38–40	33–35	51	43	43–44
8	51	32–33	47–51	44–47	41–43	36–38	52	44–46	45–47
9	52–54	34–36	52–55	48–50	44–45	39–41	53	47–50	48–51
10	55–58	37–39	56–58	51–53	46	42–43	54–55	51–55	52–54
11	59–62	40–41	59–60	54–56	47	44–45	56	56–60	55–57
12	63–66	42–43	61–63	57–58	48	46–48	57	61–63	58–60
13	–	44–45	64–65	59–60	–	49–51	–	–	–
14	–	–	66	–	–	–	–	–	–
15	–	–	–	–	–	–	–	–	–
16	–	–	–	–	–	–	–	–	–
17	–	–	–	–	–	–	–	–	–
18	–	–	–	–	–	–	–	–	–
19	–	–	–	–	–	–	–	–	–

Note. **Com** = Communication; **CU** = Community Use; **FA** = Functional Academics; **SL** = School Living; **HS** = Health and Safety; **LS** = Leisure; **SC** = Self-Care; **SD** = Self-Direction; **Soc** = Social.

Table A.1 Scaled Score Equivalents of Skill Area Raw Scores: Teacher/Daycare Provider and Teacher Forms (continued)

Teacher Form

Ages 9:0–9:3

ss	Com	CU	FA	SL	HS	LS	SC	SD	Soc
1	0-39	0-18	0-17	0-31	0-26	0-21	0-40	0-32	0-31
2	40-43	19-22	18-23	32-35	27-30	22-25	41-44	33-36	32-35
3	44-45	23-25	24-28	36-37	31-33	26-28	45-47	37-39	36-38
4	46	26-27	29-32	38	34-35	29-30	48	40	39-40
5	47-48	28-29	33-36	39-40	36	31	49	41	41
6	49	30-31	37-41	41-42	37-38	32-33	50	42-43	42
7	50-51	32-33	42-47	43-44	39-40	34-35	51	44-45	43-44
8	52-53	34-35	48-52	45-47	41-43	36-38	52-53	46-48	45-47
9	54-55	36-37	53-56	48-50	44-45	39-41	54	49-51	48-51
10	56-59	38-39	57-59	51-53	46	42-43	55	52-55	52-55
11	60-62	40-41	60-61	54-56	47	44-45	56-57	56-60	56-59
12	63-66	42-43	62-63	57-58	48	46-48	–	61-63	60
13	–	44-45	64-66	59-60	–	49-51	–	–	–
14	–	–	–	–	–	–	–	–	–
15	–	–	–	–	–	–	–	–	–
16	–	–	–	–	–	–	–	–	–
17	–	–	–	–	–	–	–	–	–
18	–	–	–	–	–	–	–	–	–
19	–	–	–	–	–	–	–	–	–

Ages 9:4–9:7

Com	CU	FA	SL	HS	LS	SC	SD	Soc	ss
0-39	0-18	0-17	0-31	0-26	0-21	0-40	0-32	0-31	1
40-43	19-22	18-23	32-35	27-30	22-25	41-44	33-36	32-35	2
44-46	23-25	24-28	36-38	31-33	26-28	45-47	37-39	36-38	3
47-48	26-27	29-32	39-40	34-35	29-30	48-49	40-41	39-40	4
49	28-29	33-36	41	36	31	50	42	41	5
50	30-31	37-41	42	37-38	32-33	51	43	42	6
51	32-33	42-47	43-44	39-40	34-35	52	44-45	43-44	7
52-53	34-35	48-52	45-47	41-43	36-38	53	46-48	45-47	8
54-55	36-37	53-56	48-50	44-45	39-41	54	49-51	48-51	9
56-59	38-39	57-59	51-53	46	42-43	55	52-55	52-55	10
60-62	40-41	60-61	54-56	47	44-45	56-57	56-60	56-59	11
63-66	42-43	62-63	57-58	48	46-48	–	61-63	60	12
–	44-45	64-66	59-60	–	49-51	–	–	–	13
–	–	–	–	–	–	–	–	–	14
–	–	–	–	–	–	–	–	–	15
–	–	–	–	–	–	–	–	–	16
–	–	–	–	–	–	–	–	–	17
–	–	–	–	–	–	–	–	–	18
–	–	–	–	–	–	–	–	–	19

Ages 9:8–9:11

ss	Com	CU	FA	SL	HS	LS	SC	SD	Soc
1	0-39	0-18	0-17	0-31	0-26	0-21	0-40	0-32	0-31
2	40-43	19-25	18-28	32-35	27-30	22-25	41-44	33-36	32-35
3	44-46	26-27	29-32	36-38	31-34	26-28	45-47	37-39	36-38
4	47-48	28-29	33-36	39-41	35-36	29-30	48-49	40-41	39-40
5	49-50	30-31	37-41	42	37-38	31	50	42-43	41-42
6	51	32-33	42-47	43-44	39-40	32-33	51	44	43
7	–	34-35	48-52	45	41-42	34-35	52	45	43-44
8	52-53	36	53	46-47	43	36-38	53	46-48	45-47
9	54-55	37	54-56	48-50	44-45	39-41	54	49-51	48-51
10	56-59	38-39	57-59	51-53	46	42-43	55	52-55	52-55
11	60-62	40-41	60-61	54-56	47	44-45	56-57	56-60	56-59
12	63-66	42-43	62-63	57-58	48	46-48	–	61-63	60
13	–	44-45	64-66	59-60	–	49-51	–	–	–
14	–	–	–	–	–	–	–	–	–
15	–	–	–	–	–	–	–	–	–
16	–	–	–	–	–	–	–	–	–
17	–	–	–	–	–	–	–	–	–
18	–	–	–	–	–	–	–	–	–
19	–	–	–	–	–	–	–	–	–

Ages 10:0–10:3

Com	CU	FA	SL	HS	LS	SC	SD	Soc	ss
0-41	0-22	0-23	0-34	0-30	0-22	0-41	0-34	0-33	1
42-45	23-25	24-32	35-38	31-33	23-26	42-45	35-38	34-37	2
46-48	26-29	33-38	39-40	34-35	27-29	46-48	39-41	38-40	3
49	30-32	39-43	41	36-37	30-31	49-50	42	41	4
50	33-34	44-47	42-43	38-39	32-33	–	43	42	5
51	–	48-50	44	40-41	34-35	51	44-45	43	6
52	35	51-52	45-46	42-43	36-37	52	46-47	44-45	7
53-54	36-37	53-55	47-48	44	38-39	53	48-49	46-48	8
55-57	38-39	56-58	49-51	45	40-42	54	50-52	49-51	9
58-61	40-41	59-60	52-54	46	43-44	55	53-56	52-55	10
62-65	42-43	61-63	55-57	47-48	45-46	56-57	57-61	56-59	11
66	44-45	64-65	58-60	–	47-48	–	62-63	60	12
–	–	66	–	–	49-51	–	–	–	13
–	–	–	–	–	–	–	–	–	14
–	–	–	–	–	–	–	–	–	15
–	–	–	–	–	–	–	–	–	16
–	–	–	–	–	–	–	–	–	17
–	–	–	–	–	–	–	–	–	18
–	–	–	–	–	–	–	–	–	19

Note. **Com** = Communication; **CU** = Community Use; **FA** = Functional Academics; **SL** = School Living; **HS** = Health and Safety; **LS** = Leisure; **SC** = Self-Care; **SD** = Self-Direction; **Soc** = Social.

Table A.1 Scaled Score Equivalents of Skill Area Raw Scores: Teacher/Daycare Provider and Teacher Forms (continued)

Teacher Form

Ages 10:4–10:7

ss	Com	CU	FA	SL	HS	LS	SC	SD	Soc	ss
1	0–41	0–25	0–32	0–34	0–30	0–22	0–41	0–34	0–33	1
2	42–45	26–29	33–38	35–38	31–34	23–26	42–45	35–38	34–37	2
3	46–48	30–32	39–43	39–41	35–37	27–29	46–48	39–41	38–40	3
4	49–50	33–34	44–47	42–43	38–39	30–31	49–50	42–43	41–42	4
5	51	–	48–50	44	40–41	32–33	–	44	–	5
6	–	35	51–52	45	42	34–35	51	45	43	6
7	52	36	53	46	43	36–37	52	46–47	44–45	7
8	53–54	37	54–55	47–48	44	38–39	53	48–49	46–48	8
9	55–57	38–39	56–58	49–51	45	40–42	54	50–52	49–51	9
10	58–61	40–41	59–60	52–54	46	43–44	55	53–56	52–55	10
11	62–65	42–43	61–63	55–57	47–48	45–46	56–57	57–61	56–59	11
12	66	44–45	64–65	58–60	–	47–48	–	62–63	60	12
13	–	–	66	–	–	49–51	–	–	–	13
14	–	–	–	–	–	–	–	–	–	14
15	–	–	–	–	–	–	–	–	–	15
16	–	–	–	–	–	–	–	–	–	16
17	–	–	–	–	–	–	–	–	–	17
18	–	–	–	–	–	–	–	–	–	18
19	–	–	–	–	–	–	–	–	–	19

Ages 10:8–10:11

ss	Com	CU	FA	SL	HS	LS	SC	SD	Soc	ss
1	0–41	0–25	0–32	0–34	0–30	0–22	0–41	0–34	0–33	1
2	42–45	26–29	33–38	35–38	31–34	23–26	42–45	35–38	34–37	2
3	46–48	30–32	39–43	39–41	35–37	27–29	46–48	39–41	38–40	3
4	49–50	33–34	44–47	42–43	38–39	30–31	49–50	42–43	41–42	4
5	51	35	48–50	44	40–41	32–33	51	44	43	5
6	52	–	51–52	45	42	34–35	–	45	–	6
7	–	36	53	46	43	36–37	52	46–47	44–45	7
8	53–54	37	54–55	47–48	44	38–39	53	48–49	46–48	8
9	55–57	38–39	56–58	49–51	45	40–42	54	50–52	49–51	9
10	58–61	40–41	59–60	52–54	46	43–44	55	53–56	52–55	10
11	62–65	42–43	61–63	55–57	47–48	45–46	56–57	57–61	56–59	11
12	66	44–45	64–65	58–60	–	47–48	–	62–63	60	12
13	–	–	66	–	–	49–51	–	–	–	13
14	–	–	–	–	–	–	–	–	–	14
15	–	–	–	–	–	–	–	–	–	15
16	–	–	–	–	–	–	–	–	–	16
17	–	–	–	–	–	–	–	–	–	17
18	–	–	–	–	–	–	–	–	–	18
19	–	–	–	–	–	–	–	–	–	19

Ages 11:0–11:3

ss	Com	CU	FA	SL	HS	LS	SC	SD	Soc	ss
1	0–42	0–26	0–32	0–35	0–31	0–22	0–42	0–34	0–34	1
2	43–46	27–30	33–38	36–39	32–35	23–26	43–46	35–38	35–38	2
3	47–49	31–33	39–43	40–42	36–38	27–29	47–49	39–41	39–41	3
4	50–51	34	44–47	43–44	39–40	30–31	50	42–43	42	4
5	–	35	48–50	–	41	32–33	51	44	43	5
6	52	36	51–52	45	42	34–35	52	45	44	6
7	53	37	53	46	43	36–37	53	46–47	45–46	7
8	54–55	38	54–55	47–48	44	38–39	54	48–49	47–48	8
9	56–58	39–40	56–58	49–51	45	40–42	55	50–52	49–51	9
10	59–61	41–42	59–61	52–55	46	43–45	56	53–57	52–55	10
11	62–65	43–44	62–64	56–59	47–48	46–48	57	58–63	56–59	11
12	66	45	65–66	60	–	49–51	–	–	60	12
13	–	–	–	–	–	–	–	–	–	13
14	–	–	–	–	–	–	–	–	–	14
15	–	–	–	–	–	–	–	–	–	15
16	–	–	–	–	–	–	–	–	–	16
17	–	–	–	–	–	–	–	–	–	17
18	–	–	–	–	–	–	–	–	–	18
19	–	–	–	–	–	–	–	–	–	19

Ages 11:4–11:7

ss	Com	CU	FA	SL	HS	LS	SC	SD	Soc	ss
1	0–42	0–26	0–32	0–35	0–31	0–22	0–42	0–34	0–34	1
2	43–46	27–30	33–38	36–39	32–35	23–26	43–46	35–38	35–38	2
3	47–49	31–33	39–43	40–42	36–38	27–29	47–49	39–41	39–41	3
4	50–51	34–35	44–47	43–44	39–40	30–31	50–51	42–43	42–43	4
5	52	–	48–50	–	41	32–33	–	44	–	5
6	–	36	51–52	45	42	34–35	52	45	44	6
7	53	37	53	46	43	36–37	53	46–47	45–46	7
8	54–55	38	54–55	47–48	44	38–39	54	48–49	47–48	8
9	56–58	39–40	56–58	49–51	45	40–42	55	50–52	49–51	9
10	59–61	41–42	59–61	52–55	46	43–45	56	53–57	52–55	10
11	62–65	43–44	62–64	56–59	47–48	46–48	57	58–63	56–59	11
12	66	45	65–66	60	–	49–51	–	–	60	12
13	–	–	–	–	–	–	–	–	–	13
14	–	–	–	–	–	–	–	–	–	14
15	–	–	–	–	–	–	–	–	–	15
16	–	–	–	–	–	–	–	–	–	16
17	–	–	–	–	–	–	–	–	–	17
18	–	–	–	–	–	–	–	–	–	18
19	–	–	–	–	–	–	–	–	–	19

Note. **Com** = Communication; **CU** = Community Use; **FA** = Functional Academics; **SL** = School Living; **HS** = Health and Safety; **LS** = Leisure; **SC** = Self-Care; **SD** = Self-Direction; **Soc** = Social.

Table A.1 Scaled Score Equivalents of Skill Area Raw Scores: Teacher/Daycare Provider and Teacher Forms (continued)

Teacher Form

Ages 11:8–11:11

ss	Com	CU	FA	SL	HS	LS	SC	SD	Soc	ss
1	0-42	0-26	0-32	0-35	0-31	0-22	0-42	0-34	0-34	1
2	43-46	27-30	33-38	36-39	32-35	23-26	43-46	35-38	35-38	2
3	47-49	31-33	39-43	40-42	36-38	27-29	47-49	39-41	39-41	3
4	50-51	34-35	44-47	43-44	39-40	30-31	50-51	42-43	42-43	4
5	52	36	48-50	–	41	32-33	52	44	44	5
6	53	–	51-52	45	42	34-35	–	45	–	6
7	54	37	53	46	43	36-37	53	46-47	45-46	7
8	55	38	54-55	47-48	44	38-39	54	48-49	47-48	8
9	56-58	39-40	56-58	49-51	45	40-42	55	50-52	49-51	9
10	59-61	41-42	59-61	52-55	46	43-45	56	53-57	52-55	10
11	62-65	43-44	62-64	56-59	47-48	46-48	57	58-63	56-59	11
12	66	45	65-66	60	–	49-51	–	–	60	12
13	–	–	–	–	–	–	–	–	–	13
14	–	–	–	–	–	–	–	–	–	14
15	–	–	–	–	–	–	–	–	–	15
16	–	–	–	–	–	–	–	–	–	16
17	–	–	–	–	–	–	–	–	–	17
18	–	–	–	–	–	–	–	–	–	18
19	–	–	–	–	–	–	–	–	–	19

Ages 12:0–12:3

ss	Com	CU	FA	SL	HS	LS	SC	SD	Soc	ss
1	0-44	0-27	0-35	0-35	0-32	0-23	0-46	0-35	0-35	1
2	45-48	28-31	36-40	36-39	33-36	24-27	47-49	36-39	36-39	2
3	49-51	32-34	41-44	40-42	37-39	28-30	50-51	40-42	40-42	3
4	52	35	45-48	43-44	40-41	31-32	–	43-44	43	4
5	53	36	49-51	–	42	33	52	45	44	5
6	54	37	52-53	45	–	34-35	53	46	45	6
7	55	–	54-55	46	43	36-37	–	47	46-47	7
8	56	38	56-57	47-48	44	38-39	54	48-49	48-49	8
9	57-58	39-40	58-59	49-51	45	40-42	55	50-52	50-52	9
10	59-61	41-43	60-61	52-55	46	43-45	56	53-57	53-55	10
11	62-65	44-45	62-64	56-59	47-48	46-48	57	58-63	56-59	11
12	66	–	65-66	60	–	49-51	–	–	60	12
13	–	–	–	–	–	–	–	–	–	13
14	–	–	–	–	–	–	–	–	–	14
15	–	–	–	–	–	–	–	–	–	15
16	–	–	–	–	–	–	–	–	–	16
17	–	–	–	–	–	–	–	–	–	17
18	–	–	–	–	–	–	–	–	–	18
19	–	–	–	–	–	–	–	–	–	19

Ages 12:4–12:7

ss	Com	CU	FA	SL	HS	LS	SC	SD	Soc	ss
1	0-44	0-27	0-35	0-35	0-32	0-23	0-46	0-35	0-35	1
2	45-48	28-31	36-40	36-39	33-36	24-27	47-49	36-39	36-39	2
3	49-51	32-34	41-44	40-42	37-39	28-30	50-51	40-42	40-42	3
4	52-53	35-36	45-48	43-44	40-41	31-32	52	43-44	43-44	4
5	54	–	49-51	–	42	33	–	45	–	5
6	–	37	52-53	45	–	34-35	53	46	45	6
7	55	38	54-55	46	43	36-37	–	47	46-47	7
8	56	38	56-57	47-48	44	38-39	54	48-49	48-49	8
9	57-58	39-40	58-59	49-51	45	40-42	55	50-52	50-52	9
10	59-61	41-43	60-61	52-55	46	43-45	56	53-57	53-55	10
11	62-65	44-45	62-64	56-59	47-48	46-48	57	58-63	56-59	11
12	66	–	65-66	60	–	49-51	–	–	60	12
13	–	–	–	–	–	–	–	–	–	13
14	–	–	–	–	–	–	–	–	–	14
15	–	–	–	–	–	–	–	–	–	15
16	–	–	–	–	–	–	–	–	–	16
17	–	–	–	–	–	–	–	–	–	17
18	–	–	–	–	–	–	–	–	–	18
19	–	–	–	–	–	–	–	–	–	19

Ages 12:8–12:11

ss	Com	CU	FA	SL	HS	LS	SC	SD	Soc	ss
1	0-44	0-27	0-35	0-35	0-32	0-23	0-46	0-35	0-35	1
2	45-48	28-31	36-40	36-39	33-36	24-27	47-49	36-39	36-39	2
3	49-51	32-34	41-44	40-42	37-39	28-30	50-51	40-42	40-42	3
4	52-53	35-36	45-48	43-44	40-41	31-32	52	43-44	43-44	4
5	54	–	49-51	–	42	33	–	45	–	5
6	–	37	52-53	45	–	34-35	53	46	45	6
7	55	–	54-55	46	43	36-37	–	47	46-47	7
8	56	38	56-57	47-48	44	38-39	54	48-49	48-49	8
9	57-58	39-40	58-59	49-51	45	40-42	55	50-52	50-52	9
10	59-61	41-43	60-61	52-55	46	43-45	56	53-57	53-55	10
11	62-65	44-45	62-64	56-59	47-48	46-48	57	58-63	56-59	11
12	66	–	65-66	60	–	49-51	–	–	60	12
13	–	–	–	–	–	–	–	–	–	13
14	–	–	–	–	–	–	–	–	–	14
15	–	–	–	–	–	–	–	–	–	15
16	–	–	–	–	–	–	–	–	–	16
17	–	–	–	–	–	–	–	–	–	17
18	–	–	–	–	–	–	–	–	–	18
19	–	–	–	–	–	–	–	–	–	19

Note. **Com** = Communication; **CU** = Community Use; **FA** = Functional Academics; **SL** = School Living; **HS** = Health and Safety; **LS** = Leisure; **SC** = Self-Care; **SD** = Self-Direction; **Soc** = Social.

Table A.1 Scaled Score Equivalents of Skill Area Raw Scores: Teacher/Daycare Provider and Teacher Forms (continued)

Age 13

ss	Com	CU	FA	SL	HS	LS	SC	SD	Soc	ss
1	0-44	0-27	0-37	0-35	0-32	0-23	0-46	0-35	0-35	1
2	45-48	28-31	38-42	36-39	33-36	24-27	47-49	36-39	36-39	2
3	49-51	32-34	43-46	40-42	37-39	28-30	50-51	40-42	40-42	3
4	52-53	35-36	47-49	43-44	40-41	31-32	52	43-44	43-44	4
5	54	-	50-52	-	42	33	-	45	-	5
6	-	37	53-54	45	-	34-35	53	46	45	6
7	55	-	55-56	46	43	36-37	-	47	46-47	7
8	56-57	38	57-58	47-48	44	38-39	54	48-50	48-49	8
9	58-59	39-40	59-60	49-51	45	40-42	55	51-54	50-52	9
10	60-62	41-43	61-62	52-55	46	43-45	56	55-59	53-55	10
11	63-66	44-45	63-64	56-60	47-48	46-48	57	60-63	56-59	11
12	-	-	65-66	-	-	49-51	-	-	60	12
13	-	-	-	-	-	-	-	-	-	13
14	-	-	-	-	-	-	-	-	-	14
15	-	-	-	-	-	-	-	-	-	15
16	-	-	-	-	-	-	-	-	-	16
17	-	-	-	-	-	-	-	-	-	17
18	-	-	-	-	-	-	-	-	-	18
19	-	-	-	-	-	-	-	-	-	19

Age 14

ss	Com	CU	FA	SL	HS	LS	SC	SD	Soc	ss
1	0-44	0-27	0-37	0-35	0-32	0-23	0-46	0-35	0-35	1
2	45-48	28-31	38-42	36-39	33-36	24-27	47-49	36-39	36-39	2
3	49-51	32-34	43-46	40-42	37-39	28-30	50-51	40-42	40-42	3
4	52-53	35-36	47-49	43-44	40-41	31-32	52	43-44	43-44	4
5	54	-	50-52	-	42	33	-	45	-	5
6	-	37	53-54	45	-	34-35	53	46	45	6
7	55	-	55-56	46	43	36-37	-	47	46-47	7
8	56-57	38	57-58	47-48	44	38-39	54	48-50	48-49	8
9	58-59	39-40	59-60	49-51	45	40-42	55	51-54	50-52	9
10	60-62	41-43	61-62	52-55	46	43-45	56	55-59	53-55	10
11	63-66	44-45	63-64	56-60	47-48	46-48	57	60-63	56-59	11
12	-	-	65-66	-	-	49-51	-	-	60	12
13	-	-	-	-	-	-	-	-	-	13
14	-	-	-	-	-	-	-	-	-	14
15	-	-	-	-	-	-	-	-	-	15
16	-	-	-	-	-	-	-	-	-	16
17	-	-	-	-	-	-	-	-	-	17
18	-	-	-	-	-	-	-	-	-	18
19	-	-	-	-	-	-	-	-	-	19

Age 15

ss	Com	CU	FA	SL	HS	LS	SC	SD	Soc	ss
1	0-44	0-27	0-37	0-36	0-32	0-23	0-46	0-35	0-35	1
2	45-48	28-31	38-42	37-40	33-36	24-27	47-49	36-39	36-39	2
3	49-51	32-34	43-46	41-43	37-39	28-30	50-51	40-42	40-42	3
4	52-53	35-36	47-49	44	40-41	31-32	52	43-44	43-44	4
5	54	-	50-52	45	42	33-34	53	45	-	5
6	-	37	53-54	46	-	35-36	-	46	45	6
7	55	-	55-56	47	43	37-38	54	47	46-47	7
8	56-57	38	57-58	48-49	44	39-40	55	48-50	48-49	8
9	58-59	39-40	59-61	50-51	45	41-43	56	51-54	50-52	9
10	60-62	41-43	62-63	52-55	46	44-46	-	55-59	53-55	10
11	63-66	44-45	64-66	56-60	47-48	47-49	57	60-63	56-59	11
12	-	-	-	-	-	50-51	-	-	60	12
13	-	-	-	-	-	-	-	-	-	13
14	-	-	-	-	-	-	-	-	-	14
15	-	-	-	-	-	-	-	-	-	15
16	-	-	-	-	-	-	-	-	-	16
17	-	-	-	-	-	-	-	-	-	17
18	-	-	-	-	-	-	-	-	-	18
19	-	-	-	-	-	-	-	-	-	19

Age 16

ss	Com	CU	FA	SL	HS	LS	SC	SD	Soc	ss
1	0-44	0-27	0-37	0-36	0-32	0-23	0-46	0-35	0-35	1
2	45-48	28-31	38-42	37-40	33-36	24-27	47-49	36-39	36-39	2
3	49-51	32-34	43-46	41-43	37-39	28-30	50-51	40-42	40-42	3
4	52-53	35-36	47-49	44-45	40-41	31-32	52	43-44	43-44	4
5	54	-	50-52	-	42	33-34	53	45	-	5
6	-	37	53-54	46	-	35-36	54	46	45	6
7	55	-	55-56	47	43	37-38	55	47	46-47	7
8	56-57	38	57-58	48-49	44	39-40	-	48-50	48-49	8
9	58-59	39-40	59-61	50-51	45	41-43	56	51-54	50-52	9
10	60-62	41-43	62-63	52-55	46	44-46	-	55-59	53-55	10
11	63-66	44-45	64-66	56-60	47-48	47-49	57	60-63	56-59	11
12	-	-	-	-	-	50-51	-	-	60	12
13	-	-	-	-	-	-	-	-	-	13
14	-	-	-	-	-	-	-	-	-	14
15	-	-	-	-	-	-	-	-	-	15
16	-	-	-	-	-	-	-	-	-	16
17	-	-	-	-	-	-	-	-	-	17
18	-	-	-	-	-	-	-	-	-	18
19	-	-	-	-	-	-	-	-	-	19

Note. **Com** = Communication; **CU** = Community Use; **FA** = Functional Academics; **SL** = School Living; **HS** = Health and Safety; **LS** = Leisure; **SC** = Self-Care; **SD** = Self-Direction; **Soc** = Social.

Table A.1 Scaled Score Equivalents of Skill Area Raw Scores: Teacher/Daycare Provider and Teacher Forms (continued)

Teacher Form — **Ages 17–21**

ss	Com	CU	FA	SL	HS	LS	SC	SD	Soc	WK	ss
1	0–44	0–27	0–41	0–36	0–33	0–24	0–48	0–35	0–36	0–27	1
2	45–48	28–31	42–44	37–40	34–36	25–28	49–50	36–39	37–40	28–33	2
3	49–51	32–34	45–47	41–43	37–39	29–31	51–52	40–42	41–43	34–38	3
4	52–53	35–36	48–49	44–45	40–41	32–33	53–54	43–44	44–45	39–42	4
5	54–55	37–38	50–52	–	42	34–35	–	45	46–47	43–45	5
6	56	39	53–55	46	–	36–37	55	46	48–49	46–49	6
7	57	40	56–57	47	43	38–39	–	47	50	50–52	7
8	58–59	41	58–59	48–49	44	40–41	56	48–50	51–52	53–55	8
9	60–61	42	60–61	50–51	45	42–44	–	51–54	53–55	56–57	9
10	62–64	43	62–63	52–55	46	45–47	–	55–59	56–57	58	10
11	65–66	44–45	64–66	56–60	47–48	48–49	57	60–63	58–59	59–60	11
12	–	–	–	–	–	50–51	–	–	60	61–63	12
13	–	–	–	–	–	–	–	–	–	–	13
14	–	–	–	–	–	–	–	–	–	–	14
15	–	–	–	–	–	–	–	–	–	–	15
16	–	–	–	–	–	–	–	–	–	–	16
17	–	–	–	–	–	–	–	–	–	–	17
18	–	–	–	–	–	–	–	–	–	–	18
19	–	–	–	–	–	–	–	–	–	–	19

Note. **Com** = Communication; **CU** = Community Use; **FA** = Functional Academics; **SL** = School Living; **HS** = Health and Safety; **LS** = Leisure; **SC** = Self-Care; **SD** = Self-Direction; **Soc** = Social; **WK** = Work.

Table A.2 GAC and Adaptive Domain Composite Equivalents of Sums of Scaled Scores: Teacher/Daycare Provider and Teacher Forms

Teacher/Daycare Provider Form — **Ages 2:0–2:5**

Composite Score	Percentile Rank	GAC	CON	SO	PR	Composite Score	Percentile Rank	GAC	CON	SO	PR
90% Confidence Interval ±		4	6	7	7	90% Confidence Interval ±		4	6	7	7
95% Confidence Interval ±		5	7	8	8	95% Confidence Interval ±		5	7	8	8
		Sums of Scaled Scores						Sums of Scaled Scores			
40	<0.1	9–10	–	–	–	101	53	94	31	–	–
41	<0.1	11	–	–	–	102	55	95–96	–	21	31
42	<0.1	12–13	–	–	–	103	58	97	32	–	–
43	<0.1	14	–	–	3	104	61	98–99	–	22	32
44	<0.1	15–16	–	–	–	105	63	100	33	–	–
45	<0.1	17	3	–	4	106	66	101–102	–	23	33
46	<0.1	18–19	–	–	–	107	68	103	34	–	–
47	<0.1	20	4	–	5	108	70	104–105	–	–	34
48	<0.1	21–22	–	–	–	109	73	106	35	24	–
49	<0.1	23	5	2	6	110	75	107–108	–	–	35
50	<0.1	24–25	–	–	–	111	77	109	36	–	–
51	0.1	26	6	3	7	112	79	110	–	–	36
52	0.1	27–28	–	–	8	113	81	111	37	25	–
53	0.1	29	7	4	–	114	82	112	–	–	37
54	0.1	30	–	–	9	115	84	113	38	–	–
55	0.1	31–32	8	5	–	116	86	114	–	26	38
56	0.2	33	–	–	10	117	87	115	39	–	–
57	0.2	34–35	9	–	–	118	88	116	–	27	39
58	0.3	36	–	6	11	119	90	117	–	–	–
59	0.3	37	10	–	–	120	91	118	40	–	40
60	0.4	38	11	–	12	121	92	119	–	28	–
61	0.5	39	–	7	–	122	93	120	41	–	41
62	1	40	12	–	13	123	94	121	–	–	–
63	1	41	–	–	–	124	95	122	–	–	42
64	1	42	13	8	14	125	95	123	42	29	–
65	1	43	–	–	–	126	96	124	–	–	43
66	1	44	14	–	15	127	96	125	–	–	–
67	1	45	–	9	–	128	97	126	43	30	–
68	2	46	15	–	16	129	97	127	–	–	44
69	2	47–48	–	–	–	130	98	128	44	–	–
70	2	49	16	10	17	131	98	129	–	31	–
71	3	50–51	–	–	–	132	98	130	–	–	45
72	3	52	17	–	18	133	99	131	45	–	–
73	4	53–54	–	11	–	134	99	132	–	–	–
74	4	55	18	–	19	135	99	133	–	32	46
75	5	56–57	–	–	–	136	99	134	46	–	–
76	5	58	19	12	20	137	99	135	–	–	–
77	6	59–60	–	–	–	138	99	136	–	33	47
78	7	61	20	–	–	139	99.5	137	47	–	–
79	8	62	–	13	21	140	99.6	138	–	–	–
80	9	63	21	–	–	141	99.7	139	–	–	48
81	10	64	–	–	22	142	99.7	140	48	34	–
82	12	65–66	22	14	–	143	99.8	141	–	–	49
83	13	67–68	–	–	–	144	99.8	142	49	–	–
84	14	69	23	–	23	145	99.9	143	–	–	50
85	16	70–71	–	15	–	146	99.9	144	50	35	–
86	18	72–73	24	–	–	147	99.9	145	–	–	–
87	19	74	–	–	24	148	99.9	146	51	–	51
88	21	75–76	25	16	–	149	99.9	147	–	36	–
89	23	77	–	–	–	150	>99.9	148	52	–	52
90	25	78–79	26	–	25	151	>99.9	149	–	–	–
91	27	80–81	–	17	–	152	>99.9	150	53	37	53
92	30	82	27	–	26	153	>99.9	151	–	–	–
93	32	83–84	–	–	–	154	>99.9	152	54	–	54
94	34	85	28	18	27	155	>99.9	153	–	38	–
95	37	86	–	–	–	156	>99.9	154	55	–	55
96	39	87	29	–	28	157	>99.9	155	–	–	–
97	42	88	–	19	–	158	>99.9	156	56	–	56
98	45	89	–	–	29	159	>99.9	157	–	–	–
99	47	90–91	30	–	–	160	>99.9	158–171	57	–	57
100	50	92–93	–	20	30						

Note. **CON** = Conceptual Adaptive Domain; **SO** = Social Adaptive Domain; **PR** = Practical Adaptive Domain.

Table A.2   GAC and Adaptive Domain Composite Equivalents of Sums of Scaled Scores: Teacher/Daycare Provider and Teacher Forms (continued)

Teacher/Daycare Provider Form   **Ages 2:6–2:11**

Composite Score	Percentile Rank	GAC	CON	SO	PR	Composite Score	Percentile Rank	GAC	CON	SO	PR
90% Confidence Interval ±		3	6	7	6	90% Confidence Interval ±		3	6	7	6
95% Confidence Interval ±		4	7	8	7	95% Confidence Interval ±		4	7	8	7
		Sums of Scaled Scores						**Sums of Scaled Scores**			
40	<0.1	9–10	–	–	–	101	53	94	31	–	–
41	<0.1	11	–	–	–	102	55	95–96	–	21	31
42	<0.1	12–13	–	–	–	103	58	97	32	–	–
43	<0.1	14	–	–	3	104	61	98–99	–	22	32
44	<0.1	15–16	–	–	–	105	63	100	33	–	–
45	<0.1	17	3	–	4	106	66	101–102	–	23	33
46	<0.1	18–19	–	–	–	107	68	103	34	–	–
47	<0.1	20	4	–	5	108	70	104–105	–	–	34
48	<0.1	21–22	–	–	–	109	73	106	35	24	–
49	<0.1	23	5	2	6	110	75	107–108	–	–	35
50	<0.1	24–25	–	–	–	111	77	109	36	–	–
51	0.1	26	6	3	7	112	79	110	–	–	36
52	0.1	27–28	–	–	8	113	81	111	37	25	–
53	0.1	29	7	4	–	114	82	112	–	–	37
54	0.1	30	–	–	9	115	84	113	38	–	–
55	0.1	31–32	8	5	–	116	86	114	–	26	38
56	0.2	33	–	–	10	117	87	115	39	–	–
57	0.2	34–35	9	–	–	118	88	116	–	27	39
58	0.3	36	–	6	11	119	90	117	–	–	–
59	0.3	37	10	–	–	120	91	118	40	–	40
60	0.4	38	11	–	12	121	92	119	–	28	–
61	0.5	39	–	7	–	122	93	120	41	–	41
62	1	40	12	–	13	123	94	121	–	–	–
63	1	41	–	–	–	124	95	122	–	–	42
64	1	42	13	8	14	125	95	123	42	29	–
65	1	43	–	–	–	126	96	124	–	–	43
66	1	44	14	–	15	127	96	125	–	–	–
67	1	45	–	9	–	128	97	126	43	30	–
68	2	46	15	–	16	129	97	127	–	–	44
69	2	47–48	–	–	–	130	98	128	44	–	–
70	2	49	16	10	17	131	98	129	–	31	–
71	3	50–51	–	–	–	132	98	130	–	–	45
72	3	52	17	–	18	133	99	131	45	–	–
73	4	53–54	–	11	–	134	99	132	–	–	–
74	4	55	18	–	19	135	99	133	–	32	46
75	5	56–57	–	–	–	136	99	134	46	–	–
76	5	58	19	12	20	137	99	135	–	–	–
77	6	59–60	–	–	–	138	99	136	–	33	47
78	7	61	20	–	–	139	99.5	137	47	–	–
79	8	62	–	13	21	140	99.6	138	–	–	–
80	9	63	21	–	–	141	99.7	139	–	–	48
81	10	64	–	–	22	142	99.7	140	48	34	–
82	12	65–66	22	14	–	143	99.8	141	–	–	49
83	13	67–68	–	–	–	144	99.8	142	49	–	–
84	14	69	23	–	23	145	99.9	143	–	–	50
85	16	70–71	–	15	–	146	99.9	144	50	35	–
86	18	72–73	24	–	–	147	99.9	145	–	–	–
87	19	74	–	–	24	148	99.9	146	51	–	51
88	21	75–76	25	16	–	149	99.9	147	–	36	–
89	23	77	–	–	–	150	>99.9	148	52	–	52
90	25	78–79	26	–	25	151	>99.9	149	–	–	–
91	27	80–81	–	17	–	152	>99.9	150	53	37	53
92	30	82	27	–	26	153	>99.9	151	–	–	–
93	32	83–84	–	–	–	154	>99.9	152	54	–	54
94	34	85	28	18	27	155	>99.9	153	–	38	–
95	37	86	–	–	–	156	>99.9	154	55	–	55
96	39	87	29	–	28	157	>99.9	155	–	–	–
97	42	88	–	19	–	158	>99.9	156	56	–	56
98	45	89	–	–	29	159	>99.9	157	–	–	–
99	47	90–91	30	–	–	160	>99.9	158–171	57	–	57
100	50	92–93	–	20	30						

Note. **CON** = Conceptual Adaptive Domain; **SO** = Social Adaptive Domain; **PR** = Practical Adaptive Domain.

187

Table A.2 GAC and Adaptive Domain Composite Equivalents of Sums of Scaled Scores: Teacher/Daycare Provider and Teacher Forms *(continued)*

Teacher/Daycare Provider Form   **Ages 3:0–3:5**

	GAC	CON	SO	PR			GAC	CON	SO	PR
90% Confidence Interval ±	2	4	5	5	90% Confidence Interval ±		2	4	5	5
95% Confidence Interval ±	3	5	6	6	95% Confidence Interval ±		3	5	6	6
Composite Score	**Percentile Rank**	**Sums of Scaled Scores**			**Composite Score**	**Percentile Rank**	**Sums of Scaled Scores**			
40	<0.1	9–10	–	–	–	101	53	94	31	–	–
41	<0.1	11	–	–	–	102	55	95–96	–	21	31
42	<0.1	12–13	–	–	–	103	58	97	32	–	–
43	<0.1	14	–	–	3	104	61	98–99	–	22	32
44	<0.1	15–16	–	–	–	105	63	100	33	–	–
45	<0.1	17	3	–	4	106	66	101–102	–	23	33
46	<0.1	18–19	–	–	–	107	68	103	34	–	–
47	<0.1	20	4	–	5	108	70	104–105	–	–	34
48	<0.1	21–22	–	–	–	109	73	106	35	24	–
49	<0.1	23	5	2	6	110	75	107–108	–	–	35
50	<0.1	24–25	–	–	–	111	77	109	36	–	–
51	0.1	26	6	3	7	112	79	110	–	–	36
52	0.1	27–28	–	–	8	113	81	111	37	25	–
53	0.1	29	7	4	–	114	82	112	–	–	37
54	0.1	30	–	–	9	115	84	113	38	–	–
55	0.1	31–32	8	5	–	116	86	114	–	26	38
56	0.2	33	–	–	10	117	87	115	39	–	–
57	0.2	34–35	9	–	–	118	88	116	–	27	39
58	0.3	36	–	6	11	119	90	117	–	–	–
59	0.3	37	10	–	–	120	91	118	40	–	40
60	0.4	38	11	–	12	121	92	119	–	28	–
61	0.5	39	–	7	–	122	93	120	41	–	41
62	1	40	12	–	13	123	94	121	–	–	–
63	1	41	–	–	–	124	95	122	–	–	42
64	1	42	13	8	14	125	95	123	42	29	–
65	1	43	–	–	–	126	96	124	–	–	43
66	1	44	14	–	15	127	96	125	–	–	–
67	1	45	–	9	–	128	97	126	43	30	–
68	2	46	15	–	16	129	97	127	–	–	44
69	2	47–48	–	–	–	130	98	128	44	–	–
70	2	49	16	10	17	131	98	129	–	31	–
71	3	50–51	–	–	–	132	98	130	–	–	45
72	3	52	17	–	18	133	99	131	45	–	–
73	4	53–54	–	11	–	134	99	132	–	–	–
74	4	55	18	–	19	135	99	133	–	32	46
75	5	56–57	–	–	–	136	99	134	46	–	–
76	5	58	19	12	20	137	99	135	–	–	–
77	6	59–60	–	–	–	138	99	136	–	33	47
78	7	61	20	–	–	139	99.5	137	47	–	–
79	8	62	–	13	21	140	99.6	138	–	–	–
80	9	63	21	–	–	141	99.7	139	–	–	48
81	10	64	–	–	22	142	99.7	140	48	34	–
82	12	65–66	22	14	–	143	99.8	141	–	–	49
83	13	67–68	–	–	–	144	99.8	142	49	–	–
84	14	69	23	–	23	145	99.9	143	–	–	50
85	16	70–71	–	15	–	146	99.9	144	50	35	–
86	18	72–73	24	–	–	147	99.9	145	–	–	–
87	19	74	–	–	24	148	99.9	146	51	–	51
88	21	75–76	25	16	–	149	99.9	147	–	36	–
89	23	77	–	–	–	150	>99.9	148	52	–	52
90	25	78–79	26	–	25	151	>99.9	149	–	–	–
91	27	80–81	–	17	–	152	>99.9	150	53	37	53
92	30	82	27	–	26	153	>99.9	151	–	–	–
93	32	83–84	–	–	–	154	>99.9	152	54	–	54
94	34	85	28	18	27	155	>99.9	153	–	38	–
95	37	86	–	–	–	156	>99.9	154	55	–	55
96	39	87	29	–	28	157	>99.9	155	–	–	–
97	42	88	–	19	–	158	>99.9	156	56	–	56
98	45	89	–	–	29	159	>99.9	157	–	–	–
99	47	90–91	30	–	–	160	>99.9	158–171	57	–	57
100	50	92–93	–	20	30						

Note. **CON** = Conceptual Adaptive Domain; **SO** = Social Adaptive Domain; **PR** = Practical Adaptive Domain.

Table A.2 GAC and Adaptive Domain Composite Equivalents of Sums of Scaled Scores: Teacher/Daycare Provider and Teacher Forms (continued)

Teacher/Daycare Provider Form — **Ages 3:6–3:11**

Composite Score	Percentile Rank	GAC	CON	SO	PR	Composite Score	Percentile Rank	GAC	CON	SO	PR
90% Confidence Interval ±		3	5	7	7	90% Confidence Interval ±		3	5	7	7
95% Confidence Interval ±		4	6	8	8	95% Confidence Interval ±		4	6	8	8
		Sums of Scaled Scores						Sums of Scaled Scores			
40	<0.1	9–10	–	–	–	101	53	94	31	–	–
41	<0.1	11	–	–	–	102	55	95–96	–	21	31
42	<0.1	12–13	–	–	–	103	58	97	32	–	–
43	<0.1	14	–	–	3	104	61	98–99	–	22	32
44	<0.1	15–16	–	–	–	105	63	100	33	–	–
45	<0.1	17	3	–	4	106	66	101–102	–	23	33
46	<0.1	18–19	–	–	–	107	68	103	34	–	–
47	<0.1	20	4	–	5	108	70	104–105	–	–	34
48	<0.1	21–22	–	–	–	109	73	106	35	24	–
49	<0.1	23	5	2	6	110	75	107–108	–	–	35
50	<0.1	24–25	–	–	–	111	77	109	36	–	–
51	0.1	26	6	3	7	112	79	110	–	–	36
52	0.1	27–28	–	–	8	113	81	111	37	25	–
53	0.1	29	7	4	–	114	82	112	–	–	37
54	0.1	30	–	–	9	115	84	113	38	–	–
55	0.1	31–32	8	5	–	116	86	114	–	26	38
56	0.2	33	–	–	10	117	87	115	39	–	–
57	0.2	34–35	9	–	–	118	88	116	–	27	39
58	0.3	36	–	6	11	119	90	117	–	–	–
59	0.3	37	10	–	–	120	91	118	40	–	40
60	0.4	38	11	–	12	121	92	119	–	28	–
61	0.5	39	–	7	–	122	93	120	41	–	41
62	1	40	12	–	13	123	94	121	–	–	–
63	1	41	–	–	–	124	95	122	–	–	42
64	1	42	13	8	14	125	95	123	42	29	–
65	1	43	–	–	–	126	96	124	–	–	43
66	1	44	14	–	15	127	96	125	–	–	–
67	1	45	–	9	–	128	97	126	43	30	–
68	2	46	15	–	16	129	97	127	–	–	44
69	2	47–48	–	–	–	130	98	128	44	–	–
70	2	49	16	10	17	131	98	129	–	31	–
71	3	50–51	–	–	–	132	98	130	–	–	45
72	3	52	17	–	18	133	99	131	45	–	–
73	4	53–54	–	11	–	134	99	132	–	–	–
74	4	55	18	–	19	135	99	133	–	32	46
75	5	56–57	–	–	–	136	99	134	46	–	–
76	5	58	19	12	20	137	99	135	–	–	–
77	6	59–60	–	–	–	138	99	136	–	33	47
78	7	61	20	–	–	139	99.5	137	47	–	–
79	8	62	–	13	21	140	99.6	138	–	–	–
80	9	63	21	–	–	141	99.7	139	–	–	48
81	10	64	–	–	22	142	99.7	140	48	34	–
82	12	65–66	22	14	–	143	99.8	141	–	–	49
83	13	67–68	–	–	–	144	99.8	142	49	–	–
84	14	69	23	–	23	145	99.9	143	–	–	50
85	16	70–71	–	15	–	146	99.9	144	50	35	–
86	18	72–73	24	–	–	147	99.9	145	–	–	–
87	19	74	–	–	24	148	99.9	146	51	–	51
88	21	75–76	25	16	–	149	99.9	147	–	36	–
89	23	77	–	–	–	150	>99.9	148	52	–	52
90	25	78–79	26	–	25	151	>99.9	149	–	–	–
91	27	80–81	–	17	–	152	>99.9	150	53	37	53
92	30	82	27	–	26	153	>99.9	151	–	–	–
93	32	83–84	–	–	–	154	>99.9	152	54	–	54
94	34	85	28	18	27	155	>99.9	153	–	38	–
95	37	86	–	–	–	156	>99.9	154	55	–	55
96	39	87	29	–	28	157	>99.9	155	–	–	–
97	42	88	–	19	–	158	>99.9	156	56	–	56
98	45	89	–	–	29	159	>99.9	157	–	–	–
99	47	90–91	30	–	–	160	>99.9	158–171	57	–	57
100	50	92–93	–	20	30						

Note. **CON** = Conceptual Adaptive Domain; **SO** = Social Adaptive Domain; **PR** = Practical Adaptive Domain.

Table A.2 GAC and Adaptive Domain Composite Equivalents of Sums of Scaled Scores: Teacher/Daycare Provider and Teacher Forms (continued)

Teacher/Daycare Provider Form — **Ages 4:0–4:5**

Composite Score	Percentile Rank	GAC	CON	SO	PR	Composite Score	Percentile Rank	GAC	CON	SO	PR
90% Confidence Interval ±		3	4	6	6	90% Confidence Interval ±		3	4	6	6
95% Confidence Interval ±		4	5	7	7	95% Confidence Interval ±		4	5	7	7
		Sums of Scaled Scores						Sums of Scaled Scores			
40	<0.1	9–10	–	–	–	101	53	94	31	–	–
41	<0.1	11	–	–	–	102	55	95–96	–	21	31
42	<0.1	12–13	–	–	–	103	58	97	32	–	–
43	<0.1	14	–	–	3	104	61	98–99	–	22	32
44	<0.1	15–16	–	–	–	105	63	100	33	–	–
45	<0.1	17	3	–	4	106	66	101–102	–	23	33
46	<0.1	18–19	–	–	–	107	68	103	34	–	–
47	<0.1	20	4	–	5	108	70	104–105	–	–	34
48	<0.1	21–22	–	–	–	109	73	106	35	24	–
49	<0.1	23	5	2	6	110	75	107–108	–	–	35
50	<0.1	24–25	–	–	–	111	77	109	36	–	–
51	0.1	26	6	3	7	112	79	110	–	–	36
52	0.1	27–28	–	–	8	113	81	111	37	25	–
53	0.1	29	7	4	–	114	82	112	–	–	37
54	0.1	30	–	–	9	115	84	113	38	–	–
55	0.1	31–32	8	5	–	116	86	114	–	26	38
56	0.2	33	–	–	10	117	87	115	39	–	–
57	0.2	34–35	9	–	–	118	88	116	–	27	39
58	0.3	36	–	6	11	119	90	117	–	–	–
59	0.3	37	10	–	–	120	91	118	40	–	40
60	0.4	38	11	–	12	121	92	119	–	28	–
61	0.5	39	–	7	–	122	93	120	41	–	41
62	1	40	12	–	13	123	94	121	–	–	–
63	1	41	–	–	–	124	95	122	–	–	42
64	1	42	13	8	14	125	95	123	42	29	–
65	1	43	–	–	–	126	96	124	–	–	43
66	1	44	14	–	15	127	96	125	–	–	–
67	1	45	–	9	–	128	97	126	43	30	–
68	2	46	15	–	16	129	97	127	–	–	44
69	2	47–48	–	–	–	130	98	128	44	–	–
70	2	49	16	10	17	131	98	129	–	31	–
71	3	50–51	–	–	–	132	98	130	–	–	45
72	3	52	17	–	18	133	99	131	45	–	–
73	4	53–54	–	11	–	134	99	132	–	–	–
74	4	55	18	–	19	135	99	133	–	32	46
75	5	56–57	–	–	–	136	99	134	46	–	–
76	5	58	19	12	20	137	99	135	–	–	–
77	6	59–60	–	–	–	138	99	136	–	33	47
78	7	61	20	–	–	139	99.5	137	47	–	–
79	8	62	–	13	21	140	99.6	138	–	–	–
80	9	63	21	–	–	141	99.7	139	–	–	48
81	10	64	–	–	22	142	99.7	140	48	34	–
82	12	65–66	22	14	–	143	99.8	141	–	–	49
83	13	67–68	–	–	–	144	99.8	142	49	–	–
84	14	69	23	–	23	145	99.9	143	–	–	50
85	16	70–71	–	15	–	146	99.9	144	50	35	–
86	18	72–73	24	–	–	147	99.9	145	–	–	–
87	19	74	–	–	24	148	99.9	146	51	–	51
88	21	75–76	25	16	–	149	99.9	147	–	36	–
89	23	77	–	–	–	150	>99.9	148	52	–	52
90	25	78–79	26	–	25	151	>99.9	149	–	–	–
91	27	80–81	–	17	–	152	>99.9	150	53	37	53
92	30	82	27	–	26	153	>99.9	151	–	–	–
93	32	83–84	–	–	–	154	>99.9	152	54	–	54
94	34	85	28	18	27	155	>99.9	153	–	38	–
95	37	86	–	–	–	156	>99.9	154	55	–	55
96	39	87	29	–	28	157	>99.9	155	–	–	–
97	42	88	–	19	–	158	>99.9	156	56	–	56
98	45	89	–	–	29	159	>99.9	157	–	–	–
99	47	90–91	30	–	–	160	>99.9	158–171	57	–	57
100	50	92–93	–	20	30						

Note. **CON** = Conceptual Adaptive Domain; **SO** = Social Adaptive Domain; **PR** = Practical Adaptive Domain.

Table A.2 GAC and Adaptive Domain Composite Equivalents of Sums of Scaled Scores: Teacher/Daycare Provider and Teacher Forms *(continued)*

Teacher/Daycare Provider Form — **Ages 4:6–4:11**

Composite Score	Percentile Rank	GAC	CON	SO	PR	Composite Score	Percentile Rank	GAC	CON	SO	PR
90% Confidence Interval ±		3	5	6	7	90% Confidence Interval ±		3	5	6	7
95% Confidence Interval ±		4	6	7	8	95% Confidence Interval ±		4	6	7	8
		Sums of Scaled Scores						Sums of Scaled Scores			
40	<0.1	9–10	–	–	–	101	53	94	31	–	–
41	<0.1	11	–	–	–	102	55	95–96	–	21	31
42	<0.1	12–13	–	–	–	103	58	97	32	–	–
43	<0.1	14	–	–	3	104	61	98–99	–	22	32
44	<0.1	15–16	–	–	–	105	63	100	33	–	–
45	<0.1	17	3	–	4	106	66	101–102	–	23	33
46	<0.1	18–19	–	–	–	107	68	103	34	–	–
47	<0.1	20	4	–	5	108	70	104–105	–	–	34
48	<0.1	21–22	–	–	–	109	73	106	35	24	–
49	<0.1	23	5	2	6	110	75	107–108	–	–	35
50	<0.1	24–25	–	–	–	111	77	109	36	–	–
51	0.1	26	6	3	7	112	79	110	–	–	36
52	0.1	27–28	–	–	8	113	81	111	37	25	–
53	0.1	29	7	4	–	114	82	112	–	–	37
54	0.1	30	–	–	9	115	84	113	38	–	–
55	0.1	31–32	8	5	–	116	86	114	–	26	38
56	0.2	33	–	–	10	117	87	115	39	–	–
57	0.2	34–35	9	–	–	118	88	116	–	27	39
58	0.3	36	–	6	11	119	90	117	–	–	–
59	0.3	37	10	–	–	120	91	118	40	–	40
60	0.4	38	11	–	12	121	92	119	–	28	–
61	0.5	39	–	7	–	122	93	120	41	–	41
62	1	40	12	–	13	123	94	121	–	–	–
63	1	41	–	–	–	124	95	122	–	–	42
64	1	42	13	8	14	125	95	123	42	29	–
65	1	43	–	–	–	126	96	124	–	–	43
66	1	44	14	–	15	127	96	125	–	–	–
67	1	45	–	9	–	128	97	126	43	30	–
68	2	46	15	–	16	129	97	127	–	–	44
69	2	47–48	–	–	–	130	98	128	44	–	–
70	2	49	16	10	17	131	98	129	–	31	–
71	3	50–51	–	–	–	132	98	130	–	–	45
72	3	52	17	–	18	133	99	131	45	–	–
73	4	53–54	–	11	–	134	99	132	–	–	–
74	4	55	18	–	19	135	99	133	–	32	46
75	5	56–57	–	–	–	136	99	134	46	–	–
76	5	58	19	12	20	137	99	135	–	–	–
77	6	59–60	–	–	–	138	99	136	–	33	47
78	7	61	20	–	–	139	99.5	137	47	–	–
79	8	62	–	13	21	140	99.6	138	–	–	–
80	9	63	21	–	–	141	99.7	139	–	–	48
81	10	64	–	–	22	142	99.7	140	48	34	–
82	12	65–66	22	14	–	143	99.8	141	–	–	49
83	13	67–68	–	–	–	144	99.8	142	49	–	–
84	14	69	23	–	23	145	99.9	143	–	–	50
85	16	70–71	–	15	–	146	99.9	144	50	35	–
86	18	72–73	24	–	–	147	99.9	145	–	–	–
87	19	74	–	–	24	148	99.9	146	51	–	51
88	21	75–76	25	16	–	149	99.9	147	–	36	–
89	23	77	–	–	–	150	>99.9	148	52	–	52
90	25	78–79	26	–	25	151	>99.9	149	–	–	–
91	27	80–81	–	17	–	152	>99.9	150	53	37	53
92	30	82	27	–	26	153	>99.9	151	–	–	–
93	32	83–84	–	–	–	154	>99.9	152	54	–	54
94	34	85	28	18	27	155	>99.9	153	–	38	–
95	37	86	–	–	–	156	>99.9	154	55	–	55
96	39	87	29	–	28	157	>99.9	155	–	–	–
97	42	88	–	19	–	158	>99.9	156	56	–	56
98	45	89	–	–	29	159	>99.9	157	–	–	–
99	47	90–91	30	–	–	160	>99.9	158–171	57	–	57
100	50	92–93	–	20	30						

Note. **CON** = Conceptual Adaptive Domain; **SO** = Social Adaptive Domain; **PR** = Practical Adaptive Domain.

Table A.2 GAC and Adaptive Domain Composite Equivalents of Sums of Scaled Scores: Teacher/Daycare Provider and Teacher Forms (continued)

Teacher/Daycare Provider Form

Ages 5:0–5:11

Composite Score	Percentile Rank	GAC	CON	SO	PR	Composite Score	Percentile Rank	GAC	CON	SO	PR
90% Confidence Interval ±		3	4	5	7	90% Confidence Interval ±		3	4	5	7
95% Confidence Interval ±		4	5	6	8	95% Confidence Interval ±		4	5	6	8
		\<Sums of Scaled Scores\>						\<Sums of Scaled Scores\>			
40	<0.1	9–10	–	–	–	101	53	94	31	–	–
41	<0.1	11	–	–	–	102	55	95–96	–	21	31
42	<0.1	12–13	–	–	–	103	58	97	32	–	–
43	<0.1	14	–	–	3	104	61	98–99	–	22	32
44	<0.1	15–16	–	–	–	105	63	100	33	–	–
45	<0.1	17	3	–	4	106	66	101–102	–	23	33
46	<0.1	18–19	–	–	–	107	68	103	34	–	–
47	<0.1	20	4	–	5	108	70	104–105	–	–	34
48	<0.1	21–22	–	–	–	109	73	106	35	24	–
49	<0.1	23	5	2	6	110	75	107–108	–	–	35
50	<0.1	24–25	–	–	–	111	77	109	36	–	–
51	0.1	26	6	3	7	112	79	110	–	–	36
52	0.1	27–28	–	–	8	113	81	111	37	25	–
53	0.1	29	7	4	–	114	82	112	–	–	37
54	0.1	30	–	–	9	115	84	113	38	–	–
55	0.1	31–32	8	5	–	116	86	114	–	26	38
56	0.2	33	–	–	10	117	87	115	39	–	–
57	0.2	34–35	9	–	–	118	88	116	–	27	39
58	0.3	36	–	6	11	119	90	117	–	–	–
59	0.3	37	10	–	–	120	91	118	40	–	40
60	0.4	38	11	–	12	121	92	119	–	28	–
61	0.5	39	–	7	–	122	93	120	41	–	41
62	1	40	12	–	13	123	94	121	–	–	–
63	1	41	–	–	–	124	95	122	–	–	42
64	1	42	13	8	14	125	95	123	42	29	–
65	1	43	–	–	–	126	96	124	–	–	43
66	1	44	14	–	15	127	96	125	–	–	–
67	1	45	–	9	–	128	97	126	43	30	–
68	2	46	15	–	16	129	97	127	–	–	44
69	2	47–48	–	–	–	130	98	128	44	–	–
70	2	49	16	10	17	131	98	129	–	31	–
71	3	50–51	–	–	–	132	98	130	–	–	45
72	3	52	17	–	18	133	99	131	45	–	–
73	4	53–54	–	11	–	134	99	132	–	–	–
74	4	55	18	–	19	135	99	133	–	32	46
75	5	56–57	–	–	–	136	99	134	46	–	–
76	5	58	19	12	20	137	99	135	–	–	–
77	6	59–60	–	–	–	138	99	136	–	33	47
78	7	61	20	–	–	139	99.5	137	47	–	–
79	8	62	–	13	21	140	99.6	138	–	–	–
80	9	63	21	–	–	141	99.7	139	–	–	48
81	10	64	–	–	22	142	99.7	140	48	34	–
82	12	65–66	22	14	–	143	99.8	141	–	–	49
83	13	67–68	–	–	–	144	99.8	142	49	–	–
84	14	69	23	–	23	145	99.9	143	–	–	50
85	16	70–71	–	15	–	146	99.9	144	50	35	–
86	18	72–73	24	–	–	147	99.9	145	–	–	–
87	19	74	–	–	24	148	99.9	146	51	–	51
88	21	75–76	25	16	–	149	99.9	147	–	36	–
89	23	77	–	–	–	150	>99.9	148	52	–	52
90	25	78–79	26	–	25	151	>99.9	149	–	–	–
91	27	80–81	–	17	–	152	>99.9	150	53	37	53
92	30	82	27	–	26	153	>99.9	151	–	–	–
93	32	83–84	–	–	–	154	>99.9	152	54	–	54
94	34	85	28	18	27	155	>99.9	153	–	38	–
95	37	86	–	–	–	156	>99.9	154	55	–	55
96	39	87	29	–	28	157	>99.9	155	–	–	–
97	42	88	–	19	–	158	>99.9	156	56	–	56
98	45	89	–	–	29	159	>99.9	157	–	–	–
99	47	90–91	30	–	–	160	>99.9	158–171	57	–	57
100	50	92–93	–	20	30						

Note. **CON** = Conceptual Adaptive Domain; **SO** = Social Adaptive Domain; **PR** = Practical Adaptive Domain.

Table A.2 **GAC and Adaptive Domain Composite Equivalents of Sums of Scaled Scores: Teacher/Daycare Provider and Teacher Forms** (continued)

Teacher Form

Age 5

Composite Score	Percentile Rank	GAC	CON	SO	PR	Composite Score	Percentile Rank	GAC	CON	SO	PR
90% Confidence Interval ±		3	5	5	6	90% Confidence Interval ±		3	5	5	6
95% Confidence Interval ±		4	6	6	7	95% Confidence Interval ±		4	6	6	7
		Sums of Scaled Scores						Sums of Scaled Scores			
40	<0.1	9	–	–	–	86	17.5	66	–	–	29
41	<0.1	10	–	–	4	87	19.3	67–68	21	15	30
42	<0.1	11	–	–	–	88	21.2	69–70	–	–	–
43	<0.1	12	–	–	5	89	23.2	71–72	22	–	31
44	<0.1	13	–	–	–	90	25.2	73–74	–	16	32
45	<0.1	14	–	–	6	91	27.4	75	23	–	–
46	<0.1	15	–	–	–	92	29.7	76–77	–	17	33
47	<0.1	16	–	–	7	93	32	78–79	24	–	34
48	<0.1	17	3	–	–	94	34.5	80	–	18	35
49	<0.1	18	–	–	8	95	36.9	81–82	25	–	36
50	<0.1	19	–	–	–	96	39.5	83–84	–	19	–
51	<0.1	20	4	–	9	97	42.1	85	26	–	37
52	<0.1	21	–	–	–	98	44.7	86–87	–	20	38
53	<0.1	22	5	–	10	99	47.3	88	27	–	39
54	0.1	23	–	–	–	100	50	89–90	28	21	40
55	0.1	24	6	2	11	101	52.7	91	29	–	–
56	0.2	25	–	–	–	102	55.3	92–93	–	–	41
57	0.2	26	7	–	12	103	57.9	94	30	22	42
58	0.3	27	–	3	–	104	60.5	95	–	–	43
59	0.3	28	8	–	13	105	63.1	96–97	31	23	–
60	0.4	29	–	–	–	106	65.5	98	–	–	44
61	0.5	30	9	4	14	107	68	99	–	–	45
62	0.6	31–32	–	–	–	108	70.3	100	32	24	–
63	0.7	33–34	10	–	15	109	72.6	101–102	–	–	46
64	0.8	35–36	–	5	–	110	74.8	103	33	–	47
65	1.0	37–38	11	–	16	111	76.8	104	–	–	–
66	1.2	39–40	–	6	–	112	78.8	105	34	25	48
67	1.4	41–42	12	–	17	113	80.7	106	–	–	–
68	1.6	43–44	–	7	–	114	82.5	107	–	–	49
69	1.9	45–46	13	–	18	115	84.1	108	35	–	–
70	2.3	47–48	14	8	19	116	85.7	109	–	26	50
71	2.7	49	–	–	–	117	87.1	110	36	–	–
72	3.1	50	15	9	20	118	88.5	111	–	–	–
73	3.6	51	–	–	21	119	89.7	112	37	–	51
74	4.2	52	–	–	–	120	90.9	113	–	27	–
75	4.8	53	16	10	22	121	91.9	114	38	–	52
76	5.5	54	–	–	–	122	92.9	115	–	–	–
77	6.3	55	–	–	23	123	93.7	116	39	–	–
78	7.1	56	17	11	24	124	94.5	117	–	–	53
79	8.1	57	–	–	–	125	95.2	–	40	28	–
80	9.1	58	–	–	25	126	95.8	118	–	–	–
81	10.3	59	18	12	26	127	96.4	119	41	–	54
82	11.5	60	–	–	–	128	96.9	120	42	–	–
83	12.9	61	19	13	27	129	97.3	121	43	–	–
84	14.3	62–63	–	–	28	130	>97.3	122–131	44–57	29–38	55–76
85	15.9	64–65	20	14	–						

Note. **CON** = Conceptual Adaptive Domain; **SO** = Social Adaptive Domain; **PR** = Practical Adaptive Domain.

Table A.2   GAC and Adaptive Domain Composite Equivalents of Sums of Scaled Scores: Teacher/Daycare Provider and Teacher Forms *(continued)*

Teacher Form

Age 6

Composite Score	Percentile Rank	GAC	CON	SO	PR	Composite Score	Percentile Rank	GAC	CON	SO	PR
90% Confidence Interval ±		2	4	4	4	90% Confidence Interval ±		2	4	4	4
95% Confidence Interval ±		3	5	5	5	95% Confidence Interval ±		3	5	5	5
		Sums of Scaled Scores						**Sums of Scaled Scores**			
40	<0.1	9	–	–	–	86	17.5	63–64	19	–	26
41	<0.1	10	–	–	–	87	19.3	65–66	–	14	27
42	<0.1	11	–	–	–	88	21.2	67–69	20	–	28
43	<0.1	12	–	–	4	89	23.2	70–71	–	–	29
44	<0.1	13	–	–	–	90	25.2	72	21	15	30
45	<0.1	14	–	–	5	91	27.4	73–74	–	–	31
46	<0.1	15	–	–	–	92	29.7	75–76	22	–	32
47	<0.1	16	–	–	6	93	32	77–78	–	16	33
48	<0.1	17	–	–	–	94	34.5	79	23	–	34
49	<0.1	18	3	–	7	95	36.9	80–81	–	17	35
50	<0.1	19	–	–	–	96	39.5	82–83	24	–	36
51	<0.1	20	–	–	8	97	42.1	84	25	18	37
52	<0.1	21	4	–	–	98	44.7	85	26	–	38
53	<0.1	22	–	–	9	99	47.3	86	27	19	39
54	0.1	23	–	–	–	100	50	87–88	28	–	40
55	0.1	24	5	2	10	101	52.7	89	–	20	–
56	0.2	25	–	–	–	102	55.3	90	29	–	41
57	0.2	26	6	–	11	103	57.9	91	–	–	42
58	0.3	27	–	3	–	104	60.5	92	30	21	–
59	0.3	28	7	–	12	105	63.1	93–94	31	–	43
60	0.4	29	–	–	–	106	65.5	95	–	–	–
61	0.5	30	8	4	13	107	68	96	32	–	44
62	0.6	31	–	–	–	108	70.3	97	–	22	–
63	0.7	32	9	–	14	109	72.6	98	33	–	45
64	0.8	33	–	5	–	110	74.8	99	–	–	–
65	1.0	34	10	–	15	111	76.8	100	–	–	–
66	1.2	35	–	6	–	112	78.8	101	34	23	46
67	1.4	36–37	11	–	16	113	80.7	102	–	–	–
68	1.6	38–39	–	7	–	114	82.5	103	35	–	47
69	1.9	40–41	12	–	17	115	84.1	104	–	–	–
70	2.3	42–43	13	8	18	116	85.7	105	36	24	–
71	2.7	44	–	–	–	117	87.1	106	–	–	48
72	3.1	45	14	9	19	118	88.5	107	–	–	–
73	3.6	46	–	–	–	119	89.7	108	37	–	49
74	4.2	47	–	–	–	120	90.9	109	–	–	–
75	4.8	48	15	10	20	121	91.9	110	38	25	–
76	5.5	49	–	–	–	122	92.9	111	–	–	50
77	6.3	50	–	–	–	123	93.7	112	–	–	–
78	7.1	51	16	11	21	124	94.5	113	39	–	–
79	8.1	52	–	–	–	125	95.2	–	–	–	–
80	9.1	53	–	–	–	126	95.8	114	–	26	51
81	10.3	54	17	12	22	127	96.4	115	40	–	–
82	11.5	55	–	–	–	128	96.9	116	–	–	–
83	12.9	56–57	–	–	23	129	97.3	117	–	–	52
84	14.3	58–59	18	13	24	130	>97.3	118–131	41–57	27–38	53–76
85	15.9	60–62	–	–	25						

Note. **CON** = Conceptual Adaptive Domain; **SO** = Social Adaptive Domain; **PR** = Practical Adaptive Domain.

Table A.2 GAC and Adaptive Domain Composite Equivalents of Sums of Scaled Scores: Teacher/Daycare Provider and Teacher Forms (continued)

Teacher Form — **Age 7**

Composite Score	Percentile Rank	GAC	CON	SO	PR	Composite Score	Percentile Rank	GAC	CON	SO	PR
90% Confidence Interval ±		2	4	5	5	90% Confidence Interval ±		2	4	5	5
95% Confidence Interval ±		3	5	6	6	95% Confidence Interval ±		3	5	6	6
		Sums of Scaled Scores						**Sums of Scaled Scores**			
40	<0.1	–	–	–	–	86	17.5	65–67	–	14	27
41	<0.1	9	–	–	–	87	19.3	68–69	19	–	28
42	<0.1	10	–	–	–	88	21.2	70–71	–	15	29
43	<0.1	11	–	–	4	89	23.2	72–73	20	–	30
44	<0.1	12	–	–	–	90	25.2	74–75	–	16	31
45	<0.1	13	–	–	5	91	27.4	76–77	21	–	32
46	<0.1	14	–	–	–	92	29.7	78	–	17	33
47	<0.1	15	–	–	6	93	32	79–80	22	–	34
48	<0.1	16	–	–	–	94	34.5	81–82	23	18	35
49	<0.1	17	3	–	7	95	36.9	83	24	–	36
50	<0.1	18	–	–	–	96	39.5	84–85	25	–	37
51	<0.1	19	–	–	8	97	42.1	86	26	19	38
52	<0.1	20	4	–	–	98	44.7	87	27	–	39
53	<0.1	21	–	–	9	99	47.3	88–89	28	20	40
54	0.1	22	–	–	–	100	50	90	29	–	41
55	0.1	23	5	2	10	101	52.7	91	30	21	–
56	0.2	24	–	–	–	102	55.3	92	–	–	42
57	0.2	25	6	–	11	103	57.9	93–94	31	–	–
58	0.3	26	–	3	–	104	60.5	95	–	22	43
59	0.3	27	7	–	12	105	63.1	96	32	–	–
60	0.4	28	–	–	–	106	65.5	97	–	–	44
61	0.5	29	8	4	13	107	68	98	–	–	–
62	0.6	30	–	–	–	108	70.3	99	33	23	45
63	0.7	31	9	–	14	109	72.6	100	–	–	–
64	0.8	32	–	5	–	110	74.8	101	34	–	–
65	1.0	33	10	–	15	111	76.8	102	–	–	46
66	1.2	34	–	6	–	112	78.8	103	35	–	–
67	1.4	35	11	–	16	113	80.7	104	–	24	–
68	1.6	36	–	7	–	114	82.5	105	–	–	47
69	1.9	37	12	–	17	115	84.1	106	36	–	–
70	2.3	38	13	8	18	116	85.7	107	–	–	–
71	2.7	39	–	–	–	117	87.1	108	37	–	48
72	3.1	40	14	9	19	118	88.5	109	–	–	–
73	3.6	41	–	–	–	119	89.7	110	–	25	–
74	4.2	42	–	–	–	120	90.9	–	38	–	49
75	4.8	43	15	10	20	121	91.9	111	–	–	–
76	5.5	44	–	–	–	122	92.9	112	–	–	–
77	6.3	45	–	–	–	123	93.7	113	39	–	50
78	7.1	46	16	11	21	124	94.5	114	–	–	–
79	8.1	47	–	–	–	125	95.2	115	–	26	–
80	9.1	48–49	–	–	22	126	95.8	116	40	–	51
81	10.3	50–52	17	12	–	127	96.4	–	–	–	–
82	11.5	53–56	–	–	23	128	96.9	117	41	–	52
83	12.9	57–59	–	–	24	129	97.3	118	42	–	–
84	14.3	60–61	18	13	25	130	>97.3	119–131	43–57	27–38	53–76
85	15.9	62–64	–	–	26						

Note. **CON** = Conceptual Adaptive Domain; **SO** = Social Adaptive Domain; **PR** = Practical Adaptive Domain.

Table A.2 GAC and Adaptive Domain Composite Equivalents of Sums of Scaled Scores: Teacher/Daycare Provider and Teacher Forms (continued)

Teacher Form — **Age 8**

Composite Score	Percentile Rank	GAC	CON	SO	PR	Composite Score	Percentile Rank	GAC	CON	SO	PR
90% Confidence Interval ±		2	3	4	3	90% Confidence Interval ±		2	3	4	3
95% Confidence Interval ±		3	4	5	4	95% Confidence Interval ±		3	4	5	4
		Sums of Scaled Scores						Sums of Scaled Scores			
40	<0.1	9	–	–	–	81	10	56	16	12	–
41	<0.1	10	–	–	4	82	12	57–58	–	–	24
42	<0.1	11	–	–	–	83	13	59–60	–	–	25
43	<0.1	12	–	–	5	84	14	61–63	17	13	26–27
44	<0.1	13	–	–	–	85	16	64–66	–	–	28
45	<0.1	14	–	–	6	86	18	67–68	18	14	29
46	<0.1	15	–	–	–	87	19	69–70	19	–	30–31
47	<0.1	16	–	–	7	88	21	71–72	20	15	32
48	<0.1	17	–	–	–	89	23	73–74	21	16	33
49	<0.1	18	–	–	8	90	25	75–76	22	17	34
50	<0.1	19	3	–	–	91	27	77	23	–	35
51	0.1	20	–	–	9	92	30	78–79	24	18	36
52	0.1	21	–	–	–	93	32	80	25	–	37
53	0.1	22	4	–	10	94	34	81–82	26	19	–
54	0.1	23	–	–	–	95	37	83	–	–	38
55	0.1	24	–	2	11	96	39	84–85	27	20	39
56	0.2	25	5	–	–	97	42	86	–	–	–
57	0.2	26	–	–	12	98	45	87	28	21	40
58	0.3	27	–	3	–	99	47	88	29	–	41
59	0.3	28	6	–	13	100	50	89–90	30	–	–
60	0.4	29	–	–	–	101	53	91	–	22	42
61	0.5	30	7	4	14	102	55	92	31	–	–
62	1	31	–	–	–	103	58	93	–	–	43
63	1	32	8	–	15	104	61	94	–	–	–
64	1	33	–	5	–	105	63	95	32	23	–
65	1	34–35	9	–	16	106	66	96	–	–	44
66	1	36–37	–	6	–	107	68	97	–	–	–
67	1	38–39	10	–	17	108	70	98–99	33	–	45
68	2	40–41	–	7	–	109	73	100	–	–	–
69	2	42–43	11	–	18	110	75	101	–	24	–
70	2	44–45	12	8	19	111	77	102	34	–	46
71	3	46	–	–	–	112	79	103	–	–	–
72	3	47	13	9	20	113	81	104	–	–	–
73	4	48	–	–	–	114	82	105	–	–	47
74	4	49	–	–	–	115	84	106	35	–	–
75	5	50	14	10	21	116	86	107	–	25	–
76	5	51	–	–	–	117	87	108	–	–	48
77	6	52	–	–	–	118	88	109	–	–	–
78	7	53	15	11	22	119	90	110	36	–	–
79	8	54	–	–	–	120	>90	111–131	37–57	26–38	49–76
80	9	55	–	–	23						

Note. **CON** = Conceptual Adaptive Domain; **SO** = Social Adaptive Domain; **PR** = Practical Adaptive Domain.

Table A.2 GAC and Adaptive Domain Composite Equivalents of Sums of Scaled Scores: Teacher/Daycare Provider and Teacher Forms (continued)

Teacher Form   **Age 9**

Composite Score	Percentile Rank	GAC	CON	SO	PR	Composite Score	Percentile Rank	GAC	CON	SO	PR
90% Confidence Interval ±		2	3	4	4	90% Confidence Interval ±		2	3	4	4
95% Confidence Interval ±		3	4	5	5	95% Confidence Interval ±		3	4	5	5
		Sums of Scaled Scores						**Sums of Scaled Scores**			
40	<0.1	9	–	–	–	81	10	52	16	12	22
41	<0.1	10	–	–	–	82	12	53	–	–	–
42	<0.1	11	–	–	–	83	13	54–55	–	–	23
43	<0.1	12	–	–	4	84	14	56–58	17	13	24
44	<0.1	13	–	–	–	85	16	59–61	–	–	25–26
45	<0.1	14	–	–	5	86	18	62–64	–	–	27
46	<0.1	15	–	–	–	87	19	65–67	18	14	28–29
47	<0.1	16	–	–	6	88	21	68–69	–	–	30
48	<0.1	17	–	–	–	89	23	70–71	19	15	31–32
49	<0.1	18	–	–	7	90	25	72–73	20	–	33
50	<0.1	19	3	–	–	91	27	74–75	21	16	34
51	0.1	20	–	–	8	92	30	76–77	22	–	35
52	0.1	21	–	–	–	93	32	78	23	17	36
53	0.1	22	4	–	9	94	34	79–80	24	–	37
54	0.1	23	–	–	–	95	37	81	25	18	38
55	0.1	24	–	2	10	96	39	82–83	–	19	–
56	0.2	25	5	–	–	97	42	84	26	–	39
57	0.2	26	–	–	11	98	45	85	27	20	–
58	0.3	27	–	3	–	99	47	86	28	–	40
59	0.3	28	6	–	12	100	50	87–88	29	–	41
60	0.4	29	–	–	–	101	53	89	30	21	–
61	0.5	30	7	4	13	102	55	90	–	–	42
62	1	31	–	–	–	103	58	91	31	–	–
63	1	32	8	–	14	104	61	92	–	–	–
64	1	33	–	5	–	105	63	93	–	22	43
65	1	34	9	–	15	106	66	94	32	–	–
66	1	35	–	6	–	107	68	95	–	–	44
67	1	36	10	–	16	108	70	96	–	–	–
68	2	37	–	7	–	109	73	97	33	–	–
69	2	38–39	11	–	17	110	75	98	–	23	45
70	2	40–41	12	8	18	111	77	99	–	–	–
71	3	42	–	–	–	112	79	100	34	–	–
72	3	43	13	9	19	113	81	101	–	–	46
73	4	44	–	–	–	114	82	102	–	–	–
74	4	45	–	–	–	115	84	103	35	–	–
75	5	46	14	10	20	116	86	104	–	24	–
76	5	47	–	–	–	117	87	105	–	–	47
77	6	48	–	–	–	118	88	106	–	–	–
78	7	49	15	11	21	119	90	107	36	–	–
79	8	50	–	–	–	120	>90	108–131	37–57	25–38	48–76
80	9	51	–	–	–						

Note. **CON** = Conceptual Adaptive Domain; **SO** = Social Adaptive Domain; **PR** = Practical Adaptive Domain.

Table A.2   GAC and Adaptive Domain Composite Equivalents of Sums of Scaled Scores: Teacher/Daycare Provider and Teacher Forms *(continued)*

Teacher Form

Age 10

Composite Score	Percentile Rank	GAC	CON	SO	PR		Composite Score	Percentile Rank	GAC	CON	SO	PR
90% Confidence Interval ±		2	3	4	4		90% Confidence Interval ±		2	3	4	4
95% Confidence Interval ±		3	4	5	5		95% Confidence Interval ±		3	4	5	5
		Sums of Scaled Scores							**Sums of Scaled Scores**			
40	<0.1	9	–	–	–		81	10	59	16	–	23
41	<0.1	10	–	–	–		82	12	60	–	12	24
42	<0.1	11	–	–	–		83	13	61	–	–	25–26
43	<0.1	12	–	–	4		84	14	62	17	13	27
44	<0.1	13	–	–	–		85	16	63–64	–	–	28–29
45	<0.1	14	–	–	5		86	18	65–66	–	14	30
46	<0.1	15	–	–	–		87	19	67–68	18	–	31
47	<0.1	16	–	–	6		88	21	69–70	–	15	32
48	<0.1	17	–	–	–		89	23	71–72	19	16	33
49	<0.1	18	–	–	7		90	25	73–74	–	–	34
50	<0.1	19	3	–	–		91	27	75	20	17	35
51	0.1	20	–	–	8		92	30	76–77	21	–	36
52	0.1	21	–	–	–		93	32	78	22	18	–
53	0.1	22	4	–	9		94	34	79–80	23	–	37
54	0.1	23	–	–	–		95	37	81	24	19	38
55	0.1	24	–	2	10		96	39	82	25	–	–
56	0.2	25	5	–	–		97	42	83	26	20	39
57	0.2	26	–	–	11		98	45	84–85	27–28	–	–
58	0.3	27	–	3	–		99	47	86	29	–	40
59	0.3	28	6	–	12		100	50	87	30	21	–
60	0.4	29	–	–	–		101	53	88	–	–	41
61	0.5	30	7	4	13		102	55	89	31	–	–
62	1	31–32	–	–	–		103	58	90	–	22	–
63	1	33–34	8	–	14		104	61	91–92	32	–	42
64	1	35–36	–	5	–		105	63	93	–	–	–
65	1	37–38	9	–	15		106	66	94	–	–	43
66	1	39–40	–	6	–		107	68	95	33	23	–
67	1	41–42	10	–	16		108	70	96	–	–	–
68	2	43–44	–	7	–		109	73	97	–	–	44
69	2	45–46	11	–	17		110	75	98	–	–	–
70	2	47–48	12	8	18		111	77	99	34	–	–
71	3	49	–	–	–		112	79	100	–	24	–
72	3	50	13	9	19		113	81	101	–	–	45
73	4	51	–	–	–		114	82	102	–	–	–
74	4	52	–	–	–		115	84	103	35	–	–
75	5	53	14	10	20		116	86	104	–	–	46
76	5	54	–	–	–		117	87	105	–	–	–
77	6	55	–	–	–		118	88	106	–	25	–
78	7	56	15	–	21		119	90	107	–	–	–
79	8	57	–	11	–		120	>90	108–131	36–57	26–38	47–76
80	9	58	–	–	22							

Note. **CON** = Conceptual Adaptive Domain; **SO** = Social Adaptive Domain; **PR** = Practical Adaptive Domain.

Table A.2   GAC and Adaptive Domain Composite Equivalents of Sums of Scaled Scores: Teacher/Daycare Provider and Teacher Forms (continued)

Teacher Form — **Age 11**

Composite Score	Percentile Rank	GAC	CON	SO	PR	Composite Score	Percentile Rank	GAC	CON	SO	PR
90% Confidence Interval ±		2	2	3	3	90% Confidence Interval ±		2	2	3	3
95% Confidence Interval ±		3	3	4	4	95% Confidence Interval ±		3	3	4	4
		Sums of Scaled Scores						Sums of Scaled Scores			
40	<0.1	–	–	–	–	81	10	49–50	16	12	21
41	<0.1	9	–	–	–	82	12	51–53	–	–	–
42	<0.1	10	–	–	–	83	13	54–57	–	–	22
43	<0.1	11	–	–	–	84	14	58–61	17	13	23
44	<0.1	12	–	–	–	85	16	62–64	–	–	24
45	<0.1	13	–	–	4	86	18	65–66	18	–	25
46	<0.1	14	–	–	–	87	19	67–68	–	14	26–27
47	<0.1	15	–	–	5	88	21	69–70	19	–	28–29
48	<0.1	16	–	–	–	89	23	71–72	20	15	30–31
49	<0.1	17	–	–	6	90	25	73	21	–	32
50	<0.1	18	3	–	–	91	27	74–75	22	16	33
51	0.1	19	–	–	7	92	30	76	23	17	34
52	0.1	20	–	–	–	93	32	77	24	18	35
53	0.1	21	4	–	8	94	34	78–79	25	–	36
54	0.1	22	–	–	–	95	37	80	26	19	37
55	0.1	23	–	2	9	96	39	81	27	–	38
56	0.2	24	5	–	–	97	42	82	28	–	39
57	0.2	25	–	–	10	98	45	83–84	29	20	–
58	0.3	26	–	3	–	99	47	85	–	–	40
59	0.3	27	6	–	11	100	50	86	30	–	–
60	0.4	28	–	–	–	101	53	87	–	–	–
61	0.5	29	7	4	12	102	55	88	–	21	41
62	1	30	–	–	–	103	58	89	31	–	–
63	1	31	8	–	13	104	61	90	–	–	–
64	1	32	–	5	–	105	63	91	–	–	42
65	1	33	9	–	14	106	66	92	–	–	–
66	1	34	–	6	–	107	68	93	32	22	–
67	1	35	10	–	15	108	70	94	–	–	–
68	2	36	–	7	–	109	73	95	–	–	43
69	2	37	11	–	16	110	75	96	–	–	–
70	2	38	12	8	17	111	77	97	33	–	–
71	3	39	–	–	–	112	79	98	–	23	–
72	3	40	13	9	18	113	81	99	–	–	44
73	4	41	–	–	–	114	82	100	–	–	–
74	4	42	–	–	–	115	84	101	–	–	–
75	5	43	14	10	19	116	86	102	34	–	–
76	5	44	–	–	–	117	87	103	–	–	–
77	6	45	–	–	–	118	88	104	–	24	45
78	7	46	15	11	20	119	90	105	–	–	–
79	8	47	–	–	–	120	>90	106–131	35–57	25–38	46–76
80	9	48	–	–	–						

Note. **CON** = Conceptual Adaptive Domain; **SO** = Social Adaptive Domain; **PR** = Practical Adaptive Domain.

Table A.2 GAC and Adaptive Domain Composite Equivalents of Sums of Scaled Scores: Teacher/Daycare Provider and Teacher Forms (continued)

Teacher Form — **Age 12**

Composite Score	Percentile Rank	GAC	CON	SO	PR	Composite Score	Percentile Rank	GAC	CON	SO	PR
90% Confidence Interval ±		2	3	4	3	90% Confidence Interval ±		2	3	4	3
95% Confidence Interval ±		3	4	5	4	95% Confidence Interval ±		3	4	5	4
		\multicolumn{4}{c}{Sums of Scaled Scores}			\multicolumn{4}{c}{Sums of Scaled Scores}
40	<0.1	–	–	–	–	81	10	49	16	12	21
41	<0.1	9	–	–	–	82	12	50	–	–	–
42	<0.1	10	–	–	–	83	13	51	–	–	–
43	<0.1	11	–	–	–	84	14	52–53	17	13	22
44	<0.1	12	–	–	–	85	16	54–56	–	–	–
45	<0.1	13	–	–	4	86	18	57–60	–	–	23
46	<0.1	14	–	–	–	87	19	61–63	18	14	24–25
47	<0.1	15	–	–	5	88	21	64–66	–	–	26–27
48	<0.1	16	–	–	–	89	23	67–68	19	–	28
49	<0.1	17	–	–	6	90	25	69–70	–	15	29–30
50	<0.1	18	3	–	–	91	27	71	20	–	31
51	0.1	19	–	–	7	92	30	72–73	21–22	16	32
52	0.1	20	–	–	–	93	32	74–75	23–24	–	33
53	0.1	21	4	–	8	94	34	76	25	17	34
54	0.1	22	–	–	–	95	37	77	26	18	35
55	0.1	23	–	2	9	96	39	78–79	27	–	–
56	0.2	24	5	–	–	97	42	80	28	19	36
57	0.2	25	–	–	10	98	45	81	29	–	–
58	0.3	26	–	3	–	99	47	82–83	–	–	37
59	0.3	27	6	–	11	100	50	84	30	20	38
60	0.4	28	–	–	–	101	53	85	–	–	39
61	0.5	29	7	4	12	102	55	86	–	–	–
62	1	30	–	–	–	103	58	87	31	–	40
63	1	31	8	–	13	104	61	88	–	21	–
64	1	32	–	5	–	105	63	89	–	–	41
65	1	33	9	–	14	106	66	90	–	–	–
66	1	34	–	6	–	107	68	91	32	–	–
67	1	35	10	–	15	108	70	92	–	–	42
68	2	36	–	7	–	109	73	93	–	22	–
69	2	37	11	–	16	110	75	94	–	–	–
70	2	38	12	8	17	111	77	95	33	–	43
71	3	39	–	–	–	112	79	96	–	–	–
72	3	40	13	9	18	113	81	97	–	–	–
73	4	41	–	–	–	114	82	98	–	23	–
74	4	42	–	–	–	115	84	99	–	–	44
75	5	43	14	10	19	116	86	100	34	–	–
76	5	44	–	–	–	117	87	101	–	–	–
77	6	45	–	–	–	118	88	102	–	–	–
78	7	46	15	11	20	119	90	103	–	–	45
79	8	47	–	–	–	120	>90	104–131	35–57	24–38	46–76
80	9	48	–	–	–						

Note. **CON** = Conceptual Adaptive Domain; **SO** = Social Adaptive Domain; **PR** = Practical Adaptive Domain.

Table A.2   GAC and Adaptive Domain Composite Equivalents of Sums of Scaled Scores: Teacher/Daycare Provider and Teacher Forms *(continued)*

Teacher Form

Ages 13–14

		GAC	CON	SO	PR			GAC	CON	SO	PR
90% Confidence Interval ±		2	3	4	3	90% Confidence Interval ±		2	3	4	3
95% Confidence Interval ±		3	4	5	4	95% Confidence Interval ±		3	4	5	4
Composite Score	Percentile Rank	Sums of Scaled Scores				Composite Score	Percentile Rank	Sums of Scaled Scores			
40	<0.1	9	–	–	–	81	10	59	16	12	22
41	<0.1	10	–	–	–	82	12	60	–	–	–
42	<0.1	11	–	–	–	83	13	61	–	–	23
43	<0.1	12	–	–	4	84	14	62	17	13	–
44	<0.1	13	–	–	–	85	16	63	–	–	24
45	<0.1	14	–	–	5	86	18	64	–	–	25
46	<0.1	15	–	–	–	87	19	65	18	14	26
47	<0.1	16	–	–	6	88	21	66	–	–	27
48	<0.1	17	–	–	–	89	23	67–68	19	15	28–29
49	<0.1	18	–	–	7	90	25	69–70	20	–	30
50	<0.1	19	3	–	–	91	27	71–72	21	16	31
51	0.1	20	–	–	8	92	30	73–74	22	–	32
52	0.1	21	–	–	–	93	32	75	23	17	33
53	0.1	22	4	–	9	94	34	76–77	24	18	34
54	0.1	23	–	–	–	95	37	78	25	–	35
55	0.1	24	–	2	10	96	39	79–80	26	19	36
56	0.2	25	5	–	–	97	42	81	–	–	37
57	0.2	26	–	–	11	98	45	82–83	27	–	38
58	0.3	27	–	3	–	99	47	84	28	20	39
59	0.3	28	6	–	12	100	50	85	29	–	40
60	0.4	29	–	–	–	101	53	86–87	–	–	–
61	0.5	30	7	4	13	102	55	88	30	–	41
62	1	31–32	–	–	–	103	58	89	–	21	–
63	1	33–34	8	–	14	104	61	90	31	–	–
64	1	35–36	–	5	–	105	63	91–92	–	–	42
65	1	37–38	9	–	15	106	66	93	–	–	–
66	1	39–40	–	6	–	107	68	94	32	–	–
67	1	41–42	10	–	16	108	70	95	–	22	43
68	2	43–44	–	7	–	109	73	96–97	–	–	–
69	2	45–46	11	–	17	110	75	98	–	–	–
70	2	47–48	12	8	18	111	77	99	33	–	44
71	3	49	–	–	–	112	79	100–101	–	–	–
72	3	50	13	9	19	113	81	102	–	23	–
73	4	51	–	–	–	114	82	103	–	–	45
74	4	52	–	–	–	115	84	104–105	34	–	–
75	5	53	14	10	20	116	86	106	–	–	–
76	5	54	–	–	–	117	87	107–108	–	–	–
77	6	55	–	–	–	118	88	109	–	–	46
78	7	56	15	11	21	119	90	110–111	–	24	–
79	8	57	–	–	–	120	>90	112–131	35–57	25–38	47–76
80	9	58	–	–	–						

Note. **CON** = Conceptual Adaptive Domain; **SO** = Social Adaptive Domain; **PR** = Practical Adaptive Domain.

Table A.2 GAC and Adaptive Domain Composite Equivalents of Sums of Scaled Scores: Teacher/Daycare Provider and Teacher Forms *(continued)*

Teacher Form

Ages 15–16

		GAC	CON	SO	PR			GAC	CON	SO	PR
90% Confidence Interval ±		2	2	3	3	90% Confidence Interval ±		2	2	3	3
95% Confidence Interval ±		3	3	4	4	95% Confidence Interval ±		3	3	4	4
Composite Score	Percentile Rank	Sums of Scaled Scores				Composite Score	Percentile Rank	Sums of Scaled Scores			
40	<0.1	9	–	–	–	81	10	59	16	12	21
41	<0.1	10	–	–	–	82	12	60	–	–	–
42	<0.1	11	–	–	–	83	13	61	–	–	22
43	<0.1	12	–	–	–	84	14	62	17	13	23
44	<0.1	13	–	–	–	85	16	63	–	–	24
45	<0.1	14	–	–	4	86	18	64	–	14	25–26
46	<0.1	15	–	–	–	87	19	65–66	18	–	27–28
47	<0.1	16	–	–	5	88	21	67–69	–	15	29–30
48	<0.1	17	–	–	–	89	23	70–71	19	–	31–32
49	<0.1	18	–	–	6	90	25	72–73	20	16	33
50	<0.1	19	3	–	–	91	27	74–75	21	–	34
51	0.1	20	–	–	7	92	30	76	22	17	35
52	0.1	21	–	–	–	93	32	77–78	23	–	36
53	0.1	22	4	–	8	94	34	79	24	18	37
54	0.1	23	–	–	–	95	37	80–81	25	19	38
55	0.1	24	–	2	9	96	39	82	26	–	39
56	0.2	25	5	–	–	97	42	83–84	27	20	40
57	0.2	26	–	–	10	98	45	85	28	–	–
58	0.3	27	–	3	–	99	47	86	29	–	41
59	0.3	28	6	–	11	100	50	87–88	–	21	–
60	0.4	29	–	–	–	101	53	89	30	–	–
61	0.5	30	7	4	12	102	55	90	–	–	42
62	1	31–32	–	–	–	103	58	91–92	–	–	–
63	1	33–34	8	–	13	104	61	93	31	22	–
64	1	35–36	–	5	–	105	63	94	–	–	–
65	1	37–38	9	–	14	106	66	95	–	–	43
66	1	39–40	–	6	–	107	68	96	–	–	–
67	1	41–42	10	–	15	108	70	97–98	32	–	–
68	2	43–44	–	7	–	109	73	99	–	23	–
69	2	45–46	11	–	16	110	75	100	–	–	44
70	2	47–48	12	8	17	111	77	101–102	–	–	–
71	3	49	–	–	–	112	79	103	–	–	–
72	3	50	13	9	18	113	81	104	33	–	–
73	4	51	–	–	–	114	82	105–106	–	–	45
74	4	52	–	–	–	115	84	107	–	24	–
75	5	53	14	10	19	116	86	108–109	–	–	–
76	5	54	–	–	–	117	87	110	–	–	46
77	6	55	–	–	–	118	88	111–112	34	–	–
78	7	56	15	11	20	119	90	113–115	–	–	–
79	8	57	–	–	–	120	>90	116–131	35–57	25–38	47–76
80	9	58	–	–	–						

Note. **CON** = Conceptual Adaptive Domain; **SO** = Social Adaptive Domain; **PR** = Practical Adaptive Domain.

Table A.2 GAC and Adaptive Domain Composite Equivalents of Sums of Scaled Scores: Teacher/Daycare Provider and Teacher Forms (continued)

Teacher Form

Ages 17–21

Composite Score	Percentile Rank	GAC	CON	SO	PR	Composite Score	Percentile Rank	GAC	CON	SO	PR
90% Confidence Interval ±		2	3	4	4	90% Confidence Interval ±		2	3	4	4
95% Confidence Interval ±		3	4	5	5	95% Confidence Interval ±		3	4	5	5
		Sums of Scaled Scores						Sums of Scaled Scores			
40	<0.1	–	–	–	–	81	10	56–58	18	13	26–27
41	<0.1	9	–	–	–	82	12	59–61	–	–	28–29
42	<0.1	10	–	–	–	83	13	62–63	19	–	30
43	<0.1	11	–	–	4	84	14	64–65	–	14	31
44	<0.1	12	–	–	–	85	16	66–67	20	–	32
45	<0.1	13	–	–	5	86	18	68–69	–	–	33
46	<0.1	14	–	–	–	87	19	70–71	21	15	34
47	<0.1	15	–	–	6	88	21	72–73	22	–	35
48	<0.1	16	3	–	–	89	23	74	23	–	36
49	<0.1	17	–	–	7	90	25	75–76	24	16	37
50	<0.1	18	–	–	–	91	27	77	25	–	38
51	0.1	19	4	–	8	92	30	78	26	–	–
52	0.1	20	–	–	–	93	32	79–80	27	17	39
53	0.1	21	5	–	9	94	34	81	28	–	–
54	0.1	22	–	2	–	95	37	82	–	18	40
55	0.1	23	6	–	10	96	39	83–84	29	19	–
56	0.2	24	–	–	–	97	42	85	–	–	–
57	0.2	25	7	3	11	98	45	86	–	20	41
58	0.3	26	–	–	–	99	47	87	30	–	–
59	0.3	27	8	–	12	100	50	88	–	–	–
60	0.4	28	–	4	–	101	53	89–90	–	21	–
61	0.5	29	9	–	13	102	55	91	–	–	42
62	1	30	–	5	–	103	58	92	31	–	–
63	1	31	10	–	14	104	61	93	–	–	–
64	1	32	–	6	–	105	63	94	–	22	–
65	1	33	11	–	15	106	66	95	–	–	43
66	1	34	–	7	–	107	68	96	–	–	–
67	1	35	12	–	16	108	70	97	32	–	–
68	2	36	–	8	–	109	73	98	–	–	–
69	2	37	13	–	17	110	75	99–100	–	23	–
70	2	38	14	9	18	111	77	101	–	–	44
71	3	39	–	–	–	112	79	102	–	–	–
72	3	40	15	10	19	113	81	103	–	–	–
73	4	41	–	–	–	114	82	104	33	–	–
74	4	42	–	–	–	115	84	105–106	–	–	45
75	5	43	16	11	20	116	86	107	–	24	–
76	5	44	–	–	–	117	87	108	–	–	–
77	6	45–46	–	–	21	118	88	109–110	–	–	46
78	7	47–49	17	12	22–23	119	90	111–112	34	–	–
79	8	50–52	–	–	24	120	>90	113–131	35–57	25–38	47–76
80	9	53–55	–	–	25						

Note. **CON** = Conceptual Adaptive Domain; **SO** = Social Adaptive Domain; **PR** = Practical Adaptive Domain.

Table A.3 Average Number of Items Guessed by the Standardization Sample: Teacher/Daycare Provider and Teacher Forms

Teacher/Daycare Provider Form — Age Group

Skill Areas	2:0–2:5 Mean	$SE_{\bar{x}}$	2:6–2:11 Mean	$SE_{\bar{x}}$	3:0–3:5 Mean	$SE_{\bar{x}}$	3:6–3:11 Mean	$SE_{\bar{x}}$	4:0–4:5 Mean	$SE_{\bar{x}}$	4:6–4:11 Mean	$SE_{\bar{x}}$	5:0–5:11 Mean	$SE_{\bar{x}}$
Communication	0.72	0.14	0.48	0.13	0.60	0.23	0.36	0.09	0.59	0.19	0.29	0.08	0.45	0.11
Functional Pre-Academics	0.57	0.13	0.50	0.18	0.87	0.22	0.76	0.22	0.50	0.15	0.49	0.12	0.38	0.07
School Living	0.44	0.11	0.62	0.21	0.63	0.21	0.60	0.16	0.45	0.12	0.28	0.08	0.40	0.09
Health and Safety	1.13	0.15	1.15	0.19	1.46	0.22	1.14	0.17	1.41	0.21	1.23	0.16	1.61	0.17
Leisure	0.59	0.12	0.56	0.11	0.60	0.19	0.47	0.11	0.45	0.13	0.25	0.07	0.61	0.11
Self-Care	0.53	0.11	0.38	0.11	0.50	0.14	0.46	0.13	0.56	0.21	0.53	0.11	1.16	0.22
Self-Direction	0.45	0.10	0.45	0.12	0.44	0.19	0.52	0.18	0.38	0.11	0.30	0.05	0.54	0.10
Social	0.54	0.10	0.51	0.13	0.60	0.19	0.55	0.20	0.38	0.08	0.45	0.10	0.77	0.14
Motor	0.82	0.17	0.66	0.13	0.79	0.16	0.52	0.13	0.53	0.12	0.21	0.06	0.83	0.18

Teacher Form — Age Group

Skill Areas	5 Mean	$SE_{\bar{x}}$	6 Mean	$SE_{\bar{x}}$	7 Mean	$SE_{\bar{x}}$	8 Mean	$SE_{\bar{x}}$	9 Mean	$SE_{\bar{x}}$	10 Mean	$SE_{\bar{x}}$	11 Mean	$SE_{\bar{x}}$	12 Mean	$SE_{\bar{x}}$	13–14 Mean	$SE_{\bar{x}}$	15–16 Mean	$SE_{\bar{x}}$	17–21 Mean	$SE_{\bar{x}}$
Communication	0.75	0.11	0.87	0.12	1.02	0.13	0.84	0.12	1.05	0.17	0.78	0.18	0.83	0.17	1.11	0.23	1.02	0.13	1.17	0.18	0.53	0.13
Community Use	0.75	0.11	1.25	0.14	1.72	0.15	1.88	0.17	1.88	0.19	1.77	0.20	2.58	0.25	2.69	0.24	2.48	0.19	2.49	0.31	1.03	0.16
Functional Academics	0.47	0.17	1.09	0.18	1.68	0.23	1.64	0.21	1.59	0.26	1.35	0.24	1.79	0.23	2.05	0.22	2.07	0.18	1.99	0.27	1.06	0.17
School Living	0.58	0.17	0.29	0.07	0.41	0.12	0.73	0.17	0.81	0.18	0.61	0.18	0.91	0.17	1.44	0.17	1.51	0.15	2.06	0.28	1.55	0.23
Health and Safety	0.65	0.13	1.06	0.14	0.97	0.13	1.01	0.19	1.19	0.17	1.10	0.18	1.72	0.23	2.39	0.28	2.60	0.23	2.54	0.35	1.49	0.26
Leisure	1.00	0.19	1.34	0.15	1.16	0.14	1.25	0.19	1.42	0.23	1.00	0.17	1.50	0.18	1.76	0.20	2.00	0.19	2.56	0.34	1.78	0.29
Self-Care	0.43	0.09	0.41	0.08	0.34	0.07	0.49	0.11	0.60	0.16	0.43	0.15	0.77	0.16	1.11	0.17	0.99	0.14	1.50	0.30	0.85	0.21
Self-Direction	0.55	0.14	0.39	0.10	0.76	0.16	0.53	0.13	0.51	0.16	0.47	0.17	0.70	0.16	1.03	0.17	0.81	0.11	1.06	0.19	0.67	0.16
Social	0.55	0.15	0.54	0.13	0.61	0.12	0.69	0.16	0.86	0.21	0.57	0.17	0.89	0.17	1.64	0.22	1.54	0.16	1.99	0.30	0.99	0.19
Work	–	–	–	–	–	–	–	–	–	–	–	–	–	–	–	–	–	–	–	–	2.22	0.50

Note. $SE_{\bar{x}}$ = Standard Error of the Mean.

Table A.4   Test-Age Equivalents of Skill Area Raw Scores: Teacher/Daycare Provider and Teacher Forms

Teacher/Daycare Provider Form

Test Age	Communication	Functional Pre-Academics	School Living	Health and Safety	Leisure	Self-Care	Self-Direction	Social	Motor	Test Age
2:0–2:2	44–48	13–16	33–37	34–36	48–51	52–54	41–43	46–49	58–59	2:0–2:2
2:3–2:5	49–53	17–21	38–43	37–39	52–54	55–57	44–46	50–53	60–61	2:3–2:5
2:6–2:8	54–57	22–26	44–48	40–42	55–56	58–60	47–49	54–56	62–64	2:6–2:8
2:9–2:11	58–59	27–31	49–52	43–45	57–58	61–62	50–52	57–58	65–66	2:9–2:11
3:0–3:2	60–61	32–35	53–55	46–48	59–60	63–64	53–54	59–60	67–69	3:0–3:2
3:3–3:5	62–63	36–39	56	49–51	61	65–66	55–56	61	70–72	3:3–3:5
3:6–3:8	64–67	40–44	57–60	52–53	62–63	67	57–59	62–64	73	3:6–3:8
3:9–3:11	–	45–49	–	54	64	–	60	–	74–75	3:9–3:11
4:0–4:2	68	50–52	61–62	55	65	68	–	–	76	4:0–4:2
4:3–4:5	–	53–55	63	–	–	–	61–62	65	77	4:3–4:5
4:6–4:8	69	56–57	–	56	–	–	63	66	–	4:6–4:8
4:9–4:11	–	58–59	64	57	–	–	–	67	78	4:9–4:11
5:0–5:2	70	60–63	65	–	66	69	–	–	–	5:0–5:2
5:3–5:5	–	64–65	–	–	–	–	–	–	–	5:3–5:5
5:6–5:8	–	66	–	58–59	–	–	64–66	68–69	79	5:6–5:8
5:9–5:11	–	67–68	–	60	–	70	–	–	–	5:9–5:11

Teacher Form

Test Age	Communication	Community Use	Functional Academics	School Living	Health and Safety	Leisure	Self-Care	Self-Direction	Social	Test Age
5:0–5:3	–	22–23	11–12	–	–	–	–	–	–	5:0–5:3
5:4–5:7	47–48	24–26	13–16	43–46	39	–	51	43–45	–	5:4–5:7
5:8–5:11	49	–	17–21	–	40	37	–	46	48–50	5:8–5:11
6:0–6:3	50	27–28	22–26	–	–	38–39	–	47	–	6:0–6:3
6:4–6:7	51	29	27–30	47–49	41	–	52	48	–	6:4–6:7
6:8–6:11	52	30	31–37	–	42	–	–	49	–	6:8–6:11
7:0–7:3	–	31–32	38–44	–	–	–	53	50	–	7:0–7:3
7:4–7:7	53–54	33	45–48	50	43	40–41	–	–	51	7:4–7:7
7:8–7:11	–	34	49–51	–	44	–	–	51	–	7:8–7:11
8:0–8:3	55	35–36	52–55	–	45	–	54	–	–	8:0–8:3
8:4–8:7	–	–	–	51	–	42	–	52	–	8:4–8:7
8:8–8:11	56	37	56	–	–	–	–	–	–	8:8–8:11
9:0–9:3	57	38–39	57–58	–	–	–	–	–	–	9:0–9:3
9:4–9:7	58	–	–	–	–	–	55	–	52	9:4–9:7
9:8–9:11	–	–	–	–	–	–	–	–	–	9:8–9:11
10:0–10:3	–	–	–	–	–	–	–	53–54	–	10:0–10:3
10:4–10:7	–	40	59	–	–	–	–	–	53	10:4–10:7
10:8–10:11	59	–	–	52	–	43	–	–	–	10:8–10:11
11:0–11:3	–	–	–	–	–	–	–	55	54	11:0–11:3
11:4–11:7	–	–	60	53	46	–	–	–	–	11:4–11:7
11:8–11:11	–	–	–	–	–	–	–	–	55	11:8–11:11
12:0–12:3	60–61	41	–	54	–	44	–	56	–	12:0–12:3
12:4–12:7	–	–	61	–	–	–	56	–	–	12:4–12:7
12:8–12:11	–	42	–	55	–	45	–	57	–	12:8–12:11
13:0–13:11	–	–	–	–	–	–	–	–	–	13:0–13:11
14:0–14:11	–	43	–	–	–	–	–	–	–	14:0–14:11
15:0–15:11	62	–	62	–	–	–	–	58–59	–	15:0–15:11
16:0–16:11	–	–	63	–	–	46	–	–	–	16:0–16:11
17:0–21:11	63–64	–	–	–	–	47	–	–	56–57	17:0–21:11

Table A.5 Scaled Score Equivalents of Skill Area Raw Scores: Parent/Primary Caregiver and Parent Forms

Parent/Primary Caregiver Form

Age 0:0

ss	Com	HS	LS	SC	SD	Soc	MO	ss
1	–	–	–	–	–	–	–	1
2	–	–	–	–	–	–	–	2
3	–	0	–	–	0	–	–	3
4	0	–	–	0	–	–	–	4
5	1-2	1	–	1-2	1	0	0	5
6	3	–	–	3-4	2-3	1	1	6
7	4	2	–	5	4-5	2-3	–	7
8	5	–	0	–	6	4	2	8
9	6	3	–	6	7	5	3	9
10	7-8	–	–	7	–	6-7	4	10
11	9-10	4	1	8	8	8-9	5	11
12	11	5	2-3	9-10	9-10	10-11	6	12
13	12-13	6-7	4	11	11	12-13	–	13
14	14-15	8	5-6	12	–	14-15	7	14
15	16	9	7-8	13-14	12	16	8-9	15
16	–	10	9-10	15-16	13-14	17	10-11	16
17	17	11	11	17	15	18-19	12-13	17
18	–	12	12	–	16	20-21	14	18
19	18-75	13-72	13-66	18-72	17-75	22-72	15-81	19

Age 0:1

ss	Com	HS	LS	SC	SD	Soc	MO	ss
1	–	–	–	–	–	–	–	1
2	–	–	–	–	–	–	–	2
3	0	0	–	0	0	–	–	3
4	1-2	–	–	1-2	1	0	0	4
5	3	1	–	3-4	2-3	1	1	5
6	4	–	–	5	4-5	2-3	–	6
7	5	2	–	–	6	4	2	7
8	6	3	0	6	7	5	3	8
9	7-8	–	–	7	–	6-7	4	9
10	9-10	4	1	8	8	8-9	5	10
11	11	5	2-3	9-10	9-10	10-11	6	11
12	12-13	6-7	4	11	11	12-13	7	12
13	14-15	8	5-6	12	–	14-15	8-9	13
14	16	9	7-8	13-14	12	16	10-11	14
15	–	10-11	9-10	15-16	13-14	17	12-13	15
16	17	12	11	17	15	18-19	14	16
17	–	–	12	–	16	20-21	15	17
18	18	13	13	18	17	22-24	16-17	18
19	19-75	14-72	14-66	19-72	18-75	25-72	18-81	19

Age 0:2

ss	Com	HS	LS	SC	SD	Soc	MO	ss
1	–	–	–	–	–	–	–	1
2	–	–	–	–	–	–	–	2
3	0	0	–	0	0	–	–	3
4	1-2	–	–	1-2	1	0	0	4
5	3	1	–	3-4	2-3	1	1	5
6	4	–	–	5	4-5	2-3	2	6
7	5	2	0	6	6	4-5	3-4	7
8	6	3	1	7	7	6-7	5	8
9	7-8	–	2-3	8-9	8	8-9	6	9
10	9-10	4	4	10	9-10	10-11	7	10
11	11	5	5-6	11-12	11	12-13	8-9	11
12	12-13	6-7	7-8	13-14	–	14-15	10-11	12
13	14-15	8	9-10	15-16	12-13	16	12-13	13
14	16	9	11	17	14	17-18	14	14
15	–	10-11	12	–	15	19-20	15	15
16	17	12	13	18	16-17	21-22	16-17	16
17	18-19	–	14	19	18	23-24	18	17
18	20-22	13-14	15-23	20-35	19-22	25-27	19-33	18
19	23-75	15-72	24-66	36-72	23-75	28-72	34-81	19

Age 0:3

ss	Com	HS	LS	SC	SD	Soc	MO	ss
1	–	–	–	–	–	–	–	1
2	0	–	–	0	–	–	–	2
3	1-2	0	–	1-2	0-1	0	0	3
4	3	–	–	3-4	2-3	1	1	4
5	4	1	–	5	4-5	2-3	2	5
6	5	–	0	6	6	4-5	3-4	6
7	6	2	1	7	7	6-7	5	7
8	7-8	3	2-3	8-9	8	8-9	6-7	8
9	9-10	4	4	10	9-10	10-11	8-9	9
10	11	5	5-6	11-12	11	12-13	10-11	10
11	12-13	6-7	7-8	13-14	–	14-15	12-13	11
12	14-15	8	9-10	15-16	12-13	16	14	12
13	16	9	11	17	14	17-18	15	13
14	–	10-11	12	18	15	19-20	16-17	14
15	17	12	13-14	19	16-17	21-22	18	15
16	18-19	–	15-16	20-26	18	23-24	19-24	16
17	20-22	13-14	17-23	27-35	19-22	25-27	25-33	17
18	23-31	15-20	24-35	36-48	23-33	28-39	34-51	18
19	32-75	21-72	36-66	49-72	34-75	40-72	52-81	19

Note. **Com** = Communication; **HS** = Health and Safety; **LS** = Leisure; **SC** = Self-Care; **SD** = Self-Direction; **Soc** = Social; **MO** = Motor.

Table A.5 Scaled Score Equivalents of Skill Area Raw Scores: Parent/Primary Caregiver and Parent Forms (continued)

Parent/Primary Caregiver Form — **Age 0:4**

ss	Com	HS	LS	SC	SD	Soc	MO	ss
1	–	–	–	–	–	–	–	1
2	0	–	–	0-1	0	–	–	2
3	1-2	0	–	2-4	1	0-1	0	3
4	3-4	1	–	5	2-4	2-3	1	4
5	5	–	0	6	5-6	4-5	3-5	5
6	6	2	1	7	7	6-7	6	6
7	7-8	3	2-3	8-9	8	8-9	7-8	7
8	9-10	–	4-5	10	9-10	10-11	9-10	8
9	11	4	6	11-12	11	12-13	11-12	9
10	12-13	5	7-8	13-15	–	14-15	13	10
11	14	6-7	9-10	16-17	12-13	16	14	11
12	15	8	11-12	–	14	17-18	15	12
13	16	9-10	13	18-19	15	19-20	16-17	13
14	17	11-12	14	20-22	16-17	21-22	18-20	14
15	18-19	–	15-19	23-30	18-20	23-24	21-28	15
16	20-22	13-14	20-23	31-35	21-22	25-27	29-33	16
17	23-28	15-17	24-30	36-44	23-29	28-35	34-45	17
18	29-33	18-24	31-40	45-51	30-36	36-42	46-56	18
19	34-75	25-72	41-66	52-72	37-75	43-72	57-81	19

Age 0:5

ss	Com	HS	LS	SC	SD	Soc	MO	ss
1	0	–	–	0-1	–	–	0	1
2	1-2	–	–	2-4	0-1	0-1	1	2
3	3-4	0	–	5	2-4	2-3	2	3
4	5	1	0	6	5-6	4-5	3-5	4
5	6	–	1	7	7	6-7	6-8	5
6	7-8	2	2-3	8-9	8	8-9	9-10	6
7	9-10	3	4-5	10	9-10	10-11	11-12	7
8	11	4	6	11-12	11	12-13	13	8
9	12-13	5	7-8	13-15	–	14-15	14	9
10	14	6-7	9-10	16-17	12-13	16	15	10
11	15	8	11-12	18-19	14	17-18	16-17	11
12	16	9-10	13-14	20-22	15	19-20	18-20	12
13	17	11-12	15-16	23-26	16-17	21-22	21-24	13
14	18-19	–	17-19	27-30	18-20	23-24	25-28	14
15	20-22	13-14	20-23	31-35	21-22	25-27	29-33	15
16	23-28	15-17	24-30	36-44	23-29	28-35	34-45	16
17	29-31	18-20	31-35	45-48	30-33	36-39	46-51	17
18	32-33	21-24	36-40	49-51	34-36	40-42	52-56	18
19	34-75	25-72	41-66	52-72	37-75	43-72	57-81	19

Age 0:6

ss	Com	HS	LS	SC	SD	Soc	MO	ss
1	0	–	–	0-1	–	–	0	1
2	1-2	–	–	2-4	0-1	0-1	1-2	2
3	3-4	0	0	5-6	2-4	2-3	3-5	3
4	5	1	1	7	5-6	4-6	6-8	4
5	6-7	–	2-3	8-10	7-8	7-9	9-10	5
6	8	2	4-5	11-12	9	10-11	11-12	6
7	9-10	3	6	13-15	10	12-13	13-14	7
8	11-12	4	7-8	16-17	11	14-15	15	8
9	13	5	9-10	18-19	12-13	16	16-17	9
10	14	6-7	11-12	20-22	14	17-18	18-20	10
11	15	8	13-14	23-24	15	19-20	21-24	11
12	16-17	9-10	15-16	25-27	16-17	21-22	25-28	12
13	18-19	11-12	17-19	28-30	18-20	23-24	29-33	13
14	20-22	13-15	20-23	31-35	21-22	25-27	34-35	14
15	23-25	16-17	24-26	36-40	23-25	28-31	36-39	15
16	26-28	18-19	27-30	41-44	26-29	32-35	40-45	16
17	29-31	20-21	31-35	45-48	30-33	36-39	46-51	17
18	32-33	22-24	36-40	49-51	34-36	40-42	52-56	18
19	34-75	25-72	41-66	52-72	37-75	43-72	57-81	19

Age 0:7

ss	Com	HS	LS	SC	SD	Soc	MO	ss
1	0	–	–	0-1	–	–	0	1
2	1-4	–	–	2-6	0-3	0-2	1-5	2
3	5	0	0-1	7	4-5	3-5	6-8	3
4	6-7	1	2-3	8-10	6-8	6-9	9-10	4
5	8	2	4-5	11-12	9	10-11	11-12	5
6	9-10	3	6	13-15	10	12-13	13-14	6
7	11-12	4	7-8	16-17	11	14-15	15	7
8	13	5	9-10	18-19	12-13	16	16-18	8
9	14	6-7	11-12	20-22	14	17-18	19-21	9
10	15	8	13-14	23-24	15	19-20	22-24	10
11	16-17	9-10	15-16	25-27	16-17	21-22	25-28	11
12	18-19	11-12	17-19	28-30	18-20	23-24	29-33	12
13	20-22	13-15	20-23	31-35	21-22	25-27	34-35	13
14	23-25	16-17	24-26	36-40	23-25	28-31	36-39	14
15	26-28	18-19	27-30	41-43	26-29	32-35	40-44	15
16	29-31	20-21	31-35	44-46	30-33	36-38	45-46	16
17	32-33	22-24	36-38	47-48	34-36	39-41	47-51	17
18	34-44	25-32	39-42	49-51	37-44	42-45	52-56	18
19	45-75	33-72	43-66	52-72	45-75	46-72	57-81	19

Note. **Com** = Communication; **HS** = Health and Safety; **LS** = Leisure; **SC** = Self-Care; **SD** = Self-Direction; **Soc** = Social; **MO** = Motor.

Table A.5 Scaled Score Equivalents of Skill Area Raw Scores: Parent/Primary Caregiver and Parent Forms (continued)

Parent/Primary Caregiver Form

Age 0:8

ss	Com	HS	LS	SC	SD	Soc	MO	ss
1	0-2	–	–	0-4	0-1	0-1	0-2	1
2	3-4	0	0	5-7	2-4	2-3	3-6	2
3	5	1	1	8-10	5-6	4-6	7-10	3
4	6-7	2	2-3	11-14	7-8	7-9	11-12	4
5	8	3	4-6	15-17	9-10	10-13	13-15	5
6	9-10	4	7-8	18-19	11	14-15	16-17	6
7	11-12	5	9-10	20	12-13	16	18-20	7
8	13-14	6-7	11-12	21-22	14	17-18	21-24	8
9	15	8	13-14	23-24	15	19-20	25-27	9
10	16-17	9-10	15-16	25-27	16-17	21-22	28-30	10
11	18-19	11-12	17-19	28-30	18-20	23-24	31-33	11
12	20-21	13-15	20-23	31-35	21-22	25-26	34-35	12
13	22-23	16-17	24-25	36-37	23-25	27-28	36-39	13
14	24-26	18-19	26-28	38-40	26-29	29-31	40-42	14
15	27-29	20-21	29-31	41-44	30-33	32-35	43-45	15
16	30-33	22-24	32-35	45-48	34-36	36-39	46-49	16
17	34-38	25-28	36-40	49-51	37-40	40-42	50-52	17
18	39-50	29-37	41-47	52-53	41-49	43-50	53-56	18
19	51-75	38-72	48-66	54-72	50-75	51-72	57-81	19

Age 0:9

ss	Com	HS	LS	SC	SD	Soc	MO	ss
1	0-4	–	–	0-7	0-3	0-2	0-6	1
2	5	0	0-1	8-10	4-5	3-5	7-10	2
3	6-7	1-2	2-3	11-14	6-8	6-9	11-12	3
4	8	3	4-6	15-17	9-10	10-13	13-15	4
5	9-10	4	7-8	18-19	11	14-15	16-18	5
6	11-12	5	9-10	20	12-13	16	19-21	6
7	13-14	6-7	11-12	21-22	14	17-18	22-24	7
8	15	8	13-14	23-24	15	19-20	25-27	8
9	16-17	9-10	15-16	25-27	16-17	21-22	28-30	9
10	18-19	11-12	17-19	28-30	18-20	23-24	31-33	10
11	20-21	13-15	20-23	31-35	21-22	25-26	34-35	11
12	22-23	16-17	24-25	36-37	23-25	27-28	36-39	12
13	24-26	18-19	26-28	38-40	26-29	29-31	40-42	13
14	27-29	20-21	29-31	41-43	30-33	32-35	43-44	14
15	30-33	22-24	32-35	44-46	34-36	36-38	45-46	15
16	34-38	25-28	36-38	47-48	37-40	39-41	47-49	16
17	39-44	29-32	39-42	49-51	41-44	42-45	50-52	17
18	45-50	33-37	43-47	52-53	45-49	46-50	53-56	18
19	51-75	38-72	48-66	54-72	50-75	51-72	57-81	19

Age 0:10

ss	Com	HS	LS	SC	SD	Soc	MO	ss
1	0-4	–	–	0-10	0-3	0-2	0-6	1
2	5	0	0-1	11-14	4-5	3-5	7-11	2
3	6-7	1-2	2-3	15-17	6-8	6-9	12-15	3
4	8	3-4	4-6	18-19	9-10	10-13	16-18	4
5	9-10	5	7-8	20	11-12	14-16	19-21	5
6	11-12	6-7	9-11	21-22	13-14	17-18	22-24	6
7	13-14	8	12-14	23-24	15	19-20	25-27	7
8	15-16	9-10	15-16	25-27	16-17	21-22	28-30	8
9	17-18	11-12	17-19	28-30	18-19	23	31-33	9
10	19	13-15	20-21	31-32	20-21	24	34-36	10
11	20-21	16-17	22-23	33-35	22-24	25-26	37-39	11
12	22-23	18-19	24-25	36-37	25-26	27-28	40-41	12
13	24-26	20-21	26-28	38-40	27-29	29-31	42-44	13
14	27-29	22-23	29-31	41-43	30-33	32-35	45-46	14
15	30-33	24-26	32-35	44-46	34-36	36-38	47-49	15
16	34-38	27-28	36-38	47-48	37-40	39-41	50-52	16
17	39-44	29-32	39-42	49-51	41-44	42-45	53-54	17
18	45-50	33-37	43-47	52-53	45-49	46-50	55-57	18
19	51-75	38-72	48-66	54-72	50-75	51-72	58-81	19

Age 0:11

ss	Com	HS	LS	SC	SD	Soc	MO	ss
1	0-4	–	–	0-10	0-3	0-2	0-6	1
2	5-7	0-2	0-1	11-14	4-5	3-9	7-12	2
3	8	3-4	2-3	15-17	6-8	10-13	13-17	3
4	9-10	5	4-7	18-20	9-11	14-16	18-21	4
5	11-12	6-7	8-11	21-22	12-14	17-18	22-24	5
6	13-14	8	12-14	23-24	15	19-20	25-27	6
7	15-16	9-10	15-16	25-27	16-17	21-22	28-30	7
8	17-18	11-12	17-19	28-30	18-19	23	31-33	8
9	19	13-15	20-21	31-32	20-21	24	34-36	9
10	20-21	16-17	22-23	33-35	22-24	25-26	37-39	10
11	22-23	18-19	24-25	36-37	25-26	27-28	40-41	11
12	24-26	20-21	26-28	38-40	27-29	29-31	42-44	12
13	27-29	22-23	29-31	41-43	30-33	32-35	45-46	13
14	30-33	24-26	32-35	44-46	34-36	36-38	47-49	14
15	34-38	27-28	36-38	47-48	37-40	39-41	50-52	15
16	39-44	29-32	39-42	49-51	41-44	42-45	53-54	16
17	45-50	33-37	43-47	52-53	45-49	46-50	55-57	17
18	51-56	38-46	48-50	54-57	50-53	51-55	58-66	18
19	57-75	47-72	51-66	58-72	54-75	56-72	67-81	19

Note. **Com** = Communication; **HS** = Health and Safety; **LS** = Leisure; **SC** = Self-Care; **SD** = Self-Direction; **Soc** = Social; **MO** = Motor.

Table A.5 Scaled Score Equivalents of Skill Area Raw Scores: Parent/Primary Caregiver and Parent Forms (continued)

Parent/Primary Caregiver Form

Ages 1:0–1:1

ss	Com	CU	FA	HL	HS	LS	SC	SD	Soc	MO	ss
1	0-5	-	-	-	0	-	0-10	0-4	0-5	0-11	1
2	6-7	-	-	-	1-2	0-3	11-15	5-8	6-9	12-15	2
3	8-10	-	-	-	3-4	4-6	16-19	9-10	10-13	16-18	3
4	11-12	-	-	-	5-6	7-8	20	11-12	14-17	19-23	4
5	13-14	-	-	-	7-8	9-11	21-24	13-14	18-20	24-28	5
6	15-16	-	-	0	9-10	12-14	25-28	15-17	21-22	29-32	6
7	17-18	-	0	1	11-12	15-18	29-31	18-19	23-24	33-36	7
8	19-20	0	-	2-3	13-15	19-21	32-34	20-22	25-26	37-39	8
9	21-22	-	1	4-6	16-18	22-23	35-37	23-25	27-28	40-41	9
10	23-25	1	-	7-10	19-21	24-25	38-40	26-28	29-31	42-44	10
11	26-28	2-3	2	11-14	22-23	26-28	41-42	29-30	32-33	45-46	11
12	29-31	4-5	3	15-19	24-26	29-32	43-44	31-33	34-35	47-49	12
13	32-35	6-8	4-5	20-25	27-28	33-35	45-46	34-36	36-38	50-52	13
14	36-38	9-11	6-8	26-30	29-30	36-38	47-48	37-39	39-42	53-54	14
15	39-41	12-15	9-12	31-36	31-33	39-41	49-50	40-42	43-46	55-57	15
16	42-45	16-20	13-17	37-42	34-37	42-44	51-52	43-46	47-49	58-59	16
17	46-50	21-26	18-22	43-49	38-41	45-47	53-54	47-49	50-52	60-62	17
18	51-61	27-33	23-26	50-56	42-50	48-52	55-61	50-57	53-58	63-69	18
19	62-75	34-66	27-69	57-75	51-72	53-66	62-72	58-75	59-72	70-81	19

Ages 1:2–1:3

Com	CU	FA	HL	HS	LS	SC	SD	Soc	MO	ss
0-7	-	-	-	0-2	-	0-10	0-4	0-9	0-12	1
8-10	-	-	-	3-4	0-3	11-15	5-8	10-13	13-17	2
11-13	-	-	-	5-6	4-7	16-24	9-11	14-18	18-24	3
14	-	-	-	7-8	8-11	25	12-14	19-20	25-30	4
15-16	-	-	0-1	9-10	12-14	26-28	15-17	21-23	31-35	5
17-18	-	0	2-3	11-13	15-18	29-31	18-19	24-26	36-39	6
19-21	0	1	4-6	14-17	19-21	32-34	20-22	27-28	40-41	7
22-24	-	-	7-10	18-20	22-24	35-38	23-25	29-31	42-44	8
25-27	1-2	2	11-14	21-23	25-27	39-41	26-28	32-33	45-47	9
28-30	3-4	3	15-19	24-26	28-30	42-43	29-31	34-35	48-50	10
31-33	5-6	4-5	20-25	27-28	31-33	44-45	32-34	36-38	51-52	11
34-36	7-9	6	26-30	29-30	34-36	46-47	35-37	39-41	53-54	12
37-39	10-12	7-8	31-36	31-33	37-38	48-49	38-40	42-44	55-57	13
40-42	13-16	9-12	37-39	34-37	39-41	50-52	41-43	45-46	58-59	14
43-45	17-20	13-17	40-43	38-40	42-44	53-54	44-46	47-49	60-61	15
46-50	21-26	18-22	44-49	41-42	45-47	55-56	47-49	50-52	62-63	16
51-56	27-32	23-26	50-56	43-46	48-50	57-59	50-53	53-55	64-66	17
57-61	33-39	27-29	57-62	47-50	51-52	60-61	54-57	56-58	67-69	18
62-75	40-66	30-69	63-75	51-72	53-66	62-72	58-75	59-72	70-81	19

Ages 1:4–1:5

ss	Com	CU	FA	HL	HS	LS	SC	SD	Soc	MO	ss
1	0-10	-	-	-	0-3	0-3	0-15	0-7	0-13	0-17	1
2	11-13	-	-	-	4-6	4-7	16-24	8-10	14-18	18-24	2
3	14	-	-	-	7-8	8-11	25	11-14	19-20	25-30	3
4	15-16	-	-	0-1	9-10	12-14	26-28	15-17	21-23	31-35	4
5	17-18	-	0	2-4	11-13	15-18	29-31	18-19	24-26	36-39	5
6	19-21	0	1	5-8	14-17	19-21	32-34	20-22	27-28	40-42	6
7	22-24	-	2	9-12	18-20	22-24	35-38	23-25	29-31	43-46	7
8	25-27	1-2	3	13-16	21-23	25-27	39-41	26-28	32-33	47-49	8
9	28-30	3-4	4	17-21	24-26	28-30	42-43	29-31	34-36	50-52	9
10	31-33	5-6	5	22-27	27-29	31-33	44-45	32-34	37-39	53-54	10
11	34-36	7-9	6	28-32	30-32	34-36	46-47	35-37	40-41	55-56	11
12	37-39	10-12	7-8	33-36	33-34	37-38	48-49	38-40	42-44	57	12
13	40-42	13-16	9-12	37-39	35-37	39-41	50-52	41-43	45-46	58-59	13
14	43-45	17-20	13-17	40-43	38-40	42-44	53-54	44-46	47-49	60-61	14
15	46-50	21-26	18-22	44-49	41-42	45-47	55-56	47-49	50-52	62-63	15
16	51-54	27-30	23-26	50-56	43-46	48-50	57-59	50-53	53-55	64-66	16
17	55-58	31-35	27-29	57-62	47-50	51-52	60-61	54-57	56-58	67-69	17
18	59-61	36-41	30-40	63-74	51-57	53-56	62-64	58-60	59-62	70-71	18
19	62-75	42-66	41-69	75	58-72	57-66	65-72	61-75	63-72	72-81	19

Ages 1:6–1:7

Com	CU	FA	HL	HS	LS	SC	SD	Soc	MO	ss
0-13	-	-	-	0-3	0-7	0-24	0-7	0-18	0-24	1
14	-	-	-	4-6	8-11	25	8-10	19-20	25-30	2
15-16	-	-	0-1	7-9	12-14	26-30	11-14	21-23	31-35	3
17-18	-	0	2-4	10-13	15-17	31-34	15-19	24-26	36-39	4
19-21	-	1	5-8	14-17	18-20	35-37	20-23	27-28	40-43	5
22-24	0	2	9-13	18-20	21-24	38-39	24-26	29-31	44-47	6
25-27	1-2	3	14-18	21-23	25-28	40-41	27-29	32-33	48-51	7
28-30	3-4	4	19-24	24-27	29-31	42-43	30-32	34-36	52-54	8
31-33	5-6	5	25-29	28-30	32-34	44-45	33-34	37-39	55-56	9
34-36	7-9	6	30-33	31-32	35-36	46-48	35-37	40-42	57	10
37-39	10-12	7-8	34-37	33-34	37-39	49-50	38-40	43-44	58	11
40-42	13-16	9-11	38-41	35-37	40-41	51-53	41-43	45-46	59	12
43-45	17-20	12-14	42-46	38-40	42-44	54-55	44-46	47-49	60-61	13
46-48	21-23	15-18	47-50	41-42	45-47	56-57	47-49	50-52	62-63	14
49-52	24-26	19-23	51-54	43-45	48-49	58-59	50-52	53-55	64-65	15
53-55	27-32	24-29	55-59	46-48	50-52	60-61	53-55	56-58	66-67	16
56-58	33-39	30-34	60-66	49-52	53-54	62-63	56-58	59-60	68-69	17
59-62	40-45	35-40	67-74	53-57	55-56	64-65	59-60	61-62	70-71	18
63-75	46-66	41-69	75	58-72	57-66	66-72	61-75	63-72	72-81	19

Note. **Com** = Communication; **CU** = Community Use; **FA** = Functional Pre-Academics; **HL** = Home Living; **HS** = Health and Safety; **LS** = Leisure; **SC** = Self-Care; **SD** = Self-Direction; **Soc** = Social; **MO** = Motor.

Table A.5 Scaled Score Equivalents of Skill Area Raw Scores: Parent/Primary Caregiver and Parent Forms (continued)

Parent/Primary Caregiver Form

Ages 1:8–1:9

ss	Com	CU	FA	HL	HS	LS	SC	SD	Soc	MO	ss
1	0-13	-	-	-	0-3	0-10	0-25	0-10	0-19	0-30	1
2	14-16	-	-	0-1	4-8	11-14	26-30	11-14	20-23	31-35	2
3	17-18	-	0	2-4	9-13	15-17	31-34	15-19	24-26	36-39	3
4	19-21	-	1	5-8	14-17	18-20	35-37	20-23	27-28	40-43	4
5	22-24	0	2	9-13	18-20	21-24	38-39	24-26	29-31	44-47	5
6	25-27	1-2	3	14-18	21-23	25-28	40-41	27-29	32-33	48-51	6
7	28-30	3-4	4	19-24	24-27	29-31	42-43	30-32	34-36	52-54	7
8	31-33	5-6	5	25-29	28-30	32-34	44-45	33-34	37-39	55-56	8
9	34-36	7-9	6	30-33	31-32	35-36	46-48	35-37	40-42	57	9
10	37-39	10-12	7-8	34-37	33-34	37-39	49-50	38-40	43-44	58	10
11	40-42	13-16	9-11	38-41	35-37	40-41	51-53	41-43	45-46	59	11
12	43-45	17-20	12-14	42-46	38-40	42-44	54-55	44-46	47-49	60-61	12
13	46-48	21-23	15-18	47-50	41-42	45-47	56-57	47-49	50-52	62-63	13
14	49-52	24-26	19-23	51-54	43-45	48-49	58-59	50-52	53-55	64-65	14
15	53-55	27-32	24-29	55-59	46-48	50-52	60-61	53-55	56-58	66-67	15
16	56-58	33-39	30-34	60-65	49-52	53-54	62-63	56-58	59-60	68-69	16
17	59-62	40-45	35-40	66-69	53-57	55-56	64-65	59-60	61-62	70-71	17
18	63-71	46-55	41-52	70-74	58-66	57-61	66-70	61-67	63-69	72-74	18
19	72-75	56-66	53-69	75	67-72	62-66	71-72	68-75	70-72	75-81	19

Ages 1:10–1:11

ss	Com	CU	FA	HL	HS	LS	SC	SD	Soc	MO	ss
1	0-13	-	-	-	0-3	0-10	0-30	0-14	0-19	0-32	1
2	14-16	-	0	0-3	4-8	11-15	31-34	15-19	20-23	33-38	2
3	17-19	-	1	4-8	9-13	16-20	35-37	20-23	24-27	39-43	3
4	20-22	0-1	2	9-13	14-18	21-24	38-39	24-26	28-30	44-47	4
5	23-26	2-3	3	14-18	19-23	25-28	40-41	27-29	31-32	48-51	5
6	27-30	4-6	4-5	19-24	24-27	29-31	42-43	30-32	33-35	52-54	6
7	31-34	7-9	6	25-29	28-30	32-34	44-45	33-34	36-39	55-56	7
8	35-38	10-11	7-8	30-33	31-33	35-36	46-48	35-37	40-42	57	8
9	39-42	12-14	9-10	34-37	34-37	37-39	49-51	38-39	43-44	58	9
10	43-45	15-17	11-12	38-42	38-40	40-42	52-54	40-42	45-47	59-60	10
11	46-48	18-21	13-15	43-46	41-42	43-45	55-56	43-46	48-50	61-62	11
12	49-52	22-26	16-19	47-50	43-45	46-48	57-58	47-50	51-53	63-64	12
13	53-55	27-32	20-24	51-54	46-48	49-51	59-60	51-53	54-56	65-66	13
14	56-58	33-38	25-30	55-58	49-51	52-54	61-62	54-56	57-59	67-68	14
15	59-62	39-43	31-34	59-61	52-55	55-56	63-65	57-59	60-62	69	15
16	63-67	44-47	35-38	62-65	56-58	57-59	66-67	60-62	63-65	70-71	16
17	68-70	48-50	39-45	66-69	59-60	60-61	68-69	63-64	66-67	72	17
18	71-72	51-55	46-52	70-74	61-66	62	70	65-67	68-69	73-74	18
19	73-75	56-66	53-69	75	67-72	63-66	71-72	68-75	70-72	75-81	19

Ages 2:0–2:2

ss	Com	CU	FA	HL	HS	LS	SC	SD	Soc	MO	ss
1	0-13	-	-	-	0-3	0-10	0-30	0-19	0-19	0-38	1
2	14-18	-	0-1	0-5	4-10	11-17	31-34	20-23	20-24	39-43	2
3	19-22	0-1	2	6-11	11-17	18-23	35-37	24-26	25-29	44-47	3
4	23-26	2-3	3	12-18	18-23	24-28	38-41	27-29	30-32	48-51	4
5	27-30	4-6	4-5	19-24	24-27	29-31	42-43	30-32	33-35	52-53	5
6	31-34	7-9	6	25-29	28-30	32-34	44-45	33-34	36-39	54-56	6
7	35-38	10-11	7-8	30-33	31-33	35-36	46-48	35-37	40-42	57	7
8	39-42	12-14	9-11	34-37	34-37	37-39	49-51	38-39	43-44	58	8
9	43-46	15-18	12-14	38-42	38-40	40-42	52-54	40-42	45-47	59-60	9
10	47-51	19-22	15-18	43-46	41-42	43-45	55-56	43-46	48-50	61-62	10
11	52-55	23-27	19-22	47-50	43-45	46-48	57-58	47-50	51-53	63-64	11
12	56-58	28-32	23-26	51-54	46-48	49-51	59-60	51-53	54-56	65-66	12
13	59-62	33-38	27-30	55-58	49-52	52-54	61-62	54-56	57-59	67-68	13
14	63-65	39-43	31-34	59-61	53-55	55-57	63-65	57-59	60-62	69	14
15	66-68	44-47	35-38	62-65	56-58	58-59	66-67	60-62	63-65	70-71	15
16	69-70	48-50	39-45	66-69	59-60	60-61	68-69	63-64	66-67	72	16
17	71-72	51-55	46-52	70-71	61-66	62	70	65-67	68-69	73-74	17
18	73-74	56-57	53-62	72-74	67-68	63-66	71	68-71	70-72	75-77	18
19	75	58-66	63-69	75	69-72	-	72	72-75	-	78-81	19

Ages 2:3–2:5

ss	Com	CU	FA	HL	HS	LS	SC	SD	Soc	MO	ss
1	0-13	-	-	-	0-3	0-10	0-30	0-20	0-19	0-39	1
2	14-18	0-1	0-1	0-5	4-10	11-17	31-34	21-24	20-24	40-44	2
3	19-23	2-3	2-3	6-11	11-17	18-23	35-37	25-28	25-29	45-48	3
4	24-29	4-6	4-5	12-18	18-23	24-28	38-41	29-31	30-33	49-51	4
5	30-34	7-9	6	19-25	24-28	29-32	42-45	32-33	34-37	52-53	5
6	35-38	10-11	7-8	26-31	29-33	33-36	46-48	34-36	38-40	54-56	6
7	39-42	12-14	9-11	32-37	34-37	37-39	49-51	37-39	41-43	57-58	7
8	43-46	15-18	12-14	38-42	38-40	40-42	52-55	40-43	44-47	59-60	8
9	47-51	19-23	15-18	43-46	41-42	43-45	56-58	44-46	48-50	61-62	9
10	52-55	24-28	19-22	47-50	43-45	46-48	59-60	47-50	51-53	63-64	10
11	56-59	29-33	23-26	51-54	46-48	49-51	61-62	51-53	54-56	65-66	11
12	60-62	34-38	27-30	55-58	49-52	52-54	63	54-56	57-58	67-68	12
13	63-65	39-43	31-34	59-61	53-55	55-57	64-65	57-59	59-60	69	13
14	66-68	44-47	35-38	62-64	56-58	58-59	66-67	60-62	61-62	70-71	14
15	69-70	48-50	39-43	65-67	59-60	60-61	68-69	63-64	63-65	72	15
16	71-72	51-52	44-49	68-69	61-63	62	70	65-67	66-67	73-74	16
17	73	53-55	50-55	70-71	64-66	63-64	71	68-69	68-69	75-76	17
18	74	56-57	56-62	72-74	67-68	65-66	-	70-71	70-71	77	18
19	75	58-66	63-69	75	69-72	-	72	72-75	72	78-81	19

Note. Com = Communication; CU = Community Use; FA = Functional Pre-Academics; HL = Home Living; HS = Health and Safety; LS = Leisure; SC = Self-Care; SD = Self-Direction; Soc = Social; MO = Motor.

Table A.5   Scaled Score Equivalents of Skill Area Raw Scores: Parent/Primary Caregiver and Parent Forms *(continued)*

Parent/Primary Caregiver Form

Ages 2:6–2:8

ss	Com	CU	FA	HL	HS	LS	SC	SD	Soc	MO
1	0-16	-	0	0-5	0-10	0-17	0-34	0-24	0-23	0-39
2	17-21	0-1	1-2	6-10	11-16	18-23	35-37	25-28	24-28	40-44
3	22-27	2-5	3-5	11-16	17-23	24-28	38-41	29-31	29-33	45-48
4	28-34	6-9	6	17-23	24-28	29-32	42-45	32-33	34-37	49-53
5	35-38	10-11	7-8	24-30	29-33	33-36	46-48	34-36	38-40	54-56
6	39-42	12-14	9-11	31-36	34-37	37-39	49-51	37-39	41-43	57-58
7	43-46	15-18	12-14	37-42	38-40	40-42	52-55	40-43	44-47	59-60
8	47-51	19-23	15-18	43-46	41-42	43-45	56-58	44-46	48-50	61-62
9	52-55	24-28	19-22	47-50	43-45	46-48	59-60	47-50	51-53	63-64
10	56-59	29-33	23-26	51-54	46-48	49-51	61-62	51-53	54-56	65-66
11	60-62	34-38	27-30	55-58	49-52	52-54	63	54-56	57-59	67-68
12	63-65	39-43	31-34	59-60	53-55	55-57	64-65	57-59	60-62	69
13	66-68	44-47	35-38	61-62	56-58	58-59	66-67	60-61	63-65	70-71
14	69-70	48-50	39-43	63-64	59-60	60	68-69	62-63	66-67	72-73
15	71-72	51-52	44-49	65-67	61-63	61	70	64-65	68	74
16	-	53-55	50-53	68-70	64-66	62	71	66-67	69-70	75-76
17	73	56-57	54-57	71-72	67-68	63-64	-	68-69	71	77
18	74	58-63	58-62	73-74	69-70	65-66	72	70-71	72	78-79
19	75	64-66	63-69	75	71-72	-	-	72-75	-	80-81

Ages 2:9–2:11

ss	Com	CU	FA	HL	HS	LS	SC	SD	Soc	MO
1	0-16	-	0	0-5	0-10	0-22	0-34	0-27	0-23	0-39
2	17-21	0-1	1-2	6-10	11-16	23-26	35-39	28-29	24-28	40-44
3	22-27	2-5	3-5	11-16	17-23	27-30	40-44	30-32	29-33	45-48
4	28-34	6-9	6-8	17-23	24-29	31-33	45-48	33-36	34-38	49-53
5	35-40	10-13	9-11	24-30	30-34	34-37	49-51	37-39	39-43	54-57
6	41-46	14-18	12-14	31-36	35-38	38-41	52-55	40-43	44-47	58-60
7	47-51	19-23	15-18	37-42	39-42	42-44	56-58	44-46	48-50	61-62
8	52-55	24-28	19-21	43-47	43-45	45-48	59-60	47-49	51-53	63
9	56-59	29-33	22-25	48-51	46-48	49-51	61-62	50-52	54-55	64-65
10	60-62	34-37	26-30	52-55	49-50	52-53	63-65	53-55	56-58	66-67
11	63-65	38-40	31-34	56-58	51-53	54-55	66-67	56-57	59-60	68-69
12	66-67	41-44	35-38	59-60	54-56	56-58	68	58-59	61-63	70-71
13	68-69	45-48	39-42	61-62	57-60	59-60	69	60-62	64-65	72-73
14	70-71	49-51	43-46	63-65	61-63	61	70	63-64	66-67	74
15	72	52-54	47-49	66-68	64-66	62	71	65-66	68	75-76
16	-	55-57	50-53	69-70	67-68	63-64	-	67	69-70	77
17	73	58-60	54-57	71-72	69	65	72	68-69	71	78
18	74	61-63	58-62	73-74	70	66	-	70-71	72	79
19	75	64-66	63-69	75	71-72	-	-	72-75	-	80-81

Ages 3:0–3:2

ss	Com	CU	FA	HL	HS	LS	SC	SD	Soc	MO
1	0-21	-	0-2	0-10	0-10	0-22	0-34	0-27	0-23	0-43
2	22-25	0-1	3	11-15	11-17	23-26	35-40	28-29	24-29	44-46
3	26-30	2-7	4-5	16-21	18-24	27-30	41-45	30-32	30-35	47-50
4	31-36	8-13	6-8	22-27	25-30	31-34	46-50	33-36	36-40	51-54
5	37-42	14-18	9-12	28-33	31-36	35-39	51-54	37-40	41-45	55-57
6	43-48	19-23	13-16	34-40	37-41	40-44	55-58	41-44	46-49	58-60
7	49-54	24-28	17-21	41-46	42-45	45-48	59-60	45-48	50-53	61-63
8	55-59	29-33	22-25	47-51	46-48	49-51	61-62	49-52	54-55	64-65
9	60-62	34-37	26-30	52-55	49-50	52-53	63-65	53-55	56-58	66-67
10	63-65	38-40	31-34	56-58	51-53	54-55	66-67	56-57	59-60	68-69
11	66-67	41-44	35-38	59-60	54-56	56-58	68	58-59	61-63	70-71
12	68-69	45-48	39-42	61-62	57-60	59-60	69	60-62	64-65	72-73
13	70	49-51	43-46	63-65	61-63	61	70	63-64	66-67	74
14	71	52-54	47-49	66-68	64-66	62	71	65-66	68	75-76
15	72	55-57	50-53	69-70	67-68	63-64	-	67	69-70	77
16	73	58-59	54-57	71-72	69	65	72	68-69	71	78
17	74	60-61	58-60	73	70	66	-	70-71	72	79
18	-	62-63	61-63	74	71-72	-	-	72-75	-	80-81
19	75	64-66	64-69	75	-	-	-	-	-	-

Ages 3:3–3:5

ss	Com	CU	FA	HL	HS	LS	SC	SD	Soc	MO
1	0-21	-	0-2	0-10	0-10	0-22	0-34	0-27	0-23	0-43
2	22-25	0-1	3	11-15	11-17	23-26	35-40	28-29	24-29	44-46
3	26-30	2-7	4-5	16-21	18-24	27-31	41-45	30-32	30-35	47-50
4	31-36	8-15	6-8	22-27	25-30	32-34	46-50	33-36	36-40	51-54
5	37-43	16-22	9-12	28-33	31-36	35-39	51-54	37-40	41-45	55-57
6	44-49	23-28	13-16	34-40	37-41	40-44	55-58	41-44	46-49	58-60
7	50-54	29-33	17-21	41-46	42-45	45-48	59-62	45-48	50-53	61-63
8	55-59	34-37	22-26	47-51	46-49	49-51	63-65	49-52	54-56	64-65
9	60-63	38-40	27-31	52-55	50-53	52-55	66-67	53-55	57-59	66-68
10	64-66	41-43	32-36	56-59	54-56	56-58	68	56-59	60-61	68-69
11	67-68	44-46	37-41	60-62	57-58	59-60	69	60-62	62-63	71-72
12	69	47-49	42-45	63-65	59-60	61	70	63-64	64-65	73-74
13	70	50-52	46-49	66-68	61-63	62	-	65-66	66-67	75
14	71	53-55	50-53	69-70	64-66	63-64	71	67	68-69	76
15	72	56-57	54-56	71	67-68	65	72	68-69	70	77-78
16	73	58-59	57-58	72	69-70	66	-	70-71	71	79
17	74	60-61	59-60	73	71	-	-	72-73	72	80
18	-	62-63	61-63	74	72	-	-	74-75	-	81
19	75	64-66	64-69	75	-	-	-	-	-	-

Note. **Com** = Communication; **CU** = Community Use; **FA** = Functional Pre-Academics; **HL** = Home Living; **HS** = Health and Safety; **LS** = Leisure; **SC** = Self-Care; **SD** = Self-Direction; **Soc** = Social; **MO** = Motor.

Table A.5 Scaled Score Equivalents of Skill Area Raw Scores: Parent/Primary Caregiver and Parent Forms (continued)

Parent/Primary Caregiver Form

Ages 3:6–3:8

ss	Com	CU	FA	HL	HS	LS	SC	SD	Soc	MO
1	0-25	0-1	0-3	0-15	0-17	0-26	0-40	0-27	0-28	0-46
2	26-30	2-7	4-5	16-21	18-24	27-31	41-45	28-32	29-33	47-50
3	31-36	8-15	6-8	22-27	25-30	32-34	46-50	33-36	34-37	51-54
4	37-43	16-22	9-12	28-33	31-36	35-39	51-54	37-40	38-42	55-57
5	44-49	23-28	13-16	34-40	37-41	40-44	55-58	41-44	43-47	58-60
6	50-54	29-33	17-21	41-46	42-45	45-47	59-62	45-48	48-51	61-63
7	55-59	34-37	22-26	47-51	46-49	48-50	63-65	49-52	52-55	64-65
8	60-63	38-40	27-31	52-55	50-53	51-54	66-67	53-55	56-58	66-68
9	64-65	41-43	32-36	56-59	54-56	55-57	68	56-58	59-60	69-70
10	66-67	44-46	37-41	60-62	57-58	58-59	69	59-60	61-62	71-72
11	68-69	47-49	42-45	63-64	59-60	60	70	61-62	63-64	73-74
12	70	50-52	46-49	65-66	61-63	61	–	63-64	65-66	75
13	71	53-54	50-53	67-68	64-66	62-63	71	65-66	67	76
14	72	55-56	54-56	69-70	67-68	64	72	67	68-69	77-78
15	73	57-58	57-58	71-72	69-70	65	–	68-69	70	79
16	74	59-60	59-60	73	71	66	–	70-71	71	80
17	–	61-62	61-63	74	72	–	–	72-73	72	81
18	75	63-64	64-66	–	–	–	–	74-75	–	–
19	–	65-66	67-69	75	–	–	–	–	–	–

Ages 3:9–3:11

ss	Com	CU	FA	HL	HS	LS	SC	SD	Soc	MO
1	0-28	0-7	0-3	0-19	0-24	0-31	0-45	0-27	0-28	0-50
2	29-36	8-15	4-6	20-25	25-30	32-33	46-48	28-32	29-33	51-52
3	37-43	16-22	7-10	26-32	31-39	34-36	49-51	33-37	34-40	53-55
4	44-49	23-28	11-15	33-38	40-42	37-40	52-54	38-42	41-44	56-59
5	50-54	29-33	16-21	39-43	43-44	41-44	55-58	43-47	45-47	60-62
6	55-58	34-37	22-26	44-48	45-47	45-47	59-62	48-51	48-51	63-65
7	59-61	38-40	27-31	49-52	48-51	48-50	63-65	52-54	52-55	66-68
8	62-63	41-42	32-36	53-56	52-55	51-54	66-67	55-56	56-58	69-70
9	64-65	43-45	37-41	57-59	56-58	55-57	68	57-58	59-60	71-72
10	66-67	46-47	42-45	60-62	59-60	58-59	69	59-60	61-62	73-74
11	68-69	48-50	46-49	63-64	61-62	60	70	61-62	63-64	75
12	70	51-52	50-53	65-66	63-64	61	–	63-64	65-66	76-77
13	71	53-54	54-56	67-68	65-66	62-63	71	65-66	67	78
14	72	55-56	57-59	69-70	67-68	64	72	67	68-69	79
15	73	57-58	60-61	71-72	69-70	65	–	68-69	70	–
16	74	59-61	62-63	73	71	66	–	70-71	71	80
17	–	62-63	64-65	74	72	–	–	72-73	72	81
18	75	64-65	66	–	–	–	–	74-75	–	–
19	–	66	67-69	75	–	–	–	–	–	–

Ages 4:0–4:2

ss	Com	CU	FA	HL	HS	LS	SC	SD	Soc	MO
1	0-36	0-7	0-6	0-23	0-30	0-33	0-48	0-32	0-33	0-52
2	37-43	8-15	7-10	24-29	31-39	34-36	49-51	33-37	34-40	53-55
3	44-47	16-22	11-15	30-35	40-42	37-40	52-54	38-41	41-44	56-59
4	48-51	23-29	16-21	36-41	43-44	41-44	55-57	42-46	45-47	60-62
5	52-54	30-35	22-26	42-46	45-47	45-47	58-61	47-50	48-51	63-65
6	55-58	36-40	27-31	47-51	48-51	48-50	62-64	51-53	52-54	66-68
7	59-61	41-42	32-36	52-55	52-54	51-53	65-66	54-55	55-57	69-70
8	62-63	43-45	37-41	56-58	55-57	54-56	67-68	56-57	58-59	71-72
9	64-65	46-47	42-45	59-61	58-59	57-58	69	58-60	60-62	73-74
10	66-67	48-50	46-49	62-64	60-62	59-60	70	61-62	63-64	75
11	68-69	51-52	50-53	65-66	63-64	61	–	63-64	65-66	76-77
12	70	53-54	54-56	67-68	65-66	62-63	71	65-66	67	78
13	71-72	55-56	57-59	69-70	67-68	64	–	67	68-69	79
14	73	57-58	60-61	71-72	69-70	65	72	68-69	70	–
15	74	59-61	62-63	73	71	66	–	70-71	71	80
16	–	62-63	64-65	74	72	–	–	72-73	72	81
17	75	64-65	66	75	–	–	–	74-75	–	–
18	–	66	67-68	–	–	–	–	–	–	–
19	–	–	69	–	–	–	–	–	–	–

Ages 4:3–4:5

ss	Com	CU	FA	HL	HS	LS	SC	SD	Soc	MO
1	0-38	0-7	0-9	0-23	0-39	0-36	0-50	0-33	0-40	0-55
2	39-43	8-15	10-15	24-29	40-42	37-40	51-52	34-37	41-44	56-59
3	44-49	16-22	16-21	30-35	43-44	41-43	53-54	38-41	45-47	60-62
4	50-51	23-29	22-26	36-41	45-46	44-46	55-57	42-46	48-49	63-65
5	52-54	30-35	27-31	42-46	47-48	47-49	58-61	47-50	50-52	66-67
6	55-58	36-40	32-36	47-51	49-51	50-51	62-64	51-53	53-54	68-69
7	59-61	41-44	37-40	52-55	52-54	52-53	65-66	54-55	55-57	70-71
8	62-63	45-47	41-44	56-58	55-57	54-56	67-68	56-57	58-59	72-73
9	64-65	48-50	45-49	59-61	58-59	57-58	69	58-60	60-62	74-75
10	66-67	51-52	50-53	62-64	60-62	59-60	70	61-63	63-64	76-77
11	68-69	53-54	54-56	65-66	63-65	61-62	–	64-65	65-66	78
12	70	55-56	57-59	67-68	66-67	63	71	66-67	67-68	79
13	71-72	57-58	60-61	69-71	68	64	–	68-69	69-70	–
14	73	59-61	62-63	72-73	69-70	65	72	70-71	71	80
15	74	62-63	64-65	74	71	66	–	72-73	–	81
16	–	64-65	66	–	72	–	–	74	72	–
17	75	66	67	75	–	–	–	75	–	–
18	–	–	68	–	–	–	–	–	–	–
19	–	–	69	–	–	–	–	–	–	–

212

Note. **Com** = Communication; **CU** = Community Use; **FA** = Functional Pre-Academics; **HL** = Home Living; **HS** = Health and Safety; **LS** = Leisure; **SC** = Self-Care; **SD** = Self-Direction; **Soc** = Social; **MO** = Motor.

Table A.5 Scaled Score Equivalents of Skill Area Raw Scores: Parent/Primary Caregiver and Parent Forms (continued)

Parent/Primary Caregiver Form — Ages 4:6–4:8

ss	Com	CU	FA	HL	HS	LS	SC	SD	Soc	MO
1	0-43	0-15	0-9	0-28	0-39	0-40	0-51	0-33	0-42	0-59
2	44-49	16-22	10-16	29-33	40-42	41-42	52-54	34-37	43-44	60-62
3	50-51	23-29	17-23	34-38	43-45	43-44	55-57	38-41	45-47	63-65
4	52-53	30-33	24-29	39-43	46-48	45-47	58-61	42-46	48-49	66-67
5	54-56	34-37	30-35	44-48	49-51	48-50	62-64	47-50	50-52	68-69
6	57-59	38-41	36-40	49-53	52-54	51-53	65-66	51-53	53-56	70-71
7	60-62	42-45	41-44	54-57	55-57	54-56	67-68	54-56	57-59	72-73
8	63-65	46-48	45-49	58-60	58-59	57-58	69	57-59	60-61	74-75
9	66-67	49-51	50-53	61-63	60-62	59-60	70	60-62	62-63	76-77
10	68-69	52-53	54-56	64-66	63-65	61-62	-	63-64	64-65	78
11	70	54-56	57-59	67-68	66-67	63	71	65-66	66	79
12	71-72	57-58	60-61	69-70	68	64	-	67	67-68	-
13	73	59-60	62-63	71-72	69	65	72	68-69	69-70	80
14	-	61-62	64-65	73	70	-	-	70-71	71	-
15	74	63-64	66	74	71	66	-	72-73	-	81
16	-	65	67	75	72	-	-	74	72	-
17	75	66	68	-	-	-	-	75	-	-
18	-	-	69	-	-	-	-	-	-	-
19	-	-	-	-	-	-	-	-	-	-

Ages 4:9–4:11

Com	CU	FA	HL	HS	LS	SC	SD	Soc	MO	ss
0-49	0-22	0-9	0-28	0-39	0-41	0-51	0-33	0-42	0-61	1
50	23-25	10-16	29-33	40-42	42	52-56	34-37	43-44	62-63	2
51	26-29	17-23	34-38	43-45	43-44	57-60	38-41	45-47	64-65	3
52-53	30-33	24-32	39-43	46-48	45-47	61-63	42-46	48-49	66-67	4
54-56	34-37	33-35	44-48	49-51	48-50	64-65	47-50	50-52	68-70	5
57-59	38-41	36-40	49-53	52-54	51-53	66-67	51-53	53-56	71-72	6
60-62	42-45	41-45	54-57	55-57	54-56	68	54-56	57-59	73-74	7
63-65	46-48	46-49	58-60	58-60	57-59	69	57-59	60-61	75	8
66-68	49-51	50-54	61-63	61-63	60-61	70	60-62	62-63	76-77	9
69-70	52-53	55-58	64-66	64-65	62	-	63-64	64-65	78	10
71	54-56	59-61	67-68	66-67	63	71	65-66	66	79	11
72	57-58	62-63	69-70	68	64	-	67	67-68	-	12
73	59-60	64-65	71-72	69	65	72	68-69	69-70	80	13
-	61-62	66	73	70	-	-	70-71	71	-	14
74	63-64	67	74	71	66	-	72-73	-	81	15
-	65	68	75	72	-	-	74	72	-	16
75	66	69	-	-	-	-	75	-	-	17
-	-	-	-	-	-	-	-	-	-	18
-	-	-	-	-	-	-	-	-	-	19

Ages 5:0–5:2

ss	Com	CU	FA	HL	HS	LS	SC	SD	Soc	MO
1	0-49	0-22	0-9	0-28	0-39	0-41	0-51	0-33	0-42	0-61
2	50	23-26	10-23	29-38	40-43	42	52-56	34-39	43-47	62-63
3	51	27-31	24-32	39-43	44-46	43-44	57-60	40-43	48-49	64-65
4	52-53	32-36	33-35	44-46	47-48	45-47	61-63	44-47	50-52	66-67
5	54-56	37-40	36-40	47-50	49-51	48-50	64-65	48-50	53-54	68-70
6	57-60	41-44	41-45	51-53	52-54	51-53	66-67	51-53	55-56	71-72
7	61-63	45-47	46-49	54-57	55-57	54-56	68	54-56	57-59	73-74
8	64-65	48-50	50-54	58-60	58-60	57-59	69	57-59	60-61	75
9	66-68	51-52	55-58	61-63	61-63	60-61	70	60-62	62-63	76-77
10	69-70	53-54	59-61	64-66	64-65	62	-	63-64	64-65	78
11	71	55-56	62-63	67-68	66-67	63	71	65-66	66-67	79
12	72	57-58	64-65	69-70	68	64	-	67-68	68-69	-
13	73	59-60	66	71-72	69	65	72	69-70	70	80
14	-	61-62	67	73	70	-	-	71-72	71	81
15	74	63-64	68	74	71	66	-	73-74	-	-
16	-	65	69	75	72	-	-	75	72	-
17	75	66	-	-	-	-	-	-	-	-
18	-	-	-	-	-	-	-	-	-	-
19	-	-	-	-	-	-	-	-	-	-

Ages 5:3–5:5

Com	CU	FA	HL	HS	LS	SC	SD	Soc	MO	ss
0-49	0-26	0-23	0-38	0-43	0-41	0-52	0-39	0-47	0-61	1
50-51	27-31	24-32	39-43	44-46	42	53-57	40-43	48-49	62-63	2
52-53	32-36	33-35	44-46	47-48	43-44	58-61	44-47	50-52	64-65	3
54-56	37-40	36-40	47-50	49-50	45-47	62-64	48-50	53-54	66-68	4
57-60	41-44	41-45	51-53	51-53	48-50	65-66	51-53	55-56	69-71	5
61-63	45-47	46-49	54-56	54-56	51-53	67	54-55	57-58	72-73	6
64-65	48-50	50-54	57-59	57-59	54-56	68	56-57	59-60	74-75	7
66-67	51-52	55-58	60-62	60-62	57-59	69	58-60	61-62	76-77	8
68-69	53-54	59-61	63-65	63-64	60-61	70	61-63	63-64	78	9
70-71	55-56	62-63	66-67	65-66	62-63	-	64-65	65-67	79	10
72	57-58	64-65	68	67-68	64	71	66-68	66-67	-	11
73	59-60	66	69-70	69	65	-	69-70	68-69	80	12
-	61-62	67	71-72	70	-	72	71-72	70	81	13
74	63	68	73	71	66	-	73-74	71	-	14
-	64	69	74	72	-	-	75	72	-	15
75	65	-	75	-	-	-	-	-	-	16
-	66	-	-	-	-	-	-	-	-	17
-	-	-	-	-	-	-	-	-	-	18
-	-	-	-	-	-	-	-	-	-	19

Note. **Com** = Communication; **CU** = Community Use; **FA** = Functional Pre-Academics; **HL** = Home Living; **HS** = Health and Safety; **LS** = Leisure; **SC** = Self-Care; **SD** = Self-Direction; **Soc** = Social; **MO** = Motor.

Table A.5 Scaled Score Equivalents of Skill Area Raw Scores: Parent/Primary Caregiver and Parent Forms (continued)

Parent/Primary Caregiver Form

Ages 5:6–5:8

ss	Com	CU	FA	HL	HS	LS	SC	SD	Soc	MO	ss
1	0-49	0-26	0-32	0-40	0-43	0-41	0-52	0-39	0-47	0-61	1
2	50-51	27-31	33-34	41-43	44-46	42	53-57	40-43	48-49	62-63	2
3	52-53	32-36	35-37	44-46	47-48	43-44	58-61	44-47	50-52	64-65	3
4	54-56	37-40	38-41	47-50	49-50	45-47	62-64	48-50	53-54	66-68	4
5	57-60	41-44	42-45	51-53	51-53	48-50	65-66	51-53	55-56	69-71	5
6	61-63	45-47	46-49	54-56	54-56	51-53	67	54-55	57-58	72-73	6
7	64-65	48-50	50-54	57-59	57-59	54-56	68	56-57	59-60	74-75	7
8	66-67	51-52	55-58	60-62	60-62	57-59	69	58-60	61-62	76-77	8
9	68-69	53-54	59-61	63-65	63-64	60-61	70	61-63	63-64	78	9
10	70-71	55-56	62-63	66-67	65-66	62-63	–	64-65	65-67	79	10
11	72	57-58	64-65	68	67-68	64	71	66-68	68-69	–	11
12	73	59-60	66	69-70	69	65	–	69-70	70	80	12
13	–	61-62	67	71-72	70	–	72	71-72	71	81	13
14	74	63	68-69	73	71	66	–	73-74	–	–	14
15	–	64	–	74	72	–	–	75	72	–	15
16	75	65	–	75	–	–	–	–	–	–	16
17	–	66	–	–	–	–	–	–	–	–	17
18	–	–	–	–	–	–	–	–	–	–	18
19	–	–	–	–	–	–	–	–	–	–	19

Ages 5:9–5:11

ss	Com	CU	FA	HL	HS	LS	SC	SD	Soc	MO	ss
1	0-49	0-31	0-34	0-43	0-46	0-41	0-52	0-43	0-49	0-61	1
2	50-51	32-36	35-37	44-46	47	42	53-57	44-46	50-52	62-63	2
3	52-53	37-40	38-41	47-49	48	43-44	58-61	47-48	53-54	64-65	3
4	54-56	41-44	42-45	50-51	49-50	45-47	62-64	49-50	55	66-68	4
5	57-60	45-47	46-49	52-53	51-53	48-50	65-66	51-53	56	69-71	5
6	61-63	48-50	50-54	54-56	54-56	51-53	67	54-55	57-58	72-73	6
7	64-65	51-52	55-58	57-59	57-59	54-56	68	56-57	59-60	74-75	7
8	66-67	53-54	59-61	60-62	60-62	57-59	69	58-60	61-63	76-77	8
9	68-69	55	62-63	63-65	63-64	60-61	70	61-64	64-66	78	9
10	70-71	56	64-65	66-67	65-66	62-63	–	65-67	67-68	79	10
11	72	57-58	66	68	67-68	64	71	68-70	69	80	11
12	73	59-60	67	69-70	69	65	–	71-72	70	81	12
13	–	61-62	68-69	71-72	70	–	72	73-74	71	–	13
14	74	63	–	73	71	66	–	75	–	–	14
15	–	64	–	74	72	–	–	–	72	–	15
16	75	65	–	75	–	–	–	–	–	–	16
17	–	66	–	–	–	–	–	–	–	–	17
18	–	–	–	–	–	–	–	–	–	–	18
19	–	–	–	–	–	–	–	–	–	–	19

Note. **Com** = Communication; **CU** = Community Use; **FA** = Functional Pre-Academics; **HL** = Home Living; **HS** = Health and Safety; **LS** = Leisure; **SC** = Self-Care; **SD** = Self-Direction; **Soc** = Social; **MO** = Motor.

Table A.5 Scaled Score Equivalents of Skill Area Raw Scores: Parent/Primary Caregiver and Parent Forms (continued)

Parent Form

Ages 5:0–5:3

ss	Com	CU	FA	HL	HS	LS	SC	SD	Soc	ss
1	0-25	0	–	0-6	0-19	0-6	0-5	0-1	0-10	1
2	26-29	1-4	0-3	7-10	20-23	7-12	6-14	2-4	11-18	2
3	30-32	5-7	4-6	11-13	24-26	13-17	15-22	5-7	19-25	3
4	33-34	8-9	7-8	14-17	27-28	18-21	23-29	8-11	26-31	4
5	35-36	–	–	18-20	–	22-24	30-35	12-14	32-36	5
6	37-39	–	9	21-23	29	25-28	36-40	15-18	37-40	6
7	40-42	10	–	24-26	30	29-32	41-44	19-22	41-44	7
8	43-46	11	10	27-29	31-32	33-35	45-48	23-26	45-47	8
9	47-49	12	11-12	30-32	33-35	36-39	49-52	27-31	48-51	9
10	50-53	13-19	13-15	33-35	36-41	40-43	53-55	32-35	52-54	10
11	54-56	20-24	16-19	36-38	42-44	44-46	56-58	36-39	55-56	11
12	57-59	25-29	20-24	39-42	45-48	47-50	59-61	40-44	57-59	12
13	60-62	30-35	25-30	43-46	49-51	51-53	62-64	45-48	60-62	13
14	63-65	36-42	31-37	47-50	52-54	54-56	65-67	49-53	63-65	14
15	66-68	43-50	38-54	51-55	55-58	57-59	68-70	54-58	66-67	15
16	69-71	51-59	55-64	56-61	59-62	60-62	71-72	59-63	68-69	16
17	72	60-69	65-69	62-68	63-66	63-64	–	64-69	–	17
18	–	–	–	69-75	–	65-66	–	70-75	–	18
19	–	–	–	–	–	–	–	–	–	19

Ages 5:4–5:7

ss	Com	CU	FA	HL	HS	LS	SC	SD	Soc	ss
1	0-25	0	–	0-6	0-19	0-6	0-5	0-1	0-10	1
2	26-29	1-4	0-3	7-10	20-23	7-12	6-14	2-4	11-18	2
3	30-32	5-7	4-6	11-13	24-26	13-17	15-22	5-7	19-25	3
4	33-34	8-9	7-8	14-17	27-28	18-21	23-29	8-11	26-31	4
5	35-36	–	9	18-20	29	22-24	30-35	12-14	32-36	5
6	37-39	10	–	21-23	30	25-28	36-40	15-18	37-40	6
7	40-42	11	10	24-26	31-32	29-32	41-44	19-22	41-44	7
8	43-46	12	11-12	27-29	33-35	33-35	45-48	23-26	45-47	8
9	47-49	13-15	13-15	30-32	36-38	36-39	49-52	27-31	48-51	9
10	50-53	16-19	16-19	33-35	39-41	40-43	53-55	32-35	52-54	10
11	54-56	20-24	20-24	36-38	42-44	44-46	56-58	36-39	55-56	11
12	57-59	25-29	25-30	39-42	45-48	47-50	59-61	40-44	57-59	12
13	60-62	30-35	31-37	43-46	49-51	51-53	62-64	45-48	60-62	13
14	63-65	36-42	38-45	47-50	52-54	54-56	65-67	49-53	63-65	14
15	66-68	43-50	46-54	51-55	55-58	57-59	68-70	54-58	66-67	15
16	69-71	51-59	55-64	56-61	59-62	60-62	71-72	59-63	68-69	16
17	72	60-69	65-69	62-68	63-66	63-64	–	64-69	–	17
18	–	–	–	69-75	–	65-66	–	70-75	–	18
19	–	–	–	–	–	–	–	–	–	19

Ages 5:8–5:11

ss	Com	CU	FA	HL	HS	LS	SC	SD	Soc	ss
1	0-25	0	–	0-6	0-19	0-6	0-5	0-1	0-10	1
2	26-29	1-4	0-6	7-10	20-26	7-12	6-22	2-4	11-20	2
3	30-32	5-8	7-8	11-13	27-28	13-18	23-29	5-7	21-27	3
4	33-34	9	9	14-17	29	19-23	30-35	8-12	28-33	4
5	35-36	10	10	18-20	30	24-27	36-40	13-17	34-38	5
6	37-40	11	11-12	21-24	31-33	28-31	41-44	18-22	39-42	6
7	41-44	12-13	13-15	25-27	34-35	32-34	45-48	23-26	43-45	7
8	45-48	14-15	16-17	28-31	36-38	35-37	49-52	27-31	46-48	8
9	49-51	16-19	18-20	32-34	39-41	38-41	53-55	32-35	49-51	9
10	52-55	20-24	21-24	35-38	42-44	42-44	56-57	36-39	52-54	10
11	56-58	25-28	25-30	39-41	45-47	45-47	58-60	40-44	55-57	11
12	59-61	29-33	31-37	42-45	48-49	48-50	61-62	45-48	58-59	12
13	62-64	34-39	38-45	46-49	50-52	51-53	63-65	49-53	60-62	13
14	65-67	40-45	46-50	50-54	53-55	54-57	66-68	54-58	63-65	14
15	68-71	46-52	51-55	55-59	56-58	58-60	69-71	59-63	66-67	15
16	72	53-60	56-64	60-65	59-62	61-64	72	64-69	68-69	16
17	–	61-69	65-69	66-72	63-66	65-66	–	70-75	–	17
18	–	–	–	73-75	–	–	–	–	–	18
19	–	–	–	–	–	–	–	–	–	19

Ages 6:0–6:3

ss	Com	CU	FA	HL	HS	LS	SC	SD	Soc	ss
1	0-26	0-4	0-3	0-7	0-23	0-12	0-14	0-2	0-18	1
2	27-30	5-7	4-6	8-12	24-26	13-17	15-27	3-7	19-25	2
3	31-33	8-9	7-9	13-16	27-30	18-21	28-33	8-11	26-31	3
4	34-36	10-11	10	17-20	31-32	22-24	34-38	12-14	32-36	4
5	37-39	12	11-13	21-23	33-35	25-28	39-42	15-18	37-40	5
6	40-42	13-14	14-15	24-26	36	29-32	43-46	19-22	41-44	6
7	43-46	15	16-19	27-29	37	33-35	47-49	23-27	45-47	7
8	47-49	16-17	20-23	30-32	38-39	36-39	50-52	28-31	48-51	8
9	50-53	18-20	24-27	33-35	40-42	40-43	53-55	32-36	52-54	9
10	54-56	21-24	28-32	36-38	43-44	44-46	56-58	37-40	55-56	10
11	57-59	25-29	33-36	39-42	45-48	47-50	59-61	41-44	57-59	11
12	60-62	30-35	37-41	43-46	49-51	51-53	62-64	45-48	60-62	12
13	63-65	36-42	42-45	47-50	52-54	54-56	65-67	49-53	63-65	13
14	66-68	43-50	46-54	51-55	55-58	57-59	68-70	54-58	66-67	14
15	69-71	51-59	55-61	56-61	59-61	60-62	71-72	59-64	68-69	15
16	72	60-69	62-67	62-68	62-65	63-64	–	65-71	–	16
17	–	–	68-69	69-75	66	65-66	–	72-75	–	17
18	–	–	–	–	–	–	–	–	–	18
19	–	–	–	–	–	–	–	–	–	19

Note. **Com** = Communication; **CU** = Community Use; **FA** = Functional Academics; **HL** = Home Living; **HS** = Health and Safety; **LS** = Leisure; **SC** = Self-Care; **SD** = Self-Direction; **Soc** = Social.

Table A.5 Scaled Score Equivalents of Skill Area Raw Scores: Parent/Primary Caregiver and Parent Forms (continued)

Parent Form

Ages 6:4-6:7

ss	Com	CU	FA	HL	HS	LS	SC	SD	Soc	ss
1	0-26	0-4	0-6	0-7	0-26	0-12	0-27	0-2	0-20	1
2	27-30	5-8	7-10	8-12	27-30	13-18	28-33	3-7	21-27	2
3	31-33	9-11	11-13	13-16	31-33	19-23	34-38	8-12	28-33	3
4	34-36	12-13	14-15	17-20	34-35	24-27	39-42	13-17	34-38	4
5	37-40	14	16-17	21-24	36	28-31	43-46	18-22	39-42	5
6	41-44	15	18-20	25-27	37	32-34	47-49	23-27	43-45	6
7	45-48	16-17	21-23	28-31	38-39	35-37	50-52	28-31	46-48	7
8	49-51	18-20	24-27	32-34	40-42	38-41	53-55	32-36	49-51	8
9	52-55	21-24	28-32	35-38	43-44	42-44	56-57	37-40	52-54	9
10	56-58	25-28	33-36	39-41	45-47	45-47	58-60	41-44	55-57	10
11	59-61	29-33	37-41	42-45	48-49	48-50	61-62	45-48	58-59	11
12	62-64	34-39	42-45	46-49	50-52	51-53	63-65	49-53	60-62	12
13	65-67	40-45	46-50	50-54	53-55	54-57	66-68	54-58	63-65	13
14	68-71	46-52	51-55	55-59	56-58	58-60	69-71	59-64	66-67	14
15	72	53-60	56-61	60-65	59-61	61-64	72	65-71	68-69	15
16	-	61-69	62-67	66-72	62-65	65-66	-	72-75	-	16
17	-	-	68-69	73-75	66	-	-	-	-	17
18	-	-	-	-	-	-	-	-	-	18
19	-	-	-	-	-	-	-	-	-	19

Ages 6:8-6:11

ss	Com	CU	FA	HL	HS	LS	SC	SD	Soc	ss
1	0-26	0-4	0-6	0-7	0-26	0-12	0-27	0-2	0-20	1
2	27-33	5-8	7-13	8-16	27-30	13-18	28-33	3-12	21-33	2
3	34-36	9-12	14-15	17-20	31-33	19-23	34-38	13-17	34-38	3
4	37-40	13-14	16-17	21-24	34-35	24-27	39-42	18-24	39-42	4
5	41-44	15	18-20	25-27	36	28-31	43-46	25-28	43-45	5
6	45-48	16-17	21-23	28-31	37	32-35	47-50	29-31	46-48	6
7	49-50	18-20	24-27	32-34	38-39	36-38	51-53	32-36	49-50	7
8	51-52	21-22	28-32	35-36	40-42	39-41	54-56	37-39	51-52	8
9	53-55	23-25	33-36	37-38	43-45	42-44	57-59	40-42	53-54	9
10	56-58	26-29	37-41	39-41	46-48	45-47	60-61	43-46	55-57	10
11	59-61	30-33	42-45	42-45	49-50	48-50	62-63	47-49	58-59	11
12	62-64	34-39	46-50	46-49	51-53	51-53	64-65	50-53	60-62	12
13	65-67	40-45	51-54	50-54	54-55	54-57	66-68	54-58	63-65	13
14	68-71	46-52	55-57	55-59	56-58	58-60	69-71	59-64	66-67	14
15	72	53-60	58-61	60-65	59-61	61-64	72	65-71	68-69	15
16	-	61-69	62-67	66-72	62-65	65-66	-	72-75	-	16
17	-	-	68-69	73-75	66	-	-	-	-	17
18	-	-	-	-	-	-	-	-	-	18
19	-	-	-	-	-	-	-	-	-	19

Ages 7:0-7:3

ss	Com	CU	FA	HL	HS	LS	SC	SD	Soc	ss
1	0-30	0-8	0-10	0-12	0-26	0-17	0-28	0-7	0-27	1
2	31-38	9-11	11-13	13-19	27-30	18-22	29-35	8-22	28-34	2
3	39-42	12-13	14-17	20-24	31-33	23-26	36-41	23-27	35-39	3
4	43-45	14-15	18-20	25-28	34-35	27-31	42-46	28-31	40-43	4
5	46-47	16-17	21-22	29-31	36-37	32-34	47-49	32-33	44-46	5
6	48	18	23-25	32-33	38-39	35-37	50-52	34-35	47-48	6
7	49-51	19-20	26-29	34	40-42	38-41	53-55	36-37	49-51	7
8	52-55	21-24	30-33	35-38	43-44	42-44	56-57	38-40	52-54	8
9	56-58	25-28	34-37	39-41	45-47	45-47	58-60	41-44	55-56	9
10	59-60	29-32	38-42	42-44	48-49	48-50	61-62	45-48	57-59	10
11	61-63	33-36	43-46	45-48	50-52	51-53	63-65	49-52	60-61	11
12	64-65	37-41	47-50	49-52	53-55	54-55	66-67	53-56	62-63	12
13	66-68	42-47	51-55	53-57	56-57	56-58	68-69	57-60	64-65	13
14	69-71	48-54	56-60	58-62	58-59	59-61	70-71	61-65	66-68	14
15	72	55-62	61-64	63-68	60-62	62-64	72	66-71	69	15
16	-	63-69	65-67	69-75	63-65	65-66	-	72-75	-	16
17	-	-	68-69	-	66	-	-	-	-	17
18	-	-	-	-	-	-	-	-	-	18
19	-	-	-	-	-	-	-	-	-	19

Ages 7:4-7:7

ss	Com	CU	FA	HL	HS	LS	SC	SD	Soc	ss
1	0-38	0-8	0-13	0-19	0-26	0-17	0-28	0-24	0-34	1
2	39-42	9-12	14-17	20-24	27-30	18-22	29-35	25-28	35-39	2
3	43-45	13-15	18-20	25-28	31-33	23-26	36-41	29-31	40-43	3
4	46-47	16-17	21-22	29-31	34-35	27-31	42-46	32-33	44-46	4
5	48	18	23-25	32-33	36-37	32-35	47-50	34-35	47-48	5
6	49-50	19-20	26-29	34	38-39	36-38	51-53	36-37	49-50	6
7	51-52	21-22	30-33	35-36	40-42	39-41	54-56	38-39	51-52	7
8	53-55	23-25	34-37	37-38	43-45	42-44	57-59	40-42	53-54	8
9	56-58	26-29	38-42	39-41	46-48	45-47	60-61	43-46	55-56	9
10	59-60	30-32	43-46	42-44	49-50	48-50	62-63	47-49	57-59	10
11	61-63	33-36	47-50	45-48	51-53	51-53	64-65	50-52	60-61	11
12	64-65	37-41	51-54	49-52	54-55	54-55	66-67	53-56	62-63	12
13	66-68	42-47	55-57	53-57	56-57	56-58	68-69	57-60	64-65	13
14	69-71	48-54	58-60	58-62	58-59	59-61	70-71	61-65	66-68	14
15	72	55-62	61-64	63-68	60-62	62-64	72	66-71	69	15
16	-	63-69	65-67	69-75	63-65	65-66	-	72-75	-	16
17	-	-	68-69	-	66	-	-	-	-	17
18	-	-	-	-	-	-	-	-	-	18
19	-	-	-	-	-	-	-	-	-	19

Note. **Com** = Communication; **CU** = Community Use; **FA** = Functional Academics; **HL** = Home Living; **HS** = Health and Safety; **LS** = Leisure; **SC** = Self-Care; **SD** = Self-Direction; **Soc** = Social.

Table A.5 Scaled Score Equivalents of Skill Area Raw Scores: Parent/Primary Caregiver and Parent Forms (continued)

Parent Form

Ages 7:8–7:11

ss	Com	CU	FA	HL	HS	LS	SC	SD	Soc	ss
1	0-38	0-8	0-13	0-19	0-26	0-17	0-28	0-24	0-34	1
2	39-42	9-12	14-17	20-24	27-30	18-26	29-35	25-28	35-39	2
3	43-45	13-15	18-21	25-28	31-33	27-31	36-41	29-31	40-43	3
4	46-47	16-17	22-24	29-32	34-35	32-35	42-46	32-34	44-46	4
5	48	18	25-26	33-34	36-37	36-37	47-50	35-37	47-48	5
6	49-50	19-20	27-29	35-36	38-39	38-39	51-53	38-39	49-50	6
7	51-52	21-22	30-33	37-38	40-42	40-41	54-56	40	51-52	7
8	53-55	23-25	34-38	39-40	43-45	42-44	57-59	41-42	53-54	8
9	56-58	26-29	39-43	41-42	46-48	45-47	60-61	43-46	55-56	9
10	59-60	30-32	44-48	43-45	49-50	48-50	62-63	47-49	57-59	10
11	61-63	33-36	49-52	46-48	51-53	51-53	64-65	50-52	60-61	11
12	64-65	37-41	53-55	49-52	54-55	54-56	66-67	53-56	62-63	12
13	66-68	42-47	56-58	53-57	56-57	57-58	68-69	57-60	64-65	13
14	69-71	48-54	59-61	58-62	58-60	59-61	70-71	61-65	66-68	14
15	72	55-62	62-64	63-68	61-62	62-64	72	66-71	69	15
16	–	63-69	65-67	69-75	63-65	65-66	–	72-75	–	16
17	–	–	68-69	–	66	–	–	–	–	17
18	–	–	–	–	–	–	–	–	–	18
19	–	–	–	–	–	–	–	–	–	19

Ages 8:0–8:3

ss	Com	CU	FA	HL	HS	LS	SC	SD	Soc	ss
1	0-38	0-8	0-17	0-23	0-27	0-22	0-28	0-25	0-39	1
2	39-42	9-12	18-20	24-28	28-31	23-28	29-35	26-30	40-43	2
3	43-45	13-15	21-22	29-31	32-34	29-32	36-41	31-33	44-46	3
4	46-47	16-17	23-25	32-33	35-36	33-35	42-46	34-35	47-48	4
5	48-49	18	26-29	34-35	37-38	36-38	47-51	36-37	49	5
6	50-51	19-20	30-33	36-37	39-41	39-41	52-55	38-39	50	6
7	52-54	21-23	34-37	38-39	42-44	42-44	56-58	40-42	51-52	7
8	55-57	24-27	38-42	40-41	45-47	45-47	59-61	43-45	53-55	8
9	58-60	28-32	43-46	42-44	48-49	48-50	62-63	46-48	56-57	9
10	61-63	33-36	47-50	45-48	50-52	51-53	64-65	49-52	58-60	10
11	64-65	37-40	51-54	49-52	53-55	54-55	66-67	53-55	61-63	11
12	66-67	41-44	55-57	53-57	56-57	56-58	68	56-59	64-65	12
13	68-69	45-49	58-60	58-62	58-59	59-61	69-70	60-63	66-68	13
14	70-72	50-55	61-63	63-67	60-62	62-63	71	64-68	69	14
15	–	56-62	64-65	68-73	63-64	64-65	72	69-74	–	15
16	–	63-69	66-67	74-75	65-66	66	–	75	–	16
17	–	–	68-69	–	–	–	–	–	–	17
18	–	–	–	–	–	–	–	–	–	18
19	–	–	–	–	–	–	–	–	–	19

Ages 8:4–8:7

ss	Com	CU	FA	HL	HS	LS	SC	SD	Soc	ss
1	0-38	0-8	0-17	0-23	0-27	0-28	0-28	0-25	0-39	1
2	39-42	9-12	18-21	24-28	28-31	29-32	29-35	26-30	40-43	2
3	43-45	13-15	22-24	29-32	32-34	33-35	36-41	31-34	44-46	3
4	46-47	16-17	25-26	33-35	35-36	36-37	42-46	35-37	47-48	4
5	48-49	18	27-29	36-37	37-38	38-39	47-51	38-39	49	5
6	50-51	19-20	30-33	38-41	39-41	40-41	52-55	40	50	6
7	52-54	21-23	34-38	40	42-44	42-44	56-58	41-42	51-52	7
8	55-57	24-27	39-43	41-42	45-47	45-47	59-61	43-45	53-55	8
9	58-60	28-32	44-48	43-45	48-49	48-50	62-63	46-48	56-57	9
10	61-63	33-36	49-52	46-48	50-52	51-53	64-65	49-52	58-60	10
11	64-65	37-40	53-55	49-52	53-55	54-56	66-67	53-55	61-63	11
12	66-67	41-44	56-58	53-57	56-57	57-58	68	56-59	64-65	12
13	68-69	45-49	59-61	58-62	58-60	59-61	69-70	60-63	66-68	13
14	70-72	50-55	62-63	63-67	61-62	62-63	71	64-68	69	14
15	–	56-62	64-65	68-73	63-64	64-65	72	69-74	–	15
16	–	63-69	66-67	74-75	65-66	66	–	75	–	16
17	–	–	68-69	–	–	–	–	–	–	17
18	–	–	–	–	–	–	–	–	–	18
19	–	–	–	–	–	–	–	–	–	19

Ages 8:8–8:11

ss	Com	CU	FA	HL	HS	LS	SC	SD	Soc	ss
1	0-38	0-8	0-17	0-23	0-27	0-28	0-28	0-25	0-39	1
2	39-42	9-12	18-21	24-32	28-31	29-32	29-40	26-32	40-43	2
3	43-45	13-15	22-26	33-35	32-34	33-35	41-46	33-36	44-46	3
4	46-47	16-17	27-29	36-37	35-36	36-37	47-51	37-39	47-48	4
5	48-49	18	30-33	38-39	37-38	38-39	52-55	40	49-50	5
6	50-51	19-20	34-38	40	39-41	40-41	56-58	41-42	51	6
7	52-54	21-24	39-43	41-42	42-44	42-44	59-60	43-44	52-53	7
8	55-57	25-29	44-48	43-45	45-47	45-47	61-62	45-47	54-55	8
9	58-60	30-34	49-52	46-47	48-49	48-50	63-64	48-50	56-57	9
10	61-63	35-38	53-54	48-50	50-52	51-53	65	51-53	58-60	10
11	64-65	39-42	55-57	51-53	53-55	54-56	66-67	54-56	61-63	11
12	66-67	43-46	58-59	54-57	56-57	57-58	68	57-59	64-65	12
13	68-69	47-50	60-62	58-62	58-60	59-61	69-70	60-63	66-68	13
14	70-72	51-55	63-64	63-67	61-62	62-63	71	64-68	69	14
15	–	56-62	65-66	68-73	63-64	64-65	72	69-74	–	15
16	–	63-69	67-68	74-75	65-66	66	–	75	–	16
17	–	–	69	–	–	–	–	–	–	17
18	–	–	–	–	–	–	–	–	–	18
19	–	–	–	–	–	–	–	–	–	19

Note. **Com** = Communication; **CU** = Community Use; **FA** = Functional Academics; **HL** = Home Living; **HS** = Health and Safety; **LS** = Leisure; **SC** = Self-Care; **SD** = Self-Direction; **Soc** = Social.

Table A.5 Scaled Score Equivalents of Skill Area Raw Scores: Parent/Primary Caregiver and Parent Forms (continued)

Parent Form

Ages 9:0–9:3

ss	Com	CU	FA	HL	HS	LS	SC	SD	Soc	ss
1	0-38	0-8	0-20	0-28	0-27	0-28	0-35	0-30	0-41	1
2	39-42	9-12	21-24	29-32	28-31	29-32	36-41	31-34	42-45	2
3	43-45	13-15	25-27	33-36	32-34	33-35	42-46	35-37	46-48	3
4	46-47	16-17	28-33	37-39	35-36	36-37	47-51	38-39	49	4
5	48-50	18-20	34-38	40-41	37-38	38-40	52-55	40-41	50	5
6	51-54	21-23	39-42	42	39-41	41-44	56-58	42	51-52	6
7	55-57	24-27	43-45	43	42-45	45-47	59-61	43-45	53-55	7
8	58-60	28-32	46-49	44-45	46-49	48-49	62-63	46-48	56-57	8
9	61-62	33-36	50-52	46-48	50-52	50-52	64-65	49-52	58-59	9
10	63-64	37-40	53-55	49-52	53-55	53-54	66-67	53-55	60-61	10
11	65-66	41-44	56-58	53-56	56-57	55-56	68	56-59	62-63	11
12	67-68	45-49	59-61	57-59	58-59	57-59	69	60-62	64-65	12
13	69-70	50-55	62-63	60-63	60-61	60-61	70	63-65	66-68	13
14	71-72	56-59	64-65	64-68	62-63	62-64	71	66-69	69	14
15	–	60-64	66-67	69-74	64-65	65-66	72	70-74	–	15
16	–	65-69	68-69	75	66	–	–	75	–	16
17	–	–	–	–	–	–	–	–	–	17
18	–	–	–	–	–	–	–	–	–	18
19	–	–	–	–	–	–	–	–	–	19

Ages 9:4–9:7

ss	Com	CU	FA	HL	HS	LS	SC	SD	Soc	ss
1	0-38	0-8	0-20	0-32	0-27	0-28	0-40	0-32	0-41	1
2	39-42	9-12	21-27	33-36	28-31	29-32	41-46	33-36	42-45	2
3	43-45	13-15	28-33	37-39	32-34	33-35	47-51	37-39	46-48	3
4	46-47	16-17	34-38	40-41	35-36	36-37	52-55	40-41	49-50	4
5	48-50	18-20	39-42	42	37-38	38-40	56-58	42	51	5
6	51-54	21-24	43-45	43	39-41	41-44	59-60	43-44	52-53	6
7	55-57	25-29	46-49	44-45	42-45	45-47	61-62	45-47	54-55	7
8	58-60	30-34	50-52	46-47	46-49	48-49	63-64	48-50	56-57	8
9	61-62	35-38	53-54	48-50	50-52	50-52	65	51-53	58-59	9
10	63-64	39-42	55-57	51-53	53-55	53-54	66-67	54-56	60-61	10
11	65-66	43-46	58-59	54-56	56-57	55-56	68	57-59	62-63	11
12	67-68	47-50	60-62	57-59	58-59	57-59	69	60-62	64-65	12
13	69-70	51-55	63-64	60-63	60-61	60-61	70	63-65	66-68	13
14	71-72	56-59	65-66	64-68	62-63	62-64	71	66-69	69	14
15	–	60-64	67-68	69-74	64-65	65-66	72	70-74	–	15
16	–	65-69	69	75	66	–	–	75	–	16
17	–	–	–	–	–	–	–	–	–	17
18	–	–	–	–	–	–	–	–	–	18
19	–	–	–	–	–	–	–	–	–	19

Ages 9:8–9:11

ss	Com	CU	FA	HL	HS	LS	SC	SD	Soc	ss
1	0-38	0-8	0-20	0-32	0-27	0-28	0-40	0-32	0-41	1
2	39-42	9-13	21-27	33-36	28-31	29-32	41-46	33-36	42-45	2
3	43-45	14-17	28-33	37-39	32-34	33-35	47-51	37-39	46-48	3
4	46-47	18-20	34-38	40-41	35-36	36-37	52-55	40-42	49-50	4
5	48-50	21-22	39-42	42-43	37-40	38-40	56-58	43-44	51	5
6	51-54	23-25	43-45	44	41-44	41-44	59-60	45	52-53	6
7	55-57	26-29	46-49	45	45-47	45-47	61-62	46-47	54-55	7
8	58-60	30-34	50-52	46-47	48-50	48-49	63-64	48-50	56-57	8
9	61-62	35-39	53-55	48-50	51-52	50-52	65	51-53	58-59	9
10	63-64	40-43	56-58	51-54	53-55	53-54	66-67	54-56	60-61	10
11	65-66	44-47	59-60	55-57	56-57	55-56	68	57-59	62-63	11
12	67-68	48-50	61-62	58-60	58-59	57-59	69	60-62	64-65	12
13	69-70	51-55	63-64	61-63	60-61	60-61	70	63-65	66-68	13
14	71-72	56-59	65-66	64-68	62-63	62-64	71	66-69	69	14
15	–	60-64	67-68	69-74	64-65	65-66	72	70-74	–	15
16	–	65-69	69	75	66	–	–	75	–	16
17	–	–	–	–	–	–	–	–	–	17
18	–	–	–	–	–	–	–	–	–	18
19	–	–	–	–	–	–	–	–	–	19

Ages 10:0–10:3

ss	Com	CU	FA	HL	HS	LS	SC	SD	Soc	ss
1	0-39	0-12	0-20	0-34	0-28	0-30	0-44	0-35	0-41	1
2	40-43	13-15	21-27	35-38	29-32	31-33	45-49	36-39	42-45	2
3	44-46	16-17	28-33	39-41	33-36	34-35	50-53	40-41	46-48	3
4	47-48	18-20	34-38	42	37-38	36-38	54-56	42	49-50	4
5	49-51	21-24	39-43	43	39-41	39-41	57-58	43-44	51-52	5
6	52-55	25-29	44-48	44-45	42-44	42-44	59-61	45-47	53	6
7	56-58	30-34	49-52	46-47	46-49	45-47	62-63	48-49	54-55	7
8	59-61	35-38	53-54	48-50	50-52	48-50	64-65	50-52	56-57	8
9	62-63	39-42	55-57	51-53	53-54	51-52	66	53-56	58-59	9
10	64-65	43-46	58-59	54-56	55-56	53-55	67-68	57-59	60-62	10
11	66-67	47-50	60-62	57-59	57-58	56-57	69	60-62	63-64	11
12	68-69	51-53	63-64	60-63	59-60	58-60	70	63-65	65-66	12
13	70-71	54-56	65	64-66	61-62	61-62	71	66-68	67-68	13
14	72	57-60	66-67	67-70	63	63-64	72	69-71	69	14
15	–	61-64	68	71-74	64-65	65-66	–	72-75	–	15
16	–	65-69	69	75	66	–	–	–	–	16
17	–	–	–	–	–	–	–	–	–	17
18	–	–	–	–	–	–	–	–	–	18
19	–	–	–	–	–	–	–	–	–	19

Note. **Com** = Communication; **CU** = Community Use; **FA** = Functional Academics; **HL** = Home Living; **HS** = Health and Safety; **LS** = Leisure; **SC** = Self-Care; **SD** = Self-Direction; **Soc** = Social.

Table A.5 Scaled Score Equivalents of Skill Area Raw Scores: Parent/Primary Caregiver and Parent Forms (continued)

Parent Form

Ages 10:4–10:7

ss	Com	CU	FA	HL	HS	LS	SC	SD	Soc
1	0-39	0-17	0-20	0-34	0-28	0-30	0-44	0-35	0-41
2	40-43	14-17	21-27	35-38	29-32	31-33	45-49	36-39	42-45
3	44-46	18-20	28-33	39-41	33-36	34-35	50-53	40-42	46-48
4	47-48	21-22	34-38	42-43	37-40	36-38	54-56	43-44	49-50
5	49-51	23-25	39-43	44	41-44	39-41	57-58	45	51-52
6	52-55	26-29	44-48	45	45-47	42-44	59-61	46-47	53
7	56-58	30-34	49-52	46-47	48-50	45-47	62-63	48-49	54-55
8	59-61	35-39	53-55	48-50	51-52	48-50	64-65	50-52	56-57
9	62-63	40-43	56-58	51-54	53-54	51-52	66	53-56	58-59
10	64-65	44-47	59-60	55-57	55-56	53-55	67-68	57-59	60-62
11	66-67	48-50	61-62	58-60	57-58	56-57	69	60-62	63-64
12	68-69	51-53	63-64	61-63	59-60	58-60	70	63-65	65-66
13	70-71	54-56	65	64-66	61-62	61-62	71	66-68	67-68
14	72	57-60	66-67	67-70	63	63-64	72	69-71	69
15	–	61-64	68	71-74	64-65	65-66	–	72-75	–
16	–	65-69	69	75	66	–	–	–	–
17	–	–	–	–	–	–	–	–	–
18	–	–	–	–	–	–	–	–	–
19	–	–	–	–	–	–	–	–	–

Ages 10:8–10:11

ss	Com	CU	FA	HL	HS	LS	SC	SD	Soc
1	0-39	0-13	0-20	0-34	0-28	0-30	0-44	0-35	0-41
2	40-43	14-18	21-27	35-38	29-32	31-33	45-49	36-39	42-45
3	44-46	19-22	28-33	39-41	33-36	34-35	50-53	40-42	46-48
4	47-48	23-25	34-38	42-44	37-40	36-38	54-56	43-44	49-50
5	49-51	26-27	39-43	45	41-44	39-41	57-58	45-47	51-52
6	52-55	28-30	44-48	46-47	45-47	42-44	59-61	48-49	53
7	56-58	31-34	49-52	48	48-50	45-47	62-63	50	54-55
8	59-61	35-39	53-55	49-50	51-52	48-50	64-65	51-52	56-57
9	62-63	40-43	56-58	51-54	53-54	51-52	66	53-56	58-59
10	64-65	44-47	59-60	55-57	55-56	53-55	67-68	57-59	60-62
11	66-67	48-50	61-62	58-60	57-58	56-57	69	60-62	63-64
12	68-69	51-53	63-64	61-63	59-60	58-60	70	63-65	65-66
13	70-71	54-56	65	64-66	61-62	61-62	71	66-68	67-68
14	72	57-60	66-67	67-70	63	63-64	72	69-71	69
15	–	61-64	68	71-74	64-65	65-66	–	72-75	–
16	–	65-69	69	75	66	–	–	–	–
17	–	–	–	–	–	–	–	–	–
18	–	–	–	–	–	–	–	–	–
19	–	–	–	–	–	–	–	–	–

Ages 11:0–11:3

ss	Com	CU	FA	HL	HS	LS	SC	SD	Soc
1	0-40	0-17	0-20	0-37	0-29	0-31	0-45	0-36	0-43
2	41-44	18-20	21-27	38-41	30-35	32-34	46-49	37-40	44-47
3	45-47	21-22	28-33	42-43	36-40	35-37	50-54	41-44	48-50
4	48-49	23-25	34-38	44	41-44	38-39	55-58	45-47	51-52
5	50-52	26-29	39-44	45-46	45-47	40-42	59-61	46-47	53
6	53-56	30-34	45-49	47	48-49	43-45	62-63	48-49	54
7	57-59	35-39	50-53	48-50	50-52	46-48	64-65	50-52	55-56
8	60-61	40-43	54-56	51-52	53-54	49-51	66	53-55	57-58
9	62-64	44-46	57-59	53-55	55-56	52-53	67-68	56-58	59-60
10	65-66	47-49	60-61	56-58	57-58	54-55	69	59-61	61-62
11	67-68	50-52	62-63	59-62	59-60	56-58	70	62-64	63-64
12	69-70	53-56	64-65	63-65	61	59-60	71	65-67	65-66
13	71-72	57-59	66	66-69	62-63	61-63	72	68-70	67-68
14	–	60-63	67-68	70-74	64	64-66	–	71-72	69
15	–	64-68	69	75	65-66	–	–	73-75	–
16	–	69	–	–	–	–	–	–	–
17	–	–	–	–	–	–	–	–	–
18	–	–	–	–	–	–	–	–	–
19	–	–	–	–	–	–	–	–	–

Ages 11:4–11:7

ss	Com	CU	FA	HL	HS	LS	SC	SD	Soc
1	0-40	0-18	0-20	0-37	0-29	0-31	0-45	0-36	0-43
2	41-44	19-22	21-27	38-41	30-35	32-34	46-49	37-40	44-47
3	45-47	23-25	28-33	42-44	36-40	35-37	50-54	41-44	48-50
4	48-49	26-27	34-38	45-46	41-44	38-39	55-58	45-47	51-52
5	50-52	28-30	39-44	47	45-47	40-42	59-61	48-49	53
6	53-56	31-34	45-49	48	48-49	43-45	62-63	50	54
7	57-59	35-39	50-53	49-50	50-52	46-48	64-65	51-52	55-56
8	60-61	40-43	54-56	51-52	53-54	49-51	66	53-55	57-58
9	62-64	44-46	57-59	53-55	55-56	52-53	67-68	56-58	59-60
10	65-66	47-49	60-61	56-58	57-58	54-55	69	59-61	61-62
11	67-68	50-52	62-63	59-62	59-60	56-58	70	62-64	63-64
12	69-70	53-56	64-65	63-65	61	59-60	71	65-67	65-66
13	71-72	57-59	66	66-69	62-63	61-63	72	68-70	67-68
14	–	60-63	67-68	70-74	64	64-66	–	71-72	69
15	–	64-68	69	75	65-66	–	–	73-75	–
16	–	69	–	–	–	–	–	–	–
17	–	–	–	–	–	–	–	–	–
18	–	–	–	–	–	–	–	–	–
19	–	–	–	–	–	–	–	–	–

Note. **Com** = Communication; **CU** = Community Use; **FA** = Functional Academics; **HL** = Home Living; **HS** = Health and Safety; **LS** = Leisure; **SC** = Self-Care; **SD** = Self-Direction; **Soc** = Social.

A Parent Ages 5–21

Table A.5 Scaled Score Equivalents of Skill Area Raw Scores: Parent/Primary Caregiver and Parent Forms (continued)

Parent Form

Ages 11:8–11:11

ss	Com	CU	FA	HL	HS	LS	SC	SD	Soc	ss
1	0-40	0-18	0-20	0-37	0-29	0-31	0-45	0-36	0-43	1
2	41-44	19-24	21-27	38-41	30-39	32-34	46-52	37-40	44-47	2
3	45-47	25-27	28-33	42-44	40-43	35-37	53-56	41-44	48-50	3
4	48-49	28-30	34-38	45-46	44-46	38-39	57-59	45-47	51-52	4
5	50-52	31-33	39-44	47-48	47-48	40-42	60-61	48-49	53	5
6	53-56	34-35	45-49	49	49-50	43-45	62-63	50	54	6
7	57-59	36-39	50-53	50-51	51-52	46-48	64-65	51-52	55-56	7
8	60-61	40-43	54-56	52-53	53-54	49-51	66	53-55	57-58	8
9	62-64	44-46	57-59	54-55	55-56	52-53	67-68	56-58	59-60	9
10	65-66	47-49	60-61	56-58	57-58	54-55	69	59-61	61-62	10
11	67-68	50-52	62-63	59-62	59-60	56-58	70	62-64	63-64	11
12	69-70	53-56	64-65	63-65	61	59-60	71	65-67	65-66	12
13	71-72	57-59	66	66-69	62-63	61-63	72	68-70	67-68	13
14	–	60-63	67-68	70-74	64-65	64-66	–	71-72	69	14
15	–	64-68	69	75	66	–	–	73-75	–	15
16	–	69	–	–	–	–	–	–	–	16
17	–	–	–	–	–	–	–	–	–	17
18	–	–	–	–	–	–	–	–	–	18
19	–	–	–	–	–	–	–	–	–	19

Ages 12:0–12:3

ss	Com	CU	FA	HL	HS	LS	SC	SD	Soc	ss
1	0-41	0-22	0-20	0-37	0-35	0-31	0-49	0-36	0-43	1
2	42-45	23-25	21-27	38-41	36-40	32-34	50-54	37-40	44-47	2
3	46-48	26-28	28-33	42-45	41-44	35-37	55-58	41-44	48-50	3
4	49-50	29-31	34-38	46-47	45-47	38-39	59-61	45-47	51-52	4
5	51-53	32-34	39-44	48	48-49	40-42	62	48-49	53	5
6	54-56	35-38	45-50	49-50	50-51	43-45	63	50	54	6
7	57-59	39-42	51-54	51-52	52-53	46-48	64-65	51-52	55-56	7
8	60-61	43-45	55-57	53-55	54-55	49-51	66	53-55	57-58	8
9	62-64	46-48	58-60	56-57	56-57	52-54	67-68	56-58	59-60	9
10	65-66	49-51	61-62	58-60	58-59	55-57	69-70	59-61	61-63	10
11	67-69	52-54	63-64	61-64	60-61	58-59	71	62-64	64-65	11
12	70-71	55-57	65	65-68	62-63	60-61	72	65-68	66-68	12
13	72	58-60	66-67	69-73	64	62-64	–	69-72	69	13
14	–	61-64	68	74-75	65-66	65-66	–	73-75	–	14
15	–	65-68	69	–	–	–	–	–	–	15
16	–	69	–	–	–	–	–	–	–	16
17	–	–	–	–	–	–	–	–	–	17
18	–	–	–	–	–	–	–	–	–	18
19	–	–	–	–	–	–	–	–	–	19

Ages 12:4–12:7

ss	Com	CU	FA	HL	HS	LS	SC	SD	Soc	ss
1	0-41	0-24	0-20	0-37	0-39	0-31	0-52	0-36	0-43	1
2	42-45	25-28	21-27	38-41	40-43	32-34	53-56	37-40	44-47	2
3	46-48	29-31	28-33	42-45	44-46	35-37	57-59	41-44	48-50	3
4	49-50	32-33	34-38	46-48	47-48	38-39	60-61	45-47	51-52	4
5	51-53	34-35	39-44	49	49-50	40-42	62	48-49	53	5
6	54-56	36-38	45-50	50-51	51	43-45	63	50	54	6
7	57-59	39-42	51-54	52-53	52-53	46-48	64-65	51-52	55-56	7
8	60-61	43-45	55-57	54-55	54-55	49-51	66	53-55	57-58	8
9	62-64	46-48	58-60	56-57	56-57	52-54	67-68	56-58	59-60	9
10	65-66	49-51	61-62	58-60	58-59	55-57	69-70	59-61	61-63	10
11	67-69	52-54	63-64	61-64	60-61	58-59	71	62-64	64-65	11
12	70-71	55-57	65	65-68	62-63	60-61	72	65-68	66-68	12
13	72	58-60	66-67	69-73	64-65	62-64	–	69-72	69	13
14	–	61-64	68	74-75	66	65-66	–	73-75	–	14
15	–	65-68	69	–	–	–	–	–	–	15
16	–	69	–	–	–	–	–	–	–	16
17	–	–	–	–	–	–	–	–	–	17
18	–	–	–	–	–	–	–	–	–	18
19	–	–	–	–	–	–	–	–	–	19

Ages 12:8–12:11

ss	Com	CU	FA	HL	HS	LS	SC	SD	Soc	ss
1	0-41	0-24	0-20	0-37	0-39	0-31	0-52	0-36	0-43	1
2	42-45	25-28	21-27	38-41	40-43	32-34	53-56	37-40	44-47	2
3	46-48	29-31	28-33	42-45	44-46	35-37	57-59	41-44	48-50	3
4	49-50	32-33	34-38	46-48	47-48	38-39	60-61	45-47	51-52	4
5	51-53	34-35	39-44	49	49-50	40-42	62	48-49	53	5
6	54-56	36-38	45-50	50-51	51	43-45	63-64	50	54	6
7	57-59	39-42	51-54	52-53	52-53	46-48	65	51-52	55-56	7
8	60-61	43-45	55-57	54-55	54-55	49-51	66	53-55	57-58	8
9	62-64	46-48	58-60	56-57	56-57	52-54	67-68	56-58	59-60	9
10	65-66	49-51	61-62	58-60	58-59	55-57	69-70	59-61	61-63	10
11	67-69	52-54	63-64	61-64	60-61	58-59	71	62-64	64-65	11
12	70-71	55-57	65	65-68	62-63	60-61	72	65-68	66-68	12
13	72	58-60	66-67	69-73	64-65	62-64	–	69-72	69	13
14	–	61-64	68	74-75	66	65-66	–	73-75	–	14
15	–	65-68	69	–	–	–	–	–	–	15
16	–	69	–	–	–	–	–	–	–	16
17	–	–	–	–	–	–	–	–	–	17
18	–	–	–	–	–	–	–	–	–	18
19	–	–	–	–	–	–	–	–	–	19

Note. **Com** = Communication; **CU** = Community Use; **FA** = Functional Academics; **HL** = Home Living; **HS** = Health and Safety; **LS** = Leisure; **SC** = Self-Care; **SD** = Self-Direction; **Soc** = Social.

Table A.5 Scaled Score Equivalents of Skill Area Raw Scores: Parent/Primary Caregiver and Parent Forms (*continued*)

Parent Form

Age 13

ss	Com	CU	FA	HL	HS	LS	SC	SD	Soc	ss
1	0-41	0-24	0-27	0-41	0-41	0-31	0-55	0-39	0-43	1
2	42-45	25-28	28-33	42-45	42-45	32-34	56-59	40-43	44-47	2
3	46-48	29-31	34-38	46-48	46-48	35-37	60-61	44-46	48-50	3
4	49-50	32-33	39-44	49	49-50	38-39	62	47-48	51-52	4
5	51-53	34-36	45-50	50-51	51	40-42	63-64	49	53	5
6	54-57	37-40	51-54	52	52	43-46	65	50-51	54	6
7	58-60	41-45	55-57	53-54	53-54	47-50	66	52-53	55-56	7
8	61-62	46-48	58-60	55-56	55-56	51-53	67-68	54-56	57-58	8
9	63-65	49-51	61-62	57-58	57-58	54-56	69	57-59	59-60	9
10	66-67	52-54	63-64	60-62	59-60	57-58	70	60-62	61-63	10
11	68-69	55-57	65	63-65	61-62	59-60	71	63-65	64-65	11
12	70-71	58-60	66	66-69	63-64	61-62	72	66-68	66-68	12
13	72	61-64	67	70-73	65	63-64	–	69-72	69	13
14	–	65-68	68	74-75	66	65-66	–	73-75	–	14
15	–	69	69	–	–	–	–	–	–	15
16	–	–	–	–	–	–	–	–	–	16
17	–	–	–	–	–	–	–	–	–	17
18	–	–	–	–	–	–	–	–	–	18
19	–	–	–	–	–	–	–	–	–	19

Age 14

ss	Com	CU	FA	HL	HS	LS	SC	SD	Soc	ss
1	0-41	0-24	0-29	0-42	0-41	0-31	0-55	0-39	0-43	1
2	42-45	25-28	30-36	43-46	42-45	32-34	56-59	40-43	44-47	2
3	46-48	29-31	37-42	47-49	46-48	35-37	60-62	44-46	48-50	3
4	49-50	32-33	43-47	50-51	49-50	38-39	63-64	47-48	51-52	4
5	51-53	34-36	48-51	–	51	40-42	–	49	53	5
6	54-57	37-40	52-55	52	52	43-46	65	50-51	54	6
7	58-60	41-45	56-58	53-54	53-54	47-50	66	52-53	55-56	7
8	61-62	46-49	59-60	55-56	55-56	51-53	67-68	54-56	57-58	8
9	63-65	49-51	61-62	57-59	57-58	54-56	69	57-59	59-60	9
10	66-67	54-56	63-64	60-62	59-60	57-58	70	60-62	61-63	10
11	68-69	57-59	65	63-65	61-62	59-60	71	63-65	64-65	11
12	70-71	60-62	66	66-69	63-64	61-62	72	66-68	66-68	12
13	72	63-65	67	70-73	65	63-64	–	69-72	69	13
14	–	66-68	68	74-75	66	65-66	–	73-75	–	14
15	–	69	69	–	–	–	–	–	–	15
16	–	–	–	–	–	–	–	–	–	16
17	–	–	–	–	–	–	–	–	–	17
18	–	–	–	–	–	–	–	–	–	18
19	–	–	–	–	–	–	–	–	–	19

Age 15

ss	Com	CU	FA	HL	HS	LS	SC	SD	Soc	ss
1	0-41	0-24	0-32	0-42	0-41	0-32	0-59	0-39	0-43	1
2	42-45	25-28	33-39	43-46	42-45	33-35	60-62	40-43	44-47	2
3	46-48	29-31	40-45	47-49	46-48	36-38	63	44-46	48-50	3
4	49-50	32-33	46-50	50-51	49-50	39-40	64	47-48	51-52	4
5	51-53	34-36	51-54	–	51-52	41-43	65	49	53	5
6	54-57	37-40	55-57	52	53-54	44-47	66	50-51	54	6
7	58-61	41-45	58-60	53-54	55-56	48-51	67-68	52-54	55-56	7
8	62-64	46-50	61-62	55-57	57-58	52-54	69	55-58	57-59	8
9	65-66	51-55	63-64	58-61	59-60	55-57	70	59-61	60-61	9
10	67-68	56-59	65	62-64	61-62	58-59	–	62-64	62-64	10
11	69-70	60-62	66	65-67	63-64	60-61	71	65-67	65-66	11
12	71	63-64	67	68-70	65	62-63	72	68-70	67-68	12
13	72	65-66	68	71-73	66	64-65	–	71-74	69	13
14	–	67-68	69	74-75	–	66	–	75	–	14
15	–	69	–	–	–	–	–	–	–	15
16	–	–	–	–	–	–	–	–	–	16
17	–	–	–	–	–	–	–	–	–	17
18	–	–	–	–	–	–	–	–	–	18
19	–	–	–	–	–	–	–	–	–	19

Age 16

ss	Com	CU	FA	HL	HS	LS	SC	SD	Soc	ss
1	0-41	0-24	0-32	0-42	0-41	0-32	0-61	0-39	0-43	1
2	42-45	25-28	33-39	43-46	42-45	33-35	62	40-43	44-47	2
3	46-48	29-31	40-45	47-49	46-48	36-38	63	44-46	48-50	3
4	49-50	32-33	46-50	50-51	49-50	39-40	64	47-48	51-52	4
5	51-53	34-36	51-54	–	51-52	41-43	65	49	53	5
6	54-57	37-40	55-57	52	53-54	44-47	66	50-51	54	6
7	58-61	41-45	58-60	53-54	55-57	48-51	67-68	52-54	55-56	7
8	62-64	46-50	61-62	55-57	58-59	52-54	69	55-58	57-59	8
9	65-66	51-55	63-64	58-61	60	55-57	70	59-61	60-61	9
10	67-68	56-59	65	62-64	61-62	58-59	–	62-64	62-64	10
11	69-70	60-62	66-67	65-67	63-64	60-61	71	65-67	65-66	11
12	71	63-64	68	68-70	65	62-63	72	68-70	67-68	12
13	72	65-66	69	71-73	66	64-65	–	71-74	69	13
14	–	67-68	–	74-75	–	66	–	75	–	14
15	–	69	–	–	–	–	–	–	–	15
16	–	–	–	–	–	–	–	–	–	16
17	–	–	–	–	–	–	–	–	–	17
18	–	–	–	–	–	–	–	–	–	18
19	–	–	–	–	–	–	–	–	–	19

Note. **Com** = Communication; **CU** = Community Use; **FA** = Functional Academics; **HL** = Home Living; **HS** = Health and Safety; **LS** = Leisure; **SC** = Self-Care; **SD** = Self-Direction; **Soc** = Social.

A
Parent
Ages 5–21

Table A.5   Scaled Score Equivalents of Skill Area Raw Scores:
Parent/Primary Caregiver and Parent Forms *(continued)*

Parent Form

Ages 17–21

ss	Com	CU	FA	HL	HS	LS	SC	SD	Soc	WK	ss
1	0–41	0–30	0–32	0–42	0–41	0–32	0–61	0–39	0–43	0–39	1
2	42–45	31–32	33–39	43–46	42–45	33–35	62	40–43	44–47	40–44	2
3	46–48	33–34	40–45	47–49	46–48	36–38	63	44–46	48–50	45–48	3
4	49–50	35–36	46–50	50–51	49–50	39–40	64	47–48	51–52	49–51	4
5	51–53	37–39	51–54	–	51–52	41–43	65	49–50	53	52–53	5
6	54–57	40–43	55–58	52	53–55	44–47	66	51–53	54–55	54	6
7	58–61	44–48	59–61	53–54	56–58	48–51	67–68	54–56	56–58	55–56	7
8	62–65	49–53	62–63	55–57	59–60	52–55	69	57–60	59–61	57–58	8
9	66–68	54–58	64–65	58–61	61–62	56–58	70	61–64	62–64	59	9
10	69–70	59–62	66	62–65	63	59–61	–	65–67	65–66	60	10
11	71	63–65	67	66–69	64	62–63	71	68–70	67–68	61	11
12	72	66–67	68–69	70–72	65–66	64	72	71–73	69	62	12
13	–	68	–	73–75	–	65–66	–	74–75	–	63	13
14	–	69	–	–	–	–	–	–	–	–	14
15	–	–	–	–	–	–	–	–	–	–	15
16	–	–	–	–	–	–	–	–	–	–	16
17	–	–	–	–	–	–	–	–	–	–	17
18	–	–	–	–	–	–	–	–	–	–	18
19	–	–	–	–	–	–	–	–	–	–	19

Note. **Com** = Communication; **CU** = Community Use; **FA** = Functional Academics; **HL** = Home Living;
HS = Health and Safety; **LS** = Leisure; **SC** = Self-Care; **SD** = Self-Direction; **Soc** = Social; **WK** = Work.

Table A.6 GAC and Adaptive Domain Composite Equivalents of Sums of Scaled Scores: Parent/Primary Caregiver and Parent Forms

Parent/Primary Caregiver Form — Ages 0:0–0:3

	GAC	CON	SO	PR
90% Confidence Interval ±	9	14	11	15
95% Confidence Interval ±	11	16	13	17

Composite Score	Percentile Rank	GAC	CON	SO	PR	Composite Score	Percentile Rank	GAC	CON	SO	PR
40	<0.1	7–16	–	–	–	101	53	72	–	–	–
41	<0.1	17	–	–	–	102	55	73	–	21	–
42	<0.1	18	–	–	–	103	58	74	–	–	21
43	<0.1	19	–	–	–	104	61	75	21	–	–
44	<0.1	20	–	–	–	105	63	76	–	22	–
45	<0.1	21	–	–	–	106	66	–	–	–	–
46	<0.1	22	–	–	–	107	68	77	–	–	22
47	<0.1	23	–	–	–	108	70	78	22	23	–
48	<0.1	24	–	2	–	109	73	–	–	–	–
49	<0.1	25	–	–	–	110	75	79	–	–	23
50	<0.1	26	2	3	2	111	77	80	23	24	–
51	0.1	27	–	–	–	112	79	81	–	–	–
52	0.1	–	–	4	3	113	81	–	–	25	24
53	0.1	28	3	–	–	114	82	82	24	–	–
54	0.1	29	–	5	–	115	84	83	–	–	–
55	0.1	–	4	–	4	116	86	–	–	26	25
56	0.2	30	–	6	–	117	87	84	25	–	–
57	0.2	31	5	–	5	118	88	85	–	27	–
58	0.3	32	–	–	–	119	90	86	–	–	26
59	0.3	33	6	7	6	120	91	87	26	–	–
60	0.4	34	–	–	–	121	92	88	–	28	–
61	0.5	35	7	–	7	122	93	89	–	–	27
62	1	36	–	8	–	123	94	90	27	–	–
63	1	37	8	–	8	124	95	91	–	29	–
64	1	38	–	–	–	125	95	92	–	–	28
65	1	39	9	9	–	126	96	93	28	–	–
66	1	40	–	–	9	127	96	94–95	–	30	–
67	1	41	–	–	–	128	97	96	–	–	29
68	2	42	10	10	–	129	97	97	29	–	–
69	2	43	–	–	10	130	98	98	–	31	–
70	2	44	–	–	–	131	98	99	–	–	30
71	3	45	11	11	11	132	98	100	30	–	–
72	3	46	–	–	–	133	99	101–102	–	32	–
73	4	47	–	–	–	134	99	103–104	–	–	31
74	4	48	12	12	12	135	99	105	31	–	–
75	5	49	–	–	–	136	99	106	–	33	32
76	5	50	–	–	–	137	99	107	32	–	–
77	6	51	13	13	13	138	99	108	–	–	33
78	7	52	–	–	–	139	99.5	109	33	34	–
79	8	53	–	–	–	140	99.6	110	–	–	34
80	9	54	14	14	14	141	99.7	111	34	–	–
81	10	55	–	–	–	142	99.7	112	–	35	–
82	12	56	–	–	–	143	99.8	113	35	–	35
83	13	57	15	15	15	144	99.8	114	–	–	–
84	14	58	–	–	–	145	99.9	115	–	36	36
85	16	59	–	–	–	146	99.9	116	36	–	–
86	18	60	16	–	16	147	99.9	117	–	–	37
87	19	61	–	16	–	148	99.9	118	37	37	–
88	21	62	–	–	–	149	99.9	119	–	–	38
89	23	–	17	–	17	150	>99.9	120	38	–	–
90	25	63	–	17	–	151	>99.9	121	–	38	–
91	27	64	–	–	–	152	>99.9	122	–	–	–
92	30	–	–	–	18	153	>99.9	123	–	–	–
93	32	65	18	18	–	154	>99.9	124	–	–	–
94	34	66	–	–	–	155	>99.9	125	–	–	–
95	37	67	–	–	19	156	>99.9	126	–	–	–
96	39	68	19	19	–	157	>99.9	127	–	–	–
97	42	–	–	–	–	158	>99.9	128	–	–	–
98	45	69	–	–	–	159	>99.9	129	–	–	–
99	47	70	–	20	20	160	>99.9	130–133	–	–	–
100	50	71	20	–	–						

Note. **CON** = Conceptual Adaptive Domain; **SO** = Social Adaptive Domain; **PR** = Practical Adaptive Domain.

Table A.6 GAC and Adaptive Domain Composite Equivalents of Sums of Scaled Scores: Parent/Primary Caregiver and Parent Forms (continued)

Parent/Primary Caregiver Form — **Ages 0:4–0:7**

Composite Score	Percentile Rank	GAC	CON	SO	PR	Composite Score	Percentile Rank	GAC	CON	SO	PR
90% Confidence Interval ±		6	11	9	9	90% Confidence Interval ±		6	11	9	9
95% Confidence Interval ±		7	13	10	11	95% Confidence Interval ±		7	13	10	11
		Sums of Scaled Scores						*Sums of Scaled Scores*			
40	<0.1	7–16	–	–	–	101	53	72	–	–	–
41	<0.1	17	–	–	–	102	55	73	–	21	–
42	<0.1	18	–	–	–	103	58	74	–	–	21
43	<0.1	19	–	–	–	104	61	75	21	–	–
44	<0.1	20	–	–	–	105	63	76	–	22	–
45	<0.1	21	–	–	–	106	66	–	–	–	–
46	<0.1	22	–	–	–	107	68	77	–	–	22
47	<0.1	23	–	–	–	108	70	78	22	23	–
48	<0.1	24	–	2	–	109	73	–	–	–	–
49	<0.1	25	–	–	–	110	75	79	–	–	23
50	<0.1	26	2	3	2	111	77	80	23	24	–
51	0.1	27	–	–	–	112	79	81	–	–	–
52	0.1	–	–	4	3	113	81	–	–	25	24
53	0.1	28	3	–	–	114	82	82	24	–	–
54	0.1	29	–	5	–	115	84	83	–	–	–
55	0.1	–	4	–	4	116	86	–	–	26	25
56	0.2	30	–	6	–	117	87	84	25	–	–
57	0.2	31	5	–	5	118	88	85	–	27	–
58	0.3	32	–	–	–	119	90	86	–	–	26
59	0.3	33	6	7	6	120	91	87	26	–	–
60	0.4	34	–	–	–	121	92	88	–	28	–
61	0.5	35	7	–	7	122	93	89	–	–	27
62	1	36	–	8	–	123	94	90	27	–	–
63	1	37	8	–	8	124	95	91	–	29	–
64	1	38	–	–	–	125	95	92	–	–	28
65	1	39	9	9	–	126	96	93	28	–	–
66	1	40	–	–	9	127	96	94–95	–	30	–
67	1	41	–	–	–	128	97	96	–	–	29
68	2	42	10	10	–	129	97	97	29	–	–
69	2	43	–	–	10	130	98	98	–	31	–
70	2	44	–	–	–	131	98	99	–	–	30
71	3	45	11	11	11	132	98	100	30	–	–
72	3	46	–	–	–	133	99	101–102	–	32	–
73	4	47	–	–	–	134	99	103–104	–	–	31
74	4	48	12	12	12	135	99	105	31	–	–
75	5	49	–	–	–	136	99	106	–	33	32
76	5	50	–	–	–	137	99	107	32	–	–
77	6	51	13	13	13	138	99	108	–	–	33
78	7	52	–	–	–	139	99.5	109	33	34	–
79	8	53	–	–	–	140	99.6	110	–	–	34
80	9	54	14	14	14	141	99.7	111	34	–	–
81	10	55	–	–	–	142	99.7	112	–	35	–
82	12	56	–	–	–	143	99.8	113	35	–	35
83	13	57	15	15	15	144	99.8	114	–	–	–
84	14	58	–	–	–	145	99.9	115	–	36	36
85	16	59	–	–	–	146	99.9	116	36	–	–
86	18	60	16	–	16	147	99.9	117	–	–	37
87	19	61	–	16	–	148	99.9	118	37	37	–
88	21	62	–	–	–	149	99.9	119	–	–	38
89	23	–	17	–	17	150	>99.9	120	38	–	–
90	25	63	–	17	–	151	>99.9	121	–	38	–
91	27	64	–	–	–	152	>99.9	122	–	–	–
92	30	–	–	–	18	153	>99.9	123	–	–	–
93	32	65	18	18	–	154	>99.9	124	–	–	–
94	34	66	–	–	–	155	>99.9	125	–	–	–
95	37	67	–	–	19	156	>99.9	126	–	–	–
96	39	68	19	19	–	157	>99.9	127	–	–	–
97	42	–	–	–	–	158	>99.9	128	–	–	–
98	45	69	–	–	–	159	>99.9	129	–	–	–
99	47	70	–	20	20	160	>99.9	130–133	–	–	–
100	50	71	20	–	–						

Note. **CON** = Conceptual Adaptive Domain; **SO** = Social Adaptive Domain; **PR** = Practical Adaptive Domain.

Parent/Primary Caregiver Ages 0–5

A

Table A.6 GAC and Adaptive Domain Composite Equivalents of Sums of Scaled Scores: Parent/Primary Caregiver and Parent Forms (continued)

Parent/Primary Caregiver Form — **Ages 0:8–0:11**

		GAC	CON	SO	PR
90% Confidence Interval ±		6	10	8	10
95% Confidence Interval ±		7	12	10	12

Composite Score	Percentile Rank	Sums of Scaled Scores			
		GAC	CON	SO	PR
40	<0.1	7–16	–	–	–
41	<0.1	17	–	–	–
42	<0.1	18	–	–	–
43	<0.1	19	–	–	–
44	<0.1	20	–	–	–
45	<0.1	21	–	–	–
46	<0.1	22	–	–	–
47	<0.1	23	–	–	–
48	<0.1	24	–	2	–
49	<0.1	25	–	–	–
50	<0.1	26	2	3	2
51	0.1	27	–	–	–
52	0.1	–	–	4	3
53	0.1	28	3	–	–
54	0.1	29	–	5	–
55	0.1	–	4	–	4
56	0.2	30	–	6	–
57	0.2	31	5	–	5
58	0.3	32	–	–	–
59	0.3	33	6	7	6
60	0.4	34	–	–	–
61	0.5	35	7	–	7
62	1	36	–	8	–
63	1	37	8	–	8
64	1	38	–	–	–
65	1	39	9	9	–
66	1	40	–	–	9
67	1	41	–	–	–
68	2	42	10	10	–
69	2	43	–	–	10
70	2	44	–	–	–
71	3	45	11	11	11
72	3	46	–	–	–
73	4	47	–	–	–
74	4	48	12	12	12
75	5	49	–	–	–
76	5	50	–	–	–
77	6	51	13	13	13
78	7	52	–	–	–
79	8	53	–	–	–
80	9	54	14	14	14
81	10	55	–	–	–
82	12	56	–	–	–
83	13	57	15	15	15
84	14	58	–	–	–
85	16	59	–	–	–
86	18	60	16	–	16
87	19	61	–	16	–
88	21	62	–	–	–
89	23	–	17	–	17
90	25	63	–	17	–
91	27	64	–	–	–
92	30	–	–	–	18
93	32	65	18	18	–
94	34	66	–	–	–
95	37	67	–	–	19
96	39	68	19	19	–
97	42	–	–	–	–
98	45	69	–	–	–
99	47	70	–	20	20
100	50	71	20	–	–

		GAC	CON	SO	PR
90% Confidence Interval ±		6	10	8	10
95% Confidence Interval ±		7	12	10	12

Composite Score	Percentile Rank	Sums of Scaled Scores			
		GAC	CON	SO	PR
101	53	72	–	–	–
102	55	73	–	21	–
103	58	74	–	–	21
104	61	75	21	–	–
105	63	76	–	22	–
106	66	–	–	–	–
107	68	77	–	–	22
108	70	78	22	23	–
109	73	–	–	–	–
110	75	79	–	–	23
111	77	80	23	24	–
112	79	81	–	–	–
113	81	–	–	25	24
114	82	82	24	–	–
115	84	83	–	–	–
116	86	–	–	26	25
117	87	84	25	–	–
118	88	85	–	27	–
119	90	86	–	–	26
120	91	87	26	–	–
121	92	88	–	28	–
122	93	89	–	–	27
123	94	90	27	–	–
124	95	91	–	29	–
125	95	92	–	–	28
126	96	93	28	–	–
127	96	94–95	–	30	–
128	97	96	–	–	29
129	97	97	29	–	–
130	98	98	–	31	–
131	98	99	–	–	30
132	98	100	30	–	–
133	99	101–102	–	32	–
134	99	103–104	–	–	31
135	99	105	31	–	–
136	99	106	–	33	32
137	99	107	32	–	–
138	99	108	–	–	33
139	99.5	109	33	34	–
140	99.6	110	–	–	34
141	99.7	111	34	–	–
142	99.7	112	–	35	–
143	99.8	113	35	–	35
144	99.8	114	–	–	–
145	99.9	115	–	36	36
146	99.9	116	36	–	–
147	99.9	117	–	–	37
148	99.9	118	37	37	–
149	99.9	119	–	–	38
150	>99.9	120	38	–	–
151	>99.9	121	–	38	–
152	>99.9	122	–	–	–
153	>99.9	123	–	–	–
154	>99.9	124	–	–	–
155	>99.9	125	–	–	–
156	>99.9	126	–	–	–
157	>99.9	127	–	–	–
158	>99.9	128	–	–	–
159	>99.9	129	–	–	–
160	>99.9	130–133	–	–	–

Note. **CON** = Conceptual Adaptive Domain; **SO** = Social Adaptive Domain; **PR** = Practical Adaptive Domain.

A
Parent/Primary Caregiver
Ages 0–5

Table A.6 GAC and Adaptive Domain Composite Equivalents of Sums of Scaled Scores: Parent/Primary Caregiver and Parent Forms (continued)

Parent/Primary Caregiver Form   **Ages 1:0–1:3**

		GAC	CON	SO	PR			GAC	CON	SO	PR
90% Confidence Interval ±		4	7	7	6	90% Confidence Interval ±		4	7	7	6
95% Confidence Interval ±		5	8	9	7	95% Confidence Interval ±		5	8	9	7
Composite Score	Percentile Rank	GAC	CON	SO	PR	Composite Score	Percentile Rank	GAC	CON	SO	PR
40	<0.1	10	–	–	–	101	53	103–104	31	–	41
41	<0.1	11–12	–	–	4	102	55	105	–	21	42
42	<0.1	13	–	–	–	103	58	106–107	32	–	43
43	<0.1	14	–	–	5	104	61	108	–	–	–
44	<0.1	15	–	–	–	105	63	109–110	33	22	44
45	<0.1	16–17	3	–	6	106	66	111–112	–	–	45
46	<0.1	18–19	–	–	–	107	68	113	34	–	46
47	<0.1	20–21	4	–	7	108	70	114–115	–	23	–
48	<0.1	22–23	–	2	–	109	73	116	35	–	47
49	<0.1	24–25	5	–	8	110	75	117	–	–	–
50	<0.1	26–27	6	3	9	111	77	118–119	36	24	48
51	0.1	28–29	–	–	–	112	79	120	–	–	49
52	0.1	30–31	7	4	10	113	81	121–122	37	25	–
53	0.1	32–33	8	–	11	114	82	123–124	–	–	50
54	0.1	34–35	–	5	–	115	84	125–126	38	–	–
55	0.1	36–37	9	–	12	116	86	127	–	26	51
56	0.2	38–39	10	6	13	117	87	128	39	–	–
57	0.2	40–41	11	–	–	118	88	129	–	27	52
58	0.3	42–43	–	–	14	119	90	130–131	40	–	–
59	0.3	44–45	12	7	15	120	91	132–133	–	–	53
60	0.4	46–47	–	–	–	121	92	134–135	41	28	–
61	0.5	48–49	13	–	16	122	93	136	–	–	54
62	1	50–51	–	8	17	123	94	137	42	–	55
63	1	52–53	14	–	–	124	95	138	–	29	56
64	1	54–55	–	–	18	125	95	139	43	–	–
65	1	56–57	15	9	19	126	96	140–141	–	–	57
66	1	58–59	–	–	–	127	96	142–143	44	30	58
67	1	60–61	16	–	20	128	97	144	–	–	–
68	2	62	–	10	21	129	97	145	45	–	59
69	2	63	17	–	–	130	98	146	–	31	–
70	2	64	–	–	22	131	98	147	46	–	60
71	3	65	18	11	23	132	98	148–149	–	–	–
72	3	66	–	–	–	133	99	150–151	47	32	61
73	4	67	19	–	24	134	99	152–153	–	–	–
74	4	68	–	12	25	135	99	154–155	48	–	62
75	5	69	–	–	–	136	99	156–157	–	33	–
76	5	70	20	–	26	137	99	158	49	–	63
77	6	71	–	13	27	138	99	159	–	–	64
78	7	72	–	–	–	139	99.5	160–161	50	34	–
79	8	73	21	–	28	140	99.6	162–163	–	–	65
80	9	74	–	14	29	141	99.7	164	51	–	–
81	10	75	–	–	–	142	99.7	165–166	–	35	66
82	12	76	22	–	30	143	99.8	167	–	–	67
83	13	77	–	15	31	144	99.8	168–169	52	–	–
84	14	78	23	–	32	145	99.9	170	–	36	68
85	16	79–80	–	–	–	146	99.9	171	53	–	–
86	18	81	24	–	33	147	99.9	172–173	–	–	69
87	19	82–83	–	16	–	148	99.9	174–175	54	37	70
88	21	84	25	–	34	149	99.9	176–177	–	–	–
89	23	85–86	–	–	–	150	>99.9	178	55	–	71
90	25	87	26	17	35	151	>99.9	179	–	38	–
91	27	88	–	–	–	152	>99.9	180–181	56	–	72
92	30	89–90	–	–	36	153	>99.9	182	–	–	73
93	32	91–92	27	18	–	154	>99.9	183–184	–	–	–
94	34	93	–	–	37	155	>99.9	185	57	–	74
95	37	94	28	–	–	156	>99.9	186	–	–	–
96	39	95	–	19	38	157	>99.9	187	–	–	75
97	42	96	29	–	–	158	>99.9	188	–	–	76
98	45	97–98	–	–	39	159	>99.9	189	–	–	–
99	47	99–100	30	20	40	160	>99.9	190	–	–	–
100	50	101–102	–	–	–						

Note. **CON** = Conceptual Adaptive Domain; **SO** = Social Adaptive Domain; **PR** = Practical Adaptive Domain.

Parent/Primary Caregiver Form — **Ages 1:4–1:7**

Composite Score	Percentile Rank	GAC	CON	SO	PR	Composite Score	Percentile Rank	GAC	CON	SO	PR
	90% Confidence Interval ±	3	6	8	6		90% Confidence Interval ±	3	6	8	6
	95% Confidence Interval ±	4	7	10	7		95% Confidence Interval ±	4	7	10	7
		Sums of Scaled Scores						Sums of Scaled Scores			
40	<0.1	10	–	–	–	101	53	103–104	31	–	41
41	<0.1	11–12	–	–	4	102	55	105	–	21	42
42	<0.1	13	–	–	–	103	58	106–107	32	–	43
43	<0.1	14	–	–	5	104	61	108	–	–	–
44	<0.1	15	–	–	–	105	63	109–110	33	22	44
45	<0.1	16–17	3	–	6	106	66	111–112	–	–	45
46	<0.1	18–19	–	–	–	107	68	113	34	–	46
47	<0.1	20–21	4	–	7	108	70	114–115	–	23	–
48	<0.1	22–23	–	2	–	109	73	116	35	–	47
49	<0.1	24–25	5	–	8	110	75	117	–	–	–
50	<0.1	26–27	6	3	9	111	77	118–119	36	24	48
51	0.1	28–29	–	–	–	112	79	120	–	–	49
52	0.1	30–31	7	4	10	113	81	121–122	37	25	–
53	0.1	32–33	8	–	11	114	82	123–124	–	–	50
54	0.1	34–35	–	5	–	115	84	125–126	38	–	–
55	0.1	36–37	9	–	12	116	86	127	–	26	51
56	0.2	38–39	10	6	13	117	87	128	39	–	–
57	0.2	40–41	11	–	–	118	88	129	–	27	52
58	0.3	42–43	–	–	14	119	90	130–131	40	–	–
59	0.3	44–45	12	7	15	120	91	132–133	–	–	53
60	0.4	46–47	–	–	–	121	92	134–135	41	28	–
61	0.5	48–49	13	–	16	122	93	136	–	–	54
62	1	50–51	–	8	17	123	94	137	42	–	55
63	1	52–53	14	–	–	124	95	138	–	29	56
64	1	54–55	–	–	18	125	95	139	43	–	–
65	1	56–57	15	9	19	126	96	140–141	–	–	57
66	1	58–59	–	–	–	127	96	142–143	44	30	58
67	1	60–61	16	–	20	128	97	144	–	–	–
68	2	62	–	10	21	129	97	145	45	–	59
69	2	63	17	–	–	130	98	146	–	31	–
70	2	64	–	–	22	131	98	147	46	–	60
71	3	65	18	11	23	132	98	148–149	–	–	–
72	3	66	–	–	–	133	99	150–151	47	32	61
73	4	67	19	–	24	134	99	152–153	–	–	–
74	4	68	–	12	25	135	99	154–155	48	–	62
75	5	69	–	–	–	136	99	156–157	–	33	–
76	5	70	20	–	26	137	99	158	49	–	63
77	6	71	–	13	27	138	99	159	–	–	64
78	7	72	–	–	–	139	99.5	160–161	50	34	–
79	8	73	21	–	28	140	99.6	162–163	–	–	65
80	9	74	–	14	29	141	99.7	164	51	–	–
81	10	75	–	–	–	142	99.7	165–166	–	35	66
82	12	76	22	–	30	143	99.8	167	–	–	67
83	13	77	–	15	31	144	99.8	168–169	52	–	–
84	14	78	23	–	32	145	99.9	170	–	36	68
85	16	79–80	–	–	–	146	99.9	171	53	–	–
86	18	81	24	–	33	147	99.9	172–173	–	–	69
87	19	82–83	–	16	–	148	99.9	174–175	54	37	70
88	21	84	25	–	34	149	99.9	176–177	–	–	–
89	23	85–86	–	–	–	150	>99.9	178	55	–	71
90	25	87	26	17	35	151	>99.9	179	–	38	–
91	27	88	–	–	–	152	>99.9	180–181	56	–	72
92	30	89–90	–	–	36	153	>99.9	182	–	–	73
93	32	91–92	27	18	–	154	>99.9	183–184	–	–	–
94	34	93	–	–	37	155	>99.9	185	57	–	74
95	37	94	28	–	–	156	>99.9	186	–	–	–
96	39	95	–	19	38	157	>99.9	187	–	–	75
97	42	96	29	–	–	158	>99.9	188	–	–	76
98	45	97–98	–	–	39	159	>99.9	189	–	–	–
99	47	99–100	30	20	40	160	>99.9	190	–	–	–
100	50	101–102	–	–	–						

Note. **CON** = Conceptual Adaptive Domain; **SO** = Social Adaptive Domain; **PR** = Practical Adaptive Domain.

A
Parent/Primary Caregiver
Ages 0–5

Table A.6 GAC and Adaptive Domain Composite Equivalents of Sums of Scaled Scores: Parent/Primary Caregiver and Parent Forms (continued)

Parent/Primary Caregiver Form — Ages 1:8–1:11

		GAC	CON	SO	PR			GAC	CON	SO	PR
90% Confidence Interval ±		4	7	8	6	90% Confidence Interval ±		4	7	8	6
95% Confidence Interval ±		5	8	9	7	95% Confidence Interval ±		5	8	9	7
Composite Score	Percentile Rank	Sums of Scaled Scores				Composite Score	Percentile Rank	Sums of Scaled Scores			
40	<0.1	10	–	–	–	101	53	103–104	31	–	41
41	<0.1	11–12	–	–	4	102	55	105	–	21	42
42	<0.1	13	–	–	–	103	58	106–107	32	–	43
43	<0.1	14	–	–	5	104	61	108	–	–	–
44	<0.1	15	–	–	–	105	63	109–110	33	22	44
45	<0.1	16–17	3	–	6	106	66	111–112	–	–	45
46	<0.1	18–19	–	–	–	107	68	113	34	–	46
47	<0.1	20–21	4	–	7	108	70	114–115	–	23	–
48	<0.1	22–23	–	2	–	109	73	116	35	–	47
49	<0.1	24–25	5	–	8	110	75	117	–	–	–
50	<0.1	26–27	6	3	9	111	77	118–119	36	24	48
51	0.1	28–29	–	–	–	112	79	120	–	–	49
52	0.1	30–31	7	4	10	113	81	121–122	37	25	–
53	0.1	32–33	8	–	11	114	82	123–124	–	–	50
54	0.1	34–35	–	5	–	115	84	125–126	38	–	–
55	0.1	36–37	9	–	12	116	86	127	–	26	51
56	0.2	38–39	10	6	13	117	87	128	39	–	–
57	0.2	40–41	11	–	–	118	88	129	–	27	52
58	0.3	42–43	–	–	14	119	90	130–131	40	–	–
59	0.3	44–45	12	7	15	120	91	132–133	–	–	53
60	0.4	46–47	–	–	–	121	92	134–135	41	28	–
61	0.5	48–49	13	–	16	122	93	136	–	–	54
62	1	50–51	–	8	17	123	94	137	42	–	55
63	1	52–53	14	–	–	124	95	138	–	29	56
64	1	54–55	–	–	18	125	95	139	43	–	–
65	1	56–57	15	9	19	126	96	140–141	–	–	57
66	1	58–59	–	–	–	127	96	142–143	44	30	58
67	1	60–61	16	–	20	128	97	144	–	–	–
68	2	62	–	10	21	129	97	145	45	–	59
69	2	63	17	–	–	130	98	146	–	31	–
70	2	64	–	–	22	131	98	147	46	–	60
71	3	65	18	11	23	132	98	148–149	–	–	–
72	3	66	–	–	–	133	99	150–151	47	32	61
73	4	67	19	–	24	134	99	152–153	–	–	–
74	4	68	–	12	25	135	99	154–155	48	–	62
75	5	69	–	–	–	136	99	156–157	–	33	–
76	5	70	20	–	26	137	99	158	49	–	63
77	6	71	–	13	27	138	99	159	–	–	64
78	7	72	–	–	–	139	99.5	160–161	50	34	–
79	8	73	21	–	28	140	99.6	162–163	–	–	65
80	9	74	–	14	29	141	99.7	164	51	–	–
81	10	75	–	–	–	142	99.7	165–166	–	35	66
82	12	76	22	–	30	143	99.8	167	–	–	67
83	13	77	–	15	31	144	99.8	168–169	52	–	–
84	14	78	23	–	32	145	99.9	170	–	36	68
85	16	79–80	–	–	–	146	99.9	171	53	–	–
86	18	81	24	–	33	147	99.9	172–173	–	–	69
87	19	82–83	–	16	–	148	99.9	174–175	54	37	70
88	21	84	25	–	34	149	99.9	176–177	–	–	–
89	23	85–86	–	–	–	150	>99.9	178	55	–	71
90	25	87	26	17	35	151	>99.9	179	–	38	–
91	27	88	–	–	–	152	>99.9	180–181	56	–	72
92	30	89–90	–	–	36	153	>99.9	182	–	–	73
93	32	91–92	27	18	–	154	>99.9	183–184	–	–	–
94	34	93	–	–	37	155	>99.9	185	57	–	74
95	37	94	28	–	–	156	>99.9	186	–	–	–
96	39	95	–	19	38	157	>99.9	187	–	–	75
97	42	96	29	–	–	158	>99.9	188	–	–	76
98	45	97–98	–	–	39	159	>99.9	189	–	–	–
99	47	99–100	30	20	40	160	>99.9	190	–	–	–
100	50	101–102	–	–	–						

Note. **CON** = Conceptual Adaptive Domain; **SO** = Social Adaptive Domain; **PR** = Practical Adaptive Domain.

Table A.6 GAC and Adaptive Domain Composite Equivalents of Sums of Scaled Scores: Parent/Primary Caregiver and Parent Forms (continued)

Parent/Primary Caregiver Form   **Ages 2:0–2:5**

		GAC	CON	SO	PR			GAC	CON	SO	PR
90% Confidence Interval ±		3	5	6	5	90% Confidence Interval ±		3	5	6	5
95% Confidence Interval ±		4	6	7	6	95% Confidence Interval ±		4	6	7	6
Composite Score	Percentile Rank	\<Sums of Scaled Scores				Composite Score	Percentile Rank	Sums of Scaled Scores			
40	<0.1	10	–	–	–	101	53	103–104	31	–	41
41	<0.1	11–12	–	–	4	102	55	105	–	21	42
42	<0.1	13	–	–	–	103	58	106–107	32	–	43
43	<0.1	14	–	–	5	104	61	108	–	–	–
44	<0.1	15	–	–	–	105	63	109–110	33	22	44
45	<0.1	16–17	3	–	6	106	66	111–112	–	–	45
46	<0.1	18–19	–	–	–	107	68	113	34	–	46
47	<0.1	20–21	4	–	7	108	70	114–115	–	23	–
48	<0.1	22–23	–	2	–	109	73	116	35	–	47
49	<0.1	24–25	5	–	8	110	75	117	–	–	–
50	<0.1	26–27	6	3	9	111	77	118–119	36	24	48
51	0.1	28–29	–	–	–	112	79	120	–	–	49
52	0.1	30–31	7	4	10	113	81	121–122	37	25	–
53	0.1	32–33	8	–	11	114	82	123–124	–	–	50
54	0.1	34–35	–	5	–	115	84	125–126	38	–	–
55	0.1	36–37	9	–	12	116	86	127	–	26	51
56	0.2	38–39	10	6	13	117	87	128	39	–	–
57	0.2	40–41	11	–	–	118	88	129	–	27	52
58	0.3	42–43	–	–	14	119	90	130–131	40	–	–
59	0.3	44–45	12	7	15	120	91	132–133	–	–	53
60	0.4	46–47	–	–	–	121	92	134–135	41	28	–
61	0.5	48–49	13	–	16	122	93	136	–	–	54
62	1	50–51	–	8	17	123	94	137	42	–	55
63	1	52–53	14	–	–	124	95	138	–	29	56
64	1	54–55	–	–	18	125	95	139	43	–	–
65	1	56–57	15	9	19	126	96	140–141	–	–	57
66	1	58–59	–	–	–	127	96	142–143	44	30	58
67	1	60–61	16	–	20	128	97	144	–	–	–
68	2	62	–	10	21	129	97	145	45	–	59
69	2	63	17	–	–	130	98	146	–	31	–
70	2	64	–	–	22	131	98	147	46	–	60
71	3	65	18	11	23	132	98	148–149	–	–	–
72	3	66	–	–	–	133	99	150–151	47	32	61
73	4	67	19	–	24	134	99	152–153	–	–	–
74	4	68	–	12	25	135	99	154–155	48	–	62
75	5	69	–	–	–	136	99	156–157	–	33	–
76	5	70	20	–	26	137	99	158	49	–	63
77	6	71	–	13	27	138	99	159	–	–	64
78	7	72	–	–	–	139	99.5	160–161	50	34	–
79	8	73	21	–	28	140	99.6	162–163	–	–	65
80	9	74	–	14	29	141	99.7	164	51	–	–
81	10	75	–	–	–	142	99.7	165–166	–	35	66
82	12	76	22	–	30	143	99.8	167	–	–	67
83	13	77	–	15	31	144	99.8	168–169	52	–	–
84	14	78	23	–	32	145	99.9	170	–	36	68
85	16	79–80	–	–	–	146	99.9	171	53	–	–
86	18	81	24	–	33	147	99.9	172–173	–	–	69
87	19	82–83	–	16	–	148	99.9	174–175	54	37	70
88	21	84	25	–	34	149	99.9	176–177	–	–	–
89	23	85–86	–	–	–	150	>99.9	178	55	–	71
90	25	87	26	17	35	151	>99.9	179	–	38	–
91	27	88	–	–	–	152	>99.9	180–181	56	–	72
92	30	89–90	–	–	36	153	>99.9	182	–	–	73
93	32	91–92	27	18	–	154	>99.9	183–184	–	–	–
94	34	93	–	–	37	155	>99.9	185	57	–	74
95	37	94	28	–	–	156	>99.9	186	–	–	–
96	39	95	–	19	38	157	>99.9	187	–	–	75
97	42	96	29	–	–	158	>99.9	188	–	–	76
98	45	97–98	–	–	39	159	>99.9	189	–	–	–
99	47	99–100	30	20	40	160	>99.9	190	–	–	–
100	50	101–102	–	–	–						

Note. **CON** = Conceptual Adaptive Domain; **SO** = Social Adaptive Domain; **PR** = Practical Adaptive Domain.

Table A.6 GAC and Adaptive Domain Composite Equivalents of Sums of Scaled Scores: Parent/Primary Caregiver and Parent Forms (continued)

Parent/Primary Caregiver Form   **Ages 2:6–2:11**

		GAC	CON	SO	PR
90% Confidence Interval ±		4	6	7	6
95% Confidence Interval ±		5	7	9	7
Composite Score	Percentile Rank	Sums of Scaled Scores			

Composite Score	Percentile Rank	GAC	CON	SO	PR
40	<0.1	10	–	–	–
41	<0.1	11–12	–	–	4
42	<0.1	13	–	–	–
43	<0.1	14	–	–	5
44	<0.1	15	–	–	–
45	<0.1	16–17	3	–	6
46	<0.1	18–19	–	–	–
47	<0.1	20–21	4	–	7
48	<0.1	22–23	–	2	–
49	<0.1	24–25	5	–	8
50	<0.1	26–27	6	3	9
51	0.1	28–29	–	–	–
52	0.1	30–31	7	4	10
53	0.1	32–33	8	–	11
54	0.1	34–35	–	5	–
55	0.1	36–37	9	–	12
56	0.2	38–39	10	6	13
57	0.2	40–41	11	–	–
58	0.3	42–43	–	–	14
59	0.3	44–45	12	7	15
60	0.4	46–47	–	–	–
61	0.5	48–49	13	–	16
62	1	50–51	–	8	17
63	1	52–53	14	–	–
64	1	54–55	–	–	18
65	1	56–57	15	9	19
66	1	58–59	–	–	–
67	1	60–61	16	–	20
68	2	62	–	10	21
69	2	63	17	–	–
70	2	64	–	–	22
71	3	65	18	11	23
72	3	66	–	–	–
73	4	67	19	–	24
74	4	68	–	12	25
75	5	69	–	–	–
76	5	70	20	–	26
77	6	71	–	13	27
78	7	72	–	–	–
79	8	73	21	–	28
80	9	74	–	14	29
81	10	75	–	–	–
82	12	76	22	–	30
83	13	77	–	15	31
84	14	78	23	–	32
85	16	79–80	–	–	–
86	18	81	24	–	33
87	19	82–83	–	16	–
88	21	84	25	–	34
89	23	85–86	–	–	–
90	25	87	26	17	35
91	27	88	–	–	–
92	30	89–90	–	–	36
93	32	91–92	27	18	–
94	34	93	–	–	37
95	37	94	28	–	–
96	39	95	–	19	38
97	42	96	29	–	–
98	45	97–98	–	–	39
99	47	99–100	30	20	40
100	50	101–102	–	–	–

		GAC	CON	SO	PR
90% Confidence Interval ±		4	6	7	6
95% Confidence Interval ±		5	7	9	7

Composite Score	Percentile Rank	GAC	CON	SO	PR
101	53	103–104	31	–	41
102	55	105	–	21	42
103	58	106–107	32	–	43
104	61	108	–	–	–
105	63	109–110	33	22	44
106	66	111–112	–	–	45
107	68	113	34	–	46
108	70	114–115	–	23	–
109	73	116	35	–	47
110	75	117	–	–	–
111	77	118–119	36	24	48
112	79	120	–	–	49
113	81	121–122	37	25	–
114	82	123–124	–	–	50
115	84	125–126	38	–	–
116	86	127	–	26	51
117	87	128	39	–	–
118	88	129	–	27	52
119	90	130–131	40	–	–
120	91	132–133	–	–	53
121	92	134–135	41	28	–
122	93	136	–	–	54
123	94	137	42	–	55
124	95	138	–	29	56
125	95	139	43	–	–
126	96	140–141	–	–	57
127	96	142–143	44	30	58
128	97	144	–	–	–
129	97	145	45	–	59
130	98	146	–	31	–
131	98	147	46	–	60
132	98	148–149	–	–	–
133	99	150–151	47	32	61
134	99	152–153	–	–	–
135	99	154–155	48	–	62
136	99	156–157	–	33	–
137	99	158	49	–	63
138	99	159	–	–	64
139	99.5	160–161	50	34	–
140	99.6	162–163	–	–	65
141	99.7	164	51	–	–
142	99.7	165–166	–	35	66
143	99.8	167	–	–	67
144	99.8	168–169	52	–	–
145	99.9	170	–	36	68
146	99.9	171	53	–	–
147	99.9	172–173	–	–	69
148	99.9	174–175	54	37	70
149	99.9	176–177	–	–	–
150	>99.9	178	55	–	71
151	>99.9	179	–	38	–
152	>99.9	180–181	56	–	72
153	>99.9	182	–	–	73
154	>99.9	183–184	–	–	–
155	>99.9	185	57	–	74
156	>99.9	186	–	–	–
157	>99.9	187	–	–	75
158	>99.9	188	–	–	76
159	>99.9	189	–	–	–
160	>99.9	190	–	–	–

Note. **CON** = Conceptual Adaptive Domain; **SO** = Social Adaptive Domain; **PR** = Practical Adaptive Domain.

Table A.6 GAC and Adaptive Domain Composite Equivalents of Sums of Scaled Scores: Parent/Primary Caregiver and Parent Forms (continued)

Parent/Primary Caregiver Form | **Ages 3:0–3:5**

		GAC	CON	SO	PR			GAC	CON	SO	PR
90% Confidence Interval ±		3	5	6	4	90% Confidence Interval ±		3	5	6	4
95% Confidence Interval ±		4	6	7	5	95% Confidence Interval ±		4	6	7	5
Composite Score	Percentile Rank	\<\-\- Sums of Scaled Scores \-\->				Composite Score	Percentile Rank	\<\-\- Sums of Scaled Scores \-\->			
40	<0.1	10	–	–	–	101	53	103–104	31	–	41
41	<0.1	11–12	–	–	4	102	55	105	–	21	42
42	<0.1	13	–	–	–	103	58	106–107	32	–	43
43	<0.1	14	–	–	5	104	61	108	–	–	–
44	<0.1	15	–	–	–	105	63	109–110	33	22	44
45	<0.1	16–17	3	–	6	106	66	111–112	–	–	45
46	<0.1	18–19	–	–	–	107	68	113	34	–	46
47	<0.1	20–21	4	–	7	108	70	114–115	–	23	–
48	<0.1	22–23	–	2	–	109	73	116	35	–	47
49	<0.1	24–25	5	–	8	110	75	117	–	–	–
50	<0.1	26–27	6	3	9	111	77	118–119	36	24	48
51	0.1	28–29	–	–	–	112	79	120	–	–	49
52	0.1	30–31	7	4	10	113	81	121–122	37	25	–
53	0.1	32–33	8	–	11	114	82	123–124	–	–	50
54	0.1	34–35	–	5	–	115	84	125–126	38	–	–
55	0.1	36–37	9	–	12	116	86	127	–	26	51
56	0.2	38–39	10	6	13	117	87	128	39	–	–
57	0.2	40–41	11	–	–	118	88	129	–	27	52
58	0.3	42–43	–	–	14	119	90	130–131	40	–	–
59	0.3	44–45	12	7	15	120	91	132–133	–	–	53
60	0.4	46–47	–	–	–	121	92	134–135	41	28	–
61	0.5	48–49	13	–	16	122	93	136	–	–	54
62	1	50–51	–	8	17	123	94	137	42	–	55
63	1	52–53	14	–	–	124	95	138	–	29	56
64	1	54–55	–	–	18	125	95	139	43	–	–
65	1	56–57	15	9	19	126	96	140–141	–	–	57
66	1	58–59	–	–	–	127	96	142–143	44	30	58
67	1	60–61	16	–	20	128	97	144	–	–	–
68	2	62	–	10	21	129	97	145	45	–	59
69	2	63	17	–	–	130	98	146	–	31	–
70	2	64	–	–	22	131	98	147	46	–	60
71	3	65	18	11	23	132	98	148–149	–	–	–
72	3	66	–	–	–	133	99	150–151	47	32	61
73	4	67	19	–	24	134	99	152–153	–	–	–
74	4	68	–	12	25	135	99	154–155	48	–	62
75	5	69	–	–	–	136	99	156–157	–	33	–
76	5	70	20	–	26	137	99	158	49	–	63
77	6	71	–	13	27	138	99	159	–	–	64
78	7	72	–	–	–	139	99.5	160–161	50	34	–
79	8	73	21	–	28	140	99.6	162–163	–	–	65
80	9	74	–	14	29	141	99.7	164	51	–	–
81	10	75	–	–	–	142	99.7	165–166	–	35	66
82	12	76	22	–	30	143	99.8	167	–	–	67
83	13	77	–	15	31	144	99.8	168–169	52	–	–
84	14	78	23	–	32	145	99.9	170	–	36	68
85	16	79–80	–	–	–	146	99.9	171	53	–	–
86	18	81	24	–	33	147	99.9	172–173	–	–	69
87	19	82–83	–	16	–	148	99.9	174–175	54	37	70
88	21	84	25	–	34	149	99.9	176–177	–	–	–
89	23	85–86	–	–	–	150	>99.9	178	55	–	71
90	25	87	26	17	35	151	>99.9	179	–	38	–
91	27	88	–	–	–	152	>99.9	180–181	56	–	72
92	30	89–90	–	–	36	153	>99.9	182	–	–	73
93	32	91–92	27	18	–	154	>99.9	183–184	–	–	–
94	34	93	–	–	37	155	>99.9	185	57	–	74
95	37	94	28	–	–	156	>99.9	186	–	–	–
96	39	95	–	19	38	157	>99.9	187	–	–	75
97	42	96	29	–	–	158	>99.9	188	–	–	76
98	45	97–98	–	–	39	159	>99.9	189	–	–	–
99	47	99–100	30	20	40	160	>99.9	190	–	–	–
100	50	101–102	–	–	–						

Note. **CON** = Conceptual Adaptive Domain; **SO** = Social Adaptive Domain; **PR** = Practical Adaptive Domain.

Parent/Primary Caregiver Form **Ages 3:6–3:11**

		GAC	CON	SO	PR			GAC	CON	SO	PR
90% Confidence Interval ±		3	6	7	6	90% Confidence Interval ±		3	6	7	6
95% Confidence Interval ±		4	7	8	7	95% Confidence Interval ±		4	7	8	7
Composite Score	Percentile Rank	Sums of Scaled Scores				Composite Score	Percentile Rank	Sums of Scaled Scores			
40	<0.1	10	–	–	–	101	53	103–104	31	–	41
41	<0.1	11–12	–	–	4	102	55	105	–	21	42
42	<0.1	13	–	–	–	103	58	106–107	32	–	43
43	<0.1	14	–	–	5	104	61	108	–	–	–
44	<0.1	15	–	–	–	105	63	109–110	33	22	44
45	<0.1	16–17	3	–	6	106	66	111–112	–	–	45
46	<0.1	18–19	–	–	–	107	68	113	34	–	46
47	<0.1	20–21	4	–	7	108	70	114–115	–	23	–
48	<0.1	22–23	–	2	–	109	73	116	35	–	47
49	<0.1	24–25	5	–	8	110	75	117	–	–	–
50	<0.1	26–27	6	3	9	111	77	118–119	36	24	48
51	0.1	28–29	–	–	–	112	79	120	–	–	49
52	0.1	30–31	7	4	10	113	81	121–122	37	25	–
53	0.1	32–33	8	–	11	114	82	123–124	–	–	50
54	0.1	34–35	–	5	–	115	84	125–126	38	–	–
55	0.1	36–37	9	–	12	116	86	127	–	26	51
56	0.2	38–39	10	6	13	117	87	128	39	–	–
57	0.2	40–41	11	–	–	118	88	129	–	27	52
58	0.3	42–43	–	–	14	119	90	130–131	40	–	–
59	0.3	44–45	12	7	15	120	91	132–133	–	–	53
60	0.4	46–47	–	–	–	121	92	134–135	41	28	–
61	0.5	48–49	13	–	16	122	93	136	–	–	54
62	1	50–51	–	8	17	123	94	137	42	–	55
63	1	52–53	14	–	–	124	95	138	–	29	56
64	1	54–55	–	–	18	125	95	139	43	–	–
65	1	56–57	15	9	19	126	96	140–141	–	–	57
66	1	58–59	–	–	–	127	96	142–143	44	30	58
67	1	60–61	16	–	20	128	97	144	–	–	–
68	2	62	–	10	21	129	97	145	45	–	59
69	2	63	17	–	–	130	98	146	–	31	–
70	2	64	–	–	22	131	98	147	46	–	60
71	3	65	18	11	23	132	98	148–149	–	–	–
72	3	66	–	–	–	133	99	150–151	47	32	61
73	4	67	19	–	24	134	99	152–153	–	–	–
74	4	68	–	12	25	135	99	154–155	48	–	62
75	5	69	–	–	–	136	99	156–157	–	33	–
76	5	70	20	–	26	137	99	158	49	–	63
77	6	71	–	13	27	138	99	159	–	–	64
78	7	72	–	–	–	139	99.5	160–161	50	34	–
79	8	73	21	–	28	140	99.6	162–163	–	–	65
80	9	74	–	14	29	141	99.7	164	51	–	–
81	10	75	–	–	–	142	99.7	165–166	–	35	66
82	12	76	22	–	30	143	99.8	167	–	–	67
83	13	77	–	15	31	144	99.8	168–169	52	–	–
84	14	78	23	–	32	145	99.9	170	–	36	68
85	16	79–80	–	–	–	146	99.9	171	53	–	–
86	18	81	24	–	33	147	99.9	172–173	–	–	69
87	19	82–83	–	16	–	148	99.9	174–175	54	37	70
88	21	84	25	–	34	149	99.9	176–177	–	–	–
89	23	85–86	–	–	–	150	>99.9	178	55	–	71
90	25	87	26	17	35	151	>99.9	179	–	38	–
91	27	88	–	–	–	152	>99.9	180–181	56	–	72
92	30	89–90	–	–	36	153	>99.9	182	–	–	73
93	32	91–92	27	18	–	154	>99.9	183–184	–	–	–
94	34	93	–	–	37	155	>99.9	185	57	–	74
95	37	94	28	–	–	156	>99.9	186	–	–	–
96	39	95	–	19	38	157	>99.9	187	–	–	75
97	42	96	29	–	–	158	>99.9	188	–	–	76
98	45	97–98	–	–	39	159	>99.9	189	–	–	–
99	47	99–100	30	20	40	160	>99.9	190	–	–	–
100	50	101–102	–	–	–						

Note. **CON** = Conceptual Adaptive Domain; **SO** = Social Adaptive Domain; **PR** = Practical Adaptive Domain.

Table A.6 GAC and Adaptive Domain Composite Equivalents of Sums of Scaled Scores: Parent/Primary Caregiver and Parent Forms (continued)

Parent/Primary Caregiver Form — **Ages 4:0–4:5**

Composite Score	Percentile Rank	GAC	CON	SO	PR	Composite Score	Percentile Rank	GAC	CON	SO	PR
90% Confidence Interval ±		3	6	7	5	90% Confidence Interval ±		3	6	7	5
95% Confidence Interval ±		4	7	8	6	95% Confidence Interval ±		4	7	8	6
40	<0.1	10	–	–	–	101	53	103–104	31	–	41
41	<0.1	11–12	–	–	4	102	55	105	–	21	42
42	<0.1	13	–	–	–	103	58	106–107	32	–	43
43	<0.1	14	–	–	5	104	61	108	–	–	–
44	<0.1	15	–	–	–	105	63	109–110	33	22	44
45	<0.1	16–17	3	–	6	106	66	111–112	–	–	45
46	<0.1	18–19	–	–	–	107	68	113	34	–	46
47	<0.1	20–21	4	–	7	108	70	114–115	–	23	–
48	<0.1	22–23	–	2	–	109	73	116	35	–	47
49	<0.1	24–25	5	–	8	110	75	117	–	–	–
50	<0.1	26–27	6	3	9	111	77	118–119	36	24	48
51	0.1	28–29	–	–	–	112	79	120	–	–	49
52	0.1	30–31	7	4	10	113	81	121–122	37	25	–
53	0.1	32–33	8	–	11	114	82	123–124	–	–	50
54	0.1	34–35	–	5	–	115	84	125–126	38	–	–
55	0.1	36–37	9	–	12	116	86	127	–	26	51
56	0.2	38–39	10	6	13	117	87	128	39	–	–
57	0.2	40–41	11	–	–	118	88	129	–	27	52
58	0.3	42–43	–	–	14	119	90	130–131	40	–	–
59	0.3	44–45	12	7	15	120	91	132–133	–	–	53
60	0.4	46–47	–	–	–	121	92	134–135	41	28	–
61	0.5	48–49	13	–	16	122	93	136	–	–	54
62	1	50–51	–	8	17	123	94	137	42	–	55
63	1	52–53	14	–	–	124	95	138	–	29	56
64	1	54–55	–	–	18	125	95	139	43	–	–
65	1	56–57	15	9	19	126	96	140–141	–	–	57
66	1	58–59	–	–	–	127	96	142–143	44	30	58
67	1	60–61	16	–	20	128	97	144	–	–	–
68	2	62	–	10	21	129	97	145	45	–	59
69	2	63	17	–	–	130	98	146	–	31	–
70	2	64	–	–	22	131	98	147	46	–	60
71	3	65	18	11	23	132	98	148–149	–	–	–
72	3	66	–	–	–	133	99	150–151	47	32	61
73	4	67	19	–	24	134	99	152–153	–	–	–
74	4	68	–	12	25	135	99	154–155	48	–	62
75	5	69	–	–	–	136	99	156–157	–	33	–
76	5	70	20	–	26	137	99	158	49	–	63
77	6	71	–	13	27	138	99	159	–	–	64
78	7	72	–	–	–	139	99.5	160–161	50	34	–
79	8	73	21	–	28	140	99.6	162–163	–	–	65
80	9	74	–	14	29	141	99.7	164	51	–	–
81	10	75	–	–	–	142	99.7	165–166	–	35	66
82	12	76	22	–	30	143	99.8	167	–	–	67
83	13	77	–	15	31	144	99.8	168–169	52	–	–
84	14	78	23	–	32	145	99.9	170	–	36	68
85	16	79–80	–	–	–	146	99.9	171	53	–	–
86	18	81	24	–	33	147	99.9	172–173	–	–	69
87	19	82–83	–	16	–	148	99.9	174–175	54	37	70
88	21	84	25	–	34	149	99.9	176–177	–	–	–
89	23	85–86	–	–	–	150	>99.9	178	55	–	71
90	25	87	26	17	35	151	>99.9	179	–	38	–
91	27	88	–	–	–	152	>99.9	180–181	56	–	72
92	30	89–90	–	–	36	153	>99.9	182	–	–	73
93	32	91–92	27	18	–	154	>99.9	183–184	–	–	–
94	34	93	–	–	37	155	>99.9	185	57	–	74
95	37	94	28	–	–	156	>99.9	186	–	–	–
96	39	95	–	19	38	157	>99.9	187	–	–	75
97	42	96	29	–	–	158	>99.9	188	–	–	76
98	45	97–98	–	–	39	159	>99.9	189	–	–	–
99	47	99–100	30	20	40	160	>99.9	190	–	–	–
100	50	101–102	–	–	–						

Note. **CON** = Conceptual Adaptive Domain; **SO** = Social Adaptive Domain; **PR** = Practical Adaptive Domain.

Table A.6 GAC and Adaptive Domain Composite Equivalents of Sums of Scaled Scores: Parent/Primary Caregiver and Parent Forms (continued)

Parent/Primary Caregiver Form   **Ages 4:6–4:11**

Composite Score	Percentile Rank	GAC	CON	SO	PR	Composite Score	Percentile Rank	GAC	CON	SO	PR
90% Confidence Interval ±		4	6	7	6	90% Confidence Interval ±		4	6	7	6
95% Confidence Interval ±		5	7	9	7	95% Confidence Interval ±		5	7	9	7
		Sums of Scaled Scores						Sums of Scaled Scores			
40	<0.1	10	–	–	–	101	53	103–104	31	–	41
41	<0.1	11–12	–	–	4	102	55	105	–	21	42
42	<0.1	13	–	–	–	103	58	106–107	32	–	43
43	<0.1	14	–	–	5	104	61	108	–	–	–
44	<0.1	15	–	–	–	105	63	109–110	33	22	44
45	<0.1	16–17	3	–	6	106	66	111–112	–	–	45
46	<0.1	18–19	–	–	–	107	68	113	34	–	46
47	<0.1	20–21	4	–	7	108	70	114–115	–	23	–
48	<0.1	22–23	–	2	–	109	73	116	35	–	47
49	<0.1	24–25	5	–	8	110	75	117	–	–	–
50	<0.1	26–27	6	3	9	111	77	118–119	36	24	48
51	0.1	28–29	–	–	–	112	79	120	–	–	49
52	0.1	30–31	7	4	10	113	81	121–122	37	25	–
53	0.1	32–33	8	–	11	114	82	123–124	–	–	50
54	0.1	34–35	–	5	–	115	84	125–126	38	–	–
55	0.1	36–37	9	–	12	116	86	127	–	26	51
56	0.2	38–39	10	6	13	117	87	128	39	–	–
57	0.2	40–41	11	–	–	118	88	129	–	27	52
58	0.3	42–43	–	–	14	119	90	130–131	40	–	–
59	0.3	44–45	12	7	15	120	91	132–133	–	–	53
60	0.4	46–47	–	–	–	121	92	134–135	41	28	–
61	0.5	48–49	13	–	16	122	93	136	–	–	54
62	1	50–51	–	8	17	123	94	137	42	–	55
63	1	52–53	14	–	–	124	95	138	–	29	56
64	1	54–55	–	–	18	125	95	139	43	–	–
65	1	56–57	15	9	19	126	96	140–141	–	–	57
66	1	58–59	–	–	–	127	96	142–143	44	30	58
67	1	60–61	16	–	20	128	97	144	–	–	–
68	2	62	–	10	21	129	97	145	45	–	59
69	2	63	17	–	–	130	98	146	–	31	–
70	2	64	–	–	22	131	98	147	46	–	60
71	3	65	18	11	23	132	98	148–149	–	–	–
72	3	66	–	–	–	133	99	150–151	47	32	61
73	4	67	19	–	24	134	99	152–153	–	–	–
74	4	68	–	12	25	135	99	154–155	48	–	62
75	5	69	–	–	–	136	99	156–157	–	33	–
76	5	70	20	–	26	137	99	158	49	–	63
77	6	71	–	13	27	138	99	159	–	–	64
78	7	72	–	–	–	139	99.5	160–161	50	34	–
79	8	73	21	–	28	140	99.6	162–163	–	–	65
80	9	74	–	14	29	141	99.7	164	51	–	–
81	10	75	–	–	–	142	99.7	165–166	–	35	66
82	12	76	22	–	30	143	99.8	167	–	–	67
83	13	77	–	15	31	144	99.8	168–169	52	–	–
84	14	78	23	–	32	145	99.9	170	–	36	68
85	16	79–80	–	–	–	146	99.9	171	53	–	–
86	18	81	24	–	33	147	99.9	172–173	–	–	69
87	19	82–83	–	16	–	148	99.9	174–175	54	37	70
88	21	84	25	–	34	149	99.9	176–177	–	–	–
89	23	85–86	–	–	–	150	>99.9	178	55	–	71
90	25	87	26	17	35	151	>99.9	179	–	38	–
91	27	88	–	–	–	152	>99.9	180–181	56	–	72
92	30	89–90	–	–	36	153	>99.9	182	–	–	73
93	32	91–92	27	18	–	154	>99.9	183–184	–	–	–
94	34	93	–	–	37	155	>99.9	185	57	–	74
95	37	94	28	–	–	156	>99.9	186	–	–	–
96	39	95	–	19	38	157	>99.9	187	–	–	75
97	42	96	29	–	–	158	>99.9	188	–	–	76
98	45	97–98	–	–	39	159	>99.9	189	–	–	–
99	47	99–100	30	20	40	160	>99.9	190	–	–	–
100	50	101–102	–	–	–						

Note. **CON** = Conceptual Adaptive Domain; **SO** = Social Adaptive Domain; **PR** = Practical Adaptive Domain.

Table A.6 GAC and Adaptive Domain Composite Equivalents of Sums of Scaled Scores: Parent/Primary Caregiver and Parent Forms *(continued)*

Parent/Primary Caregiver Form **Ages 5:0–5:11**

Composite Score	Percentile Rank	GAC (90% CI ±3, 95% CI ±4)	CON (90% CI ±6, 95% CI ±7)	SO (90% CI ±6, 95% CI ±7)	PR (90% CI ±6, 95% CI ±7)	Composite Score	Percentile Rank	GAC (90% CI ±3, 95% CI ±4)	CON (90% CI ±6, 95% CI ±7)	SO (90% CI ±6, 95% CI ±7)	PR (90% CI ±6, 95% CI ±7)
		Sums of Scaled Scores						Sums of Scaled Scores			
40	<0.1	10	–	–	–	101	53	103–104	31	–	41
41	<0.1	11–12	–	–	4	102	55	105	–	21	42
42	<0.1	13	–	–	–	103	58	106–107	32	–	43
43	<0.1	14	–	–	5	104	61	108	–	–	–
44	<0.1	15	–	–	–	105	63	109–110	33	22	44
45	<0.1	16–17	3	–	6	106	66	111–112	–	–	45
46	<0.1	18–19	–	–	–	107	68	113	34	–	46
47	<0.1	20–21	4	–	7	108	70	114–115	–	23	–
48	<0.1	22–23	–	2	–	109	73	116	35	–	47
49	<0.1	24–25	5	–	8	110	75	117	–	–	–
50	<0.1	26–27	6	3	9	111	77	118–119	36	24	48
51	0.1	28–29	–	–	–	112	79	120	–	–	49
52	0.1	30–31	7	4	10	113	81	121–122	37	25	–
53	0.1	32–33	8	–	11	114	82	123–124	–	–	50
54	0.1	34–35	–	5	–	115	84	125–126	38	–	–
55	0.1	36–37	9	–	12	116	86	127	–	26	51
56	0.2	38–39	10	6	13	117	87	128	39	–	–
57	0.2	40–41	11	–	–	118	88	129	–	27	52
58	0.3	42–43	–	–	14	119	90	130–131	40	–	–
59	0.3	44–45	12	7	15	120	91	132–133	–	–	53
60	0.4	46–47	–	–	–	121	92	134–135	41	28	–
61	0.5	48–49	13	–	16	122	93	136	–	–	54
62	1	50–51	–	8	17	123	94	137	42	–	55
63	1	52–53	14	–	–	124	95	138	–	29	56
64	1	54–55	–	–	18	125	95	139	43	–	–
65	1	56–57	15	9	19	126	96	140–141	–	–	57
66	1	58–59	–	–	–	127	96	142–143	44	30	58
67	1	60–61	16	–	20	128	97	144	–	–	–
68	2	62	–	10	21	129	97	145	45	–	59
69	2	63	17	–	–	130	98	146	–	31	–
70	2	64	–	–	22	131	98	147	46	–	60
71	3	65	18	11	23	132	98	148–149	–	–	–
72	3	66	–	–	–	133	99	150–151	47	32	61
73	4	67	19	–	24	134	99	152–153	–	–	–
74	4	68	–	12	25	135	99	154–155	48	–	62
75	5	69	–	–	–	136	99	156–157	–	33	–
76	5	70	20	–	26	137	99	158	49	–	63
77	6	71	–	13	27	138	99	159	–	–	64
78	7	72	–	–	–	139	99.5	160–161	50	34	–
79	8	73	21	–	28	140	99.6	162–163	–	–	65
80	9	74	–	14	29	141	99.7	164	51	–	–
81	10	75	–	–	–	142	99.7	165–166	–	35	66
82	12	76	22	–	30	143	99.8	167	–	–	67
83	13	77	–	15	31	144	99.8	168–169	52	–	–
84	14	78	23	–	32	145	99.9	170	–	36	68
85	16	79–80	–	–	–	146	99.9	171	53	–	–
86	18	81	24	–	33	147	99.9	172–173	–	–	69
87	19	82–83	–	16	–	148	99.9	174–175	54	37	70
88	21	84	25	–	34	149	99.9	176–177	–	–	–
89	23	85–86	–	–	–	150	>99.9	178	55	–	71
90	25	87	26	17	35	151	>99.9	179	–	38	–
91	27	88	–	–	–	152	>99.9	180–181	56	–	72
92	30	89–90	–	–	36	153	>99.9	182	–	–	73
93	32	91–92	27	18	–	154	>99.9	183–184	–	–	–
94	34	93	–	–	37	155	>99.9	185	57	–	74
95	37	94	28	–	–	156	>99.9	186	–	–	–
96	39	95	–	19	38	157	>99.9	187	–	–	75
97	42	96	29	–	–	158	>99.9	188	–	–	76
98	45	97–98	–	–	39	159	>99.9	189	–	–	–
99	47	99–100	30	20	40	160	>99.9	190	–	–	–
100	50	101–102	–	–	–						

Note. **CON** = Conceptual Adaptive Domain; **SO** = Social Adaptive Domain; **PR** = Practical Adaptive Domain.

Parent Form — **Age 5**

Composite Score	Percentile Rank	GAC	CON	SO	PR	Composite Score	Percentile Rank	GAC	CON	SO	PR
90% Confidence Interval ±		3	5	6	5	90% Confidence Interval ±		3	5	6	5
95% Confidence Interval ±		4	6	7	6	95% Confidence Interval ±		4	6	7	6
		Sums of Scaled Scores						Sums of Scaled Scores			
40	<0.1	9	–	–	4	86	17.5	67	–	–	–
41	<0.1	10	–	–	–	87	19.3	68–69	22	15	29
42	<0.1	11	–	–	5	88	21.2	70	–	–	30
43	<0.1	12	–	–	–	89	23.2	71–72	23	–	31
44	<0.1	13	–	–	6	90	25.2	73–74	–	16	–
45	<0.1	14	3	–	–	91	27.4	75	24	–	32
46	<0.1	15	–	–	7	92	29.7	76	25	17	33
47	<0.1	16	4	–	–	93	32	77–78	–	–	34
48	<0.1	17	–	–	8	94	34.5	79	26	–	–
49	<0.1	18	5	–	–	95	36.9	80–81	27	18	35
50	<0.1	19	–	–	9	96	39.5	82	–	–	36
51	<0.1	20	6	–	–	97	42.1	83–84	28	–	37
52	<0.1	21	–	–	10	98	44.7	85	–	19	–
53	<0.1	22	7	–	–	99	47.3	86–87	29	–	38
54	0.1	23	–	2	11	100	50	88	30	–	39
55	0.1	24	8	–	–	101	52.7	89–90	31	20	40
56	0.2	25	–	–	12	102	55.3	91	–	–	–
57	0.2	26	9	3	–	103	57.9	92–93	32	21	41
58	0.3	27	–	–	13	104	60.5	94	–	–	42
59	0.3	28	10	–	–	105	63.1	95	33	–	–
60	0.4	29	–	4	14	106	65.5	96–97	–	22	43
61	0.5	30	11	–	–	107	68	98	34	–	44
62	0.6	31–32	–	5	15	108	70.3	99–100	–	23	–
63	0.7	33–34	12	–	–	109	72.6	101	35	–	45
64	0.8	35–36	–	6	–	110	74.8	102–103	–	–	46
65	1.0	37–38	13	–	16	111	76.8	104	36	24	–
66	1.2	39–40	–	7	–	112	78.8	105–106	–	–	47
67	1.4	41–42	14	–	–	113	80.7	107	–	25	48
68	1.6	43–44	–	8	17	114	82.5	108–109	37	–	49
69	1.9	45–46	15	–	–	115	84.1	110	–	–	–
70	2.3	47–48	16	9	18	116	85.7	111–112	38	26	50
71	2.7	49	–	–	–	117	87.1	113	–	–	51
72	3.1	50	17	10	19	118	88.5	114–115	39	–	–
73	3.6	51	–	–	–	119	89.7	116	–	27	52
74	4.2	52	–	–	20	120	90.9	117–118	40	–	53
75	4.8	53	18	11	–	121	91.9	119	–	28	–
76	5.5	54	–	–	21	122	92.9	120–121	41	–	54
77	6.3	55	–	–	22	123	93.7	122	–	–	55
78	7.1	56	19	12	–	124	94.5	123–124	–	29	56
79	8.1	57	–	–	23	125	95.2	125	42	–	–
80	9.1	58	–	–	24	126	95.8	126–127	–	–	57
81	10.3	59–60	20	13	25	127	96.4	128	43	30	58
82	11.5	61	–	–	–	128	96.9	129–130	–	–	59
83	12.9	62–63	–	–	26	129	97.3	131–132	44	–	–
84	14.3	64	21	14	27	130	>97.3	133–152	45–57	31–38	60–76
85	15.9	65–66	–	–	28						

Note. **CON** = Conceptual Adaptive Domain; **SO** = Social Adaptive Domain; **PR** = Practical Adaptive Domain.

A
Parent
Ages 5–21

Table A.6 GAC and Adaptive Domain Composite Equivalents of Sums of Scaled Scores: Parent/Primary Caregiver and Parent Forms (continued)

Parent Form — **Age 6**

		GAC	CON	SO	PR			GAC	CON	SO	PR
90% Confidence Interval ±		3	4	6	5	90% Confidence Interval ±		3	4	6	5
95% Confidence Interval ±		4	5	7	6	95% Confidence Interval ±		4	5	7	6
Composite Score	Percentile Rank	Sums of Scaled Scores				Composite Score	Percentile Rank	Sums of Scaled Scores			
40	<0.1	9	–	–	4	86	17.5	68	–	–	29
41	<0.1	10	–	–	–	87	19.3	69–70	23	–	–
42	<0.1	11	–	–	5	88	21.2	71	–	15	30
43	<0.1	12	–	–	–	89	23.2	72	24	–	31
44	<0.1	13	–	–	6	90	25.2	73–74	–	–	32
45	<0.1	14	–	–	–	91	27.4	75	25	16	33
46	<0.1	15	–	–	7	92	29.7	76–77	–	–	–
47	<0.1	16	–	–	–	93	32	78	26	17	34
48	<0.1	17	–	–	8	94	34.5	79–80	27	–	35
49	<0.1	18	3	–	–	95	36.9	81	–	–	36
50	<0.1	19	–	–	9	96	39.5	82–83	28	18	37
51	<0.1	20	4	–	–	97	42.1	84	–	–	–
52	<0.1	21	–	–	10	98	44.7	85	29	19	38
53	<0.1	22	5	–	–	99	47.3	86–87	–	–	39
54	0.1	23	–	2	11	100	50	88	30	20	40
55	0.1	24	6	–	–	101	52.7	89–90	–	–	–
56	0.2	25	–	–	12	102	55.3	91	31	21	41
57	0.2	26	7	3	–	103	57.9	92–93	–	–	42
58	0.3	27	–	–	13	104	60.5	94	32	22	–
59	0.3	28	8	–	–	105	63.1	95–96	–	–	43
60	0.4	29–30	–	4	14	106	65.5	97	33	–	44
61	0.5	31–32	9	–	–	107	68	98–99	–	23	–
62	0.6	33–34	–	5	15	108	70.3	100	34	–	45
63	0.7	35–36	10	–	–	109	72.6	101–102	–	24	46
64	0.8	37–38	–	6	–	110	74.8	103	35	–	–
65	1.0	39–40	11	–	16	111	76.8	104–105	–	–	47
66	1.2	41–42	–	7	–	112	78.8	106	36	25	48
67	1.4	43–44	12	–	–	113	80.7	107–108	–	–	–
68	1.6	45–46	–	8	17	114	82.5	109	37	26	49
69	1.9	47–48	13	–	–	115	84.1	110–111	–	–	–
70	2.3	49–50	14	9	18	116	85.7	112–113	38	–	50
71	2.7	51	–	–	–	117	87.1	114	–	27	51
72	3.1	52	15	10	19	118	88.5	115–116	39	–	–
73	3.6	53	–	–	–	119	89.7	117–118	–	–	52
74	4.2	54	–	–	20	120	90.9	119	40	–	53
75	4.8	55	16	11	–	121	91.9	120–121	–	28	–
76	5.5	56	–	–	21	122	92.9	122–123	41	–	54
77	6.3	57	17	–	–	123	93.7	124	–	–	55
78	7.1	58	18	–	22	124	94.5	125–126	42	–	56
79	8.1	59	–	12	23	125	95.2	127–128	–	29	–
80	9.1	60	19	–	24	126	95.8	129–130	43	–	57
81	10.3	61	–	–	–	127	96.4	131–132	–	–	58
82	11.5	62	20	13	25	128	96.9	133	44	–	59
83	12.9	63–64	21	–	26	129	97.3	134–135	–	–	60
84	14.3	65	–	–	27	130	>97.3	136–152	45–57	30–38	61–76
85	15.9	66–67	22	14	28						

Note. **CON** = Conceptual Adaptive Domain; **SO** = Social Adaptive Domain; **PR** = Practical Adaptive Domain.

Parent Form

Age 7

Composite Score	Percentile Rank	GAC	CON	SO	PR	Composite Score	Percentile Rank	GAC	CON	SO	PR
90% Confidence Interval ±		3	5	6	6	90% Confidence Interval ±		3	5	6	6
95% Confidence Interval ±		4	6	7	7	95% Confidence Interval ±		4	6	7	7
		Sums of Scaled Scores						Sums of Scaled Scores			
40	<0.1	9	–	–	4	86	17.5	66–67	20	–	28
41	<0.1	10	–	–	–	87	19.3	68	21	14	29
42	<0.1	11	–	–	5	88	21.2	69–70	22	–	–
43	<0.1	12	–	–	–	89	23.2	71–72	23	15	30
44	<0.1	13	–	–	6	90	25.2	73	24	–	31
45	<0.1	14	–	–	–	91	27.4	74–75	25	16	32
46	<0.1	15	–	–	7	92	29.7	76	26	–	–
47	<0.1	16	–	–	–	93	32	77	–	17	33
48	<0.1	17	–	–	8	94	34.5	78–79	27	–	34
49	<0.1	18	–	–	–	95	36.9	80	28	18	35
50	<0.1	19	3	–	9	96	39.5	81–82	–	–	–
51	<0.1	20	–	–	–	97	42.1	83	29	19	36
52	<0.1	21	–	–	10	98	44.7	84–85	–	–	37
53	<0.1	22	4	–	–	99	47.3	86	30	–	38
54	0.1	23	–	–	11	100	50	87–88	–	20	–
55	0.1	24	–	2	–	101	52.7	89	31	–	39
56	0.2	25	5	–	12	102	55.3	90	–	21	40
57	0.2	26	–	–	–	103	57.9	91–92	32	–	41
58	0.3	27	–	3	13	104	60.5	93	–	22	–
59	0.3	28	6	–	–	105	63.1	94–95	33	–	42
60	0.4	29	–	–	14	106	65.5	96	–	–	43
61	0.5	30	7	4	–	107	68	97	34	23	44
62	0.6	31–32	–	–	15	108	70.3	98–99	–	–	–
63	0.7	33–34	8	–	–	109	72.6	100	35	–	45
64	0.8	35–36	–	5	–	110	74.8	101	–	24	46
65	1.0	37–38	9	–	16	111	76.8	102–103	–	–	47
66	1.2	39–40	–	6	–	112	78.8	104	36	–	–
67	1.4	41–42	10	–	–	113	80.7	105	–	25	48
68	1.6	43–44	–	7	17	114	82.5	106–107	37	–	49
69	1.9	45–46	11	–	–	115	84.1	108	–	–	–
70	2.3	47–48	12	8	18	116	85.7	109–110	–	26	50
71	2.7	49	–	–	–	117	87.1	111	38	–	–
72	3.1	50	13	9	19	118	88.5	112	–	–	51
73	3.6	51	–	–	–	119	89.7	113–114	–	–	52
74	4.2	52	–	–	20	120	90.9	115	39	27	–
75	4.8	53	14	10	21	121	91.9	116	–	–	53
76	5.5	54	–	–	–	122	92.9	117–118	40	–	–
77	6.3	55	–	–	22	123	93.7	119	–	–	54
78	7.1	56	15	11	23	124	94.5	120–121	–	28	–
79	8.1	57	–	–	–	125	95.2	122	41	–	55
80	9.1	58	–	–	24	126	95.8	123	–	–	–
81	10.3	59	16	12	–	127	96.4	124–125	–	–	56
82	11.5	60–61	–	–	25	128	96.9	126	42	29	–
83	12.9	62	17	–	26	129	97.3	127–128	–	–	57
84	14.3	63–64	18	13	–	130	>97.3	129–152	43–57	30–38	58–76
85	15.9	65	19	–	27						

Note. **CON** = Conceptual Adaptive Domain; **SO** = Social Adaptive Domain; **PR** = Practical Adaptive Domain.

A

Parent Ages 5–21

Table A.6 GAC and Adaptive Domain Composite Equivalents of Sums of Scaled Scores: Parent/Primary Caregiver and Parent Forms (continued)

Parent Form — **Age 8**

Composite Score	Percentile Rank	GAC	CON	SO	PR	Composite Score	Percentile Rank	GAC	CON	SO	PR
	90% Confidence Interval ±	2	4	6	4		90% Confidence Interval ±	2	4	6	4
	95% Confidence Interval ±	3	5	7	5		95% Confidence Interval ±	3	5	7	5
		Sums of Scaled Scores						**Sums of Scaled Scores**			
40	<0.1	9	–	–	4	81	10	59	17	12	25
41	<0.1	10	–	–	–	82	12	60	18	–	–
42	<0.1	11	–	–	5	83	13	61	19	–	26
43	<0.1	12	–	–	–	84	14	62–63	20	13	27
44	<0.1	13	–	–	6	85	16	64–65	–	–	28
45	<0.1	14	–	–	–	86	18	66–67	21	–	29
46	<0.1	15	–	–	7	87	19	68–69	22	14	30
47	<0.1	16	–	–	–	88	21	70–71	23	–	–
48	<0.1	17	–	–	8	89	23	72–73	–	15	31
49	<0.1	18	–	–	–	90	25	74–75	24	–	32
50	<0.1	19	3	–	9	91	27	76	–	16	33
51	0.1	20	–	–	–	92	30	77–78	25	–	–
52	0.1	21	–	–	10	93	32	79–80	26	–	34
53	0.1	22	4	–	–	94	34	81	–	17	35
54	0.1	23	–	–	11	95	37	82–83	27	–	36
55	0.1	24	–	2	–	96	39	84–85	–	18	–
56	0.2	25	5	–	12	97	42	86	28	–	37
57	0.2	26	–	–	–	98	45	87–88	–	19	38
58	0.3	27	–	3	13	99	47	89	29	–	39
59	0.3	28	6	–	–	100	50	90–91	30	20	–
60	0.4	29	–	–	14	101	53	92	31	–	40
61	0.5	30	7	4	–	102	55	93	–	21	41
62	1	31–32	–	–	15	103	58	94–95	32	–	–
63	1	33–34	8	–	–	104	61	96	–	–	42
64	1	35–36	–	5	–	105	63	97–98	33	22	43
65	1	37–38	9	–	16	106	66	99	–	–	–
66	1	39–40	–	6	–	107	68	100	34	–	44
67	1	41–42	10	–	–	108	70	101–102	–	23	45
68	2	43–44	–	7	17	109	73	103	35	–	–
69	2	45–46	11	–	–	110	75	104	–	–	46
70	2	47–48	12	8	18	111	77	105–106	–	24	–
71	3	49	–	–	–	112	79	107	36	–	47
72	3	50	13	9	19	113	81	108	–	–	–
73	4	51	–	–	–	114	82	109	37	25	–
74	4	52	–	–	–	115	84	110–111	–	–	48
75	5	53	14	10	20	116	86	112	–	–	–
76	5	54	–	–	–	117	87	113	38	–	–
77	6	55	–	–	21	118	88	114–115	–	26	49
78	7	56	15	11	22	119	90	116	–	–	–
79	8	57	–	–	23	120	>90	117–152	39–57	27–38	50–76
80	9	58	16	–	24						

Note. **CON** = Conceptual Adaptive Domain; **SO** = Social Adaptive Domain; **PR** = Practical Adaptive Domain.

**Table A.6   GAC and Adaptive Domain Composite Equivalents of Sums of Scaled Scores:
Parent/Primary Caregiver and Parent Forms** (continued)

Parent Form — **Age 9**

Composite Score	Percentile Rank	GAC	CON	SO	PR	Composite Score	Percentile Rank	GAC	CON	SO	PR
90% Confidence Interval ±		3	5	6	6	90% Confidence Interval ±		3	5	6	6
95% Confidence Interval ±		4	6	7	7	95% Confidence Interval ±		4	6	7	7
		Sums of Scaled Scores						Sums of Scaled Scores			
40	<0.1	9	–	–	4	81	10	69	–	13	28
41	<0.1	10	–	–	5	82	12	70	20	–	–
42	<0.1	11	–	–	6	83	13	71	–	–	29
43	<0.1	12	–	–	7	84	14	72	21	14	–
44	<0.1	13	–	–	8	85	16	73	22	–	30
45	<0.1	14	–	–	9	86	18	74	–	–	–
46	<0.1	15	–	–	10	87	19	75	23	15	31
47	<0.1	16	–	–	–	88	21	76	–	–	–
48	<0.1	17	–	–	11	89	23	77	24	–	32
49	<0.1	18	3	–	–	90	25	78	–	16	–
50	<0.1	19	–	–	12	91	27	79	25	–	33
51	0.1	20	4	–	–	92	30	80	–	–	–
52	0.1	21–22	–	–	13	93	32	81	26	17	34
53	0.1	23–24	5	–	–	94	34	82	27	–	–
54	0.1	25–26	–	2	14	95	37	83	–	–	35
55	0.1	27–28	6	–	–	96	39	84	28	18	–
56	0.2	29–30	–	–	15	97	42	85	–	–	36
57	0.2	31–32	7	3	–	98	45	86	29	19	37
58	0.3	33–34	–	–	16	99	47	87	–	–	–
59	0.3	35–36	8	–	–	100	50	88	30	20	38
60	0.4	37–38	–	4	17	101	53	89	–	–	39
61	0.5	39–40	9	–	–	102	55	90–91	31	21	–
62	1	41–42	–	5	18	103	58	92	–	–	40
63	1	43–44	10	–	–	104	61	93	32	22	41
64	1	45–46	–	6	–	105	63	94–95	33	–	42
65	1	47–48	11	–	19	106	66	96	–	–	–
66	1	49–50	–	7	–	107	68	97–98	34	23	43
67	1	51–52	12	–	–	108	70	99	–	–	44
68	2	53–54	–	8	20	109	73	100–101	–	–	45
69	2	55–56	13	–	–	110	75	102	35	24	–
70	2	57–58	14	9	21	111	77	103–104	–	–	46
71	3	59	–	–	–	112	79	105	–	–	–
72	3	60	15	10	22	113	81	106–107	–	–	47
73	4	61	–	–	–	114	82	108	36	25	–
74	4	62	16	–	23	115	84	109–110	–	–	–
75	5	63	–	11	–	116	86	111	–	–	48
76	5	64	17	–	24	117	87	112–113	–	–	–
77	6	65	–	–	25	118	88	114–115	37	26	–
78	7	66	18	12	26	119	90	116	–	–	49
79	8	67	–	–	27	120	>90	117–152	38–57	27–38	50–76
80	9	68	19	–	–						

Note. **CON** = Conceptual Adaptive Domain; **SO** = Social Adaptive Domain; **PR** = Practical Adaptive Domain.

Parent Form

Age 10

Composite Score	Percentile Rank	GAC	CON	SO	PR	Composite Score	Percentile Rank	GAC	CON	SO	PR
90% Confidence Interval ±		3	5	6	6	90% Confidence Interval ±		3	5	6	6
95% Confidence Interval ±		4	6	7	7	95% Confidence Interval ±		4	6	7	7
		Sums of Scaled Scores						Sums of Scaled Scores			
40	<0.1	9	–	–	4	81	10	60–61	–	12	–
41	<0.1	10	–	–	5	82	12	62–63	19	–	27
42	<0.1	11	–	–	6	83	13	64–65	20	–	28
43	<0.1	12	–	–	–	84	14	66–67	–	13	–
44	<0.1	13	–	–	7	85	16	68	21	–	29
45	<0.1	14	–	–	–	86	18	69–70	22	–	30
46	<0.1	15	–	–	8	87	19	71–72	–	14	31
47	<0.1	16	–	–	–	88	21	73	23	–	–
48	<0.1	17	–	–	9	89	23	74–75	24	15	32
49	<0.1	18	3	–	–	90	25	76	–	–	33
50	<0.1	19	–	–	10	91	27	77–78	25	16	–
51	0.1	20	4	–	–	92	30	79	26	–	34
52	0.1	21	–	–	11	93	32	80–81	–	17	35
53	0.1	22	5	–	–	94	34	82	27	–	36
54	0.1	23	–	–	12	95	37	83–84	28	18	–
55	0.1	24	6	2	–	96	39	85	–	–	37
56	0.2	25	–	–	13	97	42	86–87	29	19	38
57	0.2	26	7	–	–	98	45	88	–	–	39
58	0.3	27	–	3	14	99	47	89–90	30	20	–
59	0.3	28	8	–	–	100	50	91	31	–	40
60	0.4	29	–	–	15	101	53	92	–	21	41
61	0.5	30	9	4	–	102	55	93–94	32	–	–
62	1	31–32	–	–	16	103	58	95	–	–	42
63	1	33–34	10	–	–	104	61	96	33	22	43
64	1	35–36	–	5	–	105	63	97–98	–	–	44
65	1	37–38	11	–	17	106	66	99	34	–	–
66	1	39–40	–	6	–	107	68	100	–	23	45
67	1	41–42	12	–	–	108	70	101–102	35	–	–
68	2	43–44	–	7	18	109	73	103	–	–	46
69	2	45–46	13	–	–	110	75	104	36	24	–
70	2	47–48	14	8	19	111	77	105–106	–	–	–
71	3	49	–	–	–	112	79	107	–	–	47
72	3	50	15	9	20	113	81	108	37	–	–
73	4	51	–	–	–	114	82	109	–	25	–
74	4	52	–	–	21	115	84	110–111	–	–	–
75	5	53	16	10	22	116	86	112	38	–	48
76	5	54	–	–	23	117	87	113	–	–	–
77	6	55	–	–	24	118	88	114–115	–	26	–
78	7	56	17	11	–	119	90	116	–	–	49
79	8	57–58	–	–	25	120	>90	117–152	39–57	27–38	50–76
80	9	59	18	–	26						

Note. **CON** = Conceptual Adaptive Domain; **SO** = Social Adaptive Domain; **PR** = Practical Adaptive Domain.

A
Parent
Ages 5–21

Table A.6 GAC and Adaptive Domain Composite Equivalents of Sums of Scaled Scores: Parent/Primary Caregiver and Parent Forms (continued)

Parent Form — **Age 11**

		GAC	CON	SO	PR			GAC	CON	SO	PR
90% Confidence Interval ±		3	5	6	6	90% Confidence Interval ±		3	5	6	6
95% Confidence Interval ±		4	6	7	7	95% Confidence Interval ±		4	6	7	7
Composite Score	Percentile Rank	Sums of Scaled Scores				Composite Score	Percentile Rank	Sums of Scaled Scores			
40	<0.1	9	–	–	4	81	10	62	–	14	25
41	<0.1	10	–	–	5	82	12	63–64	19	–	26
42	<0.1	11	–	–	6	83	13	65	–	–	–
43	<0.1	12	–	–	7	84	14	66	20	15	27
44	<0.1	13	–	–	8	85	16	67–68	–	–	28
45	<0.1	14	–	–	–	86	18	69	21	–	29
46	<0.1	15	–	–	9	87	19	70	22	16	–
47	<0.1	16	–	–	–	88	21	71–72	–	–	30
48	<0.1	17	–	–	10	89	23	73	23	–	31
49	<0.1	18	3	–	–	90	25	74–75	24	17	32
50	<0.1	19	–	–	11	91	27	76	–	–	33
51	0.1	20	4	–	–	92	30	77	25	–	–
52	0.1	21	–	–	12	93	32	78–79	26	18	34
53	0.1	22	5	2	–	94	34	80	–	–	35
54	0.1	23	–	–	13	95	37	81	27	–	36
55	0.1	24	6	–	–	96	39	82–83	28	–	37
56	0.2	25	–	3	14	97	42	84	–	19	–
57	0.2	26	7	–	–	98	45	85	29	–	38
58	0.3	27	–	4	15	99	47	86–87	30	–	39
59	0.3	28	8	–	–	100	50	88	–	20	40
60	0.4	29	–	5	16	101	53	89	31	–	–
61	0.5	30	9	–	–	102	55	90–91	–	21	41
62	1	31–32	–	6	17	103	58	92	32	–	42
63	1	33–34	10	–	–	104	61	93	33	–	–
64	1	35–36	–	7	–	105	63	94–95	–	22	43
65	1	37–38	11	–	18	106	66	96	34	–	–
66	1	39–40	–	8	–	107	68	97	–	–	44
67	1	41–42	12	–	–	108	70	98–99	–	23	–
68	2	43–44	–	9	19	109	73	100	35	–	45
69	2	45–46	13	–	–	110	75	101–102	–	–	–
70	2	47–48	14	10	20	111	77	103	–	–	–
71	3	49	–	–	–	112	79	104	36	24	46
72	3	50	15	11	21	113	81	105–106	–	–	–
73	4	51	–	–	–	114	82	107	–	–	–
74	4	52	–	–	–	115	84	108	–	–	–
75	5	53–54	16	12	22	116	86	109–110	37	25	47
76	5	55	–	–	–	117	87	111	–	–	–
77	6	56	–	–	23	118	88	112–113	–	–	–
78	7	57–58	17	13	–	119	90	114	–	–	48
79	8	59	–	–	24	120	>90	115–152	38–57	26–38	49–76
80	9	60–61	18	–	–						

Note. **CON** = Conceptual Adaptive Domain; **SO** = Social Adaptive Domain; **PR** = Practical Adaptive Domain.

Table A.6 GAC and Adaptive Domain Composite Equivalents of Sums of Scaled Scores: Parent/Primary Caregiver and Parent Forms (continued)

Parent Form

Age 12

Composite Score	Percentile Rank	GAC	CON	SO	PR	Composite Score	Percentile Rank	GAC	CON	SO	PR
90% Confidence Interval ±		2	4	5	4	90% Confidence Interval ±		2	4	5	4
95% Confidence Interval ±		3	5	6	5	95% Confidence Interval ±		3	5	6	5
		Sums of Scaled Scores						**Sums of Scaled Scores**			
40	<0.1	9	–	–	4	81	10	59	18	12	–
41	<0.1	10	–	–	–	82	12	60	–	–	23
42	<0.1	11	–	–	5	83	13	61	19	–	24
43	<0.1	12	–	–	–	84	14	62–63	–	13	25
44	<0.1	13	–	–	6	85	16	64–65	20	–	26
45	<0.1	14	–	–	–	86	18	66–67	21	–	27
46	<0.1	15	–	–	7	87	19	68–69	–	14	28
47	<0.1	16	–	–	–	88	21	70–71	22	–	–
48	<0.1	17	–	–	8	89	23	72–73	23	–	29
49	<0.1	18	3	–	–	90	25	74–75	–	15	30
50	<0.1	19	–	–	9	91	27	76	24	–	31
51	0.1	20	4	–	–	92	30	77–78	–	16	–
52	0.1	21	–	–	10	93	32	79	25	–	32
53	0.1	22	5	–	–	94	34	80–81	26	17	33
54	0.1	23	–	–	11	95	37	82	–	–	34
55	0.1	24	6	2	–	96	39	83–84	27	18	35
56	0.2	25	–	–	12	97	42	85	–	–	36
57	0.2	26	7	–	–	98	45	86	28	19	37
58	0.3	27	–	3	13	99	47	87	29	–	38
59	0.3	28	8	–	–	100	50	88–89	30	20	39
60	0.4	29	–	–	14	101	53	90	31	–	40
61	0.5	30	9	4	–	102	55	91	–	21	41
62	1	31–32	–	–	15	103	58	92	32	–	–
63	1	33–34	10	–	–	104	61	93	–	–	42
64	1	35–36	–	5	–	105	63	94–95	–	22	–
65	1	37–38	11	–	16	106	66	96	33	–	43
66	1	39–40	–	6	–	107	68	97	–	–	44
67	1	41–42	12	–	–	108	70	98	–	23	–
68	2	43–44	–	7	17	109	73	99	34	–	45
69	2	45–46	13	–	–	110	75	100	–	–	–
70	2	47–48	14	8	18	111	77	101	–	–	46
71	3	49	–	–	–	112	79	102	35	24	–
72	3	50	15	9	19	113	81	103	–	–	47
73	4	51	–	–	–	114	82	104	–	–	–
74	4	52	–	–	–	115	84	105–106	36	–	48
75	5	53	16	10	20	116	86	107	–	25	–
76	5	54	–	–	–	117	87	108	–	–	49
77	6	55	–	–	–	118	88	109	37	–	–
78	7	56	17	11	21	119	90	110	–	–	–
79	8	57	–	–	–	120	>90	111–152	38–57	26–38	50–76
80	9	58	–	–	22						

Note. **CON** = Conceptual Adaptive Domain; **SO** = Social Adaptive Domain; **PR** = Practical Adaptive Domain.

A

Parent
Ages 5–21

243

Table A.6 GAC and Adaptive Domain Composite Equivalents of Sums of Scaled Scores: Parent/Primary Caregiver and Parent Forms *(continued)*

Parent Form **Ages 13–14**

Composite Score	Percentile Rank	GAC	CON	SO	PR	Composite Score	Percentile Rank	GAC	CON	SO	PR
90% Confidence Interval ±		3	4	5	5	90% Confidence Interval ±		3	4	5	5
95% Confidence Interval ±		4	5	6	6	95% Confidence Interval ±		4	5	6	6
		Sums of Scaled Scores						*Sums of Scaled Scores*			
40	<0.1	9	–	–	4	81	10	59–60	–	12	25
41	<0.1	10	–	–	–	82	12	61–62	19	–	26
42	<0.1	11	–	–	5	83	13	63–64	20	–	27
43	<0.1	12	–	–	–	84	14	65–66	–	13	28
44	<0.1	13	–	–	6	85	16	67–68	21	–	29
45	<0.1	14	–	–	–	86	18	69–70	22	–	–
46	<0.1	15	–	–	7	87	19	71	23	14	30
47	<0.1	16	–	–	–	88	21	72–73	–	–	31
48	<0.1	17	–	–	8	89	23	74–75	24	–	32
49	<0.1	18	3	–	–	90	25	76	–	15	33
50	<0.1	19	–	–	9	91	27	77–78	25	–	34
51	0.1	20	4	–	–	92	30	79	26	16	–
52	0.1	21	–	–	10	93	32	80–81	–	17	35
53	0.1	22	5	–	–	94	34	82	27	–	36
54	0.1	23	–	–	11	95	37	83–84	–	18	37
55	0.1	24	6	2	–	96	39	85	28	–	–
56	0.2	25	–	–	12	97	42	86	–	19	38
57	0.2	26	7	–	–	98	45	87–88	29	20	39
58	0.3	27	–	3	13	99	47	89	–	–	–
59	0.3	28	8	–	–	100	50	90	30	21	40
60	0.4	29	–	–	14	101	53	91	31	–	41
61	0.5	30	9	4	–	102	55	92–93	–	–	–
62	1	31–32	–	–	15	103	58	94	32	22	42
63	1	33–34	10	–	–	104	61	95	–	–	43
64	1	35–36	–	5	–	105	63	96	33	–	–
65	1	37–38	11	–	16	106	66	97	–	–	44
66	1	39–40	–	6	–	107	68	98	–	23	–
67	1	41–42	12	–	–	108	70	99–100	34	–	45
68	2	43–44	–	7	17	109	73	101	–	–	46
69	2	45–46	13	–	–	110	75	102	35	–	–
70	2	47–48	14	8	18	111	77	103	–	24	47
71	3	49	–	–	–	112	79	104	36	–	–
72	3	50	15	9	19	113	81	105	–	–	48
73	4	51	–	–	–	114	82	106	37	–	–
74	4	52	–	–	–	115	84	107–108	–	25	–
75	5	53	16	10	20	116	86	109	–	–	49
76	5	54	–	–	–	117	87	110	38	–	–
77	6	55	–	–	21	118	88	111	–	–	–
78	7	56	17	11	22	119	90	112	39	–	–
79	8	57	–	–	23	120	>90	113–152	40–57	26–38	50–76
80	9	58	18	–	24						

Note. **CON** = Conceptual Adaptive Domain; **SO** = Social Adaptive Domain; **PR** = Practical Adaptive Domain.

Table A.6 GAC and Adaptive Domain Composite Equivalents of Sums of Scaled Scores: Parent/Primary Caregiver and Parent Forms (continued)

Parent Form

Ages 15–16

Composite Score	Percentile Rank	GAC	CON	SO	PR	Composite Score	Percentile Rank	GAC	CON	SO	PR
90% Confidence Interval ±		3	4	5	5	90% Confidence Interval ±		3	4	5	5
95% Confidence Interval ±		4	5	6	6	95% Confidence Interval ±		4	5	6	6
		Sums of Scaled Scores						Sums of Scaled Scores			
40	<0.1	9	–	–	4	81	10	66–67	19	12	27
41	<0.1	10	–	–	5	82	12	68	20	–	28
42	<0.1	11	–	–	6	83	13	69–70	–	–	29
43	<0.1	12	–	–	7	84	14	71	21	13	30
44	<0.1	13	–	–	8	85	16	72–73	–	–	–
45	<0.1	14	–	–	–	86	18	74	22	–	31
46	<0.1	15	–	–	9	87	19	75–76	23	14	32
47	<0.1	16	–	–	–	88	21	77	–	–	33
48	<0.1	17	–	–	10	89	23	78	24	15	34
49	<0.1	18	3	–	–	90	25	79	25	–	35
50	<0.1	19	–	–	11	91	27	80–81	–	16	36
51	0.1	20	4	–	–	92	30	82	26	–	–
52	0.1	21	–	–	12	93	32	83	27	17	37
53	0.1	22	5	–	–	94	34	84	–	18	38
54	0.1	23	–	–	13	95	37	85	28	–	39
55	0.1	24	6	2	–	96	39	86	29	19	40
56	0.2	25–26	–	–	14	97	42	87	–	–	–
57	0.2	27–28	7	–	–	98	45	88–89	30	20	41
58	0.3	29–30	–	3	15	99	47	90	–	–	42
59	0.3	31–32	8	–	–	100	50	91	31	–	–
60	0.4	33–34	–	–	16	101	53	92	–	21	43
61	0.5	35–36	9	4	–	102	55	93	32	–	–
62	1	37–38	–	–	17	103	58	94	–	22	44
63	1	39–40	10	–	–	104	61	95	33	–	–
64	1	41–42	–	5	–	105	63	96	–	–	45
65	1	43–44	11	–	18	106	66	97	34	23	–
66	1	45–46	–	6	–	107	68	98	–	–	46
67	1	47–48	12	–	–	108	70	–	–	–	–
68	2	49–50	–	7	19	109	73	99	35	–	–
69	2	51–52	13	–	–	110	75	100	–	24	47
70	2	53–54	14	8	20	111	77	101	–	–	–
71	3	55	–	–	–	112	79	102	36	–	–
72	3	56	15	9	21	113	81	103	–	–	48
73	4	57	–	–	–	114	82	104	–	25	–
74	4	58	–	–	22	115	84	105	–	–	–
75	5	59	16	10	23	116	86	106	37	–	49
76	5	60	–	–	24	117	87	107	–	–	–
77	6	61	17	–	–	118	88	108	–	–	–
78	7	62	–	11	25	119	90	109	–	26	50
79	8	63	18	–	26	120	>90	110–152	38–57	27–38	51–76
80	9	64–65	–	–	–						

Note. **CON** = Conceptual Adaptive Domain; **SO** = Social Adaptive Domain; **PR** = Practical Adaptive Domain.

A
Parent
Ages 5–21

Parent Form — **Ages 17–21**

Composite Score	Percentile Rank	GAC	CON	SO	PR	Composite Score	Percentile Rank	GAC	CON	SO	PR
90% Confidence Interval ±		2	3	5	3	90% Confidence Interval ±		2	3	5	3
95% Confidence Interval ±		3	4	6	4	95% Confidence Interval ±		3	4	6	4
		Sums of Scaled Scores						Sums of Scaled Scores			
40	<0.1	9	–	–	4	81	10	61–63	19	–	27
41	<0.1	10	–	–	–	82	12	64–65	–	13	28
42	<0.1	11	–	–	5	83	13	66–67	20	–	29
43	<0.1	12	–	–	–	84	14	68–69	21	14	30
44	<0.1	13	–	–	6	85	16	70	22	–	31
45	<0.1	14	–	–	–	86	18	71–72	23	15	32
46	<0.1	15	–	–	7	87	19	73–74	–	–	33
47	<0.1	16	–	–	–	88	21	75	24	16	34
48	<0.1	17	–	–	8	89	23	76–77	25	–	35
49	<0.1	18	3	–	–	90	25	78–79	26	17	36
50	<0.1	19	–	–	9	91	27	80	–	–	37
51	0.1	20	4	–	–	92	30	81	27	18	38
52	0.1	21	–	–	10	93	32	82–83	–	–	–
53	0.1	22	5	–	–	94	34	84	28	–	39
54	0.1	23	–	–	11	95	37	85–86	–	19	40
55	0.1	24	6	2	–	96	39	87	29	–	–
56	0.2	25	–	–	12	97	42	88	–	–	41
57	0.2	26	7	–	–	98	45	89	30	20	42
58	0.3	27	–	3	13	99	47	90–91	31	–	–
59	0.3	28	8	–	–	100	50	92	–	–	43
60	0.4	29	–	–	14	101	53	93	32	21	–
61	0.5	30	9	4	–	102	55	94	–	–	44
62	1	31–32	–	–	15	103	58	95–96	–	–	–
63	1	33–34	10	–	–	104	61	97	33	–	45
64	1	35–36	–	5	–	105	63	98	–	22	–
65	1	37–38	11	–	16	106	66	99	–	–	46
66	1	39–40	–	6	–	107	68	100	34	–	–
67	1	41–42	12	–	–	108	70	101–102	–	–	–
68	2	43–44	–	7	17	109	73	103	–	23	47
69	2	45–46	13	–	–	110	75	104	–	–	–
70	2	47–48	14	8	18	111	77	105	35	–	48
71	3	49	–	–	–	112	79	106	–	–	–
72	3	50	15	9	19	113	81	107	–	–	–
73	4	51	–	–	–	114	82	108–109	–	24	49
74	4	52	–	–	20	115	84	110	36	–	–
75	5	53	16	10	–	116	86	111	–	–	–
76	5	54	–	–	21	117	87	112	–	–	50
77	6	55	–	–	22	118	88	113–114	–	–	–
78	7	56	17	11	23	119	90	115	–	25	–
79	8	57–58	–	–	24	120	>90	116–152	37–57	26–38	51–76
80	9	59–60	18	12	25–26						

Note. **CON** = Conceptual Adaptive Domain; **SO** = Social Adaptive Domain; **PR** = Practical Adaptive Domain.

A

Parent
Ages 5–21

Table A.7 Average Number of Items Guessed by the Standardization Sample: Parent/Primary Caregiver and Parent Forms

Parent/Primary Caregiver Form

Skill Areas	0:0–0:3		0:4–0:7		0:8–0:11		1:0–1:3		1:4–1:7		1:8–1:11		2:0–2:5		2:6–2:11		3:0–3:5		3:6–3:11		4:0–4:5		4:6–4:11		5:0–5:11	
	Mean	$SE_{\bar{x}}$	Mean	$SE_{\bar{x}}$	Mean	$SE_{\bar{x}}$	Mean	$SE_{\bar{x}}$	Mean	$SE_{\bar{x}}$	Mean	$SE_{\bar{x}}$	Mean	$SE_{\bar{x}}$	Mean	$SE_{\bar{x}}$	Mean	$SE_{\bar{x}}$	Mean	$SE_{\bar{x}}$	Mean	$SE_{\bar{x}}$	Mean	$SE_{\bar{x}}$	Mean	$SE_{\bar{x}}$
Communication	0.04	0.03	0.09	0.04	0.09	0.04	0.09	0.04	0.24	0.06	0.25	0.08	0.31	0.10	0.25	0.07	0.20	0.08	0.27	0.10	0.26	0.08	0.22	0.06	0.13	0.04
Community Use	–	–	–	–	–	–	0.03	0.02	0.09	0.04	0.26	0.07	0.24	0.09	0.26	0.09	0.35	0.13	0.24	0.07	0.28	0.09	0.13	0.05	0.18	0.05
Functional Pre-Academics	–	–	–	–	–	–	0.02	0.01	0.05	0.03	0.09	0.04	0.38	0.16	0.32	0.09	0.68	0.23	0.40	0.12	0.55	0.14	0.20	0.07	0.31	0.09
Home Living	–	–	–	–	–	–	0.02	0.01	0.08	0.03	0.09	0.03	0.09	0.04	0.04	0.02	0.14	0.09	0.07	0.04	0.09	0.05	0.02	0.01	0.05	0.02
Health and Safety	0.09	0.05	0.07	0.03	0.24	0.08	0.14	0.05	0.23	0.05	0.36	0.10	0.29	0.08	0.32	0.12	0.31	0.12	0.33	0.07	0.34	0.07	0.19	0.06	0.27	0.05
Leisure	0.01	0.01	0.06	0.03	0.08	0.04	0.06	0.03	0.14	0.04	0.13	0.05	0.21	0.07	0.09	0.04	0.13	0.06	0.21	0.07	0.17	0.05	0.06	0.03	0.15	0.05
Self-Care	0.10	0.04	0.08	0.03	0.04	0.02	0.10	0.03	0.07	0.03	0.06	0.02	0.10	0.03	0.09	0.05	0.04	0.02	0.02	0.01	0.04	0.02	0.01	0.01	0.03	0.02
Self-Direction	0.02	0.01	0.11	0.04	0.08	0.03	0.09	0.03	0.14	0.04	0.18	0.04	0.19	0.07	0.21	0.08	0.18	0.07	0.29	0.08	0.18	0.05	0.08	0.04	0.09	0.03
Social	0.04	0.02	0.05	0.03	0.01	0.01	0.04	0.03	0.13	0.06	0.09	0.04	0.27	0.08	0.16	0.04	0.33	0.13	0.38	0.09	0.25	0.06	0.15	0.05	0.27	0.07
Motor	0.02	0.01	0.05	0.02	0.09	0.03	0.07	0.03	0.32	0.07	0.25	0.06	0.25	0.08	0.33	0.08	0.34	0.10	0.40	0.10	0.28	0.08	0.17	0.06	0.15	0.05

The header spanning all age-group columns reads: **Age Group**

Parent Form

Skill Areas	5		6		7		8		9		10		11		12		13–14		15–16		17–21	
	Mean	$SE_{\bar{x}}$	Mean	$SE_{\bar{x}}$	Mean	$SE_{\bar{x}}$	Mean	$SE_{\bar{x}}$	Mean	$SE_{\bar{x}}$	Mean	$SE_{\bar{x}}$	Mean	$SE_{\bar{x}}$	Mean	$SE_{\bar{x}}$	Mean	$SE_{\bar{x}}$	Mean	$SE_{\bar{x}}$	Mean	$SE_{\bar{x}}$
Communication	0.39	0.09	0.45	0.10	0.32	0.08	0.46	0.10	0.33	0.07	0.35	0.07	0.23	0.06	0.21	0.05	0.23	0.05	0.21	0.06	0.14	0.04
Community Use	0.23	0.10	0.39	0.11	0.94	0.24	0.62	0.14	0.57	0.12	0.79	0.13	0.74	0.13	0.49	0.09	0.73	0.13	0.60	0.09	0.46	0.09
Functional Academics	0.24	0.06	0.58	0.12	0.93	0.18	0.51	0.10	0.37	0.07	0.41	0.09	0.53	0.13	0.31	0.08	0.39	0.10	0.33	0.06	0.29	0.06
Home Living	0.09	0.08	0.26	0.17	0.38	0.15	0.18	0.07	0.14	0.05	0.13	0.04	0.14	0.05	0.28	0.16	0.17	0.05	0.20	0.06	0.16	0.04
Health and Safety	0.42	0.10	0.62	0.14	0.87	0.13	0.41	0.08	0.57	0.10	0.54	0.10	0.69	0.14	0.42	0.09	0.71	0.14	0.51	0.11	0.37	0.08
Leisure	0.19	0.05	0.38	0.13	0.37	0.09	0.27	0.07	0.21	0.05	0.31	0.08	0.38	0.10	0.23	0.05	0.45	0.10	0.45	0.09	0.33	0.08
Self-Care	0.14	0.05	0.21	0.10	0.12	0.04	0.07	0.03	0.07	0.03	0.11	0.04	0.19	0.05	0.08	0.03	0.25	0.08	0.15	0.04	0.12	0.03
Self-Direction	0.28	0.08	0.49	0.13	0.63	0.16	0.34	0.10	0.24	0.06	0.31	0.09	0.35	0.09	0.34	0.08	0.57	0.15	0.37	0.09	0.33	0.07
Social	0.30	0.08	0.43	0.10	0.34	0.09	0.36	0.10	0.22	0.06	0.35	0.09	0.37	0.10	0.36	0.09	0.54	0.13	0.36	0.07	0.35	0.10
Work	–	–	–	–	–	–	–	–	–	–	–	–	–	–	–	–	–	–	–	–	1.44	0.26

The header spanning all age-group columns reads: **Age Group**

Note. $SE_{\bar{x}}$ = Standard Error of the Mean.

Table A.8   Test-Age Equivalents of Skill Area Raw Scores: Parent/Primary Caregiver and Parent Forms

Parent/Primary Caregiver Form

Test Age	Communication	Community Use	Functional Pre-Academics	Home Living	Health and Safety	Leisure	Self-Care	Self-Direction	Social	Motor	Test Age
0:0	7–8	–	–	–	–	–	7	–	6–7	4	0:0
0:1	9	–	–	–	4	1–2	8–9	8	8–9	5–6	0:1
0:2	10	–	–	–	–	3–4	10	9–10	10–11	7–8	0:2
0:3	11	–	–	–	5	5–6	11–12	11	12–13	9–12	0:3
0:4	12–13	–	–	–	–	7–8	13–15	–	14–15	13–14	0:4
0:5	14	–	–	–	6	9–10	16–18	12–13	16	15–16	0:5
0:6	–	–	–	–	7	11–12	19–22	14	17–18	17–21	0:6
0:7	15	–	–	–	8	13–14	23–24	15	19–20	22–26	0:7
0:8	16–17	–	–	–	9–10	15–16	25–27	16–17	21–22	27–30	0:8
0:9	18–19	–	–	–	11–12	17–19	28–30	18–20	23	31–33	0:9
0:10	–	–	–	–	13–15	20–21	31–32	21	24	34–36	0:10
0:11	20–22	–	–	–	16–18	22–23	33–36	22–25	25–27	37–40	0:11
1:0–1:1	23–26	1–2	–	7–12	19–22	24–26	37–41	26–28	28–32	41–46	1:0–1:1
1:2–1:3	27–30	3–4	3–4	13–20	23–26	27–30	42–43	29–31	33–36	47–51	1:2–1:3
1:4–1:5	31–33	5–6	5	21–28	27–30	31–34	44–45	32–34	37–39	52–55	1:4–1:5
1:6–1:7	34–36	7–9	6	29–33	31–32	35–36	46–48	35–37	40–42	56–57	1:6–1:7
1:8–1:9	37–41	10–13	7–9	34–37	33–36	37–39	49–51	38–40	43–44	58	1:8–1:9
1:10–1:11	42–46	14–18	10–13	38–42	37–40	40–42	52–54	41–42	45–47	59–60	1:10–1:11
2:0–2:2	47–51	19–23	14–18	43–46	41–42	43–45	55–57	43–46	48–50	61–62	2:0–2:2
2:3–2:5	52–55	24–28	19–22	47–50	43–45	46–48	58–60	47–50	51–53	63–64	2:3–2:5
2:6–2:8	56–59	29–33	23–26	51–53	46–48	49–51	61–62	51–53	54–56	65–66	2:6–2:8
2:9–2:11	60–62	34–37	27–30	54–55	49–50	52–53	63–65	54–55	57–58	67	2:9–2:11
3:0–3:2	63–64	38–40	31–34	56–57	51–53	54–55	66–67	56–57	59–60	68–69	3:0–3:2
3:3–3:5	65	41–43	35–36	58–59	54–56	56–57	68	58	–	70	3:3–3:5
3:6–3:8	–	44–46	37–41	60	57–58	58	69	59	61	71–72	3:6–3:8
3:9–3:11	66	47	42–45	61	59	59	–	60	62	73–74	3:9–3:11
4:0–4:2	67	48–50	46–49	62	60–61	60	70	61	63	75	4:0–4:2
4:3–4:5	–	51	50–53	63	62	–	–	62	–	76–77	4:3–4:5
4:6–4:8	68	52	54–55	64	63	61	–	63	64	–	4:6–4:8
4:9–4:11	69	53	56–58	65	64	–	–	–	–	78	4:9–4:11
5:0–5:2	–	54	59–61	66	65	62	–	64	65	–	5:0–5:2
5:3–5:5	70	55	62	–	–	–	–	–	66	–	5:3–5:5
5:6–5:8	71	56	63	67	66	63	–	65	67	79	5:6–5:8
5:9–5:11	–	–	64–65	–	–	–	–	66–67	68	–	5:9–5:11

Table A.8 Test-Age Equivalents of Skill Area Raw Scores: Parent/Primary Caregiver and Parent Forms (continued)

Parent Form

Test Age	Communication	Community Use	Functional Academics	Home Living	Health and Safety	Leisure	Self-Care	Self-Direction	Social	Test Age
5:0–5:3	50	13–15	14–15	33	36–38	40–41	49–52	27–31	–	5:0–5:3
5:4–5:7	51–53	16–19	16–20	34–35	39–41	42–43	53–55	32–35	52–54	5:4–5:7
5:8–5:11	54	20–21	21–26	36–37	42–43	44	56	36–37	–	5:8–5:11
6:0–6:3	55	22–24	27–32	38	44	–	57	38–40	–	6:0–6:3
6:4–6:7	56–57	25–26	33–36	39–40	45–46	45–46	58–59	41–42	55–56	6:4–6:7
6:8–6:11	58	27–28	37–39	41	47	47	60	43–44	–	6:8–6:11
7:0–7:3	–	29	40–42	42	48	–	61	45–46	57	7:0–7:3
7:4–7:7	59–60	30–32	43–44	43–44	49	48–50	62	47–48	–	7:4–7:7
7:8–7:11	–	–	45–47	45	–	–	63	49	58	7:8–7:11
8:0–8:3	–	33–34	48–49	46	50	–	64	50	59	8:0–8:3
8:4–8:7	61–62	35–36	50–52	47–48	51–52	51–52	65	51–52	–	8:4–8:7
8:8–8:11	–	37	53	49	–	–	–	–	–	8:8–8:11
9:0–9:3	63	38	54	50	–	–	–	53	–	9:0–9:3
9:4–9:7	–	39–40	55	51–52	53–54	53	66	54–55	60	9:4–9:7
9:8–9:11	–	41–42	56–57	53	–	–	67	56	–	9:8–9:11
10:0–10:3	64	43	58	54	55	–	–	–	–	10:0–10:3
10:4–10:7	–	44–46	59	55	56	54	68	57–58	–	10:4–10:7
10:8–10:11	–	–	–	56	–	–	–	–	–	10:8–10:11
11:0–11:3	–	47	60	57	–	–	–	–	61	11:0–11:3
11:4–11:7	65	48	–	–	57	55	–	59	–	11:4–11:7
11:8–11:11	–	49	61	58	–	–	69	–	–	11:8–11:11
12:0–12:3	66	–	–	–	58	–	–	60	62	12:0–12:3
12:4–12:7	–	50–51	62	59	–	56	–	61	–	12:4–12:7
12:8–12:11	–	–	–	60	59	57	70	–	–	12:8–12:11
13:0–13:11	67	52–53	63	–	60	–	–	–	63	13:0–13:11
14:0–14:11	–	54–55	64	61	–	58	–	62	–	14:0–14:11
15:0–15:11	68	56–57	65	62	61	–	–	63	64	15:0–15:11
16:0–16:11	–	58–59	–	63–64	62	59	–	64	–	16:0–16:11
17:0–21:11	69–70	60–62	66	65	63	60–61	–	65–67	65–66	17:0–21:11

Table A.9 Scaled Score Equivalents of Skill Area Raw Scores: Adult Form, Self Report

Ages 16–21

ss	Com	CU	FA	HL	HS	LS	SC	SD	Soc	WK	ss
1	0-31	0-29	0-43	0-27	0-22	0-24	0-51	0-28	0-34	0-33	1
2	32-38	30-35	44-47	28-34	23-29	25-31	52-55	29-35	35-40	34-40	2
3	39-44	36-40	48-50	35-40	30-35	32-37	56-60	36-41	41-45	41-46	3
4	45-49	41-44	51-54	41-45	36-40	38-42	61-64	42-46	46-49	47-51	4
5	50-53	45-47	55-58	46-49	41-44	43-46	65-67	47-50	50-53	52-55	5
6	54-56	48-51	59-62	50-53	45-47	47-49	68-69	51-54	54-56	56-59	6
7	57-59	52-54	63-65	54-56	48-49	50-52	70	55-58	57-59	60-62	7
8	60-62	55-56	66-69	57-58	50-52	53-55	71	59-61	60-62	63-64	8
9	63-65	57-59	70-72	59-61	53-54	56-58	72	62-64	63-64	65-66	9
10	66-67	60-62	73-75	62-63	55-56	59-61	73	65-66	65	67-68	10
11	68-69	63-64	76-77	64-65	57	62-64	74	67-69	66	69	11
12	70-71	65-67	78-79	66	58	65-66	75	70-71	67	70	12
13	72-73	68-69	80	67	59	67-68	–	72-73	68-69	71	13
14	74-75	70-72	–	68-69	60	69	–	74-75	–	72	14
15	–	–	81	–	–	–	–	–	–	–	15

Ages 22–29

ss	Com	CU	FA	HL	HS	LS	SC	SD	Soc	WK	ss
1	0-35	0-35	0-46	0-32	0-35	0-29	0-59	0-36	0-36	0-41	1
2	36-42	36-41	47-51	33-38	36-40	30-35	60-62	37-42	37-42	42-47	2
3	43-48	42-46	52-55	39-43	41-44	36-40	63-64	43-47	43-47	48-52	3
4	49-53	47-49	56-58	44-47	45-47	41-43	65-66	48-51	48-51	53-56	4
5	54-57	50-53	59-62	48-50	48-50	44-47	67	52-55	52-55	57-59	5
6	58-60	54-56	63-67	51-54	51-52	48-50	68-69	56-58	56-58	60-62	6
7	61-63	57-59	68-71	55-57	53	51-53	70	59-61	59-60	63-65	7
8	64-66	60-61	72-74	58-60	54-55	54-56	71	62-64	61-62	66-67	8
9	67-68	62-64	75-76	61-62	56	57-59	72	65-67	63-64	68	9
10	69-70	65-66	77	63-64	57	60-62	73	68-69	65-66	69	10
11	71	67-68	78	65-66	58	63-64	74	70-71	67	70	11
12	72-73	69-70	79	67	59	65-66	75	72-73	68	71	12
13	74-75	71-72	80	68-69	60	67-69	–	74-75	69	72	13
14	–	–	81	–	–	–	–	–	–	–	14
15	–	–	–	–	–	–	–	–	–	–	15

Ages 30–39

ss	Com	CU	FA	HL	HS	LS	SC	SD	Soc	WK	ss
1	0-35	0-35	0-46	0-32	0-35	0-29	0-59	0-36	0-36	0-44	1
2	36-42	36-41	47-51	33-38	36-40	30-35	60-62	37-42	37-42	45-50	2
3	43-48	42-46	52-55	39-44	41-44	36-40	63-64	43-47	43-47	51-55	3
4	49-53	47-49	56-59	45-49	45-47	41-43	65-66	48-52	48-51	56-59	4
5	54-57	50-53	60-63	50-53	48-50	44-47	67-68	53-56	52-55	60-62	5
6	58-61	54-56	64-68	54-56	51-52	48-50	69-70	57-59	56-58	63-64	6
7	62-65	57-59	69-72	57-59	53	51-53	71	60-63	59-60	65-66	7
8	66-68	60-61	73-75	60-62	54-55	54-56	72	64-66	61-63	67	8
9	69-70	62-64	76-77	63-64	56	57-59	73	67-68	64-65	68	9
10	71	65-67	78	65	57	60-62	74	69-70	66	69	10
11	72	68-69	79	66	58	63-65	–	71-72	67	70	11
12	73	70-71	80	67-68	59-60	66-68	75	73	68	71	12
13	74-75	72	81	69	–	69	–	74-75	69	72	13
14	–	–	–	–	–	–	–	–	–	–	14
15	–	–	–	–	–	–	–	–	–	–	15

Ages 40–49

ss	Com	CU	FA	HL	HS	LS	SC	SD	Soc	WK	ss
1	0-35	0-35	0-46	0-32	0-35	0-29	0-61	0-36	0-36	0-44	1
2	36-42	36-41	47-51	33-38	36-40	30-35	62-63	37-42	37-42	45-50	2
3	43-48	42-46	52-55	39-44	41-44	36-40	64	43-47	43-47	51-55	3
4	49-53	47-49	56-59	45-47	45-47	41-43	65-66	48-52	48-51	56-59	4
5	54-57	50-53	60-64	48-50	48-50	44-47	67-68	53-56	52-55	60-62	5
6	58-61	54-57	65-69	51-54	51-53	48-50	69-70	57-59	56-58	63-64	6
7	62-65	58-60	70-73	55-57	54-55	51-53	71	60-63	59-60	65-66	7
8	66-68	61-63	74-76	58-60	56	54-56	72	64-66	61-63	67	8
9	69-70	64-66	77-78	61-62	57	57-59	73	67-69	64-65	68	9
10	71-72	67-68	79	63-64	58	60-62	74	70-71	66	69	10
11	73	69-70	80	65-66	59	63-65	–	72	67	70	11
12	74	71	–	67	60	66-69	75	73	68	71	12
13	75	72	81	68	–	–	–	74-75	69	72	13
14	–	–	–	–	–	–	–	–	–	–	14
15	–	–	–	–	–	–	–	–	–	–	15

Note. **Com** = Communication; **CU** = Community Use; **FA** = Functional Academics; **HL** = Home Living; **HS** = Health and Safety; **LS** = Leisure; **SC** = Self-Care; **SD** = Self-Direction; **Soc** = Social; **WK** = Work.

Table A.9 Scaled Score Equivalents of Skill Area Raw Scores: Adult Form, Self Report (continued)

Ages 50-64

ss	Com	CU	FA	HL	HS	LS	SC	SD	Soc	WK	ss
1	0-35	0-35	0-46	0-32	0-36	0-29	0-61	0-36	0-36	0-44	1
2	36-42	36-41	47-51	33-38	37-41	30-35	62-63	37-42	37-42	45-50	2
3	43-48	42-46	52-55	39-44	42-45	36-40	64	43-47	43-47	51-55	3
4	49-53	47-49	56-59	45-49	46-48	41-43	65-66	48-52	48-51	56-59	4
5	54-57	50-53	60-64	50-53	49-51	44-47	67-68	53-56	52-55	60-62	5
6	58-61	54-57	65-69	54-56	52-53	48-50	69-70	57-59	56-58	63-64	6
7	62-65	58-60	70-73	57-59	54-55	51-53	71-72	60-63	59-60	65-66	7
8	66-68	61-63	74-76	60-62	56	54-56	73	64-66	61-63	67	8
9	69-70	64-66	77-78	63-64	57	57-59	-	67-69	64-65	68	9
10	71-72	67-68	79	65-66	58	60-62	74	70-71	66	69	10
11	73	69-70	80	67	59	63-66	-	72	67	70	11
12	74	71	-	68	60	67-69	75	73	68	71	12
13	75	72	81	69	-	-	-	74-75	69	72	13
14	-	-	-	-	-	-	-	-	-	-	14
15	-	-	-	-	-	-	-	-	-	-	15

Ages 65-74

ss	Com	CU	FA	HL	HS	LS	SC	SD	Soc	WK	ss
1	0-36	0-35	0-46	0-32	0-36	0-29	0-61	0-36	0-39	0-44	1
2	37-43	36-41	47-51	33-38	37-41	30-35	62-63	37-43	40-45	45-50	2
3	44-49	42-46	52-55	39-44	42-45	36-40	64-65	44-49	46-50	51-55	3
4	50-54	47-50	56-59	45-49	46-48	41-44	66-67	50-54	51-54	56-59	4
5	55-58	51-54	60-64	50-53	49-51	45-47	68-69	55-58	55-57	60-62	5
6	59-62	55-59	65-69	54-56	52-53	48-50	70-71	59-61	58-59	63-64	6
7	63-65	60-63	70-73	57-59	54-55	51-53	72	62-64	60-62	65-66	7
8	66-68	64-66	74-76	60-62	56-57	54-56	73	65-67	63-64	67-68	8
9	69-70	67-68	77-78	63-64	58	57-60	-	68-70	65	69	9
10	71-72	69	79	65-66	-	61-64	74	71-72	66	70	10
11	73	70	80	67	59	65-68	-	73	67	71	11
12	74	71	-	68	60	69	75	74	68	72	12
13	75	72	81	69	-	-	-	75	69	-	13
14	-	-	-	-	-	-	-	-	-	-	14
15	-	-	-	-	-	-	-	-	-	-	15

Ages 75-89

ss	Com	CU	FA	HL	HS	LS	SC	SD	Soc	WK	ss
1	0-41	0-12	0-32	0-12	0-21	0-6	0-52	0-25	0-39	-	1
2	42-47	13-22	33-40	13-22	22-28	7-14	53-57	26-34	40-45	-	2
3	48-52	23-31	41-47	23-31	29-34	15-21	58-61	35-42	46-50	-	3
4	53-56	32-39	48-53	32-39	35-39	22-27	62-64	43-49	51-54	-	4
5	57-60	40-46	54-58	40-46	40-43	28-32	65-67	50-55	55-57	-	5
6	61-63	47-52	59-64	47-52	44-48	33-38	68-69	56-60	58-59	-	6
7	64-65	53-57	65-69	53-57	49-52	39-43	70-71	61-64	60-62	-	7
8	66-68	58-61	70-73	58-61	53-55	44-49	72-73	65-67	63-64	-	8
9	69-70	62-64	74-76	62-64	56-57	50-54	-	68-69	65	-	9
10	71-72	65-66	77-78	65-66	58	55-58	74	70-71	66	-	10
11	73	67-68	79	67	59	59-62	-	72	67	-	11
12	74	69-70	80	68	-	63-65	75	73-74	68-69	-	12
13	75	71-72	81	69	60	66-69	-	75	-	-	13
14	-	-	-	-	-	-	-	-	-	-	14
15	-	-	-	-	-	-	-	-	-	-	15

Note. **Com** = Communication; **CU** = Community Use; **FA** = Functional Academics; **HL** = Home Living; **HS** = Health and Safety; **LS** = Leisure; **SC** = Self-Care; **SD** = Self-Direction; **Soc** = Social; **WK** = Work.

A
Adult (Self)

A

Adult (Self)

Table A.10 GAC and Adaptive Domain Composite Equivalents of Sums of Scaled Scores: Adult Form, Self Report

Ages 16–21

		GAC w/out Work	GAC w/Work	CON	SO	PR w/out Work	PR w/Work
90% Confidence Interval ±		2	2	5	5	5	4
95% Confidence Interval ±		3	3	6	6	6	5

Composite Score	Percentile Rank	GAC w/out Work	GAC w/Work	CON	SO	PR w/out Work	PR w/Work
		Sums of Scaled Scores					
40	<0.1	9	–	–	–	4	5
41	<0.1	10	10	–	–	–	–
42	<0.1	11	11	–	–	5	6
43	<0.1	12	12	–	–	–	–
44	<0.1	13	13	–	–	6	7
45	<0.1	14	14	–	–	–	–
46	<0.1	15	15	3	–	7	8
47	<0.1	16	16	–	–	–	–
48	<0.1	17	17–18	–	–	8	9
49	<0.1	18	19–20	4	–	–	–
50	<0.1	19	21–22	–	–	9	10
51	0.1	20	23–24	5	–	–	11
52	0.1	21	25–26	–	–	10	12
53	0.1	22	27–28	6	–	–	13
54	0.1	23	29–30	–	2	11	14
55	0.1	24	31–32	7	–	–	15
56	0.2	25	33–34	–	–	12	16
57	0.2	26–27	35–36	8	3	–	17
58	0.3	28–29	37–38	–	–	13	18
59	0.3	30–31	39–40	9	–	–	19
60	0.4	32–33	41–42	–	4	14	20
61	0.5	34–35	43–44	10	–	–	21
62	1	36–37	45–46	–	5	15	22
63	1	38–39	47–48	11	–	–	23
64	1	40–41	49–50	–	6	16	24
65	1	42–43	51–52	12	–	17	25
66	1	44–45	53–54	–	7	18	26
67	1	46–47	55–56	13	–	19	27
68	2	48–49	57–58	–	8	20	28
69	2	50–51	59–60	14	–	21	29
70	2	52–53	61–62	15	9	22	30
71	3	54	63	–	–	23	–
72	3	55	64	16	10	–	31
73	4	56	65	–	–	24	–
74	4	57	66	–	–	–	32
75	5	58	67	17	11	25	–
76	5	59	68	–	–	–	33
77	6	60	69	18	–	26	–
78	7	61	70	–	12	–	34
79	8	62	71	19	–	27	35
80	9	63	72	–	–	28	–

Composite Score	Percentile Rank	GAC w/out Work	GAC w/Work	CON	SO	PR w/out Work	PR w/Work
		Sums of Scaled Scores					
81	10	64	73	20	13	–	36
82	12	65	74	–	–	29	–
83	13	66	75	–	14	–	37
84	14	67–68	76	21	–	30	38
85	16	69	77–78	–	–	–	–
86	18	70–71	79	22	15	31	39
87	19	72	80–81	23	–	32	40
88	21	73–74	82	–	16	33	41
89	23	75	83–84	24	–	–	–
90	25	76	85–86	–	17	–	42
91	27	77–78	87	25	–	34	43
92	30	79	88–89	–	18	35	44
93	32	80–81	90–91	26	–	36	45
94	34	82	92	27	19	37	46
95	37	83–84	93–94	–	–	–	–
96	39	85	95	28	20	38	47
97	42	86–87	96–97	–	–	39	48
98	45	88	98–99	29	21	40	49
99	47	89–90	100	30	–	–	50
100	50	91	101–102	–	–	41	51
101	53	92	103–104	31	22	42	52
102	55	93–94	105	32	–	43	53
103	58	95–96	106–107	33	24	44	54
104	61	97	108	34	–	–	55
105	63	98–99	109–110	35	–	45	56
106	66	100	111–112	–	23	–	57
107	68	101–102	113	36	–	46	–
108	70	103–104	114–115	37	24	–	58
109	73	105	116	–	–	47	59
110	75	106–107	117–118	–	–	–	60
111	77	108	119	38	25	48	–
112	79	109	120–121	–	–	–	61
113	81	110–111	122	–	–	49	–
114	82	112	123	–	–	–	62
115	84	113–114	124–125	–	–	–	–
116	86	115	126	–	26	50	63
117	87	116	127–128	–	–	–	–
118	88	117	129	38	–	51	64
119	90	118–119	130	–	–	–	–
120	>90	120–124	131–138	39–57	27–38	52–76	65–95

Note. **CON** = Conceptual Adaptive Domain; **SO** = Social Adaptive Domain; **PR** = Practical Adaptive Domain.

Table A.10 GAC and Adaptive Domain Composite Equivalents of Sums of Scaled Scores: Adult Form, Self Report (continued)

Ages 22–29

90% Confidence Interval ±		GAC w/out Work 3	GAC w/Work 2	CON 5	SO 5	PR w/out Work 5	PR w/Work 4
95% Confidence Interval ±		GAC w/out Work 4	GAC w/Work 3	CON 6	SO 6	PR w/out Work 6	PR w/Work 5

Composite Score	Percentile Rank	GAC w/out Work	GAC w/Work	CON	SO	PR w/out Work	PR w/Work
		Sums of Scaled Scores					
40	<0.1	9	–	–	–	4	4
41	<0.1	10	–	–	–	5	5
42	<0.1	11	–	–	–	6	–
43	<0.1	12	–	–	–	6	5
44	<0.1	13	–	–	–	–	6
45	<0.1	14	–	–	–	7	6
46	<0.1	15	–	–	–	–	–
47	<0.1	16	3	–	–	8	7
48	<0.1	17	–	–	–	–	–
49	<0.1	18	4	–	–	9	8
50	<0.1	19	–	–	–	–	–
51	0.1	20	5	–	–	10	9
52	0.1	21	–	–	–	–	–
53	0.1	22	6	–	2	11	10
54	0.1	23	–	–	–	–	–
55	0.1	24	7	–	–	12	11
56	0.2	25	–	3	–	–	12
57	0.2	26	8	–	–	13	13
58	0.3	27	–	–	4	–	14
59	0.3	28	9	–	–	14	15
60	0.4	29	–	–	–	–	16
61	0.5	30–31	10	–	5	15	17
62	1	32–33	–	6	–	–	18
63	1	34–35	11	–	–	16	19
64	1	36–37	–	–	7	–	20
65	1	38–39	12	–	–	17	21
66	1	40–41	–	8	–	–	22
67	1	42–43	13	–	–	18	23
68	2	44–45	–	9	–	–	24
69	2	46–47	14	–	–	19	25
70	2	48–49	15	–	10	20	26
71	3	50	–	–	–	–	–
72	3	51	16	11	–	21	27
73	4	52	–	–	–	–	28
74	4	53	17	–	12	22	29
75	5	54	–	12	–	23	30
76	5	55	18	–	–	24	31
77	6	56	–	13	–	–	–
78	7	57–58	18	–	13	25	32
79	8	59	65–66	–	–	26	33
80	9	60	67–68	19	14	27	34

Composite Score	Percentile Rank	GAC w/out Work	GAC w/Work	CON	SO	PR w/out Work	PR w/Work
		Sums of Scaled Scores					
81	10	61–62	69	–	14	–	35
82	12	63	70–71	20	–	28	36
83	13	64–65	72–73	–	–	29	37
84	14	66	74	21	15	30	38
85	16	67–68	75–76	–	–	31	39
86	18	69	77–78	22	16	32	40
87	19	70–71	79–80	23	–	–	41
88	21	72	81	–	–	33	42
89	23	73–74	82–83	24	17	34	43
90	25	75–76	84–85	–	–	35	44–45
91	27	77–78	86–87	25	–	36	46
92	30	79	88–89	26	18	37	47
93	32	80–81	90–91	27	–	38	48
94	34	82–83	92–93	–	–	39	49
95	37	84–85	94–95	28	19	–	–
96	39	86–87	96–97	29	–	40	50
97	42	88–89	98–99	30	–	41	51
98	45	90	100–101	–	20	42	52
99	47	91–92	102–103	31	21	–	53
100	50	93–94	104–105	32	–	43	54
101	53	95–96	106–107	33	22	–	55
102	55	97–98	108–109	–	–	44	56
103	58	99	110	34	23	45	57
104	61	100–101	111–112	–	–	46	–
105	63	102–103	113–114	35	–	–	58
106	66	104	115–116	–	24	47	–
107	68	105–106	117	36	–	–	59
108	70	107	118–119	–	–	–	–
109	73	108–109	120–121	37	25	48	60
110	75	110	122	–	–	–	–
111	77	111	123	38	26	–	61
112	79	112	124–125	–	–	–	–
113	81	113	126	–	–	49	–
114	82	114	127	39	–	–	62
115	84	115	128–129	–	–	–	–
116	86	116	130	–	–	50	–
117	87	117	131	–	–	–	63
118	88	118	132	–	–	–	–
119	90	119	133	–	–	51	–
120	>90	120–124	134–138	40–57	27–38	52–76	64–95

Note. **CON** = Conceptual Adaptive Domain; **SO** = Social Adaptive Domain; **PR** = Practical Adaptive Domain.

Table A.10 GAC and Adaptive Domain Composite Equivalents of Sums of Scaled Scores: Adult Form, Self Report (continued)

Ages 30-39

		GAC w/out Work	GAC w/Work	CON	SO	PR w/out Work	PR w/Work
90% Confidence Interval ±		2	2	4	4	4	4
95% Confidence Interval ±		3	3	5	5	5	5
Composite Score	**Percentile Rank**	Sums of Scaled Scores					
40	<0.1	9	-	-	-	-	-
41	<0.1	10	10	-	-	-	-
42	<0.1	11	11	-	-	-	-
43	<0.1	12	12	-	-	4	5
44	<0.1	13	13	-	-	-	-
45	<0.1	14	14	-	-	5	6
46	<0.1	15	15	-	-	-	-
47	<0.1	16	16	-	-	6	7
48	<0.1	17	17	-	-	-	-
49	<0.1	18	18	3	-	7	8
50	<0.1	19	19	-	-	-	-
51	0.1	20	20	4	-	8	9
52	0.1	21	21	-	-	-	-
53	0.1	22	22	5	-	9	10
54	0.1	23	23	-	-	-	-
55	0.1	24	24-25	6	2	10	11
56	0.2	25	26-27	-	-	-	12
57	0.2	26	28-29	7	-	11	13
58	0.3	27	30-31	-	3	-	14
59	0.3	28	32-33	8	-	12	15
60	0.4	29	34-35	-	-	-	16
61	0.5	30-31	36-37	9	4	13	17
62	1	32-33	38-39	-	-	-	18
63	1	34-35	40-41	10	-	14	19
64	1	36-37	42-43	-	5	-	20
65	1	38-39	44-45	11	-	15	21
66	1	40-41	46-47	12	6	16	22
67	1	42-43	48-49	-	-	-	23
68	2	44-45	50-51	-	7	-	24
69	2	46-47	52-53	13	-	17	25
70	2	48-49	54-55	14	8	18	26
71	3	50	56	-	-	-	27
72	3	51	57	15	9	19	-
73	3	52	58	-	-	-	28
74	4	53	59	-	-	20	29
75	5	54	60	16	10	21	-
76	5	55	61-62	-	-	22	30
77	6	56	63	-	-	23	31
78	7	57	64-65	17	11	-	32
79	8	58	66-67	-	-	24	33
80	9	59	68	18	-	25	34

		GAC w/out Work	GAC w/Work	CON	SO	PR w/out Work	PR w/Work
90% Confidence Interval ±		2	2	4	4	4	4
95% Confidence Interval ±		3	3	5	5	5	5
Composite Score	**Percentile Rank**	Sums of Scaled Scores					
81	10	60	69-70	-	12	26	35
82	12	61	71-72	19	-	27	36
83	13	62-63	73-74	-	-	28	37
84	14	64-65	75-76	20	13	29	38
85	16	66-67	77-78	-	-	30	39-40
86	18	68-69	79-80	21	14	31-32	41
87	19	70-72	81-82	22	-	33	42-43
88	21	73-74	83-84	23	15	34	44
89	23	75-76	85-87	-	-	35	45-46
90	25	77-78	88-89	24	16	36-37	47
91	27	79-80	90-91	25	17	38	48
92	30	81-83	92-93	26	-	39	49-50
93	32	84-85	94-96	27	18	40	51
94	34	86-87	97-98	28	19	-	52
95	37	88-89	99-100	29	-	41	-
96	39	90	101-102	30	20	42	53
97	42	91-92	103-104	31	-	-	54
98	45	93-94	105-106	-	21	43	-
99	47	95	107	32	-	-	55
100	50	96	108-109	33	-	44	56
101	53	97	110	-	22	-	-
102	55	98	111	34	-	45	57
103	58	99	112	-	-	-	-
104	61	100	113	35	-	46	58
105	63	101	114	-	23	-	-
106	66	102	115	36	-	47	59
107	68	103	116	-	-	-	-
108	70	104	117	-	24	-	-
109	73	105	118	37	-	-	-
110	75	106	119	-	-	48	60
111	77	107	120	-	-	-	-
112	79	108	121	-	-	-	-
113	81	109	122	-	-	49	61
114	82	110	123	38	25	-	-
115	84	111	124	-	-	50	-
116	86	112	125	-	-	-	-
117	87	113	126	-	-	-	62
118	88	114	127	39	-	-	-
119	90	115	128	-	-	-	-
120	>90	116-124	129-138	40-57	26-38	51-76	63-95

Note. **CON** = Conceptual Adaptive Domain; **SO** = Social Adaptive Domain; **PR** = Practical Adaptive Domain.

Table A.10 GAC and Adaptive Domain Composite Equivalents of Sums of Scaled Scores: Adult Form, Self Report *(continued)*

Ages 40–49

		GAC w/out Work	GAC w/Work	CON	SO	PR w/out Work	PR w/Work
90% Confidence Interval ±		2	2	4	5	4	4
95% Confidence Interval ±		3	3	5	6	5	5
Composite Score	**Percentile Rank**	**Sums of Scaled Scores**					
40	<0.1	9	–	–	–	–	–
41	<0.1	10	10	–	–	–	–
42	<0.1	11	11	–	–	–	–
43	<0.1	12	12	–	–	4	5
44	<0.1	13	13	–	–	–	–
45	<0.1	14	14	–	–	5	6
46	<0.1	15	15	–	–	–	–
47	<0.1	16	16	–	–	6	7
48	<0.1	17	17	–	–	–	–
49	<0.1	18	18	3	–	7	8
50	<0.1	19	19	–	–	–	–
51	0.1	20	20	4	–	8	9
52	0.1	21	21–22	–	–	–	–
53	0.1	22	23–24	5	–	9	10
54	0.1	23	25–26	–	2	–	–
55	0.1	24	27–28	6	–	10	11
56	0.2	25	29–30	–	–	–	12
57	0.2	26	31–32	7	3	11	13
58	0.3	27	33–34	–	–	–	14
59	0.3	28	35–36	8	–	12	15
60	0.4	29	37–38	–	4	–	16
61	0.5	30–31	39–40	9	–	13	17
62	1	32–33	41–42	–	5	–	18
63	1	34–35	43–44	10	–	14	19
64	1	36–37	45–46	–	6	–	20
65	1	38–39	47–48	11	–	15	21
66	1	40–41	49–50	–	7	–	22
67	1	42–43	51–52	12	–	16	23
68	2	44–45	53–54	–	8	–	24
69	2	46–47	55–56	13	–	17	25
70	2	48–49	57–58	14	9	18	26
71	3	50	59	–	–	–	–
72	3	51	60	15	10	19	27
73	4	52	61	–	–	20	28
74	4	53	62	–	–	–	–
75	5	54	63	16	11	21	29
76	5	55	64	–	–	22	30
77	6	56	65	–	–	23	31
78	7	57	66	17	12	24	32
79	8	58	67	–	–	25	33
80	9	59	68	18	–	–	34

		GAC w/out Work	GAC w/Work	CON	SO	PR w/out Work	PR w/Work
90% Confidence Interval ±		2	2	4	5	4	4
95% Confidence Interval ±		3	3	5	6	5	5
Composite Score	**Percentile Rank**	**Sums of Scaled Scores**					
81	10	60	69	–	13	26	–
82	12	61	70–71	19	–	27	35
83	13	62–63	72	20	–	28	36–37
84	14	64	73–74	–	14	29	38
85	16	65–66	75–76	21	–	30	39
86	18	67–68	77–78	–	–	31	40
87	19	69–70	79–80	22	15	32	41
88	21	71–72	81–82	23	–	33	42–43
89	23	73–74	83–84	–	–	34	44
90	25	75–76	85–86	24	16	35	45
91	27	77–78	87–88	25	–	36	46–47
92	30	79–80	89–91	–	–	37	48
93	32	81	92–93	26	17	38	49
94	34	82–83	94–95	27	–	39	50
95	37	84–85	96–97	28	18	40	51
96	39	86–87	98–99	–	–	41	52
97	42	88–89	100–101	29	19	–	53
98	45	90–91	102–103	30	20	42	54
99	47	92	104–105	31	–	43	55
100	50	93–94	106–107	–	21	–	–
101	53	95–96	108	32	–	44	56
102	55	97	109–110	33	–	–	57
103	58	98–99	111–112	–	22	45	–
104	61	100	113	34	–	–	58
105	63	101–102	114–115	–	–	46	–
106	66	103	116	35	–	–	59
107	68	104	117	–	23	47	–
108	70	105	118–119	–	–	–	–
109	73	106	120	36	–	–	60
110	75	107	121	–	–	48	–
111	77	108	122	–	–	–	–
112	79	109	123	37	24	–	61
113	81	110	124	–	–	49	–
114	82	111	125	–	–	–	–
115	84	112	126	38	–	–	62
116	86	113	127	–	25	–	–
117	87	114	128	–	–	50	–
118	88	115	129	–	–	–	–
119	90	116	130	39	–	–	63
120	>90	117–124	131–138	40–57	26–38	51–76	64–95

Note. **CON** = Conceptual Adaptive Domain; **SO** = Social Adaptive Domain; **PR** = Practical Adaptive Domain.

Table A.10 GAC and Adaptive Domain Composite Equivalents of Sums of Scaled Scores: Adult Form, Self Report (continued)

Ages 50–64

		GAC w/out Work	GAC w/Work	CON	SO	PR w/out Work	PR w/Work
90% Confidence Interval ±		2	2	4	5	5	4
95% Confidence Interval ±		3	3	5	6	6	5
Composite Score	**Percentile Rank**	Sums of Scaled Scores					
40	<0.1	9	–	–	–	4	–
41	<0.1	10	10	–	–	5	5
42	<0.1	11	11	–	–	–	–
43	<0.1	12	12	–	–	6	6
44	<0.1	13	13	–	–	–	–
45	<0.1	14	14	–	–	7	7
46	<0.1	15	15	–	–	–	–
47	<0.1	16	16	–	–	8	8
48	<0.1	17	17	–	–	–	–
49	<0.1	18	18	3	–	9	9
50	<0.1	19	19	–	–	–	–
51	0.1	20	20	4	–	10	10
52	0.1	21	21	–	–	–	–
53	0.1	22	22	5	–	11	11
54	0.1	23	23	–	–	–	–
55	0.1	24	24	6	2	12	12
56	0.2	25	25–26	–	–	–	13
57	0.2	26	27–28	7	–	13	14
58	0.3	27	29–30	–	3	–	15
59	0.3	28	31–32	8	–	14	16
60	0.4	29	33–34	–	–	–	17
61	0.5	30	35–36	9	4	15	18
62	1	31	37–38	–	–	–	19
63	1	32	39–40	10	–	16	20
64	1	33–34	41–42	–	5	–	21
65	1	35–36	43–44	11	6	17	22
66	1	37–38	45–46	–	–	18	23
67	1	39–40	47–48	12	–	–	24
68	2	41–42	49–50	–	7	–	25
69	2	43–44	51–52	13	–	19	26
70	2	45–46	53–54	14	8	20	27
71	3	47	55	–	–	–	–
72	3	48	56	15	9	21	28
73	4	49	57	–	–	–	29
74	4	50	58	–	–	–	–
75	5	51	59–60	16	10	22	30
76	5	52	61	–	–	–	31
77	6	53	62–63	–	–	23	–
78	7	54	64–65	17	11	–	32
79	8	55	66–67	–	–	24	33
80	9	56	68	–	–	–	34

		GAC w/out Work	GAC w/Work	CON	SO	PR w/out Work	PR w/Work
90% Confidence Interval ±		2	2	4	5	5	4
95% Confidence Interval ±		3	3	5	6	6	5
Composite Score	**Percentile Rank**	Sums of Scaled Scores					
81	10	57	69–70	18	12	25	35
82	12	58–59	71–72	–	–	26	36
83	13	60	73–74	19	–	27	37
84	14	61–62	75–76	–	13	28	38
85	16	63	77–78	20	–	29	39
86	18	64–65	79–80	–	–	30	40
87	19	66–67	81–82	21	14	31	41–42
88	21	68	83–84	22	–	32	43
89	23	69–70	85–86	–	–	33	44–45
90	25	71–72	87–88	23	15	34–35	46
91	27	73–74	89–90	–	–	36	47
92	30	75–76	91–92	24	16	37	48
93	32	77–78	93–94	25	–	38	49–50
94	34	79–80	95–96	26	17	39	51
95	37	81–82	97–98	–	–	–	–
96	39	83–84	99–100	27	18	40	52
97	42	85–86	101	28	–	41	53
98	45	87–88	102–103	29	19	42	54
99	47	89–90	104–105	30	20	–	–
100	50	91–92	106–107	31	–	43	55
101	53	93–94	108	–	21	–	56
102	55	95–96	109–110	32	–	44	–
103	58	97–98	111	33	–	45	57
104	61	99	112–113	–	22	–	–
105	63	100–101	114	34	–	–	58
106	66	102	115–116	35	23	46	59
107	68	103–104	117	–	–	–	–
108	70	105	118	–	–	–	–
109	73	106	119	–	–	–	60
110	75	107	120	36	24	47	–
111	77	108	121	–	–	–	–
112	79	109	122	–	–	–	–
113	81	110	123	37	25	48	–
114	82	111	124	–	–	–	61
115	84	112	125	–	–	–	–
116	86	113	126	38	–	49	–
117	87	114	127	–	–	–	–
118	88	115	128	–	–	–	62
119	90	116	129	39	–	50	–
120	>90	117–124	130–138	40–57	26–38	51–76	63–95

Note. **CON** = Conceptual Adaptive Domain; **SO** = Social Adaptive Domain; **PR** = Practical Adaptive Domain.

Table A.10 GAC and Adaptive Domain Composite Equivalents of Sums of Scaled Scores: Adult Form, Self Report (continued)

Ages 65–74

Composite Score	Percentile Rank	GAC w/out Work	GAC w/Work	CON	SO	PR w/out Work	PR w/Work
90% Confidence Interval ±		2	2	4	4	4	3
95% Confidence Interval ±		3	3	5	5	5	4
		Sums of Scaled Scores					
40	<0.1	9	–	–	–	–	–
41	<0.1	10	10	–	–	–	–
42	<0.1	11	11	–	–	–	–
43	<0.1	12	12	–	–	4	5
44	<0.1	13	13	–	–	–	–
45	<0.1	14	14	–	–	5	6
46	<0.1	15	15	–	–	–	–
47	<0.1	16	16	–	–	6	7
48	<0.1	17	17	3	–	–	–
49	<0.1	18	18	–	–	7	8
50	<0.1	19	19	–	–	–	–
51	0.1	20	20	4	–	8	9
52	0.1	21	21	–	–	–	–
53	0.1	22	22	5	–	9	10
54	0.1	23	23	–	–	–	–
55	0.1	24	24	6	2	10	11
56	0.2	25	25	–	–	–	12
57	0.2	26	26	7	–	11	13
58	0.3	27	27–28	–	3	–	14
59	0.3	28	29–30	8	–	12	15
60	0.4	29	31–32	–	–	–	16
61	0.5	30	33–34	9	4	13	17
62	1	31	35–36	–	–	–	18
63	1	32	37–38	10	–	14	19
64	1	33	39–40	–	5	–	20
65	1	34	41–42	11	–	15	21
66	1	35–36	43–44	12	6	16	22
67	1	37–38	45–46	–	–	–	23
68	2	39–40	47–48	–	7	–	24
69	2	41–42	49–50	13	–	17	25
70	2	43–44	51–52	14	8	18	26
71	3	45	53	–	–	–	–
72	3	46	54	15	9	19	27
73	4	47	55	–	–	–	–
74	4	48	56	–	–	20	–
75	5	49	57	16	10	21	28
76	5	50	58	–	–	–	–
77	6	51–52	59	17	–	22	29
78	7	53	60	–	11	23	–
79	8	54–55	61	18	–	–	30
80	9	56	62	–	–	24	31

Composite Score	Percentile Rank	GAC w/out Work	GAC w/Work	CON	SO	PR w/out Work	PR w/Work
90% Confidence Interval ±		2	2	4	4	4	3
95% Confidence Interval ±		3	3	5	5	5	4
		Sums of Scaled Scores					
81	10	57–58	63–64	19	12	25	32
82	12	59–60	65–66	–	–	26	33
83	13	61	67–68	20	–	27	34
84	14	62–63	69–70	21	13	28	35
85	16	64–65	71–72	–	–	29	36–37
86	18	66–67	73–74	22	–	30	38
87	19	68–69	75–76	23	14	31	39
88	21	70	77–78	–	–	32–33	40
89	23	71–72	79–80	24	15	34	41–42
90	25	73–75	81–82	25	16	35	43
91	27	76–77	83–84	26	17	36	44
92	30	78–79	85–86	–	18	37	45–46
93	32	80–81	87–88	27	19	38	47
94	34	82–83	89–91	28	–	39	48
95	37	84–85	92–93	–	20	40	49
96	39	86–88	94–95	29	–	41	50
97	42	89–90	96–97	30	21	–	51
98	45	91–92	98–99	31	–	42	52
99	47	93–94	100–101	–	–	43	53
100	50	95–96	102–103	32	22	–	–
101	53	97–98	104–105	–	–	44	54
102	55	99–100	106–107	33	–	–	55
103	58	101	108–109	–	–	45	–
104	61	102–103	110–111	34	23	–	56
105	63	104–105	112–113	–	–	46	–
106	66	106	114–115	35	–	–	57
107	68	107	116	–	–	–	–
108	70	108	117–118	36	24	47	58
109	73	109	119–120	–	–	–	–
110	75	110	121	–	–	–	59
111	77	111	122–123	37	–	48	–
112	79	112	124	–	–	–	–
113	81	113	125	–	–	–	–
114	82	114	126–127	38	–	–	60
115	84	115	128	–	25	49	–
116	86	116	129	–	–	–	61
117	87	117	130–131	–	–	–	–
118	88	118	132	39	–	–	62
119	90	119	133	–	–	50	–
120	>90	120–124	134–138	40–57	26–38	51–76	63–95

Note. **CON** = Conceptual Adaptive Domain; **SO** = Social Adaptive Domain; **PR** = Practical Adaptive Domain.

A Adult (Self)

257

Table A.10 GAC and Adaptive Domain Composite Equivalents of Sums of Scaled Scores: Adult Form, Self Report (continued)

Ages 75–89

		Sums of Scaled Scores			
90% Confidence Interval ±		2	4	4	4
95% Confidence Interval ±		3	5	5	5
Composite Score	**Percentile Rank**	**GAC**	**CON**	**SO**	**PR**
40	<0.1	9	–	–	–
41	<0.1	10	–	–	–
42	<0.1	11	–	–	–
43	<0.1	12	–	–	4
44	<0.1	13	–	–	–
45	<0.1	14	–	–	5
46	<0.1	15	–	–	–
47	<0.1	16	3	–	6
48	<0.1	17	–	–	–
49	<0.1	18	4	–	7
50	<0.1	19	–	–	–
51	0.1	20	5	–	8
52	0.1	21	–	–	–
53	0.1	22	6	–	9
54	0.1	23	–	–	–
55	0.1	24	7	2	10
56	0.2	25	–	–	–
57	0.2	26	8	–	11
58	0.3	27	–	3	–
59	0.3	28	9	–	12
60	0.4	29	–	–	–
61	0.5	30	10	4	13
62	1	31–32	–	–	–
63	1	33–34	11	–	14
64	1	35–36	–	5	–
65	1	37–38	12	–	15
66	1	39–40	–	6	–
67	1	41–42	13	–	16
68	2	43–44	–	7	–
69	2	45–46	14	–	17
70	2	47–48	15	8	18
71	3	49	–	–	–
72	3	50	16	9	19
73	4	51	–	–	–
74	4	52	–	–	20
75	5	53	17	10	–
76	5	54	–	–	21
77	6	55	–	–	22
78	7	56	18	11	23
79	8	57	–	–	24
80	9	58	19	12	25

		Sums of Scaled Scores			
90% Confidence Interval ±		2	4	4	4
95% Confidence Interval ±		3	5	5	5
Composite Score	**Percentile Rank**	**GAC**	**CON**	**SO**	**PR**
81	10	59	–	–	26
82	12	60–61	20	13	27
83	13	62–63	–	–	28
84	14	64–65	–	14	–
85	16	66–67	21	–	29
86	18	68	–	15	30
87	19	69–70	22	–	31
88	21	71–72	23	16	32
89	23	73–74	–	–	33
90	25	75–76	24	17	34
91	27	77–78	–	–	35
92	30	79–80	25	18	36
93	32	81–82	26	–	37
94	34	83–84	27	19	38
95	37	85–86	–	–	39
96	39	87–88	28	–	40
97	42	89–90	29	20	–
98	45	91	30	–	41
99	47	92–93	31	–	42
100	50	94–95	32	21	43
101	53	96–97	33	–	44
102	55	98	–	–	–
103	58	99–100	34	22	45
104	61	101	–	–	–
105	63	102–103	35	–	46
106	66	104	–	–	47
107	68	105–106	36	23	–
108	70	107	–	–	–
109	73	108	–	–	–
110	75	109	37	–	48
111	77	110–111	–	24	–
112	79	112	–	–	49
113	81	113	–	–	–
114	82	114	38	–	–
115	84	115	–	–	50
116	86	116	–	25	–
117	87	117	39	–	–
118	88	118	–	–	51
119	90	119	–	–	–
120	>90	120–124	40–57	26–38	52–76

Note. **CON** = Conceptual Adaptive Domain; **SO** = Social Adaptive Domain; **PR** = Practical Adaptive Domain.

Table A.11 Average Number of Items Guessed by the Standardization Sample: Adult Form, Self Report

Skill Areas	Age Group												
	16–21		22–29		30–39		40–49		50–64		65–74		75–89	
	Mean	$SE_{\bar{x}}$	Mean	$SE_{\bar{x}}$	Mean	$SE_{\bar{x}}$	Mean	$SE_{\bar{x}}$	Mean	$SE_{\bar{x}}$	Mean	$SE_{\bar{x}}$	Mean	$SE_{\bar{x}}$
Communication	0.21	0.06	0.15	0.06	0.05	0.03	0.12	0.05	0.12	0.05	0.25	0.22	0.02	0.02
Community Use	0.17	0.05	0.07	0.04	0.01	0.01	0.07	0.04	0.05	0.03	0.03	0.03	0.04	0.02
Functional Academics	0.19	0.05	0.05	0.03	0.03	0.02	0.03	0.01	0.06	0.04	0.03	0.02	0.04	0.03
Home Living	0.03	0.01	0.03	0.03	0.02	0.01	0.03	0.02	0.03	0.02	0.02	0.01	0.03	0.02
Health and Safety	0.07	0.03	0.09	0.06	0.07	0.04	0.03	0.03	0.01	0.01	0.01	0.01	0.01	0.01
Leisure	0.22	0.15	0.02	0.01	0.04	0.02	0.06	0.06	0.10	0.05	0.05	0.03	0.04	0.03
Self-Care	0.03	0.01	0.09	0.07	0.04	0.02	0.02	0.01	0.04	0.03	0.02	0.02	0.02	0.01
Self-Direction	0.09	0.04	0.07	0.03	0.03	0.01	0.11	0.08	0.08	0.04	0.00	0.00	0.06	0.03
Social	0.06	0.03	0.04	0.03	0.02	0.02	0.09	0.05	0.04	0.02	0.02	0.01	0.11	0.07
Work	0.23	0.16	0.18	0.09	0.23	0.12	0.13	0.06	0.07	0.07	0.02	0.02	—	—

Note. $SE_{\bar{x}}$ = Standard Error of the Mean.

Table A.12 Scaled Score Equivalents of Skill Area Raw Scores: Adult Form, Rated by Others

Ages 16–21

ss	Com	CU	FA	HL	HS	LS	SC	SD	Soc	WK	ss
1	0-28	0-16	0-26	0-15	0-23	0-20	0-40	0-16	0-18	0-26	1
2	29-36	17-25	27-35	16-23	24-30	21-28	41-47	17-25	19-27	27-34	2
3	37-43	26-33	36-43	24-30	31-36	29-35	48-53	26-33	28-35	35-41	3
4	44-49	34-40	44-50	31-36	37-41	36-41	54-58	34-40	36-42	42-47	4
5	50-54	41-46	51-56	37-41	42-45	42-46	59-62	41-46	43-48	48-52	5
6	55-58	47-51	57-61	42-46	46-48	47-50	63-66	47-51	49-53	53-56	6
7	59-62	52-55	62-65	47-50	49-51	51-54	67-69	52-55	54-57	57-59	7
8	63-65	56-58	66-69	51-54	52-53	55-57	70-71	56-59	58-60	60-62	8
9	66-68	59-62	70-72	55-57	54-55	58-60	72	60-63	61-63	63-65	9
10	69-70	63-65	73-75	58-60	56	61-63	73	64-66	64-65	66-67	10
11	71-72	66-67	76-77	61-63	57	64-65	74	67-69	66	68-69	11
12	73-74	68-69	78-79	64-65	58	66-67	-	70-72	67	70	12
13	75	70-71	80	66-67	59-60	68	75	73-74	68	71-72	13
14	-	72	81	68	-	69	-	75	69	-	14
15	-	-	-	69	-	-	-	-	-	-	15

Ages 22–29

ss	Com	CU	FA	HL	HS	LS	SC	SD	Soc	WK	ss
1	0-30	0-20	0-30	0-15	0-23	0-20	0-44	0-23	0-30	0-30	1
2	31-38	21-29	31-39	16-23	24-30	21-28	45-51	24-31	31-37	31-38	2
3	39-45	30-37	40-47	24-30	31-36	29-35	52-57	32-38	38-43	39-45	3
4	46-51	38-44	48-54	31-37	37-41	36-41	58-62	39-44	44-48	46-51	4
5	52-56	45-50	55-60	38-43	42-46	42-46	63-66	45-49	49-52	52-56	5
6	57-60	51-55	61-65	44-48	47-50	47-50	67-69	50-54	53-56	57-60	6
7	61-64	56-59	66-69	49-52	51-53	51-54	70-71	55-58	57-59	61-63	7
8	65-67	60-62	70-73	53-56	54-55	55-57	72-73	59-62	60-61	64-66	8
9	68-70	63-65	74-76	57-60	56	58-60	74	63-66	62-64	67-68	9
10	71-72	66-67	77-78	61-63	57	61-63	-	67-69	65	69	10
11	73	68-69	79	64-65	58	64-66	-	70-71	66-67	70	11
12	74	70-71	80	66-67	59	67-68	75	72-73	68	71	12
13	75	72	81	68	60	69	-	74	69	72	13
14	-	-	-	69	-	-	-	75	-	-	14
15	-	-	-	-	-	-	-	-	-	-	15

Ages 30–39

ss	Com	CU	FA	HL	HS	LS	SC	SD	Soc	WK	ss
1	0-36	0-22	0-38	0-22	0-34	0-20	0-44	0-25	0-35	0-41	1
2	37-43	23-31	39-46	23-30	35-40	21-29	45-51	26-34	36-41	42-47	2
3	44-49	32-39	47-53	31-37	41-45	30-36	52-57	35-42	42-46	48-52	3
4	50-54	40-46	54-59	38-43	46-49	37-41	58-62	43-49	47-50	53-56	4
5	55-58	47-52	60-64	44-48	50-52	42-46	63-66	50-55	51-53	57-59	5
6	59-62	53-57	65-68	49-52	53-54	47-50	67-69	56-60	54-56	60-62	6
7	63-66	58-61	69-71	53-56	55	51-54	70-71	61-64	57-59	63-65	7
8	67-69	62-64	72-74	57-60	56	55-57	72-73	65-67	60-62	66-67	8
9	70-71	65-67	75-76	61-63	57	58-60	74	68-69	63-64	68-69	9
10	72	68-69	77-78	64-65	58	61-63	-	70-71	65-66	70	10
11	73	70	79	66	59	64-66	-	72-73	67	71	11
12	74	71	80	67	60	67-68	75	74	68	72	12
13	75	72	81	68-69	-	69	-	75	69	-	13
14	-	-	-	-	-	-	-	-	-	-	14
15	-	-	-	-	-	-	-	-	-	-	15

Ages 40–49

ss	Com	CU	FA	HL	HS	LS	SC	SD	Soc	WK	ss
1	0-38	0-29	0-39	0-22	0-34	0-20	0-45	0-30	0-35	0-41	1
2	39-45	30-37	40-47	23-30	35-40	21-27	46-52	31-38	36-41	42-47	2
3	46-51	38-44	48-54	31-37	41-45	28-33	53-58	39-45	42-46	48-52	3
4	52-56	45-50	55-60	38-43	46-49	34-39	59-63	46-51	47-50	53-56	4
5	57-60	51-55	61-65	44-48	50-52	40-44	64-67	52-56	51-53	57-59	5
6	61-63	56-59	66-69	49-52	53-54	45-48	68-70	57-61	54-57	60-63	6
7	64-66	60-62	70-72	53-56	55	49-52	71-72	62-65	58-60	64-66	7
8	67-69	63-65	73-75	57-60	56	53-56	73	66-68	61-63	67-68	8
9	70-71	66-67	76-77	61-63	57	57-59	74	69-70	64-65	69	9
10	72	68-69	78	64-65	58	60-62	-	71-72	66	70	10
11	73	70	79	66	59	63-65	-	73	67	71	11
12	74	71	80	67	60	66-67	75	74	68	72	12
13	75	72	81	68-69	-	68-69	-	75	69	-	13
14	-	-	-	-	-	-	-	-	-	-	14
15	-	-	-	-	-	-	-	-	-	-	15

Note. **Com** = Communication; **CU** = Community Use; **FA** = Functional Academics; **HL** = Home Living; **HS** = Health and Safety; **LS** = Leisure; **SC** = Self-Care; **SD** = Self-Direction; **Soc** = Social; **WK** = Work.

Table A.12 Scaled Score Equivalents of Skill Area Raw Scores: Adult Form, Rated by Others *(continued)*

Ages 50–64

ss	Com	CU	FA	HL	HS	LS	SC	SD	Soc	WK
1	0-39	0-29	0-32	0-17	0-34	0-11	0-45	0-30	0-35	0-41
2	40-46	30-37	33-41	18-26	35-40	12-19	46-52	31-38	36-41	42-47
3	47-52	38-44	42-49	27-34	41-45	20-26	53-58	39-45	42-46	48-52
4	53-57	45-50	50-56	35-41	46-49	27-32	59-63	46-51	47-50	53-56
5	58-61	51-55	57-62	42-47	50-52	33-37	64-67	52-56	51-53	57-59
6	62-64	56-59	63-67	48-52	53-54	38-43	68-70	57-61	54-57	60-63
7	65-66	60-62	68-71	53-56	55	44-48	71-72	62-65	58-60	64-66
8	67-69	63-65	72-74	57-59	56	49-52	73	66-68	61-63	67-68
9	70-71	66-67	75-76	60-61	57	53-56	74	69-70	64-65	69
10	72	68-69	77	62-64	58	57-60	-	71-72	66	70
11	73	70	78	65-66	59	61-63	-	73	67	71
12	74	71	79-80	67	60	64-66	75	74	68	-
13	75	72	81	68-69	-	67-68	-	75	69	72
14	-	-	-	-	-	69	-	-	-	-
15	-	-	-	-	-	-	-	-	-	-

Ages 65–74

ss	Com	CU	FA	HL	HS	LS	SC	SD	Soc	WK
1	0-41	0-29	0-32	0-17	0-34	0-11	0-54	0-39	0-35	0-33
2	42-48	30-37	33-41	18-26	35-40	12-19	55-59	40-46	36-41	34-41
3	49-54	38-44	42-49	27-34	41-45	20-26	60-63	47-52	42-46	42-48
4	55-59	45-50	50-56	35-41	46-49	27-32	64-66	53-57	47-50	49-54
5	60-63	51-55	57-62	42-47	50-52	33-37	67-69	58-61	51-53	55-59
6	64-66	56-59	63-67	48-52	53-54	38-43	70-71	62-65	54-57	60-63
7	67-69	60-62	68-71	53-56	55	44-48	72-73	66-68	58-60	64-66
8	70-71	63-65	72-74	57-59	56	49-52	74	69-70	61-63	67-68
9	72	66-68	75-76	60-61	57	53-56	-	71	64-65	69
10	73	69	77	62-64	58	57-60	-	72	66	70
11	74	70	78	65-66	59	61-63	-	73	67	71
12	75	71	79-80	67	60	64-66	75	74	68	-
13	-	72	81	68-69	-	67-68	-	75	69	72
14	-	-	-	-	-	69	-	-	-	-
15	-	-	-	-	-	-	-	-	-	-

Ages 75–89

ss	Com	CU	FA	HL	HS	LS	SC	SD	Soc	WK
1	0-6	-	-	-	-	-	0-27	-	0	-
2	7-17	-	0-4	0-1	0-3	-	28-36	-	1-11	-
3	18-27	0-6	5-16	2-12	4-13	-	37-44	0-9	12-21	-
4	28-36	7-17	17-27	13-22	14-22	0-3	45-51	10-20	22-30	-
5	37-44	18-27	28-37	23-31	23-30	4-12	52-57	21-30	31-38	-
6	45-51	28-36	38-46	32-39	31-37	13-22	58-62	31-39	39-45	-
7	52-57	37-44	47-54	40-46	38-43	23-31	63-66	40-47	46-51	-
8	58-62	45-51	55-61	47-52	44-48	32-39	67-69	48-54	52-56	-
9	63-66	52-57	62-67	53-57	49-52	40-46	70-71	55-60	57-60	-
10	67-69	58-62	68-72	58-61	53-55	47-52	72-73	61-65	61-63	-
11	70-72	63-66	73-76	62-64	56-57	53-57	74	66-69	64-65	-
12	73-74	67-69	77-79	65-66	58-60	58-61	75	70-72	66-67	-
13	75	70-72	80-81	67-69	-	62-65	-	73-74	68	-
14	-	-	-	-	-	66-68	-	75	69	-
15	-	-	-	-	-	69	-	-	-	-

Note. **Com** = Communication; **CU** = Community Use; **FA** = Functional Academics; **HL** = Home Living; **HS** = Health and Safety; **LS** = Leisure; **SC** = Self-Care; **SD** = Self-Direction; **Soc** = Social; **WK** = Work.

Table A.13 GAC and Adaptive Domain Composite Equivalents of Sums of Scaled Scores: Adult Form, Rated by Others

Ages 16–21

	GAC w/out Work	GAC w/Work	CON	SO	PR w/out Work	PR w/Work
90% Confidence Interval ±	2	2	3	5	3	3
95% Confidence Interval ±	3	3	4	6	4	4

Composite Score	Percentile Rank	Sums of Scaled Scores					
		GAC w/out Work	GAC w/Work	CON	SO	PR w/out Work	PR w/Work
40	<0.1	9	10	–	–	–	5
41	<0.1	10	11	–	–	–	–
42	<0.1	11	12	–	–	–	6
43	<0.1	12	13	–	–	4	–
44	<0.1	13	14	–	–	–	7
45	<0.1	14	15	–	–	5	–
46	<0.1	15	16	–	–	–	8
47	<0.1	16	17	–	–	6	–
48	<0.1	17	18	–	–	–	9
49	<0.1	18	19	3	–	7	–
50	<0.1	19	20	–	–	–	10
51	0.1	20	21	4	–	8	11
52	0.1	21	22	–	–	–	12
53	0.1	22	23	5	–	9	13
54	0.1	23–24	24	–	2	–	14
55	0.1	25–26	25–26	6	–	10	15
56	0.2	27–28	27–28	–	–	–	16
57	0.2	29–30	29–30	7	3	11	17
58	0.3	31–32	31–32	–	–	–	18
59	0.3	33–34	33–34	8	–	12	19
60	0.4	35–36	35–36	–	4	–	20
61	0.5	37–38	37–38	9	–	13	21
62	1	39–40	39–40	–	5	–	22
63	1	41–42	41–42	10	–	14	23
64	1	43–44	43–44	–	6	–	24
65	1	45–46	45–46	11	–	15	25
66	1	47–48	47–48	–	7	–	26
67	1	49–50	49–50	12	–	16	27
68	2	51–52	51–52	–	8	–	28
69	2	53–54	53–54	13	–	17	29
70	2	55–56	55–56	14	9	18	30
71	3	57	57–58	–	–	–	–
72	3	58	59–60	15	10	19	31
73	4	59	61–62	–	–	–	32
74	4	60	63–64	16	–	20	–
75	5	61	65	–	11	21	33
76	5	62	66–67	17	–	22	34
77	6	63	68–69	–	–	23	–
78	7	64	70–71	18	12	24	35
79	8	65	72	–	–	25	36
80	9	66	73–74	19	–	26	–

	GAC w/out Work	GAC w/Work	CON	SO	PR w/out Work	PR w/Work
90% Confidence Interval ±	2	2	3	5	3	3
95% Confidence Interval ±	3	3	4	6	4	4

Composite Score	Percentile Rank	Sums of Scaled Scores					
		GAC w/out Work	GAC w/Work	CON	SO	PR w/out Work	PR w/Work
81	10	67	75–76	–	13	–	37
82	12	68	77–78	20	–	27	38
83	13	69	79	21	–	28	39
84	14	70	80–81	–	14	29	40
85	16	71	82–83	22	–	30	–
86	18	72	84	–	15	31	41
87	19	73	85–86	23	–	32	42
88	21	74	87–88	–	–	33	–
89	23	75	89	24	16	34	43
90	25	76	90–91	25	–	–	44
91	27	77	92–93	–	17	35	45
92	30	78–79	94	26	–	36	46
93	32	80–81	95–96	–	–	37	47
94	34	82–83	97	27	18	38	48
95	37	84–85	98–99	28	–	39	49
96	39	86–87	100	–	19	–	50
97	42	88–89	101–102	29	–	40	51
98	45	90–91	103	–	20	41	–
99	47	92–93	104–105	30	–	42	52
100	50	94	106	31	21	–	53
101	53	95–96	107–108	–	–	43	54
102	55	97	109	32	–	44	55
103	58	98	110–111	–	22	–	56
104	61	99–100	112	33	–	45	57
105	63	101	113	–	–	–	–
106	66	102	114	34	23	46	58
107	68	103–104	115–116	–	–	–	–
108	70	105	117	35	–	47	59
109	73	106	118	–	24	–	60
110	75	107	119	36	–	48	–
111	77	108–109	120	–	–	–	61
112	79	110	121–122	37	25	49	–
113	81	111	123	–	–	–	62
114	82	112	124	–	–	50	–
115	84	113	125	38	26	–	–
116	86	114	126	–	–	51	63
117	87	115	127	–	–	–	–
118	88	116	128	–	–	52	–
119	90	117	129	39	–	–	–
120	>90	118–125	130–138	40–57	27–38	53–76	64–95

Note. **CON** = Conceptual Adaptive Domain; **SO** = Social Adaptive Domain; **PR** = Practical Adaptive Domain.

Table A.13 GAC and Adaptive Domain Composite Equivalents of Sums of Scaled Scores: Adult Form, Rated by Others (continued)

Ages 22–29

		GAC w/out Work	GAC w/Work	CON	SO	PR w/out Work	PR w/Work
90% Confidence Interval ±		2	2	3	4	3	3
95% Confidence Interval ±		3	3	4	5	4	4

Composite Score	Percentile Rank	GAC w/out Work	GAC w/Work	CON	SO	PR w/out Work	PR w/Work
		Sums of Scaled Scores					
40	<0.1	9	10	–	–	–	–
41	<0.1	10	11	–	–	–	5
42	<0.1	11	12	–	–	–	–
43	<0.1	12	13	–	–	4	6
44	<0.1	13	14	–	–	–	–
45	<0.1	14	15	–	–	5	7
46	<0.1	15	16	–	–	–	–
47	<0.1	16	17	–	–	6	8
48	<0.1	17	18	–	–	–	–
49	<0.1	18	19	3	–	7	9
50	<0.1	19	20	4	–	8	10
51	0.1	20	21	–	–	–	–
52	0.1	21	22	5	–	9	11
53	0.1	22–23	23	–	–	–	–
54	0.1	24–25	24	–	2	–	–
55	0.1	26–27	25–26	6	–	10	12
56	0.2	28–29	27–28	–	–	–	–
57	0.2	30–31	29–30	7	3	11	13
58	0.3	32–33	31–32	–	–	–	14
59	0.3	34–35	33–34	8	–	12	15
60	0.4	36–37	35–36	–	4	–	16
61	0.5	38–39	37–38	9	–	13	17
62	1	40–41	39–40	–	5	–	18
63	1	42–43	41–42	10	–	14	19
64	1	44–45	43–44	–	6	–	20
65	1	46–47	45–46	11	–	15	21
66	1	48–49	47–48	–	7	16	22
67	1	50–51	49–50	12	–	–	23
68	2	52–53	51–52	–	8	17	24
69	2	54–55	53–54	13	–	–	25
70	2	56–57	55–56	14	9	18	26
71	3	58	57	–	–	–	–
72	3	59	58	15	10	19	27
73	4	60	59	–	–	20	–
74	4	61	60	–	–	–	–
75	5	62	61	16	11	21	28
76	5	63	62	–	–	22	–
77	6	64	63	17	–	23	29
78	7	65	64	–	12	24	–
79	8	66	65	18	–	25	30
80	9	67	66	–	–	–	31

		GAC w/out Work	GAC w/Work	CON	SO	PR w/out Work	PR w/Work
90% Confidence Interval ±		2	2	3	4	3	3
95% Confidence Interval ±		3	3	4	5	4	4

Composite Score	Percentile Rank	GAC w/out Work	GAC w/Work	CON	SO	PR w/out Work	PR w/Work
		Sums of Scaled Scores					
81	10	68	67	19	13	26	32–33
82	12	69	68	20	–	27	34
83	13	70	69–70	–	–	28	35
84	14	71	71–72	21	14	29	36
85	16	72	73–75	22	–	30	37
86	18	73	76–77	–	–	31	38–39
87	19	74	78–80	23	15	32	40
88	21	75	81–82	24	–	33	41
89	23	76	83–84	–	–	34	42
90	25	77–78	85–87	25	16	35	43
91	27	79–80	88–89	26	–	36	44–45
92	30	81–82	90–91	27	17	37	46
93	32	83–84	92–94	–	–	–	47
94	34	85–86	95–96	28	18	38	48
95	37	87–88	97–98	29	19	39	49
96	39	89–90	99–100	30	–	40	50
97	42	91	101–102	31	20	41	51
98	45	92–93	103–104	–	–	42	52
99	47	94–95	105	–	21	–	53
100	50	96	106–107	32	–	43	–
101	53	97–98	108–109	33	–	44	54
102	55	99	110	–	22	–	55
103	58	100–101	111–112	34	–	45	56
104	61	102	113	–	–	–	–
105	63	103	114–115	–	23	46	57
106	66	104	116	35	–	–	58
107	68	105	117–118	–	–	47	–
108	70	106	119	36	–	–	59
109	73	107	120	–	24	48	–
110	75	108	121	–	–	–	60
111	77	109	122	37	–	49	61
112	79	110	123	–	–	–	–
113	81	111	124	–	25	–	62
114	82	112	125	38	–	50	–
115	84	113	126	–	–	–	63
116	86	114	127	–	–	–	–
117	87	115	128	–	–	51	–
118	88	116	129	39	26	–	64
119	90	117	130	–	–	–	–
120	>90	118–125	131–138	40–57	27–38	52–76	65–95

Note. CON = Conceptual Adaptive Domain; SO = Social Adaptive Domain; PR = Practical Adaptive Domain.

A

Adult (Others)

Table A.13 GAC and Adaptive Domain Composite Equivalents of Sums of Scaled Scores: Adult Form, Rated by Others (continued)

Ages 30–39

		GAC w/out Work	GAC w/Work	CON	SO	PR w/out Work	PR w/Work
90% Confidence Interval ±		2	2	3	5	3	3
95% Confidence Interval ±		3	3	4	6	4	4
Composite Score	**Percentile Rank**	Sums of Scaled Scores					
40	<0.1	9	10	–	–	–	–
41	<0.1	10	11	–	–	–	5
42	<0.1	11	12	–	–	–	–
43	<0.1	12	13	–	–	4	6
44	<0.1	13	14	–	–	–	–
45	<0.1	14	15	–	–	5	7
46	<0.1	15	16	–	–	–	–
47	<0.1	16	17	–	–	6	8
48	<0.1	17	18	–	–	–	–
49	<0.1	18	19	3	–	7	9
50	<0.1	19	20	–	–	–	–
51	0.1	20	21	4	–	8	10
52	0.1	21	22	–	–	–	–
53	0.1	22	23	5	–	9	11
54	0.1	23	24	–	2	–	–
55	0.1	24	25	6	–	10	12
56	0.2	25	26	–	–	–	–
57	0.2	26	27–28	7	3	11	13
58	0.3	27	29–30	–	–	–	14
59	0.3	28	31–32	8	–	12	15
60	0.4	29–30	33–34	–	4	–	16
61	0.5	31–32	35–36	9	–	13	17
62	1	33–34	37–38	–	5	–	18
63	1	35–36	39–40	10	–	14	19
64	1	37–38	41–42	–	6	–	20
65	1	39–40	43–44	11	–	15	21
66	1	41–42	45–46	–	7	–	22
67	1	43–44	47–48	12	–	16	23
68	2	45–46	49–50	–	8	–	24
69	2	47–48	51–52	13	–	17	25
70	2	49–50	53–54	14	9	18	26
71	3	51	55	–	–	–	27
72	3	52	56–57	15	10	19	–
73	4	53	58	–	–	20	28
74	4	54	59–60	–	–	21	29
75	5	55	61	16	11	22	30
76	5	56	62–63	–	–	23	31
77	6	57	64	17	–	24	–
78	7	58	65–66	–	12	25	32
79	8	59	67–68	18	–	–	33
80	9	60	69	19	–	26	34

		GAC w/out Work	GAC w/Work	CON	SO	PR w/out Work	PR w/Work
90% Confidence Interval ±		2	2	3	5	3	3
95% Confidence Interval ±		3	3	4	6	4	4
Composite Score	**Percentile Rank**	Sums of Scaled Scores					
81	10	61	70–71	–	13	27	35
82	12	62–63	72–73	20	–	28	36
83	13	64–65	74	–	–	29	37
84	14	66–67	75–76	21	14	30	38
85	16	68–69	77–78	22	–	31	39
86	18	70–71	79	–	–	32	40
87	19	72–73	80–81	23	15	33	41
88	21	74–75	82–83	24	–	34	42
89	23	76–77	84–85	–	16	–	43
90	25	78–79	86–87	25	17	35	44
91	27	80	88–89	26	–	36	45
92	30	81–82	90–91	27	18	37	46
93	32	83–84	92–93	–	–	38	47
94	34	85–86	94–95	28	19	–	48
95	37	87	96–97	29	20	39	49
96	39	88–89	98–99	30	–	40	50
97	42	90–91	100–101	–	21	41	51
98	45	92	102–103	31	–	42	52
99	47	93–94	104–105	32	–	–	–
100	50	95–96	106	–	22	43	53
101	53	97	107–108	33	–	44	54
102	55	98–99	109–110	34	23	45	–
103	58	100	111–112	–	–	–	55
104	61	101	113	35	24	46	56
105	63	102–103	114–115	–	–	47	–
106	66	104	116–117	36	25	–	57
107	68	105	118	–	–	48	–
108	70	106–107	119	37	26	–	58
109	73	108	120–121	–	–	49	–
110	75	109	122	38	–	–	59
111	77	110	123	–	–	–	–
112	79	111–112	124	39	–	–	60
113	81	113	125	–	–	50	–
114	82	114	126	–	–	–	–
115	84	115	127	–	–	–	–
116	86	116	128	–	–	–	61
117	87	117	129	–	–	–	–
118	88	118	130	–	–	–	–
119	90	119	131	–	–	–	–
120	>90	120–125	132–138	40–57	27–38	51–76	62–95

Note. **CON** = Conceptual Adaptive Domain; **SO** = Social Adaptive Domain; **PR** = Practical Adaptive Domain.

Table A.13 GAC and Adaptive Domain Composite Equivalents of Sums of Scaled Scores: Adult Form, Rated by Others (continued)

Ages 40–49

Confidence Interval	GAC w/out Work	GAC w/Work	CON	SO	PR w/out Work	PR w/Work
90% Confidence Interval ±	2	2	3	4	3	3
95% Confidence Interval ±	3	3	4	5	4	4

Composite Score	Percentile Rank	GAC w/out Work	GAC w/Work	CON	SO	PR w/out Work	PR w/Work
				Sums of Scaled Scores			
40	<0.1	9	10	–	–	–	–
41	<0.1	10	11	–	–	–	5
42	<0.1	11	12	–	–	–	–
43	<0.1	12	13	–	–	4	6
44	<0.1	13	14	–	–	–	–
45	<0.1	14	15	–	–	5	7
46	<0.1	15	16	–	–	6	–
47	<0.1	16	17	–	–	–	8
48	<0.1	17	18	–	–	–	–
49	<0.1	18	19	3	–	7	9
50	<0.1	19	20	–	–	–	–
51	0.1	20–21	21	4	–	8	10
52	0.1	22–23	22	–	–	–	–
53	0.1	24–25	23	5	–	9	11
54	0.1	26–27	24	–	2	–	–
55	0.1	28–29	25	6	–	10	12
56	0.2	30–31	26	–	–	–	–
57	0.2	32–33	27	7	3	11	13
58	0.3	34–35	28	–	–	–	14
59	0.3	36–37	29	8	–	12	15
60	0.4	38–39	30	–	4	–	16
61	0.5	40–41	31	9	–	13	17
62	1	42–43	32	–	5	–	18
63	1	44–45	33	10	–	14	19
64	1	46–47	34	–	6	–	20
65	1	48–49	35–36	11	7	15	21
66	1	50–51	37–38	–	–	–	22
67	1	52–53	39–40	12	8	16	23
68	2	54–55	41–42	–	–	–	24
69	2	56–57	43–44	13	–	17	25
70	2	58–59	45–46	14	9	18	26
71	3	60	47	–	–	–	–
72	3	61	48–49	15	10	19	27
73	4	62	50–52	–	–	20	–
74	4	63	53–54	–	–	21	28
75	5	64	55–56	16	11	–	–
76	5	65	57–58	–	–	22	29
77	6	66	59–60	–	–	23	30
78	7	67	61–62	17	–	24	31
79	8	68	63–65	–	12	25	32
80	9	69	66–67	18	–	26	33
81	10	70	68–69	19	–	27	34–35
82	12	71	70–71	–	13	28	36
83	13	72	72–74	20	–	29	37
84	14	73	75–76	21	14	30	38
85	16	74	77–78	–	–	31	39–40
86	18	75	79–80	22	15	32	41
87	19	76	81–82	23	–	33	42
88	21	77	83–85	24	16	34	43
89	23	78	86–87	25	–	35	44
90	25	79	88–89	26	–	36	45
91	27	80–81	90–91	–	17	37	46
92	30	82–83	92–93	27	–	38	47
93	32	84–85	94–95	28	18	39	48
94	34	86–87	96–97	29	–	40	49
95	37	88–89	98–99	30	19	–	50
96	39	90	100–101	–	–	41	51
97	42	91–92	102–103	31	20	42	52
98	45	93–94	104–105	32	–	–	–
99	47	95	106	–	21	43	53
100	50	96–97	107–108	33	–	–	54
101	53	98	109–110	–	22	44	–
102	55	99–100	111	34	–	–	55
103	58	101	112–113	–	–	45	56
104	61	102	114	35	23	–	–
105	63	103	115–116	–	–	46	57
106	66	104	117	–	–	–	–
107	68	105	118	36	24	47	58
108	70	106	119–120	–	–	–	–
109	73	107	121	–	–	–	59
110	75	108	122	37	–	–	–
111	77	109	123	–	–	48	–
112	79	110	124	–	25	–	60
113	81	111	125	–	–	–	–
114	82	112	126	38	–	49	61
115	84	113	127	–	–	–	–
116	86	114	128	–	26	50	–
117	87	115	129	39	–	–	62
118	88	116	130	–	–	–	–
119	90	117	131	–	–	–	–
120	>90	118–125	132–138	40–57	27–38	51–76	63–95

Note. **CON** = Conceptual Adaptive Domain; **SO** = Social Adaptive Domain; **PR** = Practical Adaptive Domain.

A Adult (Others)

Table A.13 GAC and Adaptive Domain Composite Equivalents of Sums of Scaled Scores: Adult Form, Rated by Others (continued)

Ages 50–64

		90% Confidence Interval ±	95% Confidence Interval ±
	GAC w/out Work	2	3
	GAC w/Work	2	3
	CON	3	4
	SO	4	5
	PR w/out Work	3	4
	PR w/Work	3	4

Composite Score	Percentile Rank	GAC w/out Work	GAC w/Work	CON	SO	PR w/out Work	PR w/Work
		Sums of Scaled Scores					
40	<0.1	9	10	–	–	–	–
41	<0.1	10	11	–	–	4	5
42	<0.1	11	12	–	–	–	–
43	<0.1	12	13	–	–	5	6
44	<0.1	13	14	–	–	–	–
45	<0.1	14	15	–	–	6	7
46	<0.1	15	16	–	–	–	–
47	<0.1	16	17	–	–	7	8
48	<0.1	17	18	–	–	–	–
49	<0.1	18	19	3	–	8	9
50	<0.1	19	20	–	–	–	–
51	0.1	20	21	4	–	9	10
52	0.1	21–22	22	–	–	–	–
53	0.1	23–24	23	5	–	10	11
54	0.1	25–26	24	–	2	–	–
55	0.1	27–28	25	6	–	11	12
56	0.2	29–30	26	–	–	–	–
57	0.2	31–32	27	7	3	12	13
58	0.3	33–34	28	–	–	–	14
59	0.3	35–36	29	8	–	13	15
60	0.4	37–38	30	–	4	–	16
61	0.5	39–40	31	9	–	14	17
62	1	41–42	32	–	5	–	18
63	1	43–44	33	10	–	15	19
64	1	45–46	34	–	6	–	20
65	1	47–48	35–36	11	–	16	21
66	1	49–50	37–38	–	7	–	22
67	1	51–52	39–40	12	–	17	23
68	2	53–54	41–42	–	8	–	24
69	2	55–56	43–44	13	–	18	25
70	2	57–58	45–46	14	9	19	26
71	3	59	47	–	–	20	–
72	3	60	48–49	15	10	–	27
73	4	61	50–52	–	–	21	–
74	4	62	53–54	–	–	22	28
75	5	63	55–57	16	11	23	–
76	5	64	58–59	–	–	–	29
77	6	65	60–62	–	–	24	30
78	7	66	63–64	17	12	25	31
79	8	67	65–66	–	–	26	32
80	9	68	67–69	18	–	–	33–34

		90% Confidence Interval ±	95% Confidence Interval ±
	GAC w/out Work	2	3
	GAC w/Work	2	3
	CON	3	4
	SO	4	5
	PR w/out Work	3	4
	PR w/Work	3	4

Composite Score	Percentile Rank	GAC w/out Work	GAC w/Work	CON	SO	PR w/out Work	PR w/Work
		Sums of Scaled Scores					
81	10	69	70–71	–	–	27	35
82	12	70	72–73	19	13	28	–
83	13	71	74–75	–	–	29	36
84	14	72	76–77	20	14	–	37
85	16	73	78–79	21	–	30	38
86	18	74	80–81	–	15	31	39
87	19	75	82–83	22	–	32	40
88	21	76	84	23	–	–	41
89	23	77	85–86	–	16	33	42
90	25	78	87–88	24	–	34	43
91	27	79	89–90	25	17	–	44
92	30	80	91–92	–	–	35	45
93	32	81	93	26	18	36	46
94	34	82	94–95	27	–	37	47
95	37	83–84	96–97	28	19	–	–
96	39	85–86	98	–	–	38	48
97	42	87–88	99–100	29	20	39	49
98	45	89	101	30	–	–	50
99	47	90–91	102–103	–	21	40	51
100	50	92	104–105	31	–	41	–
101	53	93–94	106	32	–	–	52
102	55	95	107–108	–	22	42	53
103	58	96–97	109	33	–	43	54
104	61	98	110–111	–	–	–	–
105	63	99	112	34	23	44	55
106	66	100–101	113–114	–	–	–	56
107	68	102	115	35	–	45	57
108	70	103	116	–	24	46	–
109	73	104–105	117–118	36	–	–	58
110	75	106	119	–	–	47	59
111	77	107	120–121	–	25	48	60
112	79	108–109	122	37	–	–	–
113	81	110	123	–	–	–	–
114	82	111	124–125	–	–	–	61
115	84	112	126	38	–	49	–
116	86	113	127	–	26	–	62
117	87	114–115	128–129	–	–	–	–
118	88	116	130	–	–	50	63
119	90	117	131	39	–	–	–
120	>90	118–125	132–138	40–57	27–38	51–76	64–95

Note. **CON** = Conceptual Adaptive Domain; **SO** = Social Adaptive Domain; **PR** = Practical Adaptive Domain.

Table A.13 GAC and Adaptive Domain Composite Equivalents of Sums of Scaled Scores: Adult Form, Rated by Others (continued)

Ages 65–74

Composite Score	Percentile Rank	GAC w/out Work	GAC w/Work	CON	SO	PR w/out Work	PR w/Work
90% Confidence Interval ±		2	2	4	4	5	4
95% Confidence Interval ±		3	3	5	5	6	5
		Sums of Scaled Scores					
40	<0.1	9	10	–	–	–	–
41	<0.1	10	11	–	–	–	5
42	<0.1	11	12	–	–	–	–
43	<0.1	12	13	–	–	4	–
44	<0.1	13	14	–	–	–	–
45	<0.1	14	15	–	–	5	6
46	<0.1	15	16	–	–	–	–
47	<0.1	16	17	–	–	6	–
48	<0.1	17	18	–	–	–	7
49	<0.1	18	19	3	–	7	–
50	0.1	19	20	–	–	–	–
51	0.1	20	21	4	–	–	8
52	0.1	21	22	–	–	8	–
53	0.1	22	23	5	–	–	9
54	0.1	23	24	–	–	9	–
55	0.1	24	25	6	2	–	10
56	0.2	25	26	–	–	–	–
57	0.2	26	27	7	3	10	11
58	0.3	27	28	–	–	–	–
59	0.3	28	29	8	–	11	12
60	0.4	29-30	30	–	–	–	–
61	0.5	31-32	31	9	4	12	13
62	1	33-34	32	–	–	13	–
63	1	35-36	33	10	–	–	14
64	1	37-38	34	–	5	14	–
65	1	39-40	35-36	11	–	15	15
66	1	41-42	37-38	–	6	16	–
67	1	43-44	39-40	12	7	–	16
68	2	45-46	41-42	–	–	17	–
69	2	47-48	43-44	13	–	–	17
70	2	49-50	45-46	14	8	18	18
71	3	51	47	–	–	–	–
72	3	52	48	15	–	19	19
73	4	53	49	–	9	20	–
74	4	54	50	–	–	21	–
75	5	55	51	16	10	22-23	–
76	5	56	52	–	–	24	–
77	6	57	53-54	17	–	25	27
78	7	58-59	55-57	–	11	26	29
79	8	60-61	58-61	–	–	27	30
80	9	62-63	62-65	18	12	28	31-32

Composite Score	Percentile Rank	GAC w/out Work	GAC w/Work	CON	SO	PR w/out Work	PR w/Work
90% Confidence Interval ±		2	2	4	4	5	4
95% Confidence Interval ±		3	3	5	5	6	5
		Sums of Scaled Scores					
81	10	64-65	66-68	19	–	29	33
82	12	66-67	69-71	20	13	30	34
83	13	68-69	72-75	21	14	31	35
84	14	70-71	76-78	22	–	32	36-37
85	16	72-73	79-81	23	15	33	38
86	18	74-76	82-83	24	16	34	39-40
87	19	77-78	84-86	25	–	35	41
88	21	79-80	87-88	26	17	36	42
89	23	81-82	89-91	27	18	–	43
90	25	83	92-93	28	–	37	44
91	27	84-85	94-95	29	19	38	45
92	30	86-87	96-97	30	–	39	46
93	32	88-89	98-99	–	20	–	47
94	34	90	100	31	–	40	48
95	37	91-92	101-102	–	21	–	49
96	39	93	103-104	32	–	41	50
97	42	94-95	105	–	–	42	51
98	45	96	106-107	33	22	–	52
99	47	97	108	–	–	43	53
100	50	98	109	–	–	–	54
101	53	99	110	34	–	44	55
102	55	100	111	–	23	–	–
103	58	101	112	–	–	45	56
104	61	102	113	35	–	–	–
105	63	103	114	–	–	46	57
106	66	104	115	–	24	–	58
107	68	105	116	36	–	47	–
108	70	106	117	–	–	–	59
109	73	107	118	–	–	–	–
110	75	108	119	–	–	48	60
111	77	109	120	–	25	–	–
112	79	110	121	–	–	–	–
113	81	111	122	37	–	49	61
114	82	112	123	–	–	–	–
115	84	113	124	–	–	–	62
116	86	114	125	–	26	50	–
117	87	115	126	–	–	–	63
118	88	116	127	38	–	–	–
119	90	117	128	–	–	–	–
120	>90	118-125	129-138	39-57	27-38	51-76	64-95

Note. **CON** = Conceptual Adaptive Domain; **SO** = Social Adaptive Domain; **PR** = Practical Adaptive Domain.

A Adult (Others)

Table A.13 GAC and Adaptive Domain Composite Equivalents of Sums of Scaled Scores: Adult Form, Rated by Others (continued)

Ages 75–89

		GAC	CON	SO	PR
90% Confidence Interval ±		2	2	3	2
95% Confidence Interval ±		3	3	4	3
Composite Score	Percentile Rank	Sums of Scaled Scores			
		GAC	CON	SO	PR
40	<0.1	9	–	–	–
41	<0.1	10	–	–	–
42	<0.1	11	–	–	–
43	<0.1	12	–	–	–
44	<0.1	13	–	–	–
45	<0.1	14	–	–	4
46	<0.1	15	–	–	–
47	<0.1	16	–	–	–
48	<0.1	17	–	–	5
49	<0.1	18	–	–	–
50	<0.1	19	3	–	–
51	0.1	20	–	–	6
52	0.1	21	–	–	–
53	0.1	22	4	–	7
54	0.1	23	–	–	–
55	0.1	24	5	2	8
56	0.2	25	–	–	–
57	0.2	26	6	3	9
58	0.3	27–28	–	–	–
59	0.3	29–30	7	–	10
60	0.4	31–32	–	–	–
61	0.5	33–34	8	4	11
62	1	35–36	–	–	–
63	1	37–38	9	–	12
64	1	39–40	–	5	–
65	1	41–42	10	–	13
66	1	43–44	–	6	–
67	1	45–46	11	–	14
68	2	47–48	–	7	–
69	2	49–50	12	–	15
70	2	51–52	13	8	16
71	3	53	–	–	–
72	3	54	14	9	17
73	4	55	–	–	–
74	4	56	–	–	–
75	5	57	15	10	18
76	5	58	–	–	–
77	6	59	–	–	–
78	7	60	16	–	19
79	8	61	–	11	–
80	9	62	–	–	–

		GAC	CON	SO	PR
90% Confidence Interval ±		2	2	3	2
95% Confidence Interval ±		3	3	4	3
Composite Score	Percentile Rank	Sums of Scaled Scores			
		GAC	CON	SO	PR
81	10	63	17	–	20
82	12	64	–	12	–
83	13	65	–	–	21
84	14	66	18	13	–
85	16	67	–	–	22
86	18	68	19	14	23
87	19	69	–	–	24
88	21	70	20	–	25
89	23	71	–	15	26
90	25	72–73	21	–	27
91	27	74–75	22	16	28
92	30	76–77	23	–	29
93	32	78–79	24	17	30
94	34	80–81	25	–	31–32
95	37	82–83	26	18	33–34
96	39	84–85	27	–	35–36
97	42	86–87	28	–	37–38
98	45	88–89	29	19	39–40
99	47	90–91	30	–	41
100	50	92–93	31	20	42
101	53	94–95	32	–	–
102	55	96–97	33	21	43
103	58	98–99	–	–	44
104	61	100–101	34	22	–
105	63	102	–	–	45
106	66	103–104	35	23	–
107	68	105	–	–	46
108	70	106	36	–	–
109	73	107–108	–	24	47
110	75	109	37	–	–
111	77	110	–	–	48
112	79	111	–	–	–
113	81	112	38	25	–
114	82	113	–	–	49
115	84	114	–	–	–
116	86	115	39	–	–
117	87	116	–	26	50
118	88	117	–	–	–
119	90	118	40	–	–
120	>90	119–125	41–57	27–38	51–76

Note. CON = Conceptual Adaptive Domain; SO = Social Adaptive Domain; PR = Practical Adaptive Domain.

Table A.14   Average Number of Items Guessed by the Standardization Sample: Adult Form, Rated by Others

Skill Areas	Age Group 16–21 Mean	$SE_{\bar{x}}$	22–29 Mean	$SE_{\bar{x}}$	30–39 Mean	$SE_{\bar{x}}$	40–49 Mean	$SE_{\bar{x}}$	50–64 Mean	$SE_{\bar{x}}$	65–74 Mean	$SE_{\bar{x}}$	75–89 Mean	$SE_{\bar{x}}$
Communication	0.29	0.11	0.16	0.07	0.06	0.03	0.10	0.04	0.15	0.06	0.12	0.05	0.19	0.08
Community Use	0.80	0.19	0.24	0.08	0.25	0.10	0.16	0.06	0.22	0.07	0.25	0.09	0.28	0.08
Functional Academics	0.61	0.15	0.26	0.09	0.28	0.10	0.23	0.09	0.23	0.07	0.32	0.10	0.39	0.11
Home Living	0.49	0.14	0.14	0.06	0.21	0.13	0.11	0.05	0.14	0.07	0.27	0.12	0.09	0.03
Health and Safety	0.68	0.15	0.31	0.09	0.24	0.09	0.24	0.06	0.31	0.09	0.23	0.10	0.34	0.12
Leisure	0.51	0.14	0.37	0.15	0.16	0.05	0.26	0.08	0.21	0.06	0.54	0.22	0.36	0.12
Self-Care	0.28	0.09	0.22	0.06	0.23	0.11	0.22	0.06	0.33	0.13	0.21	0.07	0.18	0.05
Self-Direction	0.76	0.19	0.48	0.16	0.16	0.10	0.25	0.08	0.21	0.06	0.31	0.13	0.42	0.11
Social	0.51	0.15	0.24	0.08	0.08	0.03	0.18	0.06	0.12	0.04	0.15	0.06	0.23	0.09
Work	1.58	0.42	1.25	0.30	1.15	0.30	1.47	0.30	1.16	0.29	0.51	0.21	—	—

Note. $SE_{\bar{x}}$ = Standard Error of the Mean.

Appendix B

Supplementary Tables

When consulting data tables, refer carefully to the table subheadings (upper left side of tables) to ensure that you are consulting the correct section of the table for the rating form you are using.

Teacher/Daycare Provider and Teacher Forms

Parent/Primary Caregiver and Parent Forms

Adult Form, Self Report

Adult Form, Rated by Others

Table B.1   Differences Between Single Skill Area Scaled Scores and Average Scaled Scores Required for Statistical Significance (Critical Values) and Differences Obtained by Various Percentages of the Standardization Sample (Base Rates): Teacher/Daycare Provider and Teacher Forms

Teacher/Daycare Provider Form (Ages 2–5)

Mean of Conceptual Domain

Skill Area	Significance Level		Base Rate				
	0.15	0.05	1%	2%	5%	10%	25%
Communication	1.32	1.62	4.67	4.00	3.33	3.00	2.00
Functional Pre-Academics	1.33	1.63	4.67	4.00	3.33	3.00	2.00
Self-Direction	1.35	1.66	4.67	4.00	3.00	2.67	2.00

Mean of Practical Domain

Skill Area	Significance Level		Base Rate				
	0.15	0.05	1%	2%	5%	10%	25%
School Living	1.47	1.80	4.33	3.83	3.00	2.33	1.67
Health and Safety	1.75	2.15	4.33	4.00	3.00	2.33	1.67
Self-Care	1.91	2.34	4.67	4.17	3.33	3.00	2.00

Mean of 9 Skill Areas

Skill Area	Significance Level		Base Rate				
	0.15	0.05	1%	2%	5%	10%	25%
Communication	1.89	2.20	6.33	4.67	3.89	3.33	2.22
Functional Pre-Academics	1.90	2.23	5.78	5.28	4.44	3.61	2.44
School Living	1.72	2.01	4.78	3.89	3.33	2.78	2.00
Health and Safety	2.47	2.89	5.56	4.44	3.44	2.78	1.89
Leisure	2.21	2.59	4.44	4.17	3.22	2.67	1.89
Self-Care	2.85	3.33	5.44	5.17	4.33	3.56	2.44
Self-Direction	1.96	2.29	4.56	3.89	3.22	2.56	1.78
Social	2.04	2.38	4.67	3.94	3.22	2.56	1.89
Motor	2.67	3.12	5.44	5.11	4.11	3.50	2.44

Note. The differences required for statistical significance are based on the average standard error of measurement across all ages and calculated with the following formula provided by Davis (1959):

$$\text{Difference Score} = Z \sqrt{(SEM_t^2)/K^2 + [(K-2)/K](SEM_i^2)}$$

where Z is the normal curve value associated with the desired significance level derived with the Bonferroni correction of multiple comparisons, K is the number of skill areas in comparison, SEM_t^2 is the sum of the squared standard errors of measurement for all skill areas in the comparison, and SEM_i^2 is the squared standard error of measurement for the skill area of interest.

Table B.1 **Differences Between Single Skill Area Scaled Scores and Average Scaled Scores Required for Statistical Significance (Critical Values) and Differences Obtained by Various Percentages of the Standardization Sample (Base Rates): Teacher/Daycare Provider and Teacher Forms** (continued)

Teacher Form (Ages 5–21)

Mean of Conceptual Domain

| Skill Area | Significance Level | | Base Rate | | | | |
	0.15	0.05	1%	2%	5%	10%	25%
Communication	1.10	1.35	4.33	4.00	3.00	2.33	1.33
Functional Academics	1.02	1.25	4.67	4.00	3.33	2.67	1.67
Self-Direction	1.01	1.24	4.67	4.33	3.33	2.67	1.33

Mean of Practical Domain

| Skill Area | Significance Level | | Base Rate | | | | |
	0.15	0.05	1%	2%	5%	10%	25%
Community Use	1.74	2.10	5.50	5.00	4.00	3.00	1.75
School Living	1.38	1.66	5.00	4.25	3.25	2.50	1.50
Health and Safety	1.43	1.72	4.50	4.00	3.25	2.50	1.50
Self-Care	1.49	1.79	5.75	5.25	4.25	3.50	1.75

Mean of 9 Skill Areas

| Skill Area | Significance Level | | Base Rate | | | | |
	0.15	0.05	1%	2%	5%	10%	25%
Communication	1.64	1.92	5.44	4.89	3.67	2.78	1.67
Community Use	2.23	2.61	5.89	5.11	4.22	3.22	1.78
Functional Academics	1.43	1.67	5.78	5.11	4.00	3.17	2.00
School Living	1.64	1.92	5.11	4.44	3.33	2.67	1.56
Health and Safety	1.72	2.01	5.11	4.44	3.44	2.78	1.56
Leisure	1.70	1.98	4.44	3.78	3.11	2.56	1.67
Self-Care	1.82	2.12	6.56	5.89	4.78	3.78	2.11
Self-Direction	1.41	1.65	5.67	4.78	3.78	3.00	1.56
Social	1.48	1.73	5.00	4.22	3.33	2.67	1.56

Note. The differences required for statistical significance are based on the average standard error of measurement across all ages and calculated with the following formula provided by Davis (1959):

Difference Score $= Z \sqrt{(SEM_t^2)/K^2 + [(K-2)/K](SEM_i^2)}$

where Z is the normal curve value associated with the desired significance level derived with the Bonferroni correction of multiple comparisons, K is the number of skill areas in comparison, SEM_t^2 is the sum of the squared standard errors of measurement for all skill areas in the comparison, and SEM_i^2 is the squared standard error of measurement for the skill area of interest.

Table B.2 **Pairwise Comparison: Values Required for Statistical Significance (Critical Values) at the 15 and 5% Levels When Comparing Each Scaled Score With Every Other Scaled Score: Teacher/Daycare Provider and Teacher Forms**

Teacher/Daycare Provider Form (Ages 2–5) — Skill Area

Skill Area	Com	FA	SL	HS	LS	SC	SD	Soc	MO
Communication	–	1.68	1.58	2.00	1.85	2.23	1.71	1.75	2.12
Functional Pre-Academics	2.29	–	1.59	2.01	1.86	2.23	1.72	1.76	2.12
School Living	2.15	2.17	–	1.93	1.77	2.16	1.62	1.67	2.05
Health and Safety	2.72	2.73	2.62	–	2.15	2.48	2.03	2.07	2.38
Leisure	2.52	2.53	2.41	2.93	–	2.36	1.89	1.93	2.26
Self-Care	3.03	3.04	2.94	3.38	3.22	–	2.26	2.29	2.58
Self-Direction	2.33	2.34	2.21	2.77	2.57	3.07	–	1.79	2.15
Social	2.39	2.40	2.27	2.82	2.62	3.12	2.44	–	2.18
Motor	2.88	2.89	2.79	3.25	3.08	3.51	2.93	2.97	–

Teacher Form (Ages 5–21) — Skill Area

Skill Area	Com	CU	FA	SL	HS	LS	SC	SD	Soc
Communication	–	1.82	1.38	1.49	1.53	1.52	1.58	1.37	1.41
Community Use	2.47	–	1.73	1.82	1.85	1.84	1.90	1.72	1.75
Functional Academics	1.88	2.36	–	1.38	1.42	1.41	1.48	1.25	1.29
School Living	2.02	2.47	1.88	–	1.53	1.52	1.58	1.37	1.41
Health and Safety	2.08	2.52	1.94	2.08	–	1.56	1.62	1.41	1.45
Leisure	2.07	2.51	1.92	2.07	2.12	–	1.61	1.40	1.44
Self-Care	2.15	2.58	2.01	2.15	2.20	2.19	–	1.47	1.51
Self-Direction	1.86	2.35	1.70	1.86	1.93	1.91	2.00	–	1.28
Social	1.92	2.39	1.76	1.92	1.98	1.96	2.05	1.75	–

Note. **Com** = Communication; **CU** = Community Use; **FA** = Functional (Pre-)Academics; **SL** = School Living; **HS** = Health and Safety; **LS** = Leisure; **SC** = Self-Care; **SD** = Self-Direction; **Soc** = Social; **MO** = Motor.

Differences between skill area scores required for signficance at the .15 level appear above the diagonal, and the differences significant at the .05 level appear below the diagonal.

The differences for statistical significance are based on the average standard error of measurement across all ages for each skill area and calculated with the following formula:

$$\text{Difference Score} = Z \sqrt{SEM_a^2 + SEM_b^2}$$

where Z is the normal curve value associated with the desired signficance level and SEM_a and SEM_b are the standard errors of measurement of the skill area scores.

Table B.3   Cumulative Percentages of Inter-Skill Area Scatter Within 9 Skill Areas and 3 Adaptive Domains: Teacher/Daycare Provider and Teacher Forms

Teacher/Daycare Provider Form (Ages 2–5)

Scatter	GAC (9 skill areas)	Conceptual (3 skill areas)	Social (2 skill areas)	Practical (3 skill areas)
17	0.0	0.0	0.0	0.0
16	0.1	0.0	0.0	0.1
15	0.3	0.0	0.0	0.1
14	0.3	0.0	0.0	0.1
13	1.1	0.1	0.0	0.1
12	1.6	0.3	0.0	0.3
11	2.5	0.5	0.0	0.7
10	5.7	1.2	0.0	0.8
9	9.3	1.9	0.3	1.6
8	16.5	3.1	0.8	2.8
7	29.1	7.2	1.6	6.1
6	48.5	14.5	3.2	10.9
5	70.5	29.3	5.9	21.9
4	88.4	45.7	11.6	38.0
3	96.4	64.4	24.3	58.4
2	99.7	84.4	50.1	82.9
1	100.0	97.3	79.1	96.9
0	100.0	100.0	100.0	100.0
Mean	5.7	3.5	1.8	3.2
SD	2.1	2.0	1.6	2.0
Median	5.0	3.0	2.0	3.0

Teacher Form (Ages 5–21)

Scatter	GAC (9 skill areas)	Conceptual (3 skill areas)	Social (2 skill areas)	Practical (4 skill areas)
13	0.0	0.0	0.0	0.0
12	0.2	0.0	0.1	0.1
11	0.8	0.0	0.1	0.2
10	4.1	0.2	0.1	1.3
9	11.1	1.2	0.2	4.9
8	20.3	3.4	0.7	10.2
7	28.9	7.8	1.1	14.4
6	37.9	13.1	2.4	20.4
5	47.9	19.6	4.8	28.4
4	61.0	29.6	9.8	36.8
3	73.0	42.7	17.8	50.4
2	87.9	63.7	34.8	67.3
1	99.0	88.6	69.3	84.9
0	100.0	100.0	100.0	100.0
Mean	4.7	2.7	1.4	3.2
SD	2.7	2.2	1.5	2.7
Median	4.0	2.0	1.0	3.0

Table B.4   Percentage of Standardization Sample Obtaining Various Skill Area Scaled Scores 2 or More Standard Deviations Below the Mean: Teacher/Daycare Provider and Teacher Forms

Teacher/Daycare Provider Form	Number of Skill Areas at Least 2 *SD* Below the Mean							
Age Group	=9	≥8	≥7	≥6	≥5	≥4	≥3	≥2
2:0–2:5	0.0	0.0	1.0	1.0	1.0	1.0	2.0	3.0
2:6–2:11	0.0	0.0	1.0	1.0	2.0	3.0	3.0	7.0
3:0–3:5	1.0	1.0	2.0	3.0	3.0	3.0	4.0	5.0
3:6–3:11	0.0	0.0	0.0	0.0	1.0	2.0	4.0	4.0
4:0–4:5	0.0	0.0	0.0	0.0	2.0	4.0	4.0	7.0
4:6–4:11	1.0	1.0	1.0	1.0	1.0	1.0	1.0	5.0
5:0–5:11	0.7	0.7	2.0	2.0	2.0	2.7	4.0	8.0

Teacher Form	Number of Skill Areas at Least 2 *SD* Below the Mean							
Age Group	=9	≥8	≥7	≥6	≥5	≥4	≥3	≥2
5	1.3	1.3	1.3	2.7	6.0	7.3	10.0	16.0
6	3.6	4.3	5.0	6.4	7.1	8.6	11.4	20.7
7	0.7	2.1	4.3	5.7	7.9	9.3	10.7	15.7
8	1.3	4.7	5.3	5.3	8.7	10.7	14.0	20.0
9	0.0	2.7	6.0	8.7	14.0	15.3	18.7	22.0
10	0.7	4.0	4.7	8.0	8.7	13.3	17.3	23.3
11	4.7	6.7	10.0	11.3	12.0	14.7	18.7	24.7
12	2.7	5.3	9.3	12.7	16.7	20.0	26.0	32.0
13–14	2.4	4.8	7.2	9.6	11.2	15.6	24.4	30.0
15–16	3.6	7.9	8.6	10.7	13.6	15.7	20.7	27.9
17–21	1.7	3.3	4.2	6.7	9.2	10.8	13.3	19.2

Table B.5 Differences Between Adaptive Domain Composite Scores Required for Statistical Significance (Critical Values) at the 15 and 5% Levels, by Age Group and Overall Standardization Sample: Teacher/Daycare Provider and Teacher Forms

Teacher/Daycare Provider Form

Age Group	Significance Level	CON-SO	CON-PR	SO-PR
2:0–2:5	0.15	7.48	7.48	8.08
	0.05	10.18	10.18	11.00
2:6–2:11	0.15	7.78	6.82	7.78
	0.05	10.59	9.29	10.59
3:0–3:5	0.15	5.72	5.72	6.11
	0.05	7.78	7.78	8.32
3:6–3:11	0.15	7.17	7.17	8.08
	0.05	9.75	9.75	11.00
4:0–4:5	0.15	6.11	6.48	7.16
	0.05	8.31	8.82	9.74
4:6–4:11	0.15	6.48	7.48	7.78
	0.05	8.81	10.18	10.59
5:0–5:11	0.15	5.72	6.83	7.17
	0.05	7.78	9.30	9.75
Overall Sample	0.15	6.68	6.88	7.48
	0.05	9.09	9.37	10.18

Teacher Form

Age Group	Significance Level	CON-SO	CON-PR	SO-PR
5	0.15	6.11	6.48	6.48
	0.05	8.32	8.81	8.81
6	0.15	5.29	5.29	5.29
	0.05	7.21	7.21	7.21
7	0.15	5.72	5.72	6.11
	0.05	7.78	7.78	8.32
8	0.15	4.83	4.32	4.83
	0.05	6.58	5.88	6.58
9	0.15	4.83	4.83	5.29
	0.05	6.58	6.58	7.21
10	0.15	4.83	4.83	5.29
	0.05	6.58	6.58	7.21
11	0.15	3.74	3.74	4.32
	0.05	5.09	5.09	5.88
12	0.15	4.83	4.32	4.83
	0.05	6.58	5.88	6.58
13–14	0.15	4.83	4.32	4.83
	0.05	6.58	5.88	6.58
15–16	0.15	3.74	3.74	4.32
	0.05	5.09	5.09	5.88
17–21	0.15	4.83	4.83	5.29
	0.05	6.58	6.58	7.21
Overall Sample	0.15	4.92	4.84	5.21
	0.05	6.70	6.58	7.10

Note. The differences for statistical significance are based on the average standard errors of measurement by age group and overall sample for each adaptive domain and calculated with the following formula:

$$\text{Difference Score} = Z \sqrt{SEM_a^2 + SEM_b^2}$$

where Z is the normal curve value associated with the desired significance level and SEM_a and SEM_b are the standard errors of measurement of the adaptive domain scores.

Table B.6 Differences Between Adaptive Domain Composite Scores Obtained by Various Percentages of the Standardization Sample (Base Rates): Teacher/Daycare Provider and Teacher Forms

Teacher/Daycare Provider Form (Ages 2–5) **Composite Pair**

Amount of Discrepancy	CON-SO CON<SO (−)	CON-SO CON>SO (+)	CON-PR CON<PR (−)	CON-PR CON>PR (+)	SO-PR SO<PR (−)	SO-PR SO>PR (+)	Amount of Discrepancy
≥40	0.0	0.0	0.0	0.0	0.0	0.0	≥40
39	0.0	0.0	0.1	0.0	0.0	0.0	39
38	0.0	0.0	0.3	0.0	0.0	0.0	38
37	0.0	0.0	0.3	0.1	0.0	0.0	37
36	0.0	0.0	0.3	0.3	0.0	0.0	36
35	0.0	0.0	0.3	0.4	0.1	0.1	35
34	0.0	0.0	0.3	0.4	0.1	0.1	34
33	0.0	0.0	0.4	0.4	0.1	0.1	33
32	0.1	0.1	0.4	0.4	0.1	0.3	32
31	0.1	0.1	0.5	0.4	0.4	0.3	31
30	0.4	0.1	0.7	0.5	0.4	0.3	30
29	0.4	0.3	0.7	0.7	0.4	0.3	29
28	0.5	0.3	0.7	0.7	0.7	0.3	28
27	0.7	0.3	0.7	0.8	0.8	0.4	27
26	1.2	0.4	0.8	1.1	0.9	0.8	26
25	2.0	0.7	0.9	1.1	1.3	1.1	25
24	2.1	0.8	1.2	1.6	1.6	2.0	24
23	2.3	0.8	1.6	2.0	1.9	2.7	23
22	2.9	0.9	2.1	2.8	2.3	2.7	22
21	3.1	1.3	2.7	2.8	2.5	3.2	21
20	4.0	2.0	3.3	3.2	2.7	3.5	20
19	4.4	2.3	3.7	3.6	3.5	4.0	19
18	5.1	3.1	4.4	4.9	4.7	5.3	18
17	5.5	3.7	6.0	5.7	5.7	6.0	17
16	6.5	4.4	6.9	6.9	6.3	6.4	16
15	7.5	5.5	9.1	7.5	7.1	7.6	15
14	8.5	7.5	10.0	9.5	8.5	8.8	14
13	10.0	9.1	11.1	10.8	9.9	9.3	13
12	11.7	10.3	12.8	13.2	12.5	12.7	12
11	13.3	13.5	14.7	14.8	14.3	14.0	11
10	16.7	15.6	17.5	17.1	15.2	16.5	10
9	17.7	20.3	20.1	19.7	18.0	20.4	9
8	21.5	21.9	23.1	22.4	20.0	20.8	8
7	24.0	25.1	26.8	24.3	23.9	23.9	7
6	29.2	28.4	29.9	29.6	27.1	27.2	6
5	32.4	32.3	34.3	31.2	31.7	31.9	5
4	35.5	36.1	39.2	35.9	34.4	33.5	4
3	39.5	38.3	42.8	38.9	40.3	38.9	3
2	41.6	42.7	44.7	42.8	44.5	43.7	2
1	48.9	47.7	50.0	46.7	46.8	45.5	1
Mean	8.2	7.9	8.5	8.7	8.3	8.7	Mean
SD	6.5	5.6	6.4	6.6	6.3	6.4	SD
Median	6.0	7.0	7.0	7.0	7.0	7.0	Median

Table B.6 Differences Between Adaptive Domain Composite Scores Obtained by Various Percentages of the Standardization Sample (Base Rates): Teacher/Daycare Provider and Teacher Forms *(continued)*

Teacher Form (Ages 5–21)			Composite Pair				
	CON-SO		CON-PR		SO-PR		
Amount of Discrepancy	CON<SO (−)	CON>SO (+)	CON<PR (−)	CON>PR (+)	SO<PR (−)	SO>PR (+)	Amount of Discrepancy
≥40	0.1	0.0	0.1	0.0	0.0	0.0	≥40
39	0.1	0.0	0.1	0.0	0.0	0.0	39
38	0.1	0.0	0.1	0.0	0.1	0.0	38
37	0.1	0.1	0.2	0.0	0.1	0.0	37
36	0.2	0.1	0.2	0.0	0.1	0.0	36
35	0.2	0.1	0.2	0.0	0.2	0.0	35
34	0.5	0.1	0.2	0.1	0.3	0.0	34
33	0.7	0.1	0.2	0.1	0.3	0.1	33
32	0.8	0.1	0.3	0.1	0.5	0.1	32
31	1.1	0.1	0.4	0.1	0.5	0.2	31
30	1.2	0.2	0.5	0.2	0.6	0.2	30
29	1.5	0.4	0.8	0.2	0.6	0.2	29
28	1.7	0.4	0.9	0.2	0.8	0.2	28
27	2.1	0.6	1.2	0.2	0.9	0.2	27
26	2.6	0.7	1.8	0.3	1.1	0.4	26
25	3.0	0.9	2.2	0.4	1.4	0.4	25
24	3.4	1.3	3.3	0.5	1.8	0.7	24
23	3.8	1.6	3.7	0.8	2.3	0.8	23
22	4.1	2.2	4.7	0.9	2.9	1.3	22
21	4.7	2.6	5.4	1.4	3.4	1.6	21
20	5.8	3.1	6.2	1.4	3.8	2.0	20
19	6.5	3.8	7.1	1.9	4.8	2.6	19
18	7.6	4.7	8.2	2.5	5.9	3.5	18
17	9.1	6.1	9.5	3.3	6.4	4.3	17
16	10.0	7.2	11.1	4.0	7.3	5.1	16
15	12.1	8.3	12.4	5.0	8.3	6.3	15
14	13.3	9.8	13.5	6.2	9.6	7.9	14
13	14.9	11.1	15.1	7.1	11.8	9.8	13
12	16.7	12.4	16.7	8.9	13.3	11.1	12
11	18.3	14.1	18.0	10.5	14.6	13.4	11
10	21.0	15.5	19.9	12.4	15.9	15.6	10
9	23.3	17.3	22.0	14.9	18.3	18.2	9
8	26.0	20.2	23.9	18.2	20.1	20.2	8
7	29.1	23.3	26.9	23.6	22.1	23.1	7
6	31.5	24.9	29.1	26.3	25.1	31.5	6
5	33.6	27.0	30.9	29.1	28.3	35.2	5
4	35.8	31.6	33.8	37.1	32.5	38.0	4
3	40.4	34.6	37.3	41.5	35.4	41.2	3
2	46.4	39.1	41.8	44.8	38.9	44.6	2
1	49.7	45.5	46.0	47.9	43.0	50.4	1
Mean	9.7	8.2	9.9	7.3	8.9	7.7	Mean
SD	7.7	6.7	7.7	5.2	7.0	5.6	SD
Median	8.0	7.0	8.0	6.0	7.0	6.0	Median

Table B.7 **Percentage of Standardization Sample Obtaining One or More Adaptive Domain Composites or the GAC 2 or More Standard Deviations Below the Mean: Teacher/Daycare Provider and Teacher Forms**

Teacher/Daycare Provider Form

Age Group	Number of Composites at Least 2 SD Below the Mean			GAC at Least 2 SD Below the Mean
	=3	≥2	≥1	
2:0–2:5	1.0	1.0	4.0	2.0
2:6–2:11	2.0	3.0	8.0	3.0
3:0–3:5	3.0	3.0	6.0	3.0
3:6–3:11	1.0	3.0	4.0	3.0
4:0–4:5	3.0	5.0	10.0	4.0
4:6–4:11	1.0	1.0	6.0	1.0
5:0–5:11	3.3	5.3	9.3	4.7

Teacher Form

Age Group	Number of Composites at Least 2 SD Below the Mean			GAC at Least 2 SD Below the Mean
	=3	≥2	≥1	
5	2.7	6.0	13.3	6.0
6	5.7	7.1	15.7	6.4
7	3.6	8.6	14.3	6.4
8	4.7	9.3	20.7	8.0
9	7.3	12.7	18.0	12.7
10	4.0	9.3	20.0	9.3
11	9.3	12.0	17.3	11.3
12	7.3	14.0	22.7	10.7
13–14	6.8	12.0	22.8	12.8
15–16	6.4	11.4	22.1	12.1
17–21	2.5	7.5	14.2	5.0

Table B.8 Differences Between Single Skill Area Scaled Scores and Average Scaled Scores Required for Statistical Significance (Critical Values) and Differences Obtained by Various Percentages of the Standardization Sample (Base Rates): Parent/Primary Caregiver and Parent Forms

Parent/Primary Caregiver Form

Ages 0:0–0:11

Mean of 7 Skill Areas

Skill Area	Significance Level		Base Rate				
	0.15	0.05	1%	2%	5%	10%	25%
Communication	3.30	3.88	6.43	5.07	4.14	3.43	2.57
Health and Safety	3.67	4.32	5.79	5.50	4.36	3.57	2.64
Leisure	3.11	3.65	4.93	4.07	3.36	2.79	2.14
Self-Care	3.35	3.94	4.71	4.36	3.71	3.14	2.00
Self-Direction	3.35	3.94	5.57	4.79	3.93	3.14	2.29
Social	2.91	3.42	4.50	4.00	3.43	3.00	1.86
Motor	3.04	3.57	6.00	5.07	4.14	3.29	2.21

Ages 1–5

Mean of Conceptual Domain

Skill Area	Significance Level		Base Rate				
	0.15	0.05	1%	2%	5%	10%	25%
Communication	1.61	1.97	5.00	4.33	3.33	3.00	1.67
Functional Pre-Academics	1.55	1.91	4.33	4.00	3.33	3.00	2.00
Self-Direction	1.67	2.04	5.00	4.00	3.33	2.67	2.00

Mean of Practical Domain

Skill Area	Significance Level		Base Rate				
	0.15	0.05	1%	2%	5%	10%	25%
Community Use	1.85	2.23	4.75	4.00	3.25	2.75	2.00
Home Living	1.70	2.04	4.25	3.75	3.25	2.50	1.75
Health and Safety	2.06	2.47	4.25	3.75	3.00	2.50	1.75
Self-Care	2.23	2.68	5.25	4.50	3.75	3.00	2.25

Mean of 10 Skill Areas

Skill Area	Significance Level		Base Rate				
	0.15	0.05	1%	2%	5%	10%	25%
Communication	2.34	2.71	5.30	4.85	3.90	3.20	2.30
Community Use	2.32	2.68	5.20	4.40	3.50	2.90	2.10
Functional Pre-Academics	2.20	2.55	5.60	5.10	4.40	3.60	2.50
Home Living	2.04	2.36	5.20	4.60	3.70	3.00	2.10
Health and Safety	2.67	3.09	4.70	4.10	3.50	2.80	2.00
Leisure	2.48	2.87	5.30	4.60	3.80	3.10	2.00
Self-Care	2.96	3.42	5.50	4.95	3.90	3.30	2.40
Self-Direction	2.48	2.87	4.50	4.10	3.30	2.70	1.80
Social	2.48	2.87	4.30	3.90	3.30	2.80	1.90
Motor	2.96	3.42	5.70	5.05	4.30	3.50	2.30

Note. The differences required for statistical significance are based on the average standard error of measurement across all ages and calculated with the following formula provided by Davis (1959):

$$\text{Difference Score} = Z \sqrt{(SEM_t^2)/K^2 + [(K-2)/K](SEM_i^2)}$$

where Z is the normal curve value associated with the desired significance level derived with the Bonferroni correction of multiple comparisons, K is the number of skill areas in comparison, SEM_t^2 is the sum of the squared standard errors of measurement for all skill areas in the comparison, and SEM_i^2 is the squared standard error of measurement for the skill area of interest.

Table B.8 **Differences Between Single Skill Area Scaled Scores and Average Scaled Scores Required for Statistical Significance (Critical Values) and Differences Obtained by Various Percentages of the Standardization Sample (Base Rates): Parent/Primary Caregiver and Parent Forms** (continued)

Parent Form (Ages 5–21)

Mean of Conceptual Domain

Skill Area	Significance Level		Base Rate				
	0.15	0.05	1%	2%	5%	10%	25%
Communication	1.36	1.66	4.00	3.67	3.00	2.33	1.67
Functional Academics	1.32	1.61	4.00	3.67	3.00	2.33	1.67
Self-Direction	1.31	1.60	4.33	4.00	3.33	2.67	1.67

Mean of Practical Domain

Skill Area	Significance Level		Base Rate				
	0.15	0.05	1%	2%	5%	10%	25%
Community Use	1.66	2.00	5.25	4.75	3.75	3.00	2.00
Home Living	1.61	1.93	5.75	5.25	4.25	3.50	2.00
Health and Safety	1.94	2.33	4.75	4.25	3.25	2.50	1.75
Self-Care	1.94	2.33	5.25	4.50	3.75	3.00	2.00

Mean of 9 Skill Areas

Skill Area	Significance Level		Base Rate				
	0.15	0.05	1%	2%	5%	10%	25%
Communication	1.96	2.29	4.89	4.33	3.44	2.89	2.00
Community Use	2.00	2.33	5.56	5.00	3.89	3.11	2.00
Functional Academics	1.86	2.17	5.00	4.56	3.56	2.89	1.89
Home Living	1.90	2.22	6.67	6.22	5.22	4.22	2.44
Health and Safety	2.45	2.86	4.78	4.22	3.44	2.72	1.89
Leisure	1.98	2.31	4.56	4.11	3.22	2.67	1.78
Self-Care	2.45	2.86	5.67	5.00	4.11	3.33	2.22
Self-Direction	1.84	2.15	5.00	4.44	3.44	2.78	1.89
Social	1.90	2.22	5.78	5.11	4.11	3.33	2.11

Note. The differences required for statistical significance are based on the average standard error of measurement across all ages and calculated with the following formula provided by Davis (1959):

$$\text{Difference Score} = Z \sqrt{(SEM_t^2)/K^2 + [(K-2)/K](SEM_i^2)}$$

where Z is the normal curve value associated with the desired significance level derived with the Bonferroni correction of multiple comparisons, K is the number of skill areas in comparison, SEM_t^2 is the sum of the squared standard errors of measurement for all skill areas in the comparison, and SEM_i^2 is the squared standard error of measurement for the skill area of interest.

Table B.9   Pairwise Comparison: Values Required for Statistical Significance (Critical Values) at the 15 and 5% Levels When Comparing Each Scaled Score With Every Other Scaled Score: Parent/Primary Caregiver and Parent Forms

Parent/Primary Caregiver Form (Ages 0–5) — Skill Area

Skill Area	Com	CU	FA	HL	HS	LS	SC	SD	Soc	MO
Communication	–	2.21	2.15	2.08	2.55	2.38	2.60	2.42	2.35	2.55
Community Use	3.00	–	1.98	1.90	2.41	2.23	2.45	2.27	2.19	2.41
Functional Pre-Academics	2.93	2.69	–	1.83	2.36	2.17	2.40	2.22	2.14	2.36
Home Living	2.83	2.59	2.50	–	2.29	2.10	2.34	2.15	2.07	2.29
Health and Safety	3.47	3.28	3.21	3.12	–	2.57	2.77	2.61	2.54	2.73
Leisure	3.24	3.03	2.96	2.86	3.50	–	2.61	2.44	2.37	2.57
Self-Care	3.53	3.34	3.27	3.19	3.77	3.56	–	2.65	2.59	2.77
Self-Direction	3.30	3.09	3.02	2.93	3.55	3.33	3.61	–	2.41	2.61
Social	3.20	2.99	2.91	2.81	3.46	3.23	3.52	3.29	–	2.54
Motor	3.47	3.28	3.21	3.12	3.71	3.50	3.77	3.55	3.46	–

Parent Form (Ages 5–21) — Skill Area

Skill Area	Com	CU	FA	HL	HS	LS	SC	SD	Soc
Communication	–	1.79	1.72	1.74	2.04	1.78	2.04	1.71	1.74
Community Use	2.44	–	1.74	1.76	2.06	1.80	2.06	1.73	1.76
Functional Academics	2.34	2.37	–	1.69	2.00	1.73	2.00	1.66	1.69
Home Living	2.37	2.40	2.30	–	2.02	1.75	2.02	1.68	1.71
Health and Safety	2.78	2.80	2.72	2.74	–	2.05	2.28	1.99	2.02
Leisure	2.43	2.45	2.36	2.38	2.79	–	2.05	1.72	1.75
Self-Care	2.78	2.80	2.72	2.74	3.10	2.79	–	1.99	2.02
Self-Direction	2.33	2.36	2.26	2.29	2.71	2.34	2.71	–	1.68
Social	2.37	2.40	2.30	2.33	2.74	2.38	2.74	2.29	–

Note. **Com** = Communication; **CU** = Community Use; **FA** = Functional (Pre-)Academics; **HL** = Home Living; **HS** = Health and Safety; **LS** = Leisure; **SC** = Self-Care; **SD** = Self-Direction; **Soc** = Social; **MO** = Motor.

Differences between skill area scores required for signficance at the .15 level appear above the diagonal, and the differences significant at the .05 level appear below the diagonal.

The differences for statistical significance are based on the average standard error of measurement across all ages for each skill area and calculated with the following formula:

$$\text{Difference Score} = Z \sqrt{SEM_a^2 + SEM_b^2}$$

where Z is the normal curve value associated with the desired signficance level and SEM_a and SEM_b are the standard errors of measurement of the skill area scores.

Table B.10 Cumulative Percentages of Inter-Skill Area Scatter Within 7, 9, or 10 Skill Areas and 3 Adaptive Domains: Parent/Primary Caregiver and Parent Forms

Parent/Primary Caregiver Form

Ages 0:0–0:11

Scatter	GAC (7 skill areas)	Conceptual (2 skill areas)	Social (2 skill areas)	Practical (2 skill areas)
18	0.0	0.0	0.0	0.0
17	0.3	0.0	0.0	0.0
16	0.7	0.0	0.0	0.0
15	0.7	0.0	0.0	0.0
14	0.7	0.3	0.0	0.3
13	0.7	0.3	0.0	0.3
12	1.0	0.3	0.0	0.3
11	2.0	0.7	0.0	0.3
10	3.0	1.0	0.3	0.3
9	9.3	2.7	0.7	0.3
8	20.0	3.0	1.0	0.7
7	29.7	5.7	1.3	2.3
6	44.3	11.0	2.0	5.3
5	65.3	15.7	9.0	11.7
4	84.7	30.0	16.7	24.3
3	95.0	43.7	30.3	38.7
2	100.0	64.7	56.7	59.7
1	100.0	88.0	83.0	84.3
0	100.0	100.0	100.0	100.0
Mean	5.6	2.7	2.0	2.3
SD	2.2	2.2	1.6	1.9
Median	5.0	2.0	2.0	2.0

Parent/Primary Caregiver Form

Ages 1–5

Scatter	GAC (10 skill areas)	Conceptual (3 skill areas)	Social (2 skill areas)	Practical (4 skill areas)
15	0.0	0.0	0.0	0.0
14	0.2	0.0	0.0	0.0
13	0.7	0.1	0.0	0.0
12	1.7	0.2	0.0	0.2
11	3.1	0.6	0.0	0.6
10	5.3	1.1	0.1	0.9
9	9.8	2.1	0.3	2.0
8	18.0	3.8	0.8	5.0
7	34.3	7.8	1.5	8.5
6	57.3	15.8	3.7	17.0
5	77.2	26.2	7.5	31.8
4	93.4	41.2	15.3	54.5
3	98.6	64.1	30.8	78.0
2	100.0	85.0	52.7	94.5
1	100.0	97.9	84.0	99.4
0	100.0	100.0	100.0	100.0
Mean	6.0	3.5	2.0	3.9
SD	2.0	2.0	1.6	1.8
Median	6.0	3.0	2.0	4.0

Table B.10 **Cumulative Percentages of Inter-Skill Area Scatter Within 7, 9, or 10 Skill Areas and 3 Adaptive Domains: Parent/Primary Caregiver and Parent Forms** *(continued)*

Parent Form (Ages 5–21)

Scatter	GAC (9 skill areas)	Conceptual (3 skill areas)	Social (2 skill areas)	Practical (4 skill areas)
16	0.0	0.0	0.0	0.0
15	0.1	0.0	0.0	0.0
14	0.1	0.0	0.0	0.0
13	0.7	0.0	0.0	0.2
12	1.8	0.0	0.1	0.7
11	2.9	0.2	0.2	1.0
10	6.7	0.4	0.2	2.5
9	12.3	1.0	0.4	5.1
8	21.1	2.2	0.8	9.2
7	31.6	4.4	1.7	15.1
6	45.3	9.3	3.8	24.3
5	63.2	18.4	7.2	35.1
4	79.4	31.8	14.6	52.4
3	93.8	52.3	27.0	72.5
2	99.3	76.8	47.2	91.4
1	99.9	96.0	82.4	99.2
0	100.0	100.0	100.0	100.0
Mean	5.6	2.9	1.9	4.1
SD	2.4	1.8	1.7	2.3
Median	5.0	3.0	1.0	4.0

Table B.11 **Percentage of Standardization Sample Obtaining Various Skill Area Scaled Scores 2 or More Standard Deviations Below the Mean: Parent/Primary Caregiver and Parent Forms**

Parent/Primary Caregiver Form	Number of Skill Areas at Least 2 SD Below the Mean							
Age Group	≥9	≥8	≥7	≥6	≥5	≥4	≥3	≥2
0:0–0:3	0.0	0.0	0.0	0.0	0.0	0.0	3.0	5.0
0:4–0:7	0.0	0.0	0.0	0.0	0.0	1.0	1.0	1.0
0:8–0:11	0.0	0.0	0.0	0.0	1.0	1.0	2.0	3.0
1:0–1:3	0.0	0.0	0.0	0.0	0.0	0.0	1.0	1.0
1:4–1:7	0.0	0.0	1.0	1.0	1.0	1.0	3.0	4.0
1:8–1:11	0.0	0.0	1.0	1.0	2.0	2.0	3.0	6.0
2:0–2:5	0.0	1.0	1.0	1.0	1.0	1.0	1.0	2.0
2:6–2:11	1.0	2.0	2.0	2.0	2.0	2.0	3.0	3.0
3:0–3:5	0.0	1.0	2.0	3.0	4.0	4.0	4.0	6.0
3:6–3:11	0.0	1.0	1.0	1.0	1.0	2.0	2.0	5.0
4:0–4:5	0.0	0.0	0.0	0.0	1.0	2.0	4.0	6.0
4:6–4:11	0.0	0.0	1.0	2.0	2.0	3.0	7.0	8.0
5:0–5:11	0.0	0.0	0.0	0.7	1.3	2.7	3.3	6.7

Parent Form	Number of Skill Areas at Least 2 SD Below the Mean							
Age Group	=9	≥8	≥7	≥6	≥5	≥4	≥3	≥2
5	0.0	0.8	1.7	2.5	3.3	5.0	10.0	17.5
6	0.0	0.0	0.8	1.5	2.3	3.8	6.2	12.3
7	0.0	0.0	0.8	3.3	5.0	9.2	11.7	18.3
8	2.0	2.0	3.3	5.3	5.3	8.0	10.7	15.3
9	0.0	0.0	0.0	0.7	0.7	1.3	3.3	12.7
10	0.0	0.7	0.7	0.7	3.3	4.7	7.3	11.3
11	0.0	0.0	0.0	0.0	1.3	4.7	7.3	14.7
12	1.3	2.7	3.3	3.3	7.3	10.7	15.3	20.7
13–14	0.7	1.3	2.7	3.3	4.7	7.3	12.0	18.0
15–16	1.0	1.0	1.0	1.5	2.5	2.5	6.5	14.0
17–21	0.5	2.0	2.5	3.5	3.5	5.5	8.5	12.5

Table B.12 Differences Between Adaptive Domain Composite Scores Required for Statistical Significance (Critical Values) at the 15 and 5% Levels, by Age Group and Overall Standardization Sample: Parent/Primary Caregiver and Parent Forms

Parent/Primary Caregiver Form		Composite Pair		
Age Group	Significance Level	CON-SO	CON-PR	SO-PR
0:0–0:3	0.15	15.13	17.41	15.87
	0.05	20.59	23.70	21.60
0:4–0:7	0.15	12.41	12.77	11.02
	0.05	16.89	17.38	14.99
0:8–0:11	0.15	11.22	12.59	11.62
	0.05	15.27	17.14	15.82
1:0–1:3	0.15	8.90	8.08	8.36
	0.05	12.12	10.99	11.38
1:4–1:7	0.15	8.90	7.16	8.63
	0.05	12.11	9.74	11.75
1:8–1:11	0.15	8.90	7.79	8.63
	0.05	12.12	10.60	11.75
2:0–2:5	0.15	6.83	6.11	6.83
	0.05	9.29	8.32	9.29
2:6–2:11	0.15	8.36	7.16	8.08
	0.05	11.38	9.74	11.00
3:0–3:5	0.15	6.83	5.72	6.48
	0.05	9.29	7.78	8.82
3:6–3:11	0.15	7.78	7.16	8.08
	0.05	10.59	9.74	10.99
4:0–4:5	0.15	8.08	6.83	7.48
	0.05	10.99	9.29	10.18
4:6–4:11	0.15	8.08	7.16	8.36
	0.05	11.00	9.74	11.38
5:0–5:11	0.15	7.47	7.47	7.47
	0.05	10.17	10.17	10.17
Overall	0.15	9.43	9.32	9.32
Sample	0.05	12.83	12.68	12.68

Note. The differences for statistical significance are based on the average standard errors of measurement by age group and overall sample for each adaptive domain and calculated with the following formula:

$$\text{Difference Score} = Z \sqrt{SEM_a^2 + SEM_b^2}$$

where Z is the normal curve value associated with the desired signficance level and SEM_a and SEM_b are the standard errors of measurement of the adaptive domain scores.

Table B.12 **Differences Between Adaptive Domain Composite Scores Required for Statistical Significance (Critical Values) at the 15 and 5% Levels, by Age Group and Overall Standardization Sample: Parent/Primary Caregiver and Parent Forms** (continued)

Parent Form Age Group	Significance Level	Composite Pair		
		CON-SO	CON-PR	SO-PR
5	0.15	6.83	6.11	6.83
	0.05	9.29	8.32	9.29
6	0.15	6.11	5.72	6.48
	0.05	8.31	7.78	8.81
7	0.15	6.83	6.48	7.16
	0.05	9.29	8.81	9.74
8	0.15	6.11	5.29	6.11
	0.05	8.31	7.21	8.31
9	0.15	6.48	6.83	7.16
	0.05	8.81	9.29	9.74
10	0.15	6.48	6.48	6.82
	0.05	8.81	8.81	9.29
11	0.15	6.48	6.48	6.82
	0.05	8.81	8.81	9.29
12	0.15	5.72	5.29	5.72
	0.05	7.78	7.21	7.78
13–14	0.15	5.72	5.72	6.11
	0.05	7.78	7.78	8.32
15–16	0.15	5.72	5.72	6.11
	0.05	7.78	7.78	8.32
17–21	0.15	5.29	4.32	5.29
	0.05	7.20	5.88	7.20
Overall Sample	0.15	6.17	5.89	6.44
	0.05	8.40	8.02	8.77

Note. The differences for statistical significance are based on the average standard errors of measurement by age group and overall sample for each adaptive domain and calculated with the following formula:

Difference Score = $Z \sqrt{SEM_a^2 + SEM_b^2}$

where Z is the normal curve value associated with the desired signficance level and SEM_a and SEM_b are the standard errors of measurement of the adaptive domain scores.

Table B.13 Differences Between Adaptive Domain Composite Scores Obtained by Various Percentages of the Standardization Sample (Base Rates): Parent/Primary Caregiver and Parent Forms

Parent/Primary Caregiver Form (Ages 0–5)			Composite Pair				
	CON-SO		CON-PR		SO-PR		
Amount of Discrepancy	CON<SO (−)	CON>SO (+)	CON<PR (−)	CON>PR (+)	SO<PR (−)	SO>PR (+)	Amount of Discrepancy
≥40	0.1	0.1	0.3	0.1	0.0	0.2	≥40
39	0.1	0.1	0.3	0.3	0.0	0.3	39
38	0.2	0.1	0.3	0.4	0.0	0.4	38
37	0.3	0.1	0.4	0.4	0.1	0.4	37
36	0.4	0.1	0.7	0.4	0.1	0.5	36
35	0.4	0.1	1.0	0.4	0.1	0.6	35
34	0.4	0.1	1.2	0.4	0.3	0.7	34
33	0.5	0.1	1.2	0.5	0.4	0.7	33
32	0.7	0.1	1.2	0.5	0.4	0.9	32
31	0.7	0.1	1.5	0.5	0.5	1.0	31
30	0.7	0.1	1.6	0.5	0.7	1.0	30
29	0.8	0.1	1.8	0.7	1.0	1.0	29
28	0.9	0.2	1.9	1.0	1.0	1.2	28
27	1.1	0.5	2.0	1.1	1.1	1.2	27
26	1.4	0.7	2.1	1.4	1.6	1.3	26
25	1.8	0.9	2.2	1.8	1.9	1.7	25
24	2.1	1.2	2.4	2.4	2.0	2.3	24
23	2.4	1.4	2.9	2.7	2.1	2.6	23
22	2.8	2.2	3.2	3.3	2.8	2.9	22
21	3.3	2.6	3.3	3.8	3.4	3.5	21
20	3.9	3.1	3.5	4.4	3.7	3.7	20
19	4.7	3.8	4.3	4.9	4.5	4.0	19
18	5.3	4.5	5.0	5.7	5.2	4.4	18
17	6.0	5.6	5.9	6.4	6.0	5.7	17
16	6.5	6.1	7.0	7.9	7.9	6.6	16
15	7.6	7.8	8.5	8.8	8.7	8.9	15
14	9.2	9.1	10.4	10.1	10.1	10.1	14
13	11.0	10.7	12.7	11.3	11.9	11.9	13
12	13.5	12.8	14.1	13.9	13.2	13.9	12
11	15.7	16.1	16.7	16.1	15.6	15.5	11
10	19.1	17.9	19.8	19.6	18.1	18.4	10
9	21.2	20.1	21.0	21.3	20.0	21.0	9
8	23.9	24.0	23.3	24.7	23.3	23.4	8
7	25.9	27.3	26.7	27.8	27.6	27.4	7
6	29.1	30.0	29.8	30.7	29.9	29.7	6
5	32.4	33.0	32.8	33.0	33.0	34.2	5
4	35.6	37.3	36.1	37.3	37.1	37.7	4
3	41.3	39.6	41.9	40.2	40.9	41.6	3
2	43.4	43.6	43.2	43.4	44.2	45.9	2
1	48.9	47.6	47.6	48.1	46.7	49.2	1
Mean	8.7	8.6	9.3	9.1	9.2	8.9	Mean
SD	6.9	6.1	7.5	7.0	6.7	7.0	SD
Median	7.0	8.0	7.0	8.0	7.0	7.0	Median

Table B.13 Differences Between Adaptive Domain Composite Scores Obtained by Various Percentages of the Standardization Sample (Base Rates): Parent/Primary Caregiver and Parent Forms (continued)

Parent Form (Ages 5–21)			Composite Pair				
	CON-SO		CON-PR		SO-PR		
Amount of Discrepancy	CON<SO (–)	CON>SO (+)	CON<PR (–)	CON>PR (+)	SO<PR (–)	SO>PR (+)	Amount of Discrepancy
≥40	0.1	0.1	0.3	0.1	0.2	0.2	≥40
39	0.2	0.1	0.4	0.1	0.2	0.2	39
38	0.3	0.1	0.4	0.1	0.3	0.3	38
37	0.4	0.1	0.4	0.1	0.4	0.3	37
36	0.4	0.1	0.5	0.2	0.4	0.3	36
35	0.5	0.1	0.5	0.2	0.4	0.3	35
34	0.7	0.1	0.6	0.2	0.5	0.4	34
33	0.7	0.1	0.7	0.2	0.5	0.4	33
32	0.8	0.1	0.7	0.3	0.7	0.6	32
31	1.0	0.1	0.9	0.4	0.8	0.9	31
30	1.0	0.1	1.0	0.4	1.0	1.0	30
29	1.1	0.1	1.1	0.4	1.1	1.1	29
28	1.2	0.1	1.3	0.4	1.3	1.5	28
27	1.4	0.4	1.4	0.5	1.4	1.9	27
26	1.5	0.5	1.7	0.6	1.7	2.2	26
25	1.7	0.7	1.8	1.0	2.3	2.7	25
24	2.0	1.1	2.2	1.3	2.6	3.1	24
23	2.9	1.4	2.9	1.7	3.2	4.0	23
22	3.1	1.9	3.1	2.3	3.8	4.6	22
21	3.7	2.5	3.4	2.6	4.4	5.0	21
20	4.3	3.0	4.0	3.1	5.3	5.7	20
19	5.2	3.5	4.8	3.8	6.3	6.6	19
18	5.8	4.3	5.6	5.0	6.9	7.1	18
17	6.9	5.4	6.2	6.0	8.2	8.4	17
16	8.1	6.4	7.2	7.1	9.2	9.2	16
15	9.2	7.7	8.9	7.8	10.5	10.8	15
14	10.4	9.3	10.7	9.0	12.0	12.3	14
13	12.8	10.7	12.0	10.1	13.7	13.8	13
12	14.4	11.9	13.7	11.8	16.7	15.2	12
11	15.9	14.2	16.2	13.6	18.5	17.3	11
10	18.1	16.0	18.9	15.8	20.3	19.6	10
9	20.8	18.0	21.1	18.3	22.0	22.5	9
8	23.4	20.2	23.2	20.8	24.4	24.7	8
7	26.0	23.2	27.1	22.6	27.0	26.9	7
6	28.9	25.9	29.8	25.3	28.9	30.9	6
5	32.5	28.4	33.5	28.3	32.3	33.2	5
4	35.5	31.7	36.6	31.4	35.3	35.9	4
3	39.9	34.6	40.0	35.4	37.7	38.6	3
2	44.0	38.1	43.2	39.4	41.4	41.9	2
1	48.5	41.1	47.1	43.0	44.1	44.9	1
Mean	9.0	8.8	9.2	8.6	10.2	10.2	Mean
SD	7.3	6.3	7.2	6.6	7.5	7.6	SD
Median	7.0	7.0	7.0	7.0	8.5	8.5	Median

Table B.14 Percentage of Standardization Sample Obtaining One or More Adaptive Domain Composites or the GAC 2 or More Standard Deviations Below the Mean: Parent/Primary Caregiver and Parent Forms

Parent/Primary Caregiver Form

Age Group	Number of Composites at Least 2 SD Below the Mean			GAC at Least 2 SD Below the Mean
	=3	≥2	≥1	
0:0–0:3	0.0	0.0	9.0	4.0
0:4–0:7	0.0	1.0	3.0	1.0
0:8–0:11	2.0	2.0	3.0	2.0
1:0–1:3	0.0	0.0	2.0	0.0
1:4–1:7	1.0	3.0	4.0	3.0
1:8–1:11	1.0	3.0	4.0	2.0
2:0–2:5	1.0	1.0	1.0	1.0
2:6–2:11	2.0	2.0	3.0	2.0
3:0–3:5	2.0	4.0	9.0	5.0
3:6–3:11	1.0	2.0	3.0	2.0
4:0–4:5	0.0	1.0	5.0	2.0
4:6–4:11	2.0	4.0	8.0	4.0
5:0–5:11	0.0	2.0	8.0	2.7

Parent Form

Age Group	Number of Composites at Least 2 SD Below the Mean			GAC at Least 2 SD Below the Mean
	=3	≥2	≥1	
5	1.7	5.0	12.5	5.8
6	0.8	2.3	5.4	5.4
7	0.8	1.7	9.2	9.2
8	2.7	6.7	8.0	7.3
9	0.0	2.0	13.3	5.3
10	0.7	3.3	7.3	5.3
11	2.0	7.3	18.0	6.0
12	2.7	7.3	9.3	10.0
13–14	1.3	3.3	8.0	6.0
15–16	1.5	3.0	5.5	5.0
17–21	2.5	3.5	9.5	5.5

Table B.15 Differences Between Single Skill Area Scaled Scores and Average Scaled Scores Required for Statistical Significance (Critical Values) and Differences Obtained by Various Percentages of the Standardization Sample (Base Rates): Adult Form, Self Report

| | **Mean of Conceptual Domain** | | | | | | |
| Skill Area | **Significance Level** | | **Base Rate** | | | | |
	0.15	0.05	1%	2%	5%	10%	25%
Communication	1.32	1.62	4.00	3.67	3.00	2.33	1.33
Functional Academics	1.32	1.62	3.33	3.00	2.67	2.00	1.33
Self-Direction	1.23	1.51	4.00	3.67	3.00	2.33	1.67

| | **Mean of Practical Domain (without Work)** | | | | | | |
| Skill Area | **Significance Level** | | **Base Rate** | | | | |
	0.15	0.05	1%	2%	5%	10%	25%
Community Use	1.57	1.89	4.25	4.00	3.25	2.75	1.50
Home Living	1.50	1.80	5.00	4.25	3.00	2.50	1.75
Health and Safety	1.74	2.09	3.75	3.25	2.75	2.25	1.50
Self-Care	1.80	2.16	4.50	4.00	3.25	2.75	1.50

| | **Mean of Practical Domain (with Work)** | | | | | | |
| Skill Area | **Significance Level** | | **Base Rate** | | | | |
	0.15	0.05	1%	2%	5%	10%	25%
Community Use	1.66	1.99	4.60	4.20	3.60	2.80	1.70
Home Living	1.57	1.89	5.00	4.60	3.40	2.60	1.60
Health and Safety	1.86	2.23	4.00	3.60	3.20	2.40	1.40
Self-Care	1.93	2.32	4.80	4.00	3.40	2.60	1.60
Work	1.66	1.99	4.80	4.60	3.60	3.20	2.00

| | **Mean of 9 Skill Areas (GAC without Work)** | | | | | | |
| Skill Area | **Significance Level** | | **Base Rate** | | | | |
	0.15	0.05	1%	2%	5%	10%	25%
Communication	1.91	2.22	4.89	4.22	3.56	2.78	1.78
Community Use	1.91	2.22	4.22	3.67	2.89	2.33	1.56
Functional Academics	1.91	2.22	4.11	3.78	3.00	2.44	1.56
Home Living	1.79	2.08	5.78	5.22	3.89	3.00	1.89
Health and Safety	2.19	2.54	4.33	3.89	3.22	2.67	1.67
Leisure	1.56	1.82	5.67	4.56	3.78	2.67	1.67
Self-Care	2.29	2.66	5.33	4.78	3.78	3.06	1.89
Self-Direction	1.68	1.95	4.00	3.67	3.00	2.44	1.67
Social	1.91	2.22	5.22	4.22	3.33	2.67	1.78

| | **Mean of 10 Skill Areas (GAC with Work)** | | | | | | |
| Skill Area | **Significance Level** | | **Base Rate** | | | | |
	0.15	0.05	1%	2%	5%	10%	25%
Communication	1.95	2.26	5.00	4.30	3.60	2.90	1.80
Community Use	1.95	2.26	4.30	3.80	3.00	2.50	1.60
Functional Academics	1.95	2.26	4.40	3.90	3.00	2.50	1.60
Home Living	1.83	2.12	5.60	4.90	4.00	3.00	1.80
Health and Safety	2.24	2.59	4.40	3.90	3.30	2.60	1.60
Leisure	1.59	1.84	5.70	4.60	3.80	2.70	1.70
Self-Care	2.34	2.71	5.30	4.70	3.70	3.00	1.85
Self-Direction	1.71	1.98	4.10	3.70	3.00	2.30	1.65
Social	1.95	2.26	5.20	4.10	3.10	2.50	1.70
Work	1.95	2.26	5.60	4.90	4.00	3.30	2.10

Note. The differences required for statistical significance are based on the average standard error of measurement across all ages and calculated with the following formula provided by Davis (1959):

$$\text{Difference Score} = Z \sqrt{(SEM_t^2)/K^2 + [(K-2)/K](SEM_i^2)}$$

where Z is the normal curve value associated with the desired significance level derived with the Bonferroni correction of multiple comparisons, K is the number of skill areas in comparison, SEM_t^2 is the sum of the squared standard errors of measurement for all skill areas in the comparison, and SEM_i^2 is the squared standard error of measurement for the skill area of interest.

Table B.16   Pairwise Comparison: Values Required for Statistical Significance (Critical Values) at the 15 and 5% Levels When Comparing Each Scaled Score With Every Other Scaled Score: Adult Form, Self Report

| Skill Area | Skill Area | | | | | | | | | |
	Com	CU	FA	HL	HS	LS	SC	SD	Soc	WK
Communication	–	1.73	1.73	1.67	1.88	1.56	1.93	1.61	1.73	1.73
Community Use	2.36	–	1.73	1.67	1.88	1.56	1.93	1.61	1.73	1.73
Functional Academics	2.36	2.36	–	1.67	1.88	1.56	1.93	1.61	1.73	1.73
Home Living	2.27	2.27	2.27	–	1.82	1.49	1.88	1.55	1.67	1.67
Health and Safety	2.56	2.56	2.56	2.48	–	1.72	2.07	1.77	1.88	1.88
Leisure	2.12	2.12	2.12	2.03	2.34	–	1.78	1.43	1.56	1.56
Self-Care	2.63	2.63	2.63	2.56	2.81	2.42	–	1.83	1.93	1.93
Self-Direction	2.20	2.20	2.20	2.11	2.41	1.94	2.49	–	1.61	1.61
Social	2.36	2.36	2.36	2.27	2.56	2.12	2.63	2.20	–	1.73
Work	2.36	2.36	2.36	2.27	2.56	2.12	2.63	2.20	2.36	–

Note. **Com** = Communication; **CU** = Community Use; **FA** = Functional Academics; **HL** = Home Living; **HS** = Health and Safety; **LS** = Leisure; **SC** = Self-Care; **SD** = Self-Direction; **Soc** = Social; **WK** = Work.

Differences between skill area scores required for signficance at the .15 level appear above the diagonal, and the differences significant at the .05 level appear below the diagonal.

The differences for statistical significance are based on the average standard error of measurement across all ages for each skill area and calculated with the following formula:

Difference Score $= Z \sqrt{SEM_a^2 + SEM_b^2}$

where Z is the normal curve value associated with the desired signficance level and SEM_a and SEM_b are the standard errors of measurement of the skill area scores.

Table B.17   Cumulative Percentages of Inter-Skill Area Scatter Within 9 or 10 Skill Areas and 3 Adaptive Domains: Adult Form, Self Report

Scatter	GAC (9 skill areas)	GAC (10 skill areas)	Conceptual (3 skill areas)	Social (2 skill areas)	Practical (4 skill areas)	Practical (5 skill areas)
14	0.0	0.0	0.0	0.0	0.0	0.0
13	0.1	0.1	0.0	0.0	0.0	0.0
12	0.1	0.3	0.0	0.0	0.0	0.2
11	0.8	1.0	0.0	0.0	0.1	0.4
10	2.0	2.5	0.0	0.2	0.6	0.9
9	5.2	6.7	0.4	0.3	1.6	2.5
8	10.9	12.7	1.2	1.1	2.9	4.7
7	19.5	21.7	3.6	2.0	6.4	10.3
6	31.8	35.4	7.1	3.7	15.6	20.2
5	49.6	53.8	13.7	7.8	25.5	33.1
4	66.3	69.0	24.9	14.4	38.5	47.9
3	77.3	78.4	42.2	25.1	55.4	63.1
2	87.0	87.4	61.8	40.4	72.4	76.9
1	100.0	100.0	83.4	79.4	99.1	99.8
0	100.0	100.0	100.0	100.0	100.0	100.0
Mean	4.5	4.7	2.4	1.7	3.2	3.6
SD	2.3	2.4	1.9	1.7	2.0	2.2
Median	4.0	5.0	2.0	1.0	3.0	3.0

Table B.18   Percentage of Standardization Sample Obtaining Various Skill Area Scaled Scores 2 or More Standard Deviations Below the Mean: Adult Form, Self Report

Participants with the Work Skill Area

	Number of Skill Areas at Least 2 SD Below the Mean							
Age Group	≥9	≥8	≥7	≥6	≥5	≥4	≥3	≥2
16–21	1.6	1.6	1.6	1.6	2.5	2.5	3.3	4.1
22–29	0.0	0.0	0.8	0.8	1.5	3.0	6.1	10.6
30–39	0.0	0.6	0.6	1.2	1.2	2.4	4.1	7.7
40–49	0.0	0.6	0.6	0.6	2.5	2.5	4.3	8.0
50–64	0.0	0.0	0.0	1.1	2.3	4.5	8.0	11.4
65–74	0.0	0.0	0.0	5.6	7.4	7.4	11.1	14.8

Participants without the Work Skill Area

	Number of Skill Areas at Least 2 SD Below the Mean							
Age Group	=9	≥8	≥7	≥6	≥5	≥4	≥3	≥2
16–21	0.0	1.3	1.3	1.3	1.3	2.0	2.7	6.0
22–29	0.0	0.0	0.0	0.7	0.7	2.7	4.7	9.3
30–39	0.6	1.1	1.7	1.7	2.2	3.3	5.6	8.9
40–49	0.0	0.6	1.1	1.1	1.7	3.9	5.6	8.9
50–64	0.0	0.0	0.0	1.8	2.7	3.6	9.1	15.5
65–74	0.0	0.0	0.0	2.5	4.2	5.8	8.3	13.3
75–89	0.0	2.0	2.0	2.0	2.0	4.0	6.0	7.0

Table B.19 **Differences Between Adaptive Domain Composite Scores Required for Statistical Significance (Critical Values) at the 15 and 5% Levels, by Age Group and Overall Standardization Sample: Adult Form, Self Report**

Age Group	Significance Level	CON-SO	CON-PR	SO-PR
16–21	0.15	6.11	6.11	6.11
	0.05	8.32	8.32	8.32
22–29	0.15	6.11	6.11	6.11
	0.05	8.32	8.32	8.32
30–39	0.15	5.29	5.29	5.29
	0.05	7.21	7.21	7.21
40–49	0.15	5.72	5.29	5.72
	0.05	7.78	7.21	7.78
50–64	0.15	5.72	5.72	6.11
	0.05	7.78	7.78	8.32
65–74	0.15	5.29	5.29	5.29
	0.05	7.21	7.21	7.21
75–89	0.15	5.29	5.29	5.29
	0.05	7.21	7.21	7.21
Overall Sample	0.15	5.66	5.60	5.72
	0.05	7.71	7.62	7.79

Note. Practical Adaptive Domain calculated without the Work Skill Area.

The differences for statistical significance are based on the average standard errors of measurement by age group and overall sample for each adaptive domain and calculated with the following formula:

Difference Score = $Z \sqrt{SEM_a^2 + SEM_b^2}$

where Z is the normal curve value associated with the desired signficance level and SEM_a and SEM_b are the standard errors of measurement of the adaptive domain scores.

Table B.20 Differences Between Adaptive Domain Composite Scores Obtained by Various Percentages of the Standardization Sample (Base Rates): Adult Form, Self Report

Amount of Discrepancy	Composite Pair						Amount of Discrepancy
	CON-SO		CON-PR		SO-PR		
	CON<SO (−)	CON>SO (+)	CON<PR (−)	CON>PR (+)	SO<PR (−)	SO>PR (+)	
≥40	0.1	0.1	0.0	0.0	0.1	0.0	≥40
39	0.1	0.1	0.0	0.0	0.1	0.0	39
38	0.1	0.1	0.0	0.0	0.1	0.0	38
37	0.1	0.1	0.0	0.0	0.1	0.0	37
36	0.1	0.1	0.0	0.0	0.1	0.1	36
35	0.1	0.1	0.0	0.0	0.1	0.2	35
34	0.1	0.2	0.0	0.0	0.2	0.2	34
33	0.1	0.2	0.0	0.0	0.2	0.2	33
32	0.1	0.2	0.0	0.0	0.2	0.2	32
31	0.1	0.2	0.0	0.0	0.2	0.2	31
30	0.2	0.2	0.0	0.0	0.3	0.2	30
29	0.2	0.4	0.0	0.0	0.4	0.2	29
28	0.2	0.4	0.1	0.3	0.4	0.3	28
27	0.2	0.4	0.1	0.4	0.5	0.4	27
26	0.3	0.4	0.2	0.5	0.8	0.4	26
25	0.4	0.7	0.2	0.7	1.0	0.8	25
24	0.7	0.9	0.2	0.8	1.1	1.1	24
23	0.8	1.1	0.2	1.0	1.2	1.2	23
22	0.9	1.4	0.2	1.0	1.5	1.4	22
21	1.1	1.6	0.3	1.1	2.0	1.5	21
20	1.3	2.5	0.3	1.6	3.0	2.0	20
19	1.3	2.9	0.4	1.9	3.2	2.1	19
18	2.1	3.5	1.0	2.5	3.8	2.5	18
17	2.9	4.2	1.2	2.7	4.9	3.3	17
16	3.5	4.8	1.4	3.3	5.5	4.0	16
15	4.3	5.9	2.3	3.6	6.5	5.5	15
14	5.3	7.1	3.4	4.0	7.6	6.5	14
13	6.0	7.9	4.6	4.6	8.5	8.3	13
12	7.0	9.7	5.7	6.3	11.3	9.4	12
11	9.0	11.1	7.0	7.4	12.5	10.6	11
10	11.4	12.5	9.1	9.2	14.5	12.5	10
9	13.6	15.2	11.3	10.7	16.5	14.4	9
8	16.0	18.3	14.4	13.4	19.3	16.9	8
7	19.2	20.6	17.3	15.8	21.2	19.3	7
6	22.9	24.0	21.3	19.1	23.3	23.0	6
5	26.2	26.5	24.3	22.4	26.9	26.3	5
4	28.8	32.1	29.0	26.9	33.3	30.3	4
3	32.9	40.1	33.3	30.8	38.4	34.4	3
2	39.2	45.2	37.9	38.7	44.4	38.7	2
1	43.8	49.8	45.4	45.5	51.4	42.8	1
Mean	6.9	7.1	6.0	6.1	7.1	7.5	Mean
SD	5.5	5.9	4.5	5.4	6.2	5.9	SD
Median	6.0	5.0	5.0	4.0	5.0	6.0	Median

Note. Practical Adaptive Domain calculated without the Work Skill Area.

Table B.21 Percentage of Standardization Sample Obtaining One or More Adaptive Domain Composites or the GAC 2 or More Standard Deviations Below the Mean: Adult Form, Self Report

Age Group	Number of Composites at Least 2 SD Below the Mean			GAC at Least 2 SD Below the Mean
	=3	≥2	≥1	
16–21	1.3	1.3	6.0	4.0
22–29	1.3	3.3	6.0	4.0
30–39	2.2	2.8	6.1	5.0
40–49	0.6	2.8	6.1	5.0
50–64	0.9	2.7	11.8	3.6
65–74	0.8	5.8	8.3	5.0
75–89	2.0	2.0	7.0	5.0

B

Adult (Self)

Table B.22 **Differences Between Single Skill Area Scaled Scores and Average Scaled Scores Required for Statistical Significance (Critical Values) and Differences Obtained by Various Percentages of the Standardization Sample (Base Rates): Adult Form, Rated by Others**

	Mean of Conceptual Domain						
	Significance Level		Base Rate				
Skill Area	0.15	0.05	1%	2%	5%	10%	25%
Communication	1.08	1.32	3.67	3.33	2.67	2.00	1.33
Functional Academics	0.91	1.12	3.67	3.33	2.67	2.00	1.33
Self-Direction	0.97	1.19	3.67	3.33	2.67	2.17	1.33

	Mean of Practical Domain (without Work)						
	Significance Level		Base Rate				
Skill Area	0.15	0.05	1%	2%	5%	10%	25%
Community Use	1.57	1.89	4.25	3.75	3.00	2.50	1.50
Home Living	1.50	1.80	4.50	4.00	3.25	2.75	1.50
Health and Safety	1.74	2.09	3.50	3.00	2.50	2.25	1.25
Self-Care	1.80	2.16	4.50	4.00	3.00	2.50	1.50

	Mean of Practical Domain (with Work)						
	Significance Level		Base Rate				
Skill Area	0.15	0.05	1%	2%	5%	10%	25%
Community Use	1.29	1.55	4.40	4.00	3.20	2.40	1.60
Home Living	1.29	1.55	5.20	4.20	3.80	2.80	1.80
Health and Safety	1.47	1.76	3.80	3.40	2.80	2.20	1.40
Self-Care	1.47	1.76	5.00	4.20	3.00	2.60	1.80
Work	1.09	1.31	5.40	4.80	3.60	3.00	2.00

	Mean of 9 Skill Areas (GAC without Work)						
	Significance Level		Base Rate				
Skill Area	0.15	0.05	1%	2%	5%	10%	25%
Communication	1.91	2.22	4.33	4.00	3.22	2.67	1.67
Community Use	1.91	2.22	3.78	3.33	2.83	2.39	1.56
Functional Academics	1.91	2.22	4.89	4.00	2.89	2.39	1.56
Home Living	1.79	2.08	5.33	4.78	3.83	3.00	1.89
Health and Safety	2.19	2.54	3.67	3.44	2.89	2.44	1.44
Leisure	1.56	1.82	4.44	3.78	3.00	2.44	1.67
Self-Care	2.29	2.66	5.00	4.44	3.56	3.00	1.83
Self-Direction	1.68	1.95	3.67	3.33	2.78	2.33	1.56
Social	1.91	2.22	4.44	3.89	3.22	2.56	1.67

	Mean of 10 Skill Areas (GAC with Work)						
	Significance Level		Base Rate				
Skill Area	0.15	0.05	1%	2%	5%	10%	25%
Communication	1.66	1.92	4.50	4.10	3.30	2.70	1.80
Community Use	1.54	1.78	4.10	3.50	2.90	2.40	1.60
Functional Academics	1.24	1.43	5.00	4.20	3.10	2.40	1.60
Home Living	1.54	1.78	5.60	4.90	3.80	3.10	1.90
Health and Safety	1.79	2.07	4.00	3.40	3.00	2.60	1.55
Leisure	1.54	1.78	4.60	3.80	3.10	2.60	1.70
Self-Care	1.79	2.07	5.40	4.50	3.50	3.00	1.90
Self-Direction	1.40	1.62	3.70	3.30	2.80	2.30	1.50
Social	1.66	1.92	4.50	4.00	3.00	2.50	1.60
Work	1.24	1.43	6.00	5.00	3.80	3.10	1.90

Note. The differences required for statistical significance are based on the average standard error of measurement across all ages and calculated with the following formula provided by Davis (1959):

$$\text{Difference Score} = Z \sqrt{(SEM_t^2)/K^2 + [(K-2)/K](SEM_i^2)}$$

where Z is the normal curve value associated with the desired significance level derived with the Bonferroni correction of multiple comparisons, K is the number of skill areas in comparison, SEM_t^2 is the sum of the squared standard errors of measurement for all skill areas in the comparison, and SEM_i^2 is the squared standard error of measurement for the skill area of interest.

Table B.23 Pairwise Comparison: Values Required for Statistical Significance (Critical Values) at the 15 and 5% Levels When Comparing Each Scaled Score With Every Other Scaled Score: Adult Form, Rated by Others

	Skill Area									
Skill Area	Com	CU	FA	HL	HS	LS	SC	SD	Soc	WK
Communication	–	1.43	1.29	1.43	1.55	1.43	1.55	1.36	1.49	1.29
Community Use	1.94	–	1.22	1.36	1.49	1.36	1.49	1.30	1.43	1.22
Functional Academics	1.76	1.66	–	1.22	1.36	1.22	1.36	1.14	1.29	1.06
Home Living	1.94	1.86	1.66	–	1.49	1.36	1.49	1.30	1.43	1.22
Health and Safety	2.11	2.03	1.85	2.03	–	1.49	1.61	1.43	1.55	1.36
Leisure	1.94	1.86	1.66	1.86	2.03	–	1.49	1.30	1.43	1.22
Self-Care	2.11	2.03	1.85	2.03	2.19	2.03	–	1.43	1.55	1.36
Self-Direction	1.85	1.76	1.56	1.76	1.94	1.76	1.94	–	1.36	1.14
Social	2.02	1.94	1.76	1.94	2.11	1.94	2.11	1.85	–	1.29
Work	1.76	1.66	1.44	1.66	1.85	1.66	1.85	1.56	1.76	–

Note. **Com** = Communication; **CU** = Community Use; **FA** = Functional Academics; **HL** = Home Living; **HS** = Health and Safety; **LS** = Leisure; **SC** = Self-Care; **SD** = Self-Direction; **Soc** = Social; **WK** = Work.

Differences between skill area scores required for signficance at the .15 level appear above the diagonal, and the differences significant at the .05 level appear below the diagonal.

The differences for statistical significance are based on the average standard error of measurement across all ages for each skill area and calculated with the following formula:

$$\text{Difference Score} = Z \sqrt{SEM_a^2 + SEM_b^2}$$

where Z is the normal curve value associated with the desired signficance level and SEM_a and SEM_b are the standard errors of measurement of the skill area scores.

Table B.24 Cumulative Percentages of Inter-Skill Area Scatter Within 9 or 10 Skill Areas and 3 Adaptive Domains: Adult Form, Rated by Others

Scatter	GAC (9 skill areas)	GAC (10 skill areas)	Conceptual (3 skill areas)	Social (2 skill areas)	Practical (4 skill areas)	Practical (5 skill areas)
14	0.0	0.0	0.0	0.0	0.0	0.0
13	0.0	0.1	0.0	0.0	0.0	0.1
12	0.3	0.4	0.0	0.0	0.1	0.2
11	0.8	1.1	0.0	0.0	0.2	0.5
10	1.2	1.6	0.2	0.0	0.4	1.1
9	3.4	4.5	0.7	0.1	1.1	2.1
8	7.2	9.2	1.0	0.3	2.7	4.5
7	14.3	16.5	2.8	0.8	5.5	8.3
6	26.5	30.5	4.9	2.0	12.3	17.3
5	44.0	47.2	12.0	5.3	21.7	29.1
4	64.2	67.0	22.1	10.3	38.3	45.9
3	78.6	80.1	40.5	21.6	54.7	62.2
2	90.0	91.0	61.2	40.0	73.8	78.6
1	100.0	100.0	86.5	72.0	99.1	99.6
0	100.0	100.0	100.0	100.0	100.0	100.0
Mean	4.3	4.5	2.3	1.5	3.1	3.5
SD	2.1	2.2	1.8	1.5	1.9	2.1
Median	4.0	4.0	2.0	1.0	3.0	3.0

Table B.25 Percentage of Standardization Sample Obtaining Various Skill Area Scaled Scores 2 or More Standard Deviations Below the Mean: Adult Form, Rated by Others

Participants with the Work Skill Area

	Number of Skill Areas at Least 2 SD Below the Mean							
Age Group	≥9	≥8	≥7	≥6	≥5	≥4	≥3	≥2
16–21	0.0	0.0	1.5	1.5	1.5	1.5	2.9	4.4
22–29	0.8	2.3	2.3	2.3	3.9	4.7	5.4	7.8
30–39	0.0	0.0	0.7	0.7	0.7	2.1	3.4	6.9
40–49	0.0	1.8	1.8	1.8	2.4	4.1	5.9	9.4
50–64	0.0	1.6	2.3	3.1	3.1	3.1	3.9	7.8
65–74	0.0	2.6	5.1	5.1	5.1	5.1	7.7	15.4

Participants without the Work Skill Area

	Number of Skill Areas at Least 2 SD Below the Mean							
Age Group	=9	≥8	≥7	≥6	≥5	≥4	≥3	≥2
16–21	1.0	1.0	2.0	3.0	3.0	3.0	3.0	7.0
22–29	1.4	2.1	2.1	2.1	2.1	4.3	5.0	7.1
30–39	1.3	1.3	1.3	1.9	1.9	2.5	4.4	7.5
40–49	1.1	1.1	1.7	1.7	1.7	3.3	4.4	8.3
50–64	1.3	1.3	1.3	2.0	2.7	2.7	2.7	8.0
65–74	1.0	1.0	2.0	2.0	3.0	4.0	6.0	10.0
75–89	2.2	6.7	6.7	8.9	11.1	11.1	12.2	14.4

Table B.26 Differences Between Adaptive Domain Composite Scores Required for Statistical Significance (Critical Values) at the 15 and 5% Levels, by Age Group and Overall Standardization Sample: Adult Form, Rated by Others

Age Group	Significance Level	CON-SO	CON-PR	SO-PR
16–21	0.15	5.29	4.32	5.29
	0.05	7.20	5.88	7.20
22–29	0.15	4.83	4.32	4.83
	0.05	6.58	5.88	6.58
30–39	0.15	5.29	4.32	5.29
	0.05	7.20	5.88	7.20
40–49	0.15	4.83	4.32	4.83
	0.05	6.58	5.88	6.58
50–64	0.15	4.83	4.32	4.83
	0.05	6.58	5.88	6.58
65–74	0.15	5.29	5.72	5.72
	0.05	7.21	7.78	7.78
75–89	0.15	3.74	3.05	3.74
	0.05	5.09	4.16	5.09
Overall Sample	0.15	4.90	4.39	4.96
	0.05	6.67	5.97	6.75

Note. Practical Adaptive Domain calculated without the Work Skill Area.

The differences for statistical significance are based on the average standard error of measurement across all ages for each skill area and calculated with the following formula:

$$\text{Difference Score} = Z \sqrt{SEM_a^2 + SEM_b^2}$$

where Z is the normal curve value associated with the desired signficance level and SEM_a and SEM_b are the standard errors of measurement of the adaptive domain scores.

Table B.27 Differences Between Adaptive Domain Composite Scores Obtained by Various Percentages of the Standardization Sample (Base Rates): Adult Form, Rated by Others

	Composite Pair						
	CON-SO		CON-PR		SO-PR		
Amount of Discrepancy	CON<SO (−)	CON>SO (+)	CON<PR (−)	CON>PR (+)	SO<PR (−)	SO>PR (+)	Amount of Discrepancy
≥40	0.0	0.1	0.0	0.0	0.0	0.0	≥40
39	0.0	0.1	0.0	0.0	0.0	0.0	39
38	0.0	0.1	0.0	0.0	0.0	0.0	38
37	0.0	0.1	0.0	0.0	0.0	0.0	37
36	0.0	0.1	0.0	0.0	0.0	0.0	36
35	0.0	0.1	0.0	0.0	0.0	0.0	35
34	0.1	0.1	0.0	0.0	0.0	0.0	34
33	0.2	0.1	0.0	0.0	0.0	0.0	33
32	0.2	0.1	0.0	0.0	0.0	0.0	32
31	0.2	0.1	0.0	0.0	0.0	0.0	31
30	0.2	0.1	0.0	0.0	0.1	0.1	30
29	0.2	0.2	0.0	0.0	0.2	0.1	29
28	0.2	0.2	0.2	0.0	0.2	0.1	28
27	0.4	0.3	0.2	0.0	0.3	0.3	27
26	0.4	0.3	0.2	0.0	0.4	0.4	26
25	0.4	0.3	0.2	0.0	0.4	0.8	25
24	0.7	0.3	0.3	0.0	1.0	0.9	24
23	0.9	0.4	0.4	0.2	1.1	1.1	23
22	1.0	0.7	0.4	0.5	1.2	1.2	22
21	1.4	0.8	0.8	0.8	1.7	1.6	21
20	1.7	1.3	1.1	1.0	1.8	1.7	20
19	2.2	1.6	1.4	1.2	2.3	2.1	19
18	2.3	2.0	1.5	1.5	2.6	2.2	18
17	2.7	2.5	2.0	1.7	3.0	3.0	17
16	3.0	3.3	2.5	2.0	3.7	3.7	16
15	4.5	4.5	3.0	2.8	4.7	6.1	15
14	5.3	5.2	3.8	3.4	5.1	6.6	14
13	6.7	6.3	4.6	4.5	6.3	7.9	13
12	8.3	7.5	5.1	5.7	7.5	9.5	12
11	10.5	9.0	5.8	7.2	8.8	11.6	11
10	12.9	11.0	7.6	8.8	11.7	14.8	10
9	14.8	13.5	10.3	11.0	13.4	16.2	9
8	17.3	15.5	12.3	13.6	16.3	18.0	8
7	21.5	17.8	15.9	16.1	19.1	20.7	7
6	24.1	21.1	19.5	19.3	21.8	23.9	6
5	27.2	23.9	22.9	21.7	25.8	27.0	5
4	31.4	26.8	27.2	27.4	29.2	32.0	4
3	35.1	31.0	32.7	32.1	31.8	38.8	3
2	40.4	36.3	36.5	37.6	37.1	44.6	2
1	47.2	41.4	41.0	45.9	40.5	47.9	1
Mean	6.9	6.9	6.3	5.8	7.4	7.2	Mean
SD	5.5	5.5	4.8	4.7	5.6	5.6	SD
Median	6.0	6.0	5.0	4.0	6.0	5.0	Median

Note. Practical Adaptive Domain calculated without the Work Skill Area.

Table B.28 Percentage of Standardization Sample Obtaining One or More Adaptive Domain Composites or the GAC 2 or More Standard Deviations Below the Mean: Adult Form, Rated by Others

Age Group	Number of Composites at Least 2 SD Below the Mean			GAC at Least 2 SD Below the Mean
	=3	≥2	≥1	
16–21	1.3	1.3	6.0	4.0
22–29	1.3	3.3	6.0	4.0
30–39	2.2	2.8	6.1	5.0
40–49	0.6	2.8	6.1	5.0
50–64	0.9	2.7	11.8	3.6
65–74	0.8	5.8	8.3	5.0
75–89	2.0	2.0	7.0	5.0

Appendix C

Intercorrelation Tables

When consulting data tables, refer carefully to the table subheadings (upper left side of tables) to ensure that you are consulting the correct section of the table for the rating form you are using.

Table C.1 **Intercorrelations of Skill Area Scaled Scores and Sums of Scaled Scores for Adaptive Domains and the GAC: Teacher/Daycare Provider and Teacher Forms**

Teacher/Daycare Provider Form   **Ages 2:0–2:5**

Skill Area/Composite	Com	FA	SL	HS	LS	SC	SD	Soc	MO	CON[a]	SO[a]	PR[a]	GAC[b]
Communication										.60			.70
Functional Pre-Academics	.54									.54			.53
School Living	.46	.42										.58	.65
Health and Safety	.58	.28	.48									.54	.69
Leisure	.61	.42	.49	.66							.63		.75
Self-Care	.44	.37	.51	.46	.53							.56	.63
Self-Direction	.47	.39	.62	.55	.61	.59					.49		.69
Social	.64	.48	.63	.56	.63	.54	.62				.63		.78
Motor	.35	.26	.19	.43	.38	.23	.16	.35					.39
Conceptual Domain	.83	.79	.62	.59	.68	.58	.78	.73	.32				.79
Social Domain	.69	.50	.62	.67	.90	.59	.68	.91	.41	.78			.84
Practical Domain	.61	.44	.83	.80	.69	.79	.72	.71	.35	.74	.78		.80
GAC	.78	.63	.74	.76	.81	.71	.77	.84	.51	.91	.92	.91	
Mean[c]	10.03	9.91	10.36	10.14	10.30	10.08	10.40	10.35	10.29	30.34	20.65	30.58	91.86
SD	2.91	2.83	3.03	2.92	2.93	2.62	3.07	3.07	2.87	7.07	5.41	6.95	19.14

Ages 2:6–2:11

Skill Area/Composite	Com	FA	SL	HS	LS	SC	SD	Soc	MO	CON[a]	SO[a]	PR[a]	GAC[b]
Communication										.58			.68
Functional Pre-Academics	.47									.59			.60
School Living	.45	.55										.61	.73
Health and Safety	.51	.44	.65									.68	.76
Leisure	.57	.44	.56	.58							.71		.71
Self-Care	.42	.30	.41	.50	.36							.50	.51
Self-Direction	.56	.57	.70	.65	.67	.39					.66		.78
Social	.69	.52	.61	.68	.71	.41	.75				.71		.81
Motor	.50	.42	.51	.61	.46	.43	.43	.53					.63
Conceptual Domain	.82	.81	.68	.64	.68	.45	.85	.79	.54				.80
Social Domain	.68	.52	.63	.68	.92	.42	.77	.93	.54	.79			.80
Practical Domain	.56	.52	.83	.87	.60	.77	.71	.69	.63	.72	.70		.75
GAC	.75	.68	.79	.82	.78	.62	.83	.86	.72	.91	.89	.90	
Mean[c]	10.47	10.53	10.34	10.42	10.30	10.59	10.42	10.34	10.51	31.42	20.64	31.35	93.92
SD	3.09	2.91	3.09	3.09	2.88	3.05	2.94	2.95	3.11	7.42	5.40	7.61	20.66

Note. **Com** = Communication; **FA** = Functional Pre-Academics; **SL** = School Living; **HS** = Health and Safety; **LS** = Leisure; **SC** = Self-Care; **SD** = Self-Direction; **Soc** = Social; **MO** = Motor; **CON** = Conceptual Adaptive Domain; **SO** = Social Adaptive Domain; **PR** = Practical Adaptive Domain.

[a] Adaptive Domain correlations corrected by removing the skill area scaled score from the sum of the scaled scores.

[b] GAC correlations corrected by removing the skill area scaled score(s) from the sum of the scaled scores.

[c] Means and *SD*s reported under corrected adaptive domains and GAC were calculated using all skill areas included in the composite.

Table C.1 **Intercorrelations of Skill Area Scaled Scores and Sums of Scaled Scores for Adaptive Domains and the GAC: Teacher/Daycare Provider and Teacher Forms** (continued)

Teacher/Daycare Provider Form

Ages 3:0–3:5

Skill Area/Composite	Com	FA	SL	HS	LS	SC	SD	Soc	MO	CON[a]	SO[a]	PR[a]	GAC[b]
Communication										.58			.65
Functional Pre-Academics	.53									.60			.61
School Living	.50	.51										.78	.81
Health and Safety	.45	.45	.72									.68	.77
Leisure	.64	.47	.70	.74							.78		.82
Self-Care	.49	.48	.65	.52	.52							.63	.68
Self-Direction	.46	.49	.79	.77	.77	.61				.54			.82
Social	.57	.54	.77	.72	.78	.55	.79				.78		.83
Motor	.61	.57	.59	.61	.65	.64	.60	.64					.76
Conceptual Domain	.81	.83	.73	.68	.77	.64	.80	.77	.73				.86
Social Domain	.64	.53	.78	.77	.94	.56	.83	.94	.68	.82			.86
Practical Domain	.55	.56	.90	.86	.75	.84	.83	.78	.71	.79	.81		.84
GAC	.72	.70	.86	.82	.86	.75	.86	.87	.81	.93	.92	.93	
Mean[c]	10.11	9.73	9.89	10.33	10.14	10.30	9.90	10.17	10.05	29.74	20.31	30.52	90.62
SD	3.14	3.26	3.00	3.16	3.22	3.23	3.14	3.23	3.09	7.77	6.08	8.14	22.95

Ages 3:6–3:11

Skill Area/Composite	Com	FA	SL	HS	LS	SC	SD	Soc	MO	CON[a]	SO[a]	PR[a]	GAC[b]
Communication										.50			.58
Functional Pre-Academics	.45									.59			.68
School Living	.41	.62										.68	.77
Health and Safety	.50	.58	.66									.66	.75
Leisure	.43	.45	.55	.63							.62		.70
Self-Care	.42	.54	.51	.49	.45							.55	.62
Self-Direction	.44	.55	.77	.64	.67	.52				.58			.79
Social	.48	.56	.70	.61	.62	.44	.70				.62		.76
Motor	.53	.46	.49	.52	.55	.47	.51	.56					.66
Conceptual Domain	.77	.83	.75	.71	.64	.62	.82	.72	.62				.85
Social Domain	.50	.56	.69	.69	.90	.50	.76	.90	.62	.76			.80
Practical Domain	.53	.69	.86	.86	.65	.79	.77	.70	.59	.82	.75		.85
GAC	.67	.75	.83	.82	.77	.70	.84	.82	.74	.94	.89	.93	
Mean[c]	10.32	10.56	10.52	10.58	10.41	10.44	10.59	10.55	10.46	31.47	20.96	31.54	94.43
SD	2.80	2.98	2.87	2.97	2.78	2.73	2.93	2.90	2.85	7.03	5.12	7.19	19.90

Note. **Com** = Communication; **FA** = Functional Pre-Academics; **SL** = School Living; **HS** = Health and Safety; **LS** = Leisure; **SC** = Self-Care; **SD** = Self-Direction; **Soc** = Social; **MO** = Motor; **CON** = Conceptual Adaptive Domain; **SO** = Social Adaptive Domain; **PR** = Practical Adaptive Domain.

[a] Adaptive Domain correlations corrected by removing the skill area scaled score from the sum of the scaled scores.
[b] GAC correlations corrected by removing the skill area scaled score(s) from the sum of the scaled scores.
[c] Means and *SD*s reported under corrected adaptive domains and GAC were calculated using all skill areas included in the composite.

Table C.1   Intercorrelations of Skill Area Scaled Scores and Sums of Scaled Scores for Adaptive Domains and the GAC: Teacher/Daycare Provider and Teacher Forms (continued)

Teacher/Daycare Provider Form   **Ages 4:0–4:5**

Skill Area/Composite	Com	FA	SL	HS	LS	SC	SD	Soc	MO	CON[a]	SO[a]	PR[a]	GAC[b]
Communication										.58			.64
Functional Pre-Academics	.47									.60			.61
School Living	.48	.54										.69	.78
Health and Safety	.57	.38	.66									.64	.74
Leisure	.56	.49	.66	.67							.68		.80
Self-Care	.29	.42	.51	.45	.51							.53	.55
Self-Direction	.58	.60	.77	.67	.73	.51				.69			.85
Social	.61	.50	.74	.64	.68	.47	.80				.68		.80
Motor	.46	.44	.47	.58	.63	.35	.52	.46					.62
Conceptual Domain	.81	.84	.71	.64	.71	.49	.86	.76	.57				.81
Social Domain	.64	.54	.77	.71	.92	.54	.84	.92	.60	.80			.87
Practical Domain	.54	.54	.87	.84	.74	.78	.78	.74	.56	.74	.81		.81
GAC	.72	.70	.84	.80	.85	.65	.88	.84	.70	.91	.92	.92	
Mean[c]	10.07	10.20	10.06	10.08	10.20	10.13	10.10	9.89	10.26	30.37	20.09	30.27	90.99
SD	2.96	3.27	3.07	3.07	2.98	3.05	2.96	2.96	3.00	7.69	5.44	7.64	21.17

Ages 4:6–4:11

Skill Area/Composite	Com	FA	SL	HS	LS	SC	SD	Soc	MO	CON[a]	SO[a]	PR[a]	GAC[b]
Communication										.48			.59
Functional Pre-Academics	.37									.50			.56
School Living	.42	.45										.75	.78
Health and Safety	.52	.50	.76									.73	.81
Leisure	.47	.49	.66	.69							.63		.76
Self-Care	.37	.41	.56	.54	.49							.59	.61
Self-Direction	.46	.49	.80	.79	.74	.54				.58			.84
Social	.51	.33	.71	.69	.63	.40	.77				.63		.71
Motor	.54	.48	.35	.37	.42	.45	.44	.31					.54
Conceptual Domain	.77	.79	.70	.76	.72	.56	.82	.67	.62				.86
Social Domain	.55	.45	.76	.77	.90	.50	.84	.90	.41	.77			.80
Practical Domain	.51	.52	.89	.89	.71	.81	.82	.69	.45	.78	.78		.83
GAC	.69	.66	.83	.86	.82	.70	.88	.78	.64	.94	.88	.92	
Mean[c]	10.15	10.06	10.09	10.00	10.02	10.21	9.96	9.96	10.21	30.17	19.98	30.30	90.66
SD	3.06	3.09	2.93	2.95	2.92	3.01	2.92	2.92	2.99	7.17	5.27	7.67	20.34

Note. **Com** = Communication; **FA** = Functional Pre-Academics; **SL** = School Living; **HS** = Health and Safety; **LS** = Leisure; **SC** = Self-Care; **SD** = Self-Direction; **Soc** = Social; **MO** = Motor; **CON** = Conceptual Adaptive Domain; **SO** = Social Adaptive Domain; **PR** = Practical Adaptive Domain.

[a] Adaptive Domain correlations corrected by removing the skill area scaled score from the sum of the scaled scores.

[b] GAC correlations corrected by removing the skill area scaled score(s) from the sum of the scaled scores.

[c] Means and *SD*s reported under corrected adaptive domains and GAC were calculated using all skill areas included in the composite.

Table C.1   **Intercorrelations of Skill Area Scaled Scores and Sums of Scaled Scores for Adaptive Domains and the GAC: Teacher/Daycare Provider and Teacher Forms** (continued)

Teacher/Daycare Provider Form   **Ages 5:0–5:11**

Skill Area/Composite	Com	FA	SL	HS	LS	SC	SD	Soc	MO	CONᵃ	SOᵃ	PRᵃ	GACᵇ
Communication										.62			.72
Functional Pre-Academics	.48									.56			.58
School Living	.54	.49										.65	.76
Health and Safety	.61	.34	.61									.69	.73
Leisure	.66	.50	.66	.71							.72		.82
Self-Care	.50	.49	.54	.59	.61							.63	.70
Self-Direction	.59	.51	.76	.63	.75	.60				.64			.83
Social	.64	.49	.72	.62	.72	.57	.81				.72		.80
Motor	.60	.53	.52	.57	.60	.63	.57	.52					.71
Conceptual Domain	.84	.79	.72	.64	.78	.64	.85	.79	.69				.86
Social Domain	.70	.53	.74	.72	.93	.64	.84	.93	.60	.84			.87
Practical Domain	.65	.52	.84	.87	.78	.84	.78	.75	.68	.79	.82		.84
GAC	.78	.67	.81	.80	.87	.77	.87	.85	.77	.94	.92	.93	
Meanᶜ	10.04	10.00	10.09	10.05	10.20	10.10	10.13	10.02	10.35	30.17	20.22	30.24	90.98
SD	3.07	2.80	2.96	3.11	3.04	3.03	3.03	2.98	2.97	7.37	5.58	7.73	21.57

Note. **Com** = Communication; **FA** = Functional Pre-Academics; **SL** = School Living; **HS** = Health and Safety; **LS** = Leisure; **SC** = Self-Care; **SD** = Self-Direction; **Soc** = Social; **MO** = Motor; **CON** = Conceptual Adaptive Domain; **SO** = Social Adaptive Domain; **PR** = Practical Adaptive Domain.

ᵃ Adaptive Domain correlations corrected by removing the skill area scaled score from the sum of the scaled scores.
ᵇ GAC correlations corrected by removing the skill area scaled score(s) from the sum of the scaled scores.
ᶜ Means and SDs reported under corrected adaptive domains and GAC were calculated using all skill areas included in the composite.

Table C.1 Intercorrelations of Skill Area Scaled Scores and Sums of Scaled Scores for Adaptive Domains and the GAC: Teacher/Daycare Provider and Teacher Forms (continued)

Teacher Form

Age 5

Skill Area/Composite	Com	CU	FA	SL	HS	LS	SC	SD	Soc	CON[a]	SO[a]	PR[a]	GAC[b]
Communication										.51			.74
Community Use	.48											.62	.65
Functional Academics	.29	.53								.42			.49
School Living	.63	.61	.45									.77	.81
Health and Safety	.66	.55	.42	.76								.75	.81
Leisure	.73	.57	.36	.65	.67						.75		.81
Self-Care	.60	.44	.34	.53	.56	.58						.58	.63
Self-Direction	.60	.50	.46	.74	.71	.70	.42			.65			.78
Social	.68	.43	.31	.65	.72	.75	.53	.75			.75		.77
Conceptual Domain	.78	.63	.75	.76	.74	.75	.57	.85	.72				.85
Social Domain	.76	.54	.36	.70	.74	.94	.59	.77	.93	.78			.82
Practical Domain	.72	.80	.53	.87	.87	.75	.76	.72	.70	.82	.78		.85
GAC	.80	.73	.60	.85	.86	.86	.70	.83	.82	.93	.89	.95	
Mean[c]	9.66	9.05	8.94	10.09	9.80	9.72	9.91	9.15	10.25	27.75	19.97	38.85	86.57
SD	3.19	3.27	3.53	2.79	3.08	3.21	2.95	3.13	2.99	7.82	5.81	9.98	21.98

Age 6

Skill Area/Composite	Com	CU	FA	SL	HS	LS	SC	SD	Soc	CON[a]	SO[a]	PR[a]	GAC[b]
Communication										.80			.85
Community Use	.71											.63	.75
Functional Academics	.61	.62								.59			.58
School Living	.68	.60	.51									.78	.81
Health and Safety	.70	.63	.45	.77								.84	.84
Leisure	.77	.70	.49	.72	.73						.77		.85
Self-Care	.63	.49	.36	.66	.75	.63						.71	.72
Self-Direction	.79	.66	.51	.75	.78	.83	.63			.72			.86
Social	.74	.60	.42	.76	.78	.77	.74	.77			.77		.83
Conceptual Domain	.92	.77	.81	.74	.74	.80	.62	.88	.74				.86
Social Domain	.80	.69	.48	.79	.80	.94	.73	.85	.94	.82			.89
Practical Domain	.80	.81	.57	.88	.91	.81	.84	.82	.83	.84	.87		.89
GAC	.88	.81	.67	.85	.87	.88	.78	.89	.87	.94	.93	.97	
Mean[c]	8.76	8.88	9.04	9.73	9.06	9.11	9.49	8.93	9.34	26.74	18.45	37.16	82.34
SD	3.31	3.65	3.38	3.23	3.06	3.16	3.19	3.46	3.05	8.82	5.84	11.25	24.58

Note. **Com** = Communication; **CU** = Community Use; **FA** = Functional Academics; **SL** = School Living; **HS** = Health and Safety; **LS** = Leisure; **SC** = Self-Care; **SD** = Self-Direction; **Soc** = Social; **CON** = Conceptual Adaptive Domain; **SO** = Social Adaptive Domain; **PR** = Practical Adaptive Domain.

[a] Adaptive Domain correlations corrected by removing the skill area scaled score from the sum of the scaled scores.
[b] GAC correlations corrected by removing the skill area scaled score(s) from the sum of the scaled scores.
[c] Means and *SD*s reported under corrected adaptive domains and GAC were calculated using all skill areas included in the composite.

Table C.1   Intercorrelations of Skill Area Scaled Scores and Sums of Scaled Scores for Adaptive Domains and the GAC: Teacher/Daycare Provider and Teacher Forms *(continued)*

Teacher Form — **Age 7**

Skill Area/Composite	Com	CU	FA	SL	HS	LS	SC	SD	Soc	CON[a]	SO[a]	PR[a]	GAC[b]
Communication										.79			.83
Community Use	.68											.71	.78
Functional Academics	.67	.73								.67			.68
School Living	.70	.69	.60									.84	.85
Health and Safety	.67	.68	.54	.80								.81	.82
Leisure	.73	.65	.50	.72	.74						.77		.82
Self-Care	.63	.52	.46	.68	.63	.64						.67	.71
Self-Direction	.74	.64	.58	.78	.76	.78	.69			.72			.86
Social	.77	.65	.53	.72	.70	.77	.61	.82			.77		.83
Conceptual Domain	.91	.77	.85	.79	.75	.76	.67	.88	.81				.89
Social Domain	.80	.69	.55	.77	.77	.94	.67	.85	.94	.83			.86
Practical Domain	.77	.85	.68	.91	.89	.79	.81	.83	.77	.86	.83		.89
GAC	.87	.83	.75	.88	.86	.86	.77	.89	.86	.95	.92	.96	
Mean[c]	9.27	8.95	9.44	9.86	9.50	9.54	9.72	8.91	9.74	27.61	19.28	38.03	84.92
SD	3.43	3.58	3.28	3.06	2.79	2.91	3.03	3.32	2.93	8.83	5.49	10.78	23.84

Age 8

Skill Area/Composite	Com	CU	FA	SL	HS	LS	SC	SD	Soc	CON[a]	SO[a]	PR[a]	GAC[b]
Communication										.85			.86
Community Use	.77											.74	.79
Functional Academics	.77	.77								.78			.78
School Living	.75	.67	.69									.82	.88
Health and Safety	.67	.69	.63	.77								.80	.81
Leisure	.76	.72	.69	.86	.76						.84		.88
Self-Care	.74	.64	.66	.74	.67	.71						.76	.80
Self-Direction	.80	.67	.71	.85	.75	.82	.71			.81			.88
Social	.75	.64	.58	.80	.78	.84	.74	.82			.84		.85
Conceptual Domain	.94	.80	.90	.83	.75	.83	.77	.91	.79				.90
Social Domain	.79	.71	.66	.86	.80	.96	.76	.85	.96	.84			.89
Practical Domain	.83	.86	.78	.90	.88	.87	.87	.85	.84	.90	.89		.93
GAC	.90	.84	.83	.91	.85	.91	.84	.91	.88	.96	.93	.98	
Mean[c]	9.20	9.11	9.09	9.93	9.27	9.99	9.93	9.07	9.61	27.36	19.60	38.23	85.19
SD	3.44	3.11	3.11	3.09	2.83	3.04	3.01	3.22	3.08	8.96	5.87	10.58	24.40

Note. **Com** = Communication; **CU** = Community Use; **FA** = Functional Academics; **SL** = School Living; **HS** = Health and Safety; **LS** = Leisure; **SC** = Self-Care; **SD** = Self-Direction; **Soc** = Social; **CON** = Conceptual Adaptive Domain; **SO** = Social Adaptive Domain; **PR** = Practical Adaptive Domain.

[a] Adaptive Domain correlations corrected by removing the skill area scaled score from the sum of the scaled scores.
[b] GAC correlations corrected by removing the skill area scaled score(s) from the sum of the scaled scores.
[c] Means and *SD*s reported under corrected adaptive domains and GAC were calculated using all skill areas included in the composite.

Table C.1 Intercorrelations of Skill Area Scaled Scores and Sums of Scaled Scores for Adaptive Domains and the GAC: Teacher/Daycare Provider and Teacher Forms (continued)

Teacher Form

Age 9

Skill Area/Composite	Com	CU	FA	SL	HS	LS	SC	SD	Soc	CON[a]	SO[a]	PR[a]	GAC[b]
Communication										.85			.89
Community Use	.82											.75	.83
Functional Academics	.76	.78								.76			.76
School Living	.78	.72	.69									.82	.85
Health and Safety	.76	.69	.64	.76								.81	.84
Leisure	.75	.74	.65	.72	.74						.80		.84
Self-Care	.71	.62	.56	.68	.69	.58						.74	.73
Self-Direction	.80	.70	.68	.80	.76	.80	.64			.79			.88
Social	.74	.65	.56	.72	.75	.80	.65	.84			.80		.83
Conceptual Domain	.94	.84	.87	.84	.79	.81	.70	.92	.80				.92
Social Domain	.79	.73	.64	.76	.78	.95	.65	.87	.95	.85			.86
Practical Domain	.87	.86	.76	.90	.89	.79	.86	.83	.79	.90	.83		.91
GAC	.91	.86	.81	.88	.87	.87	.79	.91	.87	.97	.92	.97	
Mean[c]	8.71	9.36	9.43	9.73	9.17	9.60	9.03	8.49	8.97	26.63	18.57	37.29	82.49
SD	3.59	2.91	2.92	3.16	3.08	3.06	3.18	3.69	3.29	9.29	6.03	10.83	25.00

Age 10

Skill Area/Composite	Com	CU	FA	SL	HS	LS	SC	SD	Soc	CON[a]	SO[a]	PR[a]	GAC[b]
Communication										.88			.90
Community Use	.74											.68	.75
Functional Academics	.83	.74								.83			.82
School Living	.71	.62	.66									.74	.82
Health and Safety	.70	.64	.64	.73								.76	.78
Leisure	.74	.65	.71	.81	.64						.72		.81
Self-Care	.65	.50	.56	.54	.55	.49						.60	.63
Self-Direction	.80	.64	.74	.75	.67	.72	.55			.81			.85
Social	.79	.59	.66	.75	.72	.72	.52	.82			.72		.83
Conceptual Domain	.95	.76	.92	.76	.72	.78	.63	.91	.81				.90
Social Domain	.82	.66	.74	.84	.74	.93	.54	.83	.93	.86			.88
Practical Domain	.84	.84	.78	.87	.86	.78	.77	.78	.77	.86	.83		.88
GAC	.92	.81	.87	.86	.82	.85	.70	.89	.86	.96	.92	.96	
Mean[c]	8.64	8.91	8.97	9.65	9.33	10.14	9.49	8.89	9.39	26.50	19.53	37.39	83.41
SD	3.45	3.22	3.53	3.01	2.59	2.89	2.90	3.45	2.93	9.68	5.40	9.77	23.65

Note. **Com** = Communication; **CU** = Community Use; **FA** = Functional Academics; **SL** = School Living; **HS** = Health and Safety; **LS** = Leisure; **SC** = Self-Care; **SD** = Self-Direction; **Soc** = Social; **CON** = Conceptual Adaptive Domain; **SO** = Social Adaptive Domain; **PR** = Practical Adaptive Domain.

[a] Adaptive Domain correlations corrected by removing the skill area scaled score from the sum of the scaled scores.
[b] GAC correlations corrected by removing the skill area scaled score(s) from the sum of the scaled scores.
[c] Means and SDs reported under corrected adaptive domains and GAC were calculated using all skill areas included in the composite.

Table C.1 Intercorrelations of Skill Area Scaled Scores and Sums of Scaled Scores for Adaptive Domains and the GAC: Teacher/Daycare Provider and Teacher Forms (continued)

Teacher Form — **Age 11**

Skill Area/Composite	Com	CU	FA	SL	HS	LS	SC	SD	Soc	CON[a]	SO[a]	PR[a]	GAC[b]
Communication										.82			.89
Community Use	.78											.76	.79
Functional Academics	.79	.78								.83			.85
School Living	.78	.73	.74									.85	.88
Health and Safety	.75	.73	.73	.82								.84	.85
Leisure	.86	.77	.80	.80	.75						.82		.90
Self-Care	.69	.60	.71	.69	.66	.67						.71	.75
Self-Direction	.76	.58	.77	.78	.75	.82	.62			.81			.83
Social	.82	.66	.69	.82	.76	.82	.69	.79			.82		.86
Conceptual Domain	.92	.77	.92	.83	.81	.90	.73	.92	.84				.92
Social Domain	.88	.74	.78	.85	.79	.95	.72	.85	.96	.91			.92
Practical Domain	.85	.87	.84	.92	.91	.85	.83	.78	.83	.89	.88		.91
GAC	.91	.84	.88	.91	.88	.92	.80	.87	.89	.97	.95	.97	
Mean[c]	8.91	9.03	9.39	8.91	8.72	9.23	9.31	8.21	9.19	26.50	18.43	35.97	80.89
SD	3.30	3.20	3.05	3.29	3.29	3.02	2.79	3.52	3.22	9.09	5.95	11.13	25.22

Age 12

Skill Area/Composite	Com	CU	FA	SL	HS	LS	SC	SD	Soc	CON[a]	SO[a]	PR[a]	GAC[b]
Communication										.83			.87
Community Use	.80											.73	.80
Functional Academics	.80	.74								.83			.83
School Living	.70	.64	.66									.70	.77
Health and Safety	.71	.69	.69	.64								.75	.81
Leisure	.76	.71	.72	.64	.74						.80		.83
Self-Care	.53	.47	.46	.48	.52	.47						.56	.58
Self-Direction	.77	.67	.77	.75	.78	.74	.49			.81			.86
Social	.76	.71	.73	.69	.74	.80	.58	.78			.80		.86
Conceptual Domain	.93	.80	.92	.77	.79	.80	.54	.92	.82				.90
Social Domain	.80	.75	.76	.71	.78	.94	.56	.80	.95	.86			.88
Practical Domain	.84	.86	.78	.84	.87	.79	.72	.82	.83	.88	.85		.90
GAC	.90	.85	.86	.82	.86	.87	.65	.89	.89	.96	.93	.97	
Mean[c]	8.35	8.06	9.34	8.75	8.41	9.09	9.48	8.26	8.81	25.95	17.90	34.69	78.54
SD	3.76	3.47	3.11	3.43	3.62	3.04	2.91	3.50	3.29	9.59	6.01	11.12	25.53

Note. **Com** = Communication; **CU** = Community Use; **FA** = Functional Academics; **SL** = School Living; **HS** = Health and Safety; **LS** = Leisure; **SC** = Self-Care; **SD** = Self-Direction; **Soc** = Social; **CON** = Conceptual Adaptive Domain; **SO** = Social Adaptive Domain; **PR** = Practical Adaptive Domain.

[a] Adaptive Domain correlations corrected by removing the skill area scaled score from the sum of the scaled scores.
[b] GAC correlations corrected by removing the skill area scaled score(s) from the sum of the scaled scores.
[c] Means and SDs reported under corrected adaptive domains and GAC were calculated using all skill areas included in the composite.

Table C.1 Intercorrelations of Skill Area Scaled Scores and Sums of Scaled Scores for Adaptive Domains and the GAC: Teacher/Daycare Provider and Teacher Forms *(continued)*

Teacher Form

Ages 13–14

Skill Area/Composite	Com	CU	FA	SL	HS	LS	SC	SD	Soc	CON[a]	SO[a]	PR[a]	GAC[b]
Communication										.79			.81
Community Use	.74											.76	.79
Functional Academics	.78	.78								.81			.84
School Living	.68	.65	.70									.73	.82
Health and Safety	.65	.74	.68	.71								.79	.81
Leisure	.69	.69	.74	.71	.74						.75		.83
Self-Care	.52	.56	.56	.53	.55	.53						.61	.61
Self-Direction	.69	.56	.71	.74	.66	.70	.46			.74			.79
Social	.74	.64	.65	.75	.73	.75	.53	.81			.75		.84
Conceptual Domain	.91	.76	.91	.78	.74	.79	.57	.89	.82				.88
Social Domain	.76	.71	.74	.78	.78	.93	.57	.81	.94	.86			.88
Practical Domain	.76	.87	.80	.86	.89	.79	.77	.72	.79	.84	.84		.87
GAC	.86	.84	.87	.86	.86	.87	.69	.84	.88	.95	.93	.96	
Mean[c]	8.52	8.81	9.42	8.66	8.82	9.14	9.52	8.20	9.08	26.14	18.22	35.82	80.18
SD	3.30	3.06	2.95	3.22	3.35	3.07	2.97	3.36	3.27	8.68	5.94	10.69	24.01

Ages 15–16

Skill Area/Composite	Com	CU	FA	SL	HS	LS	SC	SD	Soc	CON[a]	SO[a]	PR[a]	GAC[b]
Communication										.80			.84
Community Use	.78											.79	.83
Functional Academics	.81	.83								.85			.85
School Living	.69	.72	.71									.77	.84
Health and Safety	.70	.77	.69	.80								.87	.85
Leisure	.75	.67	.74	.76	.70						.81		.83
Self-Care	.56	.58	.53	.49	.65	.50						.62	.60
Self-Direction	.70	.63	.76	.80	.72	.78	.47			.76			.83
Social	.78	.70	.74	.77	.75	.81	.48	.82			.81		.86
Conceptual Domain	.92	.81	.93	.80	.77	.83	.57	.90	.86				.91
Social Domain	.81	.72	.78	.81	.76	.95	.51	.84	.95	.89			.88
Practical Domain	.79	.89	.80	.88	.93	.76	.77	.76	.79	.86	.81		.86
GAC	.88	.87	.88	.88	.88	.87	.68	.87	.89	.96	.93	.96	
Mean[c]	8.44	8.74	8.88	8.87	9.14	9.29	9.42	8.51	9.64	25.83	18.93	36.16	80.92
SD	3.55	3.43	2.99	3.43	3.41	3.15	3.02	3.40	3.12	9.09	5.95	11.56	25.28

Note. **Com** = Communication; **CU** = Community Use; **FA** = Functional Academics; **SL** = School Living; **HS** = Health and Safety; **LS** = Leisure; **SC** = Self-Care; **SD** = Self-Direction; **Soc** = Social; **CON** = Conceptual Adaptive Domain; **SO** = Social Adaptive Domain; **PR** = Practical Adaptive Domain.

[a] Adaptive Domain correlations corrected by removing the skill area scaled score from the sum of the scaled scores.
[b] GAC correlations corrected by removing the skill area scaled score(s) from the sum of the scaled scores.
[c] Means and SDs reported under corrected adaptive domains and GAC were calculated using all skill areas included in the composite.

Table C.1   Intercorrelations of Skill Area Scaled Scores and Sums of Scaled Scores for Adaptive Domains and the GAC: Teacher/Daycare Provider and Teacher Forms *(continued)*

Teacher Form   **Ages 17–21**

Skill Area/Composite	Com	CU	FA	SL	HS	LS	SC	SD	Soc	CON[a]	SO[a]	PR[a]	GAC[b]
Communication										.72			.74
Community Use	.69											.68	.77
Functional Academics	.71	.79								.78			.82
School Living	.62	.65	.71									.74	.83
Health and Safety	.60	.60	.68	.76								.76	.80
Leisure	.68	.68	.67	.75	.70						.77		.82
Self-Care	.41	.47	.54	.42	.51	.32						.53	.50
Self-Direction	.63	.61	.70	.75	.72	.76	.39			.72			.84
Social	.52	.54	.54	.71	.66	.77	.36	.84			.77		.76
Conceptual Domain	.88	.78	.90	.78	.75	.80	.50	.88	.72				.89
Social Domain	.64	.65	.64	.78	.72	.94	.36	.85	.94	.80			.81
Practical Domain	.71	.82	.82	.86	.88	.75	.72	.76	.69	.86	.76		.86
GAC	.80	.82	.86	.87	.85	.87	.59	.88	.82	.95	.89	.95	
Mean[c]	8.83	9.38	9.49	9.53	9.70	9.32	9.77	8.99	9.43	27.32	18.75	38.38	84.45
SD	2.92	2.70	2.65	2.80	2.80	3.00	2.67	2.91	3.06	7.52	5.71	9.02	20.85

Note. **Com** = Communication; **CU** = Community Use; **FA** = Functional Academics; **SL** = School Living; **HS** = Health and Safety; **LS** = Leisure; **SC** = Self-Care; **SD** = Self-Direction; **Soc** = Social; **CON** = Conceptual Adaptive Domain; **SO** = Social Adaptive Domain; **PR** = Practical Adaptive Domain.

[a] Adaptive Domain correlations corrected by removing the skill area scaled score from the sum of the scaled scores.
[b] GAC correlations corrected by removing the skill area scaled score(s) from the sum of the scaled scores.
[c] Means and *SD*s reported under corrected adaptive domains and GAC were calculated using all skill areas included in the composite.

Table C.2 Intercorrelations of Skill Area Scaled Scores and Sums of Scaled Scores for Adaptive Domains and the GAC: Parent/Primary Caregiver and Parent Forms

Parent/Primary Caregiver Form   **Ages 0:0–0:3**

Skill Area/Composite	Com	HS	LS	SC	SD	Soc	MO	CON[a]	SO[a]	PR[a]	GAC[b]
Communication								.25			.45
Health and Safety	.19									.42	.32
Leisure	.32	.22							.47		.52
Self-Care	.01	.42	.32							.42	.40
Self-Direction	.25	.03	.34	.15				.25			.34
Social	.60	.31	.47	.42	.28				.47		.68
Motor	.31	.07	.24	.19	.27	.34					.37
Conceptual Domain	.77	.14	.42	.11	.81	.55	.36				
Social Domain	.55	.32	.83	.43	.36	.88	.34	.57			
Practical Domain	.12	.86	.32	.83	.11	.43	.15	.14	.44		.32
GAC	.63	.53	.66	.58	.55	.80	.56	.74	.85	.66	
Mean[c]	9.95	9.81	9.92	10.01	10.01	10.10	9.67	19.96	20.02	19.82	69.47
SD	2.69	2.82	2.29	2.62	2.88	2.74	2.62	4.40	4.31	4.58	11.43

Ages 0:4–0:7

Skill Area/Composite	Com	HS	LS	SC	SD	Soc	MO	CON[a]	SO[a]	PR[a]	GAC[b]
Communication								.15			.34
Health and Safety	.17									.53	.55
Leisure	.26	.58							.40		.64
Self-Care	.31	.53	.55							.53	.72
Self-Direction	.15	.46	.47	.55				.15			.62
Social	.34	.38	.40	.57	.55				.40		.61
Motor	.29	.22	.40	.43	.42	.32					.48
Conceptual Domain	.77	.41	.48	.57	.75	.58	.47				
Social Domain	.36	.58	.85	.67	.61	.82	.44	.64			
Practical Domain	.27	.89	.65	.85	.58	.54	.36	.56	.71		.69
GAC	.52	.70	.76	.81	.74	.73	.61	.83	.89	.86	
Mean[c]	9.92	9.81	10.81	10.46	10.48	10.73	10.30	20.40	21.54	20.27	72.51
SD	2.92	3.01	2.83	2.62	2.82	2.67	2.39	4.35	4.60	4.93	13.39

Note. **Com** = Communication; **HS** = Health and Safety; **LS** = Leisure; **SC** = Self-Care; **SD** = Self-Direction; **Soc** = Social; **MO** = Motor; **CON** = Conceptual Adaptive Domain; **SO** = Social Adaptive Domain; **PR** = Practical Adaptive Domain.

[a] Adaptive Domain correlations corrected by removing the skill area scaled score from the sum of the scaled scores.
[b] GAC correlations corrected by removing the skill area scaled score(s) from the sum of the scaled scores.
[c] Means and *SD*s reported under corrected adaptive domains and GAC were calculated using all skill areas included in the composite.

Table C.2 Intercorrelations of Skill Area Scaled Scores and Sums of Scaled Scores for Adaptive Domains and the GAC: Parent/Primary Caregiver and Parent Forms *(continued)*

Parent/Primary Caregiver Form — **Ages 0:8–0:11**

Skill Area/Composite	Com	HS	LS	SC	SD	Soc	MO	CON[a]	SO[a]	PR[a]	GAC[b]
Communication								.35			.57
Health and Safety	.45									.29	.55
Leisure	.46	.45							.72		.73
Self-Care	.27	.29	.36							.29	.45
Self-Direction	.35	.47	.68	.47				.35			.70
Social	.52	.44	.72	.33	.63				.72		.71
Motor	.46	.34	.43	.33	.42	.36					.53
Conceptual Domain	.84	.56	.69	.44	.80	.70	.54				
Social Domain	.53	.48	.93	.37	.71	.92	.43	.75			
Practical Domain	.46	.84	.51	.77	.58	.48	.42	.63	.54		.63
GAC	.71	.69	.82	.59	.79	.80	.65	.91	.87	.80	
Mean[c]	9.90	10.37	10.25	10.25	10.19	10.22	10.31	20.09	20.47	20.62	71.49
SD	2.90	2.83	2.89	2.42	2.64	2.61	2.33	4.55	5.09	4.22	13.47

Note. **Com** = Communication; **HS** = Health and Safety; **LS** = Leisure; **SC** = Self-Care; **SD** = Self-Direction; **Soc** = Social; **MO** = Motor; **CON** = Conceptual Adaptive Domain; **SO** = Social Adaptive Domain; **PR** = Practical Adaptive Domain.

Ages 1:0–1:3

Skill Area/Composite	Com	CU	FA	HL	HS	LS	SC	SD	Soc	MO	CON[a]	SO[a]	PR[a]	GAC[b]
Communication											.53			.66
Community Use	.31												.51	.53
Functional Pre-Academics	.45	.40									.50			.57
Home Living	.42	.56	.59										.64	.69
Health and Safety	.43	.41	.37	.45									.56	.58
Leisure	.49	.44	.28	.40	.50							.61		.66
Self-Care	.60	.25	.44	.44	.46	.52							.47	.67
Self-Direction	.44	.41	.40	.62	.46	.60	.50				.49			.71
Social	.62	.46	.50	.57	.44	.61	.60	.70				.61		.79
Motor	.56	.30	.38	.47	.35	.46	.57	.47	.56					.62
Conceptual Domain	.80	.47	.78	.69	.53	.58	.65	.78	.77	.59				
Social Domain	.62	.50	.43	.54	.52	.90	.62	.72	.90	.57	.75			
Practical Domain	.58	.74	.59	.81	.76	.61	.70	.66	.68	.55	.77	.72		.80
GAC	.73	.63	.66	.76	.67	.73	.74	.78	.84	.70	.92	.88	.92	
Mean[c]	10.36	10.38	10.09	9.86	10.07	10.51	10.30	10.43	10.17	10.22	30.88	20.68	40.61	102.39
SD	2.75	2.86	2.74	2.73	2.69	2.89	2.59	2.85	2.95	2.78	6.57	5.25	8.22	20.19

Note. **Com** = Communication; **CU** = Community Use; **FA** = Functional Pre-Academics; **HL** = Home Living; **HS** = Health and Safety; **LS** = Leisure; **SC** = Self-Care; **SD** = Self-Direction; **Soc** = Social; **MO** = Motor; **CON** = Conceptual Adaptive Domain; **SO** = Social Adaptive Domain; **PR** = Practical Adaptive Domain.

[a] Adaptive Domain correlations corrected by removing the skill area scaled score from the sum of the scaled scores.
[b] GAC correlations corrected by removing the skill area scaled score(s) from the sum of the scaled scores.
[c] Means and *SD*s reported under corrected adaptive domains and GAC were calculated using all skill areas included in the composite.

Table C.2 Intercorrelations of Skill Area Scaled Scores and Sums of Scaled Scores for Adaptive Domains and the GAC: Parent/Primary Caregiver and Parent Forms (continued)

Parent/Primary Caregiver Form

Ages 1:4–1:7

Skill Area/Composite	Com	CU	FA	HL	HS	LS	SC	SD	Soc	MO	CON[a]	SO[a]	PR[a]	GAC[b]
Communication											.56			.71
Community Use	.45												.68	.70
Functional Pre-Academics	.56	.64									.66			.73
Home Living	.49	.62	.67										.73	.74
Health and Safety	.66	.66	.63	.62									.76	.79
Leisure	.55	.43	.41	.41	.48							.53		.63
Self-Care	.58	.51	.56	.65	.65	.54							.69	.77
Self-Direction	.42	.63	.54	.64	.52	.60	.63					.55		.71
Social	.64	.62	.63	.60	.69	.53	.64	.56				.53		.78
Motor	.64	.37	.49	.51	.58	.51	.62	.45	.54					.67
Conceptual Domain	.80	.70	.86	.74	.74	.63	.72	.80	.74	.64				
Social Domain	.68	.60	.59	.57	.66	.88	.67	.67	.87	.60	.79			
Practical Domain	.65	.83	.74	.85	.87	.55	.83	.72	.76	.62	.86	.74		.86
GAC	.77	.76	.78	.80	.83	.70	.82	.77	.83	.73	.95	.87	.95	
Mean[c]	10.50	10.35	10.33	10.38	10.39	10.56	10.39	10.32	10.44	10.37	31.15	21.00	41.51	104.03
SD	2.83	2.97	2.91	2.85	2.98	3.02	2.99	2.94	2.85	2.95	7.12	5.14	9.97	22.85

Ages 1:8–1:11

Skill Area/Composite	Com	CU	FA	HL	HS	LS	SC	SD	Soc	MO	CON[a]	SO[a]	PR[a]	GAC[b]
Communication											.58			.61
Community Use	.33												.65	.65
Functional Pre-Academics	.58	.48									.60			.58
Home Living	.37	.71	.42										.73	.70
Health and Safety	.55	.51	.40	.54									.64	.75
Leisure	.46	.40	.44	.42	.57							.62		.65
Self-Care	.34	.38	.34	.52	.55	.43							.57	.62
Self-Direction	.41	.57	.43	.64	.62	.68	.58					.47		.76
Social	.63	.55	.55	.65	.65	.62	.61	.65				.62		.82
Motor	.45	.46	.33	.46	.63	.37	.48	.51	.50					.62
Conceptual Domain	.83	.57	.83	.59	.65	.66	.52	.76	.76	.53				
Social Domain	.61	.53	.55	.60	.68	.89	.58	.74	.90	.49	.79			
Practical Domain	.49	.80	.51	.86	.80	.56	.76	.75	.76	.63	.72	.74		.80
GAC	.69	.72	.67	.77	.81	.73	.70	.82	.86	.69	.90	.88	.93	
Mean[c]	10.05	9.65	9.75	10.40	9.98	10.42	10.36	10.51	10.29	10.19	30.31	20.71	40.39	101.60
SD	2.90	2.66	2.87	2.93	2.74	2.81	2.69	2.84	2.93	2.60	6.94	5.17	8.91	20.88

Note. **Com** = Communication; **CU** = Community Use; **FA** = Functional Pre-Academics; **HL** = Home Living; **HS** = Health and Safety; **LS** = Leisure; **SC** = Self-Care; **SD** = Self-Direction; **Soc** = Social; **MO** = Motor; **CON** = Conceptual Adaptive Domain; **SO** = Social Adaptive Domain; **PR** = Practical Adaptive Domain.

[a] Adaptive Domain correlations corrected by removing the skill area scaled score from the sum of the scaled scores.

[b] GAC correlations corrected by removing the skill area scaled score(s) from the sum of the scaled scores.

[c] Means and SDs reported under corrected adaptive domains and GAC were calculated using all skill areas included in the composite.

Table C.2   Intercorrelations of Skill Area Scaled Scores and Sums of Scaled Scores for Adaptive Domains and the GAC: Parent/Primary Caregiver and Parent Forms (continued)

Parent/Primary Caregiver Form   **Ages 2:0–2:5**

Skill Area/Composite	Com	CU	FA	HL	HS	LS	SC	SD	Soc	MO	CON[a]	SO[a]	PR[a]	GAC[b]
Communication											.72			.77
Community Use	.61												.72	.80
Functional Pre-Academics	.61	.66									.63			.62
Home Living	.54	.59	.42										.70	.73
Health and Safety	.63	.71	.49	.67									.75	.80
Leisure	.68	.65	.52	.61	.68							.69		.80
Self-Care	.54	.52	.31	.53	.51	.40							.59	.58
Self-Direction	.64	.72	.53	.74	.70	.74	.52					.65		.83
Social	.68	.68	.45	.59	.62	.69	.51	.73					.69	.77
Motor	.52	.49	.48	.51	.61	.66	.38	.51	.49					.65
Conceptual Domain	.88	.77	.84	.66	.71	.76	.53	.85	.73	.59				
Social Domain	.74	.72	.53	.65	.71	.92	.50	.80	.92	.63	.81			
Practical Domain	.70	.85	.56	.84	.87	.70	.77	.80	.72	.60	.80	.77		.84
GAC	.82	.84	.70	.79	.84	.84	.66	.87	.82	.71	.93	.90	.94	
Mean[c]	10.71	10.42	10.49	10.59	10.56	10.50	10.37	10.42	10.60	10.56	31.62	21.10	41.94	105.22
SD	3.04	2.95	3.07	2.99	2.90	3.03	3.06	3.12	3.12	2.93	7.89	5.65	9.89	23.82

Ages 2:6–2:11

Skill Area/Composite	Com	CU	FA	HL	HS	LS	SC	SD	Soc	MO	CON[a]	SO[a]	PR[a]	GAC[b]
Communication											.65			.66
Community Use	.51												.62	.78
Functional Pre-Academics	.57	.61									.61			.58
Home Living	.39	.59	.36										.66	.67
Health and Safety	.52	.54	.34	.60									.67	.71
Leisure	.56	.65	.49	.54	.61							.68		.76
Self-Care	.36	.39	.25	.41	.47	.35							.50	.49
Self-Direction	.55	.73	.50	.59	.55	.68	.48					.59		.78
Social	.52	.65	.42	.56	.55	.68	.35	.71					.68	.73
Motor	.48	.51	.42	.49	.57	.53	.33	.43	.46					.62
Conceptual Domain	.85	.74	.83	.53	.56	.69	.43	.81	.66	.53				
Social Domain	.59	.71	.49	.60	.63	.91	.38	.76	.92	.54	.73			
Practical Domain	.56	.80	.49	.82	.83	.68	.72	.74	.67	.60	.72	.74		.80
GAC	.73	.83	.66	.74	.77	.81	.59	.83	.79	.70	.89	.87	.93	
Mean[c]	10.54	10.40	10.48	10.10	10.35	10.23	10.45	10.39	10.36	10.41	31.41	20.59	41.30	103.71
SD	2.90	2.94	2.87	2.90	3.01	2.69	2.92	2.71	2.95	3.09	7.07	5.17	9.30	21.60

Note. **Com** = Communication; **CU** = Community Use; **FA** = Functional Pre-Academics; **HL** = Home Living; **HS** = Health and Safety; **LS** = Leisure; **SC** = Self-Care; **SD** = Self-Direction; **Soc** = Social; **MO** = Motor; **CON** = Conceptual Adaptive Domain; **SO** = Social Adaptive Domain; **PR** = Practical Adaptive Domain.

[a] Adaptive Domain correlations corrected by removing the skill area scaled score from the sum of the scaled scores.
[b] GAC correlations corrected by removing the skill area scaled score(s) from the sum of the scaled scores.
[c] Means and *SD*s reported under corrected adaptive domains and GAC were calculated using all skill areas included in the composite.

Table C.2 **Intercorrelations of Skill Area Scaled Scores and Sums of Scaled Scores for Adaptive Domains and the GAC: Parent/Primary Caregiver and Parent Forms** (continued)

Parent/Primary Caregiver Form

Ages 3:0–3:5

Skill Area/Composite	Com	CU	FA	HL	HS	LS	SC	SD	Soc	MO	CON[a]	SO[a]	PR[a]	GAC[b]
Communication											.67			.75
Community Use	.68												.79	.84
Functional Pre-Academics	.56	.72									.65			.69
Home Living	.58	.80	.63										.83	.83
Health and Safety	.65	.71	.52	.68									.76	.79
Leisure	.71	.67	.59	.63	.71							.71		.79
Self-Care	.55	.57	.45	.67	.61	.60							.68	.72
Self-Direction	.64	.74	.62	.78	.64	.69	.71				.71			.83
Social	.63	.75	.54	.77	.71	.71	.65	.80				.71		.84
Motor	.54	.51	.50	.58	.58	.54	.54	.49	.57					.65
Conceptual Domain	.85	.83	.84	.78	.70	.77	.67	.88	.77	.60				
Social Domain	.73	.77	.61	.76	.77	.93	.67	.80	.92	.60	.84			
Practical Domain	.71	.89	.67	.91	.86	.75	.82	.82	.83	.63	.86	.85		.90
GAC	.80	.87	.75	.87	.83	.84	.77	.87	.87	.71	.94	.93	.96	
Mean[c]	10.25	10.20	9.94	10.22	10.12	10.45	10.46	10.23	10.22	9.80	30.42	20.67	41.00	101.89
SD	3.12	3.18	3.10	3.22	3.04	3.34	3.07	3.36	3.09	2.94	8.23	5.94	10.88	25.80

Ages 3:6–3:11

Skill Area/Composite	Com	CU	FA	HL	HS	LS	SC	SD	Soc	MO	CON[a]	SO[a]	PR[a]	GAC[b]
Communication											.48			.68
Community Use	.46												.61	.68
Functional Pre-Academics	.28	.43									.36			.41
Home Living	.51	.58	.28										.71	.72
Health and Safety	.52	.62	.32	.61									.71	.75
Leisure	.72	.52	.41	.53	.60							.55		.76
Self-Care	.42	.33	.08	.54	.50	.52							.54	.57
Self-Direction	.51	.55	.35	.65	.64	.58	.50				.53			.73
Social	.46	.59	.35	.66	.55	.55	.48	.70				.55		.70
Motor	.55	.36	.28	.30	.46	.47	.44	.22	.23					.49
Conceptual Domain	.77	.62	.72	.62	.64	.74	.43	.80	.65	.46				
Social Domain	.67	.64	.43	.68	.65	.88	.57	.73	.88	.40	.79			
Practical Domain	.59	.78	.34	.85	.85	.68	.74	.73	.71	.48	.72	.79		.80
GAC	.75	.75	.53	.78	.80	.82	.66	.79	.77	.60	.90	.90	.93	
Mean[c]	10.19	10.22	10.39	10.27	10.21	9.98	9.92	10.14	10.20	10.35	30.72	20.18	40.62	101.87
SD	2.85	2.70	3.05	2.91	2.86	2.90	2.92	2.90	2.94	2.93	6.73	5.14	9.17	20.94

Note. **Com** = Communication; **CU** = Community Use; **FA** = Functional Pre-Academics; **HL** = Home Living; **HS** = Health and Safety; **LS** = Leisure; **SC** = Self-Care; **SD** = Self-Direction; **Soc** = Social; **MO** = Motor; **CON** = Conceptual Adaptive Domain; **SO** = Social Adaptive Domain; **PR** = Practical Adaptive Domain.

[a] Adaptive Domain correlations corrected by removing the skill area scaled score from the sum of the scaled scores.
[b] GAC correlations corrected by removing the skill area scaled score(s) from the sum of the scaled scores.
[c] Means and *SD*s reported under corrected adaptive domains and GAC were calculated using all skill areas included in the composite.

Table C.2   Intercorrelations of Skill Area Scaled Scores and Sums of Scaled Scores for Adaptive Domains and the GAC: Parent/Primary Caregiver and Parent Forms *(continued)*

Ages 4:0–4:5

Skill Area/Composite	Com	CU	FA	HL	HS	LS	SC	SD	Soc	MO	CON[a]	SO[a]	PR[a]	GAC[b]
Communication											.60			.68
Community Use	.55												.73	.77
Functional Pre-Academics	.48	.54									.56			.61
Home Living	.52	.68	.44										.76	.76
Health and Safety	.63	.68	.50	.69									.76	.80
Leisure	.58	.64	.47	.53	.65							.68		.76
Self-Care	.53	.54	.39	.58	.57	.59							.63	.69
Self-Direction	.55	.66	.51	.73	.72	.66	.60					.62		.81
Social	.50	.68	.45	.66	.65	.68	.63	.77					.68	.78
Motor	.53	.49	.60	.56	.55	.56	.48	.53	.47					.66
Conceptual Domain	.82	.71	.80	.69	.75	.70	.62	.84	.70	.67				
Social Domain	.59	.72	.50	.65	.71	.92	.67	.78	.92	.56	.76			
Practical Domain	.66	.86	.56	.87	.86	.71	.79	.80	.77	.61	.82	.81		.86
GAC	.75	.82	.68	.81	.84	.81	.75	.86	.82	.73	.93	.89	.95	
Mean[c]	10.03	10.43	10.53	10.19	10.07	10.10	9.96	10.21	10.13	10.44	30.77	20.23	40.65	102.09
SD	3.02	3.23	2.99	3.04	2.92	2.96	2.97	3.15	2.97	3.04	7.53	5.43	10.29	23.87

Ages 4:6–4:11

Skill Area/Composite	Com	CU	FA	HL	HS	LS	SC	SD	Soc	MO	CON[a]	SO[a]	PR[a]	GAC[b]
Communication											.49			.52
Community Use	.31												.61	.69
Functional Pre-Academics	.43	.61									.60			.66
Home Living	.32	.60	.48										.68	.68
Health and Safety	.34	.51	.43	.53									.64	.65
Leisure	.49	.45	.47	.38	.46							.53		.64
Self-Care	.45	.38	.35	.49	.51	.47							.55	.64
Self-Direction	.44	.62	.59	.63	.59	.57	.60					.61		.81
Social	.35	.66	.52	.62	.55	.53	.55	.74					.53	.76
Motor	.41	.38	.50	.47	.42	.46	.49	.49	.47					.61
Conceptual Domain	.76	.64	.84	.59	.56	.63	.57	.84	.67	.57				
Social Domain	.48	.64	.56	.57	.58	.87	.58	.75	.88	.53	.74			
Practical Domain	.45	.79	.59	.83	.80	.55	.74	.77	.75	.55	.75	.74		.80
GAC	.61	.76	.73	.75	.73	.71	.71	.85	.82	.69	.91	.87	.93	
Mean[c]	9.99	10.09	10.23	10.04	10.10	10.04	9.96	10.10	10.17	10.19	30.32	20.21	40.19	100.91
SD	2.94	3.06	3.17	3.04	2.98	2.90	2.90	3.10	3.00	2.89	7.47	5.16	9.51	22.10

Note. **Com** = Communication; **CU** = Community Use; **FA** = Functional Pre-Academics; **HL** = Home Living; **HS** = Health and Safety; **LS** = Leisure; **SC** = Self-Care; **SD** = Self-Direction; **Soc** = Social; **MO** = Motor; **CON** = Conceptual Adaptive Domain; **SO** = Social Adaptive Domain; **PR** = Practical Adaptive Domain.

[a] Adaptive Domain correlations corrected by removing the skill area scaled score from the sum of the scaled scores.
[b] GAC correlations corrected by removing the skill area scaled score(s) from the sum of the scaled scores.
[c] Means and *SD*s reported under corrected adaptive domains and GAC were calculated using all skill areas included in the composite.

Table C.2 Intercorrelations of Skill Area Scaled Scores and Sums of Scaled Scores for Adaptive Domains and the GAC: Parent/Primary Caregiver and Parent Forms (continued)

Parent/Primary Caregiver Form

Ages 5:0–5:11

Skill Area/Composite	Com	CU	FA	HL	HS	LS	SC	SD	Soc	MO	CON[a]	SO[a]	PR[a]	GAC[b]
Communication											.50			.61
Community Use	.46												.70	.76
Functional Pre-Academics	.34	.47									.43			.50
Home Living	.37	.60	.46										.63	.66
Health and Safety	.58	.63	.36	.55									.69	.74
Leisure	.51	.59	.40	.51	.54							.69		.72
Self-Care	.50	.48	.27	.42	.51	.52							.55	.62
Self-Direction	.50	.68	.41	.62	.67	.71	.56					.56		.82
Social	.45	.67	.37	.64	.62	.69	.51	.83				.69		.78
Motor	.49	.54	.40	.35	.49	.38	.47	.47	.41					.58
Conceptual Domain	.79	.68	.75	.61	.69	.69	.57	.81	.69	.58				
Social Domain	.52	.68	.42	.62	.63	.92	.56	.84	.91	.43	.75			
Practical Domain	.59	.84	.48	.80	.83	.67	.75	.79	.76	.58	.79	.77		.85
GAC	.70	.82	.60	.74	.79	.78	.70	.86	.83	.67	.92	.88	.95	
Mean[c]	10.28	10.32	10.07	10.23	10.20	10.07	10.22	10.02	10.15	10.22	30.37	20.21	40.97	101.77
SD	3.04	3.04	2.97	2.98	2.85	3.15	3.02	2.87	3.03	2.89	6.94	5.68	9.56	22.32

Note. **Com** = Communication; **CU** = Community Use; **FA** = Functional Pre-Academics; **HL** = Home Living; **HS** = Health and Safety; **LS** = Leisure; **SC** = Self-Care; **SD** = Self-Direction; **Soc** = Social; **MO** = Motor; **CON** = Conceptual Adaptive Domain; **SO** = Social Adaptive Domain; **PR** = Practical Adaptive Domain.

[a] Adaptive Domain correlations corrected by removing the skill area scaled score from the sum of the scaled scores.
[b] GAC correlations corrected by removing the skill area scaled score(s) from the sum of the scaled scores.
[c] Means and SDs reported under corrected adaptive domains and GAC were calculated using all skill areas included in the composite.

Table C.2 Intercorrelations of Skill Area Scaled Scores and Sums of Scaled Scores for Adaptive Domains and the GAC: Parent/Primary Caregiver and Parent Forms (continued)

Parent Form — **Age 5**

Skill Area/Composite	Com	CU	FA	HL	HS	LS	SC	SD	Soc	CON[a]	SO[a]	PR[a]	GAC[b]
Communication										.66			.71
Community Use	.49											.57	.65
Functional Academics	.60	.66								.70			.66
Home Living	.45	.60	.47									.75	.71
Health and Safety	.49	.49	.48	.68								.72	.74
Leisure	.68	.50	.45	.55	.63						.76		.76
Self-Care	.50	.38	.46	.55	.63	.54						.61	.67
Self-Direction	.59	.63	.65	.69	.61	.65	.59				.69		.81
Social	.61	.30	.36	.44	.62	.76	.55	.57			.76		.66
Conceptual Domain	.85	.69	.89	.61	.60	.68	.60	.85	.58				.80
Social Domain	.69	.43	.43	.53	.67	.93	.59	.65	.94	.67			.72
Practical Domain	.59	.78	.64	.86	.86	.68	.77	.77	.58	.77		.67	.80
GAC	.78	.74	.75	.78	.80	.82	.74	.85	.73	.92	.83	.94	
Mean[c]	9.81	9.15	9.46	9.95	9.71	9.98	9.93	9.99	9.88	29.26	19.87	38.74	87.87
SD	3.35	3.75	3.80	3.09	3.43	2.94	3.09	3.01	3.06	8.77	5.62	10.90	22.88

Age 6

Skill Area/Composite	Com	CU	FA	HL	HS	LS	SC	SD	Soc	CON[a]	SO[a]	PR[a]	GAC[b]
Communication										.70			.79
Community Use	.68											.67	.75
Functional Academics	.67	.68								.76			.76
Home Living	.57	.68	.61									.78	.74
Health and Safety	.66	.61	.62	.71								.78	.81
Leisure	.75	.64	.64	.59	.74						.76		.82
Self-Care	.59	.48	.52	.62	.69	.59						.68	.70
Self-Direction	.62	.67	.69	.60	.70	.70	.61				.72		.81
Social	.70	.57	.63	.55	.64	.76	.61	.73			.76		.78
Conceptual Domain	.86	.77	.90	.67	.75	.79	.65	.87	.78				.88
Social Domain	.77	.64	.68	.61	.74	.94	.64	.76	.94	.84			.84
Practical Domain	.74	.82	.71	.88	.89	.75	.81	.76	.70	.84		.78	.85
GAC	.84	.81	.82	.80	.86	.86	.77	.85	.83	.95	.90	.95	
Mean[c]	9.90	9.48	9.88	9.98	9.67	10.04	10.00	9.95	9.94	29.73	19.98	39.13	88.84
SD	2.94	3.42	3.30	2.91	3.51	3.09	3.04	2.92	3.08	8.07	5.78	10.96	23.29

Note. **Com** = Communication; **CU** = Community Use; **FA** = Functional Academics; **HL** = Home Living; **HS** = Health and Safety; **LS** = Leisure; **SC** = Self-Care; **SD** = Self-Direction; **Soc** = Social; **CON** = Conceptual Adaptive Domain; **SO** = Social Adaptive Domain; **PR** = Practical Adaptive Domain.

[a] Adaptive Domain correlations corrected by removing the skill area scaled score from the sum of the scaled scores.
[b] GAC correlations corrected by removing the skill area scaled score(s) from the sum of the scaled scores.
[c] Means and SDs reported under corrected adaptive domains and GAC were calculated using all skill areas included in the composite.

Table C.2   Intercorrelations of Skill Area Scaled Scores and Sums of Scaled Scores for Adaptive Domains and the GAC: Parent/Primary Caregiver and Parent Forms *(continued)*

Parent Form — **Age 7**

Skill Area/Composite	Com	CU	FA	HL	HS	LS	SC	SD	Soc	CON[a]	SO[a]	PR[a]	GAC[b]
Communication										.72			.76
Community Use	.45											.49	.58
Functional Academics	.64	.54								.66			.67
Home Living	.37	.45	.47									.68	.59
Health and Safety	.66	.48	.57	.62								.74	.83
Leisure	.70	.48	.53	.37	.65						.71		.74
Self-Care	.48	.35	.38	.61	.69	.49						.67	.66
Self-Direction	.63	.46	.55	.45	.67	.65	.58			.65			.76
Social	.75	.45	.50	.43	.75	.71	.55	.70			.71		.78
Conceptual Domain	.88	.56	.84	.50	.74	.73	.56	.85	.76				.82
Social Domain	.78	.50	.55	.43	.76	.91	.56	.73	.93	.81			.80
Practical Domain	.60	.71	.61	.84	.87	.61	.81	.66	.67	.73	.70		.75
GAC	.82	.67	.74	.69	.87	.80	.73	.82	.84	.92	.89	.91	
Mean[c]	9.57	9.39	9.77	9.33	9.78	9.88	9.83	9.70	9.56	29.03	19.43	38.33	86.80
SD	3.47	3.22	3.27	3.50	3.29	3.08	2.85	3.45	3.50	8.75	6.08	10.38	22.97

Age 8

Skill Area/Composite	Com	CU	FA	HL	HS	LS	SC	SD	Soc	CON[a]	SO[a]	PR[a]	GAC[b]
Communication										.75			.79
Community Use	.60											.69	.74
Functional Academics	.74	.70								.80			.80
Home Living	.53	.64	.57									.76	.70
Health and Safety	.67	.62	.68	.66								.75	.80
Leisure	.71	.64	.67	.62	.70						.76		.83
Self-Care	.63	.52	.61	.64	.64	.63						.69	.74
Self-Direction	.64	.64	.70	.56	.65	.69	.63			.72			.79
Social	.71	.53	.60	.45	.63	.76	.60	.68			.76		.75
Conceptual Domain	.89	.73	.91	.62	.75	.77	.70	.88	.75				.87
Social Domain	.76	.62	.68	.57	.71	.94	.65	.73	.94	.81			.81
Practical Domain	.71	.82	.76	.88	.86	.76	.81	.73	.64	.82	.75		.83
GAC	.84	.80	.85	.77	.84	.87	.79	.84	.81	.94	.89	.94	
Mean[c]	9.49	9.79	9.98	9.13	9.91	9.78	9.90	9.67	9.44	29.14	19.22	38.73	87.09
SD	3.43	3.20	3.29	3.80	3.21	3.29	2.93	3.52	3.47	9.13	6.35	11.13	24.78

Note. **Com** = Communication; **CU** = Community Use; **FA** = Functional Academics; **HL** = Home Living; **HS** = Health and Safety; **LS** = Leisure; **SC** = Self-Care; **SD** = Self-Direction; **Soc** = Social; **CON** = Conceptual Adaptive Domain; **SO** = Social Adaptive Domain; **PR** = Practical Adaptive Domain.

[a] Adaptive Domain correlations corrected by removing the skill area scaled score from the sum of the scaled scores.
[b] GAC correlations corrected by removing the skill area scaled score(s) from the sum of the scaled scores.
[c] Means and *SD*s reported under corrected adaptive domains and GAC were calculated using all skill areas included in the composite.

Table C.2 **Intercorrelations of Skill Area Scaled Scores and Sums of Scaled Scores for Adaptive Domains and the GAC: Parent/Primary Caregiver and Parent Forms** *(continued)*

Parent Form — **Age 9**

Skill Area/Composite	Com	CU	FA	HL	HS	LS	SC	SD	Soc	CON[a]	SO[a]	PR[a]	GAC[b]
Communication										.71			.70
Community Use	.54											.63	.73
Functional Academics	.66	.67								.68			.71
Home Living	.35	.55	.47									.66	.59
Health and Safety	.53	.70	.57	.59								.74	.77
Leisure	.59	.56	.59	.44	.63						.66		.73
Self-Care	.39	.36	.37	.50	.53	.41						.55	.55
Self-Direction	.61	.68	.58	.48	.60	.60	.46			.65			.75
Social	.65	.42	.49	.31	.50	.66	.38	.59			.66		.64
Conceptual Domain	.86	.73	.86	.51	.66	.69	.47	.86	.67				.80
Social Domain	.68	.53	.59	.41	.62	.91	.44	.65	.92	.74			.72
Practical Domain	.54	.78	.63	.85	.85	.62	.76	.67	.49	.72	.60		.71
GAC	.77	.79	.78	.70	.82	.80	.65	.82	.73	.92	.84	.91	
Mean[c]	9.93	10.15	10.04	9.00	10.40	9.93	9.91	9.73	9.69	29.71	19.63	39.47	88.80
SD	2.83	2.59	3.05	3.79	2.57	3.05	3.24	3.29	3.21	7.90	5.70	9.86	20.93

Age 10

Skill Area/Composite	Com	CU	FA	HL	HS	LS	SC	SD	Soc	CON[a]	SO[a]	PR[a]	GAC[b]
Communication										.66			.64
Community Use	.44											.67	.69
Functional Academics	.63	.64								.73			.75
Home Living	.37	.61	.56									.70	.67
Health and Safety	.48	.60	.60	.53								.66	.75
Leisure	.59	.62	.67	.54	.72						.75		.83
Self-Care	.41	.49	.50	.62	.57	.52						.67	.67
Self-Direction	.58	.55	.67	.58	.62	.77	.61			.69			.82
Social	.61	.45	.49	.50	.66	.75	.53	.74			.75		.75
Conceptual Domain	.84	.63	.88	.59	.66	.79	.59	.88	.71				.82
Social Domain	.64	.57	.62	.55	.74	.93	.56	.81	.94	.80			.82
Practical Domain	.51	.80	.69	.86	.81	.72	.82	.72	.65	.75	.73		.78
GAC	.71	.75	.80	.76	.81	.87	.74	.87	.81	.92	.90	.92	
Mean[c]	10.05	10.32	10.07	9.49	10.11	9.94	10.01	9.66	9.59	29.78	19.53	39.92	89.23
SD	2.94	2.65	2.99	3.72	3.02	3.16	3.00	3.49	3.49	8.16	6.21	10.22	22.54

Note. **Com** = Communication; **CU** = Community Use; **FA** = Functional Academics; **HL** = Home Living; **HS** = Health and Safety; **LS** = Leisure; **SC** = Self-Care; **SD** = Self-Direction; **Soc** = Social; **CON** = Conceptual Adaptive Domain; **SO** = Social Adaptive Domain; **PR** = Practical Adaptive Domain.

[a] Adaptive Domain correlations corrected by removing the skill area scaled score from the sum of the scaled scores.
[b] GAC correlations corrected by removing the skill area scaled score(s) from the sum of the scaled scores.
[c] Means and *SD*s reported under corrected adaptive domains and GAC were calculated using all skill areas included in the composite.

Table C.2   Intercorrelations of Skill Area Scaled Scores and Sums of Scaled Scores for Adaptive Domains and the GAC: Parent/Primary Caregiver and Parent Forms *(continued)*

Parent Form

Age 11

Skill Area/Composite	Com	CU	FA	HL	HS	LS	SC	SD	Soc	CON[a]	SO[a]	PR[a]	GAC[b]
Communication										.77			.77
Community Use	.66											.68	.74
Functional Academics	.72	.69								.75			.80
Home Living	.45	.55	.61									.64	.67
Health and Safety	.66	.65	.62	.55								.71	.75
Leisure	.70	.66	.69	.60	.62						.64		.80
Self-Care	.55	.54	.59	.55	.60	.60						.66	.72
Self-Direction	.69	.59	.66	.57	.62	.65	.67			.73			.80
Social	.65	.52	.65	.52	.61	.64	.62	.73			.64		.76
Conceptual Domain	.89	.72	.88	.61	.71	.76	.68	.89	.76				.87
Social Domain	.74	.64	.74	.61	.68	.88	.68	.77	.93	.84			.85
Practical Domain	.69	.82	.76	.83	.84	.75	.80	.74	.68	.82	.79		.84
GAC	.82	.80	.85	.75	.81	.84	.78	.85	.82	.94	.91	.95	
Mean[c]	9.72	10.11	10.10	9.39	9.87	9.95	9.65	9.73	9.48	29.55	19.43	39.02	88.00
SD	2.81	2.95	2.83	3.68	2.86	2.81	2.70	3.39	3.51	8.03	5.73	10.06	22.35

Age 12

Skill Area/Composite	Com	CU	FA	HL	HS	LS	SC	SD	Soc	CON[a]	SO[a]	PR[a]	GAC[b]
Communication										.73			.76
Community Use	.66											.71	.76
Functional Academics	.74	.74								.79			.81
Home Living	.53	.60	.64									.71	.74
Health and Safety	.71	.71	.71	.63								.76	.82
Leisure	.73	.63	.70	.53	.69						.68		.76
Self-Care	.45	.48	.49	.58	.57	.41						.63	.64
Self-Direction	.61	.61	.68	.68	.66	.66	.64			.69			.81
Social	.63	.59	.63	.67	.69	.68	.59	.75			.68		.80
Conceptual Domain	.87	.76	.90	.70	.78	.79	.60	.88	.76				.89
Social Domain	.74	.66	.72	.66	.75	.90	.55	.78	.93	.84			.84
Practical Domain	.70	.84	.78	.86	.87	.68	.77	.78	.76	.85	.79		.86
GAC	.81	.82	.85	.80	.86	.81	.70	.86	.85	.95	.91	.96	
Mean[c]	9.53	9.79	9.99	8.73	9.47	9.84	9.37	9.33	9.09	28.85	18.93	37.35	85.12
SD	2.99	3.22	2.88	3.78	3.44	3.04	2.90	3.48	3.50	8.26	6.00	11.16	24.00

Note. **Com** = Communication; **CU** = Community Use; **FA** = Functional Academics; **HL** = Home Living; **HS** = Health and Safety; **LS** = Leisure; **SC** = Self-Care; **SD** = Self-Direction; **Soc** = Social; **CON** = Conceptual Adaptive Domain; **SO** = Social Adaptive Domain; **PR** = Practical Adaptive Domain.

[a] Adaptive Domain correlations corrected by removing the skill area scaled score from the sum of the scaled scores.

[b] GAC correlations corrected by removing the skill area scaled score(s) from the sum of the scaled scores.

[c] Means and *SD*s reported under corrected adaptive domains and GAC were calculated using all skill areas included in the composite.

Table C.2 Intercorrelations of Skill Area Scaled Scores and Sums of Scaled Scores for Adaptive Domains and the GAC: Parent/Primary Caregiver and Parent Forms *(continued)*

Parent Form — **Ages 13–14**

Skill Area/Composite	Com	CU	FA	HL	HS	LS	SC	SD	Soc	CON[a]	SO[a]	PR[a]	GAC[b]
Communication										.77			.79
Community Use	.64											.71	.76
Functional Academics	.67	.78								.72			.80
Home Living	.52	.52	.55									.59	.65
Health and Safety	.69	.70	.71	.52								.71	.79
Leisure	.70	.70	.69	.57	.70						.71		.82
Self-Care	.57	.51	.61	.46	.55	.54						.60	.66
Self-Direction	.73	.64	.66	.64	.66	.71	.62			.76			.84
Social	.64	.46	.53	.52	.62	.71	.54	.76			.71		.73
Conceptual Domain	.89	.78	.88	.64	.77	.79	.67	.90	.73				.91
Social Domain	.72	.61	.65	.59	.71	.91	.58	.80	.94	.82			.81
Practical Domain	.74	.83	.81	.80	.85	.77	.76	.79	.66	.88	.77		.87
GAC	.83	.81	.84	.74	.84	.86	.73	.88	.80	.96	.89	.96	
Mean[c]	9.73	10.13	10.03	9.28	9.77	10.15	9.63	9.63	9.18	29.39	19.33	38.81	87.53
SD	2.71	2.82	3.16	3.71	3.34	2.81	2.89	3.29	3.42	8.15	5.77	10.34	22.87

Ages 15–16

Skill Area/Composite	Com	CU	FA	HL	HS	LS	SC	SD	Soc	CON[a]	SO[a]	PR[a]	GAC[b]
Communication										.71			.73
Community Use	.68											.67	.76
Functional Academics	.69	.75								.76			.80
Home Living	.40	.55	.50									.64	.60
Health and Safety	.59	.65	.72	.61								.72	.78
Leisure	.69	.62	.66	.46	.65						.71		.78
Self-Care	.42	.46	.52	.43	.47	.43						.52	.57
Self-Direction	.62	.60	.68	.51	.66	.71	.51			.71			.80
Social	.58	.51	.57	.46	.59	.71	.48	.73			.71		.73
Conceptual Domain	.86	.77	.89	.53	.75	.78	.55	.89	.72				.86
Social Domain	.68	.61	.66	.50	.67	.91	.50	.78	.94	.81			.79
Practical Domain	.64	.81	.76	.84	.85	.66	.71	.70	.63	.79	.70		.79
GAC	.79	.81	.84	.71	.83	.83	.65	.85	.80	.94	.88	.93	
Mean[c]	9.86	10.62	9.85	9.66	9.83	10.04	10.10	9.86	9.45	29.56	19.49	40.21	89.26
SD	2.70	2.50	2.65	3.56	2.74	2.87	2.58	3.16	3.35	7.48	5.76	9.17	20.63

Note. **Com** = Communication; **CU** = Community Use; **FA** = Functional Academics; **HL** = Home Living; **HS** = Health and Safety; **LS** = Leisure; **SC** = Self-Care; **SD** = Self-Direction; **Soc** = Social; **CON** = Conceptual Adaptive Domain; **SO** = Social Adaptive Domain; **PR** = Practical Adaptive Domain.

[a] Adaptive Domain correlations corrected by removing the skill area scaled score from the sum of the scaled scores.
[b] GAC correlations corrected by removing the skill area scaled score(s) from the sum of the scaled scores.
[c] Means and *SD*s reported under corrected adaptive domains and GAC were calculated using all skill areas included in the composite.

Table C.2 Intercorrelations of Skill Area Scaled Scores and Sums of Scaled Scores for Adaptive Domains and the GAC: Parent/Primary Caregiver and Parent Forms (continued)

Parent Form

Ages 17–21

Skill Area/Composite	Com	CU	FA	HL	HS	LS	SC	SD	Soc	CON[a]	SO[a]	PR[a]	GAC[b]
Communication										.77			.82
Community Use	.75											.78	.84
Functional Academics	.73	.80								.80			.82
Home Living	.57	.63	.62									.67	.71
Health and Safety	.73	.77	.76	.65								.81	.85
Leisure	.70	.75	.71	.62	.73						.66		.82
Self-Care	.66	.61	.59	.51	.66	.61						.66	.72
Self-Direction	.71	.72	.75	.69	.74	.76	.64			.78			.86
Social	.69	.65	.59	.57	.72	.66	.64	.77			.66		.78
Conceptual Domain	.89	.83	.91	.70	.82	.80	.69	.92	.76				.91
Social Domain	.77	.77	.71	.65	.79	.91	.69	.84	.91	.86			.88
Practical Domain	.79	.87	.80	.84	.90	.79	.81	.82	.75	.89	.85		.90
GAC	.85	.87	.85	.78	.89	.86	.78	.89	.83	.96	.93	.97	
Mean[c]	9.74	10.99	9.98	9.43	9.92	10.04	10.08	9.72	9.40	29.43	19.44	40.41	89.27
SD	2.62	2.56	2.53	3.43	2.80	2.82	2.85	3.06	2.84	7.44	5.15	9.92	21.52

Note. **Com** = Communication; **CU** = Community Use; **FA** = Functional Academics; **HL** = Home Living; **HS** = Health and Safety; **LS** = Leisure; **SC** = Self-Care; **SD** = Self-Direction; **Soc** = Social; **CON** = Conceptual Adaptive Domain; **SO** = Social Adaptive Domain; **PR** = Practical Adaptive Domain.

[a] Adaptive Domain correlations corrected by removing the skill area scaled score from the sum of the scaled scores.
[b] GAC correlations corrected by removing the skill area scaled score(s) from the sum of the scaled scores.
[c] Means and SDs reported under corrected adaptive domains and GAC were calculated using all skill areas included in the composite.

Table C.3 Intercorrelations of Skill Area Scaled Scores and Sums of Scaled Scores for Adaptive Domains and the GAC: Adult Form, Self Report

Ages 16–21

Skill Area/Composite	Com	CU	FA	HL	HS	LS	SC	SD	Soc	WK	CON[a]	SO[a]	PR-4[a]	PR-5[a]	GAC-9[b]	GAC-10[b]
Communication											.73				.75	.76
Community Use	.77												.70	.73	.84	.83
Functional Academics	.67	.80									.72				.80	.78
Home Living	.42	.52	.56										.63	.65	.64	.65
Health and Safety	.69	.73	.70	.53									.71	.71	.79	.78
Leisure	.72	.77	.72	.52	.72							.62			.82	.82
Self-Care	.31	.45	.49	.54	.46	.41							.56	.55	.55	.55
Self-Direction	.65	.70	.63	.61	.67	.73	.52				.70				.81	.83
Social	.57	.56	.52	.50	.56	.62	.49	.66				.62			.69	.68
Work	.47	.54	.48	.49	.50	.56	.42	.71	.59						.60	.66
Conceptual Domain	.88	.86	.87	.61	.78	.82	.50	.87	.67	.63					.89	.90
Social Domain	.72	.74	.69	.57	.71	.90	.50	.77	.90	.65	.83				.83	.84
Practical Domain-4	.69	.85	.80	.80	.85	.76	.73	.77	.65	.60	.86	.78		.98	.87	
Practical Domain-5	.70	.84	.78	.79	.83	.76	.70	.82	.68	.76	.87	.81	.98			.88
GAC-9	.81	.88	.85	.72	.84	.86	.63	.86	.76	.66	.96	.90	.95	.96		
GAC-10	.81	.87	.82	.72	.83	.86	.63	.87	.75	.73	.95	.90	.95	.97	1.00	
Mean[c]	9.95	9.87	9.95	9.96	10.11	10.05	10.23	9.97	10.18	10.22	29.86	20.23	40.17	50.24	90.27	100.01
SD	3.02	2.97	2.97	2.91	3.07	3.05	2.53	3.04	3.00	2.96	7.91	5.44	9.32	11.45	21.37	23.51

Ages 22–29

Skill Area/Composite	Com	CU	FA	HL	HS	LS	SC	SD	Soc	WK	CON[a]	SO[a]	PR-4[a]	PR-5[a]	GAC-9[b]	GAC-10[b]
Communication											.72				.74	.72
Community Use	.82												.67	.67	.83	.81
Functional Academics	.73	.79									.79				.80	.79
Home Living	.50	.59	.61										.71	.70	.72	.72
Health and Safety	.57	.63	.66	.66									.77	.78	.78	.79
Leisure	.64	.71	.66	.55	.61							.71			.78	.83
Self-Care	.48	.50	.51	.56	.64	.55							.65	.66	.66	.66
Self-Direction	.58	.71	.68	.67	.70	.71	.55				.68				.82	.83
Social	.58	.65	.61	.61	.64	.71	.61	.74				.71			.78	.81
Work	.47	.50	.54	.52	.63	.61	.54	.66	.71						.66	.70
Conceptual Domain	.87	.87	.92	.67	.73	.76	.58	.86	.73	.64					.88	.88
Social Domain	.66	.74	.69	.62	.68	.93	.63	.78	.92	.71	.81				.83	.87
Practical Domain-4	.71	.82	.77	.85	.88	.73	.79	.79	.75	.66	.86	.80		.98	.88	
Practical Domain-5	.69	.80	.76	.82	.87	.79	.78	.83	.81	.79	.87	.86	.98			.90
GAC-9	.80	.87	.85	.78	.83	.83	.72	.86	.83	.70	.95	.90	.96	.96		
GAC-10	.78	.85	.83	.78	.84	.86	.72	.87	.85	.76	.94	.92	.96	.97	1.00	
Mean[c]	10.03	9.74	10.27	10.17	10.38	9.92	10.49	9.94	10.21	10.55	30.24	20.13	40.77	51.24	91.14	101.36
SD	2.88	2.89	3.14	2.90	2.84	2.92	2.47	2.96	2.90	2.83	7.91	5.38	9.28	11.33	21.28	23.50

Note. **Com** = Communication; **CU** = Community Use; **FA** = Functional Academics; **HL** = Home Living; **HS** = Health and Safety; **LS** = Leisure; **SC** = Self-Care; **SD** = Self-Direction; **Soc** = Social; **WK** = Work; **CON** = Conceptual Adaptive Domain; **SO** = Social Adaptive Domain; **PR-4** = Practical Adaptive Domain without Work; **PR-5** = Practical Adaptive Domain with Work; **GAC-9** = GAC without Work; **GAC-10** = GAC with Work.

[a] Adaptive Domain correlations corrected by removing the skill area scaled score from the sum of the scaled scores.
[b] GAC correlations corrected by removing the skill area scaled score(s) from the sum of the scaled scores.
[c] Means and SDs reported under corrected adaptive domains and GAC were calculated using all skill areas included in the composite.

C
Adult (Self)

Table C.3   Intercorrelations of Skill Area Scaled Scores and Sums of Scaled Scores for Adaptive Domains and the GAC: Adult Form, Self Report (continued)

Ages 30–39

Skill Area/Composite	Com	CU	FA	HL	HS	LS	SC	SD	Soc	WK	CON[a]	SO[a]	PR-4[a]	PR-5[a]	GAC-9[b]	GAC-10[b]
Communication											.79				.80	.77
Community Use	.80												.80	.76	.89	.86
Functional Academics	.79	.84									.85				.87	.84
Home Living	.57	.70	.72										.76	.73	.75	.73
Health and Safety	.67	.72	.75	.70									.79	.74	.80	.76
Leisure	.65	.76	.69	.60	.62							.73			.79	.78
Self-Care	.68	.67	.65	.61	.65	.64							.72	.70	.75	.72
Self-Direction	.71	.77	.78	.67	.70	.71	.62					.79			.84	.83
Social	.65	.74	.70	.63	.69	.73	.67	.75					.73		.81	.80
Work	.51	.54	.56	.53	.52	.62	.59	.65	.64						.64	.68
Conceptual Domain	.91	.88	.94	.71	.77	.75	.71	.90	.76	.63					.89	.87
Social Domain	.70	.81	.75	.67	.71	.93	.70	.79	.93	.68	.81				.84	.84
Practical Domain-4	.78	.90	.85	.87	.88	.76	.83	.80	.78	.64	.88	.83		.98	.90	
Practical Domain-5	.74	.86	.82	.84	.83	.76	.79	.81	.79	.78	.87	.84	.98			.91
GAC-9	.85	.91	.90	.81	.84	.84	.80	.88	.85	.68	.96	.91	.97	.96		
GAC-10	.82	.89	.88	.78	.81	.83	.76	.87	.84	.75	.94	.90	.96	.97	1.00	
Mean[c]	10.18	9.93	9.99	10.19	10.32	9.68	10.47	10.09	10.23	10.56	30.27	19.91	40.91	52.20	91.08	103.32
SD	3.08	3.04	3.05	2.91	2.73	3.03	2.40	2.90	3.00	2.93	8.28	5.61	9.66	10.86	22.37	22.73

Ages 40–49

Skill Area/Composite	Com	CU	FA	HL	HS	LS	SC	SD	Soc	WK	CON[a]	SO[a]	PR-4[a]	PR-5[a]	GAC-9[b]	GAC-10[b]
Communication											.75				.75	.73
Community Use	.78												.79	.78	.86	.85
Functional Academics	.76	.83									.83				.87	.87
Home Living	.47	.68	.68										.74	.73	.73	.73
Health and Safety	.62	.72	.73	.67									.79	.77	.82	.81
Leisure	.55	.61	.64	.52	.57							.67			.69	.71
Self-Care	.60	.71	.70	.67	.72	.56							.79	.78	.79	.78
Self-Direction	.63	.66	.75	.66	.73	.60	.66					.74			.81	.82
Social	.69	.76	.75	.65	.76	.67	.70	.79					.67		.86	.87
Work	.51	.59	.56	.54	.60	.53	.59	.66	.67						.66	.69
Conceptual Domain	.88	.84	.93	.67	.77	.66	.73	.89	.83	.64					.88	.88
Social Domain	.68	.75	.76	.64	.73	.91	.69	.76	.91	.65	.82				.84	.85
Practical Domain-4	.70	.89	.84	.86	.88	.64	.88	.77	.82	.66	.86	.80		.98	.87	
Practical Domain-5	.69	.86	.84	.84	.85	.69	.86	.79	.84	.80	.86	.83	.98			.89
GAC-9	.81	.89	.90	.79	.86	.76	.83	.86	.89	.69	.95	.90	.96	.96		
GAC-10	.79	.88	.90	.79	.84	.77	.82	.86	.90	.76	.94	.91	.96	.97	1.00	
Mean[c]	9.90	10.06	9.88	10.06	10.16	9.31	10.24	10.06	10.02	10.63	29.83	19.33	40.51	51.71	89.67	101.68
SD	2.92	2.90	2.96	2.97	2.59	2.96	2.68	3.02	2.99	2.96	8.01	5.43	9.78	11.39	21.89	23.22

Note. **Com** = Communication; **CU** = Community Use; **FA** = Functional Academics; **HL** = Home Living; **HS** = Health and Safety; **LS** = Leisure; **SC** = Self-Care; **SD** = Self-Direction; **Soc** = Social; **WK** = Work; **CON** = Conceptual Adaptive Domain; **SO** = Social Adaptive Domain; **PR-4** = Practical Adaptive Domain without Work; **PR-5** = Practical Adaptive Domain with Work; **GAC-9** = GAC without Work; **GAC-10** = GAC with Work.

[a] Adaptive Domain correlations corrected by removing the skill area scaled score from the sum of the scaled scores.
[b] GAC correlations corrected by removing the skill area scaled score(s) from the sum of the scaled scores.
[c] Means and SDs reported under corrected adaptive domains and GAC were calculated using all skill areas included in the composite.

Table C.3 **Intercorrelations of Skill Area Scaled Scores and Sums of Scaled Scores for Adaptive Domains and the GAC: Adult Form, Self Report** (continued)

Ages 50–64

Skill Area/Composite	Com	CU	FA	HL	HS	LS	SC	SD	Soc	WK	CON[a]	SO[a]	PR-4[a]	PR-5[a]	GAC-9[b]	GAC-10[b]
Communication											.77				.81	.80
Community Use	.81												.74	.66	.82	.77
Functional Academics	.76	.72									.82				.83	.80
Home Living	.62	.66	.75										.75	.80	.78	.81
Health and Safety	.61	.70	.67	.72									.77	.75	.77	.79
Leisure	.77	.75	.70	.65	.61							.71			.83	.80
Self-Care	.50	.53	.50	.52	.51	.58							.59	.55	.64	.56
Self-Direction	.67	.66	.74	.70	.71	.74	.62				.75				.85	.84
Social	.64	.63	.66	.66	.64	.71	.60	.81				.71			.80	.83
Work	.53	.48	.58	.73	.61	.61	.53	.73	.70					.72		.74
Conceptual Domain	.90	.81	.92	.76	.73	.81	.60	.89	.78	.68					.91	.90
Social Domain	.77	.75	.74	.71	.67	.93	.63	.84	.92	.71	.86				.87	.88
Practical Domain-4	.76	.87	.79	.88	.87	.77	.74	.80	.75	.72	.87	.83		.98	.88	
Practical Domain-5	.77	.79	.78	.89	.84	.77	.68	.82	.81	.84	.88	.85	.98			.90
GAC-9	.85	.86	.87	.83	.81	.87	.70	.88	.85	.74	.96	.93	.96	.96		
GAC-10	.85	.82	.84	.85	.83	.84	.62	.87	.87	.79	.95	.93	.96	.97	1.00	
Mean[c]	9.60	9.71	9.47	9.86	9.90	8.80	10.55	10.13	10.03	10.44	29.20	18.83	40.03	51.85	88.05	101.92
SD	3.10	3.05	2.93	3.10	2.56	3.33	2.43	3.03	2.98	2.92	8.17	5.84	9.39	10.74	22.25	22.64

Ages 65–74

Skill Area/Composite	Com	CU	FA	HL	HS	LS	SC	SD	Soc	WK	CON[a]	SO[a]	PR-4[a]	PR-5[a]	GAC-9[b]	GAC-10[b]
Communication											.74				.78	.75
Community Use	.85												.75	.72	.86	.82
Functional Academics	.73	.79									.83				.84	.85
Home Living	.52	.62	.62										.71	.78	.72	.83
Health and Safety	.65	.70	.66	.60									.75	.79	.76	.78
Leisure	.70	.77	.81	.67	.71							.82			.88	.88
Self-Care	.57	.63	.60	.65	.65	.67							.74	.76	.76	.77
Self-Direction	.66	.76	.79	.71	.66	.82	.72				.78				.88	.88
Social	.65	.70	.71	.65	.62	.82	.73	.84				.82			.84	.82
Work	.45	.59	.63	.69	.66	.70	.60	.77	.68					.74		.75
Conceptual Domain	.88	.88	.93	.68	.73	.86	.70	.90	.81	.69					.91	.92
Social Domain	.71	.77	.80	.69	.69	.95	.74	.87	.95	.73	.88				.89	.89
Practical Domain-4	.76	.87	.78	.85	.85	.83	.85	.83	.79	.74	.88	.85		.99	.89	
Practical Domain-5	.75	.83	.82	.86	.87	.85	.84	.87	.81	.84	.91	.87	.99			.92
GAC-9	.83	.89	.88	.79	.81	.91	.80	.91	.88	.75	.96	.94	.96	.97		
GAC-10	.80	.85	.88	.86	.83	.91	.81	.91	.86	.80	.96	.93	.97	.98	1.00	
Mean[c]	9.99	9.64	9.82	10.19	10.04	9.31	10.45	10.37	10.50	9.81	30.18	19.81	40.33	49.74	90.31	98.69
SD	2.90	3.10	3.05	3.05	2.57	3.01	2.65	2.92	3.07	2.91	8.03	5.79	9.73	12.02	22.51	24.95

Note. **Com** = Communication; **CU** = Community Use; **FA** = Functional Academics; **HL** = Home Living; **HS** = Health and Safety; **LS** = Leisure; **SC** = Self-Care; **SD** = Self-Direction; **Soc** = Social; **WK** = Work; **CON** = Conceptual Adaptive Domain; **SO** = Social Adaptive Domain; **PR-4** = Practical Adaptive Domain without Work; **PR-5** = Practical Adaptive Domain with Work; **GAC-9** = GAC without Work; **GAC-10** = GAC with Work.

[a] Adaptive Domain correlations corrected by removing the skill area scaled score from the sum of the scaled scores.
[b] GAC correlations corrected by removing the skill area scaled score(s) from the sum of the scaled scores.
[c] Means and SDs reported under corrected adaptive domains and GAC were calculated using all skill areas included in the composite.

C
Adult (Self)

329

Table C.3   Intercorrelations of Skill Area Scaled Scores and Sums of Scaled Scores for Adaptive Domains and the GAC: Adult Form, Self Report (continued)

Ages 75–89

Skill Area/Composite	Com	CU	FA	HL	HS	LS	SC	SD	Soc	CON[a]	SO[a]	PR-4[a]	GAC-9[b]
Communication										.76			.72
Community Use	.75											.77	.87
Functional Academics	.77	.88								.85			.88
Home Living	.45	.71	.70									.82	.77
Health and Safety	.56	.72	.77	.79								.82	.84
Leisure	.72	.80	.81	.67	.73						.66		.86
Self-Care	.46	.61	.57	.65	.64	.57						.70	.68
Self-Direction	.66	.79	.78	.72	.83	.81	.63			.76			.89
Social	.54	.59	.62	.58	.64	.66	.55	.74			.66		.72
Conceptual Domain	.89	.89	.94	.69	.79	.86	.61	.90	.69				.89
Social Domain	.68	.76	.78	.68	.75	.90	.62	.85	.92	.85			.85
Practical Domain-4	.64	.88	.84	.90	.90	.79	.82	.85	.67	.86	.80		.87
GAC-9	.78	.90	.91	.82	.88	.89	.74	.91	.78	.95	.91	.96	
Mean [c]	10.13	9.86	10.02	9.81	10.20	10.02	10.37	10.05	9.84	30.20	19.86	40.24	90.30
SD	2.94	3.03	2.98	3.04	2.90	2.87	2.56	2.98	3.07	8.08	5.41	10.11	22.32

Note. **Com** = Communication; **CU** = Community Use; **FA** = Functional Academics; **HL** = Home Living; **HS** = Health and Safety; **LS** = Leisure; **SC** = Self-Care; **SD** = Self-Direction; **Soc** = Social; **CON** = Conceptual Adaptive Domain; **SO** = Social Adaptive Domain; **PR-4** = Practical Adaptive Domain without Work; **GAC-9** = GAC without Work.

[a] Adaptive Domain corrected by removing the skill area scaled score from the sum of the scaled scores.
[b] GAC corrected by removing the skill area scaled score(s) from the sum of the scaled scores.
[c] Means and *SD*s reported under corrected adaptive domains and GAC were calculated using all skill areas included in the composite.

Table C.4 **Intercorrelations of Skill Area Scaled Scores and Sums of Scaled Scores for Adaptive Domains and the GAC: Adult Form, Rated by Others**

Ages 16–21

Skill Area/Composite	Com	CU	FA	HL	HS	LS	SC	SD	Soc	WK	CON[a]	SO[a]	PR-4[a]	PR-5[a]	GAC-9[b]	GAC-10[b]
Communication											.69				.75	.68
Community Use	.68												.82	.71	.84	.78
Functional Academics	.63	.83									.75				.80	.78
Home Living	.62	.60	.60										.61	.58	.70	.61
Health and Safety	.68	.79	.76	.55									.79	.70	.84	.77
Leisure	.63	.72	.70	.60	.72							.67			.82	.76
Self-Care	.55	.72	.59	.52	.71	.66							.74	.72	.75	.71
Self-Direction	.65	.71	.73	.63	.75	.78	.70				.77				.87	.84
Social	.59	.51	.49	.59	.62	.67	.59	.78				.67			.72	.68
Work	.42	.37	.46	.57	.47	.50	.56	.65	.59					.60		.64
Conceptual Domain	.85	.84	.90	.70	.83	.79	.70	.90	.70	.59					.91	.88
Social Domain	.67	.67	.65	.65	.73	.91	.68	.85	.92	.61	.82				.83	.81
Practical Domain-4	.74	.91	.81	.78	.89	.79	.86	.81	.67	.60	.89	.80		.98	.89	
Practical Domain-5	.67	.82	.76	.74	.82	.72	.82	.79	.65	.76	.86	.78	.98			.87
GAC-9	.80	.87	.84	.76	.88	.86	.80	.90	.78	.64	.96	.90	.97	.95		
GAC-10	.74	.83	.82	.69	.82	.81	.77	.87	.75	.72	.94	.88	.95	.97	.99	
Mean[c]	9.82	9.88	10.02	9.97	10.28	10.11	10.40	10.00	10.23	10.07	29.84	20.34	40.53	51.53	90.71	102.34
SD	2.89	3.06	3.13	3.09	3.05	2.97	2.90	2.97	3.12	2.89	7.94	5.57	10.38	11.06	22.66	21.59

Ages 22–29

Skill Area/Composite	Com	CU	FA	HL	HS	LS	SC	SD	Soc	WK	CON[a]	SO[a]	PR-4[a]	PR-5[a]	GAC-9[b]	GAC-10[b]
Communication											.76				.81	.82
Community Use	.81												.83	.86	.88	.90
Functional Academics	.75	.86									.84				.86	.88
Home Living	.71	.75	.70										.81	.80	.82	.82
Health and Safety	.74	.80	.81	.75									.84	.86	.88	.88
Leisure	.73	.79	.77	.67	.73							.75			.83	.83
Self-Care	.63	.69	.64	.72	.72	.64							.78	.77	.76	.76
Self-Direction	.68	.74	.78	.75	.79	.76	.68				.78				.85	.87
Social	.67	.71	.71	.72	.76	.75	.64	.76				.75			.82	.83
Work	.64	.68	.71	.58	.71	.64	.58	.67	.66					.71		.74
Conceptual Domain	.89	.88	.93	.80	.86	.83	.72	.91	.79	.73					.93	.93
Social Domain	.75	.80	.79	.74	.79	.94	.68	.81	.93	.70	.86				.87	.88
Practical Domain-4	.81	.90	.84	.90	.91	.79	.87	.82	.79	.71	.91	.84		.98	.91	
Practical Domain-5	.81	.91	.86	.88	.92	.80	.85	.85	.81	.82	.92	.86	.98			.92
GAC-9	.85	.91	.89	.86	.90	.87	.81	.89	.86	.74	.97	.92	.97	.97		
GAC-10	.85	.92	.90	.86	.91	.87	.80	.90	.86	.80	.97	.93	.97	.98	1.00	
Mean[c]	10.19	9.96	9.96	10.20	10.46	9.80	10.00	10.27	10.11	10.25	30.43	19.91	40.62	50.43	90.96	100.23
SD	2.85	2.83	2.85	2.98	2.96	3.03	2.56	3.12	2.90	3.14	8.01	5.54	10.17	12.82	22.76	25.69

Note. **Com** = Communication; **CU** = Community Use; **FA** = Functional Academics; **HL** = Home Living; **HS** = Health and Safety; **LS** = Leisure; **SC** = Self-Care; **SD** = Self-Direction; **Soc** = Social; **WK** = Work; **CON** = Conceptual Adaptive Domain; **SO** = Social Adaptive Domain; **PR-4** = Practical Adaptive Domain without Work; **PR-5** = Practical Adaptive Domain with Work; **GAC-9** = GAC without Work; **GAC-10** = GAC with Work.

[a] Adaptive Domain correlations corrected by removing the skill area scaled score from the sum of the scaled scores.
[b] GAC correlations corrected by removing the skill area scaled score(s) from the sum of the scaled scores.
[c] Means and *SD*s reported under corrected adaptive domains and GAC were calculated using all skill areas included in the composite.

C — Adult (Others)

Table C.4 Intercorrelations of Skill Area Scaled Scores and Sums of Scaled Scores for Adaptive Domains and the GAC: Adult Form, Rated by Others (continued)

Ages 30–39

Skill Area/Composite	Com	CU	FA	HL	HS	LS	SC	SD	Soc	WK	CON[a]	SO[a]	PR-4[a]	PR-5[a]	GAC-9[b]	GAC-10[b]
Communication											.79				.80	.79
Community Use	.80												.78	.76	.87	.85
Functional Academics	.76	.84									.80				.84	.82
Home Living	.56	.67	.65										.72	.67	.74	.70
Health and Safety	.64	.75	.71	.68									.82	.79	.83	.80
Leisure	.72	.76	.75	.65	.72							.81			.85	.83
Self-Care	.56	.60	.58	.56	.67	.60							.68	.66	.68	.65
Self-Direction	.70	.73	.72	.68	.71	.72	.57				.76				.82	.83
Social	.70	.73	.66	.64	.74	.81	.58	.75				.81			.83	.81
Work	.58	.58	.61	.47	.57	.55	.52	.70	.62						.63	.69
Conceptual Domain	.91	.87	.92	.70	.76	.81	.63	.89	.78	.70					.89	.90
Social Domain	.74	.78	.74	.68	.77	.95	.62	.77	.95	.62	.83				.86	.84
Practical Domain-4	.74	.88	.81	.85	.90	.79	.81	.78	.78	.63	.86	.83		.98	.88	
Practical Domain-5	.75	.86	.80	.80	.87	.77	.77	.81	.78	.76	.88	.82	.98			.89
GAC-9	.84	.90	.88	.80	.86	.88	.74	.86	.87	.69	.95	.92	.96	.96		
GAC-10	.84	.89	.86	.76	.84	.87	.71	.86	.85	.75	.95	.90	.95	.97	1.00	
Mean[c]	10.41	10.01	10.18	10.13	10.02	9.90	10.20	9.98	10.34	9.94	30.57	20.24	40.36	50.39	91.17	101.41
SD	2.95	2.93	3.08	2.96	2.71	2.96	2.50	2.91	2.83	2.56	8.08	5.52	9.57	10.83	21.97	22.73

Ages 40–49

Skill Area/Composite	Com	CU	FA	HL	HS	LS	SC	SD	Soc	WK	CON[a]	SO[a]	PR-4[a]	PR-5[a]	GAC-9[b]	GAC-10[b]
Communication											.77				.79	.80
Community Use	.78												.76	.77	.86	.86
Functional Academics	.72	.82									.78				.82	.81
Home Living	.52	.61	.60										.72	.71	.73	.74
Health and Safety	.66	.77	.73	.68									.80	.81	.82	.82
Leisure	.75	.80	.75	.67	.74							.73			.85	.85
Self-Care	.54	.59	.57	.60	.60	.57							.67	.71	.69	.71
Self-Direction	.72	.71	.73	.69	.69	.73	.61				.78				.84	.86
Social	.70	.71	.64	.67	.70	.73	.66	.81				.73			.83	.85
Work	.62	.56	.55	.49	.61	.57	.55	.68	.68						.64	.69
Conceptual Domain	.90	.85	.91	.67	.77	.82	.63	.90	.79	.68					.89	.90
Social Domain	.78	.81	.75	.72	.77	.93	.66	.83	.93	.67	.87				.90	.91
Practical Domain-4	.74	.87	.80	.85	.90	.82	.80	.79	.80	.64	.86	.87		.98	.89	
Practical Domain-5	.76	.87	.79	.83	.89	.82	.81	.83	.83	.76	.88	.89	.98			.91
GAC-9	.84	.89	.86	.79	.86	.89	.74	.88	.87	.69	.95	.94	.96	.97		
GAC-10	.84	.89	.85	.79	.86	.88	.76	.89	.88	.75	.95	.94	.96	.97	1.00	
Mean[c]	10.41	9.97	10.32	10.26	9.99	10.06	10.50	9.94	10.20	10.08	30.66	20.26	40.72	50.68	91.64	101.42
SD	2.95	2.90	3.07	2.94	2.85	2.82	2.43	2.90	2.95	2.64	8.06	5.37	9.52	11.55	21.91	24.16

Note. **Com** = Communication; **CU** = Community Use; **FA** = Functional Academics; **HL** = Home Living; **HS** = Health and Safety; **LS** = Leisure; **SC** = Self-Care; **SD** = Self-Direction; **Soc** = Social; **WK** = Work; **CON** = Conceptual Adaptive Domain; **SO** = Social Adaptive Domain; **PR-4** = Practical Adaptive Domain without Work; **PR-5** = Practical Adaptive Domain with Work; **GAC-9** = GAC without Work; **GAC-10** = GAC with Work.

[a] Adaptive Domain correlations corrected by removing the skill area scaled score from the sum of the scaled scores.

[b] GAC correlations corrected by removing the skill area scaled score(s) from the sum of the scaled scores.

[c] Means and SDs reported under corrected adaptive domains and GAC were calculated using all skill areas included in the composite.

Table C.4   Intercorrelations of Skill Area Scaled Scores and Sums of Scaled Scores for Adaptive Domains and the GAC: Adult Form, Rated by Others (continued)

Ages 50–64

Skill Area/Composite	Com	CU	FA	HL	HS	LS	SC	SD	Soc	WK	CON[a]	SO[a]	PR-4[a]	PR-5[a]	GAC-9[b]	GAC-10[b]
Communication											.78				.79	.79
Community Use	.78												.68	.70	.81	.80
Functional Academics	.73	.79									.77				.81	.83
Home Living	.48	.48	.52										.63	.67	.65	.70
Health and Safety	.68	.75	.76	.64									.82	.82	.84	.84
Leisure	.63	.73	.73	.48	.66							.67			.78	.78
Self-Care	.55	.55	.57	.56	.63	.53							.67	.68	.69	.69
Self-Direction	.71	.68	.71	.63	.74	.72	.63				.76				.84	.86
Social	.65	.61	.58	.62	.69	.67	.62	.75				.67			.78	.81
Work	.61	.57	.65	.53	.66	.56	.59	.72	.67					.70		.74
Conceptual Domain	.90	.83	.91	.60	.81	.77	.65	.89	.73	.73					.89	.90
Social Domain	.70	.73	.72	.60	.74	.91	.63	.80	.92	.67	.82				.84	.85
Practical Domain-4	.75	.84	.79	.81	.90	.72	.80	.80	.76	.70	.87	.81		.98	.88	
Practical Domain-5	.77	.82	.82	.80	.89	.74	.78	.84	.81	.82	.89	.84	.98			.91
GAC-9	.84	.86	.86	.73	.88	.83	.75	.88	.83	.74	.95	.91	.96	.97		
GAC-10	.84	.84	.87	.77	.87	.82	.74	.89	.85	.79	.95	.91	.96	.98	1.00	
Mean[c]	10.00	9.23	9.81	10.01	9.65	10.09	10.52	9.81	10.17	10.48	29.63	20.25	39.41	49.62	89.29	99.85
SD	2.98	3.16	3.17	3.04	2.72	2.95	2.38	2.92	3.02	3.13	8.16	5.47	9.45	11.98	21.82	24.49

Ages 65–74

Skill Area/Composite	Com	CU	FA	HL	HS	LS	SC	SD	Soc	WK	CON[a]	SO[a]	PR-4[a]	PR-5[a]	GAC-9[b]	GAC-10[b]
Communication											.77				.78	.81
Community Use	.72												.69	.80	.84	.86
Functional Academics	.74	.81									.82				.83	.81
Home Living	.43	.55	.50										.65	.75	.63	.76
Health and Safety	.68	.65	.72	.65									.77	.83	.83	.84
Leisure	.61	.75	.71	.48	.68							.74			.76	.75
Self-Care	.60	.57	.55	.48	.63	.41							.65	.66	.66	.66
Self-Direction	.70	.75	.77	.64	.78	.69	.68				.79				.89	.93
Social	.70	.72	.72	.56	.70	.74	.60	.85				.74			.84	.86
Work	.66	.72	.71	.57	.64	.69	.53	.82	.78					.71		.80
Conceptual Domain	.89	.84	.93	.58	.80	.74	.67	.91	.83	.80					.90	.92
Social Domain	.70	.79	.77	.56	.74	.93	.54	.82	.93	.78	.84				.84	.83
Practical Domain-4	.73	.84	.78	.81	.88	.71	.79	.86	.77	.71	.87	.79		.98	.87	
Practical Domain-5	.82	.88	.80	.85	.89	.73	.77	.92	.84	.82	.93	.83	.98			.94
GAC-9	.82	.88	.87	.71	.86	.82	.73	.92	.88	.80	.96	.91	.96	.98		
GAC-10	.84	.89	.85	.81	.88	.80	.72	.94	.89	.84	.96	.90	.96	.98	1.00	
Mean[c]	9.96	10.02	10.54	10.45	10.10	10.62	10.62	10.40	10.46	10.67	30.90	21.08	41.19	50.56	93.17	101.08
SD	2.58	2.94	3.06	2.95	2.66	2.95	2.51	2.95	2.95	3.32	7.82	5.50	9.19	13.15	21.30	26.27

Note. **Com** = Communication; **CU** = Community Use; **FA** = Functional Academics; **HL** = Home Living; **HS** = Health and Safety; **LS** = Leisure; **SC** = Self-Care; **SD** = Self-Direction; **Soc** = Social; **WK** = Work; **CON** = Conceptual Adaptive Domain; **SO** = Social Adaptive Domain; **PR-4** = Practical Adaptive Domain without Work; **PR-5** = Practical Adaptive Domain with Work; **GAC-9** = GAC without Work; **GAC-10** = GAC with Work.

[a] Adaptive Domain correlations corrected by removing the skill area scaled score from the sum of the scaled scores.

[b] GAC correlations corrected by removing the skill area scaled score(s) from the sum of the scaled scores.

[c] Means and *SD*s reported under corrected adaptive domains and GAC were calculated using all skill areas included in the composite.

C Adult (Others)

Table C.4 Intercorrelations of Skill Area Scaled Scores and Sums of Scaled Scores for Adaptive Domains and the GAC: Adult Form, Rated by Others (continued)

Ages 75–89

Skill Area/Composite	Com	CU	FA	HL	HS	LS	SC	SD	Soc	CON[a]	SO[a]	PR-4[a]	GAC-9[b]
Communication										.87			.88
Community Use	.84											.90	.94
Functional Academics	.88	.93								.93			.95
Home Living	.81	.88	.90									.93	.92
Health and Safety	.84	.91	.94	.90								.94	.94
Leisure	.78	.85	.83	.78	.79						.83		.86
Self-Care	.78	.79	.82	.87	.87	.75						.88	.87
Self-Direction	.82	.89	.91	.88	.90	.84	.82			.89			.93
Social	.86	.86	.86	.80	.82	.83	.78	.86			.83		.89
Conceptual Domain	.94	.93	.97	.91	.94	.85	.85	.96	.90				.96
Social Domain	.86	.90	.88	.82	.85	.95	.80	.89	.96	.92			.91
Practical Domain-4	.86	.94	.94	.96	.97	.83	.93	.92	.86	.95	.88		.94
GAC-9	.91	.95	.96	.94	.96	.89	.90	.95	.91	.98	.94	.98	
Mean[c]	9.56	9.01	9.43	9.48	9.26	9.96	9.29	9.80	9.88	28.79	19.83	37.03	85.66
SD	3.12	3.47	3.59	3.68	3.19	3.11	3.49	3.58	3.32	9.84	6.15	13.15	28.41

Note. **Com** = Communication; **CU** = Community Use; **FA** = Functional Academics; **HL** = Home Living; **HS** = Health and Safety; **LS** = Leisure; **SC** = Self-Care; **SD** = Self-Direction; **Soc** = Social; **CON** = Conceptual Adaptive Domain; **SO** = Social Adaptive Domain; **PR-4** = Practical Adaptive Domain without Work; **GAC-9** = GAC without Work.

[a] Adaptive Domain correlations corrected by removing the skill area scaled score from the sum of the scaled scores.
[b] GAC correlations corrected by removing the skill area scaled score(s) from the sum of the scaled scores.
[c] Means and *SD*s reported under corrected adaptive domains and GAC were calculated using all skill areas included in the composite.

Appendix D

Examiners, Research Coordinators, Reviewers, and Consultants

Examiners, Research Coordinators, Reviewers, and Consultants

Lynne M. Adams, MSEd
Nancy K. Adams
Myrna Allen, MA
Deborah C. Almeida, MSEd
Candace Almquist, MA, CCC-SLP
Margaret Altom
Sharon D. Andrews, BS
Shana J. Asbell, MA, CCC-SLP
Ann Audley
Roseann Augat
Elizabeth Rose Avant, MA, CAGS
Rosemary Ayres
Michelle Baez
Vickie L. Bain, MA
Cary Ballesteros, MS
Margot Barth Petroskey, EdS
Mary Jo Bates, MS
Sheryl Lynn Baudendistel, MA, CCC-SLP
Jana Bennett, MEd
Sandy Benson, MA, NCSP
Sandy Benson, MA
Kathleen Bergeson, PhD
Jan Eastin Bergman, SSP/NCSP
Arlene L. Binoya Crozer, BS
Lori L. Black, MS
Candace Boan, PhD
Stanley Bodner, PhD
Barbara Boegl
Matthew D. Bogenshutz
Patricia L. Bole, MA, CCC-SLP
Angela D. Bonds, MS, SLP
John T. Boney
Tracy L. Boney
Kim Booher, MEd
Howard Boone
Debra Boos, MS
Mary Bornstein
Taunya Bos
Maureen Bosanko, MA
Linda Boulange, MS
Jodine Boyd, MA
Vicki Brands, MA, SLP-CCC
Diane Branson

Stephanie Brown, GT Facilitator
Linda Brown, EdD
Rebecca R. Brown-Johnsky, MS, CCC-SLP
Kelli W. Brunson, MS, CCC-SLP
Linda Bryant
Donna M. Burgess, MS
Maryann M. Burne, BA, MEd
Judy Butterfield
Marylin Calzadilla, PhD
Kara L. Cannon
Lorraine Cantu, BA
Nancy Carbia
Deborah Lynn Carden
Miriam Carey
Vickey J. Carlson, MA, CCC-SLP
Martha P. Carlton, PhD
Lori Carmichael
June Carter
Izreal Cary
Delia A. Casias, BBA
Jennifer Castro
Rebecca Cervantes
Polly Chan, MEd, LSSP, LPA
Kathy Chauncey, MA
Amy Chauvin, OTR/L
Camille M. Chavez, BA
Diane Cheek
Joan Cherno, MA
Linda Townsend Christ, MS, CCC-SLP
Jenny L. Clark
Mark R. Claussen, EdS
Rosemary Coffman, PhD
Ashley Cohen, PhD
Geralann K. Coldwell, MA
Lori Y. Coleman
Jennifer Collier, MSE
Sherryl Collins, MS
John Conway, MA
Susan Cooper, MA
Kelly Cosgriff, MA, CCC-SLP
Marylou Coutts, MS, CCC-SP
Blancarosa T. Craig, BA

Susan H. Cress
Mark T. Crugnale, MS
Maria C. Cruz, PhD
Susanne Cuatt
Lidia Curtev
Angela Dahncke
Cindy J. D'Alberto, MS, CCC-SLP
Dave Davenport, MS
Maria De La Sierra, MA
Ann Beth Deily, PhD
Kimberly B. Dellis, MS
Scott Dellis, MS
Rosetta H. Demming, EdS
George C. Denkowski, PhD
Lori DesJarlais
Asenath Devaney, EdS
Dorothy R. Dobbins, MA
Laura K. Dolezal, MA, CCC-SLP
Galen L. Downing, MSE
Rondi Drefs, MA, CCC-SLP
Colleen Dublin
Sarah Ducey, PhD
Joyce Eller
Joyce R. Elliot, EdS
Linda W. Ellison
Erin K. Elto, PsyD
Anne Ely, MHS, CCC-SLP/L
Nancy J. Emerick, MS
Sylvia Enriquez
Ana Estorga
Kelly Fagan, MSE
Shawna Fagnant
Helene Chaika Fausold, EdM
Gwen L. Fecht, EdS
Barbara Felix, MA
Zoila Fernandez, MAEd
Debra A. Filipiak, MS, CCC-SLP
Dana Fitz-Gale
Dennis E. Ford
Kerri Fraser
Sharon Friedman, EdD
Carrie C. Fuhrmann, MA
Maria D. Garcia, MS
Kimberly A. Garrity

Sarah Geiger, CCC-SLP

Joanne Gilchrist

William Gilchrist, EdD

Christina Gindratt, BA

Debora Gnatzig, MEd

Alma C. Godoy, BS

Diana K. Goldsberry

Jessica R. Gombert, MA

Dana Gorman

Karen M. Green

Lynn Marie Green

Irit S. Greenberg

Brenda Greer-Jennings, SSPY, LSSP, LPC

Karin Gregerson

Frieda Grigsby

Robert W. Grilli, EdD

Trinda Groff

Jean B. Gunn

Anne S. Hagen, MSW, LCSW

Glenna Hale

Sharon Hale, MSEd

Pamela A. Hamlett

Melissa A. Hancock, MA

Lori Hanson

Kathleen Hanson, MA

Karen Hardwick, PhD

Frymet S. Hare, MEd

Luci Harmon

Beatrice F. Harris

Laura J. Harris, MS, CCC-SLP

Susan K. Hart

Lori Hartley, SLP

Leslie Hathaway, MA

Pennie Hatlestad, BA

Alaina Haub, BA

Mary L. Heeringa, BSN

Diana G. Heffron

Donna L. Helm-Yost, EdD, LP

Cynthia L. Henderson

Gail Herlick-Aho, MAEd

Eleanor Herman

Donna Hibbetts, MA

Michelle Hodges, MCD

Jack Horrigan, MEd

Felicia Houston, PhD

Christie Howell, PhD

Lorraine Huffaker, MA

Patti Jackson, MEd

Ray A. James

R. Peter James, PhD

Andrew Jastrzembski

Tom Jenkins, EdS

Jen Johnston

Kathy Johnston, MS CCC-LSLP

Christine Jones, MA, CCC-SLP

Debi L. Jones

Nancy M. Jones, MS

Maria C. Juarez, MA

Sondra Kelley, BS, MA

Phyllis Kennell, MSE

Jacqueline Kay Kenyon, MS, CCC-SLP

Kimberly D. Kerlin, MA

Karen Kerns, MS

Elaine S. King

Leah M. King, MA, CCC-SLP

Edward P. Kittinger Jr., MA

Mark Klein

Gail B. Knecht, MS

Susan Knox, PhD

Perri J. Krom

Jennifer Lake

Melissa F. Lane, MEd

Julie A. Larrieu

Anita W. Latham, MA

Melissa D. Lavin

Julie LeBaron

Sherry A. Leblanc, MA

Angela B. Ledesma, MA, CCC-SLP

Joan R. Lemon, MA, CCC-LSLP

Michael Levine

Karyn Lewis-Searcy

Sandra B. Lex

Brett Liedy, BA

Lisa Lipshez, MA, CCC-SLP

Toby Lischko, MS

Patricia Litscher, OTR

Vivian Little, EdS

Nancy A. Long, EdD

Frances F. Loose, PhD

Connie Loren, MA, CCC-SLP

LoriAnn M. Lumley, MA, CCC-SLP

Linda S. Lund, EdS

Becky L. Lundeen, MA CCC-SLP

Marilyn Maldonado

June Malone

Sharyn Mann

Maureen Martin, MS

Melissa A. Martin, MA

Jacqueline Mast, MSEd, PT

Ron Mcghee, EdD

Laura Jo McKamey, MS, CCC-SLP

Kim McPherson

Maureen McQuillan, MEd

Janis Mecklenborg

Katherine Medeiros

Spears Mercer, BA

Donna Merrill

Jill Michalski

Kristie Middendorf

Pamela Mitchell, MPHIL

Melanie A. Montenora, MSEd

Jennifer Montgomery, MS

Daniel E. Moore, LP, CSP

Deborah J. Moore, EdM

Pamela P. Moore, MS

Sandra Morris, PT

Kelly L.G. Mullin, MA, CCC-SLP

Mary Mulvaney, MSW

Deborah T. Murphy, MA

Donna B. Nallett, CAGS

Elizabeth M. Neumann, PhD

Ibrahima Niang, BA

Kelly Ann Nilon, SLP

Therese M. Nugent

Alicemarie O'Connor, MEd

Marcia O'Neal, PhD

Tracy L. Otto, MEd

Phillip R. Owen

Amy Palmer, SLP

Charity Pankratz, MA

Sylvia V. Parga, BA

Donna M. Passabet, CAGS

Michele Patterson, MS

Donna J. Paul, MS

Virginia Paulson, MS, LSLP

Stephanie R. Peabody

Trixine Peart, MA, CCC-SLP

Denise Peloquin, MS

Cherri Penton, PhD

Rita Perri

Gwendolyn D. Persons

Kerri R. Phillips, MA

Sara Piper

Nasarita R. Ponce

Deneen Pond, MS, CCC-SLP

Antoine Powell, MSE

Saipin Prasertsukdee, MS

Michele R. Pratt, SLP

Rachel Pyle

Martha E. Quintanar,
MEd, NCSP

Gail Rance, SLP

Cynthia C. Randall, AA

Linda D. Reber, MA

Elsa Judith Riggin, MA

Ann E. Ritter

Melanie Rivera, MS, CCC-SLP

Jaclyn L. Rizzo, SLP

Ida L. Robbins, BSN

Joyce L. Robinson, MS

Mariam Roman

Renate Rommel

Cheryl Ann Rondinella, MS,
CCC-SLP

Tammy B. Roring, ME, CCC-SLP

Carl M. Ross, PhD

Marge Roy

Lyann Rust, MS

Mona Ryan, MS

Irene Rybicki, OTR/L

Kristin D. Saccento, MS, CCC-SLP

Luis J. Salcido

Theresa Saltzman

Sylvia B. Sanchez

Mary Sanders, EdD

Sally K. Sandlin, BS

Barry L. Sandoval, MA

Rosemary J. Santoiemma, PT

Albert Santos

Kathie Schlemper, MS, CCC-SLP

Connie Schulz

Jeanne Sergi

Flordeliz Serpa

Lenise Sgutt, MS

Toni Shahak

Susan S. Shaver, BS

D. Louise Sheard

Patsy Shepard, MEd

Melissa Shepler, MS CCC-SLP

Janice Shipbaugh, EdS

Susan M. Shires, MA

Kamelia Slankard

Dinah H. Slay

Judith L. Smith, EdD

Leighann A. Smith, MS

Pam Smith, MS

Sandra Snook

Ernest R. Solis

Martha Elena Solis, MEd

Penny L. Sprecher, PhD

Jennifer St. Clair

Sister Miriam Stadulis

Amy Stefanovic, BS

Kristi Steffel

Mary Kay Stenger, PhD

Deborah Stephenson

Art Straus, MS

Anita Sullivan

Jeanine Sunsten, MS

Donald G. Sweeney, MA

Mary Ellen Talley

Paula Taylor, M Ed

Lynn M. Thull, PhD

Stephanie Tiernan, MS, CCC-SLP

Karen Tomlinson

Cathy Torcasio, PhD

Tracy Traiger

Tracy Troeger

Kathy True, MA

Nanci Valente

Cheri Vetter, MEd

Yolanda D. Vincent, MA

Jacqueline R. Wall, MSE

Dale V. Wayman, PhD

Heather L. Webber, MA, CCC-SLP

Frances B. Weldon, MA, CCC-SLP

Alison K. Westerkamm, EdS

Susan M. White, MS

Martin J. Wiese, PhD

Brenee K. Williams, MS, MEd,
CCC-SLP

Linda Wilson, MA

Shelley Marie Windsor

Julie Yockel

John A. Yovich, MA

Joel J. Zapata, BS, MA

Eunice Zee-Chen, MS,
OTR, FAOTA

Theresa B. Ziebarth-Moritz, BA

References

Allen, M. J., & Yen, W. M. (1979). *Introduction to measurement theory.* Monterey, CA: Brooks/Cole.

American Association on Mental Retardation. (1992). *Mental retardation: Definition, classification, and systems of supports* (9th ed.). Washington, DC: Author.

American Association on Mental Retardation. (2002a). *Mental retardation: Definition, classification, and systems of support: Workbook.* Washington, DC: Author

American Association on Mental Retardation. (2002b). *Mental retardation: Definition, classification, and systems of support.* Washington, DC: Author

American Educational Research Association, American Psychological Association, & National Council on Measurement in Education. (1999). *Standards for educational and psychological testing.* Washington, DC: Author.

American Psychiatric Association. (1987). *Diagnostic and statistical manual of mental disorders* (3rd ed. rev.). Washington, DC: Author.

American Psychiatric Association. (1994). *Diagnostic and statistical manual of mental disorders* (4th ed.). Washington DC: Author.

American Psychiatric Association. (2000). *Diagnostic and statistical manual of mental disorders* (4th ed., text revision). Washington DC: Author.

Anastasi, A., & Urbina, S. (1997). *Psychological testing* (7th ed.). Upper Saddle River, NJ: Prentice Hall.

Bayley, N. (1993). *Bayley Scales of Infant Development–Second Edition.* San Antonio, TX: The Psychological Corporation.

Boan, C. H., & Harrison, P. L. (1997). Adaptive behavior assessment and individuals with mental retardation. In R. L. Taylor (Ed.), *Assessment of individuals with mental retardation* (pp. 33–53). San Diego, CA: Singular Publishing Group.

Bouffard, M., Watkinson, E. J., Thompson, L. P., Dunn, J. L. C., & Romanow, S. K. E. (1996). A test of the activity deficit hypothesis with children with movement difficulties. *Physical Activity Quarterly, 13*(1), 61–73.

Browne, M. W., & Cudeck, R. (1993). Alternative ways of assessing model fit. In K. A. Bollen & J. S. Long (Eds.), *Testing structural equation models* (pp. 136–162). Newbury Park, CA: Sage Publications.

Bruininks, R. H., McGrew, K. S., & Maruyama, G. (1988). Structure of adaptive behavior in samples with and without mental retardation. *American Journal on Mental Retardation, 93,* 265–272.

Bruininks, R. H., Woodcock, R. W., Weatherman, R. F., & Hill, B. K. (1996). *Scales of Independent Behavior–Revised.* Chicago: Riverside Publishing.

Clarke, A. M., Clarke, A. D. B., & Berg, J. M. (1985). *Mental deficiency: The changing outlook.* New York: Free Press.

Cohen, B. H. (1996). *Explaining psychological statistics.* Pacific Grove, CA: Brooks/Cole.

Davis, F. B. (1959). Interpretation of differences among averages and individual test scores. *Journal of Educational Psychology, 50*(4), 162–170.

Dunn, C. (1997). Transition assessment for secondary students with mental retardation. In R. L. Taylor (Ed.), *Assessment of individuals with mental retardation* (pp. 173–199). San Diego, CA: Singular Publishing.

Education for All Handicapped Children Act of 1975, Pub. L. No. 94–142, 89 Stat. 773 (1977).

Glutting, J. J., & Oakland, T. D. (1993). *Guide to the assessment of test session behaviors for the WISC–III and WIAT: Manual.* San Antonio, TX: The Psychological Corporation.

Gresham, F. M., & Elliott, S. N. (1990). *Social Skills Rating System Manual.* Circle Pines, MN: American Guidance Service.

Grossman, H. J. (Ed.). (1983). *Classification in mental retardation.* Washington, DC: American Association on Mental Deficiency.

Gueze, R., & Boerger, H. (1993). Children who are clumsy: Five years later. *Physical Activity Quarterly, 10*(1), 10–21.

Guilford, J. P. & Fruchter, B. (1978). *Fundamental statistics in psychology and education* (6th ed.). New York: McGraw-Hill.

Hack, M., Taylor, G., Klein, N., & Eiben, R. (1994). School-age outcomes in children with birth weights under 750 g. *New England Journal of Medicine, 331*(12), 753–759.

Harrison, P. L. (1990). Mental retardation, adaptive behavior assessment, and giftedness. In A. S. Kaufman (Ed.), *Assessing adolescent and adult intelligence* (pp. 533–585). Boston: Allyn and Bacon.

Harrison, P. L., & Boney, T. L. (2002) Adaptive behavior assessment. In A. Thomas & J. Grimes (Eds.), *Best practices in school psychology* (4th ed.) (pp. 1167–1180). Bethesda, MD: National Association of School Psychologists.

Heber, R. (1959). Modifications in the manual on terminology and classification in mental retardation [Monograph]. *American Journal of Mental Deficiency, 64* (2), 499–500.

Horn, E., & Fuchs, D. (1987). Using adaptive behavior in assessment and intervention: An overview. *The Journal of Special Education, 21*(1), 11–26.

Individuals with Disabilities Education Act Amendments of 1991, Pub. L. No. 102–150, 105 Stat. 587 (1992).

Individual with Disabilities Act of 1997, Final Regulations, 34 C.F.R. Pt. 300 and 303, *Assistance to States for the Education of Children With Disabilities and the Early Intervention Program for Infants and Toddlers with Disabilities.* (Fed. Reg. 64, 1999).

Jacobsen, J., & Mulick, J. (Eds.), (1996). *Manual on diagnosis and professional practice in mental retardation.* Washington, DC: American Psychological Association.

Jöreskog, K. G., & Sörbom, D. (1993). *LISREL 8: User's reference guide.* Chicago: Scientific Software International.

Kamphaus, R. W., & Frick, P. J. (1996). *Clinical assessment of child and adolescent personality and behavior.* Needham Heights, MA: Allyn & Bacon.

Keith, T. Z., Fehrmann, P. G., Harrison, P. L., & Pottebaum, S. M. (1987). The relation between adaptive behavior and intelligence: Testing alternative explanations. *Journal of School Psychology, 25*, 31–43.

Matarazzo, J. D. (1992). Psychological testing and assessment in the 21st Century. *American Psychologist, 47*(8), 1007–1008.

McGrew, K., & Bruininks, R. (1989) The factor structure of adaptive behavior. *School Psychology Review, 18*(1), 64–81.

Meacham, F. R., Kline, M. M., Stovall, J. A., & Sands, D. I. (1987). Adaptive behavior and low incidence handicaps: Hearing and visual impairments. *The Journal of Special Education, 21*(1), 183–196.

Naglieri, J. A. (1985). *Matrix Analogies Test–Short Form.* San Antonio, TX: The Psychological Corporation.

Niccols, G. A. (1994). Fetal alchohol syndrome: Implications for psychologists. *Clinical Psychology Review, 14*(2), 91–111.

The Psychological Corporation. (1992). *Wechsler Individual Achievement Test.* San Antonio, TX: Author.

The Psychological Corporation. (1994). *Wechsler Intelligence Scale for Children–Third Edition Writer, The Interpretive Software System: User's Guide DOS Version.* San Antonio, TX: Author.

The Psychological Corporation. (1999). *Wechsler Abbreviated Scales of Intelligence.* San Antonio, TX: Author.

Reschly, D. J. (1990). Best practices in adaptive behavior. In A. Thomas & J. Grimes (Eds.), *Best practices in school psychology–II* (pp.29–42). Washington, DC: The National Association of School Psychologists.

Reschly, D., Myers, T., & Hartel, C. (Eds). (2002). *Mental retardation: Determining eligibility for Social Security benefits.* Washington, DC: National Academy Press.

Reynolds, C. R., & Kamphaus, R. W. (1998). *Behavior Assessment System for Children.* Circle Pines, MN: American Guidance Service.

Sattler, J. M. (2001). *Assessment of children: Cognitive applications* (4th ed.). San Diego, CA: Author.

Schalock, R., & Braddock, D. (1999). *Adaptive behavior and its measurement: Implications for the field of mental retardation.* Washington, DC: American Association on Mental Retardation.

Seltzer, G. B. (1997). Adult assessment: The case for functional assessment. In R. L. Taylor (Ed.), *Assessment of individuals with mental retardation* (pp. 201–225). San Diego, CA: Singular Publishing Group.

Semel, E., Wiig, E. H., & Secord, W. A. (1994). *Clinical Evaluation of Language Fundamentals–Third Edition.* San Antonio, TX: The Psychological Corporation.

Shriver, M. D., Allen, K. D., & Mathews, J. R. (1999). Effective assessment of the shared and unique characteristics of children with autism. *School Psychology Review, 28*(4), 538–558.

Sparrow S. S., Balla, D. A., & Cicchetti, D. V. (1984). *Vineland Adaptive Behavior Scales–Interview Edition.* Circle Pines, MN: American Guidance Service.

Sparrow, S. S., Balla, D. A., & Cicchetti, D. V. (1985). *Vineland Adaptive Behavior Scales–Classroom Edition Manual.* Circle Pines, MN: American Guidance Service.

Sparrow, S. S., & Cicchetti, D. V. (1987). Adaptive behavior and the psychologically disturbed child. *The Journal of Special Education, 21*(1), 89–100.

Steiger, J. H. (1990). Structural model evaluation and modification: An interval estimation approach. *Multivariate behavioral research, 25*(2), 173–180.

Thorndike, R. L., Hagen, E. P., & Sattler, J. M. (1986). *The Stanford Binet Intelligence Scale–Fourth Edition.* Chicago: Riverside.

Tucker, L. R., & Lewis, C. (1973). A reliability coefficient for maximum likelihood factor analysis. *Psychometrika, 38*(1), 1–10.

U.S. Bureau of the Census. (1999). *Current Population Survey, March 1999* [Machine-readable data file]. Washington, DC: Bureau of the Census (Producer/Distributor).

U.S. Bureau of the Census. (2000). *Current Population Survey, October 2000* [Machine-readable data file]. Washington, DC: Bureau of the Census (Producer/Distributor).

U.S. Department of Education. (1998). *To assure the free appropriate public education of all children with disabilities: Twentieth annual report to Congress on the implementation of the Individuals with Disabilities Education Act.* Washington, DC: U.S. Government Printing Office.

U.S. Department of Education. (2001). *To assure the free appropriate public education of all children with disabilities: Twenty-third annual report to Congress on the implementation of the Individuals with Disabilities Education Act.* Washington, DC: U.S. Government Printing Office.

Wechsler, D. (1991). *Wechsler Intelligence Scale for Children–Third Edition.* San Antonio, TX: The Psychological Corporation.

Wechsler, D. (1997). *Wechsler Adult Intelligence Scale–Third Edition.* San Antonio, TX: The Psychological Corporation.

Wechsler, D. (2002). *Wechsler Preschool and Primary Scale of Intelligence–Third Edition.* San Antonio, TX: The Psychological Corporation.

Wechsler, D. (2003). *Wechsler Intelligence Scale for Children–Fourth Edition.* San Antonio, TX: The Psychological Corporation.

Weller, C., & Strawser, S. (1987) Adaptive behavior of subtypes of learning disabled individuals. *The Journal of Special Education, 21*(1), 101–116.

Wilkinson, G. S. (1993). *Wide Range Achievement Test–Revision 3.* Wilmington, DE: Jastak Associates.

World Health Organization. (1993). *International classifications of diseases.* Geneva: Author.

World Health Organization. (2001). *International classification of functioning, disability, and health.* Geneva: Author.